ADULT EDUCATIONAL PSYCHOLOGY

Adult Educational Psychology

Edited by

James A. Athanasou
University of Technology, Sydney, Australia

SENSE PUBLISHERS
ROTTERDAM / TAIPEI

A C.I.P. record for this book is available from the Library of Congress.

ISBN 978-90-8790-553-8 (paperback)
ISBN 978-90-8790-554-5 (hardback)
ISBN 978-90-8790-555-2 (e-book)

Published by: Sense Publishers,
P.O. Box 21858, 3001 AW Rotterdam, The Netherlands
http://www.sensepublishers.com

Printed on acid-free paper

TABLE OF CONTENTS

PREFACE TO THE FIRST EDITION

Welcome to *Adult Educational Psychology*. Whether you are a student, instructor or general reader, I hope that your journey through this book's various chapters is rewarding. The purpose of this text is to provide an introduction to psychology for those working and learning in adult education. A useful foundation for adult education and training is a working knowledge of behavioural science.

Background to the Text

The focus of this text is on people at the level of post-compulsory education and training. The content is designed to be relevant to learning in late adolescence (e.g., from the senior years of high school) through early, middle and late adulthood. This is an area that has been overlooked in educational psychology. For instance, most texts in educational psychology are directed towards teachers in primary or secondary education or teaching. Very few recognise that adults are also engaged in formal and informal learning on a lifelong basis and in even greater numbers than school pupils.

As a result adult education and training had to develop its own language and sets of principles to study adult learning and instruction. You will find that some concepts and ideas in adult learning such as adult learning principles, reflection or learning styles are already contained in psychology and well-researched. I hope that parts of this text will bridge the gap between adult education as a field of practice and psychology as a foundation discipline within education.

Consequently I am very pleased to be able to edit a text that is directed towards the needs of those working in higher education, technical and further education, vocational education, community education settings. The text also has application in specialised educational settings such as nursing education, religious education, careers education and in human resource development.

Structure of the Text

The text is structured around some foundation or introductory knowledge and then focuses on individual differences and the basic psychological processes associated with learning. The last section deals with the application of psychology to specific issues. In preparing their chapters, I asked each contributor to focus as much as possible on one perspective with which they were content rather than to provide a smorgasbord of psychological theories and views. This tends to bewilder the reader who is approaching psychology for the first time.

Using the Text

In using this text, you can commence at any one of the chapters and proceed only with those areas of interest to you. Alternatively, you may wish to read the chapters in sequence. Some of the early chapters provide a theoretical foundation or introduction for subsequent information. There is enough overlap between chapters, however, to ensure that your need for information is covered.

If you are new to psychology, it may help you to underline key concepts and ideas and to make notes in the margins to aid in your understanding. I do not recommend that you try to read a chapter in one sitting. Cover the chapter in a number of separate sessions as the chapters are sometimes quite comprehensive and detailed in their coverage of the subject. They try to offer the reader a densely packed and concise introduction to an area of adult educational psychology. Some of the chapters will require re-reading in order to gain full value from their content and perspective. Remember to undertake the questions and exercises at the end of each chapter as a way of checking your knowledge of the chapter contents.

Acknowledgements

In particular I acknowledge the willing cooperation of my friends and colleagues throughout Australia and overseas. All of the contributors are expert in their own area of psychology and all participated freely, giving a great deal of their valuable time. Furthermore, each allowed their chapter to be peer reviewed anonymously and independently by two reviewers. The depth and breadth of their contributions has been impressive and made me realise that it is now well beyond the capacity of any one person to cover such a diverse range of topic areas in psychology. I can do no more than acknowledge my sincere gratitude for their contributions.

I am pleased to be able to offer this text through an Australian publisher and one with whom I have dealt previously and special thanks must go to David Barlow from Social Science Press for his continuous support of Australian publications. I would like to thank Angelena Athanasou for her consistently practical advice, my colleagues Maree Joulian for assistance with preparation of the manuscript and Rory O'Brien for his excellent illustrations. I am grateful to the University of Technology, Sydney which granted me a period of study leave in which to complete this task and for the academic hospitality of the Australian Council for Educational Research and the Department of Educational Psychology at the University of Illinois at Urbana-Champaign.

Finally, I am privileged to be able to edit such a text and I trust that the final product meets your expectations. I wish you well in your journey through adult educational psychology.

James A. Athanasou
University of Technology, Sydney
November, 1998

PREFACE TO THE SECOND EDITION

I am delighted but also humbled to see the second edition of *Adult Educational Psychology* in print. In particular, I am grateful to the Sense Publishers for their faith in the book and I am also grateful to my co–contributors for agreeing to include their chapter once again. I am particularly grateful to the artist and printmaker Rory O'Brien (http://www.rory.com.au/) for permitting me to use his linoprints as distinctive illustrations once again.

For all of us this is largely a labour of love within our area of specialisation. The second edition has been produced in response to many requests for the out-of-print version and it is apparent that it has met a real need amongst students of adult education and adult educational psychology.

There are some minor changes to the chapters in this edition. I regret that the chapter from the late Michael Kaye is not included in this collection and in one sense this book is a dedication to his love of psychology which he inspired and supported as head of the School of Adult and Vocational Education at the University of Technology, Sydney. He was a firm believer in the importance of disciplinary research. Furthermore Pauline James has retired from the University of Melbourne and her chapter has not been included. In this edition I welcome the contribution of a chapter by Iasonas Lamprianou on the important topic of Rasch measurement. This challenges existing approaches to educational measurement, assessment and evaluation. It is highly recommended. I am still conscious that additional chapters could have been added to the text but there was a finite limit to the time and resources available for this second edition. Hopefully, a future editor will take up this challenge.

In order to maximise the benefit from adult educational psychology this text should be read in conjunction with other basic texts in adult education and training. I hope that you find this text useful in your study, research and work. It is my intention to retire formally later this year and in a sense this will be a parting gift to the next cohort of students and researchers. I have enjoyed teaching adult education psychology over many years and of course, I wish you well in your future studies and career.

James A. Athanasou
University of Technology, Sydney
March 2008

JAMES A. ATHANASOU

1. INTRODUCTION TO ADULT EDUCATIONAL PSYCHOLOGY

Psychology has always been a popular area of study. Many students come to this subject attracted in part by ideas of psychology as the study of the mind, or hoping that it will provide solutions for the problems in life or giving them clues to why people act in certain ways. Some have heard about the early learning experiments by Pavlov, and others may have read about the psychoanalytic work of Freud. Few people realise that psychology is a discipline with many specialties. For instance, the American Psychological Association alone publishes some 25 specialised journals for its members, covering different areas of psychology.

Psychology has become a complex field that has a background in the experimental study of human behaviour. It focuses on the study of specific behaviours from many different theoretical and applied viewpoints. The emphasis overall is on the nature of human behaviour, responding and experience – the way people develop over the lifespan, their perceptions, their thoughts, their emotions, their motivations, their learning and many other aspects of personal, social, educational and vocational adjustment. An underlying aim of this field is not only the theoretical study of behaviour but it aims also to enhance human welfare.

Indeed, there are few aspects of modern life that have not felt the impact of psychological research. Wherever you look in schools, the law, medicine, production, organisations, commerce or industry or in diverse areas such as entertainment, examinations, aviation, ergonomics, sport, selection or recruitment, public health, psychiatry, prisons, training, telecommunications or computers, you will find some application of the findings of modern psychology. Its influence is pervasive and wide-ranging. This is particularly the case in education and training where a foundational knowledge of educational psychology is considered a prerequisite in most teacher education programs.

James A Athanasou (ed.), Adult Educational Psychology, 1–8

The purpose of this chapter is to provide a broad orientation for the following sections that deal with specific topics in adult educational psychology. The different specialties within psychology are described briefly and the field of educational psychology introduced to the reader. Some details of the links between adult education and psychology are mentioned.

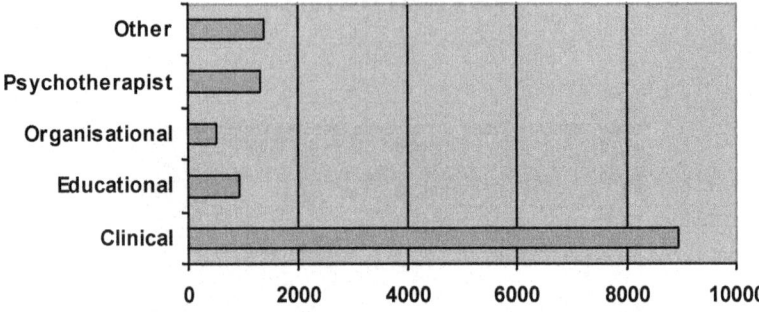

Figure 1.1 *Psychologists – Australia (Source: Australian Bureau of Statistics, Census of Population and Housing, unpublished data.)*

What Is the Work of a Psychologist?

Psychology is now a major profession of just over 13,000 in Australia (see Figure 1.1). In the last 2006 census, some 921 persons listed their occupation as educational psychologist but note this probably underestimates the total employment because many educational psychologists may be classified under other occupations such as researcher, university lecturer, teacher, guidance officer or school counsellor.

Professional psychologists now require around 6 years minimum undergraduate postgraduate study plus supervised experience usually over 2 years. While it was once the case that psychologists were able to practise with only a Bachelors degree, increasingly the requirement is for Masters Degrees and even Doctorates. There are national and international associations of psychologists such as the International Union of Psychological Science, International Association for Applied Psychology, the British Psychological Society, the American Psychological Association, and the Australian Psychological Society represents members of the profession in Australia. In most countries there are also government requirements for registration. In all Australian States and Territories there are Psychologist Registration Boards that specify the minimum period for training and experience. The reader is referred to Kostanski (2006) and O'Gorman (2007) for a more detailed picture of psychology in Australia.

Today psychologists are involved in counselling, therapy, administering tests, research, analysing working conditions, providing services to the community or acting as industrial and organisational consultants. There are many different specialties within psychology and although this text deals only with education, it may be helpful to have an introduction to some of the other areas of specialisation.

- *Clinical psychologists* diagnose, treat and prevent behaviour problems. Clinical psychologists work in private practice, hospitals, health services or specialist centres. They deal with problems such as developmental disabilities, psychiatric problems, health issues.
- *Neuropsychologists* specialise in the brain and nervous system, especially in cases where there has been a traumatic brain injury. They are involved in the diagnosis of head injury and its consequences through specialised testing. They also work in health services and private practice.
- *Counselling psychologists* offer assessment, counselling and therapy to people, couples or groups. They may deal with personal, stresses, emotional difficulties, social, educational or vocational problems.
- *Forensic psychologists* provide assessments and opinions for the courts. They operate mainly in the area of criminal behaviour, child abuse, custody matters. They work in prisons, private practice and corrective services.
- *Organisational psychologists* deal mainly with occupational and organisational behaviour. They operate in commerce and industry, specialising in areas such as human resources, selection, testing, recruitment, occupational health and safety, employment and unemployment.
- *Educational psychologists* work mainly in the areas of learning and instruction. They offer assessment, counselling and management issues for people with problems of adjustment to learning situations. They operate mainly in school settings but also in higher education. They are concerned with issues such as attention deficit disorders, hyperactivity, behaviour problems, intellectual deficits, giftedness, educational progress and career development.

The formal definition of the occupation of psychologist that is used in the Australian and New Zealand Standard Classification of occupations is set out in the insert (see Table 1.1). This provides a succinct description of the occupation in terms of education, training and duties.

Table 1.1 *Formal definition of psychologist (Source: Australian and New Zealand Standard Classification of Occupations)*

PSYCHOLOGISTS investigate, assess and provide treatment and counselling to foster optimal personal, social, educational and occupational adjustment and development.

In Australia and New Zealand:

Most occupations in this unit group have a level of skill commensurate with a bachelor degree or higher qualification. In some instances relevant experience and/or on-the-job training may be required in addition to the formal qualification. Registration or licensing may be required.

Tasks Include:

- collecting data about clients and assessing their cognitive, behavioural and emotional disorders

- administering and interpreting diagnostic tests and formulating plans for treatment

- developing, administering and evaluating individual and group treatment programs

- consulting with other professionals on details of cases and treatment plans

- conducting research studies of motivation in learning, group performance and individual differences in mental abilities and educational performance

- collecting data and analysing characteristics of students and recommending educational programs

- formulating achievement, diagnostic and predictive tests for use by teachers in planning methods and content of instruction

- developing interview techniques, psychological tests and other aids in workplace selection, placement, appraisal and promotion

- conducting surveys and research studies on job design, work groups, morale, motivation, supervision and management

- performing job analyses and establishing job requirements by observing and interviewing employees and managers

Educational Psychologists

The Australian Psychological Society also has a College of Educational and Developmental Psychologists which describes educational psychologists as being concerned with issues relating to the learning and development of people throughout their lifespan (Australian Psychological Society, 1997). For membership of the College of Educational and Developmental Psychologists, psychologists are required to undertake additional specialised training.

Some issues with which educational and developmental psychologists are concerned in adult educational psychology are listed in Table 1.2. In this table I have included late adolescence (15-19 years) in adult educational psychology quite deliberately because the focus of adult education in Australia is on the post-compulsory years of education. This encompasses adults as well as persons in their later teenage years and those who are involved in higher education, technical and further education, vocational training or even the senior years of schooling. Moreover, a demarcation between adolescence and early adulthood is not always helpful.

Table 1.2 Some situations where educational and developmental psychologists offer assistance (Source: Australian Psychological Society)

L A T E ADOLESCENCE	Adolescents, parents or others concerned with adolescents' welfare may seek help to deal with: • Conflict between adolescent and parent • Peer pressure • Career guidance • School to work transition • Sexuality issues • Drug involvement • Identity issues
ADULTHOOD	Individuals, their partners or employers may seek assistance • Parenting • Peer pressure • Career guidance • Unemployment • Sexuality issues • Drug involvement • Identity issues
SENIOR ADULTS	Elderly people or their adult children may seek information on • Healthy ageing • Decline in functioning • Dependency • Issues of loss or grief

What Is Educational Psychology?

You can see that educational psychology deals with a broad range of issues but principally those issues evolving from the areas of learning and instruction. It developed as a natural extension of the findings in general psychology and over time has developed its own identity as a field of research, study and application. It may be worthwhile to offer you a brief sketch of the background to modern educational psychology.

The beginnings of psychology come from philosophy and the personal study of mental events. The earliest approaches to the study of behaviour and learning were philosophical and this was also the Australian experience. For instance, at The University of Sydney, the first department of psychology evolved from the department of philosophy. Early researchers focused on introspection or what some would call reflection in adult education. This aspect, however, was found to be too subjective and over time psychology has tried to establish itself on a more objective basis. Experiments and various studies were introduced to provide an empirical (i.e., observational and experimental) basis for this new subject area. This emphasis distinguished it from the methods of philosophy and over time psychology emerged as a separate discipline related closely to the life sciences. Most research psychologists adopt a scientific approach to their field but it is also true that there are many other approaches that reflect changes in thinking over the last 50 years.

In the early days of psychology, it was not considered necessary for one to observe, assess, measure or to test ideas against reality. The development of psychology as an empirical field of study dated largely from the pioneering efforts of Wilhelm Wundt who established a psychological laboratory in Leipzig late last century. He set out to test ideas on introspection or self-analysis of thoughts and offered experimentation as a model for those who had an interest in studying human behaviour. Herman Ebbinghaus, for example, studied memory and in order to test recall, he developed lists of nonsense syllables such as NAV, ROC, SEB, GIX, VUF as a way of artificially studying memorisation.

This empirical approach to mental processes was adopted readily in the United States. The American psychologist William James also established a psychological laboratory at Harvard University. He applied psychology to areas such as religious experience as well as education. Edward Lee Thorndike, a student of James, is considered by many as the first educational psychologist. In 1903, he published *Educational Psychology* and some 10 years later produced a three-volume summary of empirical research in educational psychology.

The origins of educational psychology lie in attempts to apply psychological theory to classrooms. The development of intelligence tests is a good example of this effort. Alfred Binet and Henri Simon were asked by the French government to develop a method for identifying school pupils who would not benefit from regular instruction. They developed the first form of intelligence test that assessed the mental age of the pupil. Pupils attempted tasks that were designed to be as different as possible from the types of tasks learnt in school. The mental age of the pupil was dependent on being able to pass most of the tasks designed for their age group. The intelligence test was standardised and the judgement of success or failure was made more objective. This emphasis on empiricism, objectivity and standardisation are the hallmarks of modern psychology. Other pioneers in the field of educational psychology include: Jean Piaget, David Wechsler, B.F. Skinner and L.L. Thurstone.

Although learning and instruction have been the focus of educational psychology, the principal context has been learning in schools. As a result adult learning has been overlooked despite the fact that most Australians are aged 15 years and over and almost 2.5 million persons aged 15-64 are attending an educational institution (725,900 at school; 518,700 at TAFE; 928,800 in higher education; and 315,400 in other education – Source: Australian Bureau of Statistics, Education and Work, Catalogue No. 6227.0, May 2007).

What links can be made between adult education and adult educational psychology?

Adult education and educational psychology are often treated as quite unrelated and separate fields of study. Textbooks of educational psychology make little reference to adult education; and handbooks of adult and continuing education do not always make reference to educational psychology. This separation is unnecessary as well as unhelpful because there are obvious links that can be made between these disciplines especially in areas such as personal development, individual differences as well as the direct applications of psychology to adult learning situations.

Although adult education has contributed widely to social development and equality of opportunity, it may be considered able to benefit from technical models of learning and instruction that have an empirical basis as well as offering support or validity to many existing adult education approaches. Therefore educational psychology can be valuable for those working in adult education as a basis for ideas and offering support for existing practices. Educational psychology can likewise benefit not only from the applied and realistic context that adult education offers for testing its propositions but also from the experiences of adult educators.

About This Text

In this text there are chapters dealing with various aspects of educational psychology. The chapters form a sequence but you should also feel free to read those topics that are of greater interest or relevance to you.

In this book you will encounter different models of learning and behaviour. Do not be overwhelmed by these explanations because they look at behaviour from different vantage points and really operate at different levels of description. Firstly there are macro models which attempt to describe huge classes of responses and behaviours such as those in human identity. Then there are meso-level models that describe large categories of responding such as intelligence. Finally there are micro models that focus on individual responses such as stimulus response associations, memory or attention. Of course, even finer grained levels of analysis such as responding at the level of the human cell are also possible. The point is that you need to be aware that the descriptions and explanations in each chapter are by and large complementary. They view behaviour from different perspectives and at different levels of analysis. Each author has taken a particular perspective of behaviour for you that they consider pertinent to adult learning and development. There is no single unified theory of psychology that can explain, describe, predict or that can be used to control every aspect of behaviour; rather there are many models of behaviour that relate to the different topic areas. The complexity, wonder and richness of human learning and responding will be opened up by adopting these multiple viewpoints. Each one focuses in depth on one aspect and offers you some insight into how we respond to learning and instruction.

REFERENCES

Australian Psychological Society (1997). *The APS College of Educational and Developmental Psychologists* (Brochure), October 1997.

Kostanski, M. (2006). *Becoming a psychologist in Australia.* Bowen Hills, Queensland: Australian Academic Press.

O'Gorman J. M. (2007). *Psychology as a profession in Australia.* Bowen Hills, Queensland: Australian Academic Press.

James A. Athanasou
University of Technology, Sydney

MARK TENNANT

2. THE DEVELOPMENT OF IDENTITY IN THE ADULT YEARS

The desire to make sense of one's life is both powerful and widespread. What makes me the same person today as I was yesterday, last year, or perhaps twenty or thirty years ago? Have I developed and changed? In what important ways do I differ from when I was a younger? In what ways has my identity remained stable? Have there been milestones or critical events which have shaped my life, perhaps even transformed my identity? Or has my development been piecemeal and gradual, one phase of life merging imperceptibly into another? Indeed does it make sense to think of my life in terms of phases and stages? What have been the major influences in my life, those people and events which have shaped my beliefs, attitudes and values? And how do I see the continuity between my past, present and future self?

Questions such as the above are important and pertinent to individual lives, but such questions, and to varying degrees the attempted "answers", can also be found in various religious, literary, philosophical and psychological texts which attempt to set out or discover patterns to the general life course. Most commonly, the life course is described in terms of a sequence of stages through which one progresses, at least ideally. For example Aristotle proposed a three stage model, Solon divided life into nine seven-year stages, Confucius identified six stages, The Sayings of the Fathers (from the Talmud) contain fourteen stages, and Shakespeare, of course, has contributed his well known seven stages.

The psychological literature too contains propositions about the stages, tasks or phases of life. The purpose of this chapter is to explore ways of understanding the development of identity during adulthood. What are the major influences on identity formation? To what extent and how does identity change in the adult years? Can we say anything general about the way identity changes and develops as a part of the human condition irrespective of gender, history, culture, and race?

James A Athanasou (ed.), Adult Educational Psychology, 9–23
© *2008 Sense Publishers. All rights reserved.*

Part of the answer to these questions depends on what is meant by the term "identity". Rather than provide a definition of identity at the outset, this chapter progresses towards such a definition. In the first section some well known attempts in psychology to delineate the stages and phases of development are described and analysed. The second section outlines some ways in which our particular society and culture shapes our identity. The third describes a way of thinking about identity formation and change as both a psychological and social construction.

An understanding of identity in the adult years is important to the work of adult educators and trainers for a number of reasons. Firstly, adult education and training as a field of study and practice is influenced by prevailing views of adulthood (witness for example the concern with promoting autonomy and self direction and the importance placed on learning from experiences in work, family and community life). Secondly, education and training implies some kind of intervention in the lives of participants, and it is useful to locate this intervention in a lifespan framework. Indeed many adult education and training programs explicitly set out to promote personal change, often in connection with organisational or social change. Thirdly, adult education and training are integral to the concept of the lifelong learner, whose attributes are partly fashioned by our understanding of adult development. Finally, adult teaching and learning is arguably a site where there is an ongoing contestation of identities: between the teacher and learners and among learners as expectations about learning are negotiated. An understanding of identity in adulthood can assist adult educators to engage with this issue.

Life Phases

The stage, phase and task models of adult development which are most frequently cited are those of Maslow, Havighurst, Erikson, Levinson, Gould, Loevinger, and Labouvie-vief. Each of these models presents a descriptive account of development, an explanation of the fundamental processes underlying developmental progress, and a clear view of the end point of development: the mature, fully developed, psychologically healthy person.

In his early study, Levinson (1978) focused on the decade of 35-45 years. He believed that during this decade one made the shift from youth to middle age. Because he wanted to study each person intensively and examine their life in detail, he decided on a sample of only 40 subjects. He chose to study only men, partly because he acknowledged the difference between men and women and partly because he was interested in his own psychological development as a male. He divided his sample into four occupational subgroups of ten men each. He did this so that diverse sections of society could be represented and because he believed that work is of central psychological importance for the self. The four groups comprised ten hourly workers from two companies, ten executives from two companies, ten academic biologists from two universities, and ten novelists who had published at least two books. The sample comprised people from diverse social class, racial-ethnic-religious origins, and educational attainment (Levinson, 1978, pp. 12-13). Levinson described his research method as follows:

> A biographical interview combines aspects of a research interview, a clinical interview and a conversation between friends... Our essential method was to elicit the life stories of forty men, to construct biographies and to develop

generalizations based upon these biographies. ...In each case we began by immersing ourselves in the interview material and working toward an intuitive understanding of the man and his life. Gradually we tried more interpretive formulations and, going back and forth between the interviews and the analysis, came to a construction of the life course. (pp. 15-16)

Following the interviews it became apparent to Levinson that he was investigating, not only the years 35-45, but, retrospectively, the earlier years of the lives of these men. He therefore expanded the scope of his theorising to include the period from entry into adulthood until the late forties.

Levinson (1997) has since published a study of the lives of 45 women. He once again used intensive biographical interviewing: this time comprising 45 women: 15 "homemakers" and 30 "career women" divided into "businesswomen" and "academics". Despite finding important gender differences in life circumstances, the life course, and in ways of going through each developmental period (Levinson, 1997, p. 36), Levinson adhered to his general framework developed in relation to his study of men. The descriptive part of this framework is simply explained. The life cycle comprises a sequence of four eras, each lasting for approximately twenty five years. He also identified a number of developmental periods within these eras, concentrating on early and middle adulthood, as set out in Table 2.1.

Each era, according to Levinson, has its distinct and unifying character of living. Transitions between eras thus require a basic change in the character of one's life, and they may take between three and six years to complete. Within the broad eras are periods of development, each period being characterised by a set of tasks and an attempt to build or modify one's life structure. For example, in the early adult transition period the two primary tasks are, firstly, to move out of the pre-adult world and, secondly, to make a preliminary step into the adult world. Similarly during the "Culminating life structure for early adulthood" period, the two tasks are, firstly, to establish a niche in society, and, secondly, to work at making it: that is to strive for progress and advancement. A pervasive theme throughout the various periods is the existence of the "Dream": "...a vague sense of self-in-world, an imagined possibility of adult life that generates excitement and vitality" (Levinson, 1997, p.238). The place and nature of the "Dream" in one's life is constantly modified and revisited throughout the life course as the imagined self is compared with the world as it is lived.

Another fundamental process occurring throughout the life cycle is that of individuation. This refers to the changing relationship between self and the external world throughout the life course. It begins with the infant's dawning knowledge of its separate existence in a world of objects and "others". It is apparent in the tasks of the "early adult" transition; one of the principal tasks being to modify or terminate existing relationships with family and significant others and to reappraise and modify the self accordingly.

11

Table 2.1 *Eras and developmental periods (Levinson, 1997, p. 18; see also Levinson, 1978)*

Pre-adulthood: ages 0-22
Early adulthood: ages 17-45
        Early adult transition 17-22
        Entry life structure for early adulthood 22-28
        Age 30 transition 28-33
        Culminating life structure for early adulthood 33-40
Middle adulthood: ages 40-65
        Mid-life transition 40-45
        Entry life structure for middle adulthood 45-50
        Age 50 transition 50-55
        Culminating life structure for middle adulthood 55-60
Late adulthood: ages 60 - ? (late adult transition 60-65)

Indeed much of developmental progress is couched in terms of the changing nature of the relationship between self and others, such as mentor relationships, love and family relationships, and one's occupational relationships. In Mid-life, relationships are reappraised and this takes the form of a struggle between the polarities of attachment and separateness:

> We use the term 'attachment' in the broadest sense, in order to encompass all the forces that connect person and environment. To be attached is to be engaged, involved, needy, plugged in, seeking, rooted. ...At the opposite pole is separateness. This is not the same thing as isolation or aloneness. A person is separate when he is primarily involved in his inner world - a world of imagination, fantasy, play. His main interest is not in adapting to the "real world" but in constructing and exploring an imagined world, the enclosed world of his inner self. (Levinson, 1978, p.239)

Levinson (1978) viewed mid-life as a period where one needs to redress the dominance of attachment to the external world: to find a better balance between the needs of the self and the needs of society—a greater integration of separateness and attachment:

> Greater individuation allows him to be more separate from the world, to be more independent and self generating. But it also gives him the confidence and understanding to have more intense attachments in the world and to feel more fully a part of it. (Levinson, 1978, p.195)

Individuation is also apparent in the attempt to integrate polarities within the self, such as the masculine and feminine polarity, and the polarities between young and old, destruction and creation. The process of individuation is thus paradoxical: it points to a developmental move away from the world, but this independence and separateness is used to become a part of the world and to integrate previously separated aspects of the self.

In his more recent work, Levinson argued that the framework and developmental processes outlined above are common to both genders. However he did point out gender differences within this framework. For example, he developed the notion of gender splitting: the splitting of the domestic sphere from the public sphere, between the female homemaker and the male provider, between women's work and men's work, and between feminine and masculine in the individual psyche. He summarised his position thus:

> The differences between male and female are important, but so are the similarities - and so, too is the tremendous variety of individual lives, female as well as male. Even when a theme is characteristic of a particular group, there are still individual variations.... (Levinson, 1997, p. 202)

Levinson's theory has certainly helped to shape the discourse on the nature of adult development, irrespective of gender. It is for these reasons that there have been a number of subsequent studies (apart from his own) designed to evaluate the applicability of his theory to the experiences of women. But first it is worthwhile noting the position of Gilligan (1986) who was a pioneer critic of the gender bias evident in developmental theory in general. She argued that terms like "separateness", "autonomy", and "independence" are essentially male values and that females value relationships and responsibilities, empathy and attachment, and interdependence rather than independence. While the identity of boys is built upon contrast and separateness from their primary caregiver (which in most instances is female), the identity of girls is built on the perception of sameness and attachment to their primary caregiver:

> Consequently, relationships, and particularly issues of dependency, are experienced differently by women and men. For boys and men, separation and individuation are critically tied to gender identity since separation from the mother is essential for the development of masculinity. For girls and women, issues of femininity or feminine identity do not depend on the achievement of separation from the mother or on the progress of individuation. Since masculinity is defined through separation while femininity is defined through attachment, male gender identity is threatened by separation. Thus males tend to have difficulty with relationships, while females tend to have problems with individuation. The quality of embeddedness in social interaction and personal relationships that characterises women's lives in contrast to men's, however, becomes not only a descriptive difference but also a developmental liability when the milestones of childhood and adolescent development in the psychological literature are markers of increasing separation. Women's failure to separate then becomes by definition a failure to develop. (Gilligan, 1986, pp. 8-9)

Gilligan's argument is that womanhood is rarely equated with mature healthy adulthood in much of the developmental literature. This is because the idea of the healthy, developed personality is predominantly portrayed from a male perspective. What then have been the results of those studies which have explicitly aimed to validate or test Levinson's model using female subjects?

The results are rather mixed: in many cases the developmental periods described by Levinson were in fact useful as a framework for making sense of the experiences of the women studied; although there were significant differences among the women, for example, very few described a "Dream" in which career accomplishment plays a major role. Some studies found that the developmental tasks occurred within a different time frame (e.g., women resuming their undergraduate education in their 30s and 40s), or that there was greater variety in the balance of family and career commitments. Other studies did not find Levinson's developmental periods applicable to an all-female sample.

Caffarella and Olson (1993) also reviewed those studies which seek to document the life cycle of women in their own right. The results supported the view expressed by Gilligan that women, in contrast to men, place a high value on relationships and interdependence. Caffarella and Olson (1993) identified four major themes in this literature:
- The centrality of interpersonal relationships in the self-concept of women.
- The importance of role taking but uncertainty about the balancing of roles (e.g., mother, spouse, paid worker).
- Diverse and non-linear patterns of development with role discontinuities and change.
- Different cohorts with different developmental expectations (eg. young as opposed to middle-aged).

Caffarella and Olson (1993) concluded:

> A single linear pattern of psychosocial development appears to be almost the antithesis of what might be termed the "norm" for women. Rather, women's development is characterized by multiple patterns, role discontinuities, and a need to maintain a "fluid" sense of self. The importance of relationships and a sense of connectedness to others was seen as central to the overall developmental process throughout a women's lifespan. (p. 143)

This research on women's development highlights one of the limitations of the developmental literature: that it does not give sufficient emphasis to the power of social forces in shaping the course of people's lives. Indeed, most developmental psychologists portray development, in part, as a strengthening of the self in relation to the power of social forces. For example, a key term used in Levinson's description of individuation is "self generating". What is implied here is the idea that social influences on the formation of one's identity become weakened with developmental progress. That is, we become relatively liberated from the sociocultural constraints that shape our identity (Levinson referred to this as "detribalization" because it indicates the decreasing influence of the "tribe" or the family and community to which one belongs). Ultimately the test of developmental progress is the ascendancy of the self; its ability to stand apart and separate from the world.

This concept of autonomy is expressed in a variety of ways in different theories. In Maslow (1968) it is found in the construct of "self actualisation". In his words, once we have achieved a certain level of maturity we "are motivated primarily by trends to self actualisation (defined as on-going actualisation of potentials, capacities and talents, as fulfilment of a mission)" (p.25). A quality of self actualised people is their ability to transcend the environment rather than just coping with it.

Another example can be found in the work of Gould (1978) where adult development is based on our ability to separate ourselves from the false assumptions of childhood:

> By striving for a fuller, more independent adult consciousness, we trigger the angry demons of childhood consciousness. Growing and reformulating our self-definition becomes a dangerous act. It is the act of transformation.

Adult consciousness progresses between ages 16 and 50 by our mastering childhood fear, by learning to leash and modulate the childhood anger released by change. As we strive to live up to our full adult potential, we confront layer after layer of buried childhood pain. Adult consciousness then, evolves through a series of confrontations with our own primitive past. Finally, as adults we can begin to master demonic reality and rework the irrationalities of childhood. (p. 25)

Gould outlined the major false assumptions about ourselves that prevent us from being truly adult. We develop adult consciousness by shedding these assumptions. He distinguished periods in development in terms of the false assumptions which characterise the period. For example the major false assumption of the period "Leaving our parent's world" (16-22 years of age) is "I'll always belong to my parents and believe in their world". This assumption, like all the assumptions described, is a protective device which on the one hand is a source of comfort and security to the youth who is becoming independent, but on the other hand constitutes a limit on independence. From these early first steps towards independence there is a continual struggle with childhood false assumptions, until "the life of inner directedness finally prevails" at the close of mid-life. Gould (1978) remarked: "...we make the final passage from 'I am theirs' to 'I own myself'" (p. 310). Thus the self is able to transcend the world, so to speak, through transcending the false assumptions of childhood.

In the developmental stages proposed by Loevinger (1976) the theme of separation is all pervading. In the earliest stages, the pre-social and the symbiotic, the primary task is to differentiate self from non-self and to consolidate the sense of being a separate person. The impulsive stage is characterised by the attempt to impose the self on the world: because this naturally meets with resistance (often in the form of punishment), the child eventually learns some degree of self control. This self control is rather instrumental, designed to pursue impulses while protecting the self from punishment (hence the Self Protective stage). The Conformist stage occurs when the child starts to identify his or her own interests with that of the group. The child is a conformist and, at least on the surface, values niceness, helpfulness, and co-operation with others. At this point then, we can see that self identity is very much tied to social rules and regulations, but it is a rather blind conformism, without much sense of self awareness. During the Self aware and Conscientious stages which follow the child is more conscious of an inner life or self and that others have inner lives. With this awareness comes a sense of moral responsibility: "Along with the concepts of responsibility and obligations go the correlative concepts of privileges, rights and fairness. All of them imply a sense of choice rather than being a pawn of fate. The Conscientious person sees himself (herself) as the origin of his (her) own destiny." (Loevinger, 1976, p. 21).

The stages which follow; the Individualistic, Autonomous, and Integrated stages; begin with a heightened sense of individuality, one where inner conflicts and emotional dependence are recognised. During the Autonomous stage, the person finally accepts the inevitability of inner conflict and the conflict between needs and duties. There is also an acceptance of the limitations of autonomy and the inevitability of emotional interdependence. The Integrated stage brings with it a certain transcending of the conflicts apparent in the Autonomous stage, Loevinger referred to it as being similar to the concept of self-actualisation. It is interesting that Loevinger referred to autonomy as having a component of interdependence—indeed she distinguished the Individualistic from the Autonomous stage, it is thus a form of autonomy which goes beyond individualism.

Erikson (1959) is another developmental theorist who recognised that a strong sense of one's identity leads naturally to a capacity for interdependence. He described a sequence of eight stages which he terms "psychosocial stages". The first five stages are childhood stages and are basically an expansion of Freud's view of psycho sexual development, but with an explicit recognition of social influences. Erikson's view is that development occurs as the ego adjusts to meet the changing demands of society. These demands promote a struggle or crisis within the person, and it is this struggle which is the defining characteristic of a particular stage. The emotional crises, the values emerging form them, and the corresponding period of life (or "stage") are shown in Table 2.2.

Erikson (1959) spoke of the first social achievement of the infant as "his willingness to let the mother out of sight without undue anxiety or rage, because she has become an inner certainty as well as an outer predictability" (p. 61), he was referring here to the conflict between basic trust versus mistrust, and went on to explain that the state of trust "implies not only that one has learned to rely on the sameness and continuity of the outer providers, but also that one may trust oneself and the capacity of one's own organs to cope with urges" (p. 61). This is the first stage in developing a sense of identity: to trust the other and thereby trust oneself. In young adulthood the crises of intimacy versus isolation illustrates quite nicely how intimacy (read "interdependence") is predicated on a strong sense of personal identity. Intimacy is described by Erikson as a fusion of one's identity with that of others. If one avoids the experience of intimacy because of a fear of losing one's ego, then isolation and self-absorption will be the outcome. In Erikson's theory, then, once the identity crisis of adolescence has been addressed (identity versus role confusion), further developmental progress focuses on the relationship with the other rather than with the self. This is also true of the adulthood stage where there is a concern with establishing and guiding the next generation (generativity as opposed to stagnation), and the maturity stage, where the sense of ego integrity (as opposed to despair) which is cast very much in terms of the capacity to both accept oneself, and simultaneously transcend oneself and see one's personal life in its broader historical and cultural context.

All the above approaches attempt to chart the life course in terms of a sequence of phases or stages: periods of stability, equilibrium and balance alternate, in a largely predictable way, with periods of instability and transition. Accepting for the moment that the life course is indeed quite predictable and stable: what is the source of this predictability and stability? Is it the result of a natural psychological unfolding or maturation? Or is it the result of the living out of a set of largely social expectations which vary from one society to another and from one historical period to another? If the latter, to what extent do social and cultural groupings construct and then prescribe the life course patterns of their members?

Table 2.2 *Stages of Human Life (Erikson)*

Opposing Issues of Each Stage	Emerging Value	Period of Life
Basic Trust versus Mistrust	Hope	Infancy
Autonomy versus Shame and Doubt	Will	Early Childhood
Initiative versus Guilt	Purpose	Play age
Industry versus Inferiority	Competence	School Age
Identity versus Identity (Role) Confusion	Fidelity	Adolescence
Intimacy versus Isolation	Love	Young Adulthood
Generativity versus Stagnation (Self-	Care	Maturity Absorption)
Integrity versus Despair (and Disgust)	Wisdom	Old Age

Source: Based on Erikson (1978)

Social and Historical Structuring of Identity

Even the most casual observation reveals that age-graded norms, statuses and roles are a feature of social organisation. In different cultures and historical periods there are different conceptions of the stages of life, their boundaries, dimensions and divisions. There are different conceptions of what it means to be a fully developed person, the processes through which development occurs, and the significant tasks and marker events in life.

The concept of the life course with its distinct phases or stages of infancy, childhood, adolescence, adulthood and old age, is a central feature of modern western society. We live in an age graded society where much of social life is organised around socially standardised age categories. As a basic social institution, the life course may either impose external constraints on individual action (for example, sanctions for not behaving in an age-appropriate way), or, more importantly, shape the expectations we have about the proper progression of events and roles during the life course, and ultimately the way in which we experience ourselves and our relations with others. As a point of departure it is worth noting some features and propositions about age structuring and how it relates to the life course of individuals. First, age structuring is influenced by history and culture. The life course is structured in different ways in different historical periods and in different cultures. While the fact of age structuring may be universal, it takes particular forms in different cultures and historical periods.

In this sense the way in which age is structured is arbitrary rather than "natural". Secondly, age structures, like other social structures such as gender and class, become embedded in the psychology of individuals. Therefore an understanding of the life course requires an understanding of how individuals engage, and struggle with, socially prescribed age categories. Thirdly, socially constructed age categories change over time, as do the patterns of individual lives. But although individual and social changes interrelate, they are not necessarily synchronised, which means there can be disjunctions between individual and social change (for example, an individual becoming more concerned with moral and ethical issues in a society which is becoming increasingly materialist and competitive).

In western societies there is a history of state intervention and regulation which serves to maintain common life trajectories. The state legalises, standardises and provides institutional support for entry into and exit from formal education, employment, marriage, and even life itself (through birth and death certificates). There are a range of supporting mechanisms which distribute resources and opportunities to ensure an orderly progression through the various age categories and divisions within them. For example there are regulations concerning the commencement, progression and termination of schooling; funds are provided to assist with the immediate transition from secondary schooling to post-secondary education; scholarships, apprenticeships and job search schemes are often targeted towards a particular age category; mandatory retirement is combined with superannuation and other retirement schemes; and there are a host of welfare services targeted towards particular age groups. Non-state-controlled institutions also spread opportunities and resources to enhance an individual's progression through a socially approved, age-based timetable of "successful" career, family or personal development. This institutionalisation of age, and the co-option of society at large, makes it highly unlikely that individuals can chart alternative life courses, at least without considerable financial or personal cost.

There are of course forces which are moving against the continued institutionalisation of the life course such as demographic and technological change, changes in male/female relations, together with changes in the way work is organised. Thus the extent to which society continues to be age-graded in post-modern times is certainly open to question. However the essential point is that the state clearly has an interest in demarcating the roles, responsibilities and demands made upon different age categories.

In order to function effectively as members of society we need to identify correctly say, the gender and age categories to which others belong, and to assist others in identifying us as belonging to a particular gender or age category. This is because our interactions with others are partly based upon presumptions about gender or age. In the instance of gender, there are (among children at least) very few observable physical differences in most public situations. The signifiers used to position oneself as a boy or girl are dress, hairstyle, topics of conversation, choices of activity and such like. The physical differences associated with age categories are perhaps more obvious but nevertheless the same types of signifiers apply. Thus we speak of age inappropriate dress, hairstyle and activity in much the same way that we speak of these in relation to gender.

Furthermore, as with gender, one develops a posture and attitude towards oneself as belonging to an age category. By this we mean the taking on of psychological characteristics deemed to be appropriate for a given age category (for example, in old age it may be fragility, dependence, forgetfulness) which help govern relations with other age categories. Failure to act in an age appropriate manner is seen to be deviant by others, who at best will react with mild amusement, perplexity, or perhaps a few patronising comments, and at worst with anger, fear or moral outrage.

The concern here is not with why age categories seem to be a feature of social organisation, but rather with how we come to constitute ourselves as "belonging" to a particular age category. To begin with it seems reasonable to consider age category, like gender, to be primarily a social phenomenon. It has no direct physiological or biological basis and, as a social phenomenon, it is historically and culturally specific. How then is "age category" transmitted to new generations and through what processes can change occur in the way in which it is constituted? The position adopted here is that social phenomena are not transmitted genetically; they are transmitted socially and symbolically.

In the life course of any individual, social phenomena, like gender and age category, are historical givens. They are arbitrary in the sense that they are human creations, but they are nevertheless experienced as objectively real in much the same way that physical objects are experienced as real or natural. But whereas the physical world is experienced through perceiving and acting on things; the social world is experienced through interactions with others and through exposure to social institutions. In a sense we come to *know* the physical world, but we come to *be* the social world.

It is by interacting with others, and reacting to or participating in social institutions most importantly through symbolic processes, that we come to constitute ourselves as social beings. Accepting this position, our argument is that there is a discourse pertinent to "age category" in much the same way that there is a discourse pertinent to "gender". Like "gender", "age category" is sustained as a seemingly natural element of one's personal identity and subjective experience by learning the discursive practices in which all people are positioned on an age-graded continuum (see Davies, 1989). Furthermore, "gender" and "age category" intersect. The "male" life course is constructed very differently from the "female" life course and gender based relations of dominance and power are embedded in the discourse associated with age categories (see Gilligan 1986).

If discourse lies at the heart of the process, how is change possible? It seems that it is only possible through adopting new and different forms of discourse. This is precisely the issue addressed by a number of contemporary psychologists seeking to understand identity change and development from a narrative perspective (Burman, 1994; Burman & Parker, 1993; Gergen, 1997; McAdams, 1996; Shotter & Gergen, 1989; White, 1989).

Identity as an Ongoing Narrative Project in Adulthood

For McAdams (1996) identity is the sense of unity, coherence and purpose in life: it is the experience of a continuous, coherent self, a self which remains essentially the same from one situation to the next and over time; and which is unique, integrated, and different from but related to other selves. In contemporary western society, the construction of such a self has become problematic, mainly because of the constantly changing and multiple of choices we face. It is no longer true that our identity is prescribed or conferred, rather selves are made:

> one's very identity becomes a product or project that is fashioned and sculpted, not unlike a work of art moreover.. .the developing self seeks a temporal coherence. If the self keeps changing over the long journey of life, then it may be incumbent on the person to find or construct some form of life coherence and continuity to make this change make sense. (McAdams, 1996, pp. 296-297)

In this view identity is essentially a psychosocially constructed narrative which integrates the reconstructed past, perceived present, and anticipated future: in short it is a story of the self. McAdams considered identity to be the third of three levels in gaining and understanding of the person: the other two levels being personality traits (which are broad, comparative dimensions of personality e.g., extraversion, dominance, neuroticism) and personal concerns, which comprise a variety of psychological constructs such as motives, values, defence mechanism, attachment styles: strategies people use which may differ according to time, place and context (unlike traits). For example, one's achievement motivation may only come into play in sport but not in a professional context or vice versa. McAdams argued that as one moves from level one to level two, there is a movement towards a more detailed and nuanced understanding of the person over time and in particular situations. What is missing however is the concept of identity. An understanding of persons is not complete without understanding of persons' overall unity, purpose and meaning in life.

In McAdams' view, identity is self reflexively authored, made, explored and constructed (note the contrast with the more post-modern view of selves as residing in narratives which surround and define them- see Gergen, 1997). This view led him to examine the life course as a narrative or story. He defined the life story formally as: "an internalised and evolving narrative of the self that incorporates the reconstructed past, perceived present, and anticipated future" (p. 307) It is a psychosocial construction in the sense that it is jointly authored by the person and his or her defining culture. Life stories are based on fact but they go beyond mere facts by rendering past, present and future meaningful and coherent in sometimes imaginative ways. The basic function of a life story is integration - it binds together disparate elements of the self. Based on an analysis of over 200 accounts of life-story interviews, McAdams (1985, 1987, 1993) identified the following common features:

- Narrative tone - the emotional tone or attitude. e.g., pessimism, optimism, tragedy, romance, irony.
- Imagery - the metaphors and similes that provide the narrative with a distinctive feel.
- Theme - the kinds of things that are pursued in the narrative. e.g., power, love, recognition, achievement.
- Ideological setting - a moral stance or view of the "good" from which judgements are made of one's life and the lives of others.
- Nuclear episodes - scenes and events which stand out in the narrative, normally high points or low points or turning points in the narrative.
- *Imagos* - and idealised personification of the self, drawing on archetypal characters and contemporary role models.

The above features provide a way into an understanding of the life story. But of particular interest is the developmental trajectory of life stories. How do life stories change over time? Here McAdams distinguished between:

- The pre-narrative era, where infants, children and adolescents gather materials for future self stories but are not really engaged in the construction of identity proper.
- The narrative era, which runs from the beginning of the creation of a self defining life story (in late adolescence or early adulthood) and continues through most of the adult years.
- The post-narrative era, where life is reviewed and evaluated as a story which is near completion.

In the first approach to the construction of a narrative in early adulthood, the typical move is to:

- organise personal values into an ideological system

- select key scenes from the past that explain one's contemporary and anticipated future self (e.g., "it was a real turning point when the music teacher said to me 'you can do it'- it was her confidence in me which got me going and now I am embarking on a promising music career").

In their 20s and 30s, many contemporary adults fashion stories around various social roles (*imagos*), for example caregiver, partner, and worker.

Midlife brings with it concerns for harmony and reconciliation in the life story and the beginning of a creation of the end of the narrative. Identity formation may turn now to issues of generativity as people begin to define themselves in terms of their legacies. The point being made by McAdams is that for the most part of adult life, life stories are continually under construction, but that different themes and concerns emerge at different ages, and there are periods of intensive and less intensive "identity work" or "selfing". Moreover there are no dominant stories, but rather stories associated with the diverse ways in which contemporary adults live their lives. He did however stipulate the qualities of the "good" story, at least from a mental health perspective. The elements of such a story are:

- Coherence - the extent to which the story makes sense in its own terms
- Openness - tolerance for change and ambiguity
- Credibility - grounded in the real world
- Differentiation - complex and multifaceted
- Reconciliation - harmony and resolution amongst the multiplicity of self
- Generative integration - a sense of being a productive and contributing member of society.

In many ways McAdams' approach is not too dissimilar to the life stage and phase theories described earlier, after all, one of the main research tools used was the biographical interview, and so the raw data for such theories were the stories that people told about themselves. The main difference is that McAdams is not attempting to discover the "true" story of adult identity development, there are multiple ways in which people find coherence and continuity and meaning in their lives. Also, it is not as if individuals "discover" their "true" inner selves through the narratives they construct. It is not the true or authentic self which is discovered through reflection on one's life experience, instead experience is viewed as a story which can be reinterpreted and re-assessed. Indeed because the self remains situated in history and culture, it is continually open to re-inscription and re-formulation. But this doesn't mean we can ascribe any meaning to our experiences or that we can create any identity we choose. We need to give a plausible reading to our experiences, one which is credible and which, ideally, contains the essential elements of the "good" story described above.

Summary

Identity is best understood as the self's sense of continuity, coherence and meaning. Identity work or "selfing" is an ongoing project in the adult years and it involves the construction and continual reconstruction of narratives or stories about one's life. Such narratives are jointly authored by the individual and his or her culture. These narratives may reveal different concerns at different stages or phases of life, but these differences are strongly linked to cultural and historical differences. Ultimately, any practices which impact or intervene in the process of identity work, such as education, counselling and various kinds of therapy, must necessarily make judgements about what constitutes the "good" life story.

REFERENCES

Burman, E. (1994). *Deconstructing developmental psychology*. London: Routledge.

Burman, E., & Parker, I. (Eds.) (1993). *Discourse analytic research: Repertoires and readings of texts in action*. London: Routledge.

Caffarella, R., & Olson, S. (1993). Psychosocial development of women. *Adult Education Quarterly*, *43*, 125-151.

Davies, B. (1989). *Frogs and snails and feminist tales*. Sydney: Allen & Unwin

Erikson, E. H. (1959). Identity and the life cycle. *Psychological Issues, 1*, (Monograph No. 1).

Erikson, E. H. (Ed.) (1978). *Adulthood*. NY: Norton.

Gergen, M. (1997). Life stories: pieces of a dream. In Gergen, M. and Davis, S. (Eds.), *Toward a new psychology of gender* (pp.203-221). NY: Routledge.

Gilligan, C. (1986). *In a different voice*. Cambridge: Harvard University Press.

Gould, R. (1978). *Transformations: Growth and change in adult life*. NY: Simon and Schuster.

Levinson, D. (1978). *The seasons of a man's life*. NY: Knopf.

Levinson, D. (1997). *The season's of a woman's life*. NY: Ballantine.

Loevinger, J. (1976). *Ego development*. San Francisco: Jossey-Bass.

Maslow, A. (1968). *Towards of a psychology of being*. NY: Van Nostrand.

McAdams, D. (1985). *Power, intimacy and the life story: Personological inquiries into the life story*. NY: Guilford.

McAdams, D. (1987). A life-story model of identity. In R. Hogan and W. Jones (Eds.), *Perpectives in personality* (pp. 15-50). Greenwich, CT: JAI.

McAdams, D. (1993). *The stories we live by: Personal myths and the making of the self*. NY: Morrow.

McAdams, D. (1996). Personality, modernity, and the storied self: A contemporary framework for studying persons. *Psychological Inquiry, 7*, 295-321.

Shotter, J., & Gergen, K. (1989). *Texts of identity*. London: Sage.

White, M. (1989). *Selected papers*. Adelaide: Dulwich Centre Publications.

Further reading

Epston, D., & White, M. (1992). *Experience, contradiction, narrative and imagination*. Selected papers of David Epston and Michael White 1989- 1991. Adelaide: Dulwich Centre Publications.

Freeman, M. (1993). *Rewriting the self: History, memory, narrative*. London: Routledge.

Gergen, K. (1993). *Refiguring self and psychology*. Aldershot, Hants; Dartmouth.

Gergen, M., & Davis, S. (Eds.), (1997). *Toward a new psychology of gender*. NY: Routledge.

Labouvie-Vief, G. (1994). *Psyche and Eros: Mind and gender in the life course*. Cambridge: Cambridge University Press.

Tennant, M. (1997). *Psychology and adult learning* (2nd ed.). London: Routledge.

Tennant, M. & Pogson, P. (1995). *Learning and change in the adult years: A developmental perspective*. San Francisco: Jossey-Bass.

Review Questions

The following questions are designed to test your understanding of the content of this chapter. Answers can all be checked by referring to the relevant sections.

1. What is the main criticism of Levinson's notion of "individuation" as a marker of development?
2. What is a consistent finding in relation to gender differences in development?
3. What, according to Gould, is the key to developmental progress?
4. Compare and contrast Loevinger's idea of the "autonomous stage" with

Maslow's concept of "self actualisation".

5. What is the defining characteristic of each stage of Erikson's theory of development?
6. In what sense is the development of identity a "social construction"?
7. What is McAdams' view of identity and its development?
8. What, for McAdams, are the elements of the "good" life story?

Exercises

1. What kinds of expectations are placed on you as an adult educator/trainer? Are there conflicting or unrealistic expectations? How do these expectations influence your view of yourself as an adult educator/ trainer?
2. Do you have a role in promoting learner change? If so, does this involve changes to the way learners think about themselves? What techniques or methods do you use to promote such change?
3. How would you describe the "dreams" (in Levinson's sense) of your learners? How do such dreams influence your practice as an adult educator/trainer?
4. In what ways would you like your professional or personal identity to change? What does this reveal about your view of "developmental progress"?

About the Author

Mark Tennant is Professor of Adult Education at the University of Technology, Sydney. He has an international reputation in the area of adult teaching and learning. His two major books in this area are *Psychology and Adult Learning,* which won the Houle Award for literature in adult education in 1990 (Routledge, second edition, 1997); and *Learning and Change in the Adult Years: A developmental perspective* (Jossey-Bass, 1995, with Philip Pogson). In addition he has edited a book titled *Adult and Continuing Education in Australia* (Routledge, 1991), he has been an editor of the journal *Studies in Continuing Education,* and he is a consulting editor for the journal *Adult Education Quarterly.* His main concern in his writing has been on the application of the literature on adult development and learning to an understanding of adult education practice. He has held a number of honorary appointments in universities overseas, including Visiting Fellow at the University of Warwick, Visiting Scholar at Syracuse University, Visiting Professor at Hokkaido University, Visiting Professor at the University of British Columbia, and Distinguished International Visiting Professor at the University of Alaska.

Mark Tennant
University of Technology, Sydney

SHIRLEY SAUNDERS

3. SOCIAL PSYCHOLOGY OF ADULT LEARNING

In this chapter we investigate connections between the individual adult learner and the social environment in order to explore how adults learn from others in a variety of social learning contexts. We are all aware that learning from others can be extremely useful and personally relevant as well as disappointing and unproductive. Indeed what adults learn and how they feel about learning can be founded in their relationships with other people. For instance, in their interactions with other people, adults can be motivated and supported to learn successfully or can be left feeling confused and frustrated. These quite different outcomes raise a number of issues for adult education practice and shape the discussion in this chapter. How does the presence of others affect adult learning? What characteristics of the social environment influence adult learning? How can adult educators make use of research findings in social psychology to facilitate learning for adults in formal and informal social settings of learning?

To explore these questions we commence with themes that have general applicability to learning from others, both one-on-one and in groups. We then focus on themes that are particularly relevant for learning in group contexts. After an overview of research in social psychology, we discuss social learning theory, social comparison theory, social judgment theory, self disclosure, feedback and learning conversations. Next we look more closely at specific influences on learning in group settings. We investigate aspects of the nature and structural characteristics of a group which can influence adult learning. We also discuss how group contexts can facilitate or inhibit learning for adults. Finally, we develop a profile for an effective learning group which integrates earlier themes on psychological and social influences on adult learning and specific features of group learning. In addition, throughout the chapter, we consider some of the main

James A Athanasou (ed.), Adult Educational Psychology, 25–70
© 2008 Sense Publishers. All rights reserved.

research findings from studies in social psychology, including group dynamics, which have implications for adult education practice.

Learning in Social Contexts

Human beings have an innate capability for learning about self identity, techniques for survival and use of language. Much of this learning depends on interaction with other people. Indeed it has been claimed that the only way we learn who we are is by communication with others (Stewart, 1990). Two studies of children who were deprived of human contact in early childhood (one in the nineteenth century and one in the twentieth century) show that the children had no sense of identity as a human being, were only able to make crude noises and had no behaviour normally associated with human social skills (Rymer, 1993; Shattuck, 1980). Significant learning about our sense of identity and our roles comes from our social experience with others and from the way others define us (Adler & Rodman, 1994). The influence of social contexts on adult learning has been traditionally studied by social psychologists seeking to understand human learning by linking a person's innate capacities for learning to priorities for learning from the social milieu.

In 1968, Gordon Allport, in an analysis of the history of social psychology, commented that social psychologists "regard their discipline as an attempt to understand how the thought, feeling, and behaviour of individuals are influenced by the actual, imagined or implied presence of others" (Allport, 1968, p. 3). Adults learn extensively from belonging to and participating in groups of people on the job, at university and college, at home and for recreation. Even when we work on something on our own what we learn may be affected by our perceptions of the reactions of others to our individual efforts. What adults learn and remember can be greatly influenced by reinforcement from the social context of the learning and by perceptions of the social implications including those for relationships. In social interactions adults self disclose, using verbal and nonverbal communication, to give and receive feedback and to learn about themselves and others. In the next section we thus review some of the research findings from social psychology on how adults learn in complex dynamic social environments.

Adult Learning and Research in Social Psychology

How can a study of research trends in social psychology help adult educators to understand the learning process? Let us begin by looking at the scope of social psychology. "Social psychology is the scientific study of the way individuals think, feel and behave in social situations" (Brehm & Kassin, 1993, p. 5). The focus of social psychology is the study of human behaviour in social situations including how people perceive, interact, influence and learn. Consequently, research in social psychology is concerned with "the reciprocal influence of persons and their social environments" (Gold, 1997, p. 9) and the resulting impact on adult learning. Essentially, social psychologists are concerned with understanding, explaining and predicting human social behaviour so they research aspects of a person's capacity to learn and the influence of others, whether present or not, on learning. In social psychological research there is thus an interface between the psychological and the social as explanations of human behaviour and learning. Social psychologists have investigated psychological factors in learning such as motivation, attitudes, trust and self disclosure as well as social influences on learning such as the effects of group processes and the experience of solving problems and making decisions in groups.

One debate in social psychology which integrated both psychological and social approaches to the study of human behaviour was concerned with the impact of the social environment on a person's motivation for learning, selection of learning goals and resourcefulness to achieve that learning (Olson, Herman & Zanna, 1986). It was argued that any theory of human learning must take into account both the goals and the resources of the learner. The nature and extent of people's resourcefulness to take advantage of opportunities for learning can be greatly affected by the influence of their social environments. Social class, for instance, has implications for access to resources and formation of attitudes towards various types and methods of learning and development. One group in society might be oriented towards supporting learning by formal study at university while another might promote learning through apprenticeships and technical education. Adults who are supporting their own learning will make choices depending on their own and significant others' attitudes and the range of available resources. Their abilities as individuals to form learning goals, to identify and organise resources and to make decisions about learning are framed in a social context.

The dynamic process whereby the social environment influences people's motives for choosing goals and seeking learning to achieve these goals has thus been of particular interest to social psychologists. Reciprocally, people's attempts to satisfy their motives change the environment as well as themselves. The influence of motivation on learning has been conceptualised and explained in various ways. To explore these views, complete the following exercise and then discuss the relationship between individual motives, the social environment and adult learning.

Exercise

Read the following short extract on the connection between motivation and learning and then answer the questions:

> [Motives] may all be rooted in unlearned needs like hunger and thirst and the processes by which individuals become motivated may involve not only learning but also perception, cognition and so forth. However it is the necessity of their being learned and the function of the social environment in the learning process that make motives of central interest in social psychology. That motives are learnt is one of their crucial characteristics because it is partly through shaping and maintaining motives that the social environment influences the individual. Much of the pleasure and pain that individuals experience and learn to anticipate originate in their interaction with their social environments. The motives thereby engendered direct them toward one goal or another and cause them to persist in doing something or to stop doing it and start doing something else. (Gold, 1997, p. 60)

Questions
- Why are motives of interest to the social psychology of adult learning?
- How can educators take motives into account in adult learning programs?
- What are some issues which adult educators might investigate to enhance their understanding of motivation and adult learning?

Some of the questions which adult educators may explore to enhance their understanding of psychological and social influences on motivation and adult learning may include:

– What is the nature of the influence of the social environment on an adult learner's personal motivation to define and to achieve learning outcomes?
– How does an adult learner's personal motivation influence that adult's resourcefulness to achieve the learning outcome?
– How might an adult educator influence an adult's personal motivation to enhance the adult's potential for learning?
– What is the role of learning in groups for developing personal motivation and for suggesting changes in the social environment?

We shall be investigating these questions in this chapter by considering, for example, the role of the adult educator as a model for learning and by looking more closely at factors in group dynamics that make an impact on the potential for adults to learn in groups. You will also find further discussion of these issues in the later chapter in this book on motivation and adult learning. An adult's personal motives for achieving specific learning outcomes are closely related to the adult's attitudes towards learning, work and life. One experienced adult educator was heard to remark "Eighty per cent of adult education is concerned with attitude change." While this claim is purely anecdotal, it indicates an adult educator's strong view that attitudes are at the foundation of learning, performance and development of individual potential.

Historically, the study of attitudes remains "the most constant topic of social psychology" (Gold, 1997, p. 14) and again illustrates the interface between psychological and social explanations of learning. Attitude changes in individuals have been studied in group learning contexts. There have been numerous studies linking attitude change to explanations of the social construction of the self including self-conception, self-perception and self-justification (for example: Bem, 1967, 1972; Cooley, 1922; Goffman, 1959, 1967; Gordon, 1968; James, 1890; McGuire & McGuire, 1981; Mead, 1934; Sullivan, 1953). Other research in social psychology has focused on understanding various psychological features of the self which influence learning in group contexts such as the tendency to conform to group norms, personal satisfaction with groups, interpersonal relationships in groups and the use of groups as the framework for assessing one's own learning and development (Shaw, 1981). The social psychology of adult learning should therefore reflect the interaction between the psychological and the social by integrating values, attitudes, beliefs, identities, motives and perceptions with social roles, social organisation, culture, interpersonal relations and resources (Gold, 1997, p. 17).

Adults gather together in a wide variety of social groups to meet their individual needs and goals. Nevertheless, belonging to groups does not always result in productive or enjoyable learning experiences for adults. While being part of a team can be very rewarding, it is not always possible for adults to withdraw or resign from a team or group. Such people then come under the influence of a range of powerful forces in the group that inevitably affect their learning. Research on group dynamics therefore helps adult educators to understand issues such as:

– What is the nature of the interactive learning that takes place in formal and informal groups?
– What are group dynamics and how do group processes affect adult learning?

– How can adult educators facilitate adult learning in groups by applying an understanding of the dynamics of learning in groups?

Social psychologists who have focused on group dynamics have been concerned to identify and explain the characteristics of effective groups where adults can learn and develop their potential. The proliferation of team-based structures in the workplace where performances of the team and the people within it are judged and where the team is held accountable for achieving standards of productivity and quality provides a powerful incentive for adults to learn about group dynamics. How do adults facilitate group process to make an appropriate decision by consensus and how do adults learn from this experience? Adults need to learn how to learn together synergistically to produce higher quality solutions than would be possible by working and learning alone.

There is a history in social psychology from the 1930s of studies on the powerful influences exerted by groups on what individuals learn from their experience of being in a group (Cragan & Wright, 1991). Three classic experimental studies illustrate this research. One of the earliest studies of social influence was Muzafer Sherif's study in 1935 of adults' perceptions of the apparent movement of a stationary point of light. (This is known as the autokinetic effect where a stationary point of light in a darkened room appears to move between 50 and 150mm.) The results of this visual illusion showed that when people viewed the light by themselves their individual estimates of its movement varied across a range. These differences converged when people viewed the light source in groups. There seemed to be a common norm of perception in the group which persisted when people were asked again to judge the movement of the light individually. The tendency towards conformity seemed to be a function of the dynamics of the group (Sherif, 1935).

A second classic experimental study involved the deception of an unsuspecting member of a group. In the 1950s Solomon Asch conducted a series of experiments on conformity in which a naive subject was presented with a vertical line and was asked to select a matching vertical line from three others. Subjects matched the vertical line easily when working individually. However, when the naive subject was part of a group where everyone else chose an incorrect matching line, as agreed beforehand with the experimenter, approximately one third of the naive subjects went along with the group consensus and chose the incorrect line for at least half of the trials. If there was another group member who judged correctly, against the majority of the confederates in the group, then the degree of conformity of the naive subject was greatly reduced. The dynamics of the group appeared to exert conformity on the members in three ways: for some naive subjects an actual distortion of their perception seemed to occur; for some there was a realisation that their perception was different but they accepted that the group must be correct; for others there was a reluctance to appear to be different from the group in spite of believing that the group perception was wrong (Asch, 1956). These types of yielding alert us to other studies of group influence referred to by Tennant (1997): internalisation where the individual adopts the values of the group; identification where the individual wants to be like the group; and compliance where the individual conforms to the group norms to avoid rejection. All these types of group influence have the potential to affect significantly an adult's capacity for learning in a group context.

A third classic experimental study on group influence on individual decision making and attitude change was carried out by Kurt Lewin (1948). Lewin predicted from his field theory of human behaviour and learning developed in the 1930s (Lewin, 1935, 1951) that individuals would be more likely to learn and change their attitudes and behaviour if they had interacted in a group where norms were formed collaboratively. According to Lewin's field theory, behaviour and learning are considered to be a function of the interaction between the person (psychological differences among individuals) and the environment (differences among external situations). Lewin set up two separate methods of learning - discussion groups and lectures - to research a social problem identified by the US government during the Second World War: how to change American eating habits. Lewin demonstrated that the women involved in the study were more likely to consider changes in diet and to serve meals of offal (so that beef could be saved for the armed forces) if they had shared ideas and opinions in group discussions where there were group norms supporting the war effort. In contrast, women who attended a lecture on the desirability of diet change and preparation of meals using offal were much less likely to prepare the new meals. Actual preparation of the new meals a week after the learning varied from 32 % for those participating in the group discussion to 3% for those attending the lecture. Through this important study Lewin demonstrated that social psychology could be applied to the analysis and possible solution of social problems. The foundation was thus laid for the interactionist or systemic perspective on human behaviour and learning where behaviour is viewed as a function of the interaction between people and their environments or as a product of reciprocal feedback within systems (Bateson, 1979).

In summary, early research in social psychology was very much concerned with how adults can learn to change their attitudes and behaviour through participation in a variety of group learning experiences. Results showed that adults learnt a great deal and were persuaded to change their behaviour through discussions in small cohesive groups of peers more than by impersonal lectures from experts to an audience (Lewin, 1948). This research stimulated many investigations of adult learning in interactive group communication contexts where adults' experience is acknowledged to create a collaborative learning experience (Johnson & Johnson, 1997). In a spirit of cooperation adults can negotiate the topic, method and type of learning that will take place by mutual agreement or consensus, especially in a cohesive group (Jaques, 1992). Nevertheless, learning in a cohesive group is not without its problems as we shall see later in the chapter.

The vast literature on the influence of group dynamics on the thoughts, feelings, attitudes and behaviour of individual group members serves to remind us "how individual choice and independent action are shaped and constrained by groups" (Tennant, 1997, p. 113) and how group dynamics can have significant effects on adult learning in groups. American researchers Johnson & Johnson (1997) have been pre-eminent in integrating theory and practice in this area of social psychology. Their work on group theory and group skills is highly recommended for educators who wish to develop skills in group facilitation to enhance adult learning.

So far we have seen that the major research trend in social psychology from after the Second World War to the present has been to endeavour to provide dynamic explanations of human cognition and behaviour by integrating explanations of a wide variety of characteristics within the person with influences from the social situation in which the person learns. From 1946 to 1960, social psychologists investigated how the social presence of others and belonging to groups influenced learning about: prejudice and stereotyping (Allport, 1958); conformity and person perception (Asch, 1956); the need for consistency between thoughts/behaviour (cognitive dissonance) (Festinger, 1957); how we learn by comparing ourselves to other people(social comparison) (Festinger, 1954); the tendency to assign motives to others (attribution theory) and to view relationships in terms of a balance between likes and dislikes (balance theory) (Heider, 1958); attitude formation and change (Hovland, Harvey & Sherif, 1957); persuasion (Hovland, Janis & Kelley, 1953); and assessment of the rewards and costs in a social exchange (Thibaut & Kelley, 1959).

From 1961 to 1975 social psychologists extended their work on determining the effects of social influence on learning by investigating: how people thought and felt about themselves and others including their physical attractiveness (Berscheid & Walster, 1974; Dion, 1972; Schachter, 1964); how people learn from interactions in groups (Shaw, 1971); and how people are affected by social settings in terms of aggression (Bandura, 1973, 1983) and stress (Glass & Singer, 1972).

Since 1975 the social cognition approach has grown in influence on research in social psychology (Barone, Maddux & Snyder, 1997). According to cognitive theory, we can understand a person's behaviour and learning only by knowing how that person perceives the world. People are cognitive beings who form cognitive structures (that is, ways of organising experience) and a person's behaviour and learning is influenced by memories, cognitive structure and views of events in life. Cognitive researchers are particularly interested in concepts such as knowing, meaning and understanding and in the internal cognitive processes that must be inferred rather than directly observed. In cognitive theory the focus is on the study of how people perceive, remember and interpret information about themselves and others. Three areas of theory and research in social cognition relevant to our discussion are perceptions of self, perceptions of individual others and perceptions of groups (Hewes & Planalp, 1987; Shaw & Costanzo, 1982). Specific areas of research have focused on the role of inference in understanding messages (Sperber & Wilson, 1986), attribution theory (Burleson, 1986; Siebold & Spitzberg, 1981) and judgments of arguments, behaviour and attitudes (Martin & Tesser, 1992; Petty & Cacioppo, 1986).

Other recent work in social psychology has focused on motivation and emotion. The thoughts, actions and learning of human beings, as social animals, are regarded as being determined by needs and emotions. For example, in trying to explain why some people help in emergencies, social psychologists have emphasised emotional arousal as a key motivator (Piliavin, Dovidio, Gaertner & Clark, 1981). This is in contrast to the more rational, analytical aspects of human behaviour and learning captured in the social cognition approach where standards of behaviour and decision making processes are also considered as factors influencing helping (Barone, Maddux & Snyder, 1997; Coke, Batson & McDavis, 1978). In the 1990s both approaches to social psychology are influential as social psychologists attempt to take into account the whole person - who thinks, desires and feels (Brehm & Kassin, 1993, p. 10).

In this review of contemporary research in social psychology the major areas of investigation of interest to adult educators seeking to understand the process of adult learning may be summarised as:
- studies that seek to explain adult learning by linking psychological characteristics in the person to influences from the social environment;
- studies that explore the influence on adult learning of the actual or implied presence of others;
- studies of the reciprocal influence of persons and their social environments on adult learning;
- studies applying learning principles such as association and conditioning, reinforcement and reward, and imitation and modelling to adult learning in a social context;
- studies of the impact of the social environment on a person's motivation and resourcefulness for learning;
- studies of the origin and influence of needs and emotion on adult learning in social contexts;
- studies of the influence of the nature and dynamics of a group context on adult learning;
- studies of dynamics within a group that affect adult learning such as conformity, uniformity and compliance;
- studies on attitude formation and change and the influence of attitude for learning individually and in groups;
- studies of how adults learn to make judgments and develop arguments in social contexts;
- studies of how adults learn through problem solving and decision making in groups.

These are some of the research directions for a study of the social psychology of adult learning yet, even so, it is rare to find an entry on "adult learning" in the indexes of publications on social psychology (see, for example, Brehm & Kassin, 1993; Deaux & Wrightsman, 1984; Gold, 1997; McKnight & Sutton, 1994). On the other hand, it is normal to find an entry on "social learning" in these publications which is usually confined to one or two pages in contrast to whole sections on group dynamics, the social psychology of sexual behaviour and the physical environment and social behaviour. In the following section we explain what social psychologists have covered in these rather brief sections on social learning theory and how the theory applies to adult learning contexts and the role of the adult educator. Social learning theory has implications for the ways that adults learn from each other one-on-one, in groups and even from people portrayed in the visual media.

Social Learning Theory

Social learning theory is based on the assumption that people learn how to behave by observing others. The concept of "modelling" and learning through imitation are major features of the theory (Bandura, 1965, 1977, 1986; Bandura & Walters, 1963). For a fuller discussion of the nature of the theory see the chapter by Ian Cornford on "Social Learning Theory". There are many applications of the theory for adult learning. For example, implications for effective communication management and development of expertise are discussed in a later chapter by

Michael Kaye on "Interactive Learning and Human Communication". Educators, adult learners and children are all important sources of modelling in social contexts where formal and informal learning may take place. The value and process of adult learning, both formal and informal, which is facilitated in cooperative and collaborative ways particularly through social learning in the workplace and classroom, is discussed in these other chapters.

In essence, social learning theory is the view that "behaviour is learned through observation of others as well as through the direct experience of rewards and punishments" (Brehm & Kassin, 1993, p. 355). In other words, according to social learning theory, while we may learn from receiving rewards and punishments, we also learn from the example of others. In this way, social learning theory emphasises both the person and the environment as sources of learning in contrast to a needs theory of learning which explains learning in terms of a person's internal motives or needs or a behavioural modification theory of learning which focuses on contingent reinforcement from the environment (Furnham, 1997, p. 265).

The power of models to affect learning is a central tenet of social learning theory. Human role models can influence learning about pro-social, helpful behaviour and antisocial, aggressive behaviour (Bandura, 1973, 1983). While learning may take place from the example of others, a distinction needs to be made between learning and performance. Adults can learn about behaviour from human models but may not perform that behaviour, depending on perceptions of the situation including rewards and punishments. Individuals have traits, thoughts, feelings and attitudes which mediate their experience of the environment thus affecting learning. So while people learn about ideas, beliefs and behaviours from other role models, what is learnt and performed is affected by individual differences. Consequently the effect of individual differences on learning means that "not everyone is equally likely to model the behaviour of others, nor is everyone likely to serve as a model" (Furnham, 1997, p. 304).

It is also important for adult educators to recognise that social learning theory holds that attitudes can be learnt through examining the behaviour of a model. People select other people as sources of information for forming their attitudes and behaviours (Furnham, 1997, p. 304). For example, a person's attitude to job satisfaction and to learning can be highly influenced by the perceived attitudes of models such as workmates and educators. Congruency (or matching) between an educator's explanations of sound practice and the actual carrying out of that practice in the classroom or learning environment is important for the learning of appropriate attitudes by learners who may regard the educator as a model. The old adage of "practise what you preach" comes into effect and learners can become very cynical if, for example, an educator expresses an attitude advocating flexible delivery but then makes no provision for this in a teaching method.

If there is a discrepancy between espoused theory and theory in use (Schön, 1983), what is an adult likely to believe and learn from a social experience? Research on human communication where verbal communication is not supported by the accompanying nonverbal communication shows that adults are inclined to believe and learn from the action rather than the words (Burgoon, Buller & Woodall, 1989). For example, suppose I said, "I have plenty of time to talk to you" (verbal communication) while looking furtively at my watch (nonverbal communication). The inferred meaning of the contradictory nonverbal cue (I haven't really got time to talk to you) is likely to be believed and acted on by you rather than the literal message of the spoken words. What is learnt? You might have learnt that I don't really mean what I say and that you can't really depend on me or trust me. Similarly, we all scrutinise the behaviour of workmates for key learning about attitudes towards issues such as safety, restructuring and change. If workmates express their knowledge and attitudes in the shadow area of organisational communication (Egan, 1994) as "Don't quote me to management but these are shortcuts that I use and they're quite safe", then these can be very powerful learning experiences indeed as the novice is inducted by the role model.

In summary, the significance of social learning theory for the social psychology of adult learning is that adults:

– select other people as models for learning;
– pay attention to the knowledge, skills and attitudes of the models they choose;
– learn selectively from their chosen models;
– make decisions for learning based on their own perceptions of the relevance and likely application of what they have learnt from models to the adults' own contexts for application of the learning; and
– may or may not perform specific learning gained from models because of personal factors (such as levels of confidence and trust) and environmental factors (such as opportunities and resources).

For adult educators, some implications of social learning theory for adult education practice are that adult educators:

– can request information from adult learners, prior to and during a learning experience, on expectations about models and past experience, expertise and preferred ways of learning. Individual Profiles and Personal Goals Sheets can be designed to provide relevant information to help adult educators to understand and monitor adults' learning needs as adult learners may be seeking a particular type of model for learning specific knowledge, skills and attitudes;
– should monitor their own education practice and interactions with adult learners as adult learners may be closely observing the adult educator as a model for learning specific knowledge and skills;
– should carefully monitor the congruence of their espoused theory and theory of use: they should practise what they preach and communicate through congruent verbal and nonverbal means of communication;
– demonstrations of knowledge, skill and attitude should be clear and explicit and opportunities and resources for practice should be provided, as appropriate, for adult learners;
– should create a safe social learning environment where adults can practise learning in a climate of trust, confidentiality and respect;
– should model that mistakes are accepted as part of learning;
– should encourage discussions of relevance and applications of learning for the specific contexts of the adult learners and for possible future contexts;
– should represent the highest standards of their professional area. The adult educator's attitudes, for example to the topic of the learning, to the behaviour and performance of the adult learners present and to their profession, will be under scrutiny by adult learners and may be modelled by these adult learners;
– should be up to date and should model ethical behaviour. Adult educators may be mistrusted and may be regarded as inappropriate models for learning if, for example, they do not know the material, use unsuitable methods for adults to learn, do not respect confidentiality or criticise adult learners destructively; and

– should strive to model effective ways of learning. If adult educators are regarded as inappropriate models for learning then adult learners may become cynical and may lack motivation to learn, especially novice or shy adult learners who are not confident about their abilities.

Learning through models from the social environment is a very powerful way of learning. However, of course, adults do not always need to be aware of others to learn. Thus in the next section we explore factors within the individual adult learner which affect the means and potential for learning.

Individuals, Interactions and Adult Learning

We all know that we can learn some things very effectively on our own. Think of recent examples where you have learnt something by yourself and for yourself. I have learned, by myself, for example, that when I plant a garden certain species of plants cause a rash and that it is not wise for me to select them. I might be able to learn to use a new tool by trial and error. We learn from reflex reactions to the environment throughout our lives. Will that new plastic handle be hot? When I touch the ice cubes my fingers stick so I learn to twist the tray to remove them.

Our intention to try to learn something on our own may be influenced by other people's reactions and by our perceptions about the impressions that we are making on other people. I can learn to plant other species so that the neighbours will admire and approve. I might be inspired by a colleague's ability to use tools. Certainly the influence of other people, whether present or not, is a tremendous motivation and stimulation for adults to learn, to communicate and to change. What do researchers say about how individual people learn? You can compare two perspectives by trying the following exercise.

Exercise

Compare the views of these contemporary researchers:

> Those social psychologists who adopt a learning perspective prefer theories based on overt, observable behaviour which reflects our conditioning histories. Such theories are how rather than why explanations and are less interested in internal states or personal motives as influences on behaviour and, on the whole, they tend to minimise cognitive explanations. (McKnight & Sutton, 1994, pp. 8-9)

> The psychological view sees persons as entities with characteristics that lead them to behave in independent ways. It sees the single human mind as the locus for processing and understanding messages. It is hardly surprising, then, that psychological explanations have been so appealing to many communication scholars. (Littlejohn, 1996, p. 123)

Discussion Questions
– What are the differences between the two perspectives?
– What have you learnt about learning and communication according to these two views?
– What is your own view of how individuals learn?

If interactions between people are a defining feature of communication and learning, then a solely individualistic approach to explaining and understanding human communication and learning must be deficient. On the other hand, researchers acknowledge that explaining human communication only in terms of social theories is inadequate. As Littlejohn (1996, p. 124) remarked: "Although the outcome of communication may be social in nature, its ultimate genesis is individual, making psychological explanations crucial". Social psychology researchers have recently shown an interest in investigating how mutual knowledge shared by interdependent conversational partners affects learning (Planalp, 1993). Here the focus has turned to explaining how the social effect of interdependence between individuals leads to a reliance on shared knowledge and learning mutually. In an explanation of adult learning we therefore need to integrate factors at the levels of the individual, the group and the environment. These levels have been even further extended by researchers of organisational contexts of adult learning and behaviour.

In his model of how organisations function, Furnham (1997) distinguished five behavioural sciences which contributed to an analysis of the learning that takes place in organisational contexts: psychology, sociology, social psychology, anthropology and political science (Furnham, 1997, p. 4). In turn, these informing disciplines cover three levels of analysis: the individual (psychology), groups (sociology, social psychology and anthropology) and organisational systems (sociology, anthropology and political science). In Furnham's model, the contribution made by psychology at the individual level of analysis includes learning, motivation, personality, training, leadership effectiveness and other aspects related to job satisfaction. At the group level of analysis, social psychology is concerned with behavioural change, attitude change, communication, group processes and group decision-making. In this chapter we aim to link factors influencing adult learning at the individual level to features from group contexts studied by social psychology and to highlight implications for adult educators.

In summary, the significance of research on the individual level of learning for the social psychology of adult learning is that:
- it is useful to link factors in the individual to features from group contexts studied by social psychology to provide a more holistic explanation of adult learning;
- factors in the individual relevant to adult learning include motivation, personality, levels of training, leadership ability and attitudes about job satisfaction; and
- factors from group contexts relevant to adult learning include group influences on behaviour and attitude change and processes for communicating and making decisions in the group.

For adult educators, some implications of linking factors in the individual to features from group contexts to explain and predict adult learning are:
- adult educators can support adults to learn effectively on their own, for example by helping to define the scope of the learning and by suggesting resources for an individual adult learner;
- adult educators should take individualistic and group factors into account so that the planning and implementation of the learning process meets individual learning needs and uses group learning contexts appropriately;

– through specific learning experiences, adult educators can help adults to be more motivated to learn, to increase their leadership effectiveness and to develop their levels of training; and

– adult educators can facilitate group learning experiences (such as group discussions, role plays and problem solving in scenarios based on case studies) for adults to focus on behavioural and attitude change, to assist adults to learn to make decisions effectively in groups and to monitor and become more aware of the effects on learning of communication processes in groups.

As we have seen, these factors in the individual can substantially affect adult learning in social contexts. In the next section we discuss another means of learning from others where these individualistic factors have particular relevance: the tendency of adults to learn by comparing themselves to others.

Social Comparison Theory and Adult Learning

According to the theory of social comparison originally proposed by Festinger (1954), we seek other people as a means of evaluating our skills, aptitudes, values and beliefs if there is no physical or objective standard for evaluation (McKnight & Sutton, 1994). In other words, we can only evaluate many types of skill learning and our aptitudes for specific types of learning by comparing ourselves with other people. For example, you can evaluate the acuity of your eyesight by testing it against eye charts but how can you evaluate your computer skills or your aptitude for learning to play a musical instrument? In these examples you might compare your own performance to other people such as colleagues who use computers or friends and family members who play a musical instrument.

It is argued in social comparison theory that you will learn more productively, without feeling very frustrated and totally inadequate, if you choose suitable models to compare yourself with at various stages of your learning. For example, in the early stages of learning it would be more appropriate to choose someone who is more experienced on computers but not a computer scientist; an amateur and not a professional musician. Festinger called this a unidirectional drive upward in learning where an adult first chooses a person as a suitable standard and tries to match that level of performance. The adult may seek to improve further, for example by selecting someone else with even greater expertise as a model and then trying to reach a higher standard (Festinger, 1954).

What then is the effect on learning of the presence of others? In what is historically considered to be the first experiment in social psychology, Norman Tripplett, a psychologist at Indiana University in the late nineteenth century, observed that cyclists' times were faster when they were racing against each other rather than when they raced individually against the clock (Deaux & Wrightsman, 1984). Triplett (1897) studied children learning to use fishing reels and found that the children performed faster when they learnt and performed with other children than when they learnt and practised alone. The presence of other people seemed to produce a competitive effect which acted as a stimulus to learning and performance.

According to social comparison theory, we establish a basis for evaluating our own learning and performance by comparing ourselves to others who are learning with us (Gold, 1997). We can also share information with other learners and we can learn simply by observing others especially if the other learners seem to be successful in their actions. If another person is learning and doing better than we are then that person's presence may serve as a competitive cue and our own performance may improve. However, it is interesting to note that studies have shown that if another learner seems to be doing the same as we are or is vastly superior to us then we may not be stimulated to improve our performance. It has been argued that the great difference between our performance and the person who is vastly superior may make the person an inappropriate source of comparison and we may continue to learn and perform at our normal rate (Seta, 1982).

Other studies have shown that when the task is simple and has been well learned the influence of competition from the presence of others may improve performance. On the other hand, when the task is complex or less familiar competition may impair performance. Giving specific instructions which encourage learners to cooperate to learn a complex task seems to improve performance of learners (Laughlin & Jaccard, 1975).

In summary, the significance of social comparison theory for the social psychology of adult learning is that:
− adult learners use adult educators and other learners as a basis for comparison for evaluating their learning performance;
− adult learners learn more fruitfully if the person they are comparing themselves with has greater relevant expertise but is not too superior in their expertise;
− the influence of competition when people are learning in the presence of others can stimulate improvement in learning and performance, especially if the task is relatively simple; and
− if the task to be learnt is complex and people are learning in the presence of others, then a cooperative approach to learning is more likely to facilitate learning. A corollary is that people learning in a group are not likely to learn complex tasks effectively unless they cooperate to try to learn together.

For adult educators, some implications of social comparison theory for adult education practice are:
− adult educators and invited experts may perform the learning task so well that adult learners may despair about their ability to achieve at the level demonstrated, and may therefore lose motivation for learning;
− experts could be advised to demonstrate small segments of the total learning and to give opportunities for learner practice after each segment;
− adult educators can encourage adult learners to share information and to help each other to achieve specific learning outcomes;
− adult educators can provide learning opportunities for practice in small groups where adults can learn by comparing their performance to each other and where they can also give each other supportive feedback;
− if an adult educator asks a learner to perform in front of others then the adult educator should be aware that other learners will be using the performance to evaluate their own ability;
− adult learners may not wish to be exposed as models for social comparison in front of other people especially if they do not feel competent and if they lack confidence;
− adult educators might suggest appropriate models for comparison to an adult learner especially if an adult is less motivated by comparing his or her performance to a model who is significantly more competent;

– adult educators can tell learners about the models they have chosen for their own learning and how they improved their performance by comparing themselves to a range of different models over time;
– adult educators can assign adult learners to support groups based on the principles of social comparison. For example, a personal profile sheet can be designed so that each learner can provide relevant information to the adult educator. in practice groups, it may be preferable to match learners with others who are more competent. practice group membership can be rotated to give everyone a chance to work with someone who is more experienced and to act as models for those who are less experienced; and
– adult educators can give specific instructions on how adult learners could cooperate to achieve a complex learning task by working together.

While adults learn from the example of others and from making comparisons with others, in the next section we extend our discussion by looking further at how adults might be persuaded to change their attitudes and behaviours through their interactions with others.

Social Judgment Theory and Adult Learning

In contrast to the social learning and social comparison theories which focus on learning from others by example and differentiation, the emphasis in social judgment theory is on learning from others by persuasion. In other words, according to social judgment theory, adults learn to change attitudes and behaviour through persuasion by others (Granberg, 1982; O'Keefe, 1990). Initial studies concentrated on psychophysical research of people's judgments of the weight of objects and brightness of light. From these investigations Sherif and Hovland (1961) argued that people used reference points, known as anchors, as a method of comparison to make judgments. For instance, if I am familiar with the weight of a 2kg bar then I can judge the weight of an object as more or less than 2kg. Test your reference points for temperature by trying the following experiment.

Experiment
Fill three containers with water: hot; cold; lukewarm. Put your right hand in the container of hot water and your left hand in the container of cold water. After 30 seconds place both hands in the container of lukewarm water. Judge the temperature of the water in the container of lukewarm water according to perceptions from each hand. Record whether the temperature of the water feels hotter or colder according to your right or left hand. (Littlejohn, 1996, p. 152)

Your experimental results should show that you perceived that the temperature of the lukewarm water was different for your right and left hands because each hand provided a different reference point for judging the temperature. Sherif and colleagues (Sherif, Sherif, & Nebergall, 1965) argued that this principle of judgment could be applied to how adults learn to form and change attitudes and opinions. According to social judgment theory, adults develop reference points (called anchors) on which they strongly agree. These anchors are complemented by a range of latitudes of acceptance, non-commitment and rejection where adults are inclined to agree, not care or strongly disagree about an issue (as represented in Figure 3.1).

The sizes of the latitudes of acceptance, non-commitment and rejection are influenced by the amount of personal relevance of an issue or high ego (self) involvement. For example, residents in an area where an airport may be built are likely to be highly ego involved in their agreement or disagreement on the issue and are likely to have a very small latitude of non-commitment. An example from education may be where educators are highly ego involved in strong approval or disapproval of particular ways of conducting learning. Proposed changes to the way of offering a program may therefore be argued vigorously by highly committed staff whose personal philosophies of education are highly relevant to the debate and whose jobs may be directly affected by the suggested changes.

Figure 3.1 Social judgment theory.

Strongly agree	Agree	Don't care	Strongly disagree
Anchor	Latitude of Acceptance	Latitude of Non-commitment	Latitude of Rejection

High ego involvement is illustrated in Figure 3.2 where the issue is offering a program by computer rather than by weekly face to face classes. An educator whose job is directly affected by the proposed change is represented in Figure 3.2 as having a small latitude of non-commitment and larger latitudes of acceptance and rejection. The sizes of the latitudes of acceptance and rejection depend on the number of relevant statements that can be made about the issue that are accepted or rejected by a person. For example, there may be twenty statements that are clearly relevant to the issue of offering a program by computer. The educator represented in Figure 3.2 accepts seven statements, is non-committed on four and rejects nine statements. For example, one of the seven statements in the educator's latitude of acceptance is "Computers can provide interaction with educators and other learners to give feedback". One of the nine statements rejected by the educator is "Learners are expected to be computer literate and to provide their own computer". The educator is non-committed on the statement "Pro-quick software should be used".

According to social judgment theory, it may be possible to change a person's attitudes by appealing to some of the statements in the latitude of acceptance. Suppose the educator represented in Figure 3.2 is opposed to offering a particular program by computer. If we know that the educator accepts the statement that "Computers can provide interaction with educators and other learners to give feedback" then it may be possible to change that educator's negative attitude by exploring in detail how computers can provide suitable interaction and feedback for the particular program. Note that, after this discussion of interaction and feedback, the educator may even revise the reference points or anchors which determined the extent of the latitudes of acceptance, non-commitment and rejection. For example, one of the reference points or anchors with which the educator strongly agreed might have been that face to face interaction is the only suitable method for achieving the learning outcomes in certain subject areas. Further knowledge about the possibilities for interaction via modern computer technology might lead the educator to modify this reference point. This will then change the educator's latitudes of acceptance, rejection and non-commitment.

In any learning context, therefore, a person's internal anchors influence what is understood. In addition, it is predicted from the theory of social judgment that changes to strongly held attitudes and opinions are most likely to occur if a message falls within a learner's latitude of acceptance (Littlejohn, 1996). If an adult does not care about or strongly disagrees with a point of view then there is likely to be no impact on the existing anchors. The adult may learn that there is no reason to change or to experiment with new ideas or techniques. For instance, an educator may strongly disagree with the view that computers can offer suitable interaction for achieving particular learning outcomes and thus may see no reason to investigate the potential of new computer technologies.

Figure 3.2 *An educator's latitudes of acceptance, non-commitment and rejection where the issue is offering a program by computer.*

Strongly agree	Agree	Don't care	Strongly disagree
Anchor Reference points Principles for offering programs	Latitude of Acceptance 7 statements	Latitude of Non-commitment 4 statements	Latitude of Rejection 9 statements

In summary, the significance of social judgment theory for the social psychology of adult learning is that:
– adults form reference points, called anchors, on issues which are the basis of attitude formation, opinions and judgment;
– in a learning context, an adult's internal anchors influence what is understood, valued, accepted and changed;
– an adult learner's latitudes of acceptance, rejection and non-commitment about specific issues can affect learning and application of learning; and
– adult learners who hold strong values, attitudes and opinions might be persuaded to consider changing their values, attitudes and opinions if the message falls within the learner's latitude of acceptance.
For adult educators, some implications of social judgment theory for adult education practice are:
– self disclosure, feedback and empathic listening are required to share strongly
– held values, attitudes and opinions and to determine the extent of latitudes of acceptance, non-commitment and rejection;
– a supportive, safe and respectful social learning climate must be developed where adults can experiment with new behaviours to test their latitudes of acceptance, noncommitment and rejection;
– adult educators can encourage everyone to communicate to each other that the range of values, attitudes, opinions and behaviours expressed are respected within the context of the social learning environment. Adult educators can check whether there is agreement on this; and
– learning experiences which provide for small increments in knowledge, skill and attitude development may be most effective;
– if there are nonnegotiable parameters which relate to expression of attitudes or ways of conduct, then these should be clearly stated as boundaries of the

learning environment. There may be, for example, particular cultural customs and legal frameworks, such as equal employment opportunity, that define acceptable standards of behaviour and verbal and nonverbal expression in a social learning environment.

According to social judgment theory, adults may be persuaded to change their behaviours and attitudes if they are willing and able to disclose, reflect on feedback and test their ideas and assumptions in a social context. We further investigate how adults learn through self disclosure and feedback in the following sections.

Adult Learning through Self Disclosure to Others

Whether interacting one-on-one or in a group, adults disclose information about themselves to each other and learn from these reciprocal disclosures. Social psychologists Altman and Taylor (1973, 1987) have proposed the theory of social penetration to explain the type and levels of learning which result from self disclosure.

Social Penetration Theory

As relationships develop, adults learn more about the breadth and depth of each other's thoughts, feelings and attitudes through self disclosure. "Social penetration" is the term used to describe the movement from superficial levels of learning about each other to more personal, intimate levels (Altman & Taylor, 1973, 1987). The learning can be represented as parts of a circle that have both a length of arc along the circumference and a depth of radius towards the centre. Areas that a person may disclose in a relationship are arranged around the circumference of the circle. In these areas the person can disclose at various levels of depth: clichés, facts, opinions and feelings. These levels of depth of disclosure are represented in Figure 3.3. For the person represented as disclosing in a relationship in Figure 3.4 the biggest areas of disclosure are "my work ambitions" and "my hobby" while the smallest areas of disclosure are "problems about my work", "problems in my family", "our relationship" and "my friends". In the areas of work ambitions and hobby the person discloses thoughts and feelings compared to disclosures of less depth in the areas of problems at work where only clichés are disclosed and family problems where the person is willing to disclose facts but not opinions or feelings. Depth and breadth of learning in an area increases as people develop the relationship. Trust is gained as people disclose incrementally, symmetrically and reciprocally in a process known as social exchange (Kelley & Thibaut, 1978; Roloff, 1981). There is thus potential to strengthen the relationship through mutual disclosure and reciprocal learning.

According to social penetration theory there is a tendency in a relationship to learn to match the other person's level and kind of disclosure and to disclose in cycles of openness and distance. In more developed relationships over time the cycle tends to be longer as there is likely to be more disclosure. People choose the degree of openness by weighing the rewards and costs of a particular disclosure at a certain stage of the relationship. Greater disclosure has more risk. It is argued that there is rapid penetration at the beginning of relationships when the rewards are perceived to outweigh the costs. As some relationships develop the parties may find that the risks of disclosure are greater than the rewards and, rather than increasing, social penetration may decrease and the relationship may become less familiar or even end (Littlejohn, 1996).

Getting to know other people through disclosure can increase the array of topics shared by the people in the relationship, thus adding to the number of topics around the circumference of the circle. Exploring a topic more intensively increases the depth of the learning. Altman and Taylor (1973, 1987) suggested that there are four stages of learning through social exchange: orientation where very public information is disclosed; affective exploration where there is deepening of the initial exchanges of thoughts and feelings; affective exchange where there is evaluation of thoughts and feelings at a deeper level; and stable exchange where highly intimate disclosures take place allowing people to predict the response and behaviour of each other.

Figure 3.3 *Levels of depth of disclosures in a relationship as represented by Social Penetration Theory.*

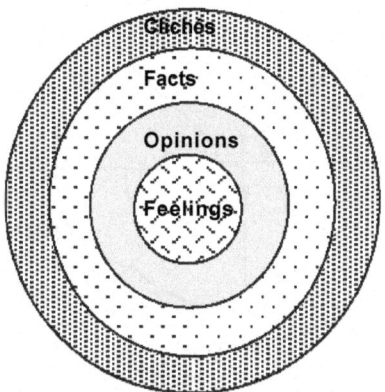

In learning groups, educators and learners learn through disclosure of information, past experience and stories. Educators may be willing to disclose their own past learning difficulties in acquiring particular knowledge or skills, to share anecdotes about applying learning and to reveal their own sources of anxiety or confusion about learning. In a social context, the type of self disclosure might be appropriate or inappropriate depending on many relationship and cultural variables. In general, appropriate self disclosure is incremental, symmetrical and reciprocal and is monitored for breadth and depth by the parties.

In summary, the significance of social penetration theory for the social psychology of adult learning is that:
- adults learn about themselves and others through self disclosure in relationships;
- adults learn to disclose in a number of areas depending on their expectations about the nature of the relationship and the social context;
- adults disclose at levels of depth: from clichés to facts to opinions to feelings;
- adults are likely to disclose incrementally, symmetrically and reciprocally; and
- some adults disclose in areas which are inappropriate for the nature of the social learning context and monopolise the time available for learning in a group.

For adult educators, some implications of social penetration theory for adult education practice are:

- adult educators can establish a range of appropriate areas for disclosure in the social learning environment by disclosing their own areas incrementally, symmetrically and reciprocally;
- adult educators can assist adult learners to express their thoughts, opinions and feelings in a safe and trusting social learning environment; and
- adult educators can monitor the appropriateness of disclosures and the time taken to express these disclosures so that some adult learners do not monopolise the time available for group learning.

Figure 3.4 *One person's breadth and depth of disclosures in a relationship as represented by Social Penetration Theory.*

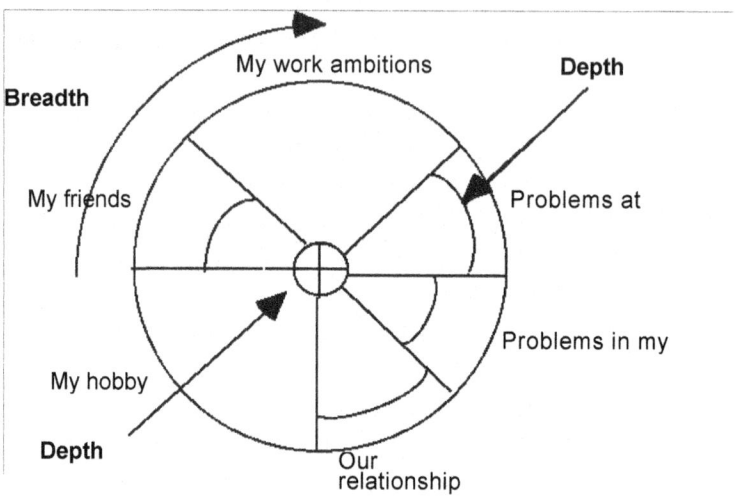

Self-Monitoring and Adult Learning

As Snyder and colleagues have noted (Snyder, 1974, 1980; Snyder & Gangestad, 1986), not all adults tend to monitor the appropriateness of their disclosures and behaviour in order to try to meet their learning goals by adjusting their responses to take into account cues from the environment. Self-monitoring has been defined as "Observing one's behaviour and the impact of that behaviour on one's progress toward a goal" (Barone, Maddux & Snyder, 1997, p. 303). In other words, self-monitoring is a tendency to "watch yourself" (Littlejohn, 1996, p. 257). In his studies of self-monitoring, Snyder determined that adults scored from low to high on his *Personal Reaction Inventory: Self-Monitoring Scale* (the scale may be completed on the web (Snyder (1974)). According to the construct of self-monitoring as reflected in Snyder's scale, low self-monitors tend to pursue their goals oblivious to feedback cues from the environment which might affect the outcome. In contrast, high self-monitors have been described as actors who tend to behave to suit what they believe is expected in the situation. For instance, high self-monitors would tend to listen to others before self disclosing and would tend to respond to try to give the most favourable impression. Low self-monitors would tend to say what they think and would tend to behave regardless of the situation. There is also a middle group identified as selective self-monitors by Snyder.

Selective self-monitors tend to monitor the social environment in a discriminating fashion according to their expectations, moods and personal goals. For example, selective self-monitors are likely to monitor the experience of a job interview very carefully in order to represent themselves favourably. In a classroom situation, selective self-monitors are likely to adjust their behaviour to cues from others so that they disclose appropriately and learn effectively in that context. Compared to high self-monitors who tend to be guarded and careful, selective self-monitors tend not to be overly concerned about making impressions that are acceptable to others. For example, selective self-monitors tend to state their views in a spirit of collaborative learning and not primarily to seek approval from others.

Snyder and his colleagues argued that selective self-monitoring of the social environment enhances learning about ourselves and others. A selective self-monitor tends to be selectively open and selectively disclosing. Thus selective self-monitors tend to be able to learn in strategic ways by paying attention to feedback. They tend to use feedback to adjust their communication to create desirable effects in accordance with their goals. In addition, communication competence has been defined as the ability to establish credibility and create a favourable impression in line with a person's goals in a communication context (Spitzberg & Cupach, 1988). It seems that selective self-monitoring, expressed as communication that relates to achieving the task and building a supportive learning climate, is beneficial for facilitating learning in group contexts.

In summary, the significance of self-monitoring for the social psychology of adult learning is that:

– the construct of self-monitoring refers to the tendency of adults to be sensitive to themselves and to be sensitive to feedback from others in order to make progress towards a goal;
– low self-monitors tend to be less concerned about the impressions they are making on others and tend to be less
– sensitive to reactions from others. They tend to behave regardless of the situation and also tend to be less sensitive to themselves;
– high self-monitors tend to be highly sensitive to the reactions of other people and tend to try constantly to adjust their responses to what they believe will suit other people; and
– selective self-monitors tend to be sensitive to themselves and to feedback from others. In a social situation they tend to adjust their behaviour taking into account their goals and the reactions of others;
– the tendency to be self-monitoring in the selective range is claimed to enhance learning. Selective self-monitors tend to be aware of how they are behaving and how others are reacting in a learning context. They tend to look for cues for learning from others and the environment to try to meet their own learning needs or goals. Thus selective self-monitors tend to adapt their behaviour to try to achieve their learning goals in social contexts.

For adult educators, some implications of self-monitoring for adult education practice are:

– adults who tend to be low self-monitors may not be aware of the potential for learning from others and the environment;

- adults who tend to be low self-monitors may behave inappropriately in social learning contexts, for example by not being aware of implicit norms of conduct and expectations for learning;
- adults who tend to be high self-monitors may seem to be learning but may be performing simply to please or impress the adult educator or others who are present;
- adult educators can encourage learners to state explicitly the norms of conduct and expectations for learning;
- adult educators can assist adult learning by being clear and specific about key points for learning and feedback on performance;
- adult educators can conduct discussions where attitudes about the value of the learning are explicitly expressed and compared;
- adult educators can arrange for learners to demonstrate learning in peer groups when the educator is not present and can encourage adult learners to determine the value of the learning according to specific criteria; and
- adult educators should be able to monitor the social learning environment in order to adjust their behaviour and educational strategies to cues from the learners and the environment.

Learning from Self Disclosure and Feedback

Humanist psychologists such as Rogers (1961) and Johnson (1993) have offered normative theories of how to communicate better in relationships (Littlejohn, 1996, p. 260) and how to learn from giving and receiving feedback. The values underlying this humanistic approach have been summarised by Bolton (1993) as:
- unconditional positive regard towards other people;
- genuineness where words match the inner feeling;
- empathy or degree of understanding of other people's perspectives; and
- a matching of intensity of affective expression, in other words, a feedback response matches the emotional intensity expressed by the other person.

Noting that Rogers inspired an ideology of "honest communication" in which interpersonal understanding and learning occurs through self-disclosure, feedback and sensitivity to the disclosures of others, Littlejohn (1996) pointed out that Rogers "did not espouse the blatant, non-adaptive self-disclosure commonly attributed to him" (Littlejohn, 1996, p. 261). Humanistic feedback guidelines are based on the precepts of mutual respect and acceptance so that the goal of accurate understanding of self and others may be sought through genuine communication. Learning about ourselves and others is impoverished by "dishonesty, lack of congruence between one's actions and feelings, poor feedback, and inhibited self-disclosure" (Littlejohn, 1996, p. 260). Constructive feedback, expressed sensitively, should promote adult learning by reducing defensiveness and maximising collaboration. Feedback can be direct without being blaming, disrespectful or destructively judgmental. Genuine and open feedback, disclosed with concern for the other person, can help adults to identify real learning needs. Effective feedback can also help adults to develop a mutually agreed upon strategy for enhanced learning and personal growth.

The following feedback guidelines are adapted from Johnson (1993). They suggest a non-threatening way of disclosing thoughts and feelings to check the accuracy of perceptions and to provide a basis for action and change. It is most important that feedback is interpreted as it was intended and that is clearly heard and understood. Feedback guidelines for constructive learning

— express what you have noticed about the behaviour of the person rather than about a characteristic of the person. "I have noticed that you joined those parts together hesitantly" rather than "I have noticed that you're nervous". It is helpful to use adverbs which describe actions ("hesitantly") rather than adjectives which describe personal qualities ("nervous");

— express what you observe rather than what you infer. "I observed that you turned off the safety switch" rather than "Obviously you don't care about safety";

— express feedback in terms of description (report) not judgment (evaluation). "You covered three out of the four steps" rather than "That was wrong. You missed a step."

— express feedback as "more or less" rather than as "either/or". "I noticed you gave more time to it today" rather than "The time you spent on it today was good." The first example is measurable feedback (in terms of more or less time) whereas the second, although positive, is vague (in terms of either good or bad use of time);

— express what you have noticed about particular behaviour in a specific situation (preferably in the present) rather than generalise about behaviour in the past. Link the feedback to time and place. "I noticed that you arrived after the 9.00 am meeting had started" rather than "You always arrive after the meeting has started."

— express feedback by sharing ideas and information rather than by giving advice. Sharing rather than telling is collaborative and empowering. "There is a two day course on presentation skills at the local

— college" rather than "I'd advise you to take that course on presentation skills at the local college";

— express feedback by exploring alternatives rather than looking for answers or solutions. "What options are there to help you to be more confident in presentations?" rather than "A course on presentations seems to be the answer to your problem."

— express feedback about what, how, when and where of what was said or done (observable) not about why things were said or done (motive). "How did you deal with the complaint?" rather than "Why did you refer the complaint to the supervisor?"

— express feedback sparingly, without overloading the other person. Check with the other person to determine how much feedback the person can use at that time; and

— express feedback at an appropriate time and place. Consider possible emotional reactions of the person initiating the feedback and the person receiving the feedback.

Self Test

To test yourself, determine whether the following statements on giving constructive feedback are True or False:

Focus feedback on the person rather than upon his or her behaviour.	True False
Focus on inferences rather than observations.	True False
Focus on description rather than judgment.	True False
Express feedback as 'more or less' instead of 'either/or'.	True False
Focus on specific behaviour in the present rather than upon general behaviour in the past.	True False
Focus on giving advice rather than sharing information.	True False
Focus feedback on seeking solutions rather than exploring alternatives.	True False
Focus on what is said rather than upon why it is said.	True False
Focus on giving as much information as you can rather than on how much the other person can use.	True False
Give feedback as soon as you observe the behaviour.	True False

Answers: F; F; T; T; T; F; F; T; F; F

These guidelines for giving and receiving constructive feedback can be practised in the model of self disclosure and feedback which is applied to collaborative learning and explained in the next section.

Adult Learning and the Johari Window Model of Self Disclosure and Feedback

American communication researchers Joseph Luft and Harry Ingham proposed a model of self disclosure based on the self as a window with four panes (Adler & Rodman, 1994; Luft, 1969; Mohan, McGregor, Saunders, & Archee, 1997; Wilson, Hantz, & Hanna, 1995). According to the Johari window model each person views their personal relationships and learning experiences from behind their window pane. (Note that the term "Johari" is derived from the authors' first names.) In the model in Figure 3.5 the four panes of the window represent the self as: Arena - the open part of the self (known to both the self and to others); Façade - the hidden part (known to the self but unknown to others); Blind Spot - the blind part (unknown to the self but known to others); and Unknown - an unknown part (unknown to both the self and to others). The open Arena pane of your Johari window would be fairly small when you meet a new person. You have not learnt to trust each other and are still cautious about self disclosure and unsure about the significance of any feedback you might receive.

Figure 3.5 Johari Window.

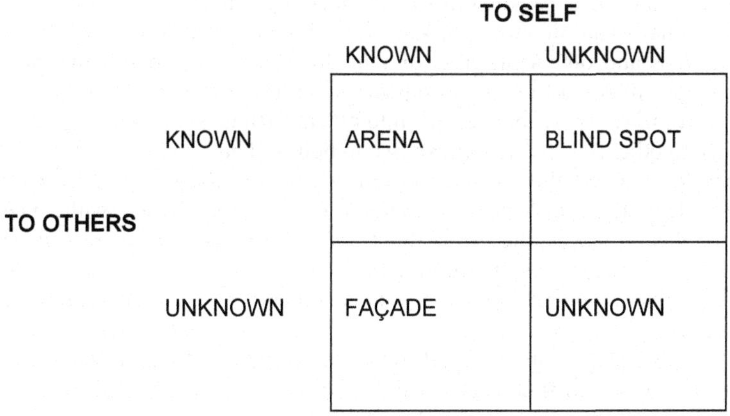

TO SELF

	KNOWN	UNKNOWN
KNOWN	ARENA	BLIND SPOT
UNKNOWN	FAÇADE	UNKNOWN

TO OTHERS

Figure 3.6. Increased self-disclosure leads to expansion of your Arena.

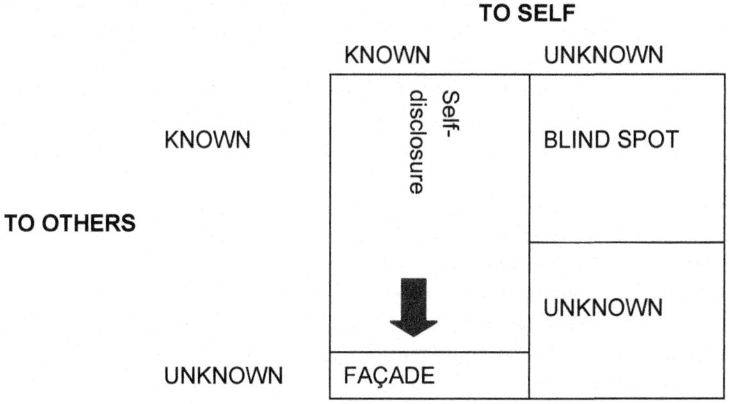

TO SELF

KNOWN UNKNOWN

KNOWN — Self-disclosure — BLIND SPOT

TO OTHERS

UNKNOWN

UNKNOWN — FAÇADE

In terms of adult learning the Johari window model highlights the influence of openness through self disclosure and giving and receiving feedback, built on increasing levels of trust, as key factors in learning in a social interaction. As shown in Figures 3.6 and 3.7 increased self-disclosure leads to a larger Arena (what others know about you). When you are receptive to feedback about yourself from others there is a reduction in your Blind Spot (you learn more about yourself). In Figure 3.8 shared learning experiences involving self-disclosure and feedback lead to an increase in the size of the Arena and enhanced potential for the quality of learning, for example in a mentoring relationship. In Figures 3.9 and 3.10 a mentoring relationship is depicted at the beginning of the relationship and at a later time where the relationship has developed through appropriate mutual disclosure and constructive feedback. In Figure 3.10 mutual learning should be enhanced in a more informed and satisfying mentoring relationship because each person has been willing to try to learn more about the other thus increasing the Arena and reducing the Façade, Blind Spot and Unknown for both people.

In summary, the significance of the Johari window model of self disclosure and feedback for the social psychology of adult learning is that:
- in the Johari window model of self disclosure and feedback adults learn about themselves and others in terms of four dimensions of the self that are either known or unknown to self and others: Arena (known to both self and others); Façade (known to self but unknown to others); Blind Spot (unknown to self but known to others); Unknown (unknown to both self and others);
- adults learn about themselves and others through disclosure and feedback in shared learning experiences. Disclosure reduces the Façade while Feedback from others reduces the Blind Spot. The Arena is thus increased and the relationship should be more informed;
- learning about yourself by disclosing to others and receiving feedback from others; and
- can be therapeutic in a social relationship where communication is non-judgemental and trust is established. Self growth can also be facilitated through modelling, comparison and mutual respect.

For adult educators, some implications of the Johari window model of self disclosure and feedback for adult education practice are:
- learning experiences where there are opportunities for adults to disclose appropriately and to give supportive feedback to each other confidentially may enhance a collaborative learning relationship;
- adult educators should encourage adult learners to build trust, to communicate in non-judgemental ways, to respect each others' self disclosures and to maintain confidentiality so that mutual learning can be enhanced in a shared learning experience;
- by modelling appropriate disclosure, providing constructive feedback to adult learners and seeking feedback from adult learners, adult educators can build a supportive social learning relationship; and
- the model is particularly relevant for facilitating a mentoring relationship.

The main features of social learning, social comparison, social judgment and social penetration theories of adult learning, applied as self disclosure and feedback in the Johari window model, can also be found in another framework for enhancing adult learning – participation in a learning conversation.

Figure 3.7 Increased feedback leads to reduction in your Blind Spot.

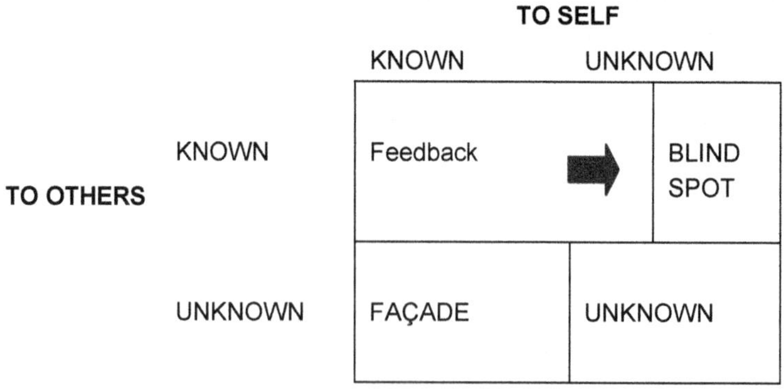

Learning Conversations and Adult Learning

The learning conversation model of adult learning in social contexts was proposed by New Zealand educational psychologist Viviane Robinson (1993). The framework was initially developed as a problem-based methodology for mentoring using critical dialogue (not in the sense of "critical theory" (Ricoeur, 1981; Pollock & Cox, 1991)) to investigate theory and practice in a collaborative partnership between the educator (experienced practitioner) and the learner (novice). Drawing on the work of Argyris and Schön (Argyris, 1982; Argyris & Schön, 1974; Schön, 1983, 1987, 1991) on educating the reflective practitioner, the learning conversation features a format for identifying and disclosing implicit theories of the world of both partners in the conversation so that feedback can be given to improve performance. The learning conversation form of dialogue can be used for giving feedback on performance in a regular, informal way and for gathering valid information for formal student assessment and performance appraisal. Learning conversations are truly conversations that promote learning for everyone involved, especially in mentoring relationships.

Figure 3.8 Shared learning experiences increase the Arena and enhance the potential for learning.

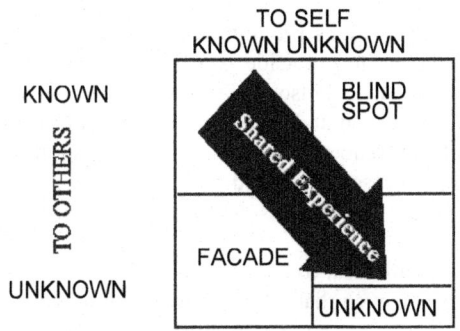

Figure 3.9 At the beginning of a
mentoring relationship.

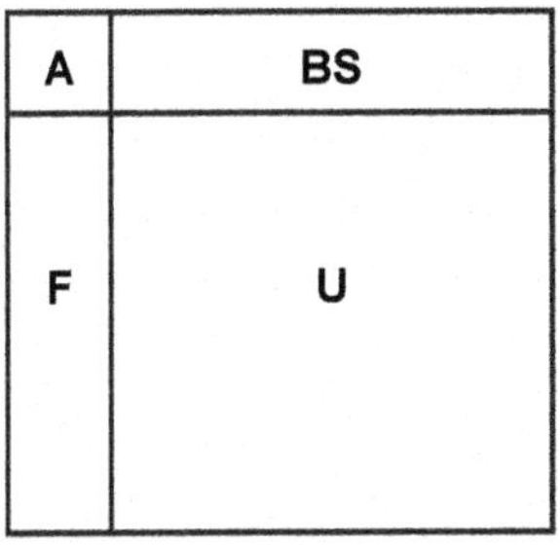

Figure 3.10 After development of a
mentoring relationship.

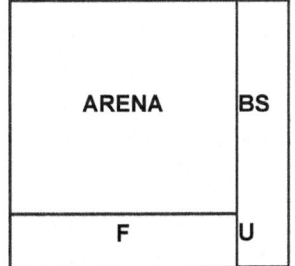

Learning conversations can be described as conversations that are simultaneously collaborative and challenging. A learning conversation between two people features:

- disclosure where both people say what they have noticed about performance and what sense they have made of it in terms of implicit theories of practice;
- testing where both people learn about each other's positions and investigate alternative theories and practices; and
- bilateral rather than unilateral power and control where both people regardless of status or experience contribute to the learning or inquiry process.

The learning conversation enables people to enhance their learning about theory and practice in their professions (and their relationships) by providing an opportunity to share ideas, identify and test assumptions, demonstrate mutual respect and achieve a balance between support and challenge. People are thus able to share rather than impose their expertise. The available time for consultation and learning together is used efficiently and effectively. The method aims to increase the quality of thinking through discussion, to increase intellectual commitment to change and to enhance mutual respect. In the learning conversation, the participants express their genuine curiosity about their observations of performance, especially when they are puzzled or are in disagreement, and they acknowledge each other's feelings about the performance and the learning process (Robinson, 1998).

In summary, learning conversations promote learning because the participants are willing to suspend judgment, to put aside power and status, to seek to clarify uncertainty and to collaborate. As Robinson (1998) explained, the participants in a learning conversation treat their own and others' views not as truths that are taken for granted but as informal and frequently implicit theories about the world that are fallible, value-laden and not necessarily shared by others. In order to uncover and discuss each others' views, the participants converse according to the following core values:

- openness so that our views are clear to ourselves and others;
- respect for the views of others so that we may learn from them and with them; and
- valid information to increase the quality of information and reasoning that informs our own and others' practice (Robinson, 1998).

The power of the learning conversation to facilitate mutual learning is summed up in Robinson's comment on these core values:

> Compare these values with those that are soft and fuzzy in the face of uncertainty, or those that deny uncertainty through domination. Both tentativeness and domination prevent learning. (Robinson, 1998)

Learning conversations are opportunities for participants to share what they think, why they think it, check their perceptions with each other and help each other to learn from mutual feedback. A framework for a learning conversation based on a teacher training scenario was developed by Robinson (1998). In the scenario used here a supervisor is giving feedback on performance of quality customer service to a trainee sales person after observing an interaction with a customer (see insert opposite).

In summary, the significance of learning conversations for the social psychology of adult learning is that:

- learning conversations provide a format for mentoring where adults can share their expertise and give specific feedback collaboratively and where mutual learning can take place by modelling, comparing and forming judgments through persuasion and disclosure;
- learning conversations are founded on disclosure, openness, respect, trust, valid information and bilateral power; and
- in the learning conversation people privately think about the feedback they wish to give and then try to identify the theory of practice which is underlying their feedback. The feedback is given directly and openly with supporting reasons and is checked for appropriateness with the other person.

For adult educators, some implications of learning conversations for adult education practice are:

- learning conversations allow a more experienced practitioner to give direct feedback on performance to someone of less experience;
- learning conversations allow both adult educators and adult learners to identify the implications for practice of their espoused theories and to test the appropriateness of their theories for practice in a process of collaborative learning; and
- Learning conversations provide a means where adult educators can interact with learners so that perspectives are not imposed but are clarified and analysed and where power is shared in a collaborative learning experience.

Stages of the Learning Conversation	**Ideas and Prompts**
A. Beginning 1. Disclose the whole agenda. 2. Invite dialogue. 3. Offer support by sharing the responsibility for improvement. 4. Check the agenda.	**A. Beginning** I want to tell you how I assessed your performance, focusing on the things I thought were strong and areas where I think more progress is needed. There may be areas where we see things differently. I want to hear your views, especially where we disagree, so that I can learn more about your views on quality customer service. One of the things I want to learn from this conversation is how to help you achieve the goals that come out of this assessment. Are you ready to start? Do you want to add anything to the agenda? Are there any questions before we talk about the assessment?

B. Disclosing and Evaluating Your Observations	B. Disclosing and Evaluating Your Observations
1. Summarise the observations you have made that are relevant to a particular heading. 2. Disclose your evaluation of what you have observed. – This involves making a professional judgment. – Show how you reached that judgment, especially if it is not obvious. – Be open to other interpretations. –	Summary of observations under headings. Say what you have noticed. Say what you make of it. Publicly check out your inference. I was troubled by the lack of customer response because it may have given you little feedback about whether the customer understood the options. Did you find out what the customer understood? I was concerned about the telephone interruption because I thought it might lower your rapport with the customer. What is your view on answering the telephone when you are with a customer?

Stages of the Learning Conversation	Ideas and Prompts

3. Ask for the other's reactions to your views.
– Value the reaction (paraphrase to check that you have understood).
– Discover why the other reacts as s/he does. This gives both parties access to his/her implicit theory of practice.
– Welcome disagreement as an opportunity for learning and to counteract unequal power.
4. Explore differences.
– Name what you agree and disagree about.
– Check you have each understood the basis of each others' views.
5. Design ways of testing and exploring the differences.
– Will more relevant data help?
– Relate the differences to a shared theory of effective professional practice
	How do you feel about what I
	   have said so far? How helpful
	   is this so far?
	   You look like you see that
	   differently. I'd like to hear what you
	   honestly think.
	How do you understand what I am
	   saying about quality customer
	   service? Note that the previous
	   question is oriented towards
	   discovering the implicit theories of
	   practice used by the person. A
	   question such as " Do you
	   understand what I am saying about
	   quality customer service?" may
	   not elicit the basis of the person's
	   views.
	5. So you are afraid that the customer
	   would shout at you if you tried to
	   find out more details?
	How does referring the customer to
	   the manual promote quality customer
	   service?

Learning conversations require an integration of appropriate self-disclosure, self-monitoring, empathic listening, astute questioning and constructive feedback. They can be conducted between two people, for example in a mentoring relationship, and by more than two people in a group learning context. When learning conversations are held in groups there may be additional factors to take into account arising from the dynamics in the group. In the following sections we therefore discuss factors which affect learning in a group and we begin by investigating research findings in social psychology specifically on group dynamics that have implications for adult learning in group contexts.

Implications of Research in Social Psychology on Group Dynamics for Adult Learning

The presence of others in a learning group can both greatly enhance and stifle opportunities for learning. While adults can benefit from the shared expertise of group members there can also be peer pressure towards conformity of ideas and conduct in a group that can lead to limits on the range of possibilities for learning. There can also be constraints on who contributes ideas and how ideas are introduced, discussed and evaluated in a group. The result can be poorer decisions and less satisfying learning experiences for members of a group.

What implications can we draw from the body of research in social psychology on group dynamics that are relevant for understanding the specific nature of group influences when adults learn in groups? Tennant (1997) has pointed out that some educators claim that:

> ...group learning is better than, say, the lecture format, because it encourages the pooling of resources, builds a sense of group belonging, allows participants to express their views, helps them to clarify their thinking, and so on. The adult educator's task is to develop an armoury of group teaching techniques, a sensitivity to the pitfalls of group work, and an ability to intervene appropriately in the group process. The ultimate aim is to establish a smoothly functioning, cohesive group in which individuals can work together and learn productively. (Tennant, 1997, p. 108)

The reservations expressed by Tennant for an unqualified endorsement of the benefits of learning in groups are supported by research on group dynamics in which social psychologists have investigated the psychological processes that occur in groups. For summaries of research on group dynamics see, for example, Cartwright & Zander, 1968; Cragan & Wright, 1991; Forsyth, 1990; Hare, 1976; Johnson & Johnson, 1997; Littlejohn, 1996; Lumsden & Lumsden, 1993; Napier & Gershenfeld, 1993; Shaw, 1981; and Williamson, 1982. The research summarised by these authors clearly shows that there are certain structural properties of groups that both advantage and disadvantage adult learning. For example, features of groups such as interdependence, composition including gender, size, structure, uniformity, conformity, power, leadership and motivation of members can influence the type and process of learning in a group. Some research findings on group dynamics relevant to our discussion of adult learning in a group are given next.

Research Findings on Group Dynamics influencing Adult Learning

1. People's opinions and attitudes are strongly influenced by the norms and goals of groups to which they belong and want to belong.
2. People are rewarded for conforming to the standards of a group and punished for deviating from them.
3. People feel a greater pressure to conform to group norms when a group meets their socio-emotional needs as well as their needs for achievement of a task. People who are most attached to a group and who identify with a group are likely to uphold group norms and resist ideas, suggestions and behaviour that conflict with group norms.
4. People have more influence or power over each other in a group when the group is high rather than low in cohesiveness.
5. A major determinant of interpersonal influence in a group is related to the frequency of communication. People who do most of the talking and who say the most positive things will usually have the most influence in a group. The size of a group affects the communication time available to each person, patterns of communication among people and the extent of a person's input to a group's learning process. The larger a group the greater the tendency for a group to be dominated by a small number of people.
6. Being part of a group can have effects on people's behaviour. For example, a group may offer a safe place where usual inhibitions are released. People can imitate others' behaviour (behavioural contagion). People can feel more anonymous (deindividuation) in a group and less personally responsible (diffusion of responsibility). These factors can lead people to behave in more antisocial and emotional ways in a group such as being aggressive, or by crying or showing affection because they are more uninhibited in a group.
7. There can be a risky shift phenomena in groups. The tendency to risky shift is where people may feel less personally responsible in groups and may make and agree to more radical or riskier decisions which they would not make on their own.
8. The communication patterns within a group affect the content of group discussion and the relationships between the people in the group. Information can be filtered out by some people or shared between people in a group. These communication patterns affect the information which is available to a group and the ways in which a group processes the information and develops relationships among the people in a group.
9. Some research findings indicate that men and women tend to behave and learn differently in groups, for example: women are less assertive and less competitive in groups than men; women use eye contact as a form of communication more frequently than men; women usually talk more in groups than men (note that this general tendency may be significantly affected by the topic under discussion); and women conform to majority opinion more than men. It has been claimed that mixed gender groups are more effective in making workable decisions than same gender groups and that people conform more in mixed gender groups than in same gender groups (Shaw, 1981).
10. When people state their opinions publicly in a group these opinions are harder to change than if they had been held privately and not made public.
11. Discussing ideas in groups and making decisions in groups help to overcome a person's resistance to persuasion.

12. The power of a majority opinion in a group to force compliance or agreement on an individual member is weakened if there is one other supporter of a minority view in a group.
13. A minority of two people can influence the majority if they are consistent and complementary in explaining their opposing point of view.
14. In highly cohesive groups, the need to maintain group consensus can lead to faulty decision making, called "groupthink" by Janis (1982), in which critical evaluation is suppressed and personal opinions are disregarded. This can result in poor quality decisions based on inadequate information and shared assumptions which are not tested for accuracy or relevance.
15. Social loafing, where some people in a group do not give their best and depend on the efforts of the others to carry them, can occur in groups if some people are low in motivation and commitment.

In summary, the significance of research in social psychology on group dynamics for adult learning in groups is that:

1. There is interdependence among the relationships of the members of a learning group and adults learn best if they can manage interpersonal relations constructively so that there is plenty of energy available in a group to learn together to achieve individual and group goals.
2. Adults can learn from the greater resources in a group. The varied experience and expertise of the members can be used to learn how to approach and solve complex problems. Adults can be stimulated to work harder and to learn more in groups because they want the group to succeed.
3. Learning groups develop norms of conduct which may facilitate or inhibit learning by individuals in a group. Individuals who value belonging to a group will tend to accept these group norms. In other words, highly cohesive groups have the power to influence the members towards a common perception of the learning that is taking place.
4. Individual members have a degree of power to influence other members of a learning group. It is important to remember that power is not always shared in a learning group.
5. How leadership functions occur in a learning group greatly affects the learning of individual members.
6. The motivation of individual group members to work cooperatively in a learning group varies according to whether the personal goals of individual group members and group goals are complementary.
7. Structures within a learning group such as communication patterns and personal influence and liking affect the satisfaction of members and their learning.
8. Men and women may behave differently in learning groups and may contribute perspectives and orientations that are extremely valuable for group learning. Gender influences in same gender and mixed gender groups may influence the type of communication interactions, ways of decision making and the development of group process.
9. Adults can learn from being involved in making group decisions. Involvement in making group decisions usually means that adults are more committed to implementation. Adults can learn a great deal from implementing group decisions and from working on issues associated with group decisions.

10. Adults can learn a lot about themselves and how others react through working in groups. Through group interaction adults may increase their personal and social awareness and may learn how to make better decisions.

11. Learning in groups can be a negative learning experience for adults depending on factors such as:
    - the suitability of the learning outcome for group learning;
    - the suitability of the size and composition of a group;
    - the ability of group members to interact well and to be prepared to take responsibility for action;
    - the degree of support for learning in a group;
    - the level of cohesiveness and whether this leads to unproductive uniformity, conformity and faulty decision making;
    - the reward system and whether the members believe that they will receive appropriate recognition for their efforts in a group;
    - the distribution of leadership and power in a group.

For adult educators, some implications of research in social psychology on group dynamics for adult education practice are:

1. Adult educators can encourage learning groups to build interdependent relationships among the members to share the work so that the group's goals and the personal goals of members are satisfied.

2. Adult educators can encourage learning groups to seek and to explore different ideas and to listen with empathy.

3. Adult educators can encourage learning groups to state explicitly their norms for conduct and to monitor and renegotiate these norms so that learning is facilitated rather than inhibited as a group develops.

4. Adult educators can facilitate adult learning in groups by assisting groups to identify means of communicating in the group that are oriented towards making progress on the task and developing harmony in a group.

5. Adult educators can encourage learning groups to share power and leadership functions to achieve maximum participation and to assist all members of a group to contribute. Group methods such as nominal group technique can help to incorporate contributions from quiet group members (Tennant, 1997; Tyson, 1989).

6. Adult educators can encourage learning groups to monitor the developing structures in a group for communication,

7. personal influence and for valuing diversity so that all members feel acknowledged and satisfied by the group learning process. Valuing diversity in a learning group can be expressed as empathic communication so that conflicts in a group are managed and members can learn constructively from the different perspectives contributed.

8. Adult educators can encourage adults to learn from the opportunities for interaction in groups where the members seek to clarify, refine and evaluate ideas.

Group Cohesiveness and Adult Learning

Do adults learn more effectively and efficiently if there is a cohesive spirit in the learning group? Researchers on group dynamics have argued that a high level of cohesiveness in a group can result in a group learning environment where there is less tension, less defensiveness about learning and change and more satisfying interpersonal relations among the group members (Tennant, 1997, p. 115). In other words, members of cohesive groups regard the group as a pleasant environment and should therefore enjoy meeting and learning together.

As we have mentioned previously, the very cohesiveness which makes the group an attractive place to learn can lead to negative effects on group learning and decision making such as pressures towards uniformity and conformity which may result in 'groupthink' (Janis, 1982). All groups need to be aware of these effects and to monitor the process of the group accordingly. Overcoming these effects is not easy for any group. It could be argued that a cohesive group that is aware of the dangers of cohesiveness on its learning process will be a more constructive and satisfying learning environment than a non-cohesive group where members have little commitment to belonging to and working in the group.

Given these findings on the positive and negative effects of group cohesiveness on learning, should adult educators facilitate the building of cohesiveness in learning groups? How can members of groups assist the group to become more cohesive? If we agree that the advantages of group cohesiveness outweigh the disadvantages, there are techniques that adults and adult educators can suggest to foster cohesiveness in groups for collaborative learning purposes, bearing in mind that these techniques should not be used for unethical, manipulative purposes (Tennant, 1997, p. 115).

What kinds of behaviour and interaction build cohesiveness in a group? The following techniques suggest a variety of communication interactions and shared group experiences that influence group identity and that can increase liking among the members of the group. These include: self disclosure of members' views and feeling; respectful communication between members; participation where members do not interrupt each other; acknowledgement of diverse viewpoints; effective listening in the group; and interactions which relieve tension in the group.

Shared group experiences can build cohesiveness by providing opportunities for success in meeting a challenging task as a group; making progress towards achieving group and individual goals; enjoying activities together as a group; and having fun. Cohesiveness is also facilitated if group members identify with a group name, if they recognise that they have things in common with other group members, if they share common goals, if they contribute to the group culture and if they relate in terms of equal status and power.

Some Techniques for Building Cohesiveness in an Adult Learning Group
- Use each other's names (check on cultural appropriateness). Provide name tags.
- Introduce members to each other: talk about who you are, your interests. Interview and introduce another member to the group.
- Make or find a location for group meetings. Have a meeting at someone's house. Contact members who miss a session. Provide support for members, for example, child care arrangements, transport.
- Treat everyone as equals. Communicate on appropriate levels. Establish an expectation that everyone should contribute. Use pauses and appropriate eye contact.
- Conduct an activity to increase/dissipate energy or tension e.g. active breathing, relaxation, stretching. Have refreshment breaks.

- Encourage appropriate self disclosure: members talk about places they have come from, other countries, cities, regions; members identify common experiences: how they were treated in the workplace; members share experiences.
- Develop trust through appropriate self disclosure or trust exercises.
- Find a common interest/ common area; something relevant to the group. Link members with other members through
- common interests. Listen to each other and network by developing common areas or ways members can help each other. Make links through transport needs.
- Discuss individual and group goals to share expectations and identify differences. Acknowledge benefits and limitations of meeting these goals through group learning.
- Do something together: an activity, game. Go on an excursion or field visit. Allocate time for socialising. Create situations where members need to contact each other.
- Recognise contributions. Delegate activities to a member or a sub group. Set a up peer support systems.
- Make contacts outside the group. Familiarise others with what the group is doing. Seek feedback from outside the group. (These techniques have been adapted from Scholtes (1993).)

Overcoming Negative Effects of Cohesiveness on Adult Learning in Groups
Janis (1982) and others (Courtright, 1978; Janis & Mann, 1977) have argued that the tendency of cohesive groups to strive for unanimity can create a pressure towards uniformity and conformity, or 'groupthink', where members start to become uncritical and blinkered in their learning and decision making (see also the section on Groupthink in the Chapter by Ray Cooksey). Cohesive groups should try to enhance the learning process by making sure that they canvass a variety of opinions on the scope of the learning, seek a wide range of information, examine all available alternatives, encourage free discussion and avoid isolation of the group. The group can invite others to join the group to contribute fresh views to the group and to challenge the group. All group members should be critical evaluators of what is being learnt and the process of learning. For instance, the group might assign a member to play the role of devil's advocate at a group meeting. Group leaders can guard against exerting too much personal influence on consensus in the group by avoiding being too directive, expressing impartiality, stating their preferences after others have had a chance to contribute and even by not attending some group meetings.

Profile of an Effective Adult Learning Group
An effective learning group can provide powerful learning experiences for adults including: developing self-understanding through shared support and mutual feedback; generating an experiential base for learning; encouraging interaction, self-determination and trust; and 'learning how to learn' (Tennant, 1997, p. 109). The following guidelines for an effective adult learning group summarise our discussion on how to promote learning within the group by self disclosing, giving and receiving feedback, modelling, comparing and persuading in an atmosphere of supportiveness and collaboration.

Guidelines for an Effective Adult Learning Group
- Encourage participation by all group members.
- Discourage domination by a few group members.
- Focus on defining and clarifying the learning issues and goals for individuals and the group.
- Suggest questions for specific learning.
- Establish ground rules for conduct in the group.
- Determine what resources the group requires.
- Collect a database for learning using reputable and appropriate methods.
- Summarise at strategic stages of the learning process.
- Be open to all ideas.
- Accept criticism of ideas.
- Express any concerns, feelings, objections and doubts.
- Reach decisions thoughtfully not hastily.
- Deal with conflict constructively.
- Identify what has been learnt about the task and relationships in the group.
- Identify areas for further learning to accomplish the task and build relationships in the group.

Conclusion

In this chapter we have investigated how adults learn in social contexts by discussing a range of explanations from social psychology. We have looked at how adults learn from selecting other people as models and how adults learn to evaluate and change their performance by comparison with others. We have discussed how adults learn through self disclosure to others by checking their thoughts, feelings and attitudes against what others reveal. Through mutual disclosure, social relationships can develop to provide supportive, empathic and trusting environments for adults to learn.

In a social relationship adults can give and receive constructive feedback to enhance mutual learning by being non-judgemental and empathic. Reciprocal and appropriate self disclosure and helpful feedback can be implemented very effectively in the learning conversation method of collaborative learning. We also discussed how the tendency to be appropriately self-monitoring in a social context may assist adults to be more sensitive to themselves and to feedback from others in order to meet their learning goals. In essence, disclosures and feedback form the basis for adults to make judgments about whether they are willing to change their existing values, beliefs and attitudes and to learn alternative ways of behaving and performing.

We then investigated the influence of group dynamics on adults' capacities to learn and to be creative and innovative in group settings. It became apparent that the same structural properties of groups that can provide a rich environment for adult learning can also lead to negative effects on a person's ability to learn constructively in a group context. We suggested how adult educators can assist groups to become cohesive through team building activities so that the experience of learning in groups is satisfying for people. Adult educators can help to facilitate adult learning in groups by understanding some of the potential negative effects of cohesiveness on group learning such as pressures towards uniformity and conformity of views and conduct and faulty decision making processes such as groupthink.

Finally, we developed a profile for an effective adult learning group that integrated earlier themes on psychological and social influences on adult learning and specific features of group learning. We recommended that adult learning groups monitor the developing norms and the learning process of the group and share leadership and power in the group. All group members should be encouraged to participate in learning collaboratively in the group. A major role for adult educators is to assist adult learning groups to build supportive learning climates. Respect, participation, trust and problem solving can be enhanced by verbal and nonverbal communication where adults express their views and feelings honestly, show empathy, relate on equal terms and are open to a range of possible interpretations and solutions. These essential attributes of effective adult learning in social contexts have been shown to be of fundamental importance to our discussion of the social psychology of adult learning.

REFERENCES

Adler, R. B., & Rodman, G. (1994). *Understanding human communication.* (5th ed.). Fort Worth: Harcourt Brace College Publishers.

Allport, G. W. (1958). *The nature of prejudice.* Garden City, NY: Doubleday Anchor.

Allport, G. W. (1968). The historical background of modern social psychology. In G. Lindzey & E. Aronson (Eds). *The handbook of social psychology,* Vol. 1, (2nd ed.). Reading, Massachusetts: Addison-Wesley.

Altman, I., & Taylor, D. A. (1973). *Social penetration: The development of interpersonal relationships.* NY: Holt, Rinehart and Winston.

Altman, I., & Taylor, D. A. (1987). Communication in interpersonal relationships: Social penetration processes. In M. Roloff and G. Miller (Eds). *Interpersonal processes: New directions in communication research* (pp.257-277). Newbury Park, California: Sage.

Argyle, M. (1974). *The social psychology of work.* Harmondsworth, Middlesex: Pelican Books.

Argyris, C. (1982). *Reasoning, learning and action.* San Francisco: Jossey-Bass.

Argyris, C., & Schön, D. (1974). *Theory in practice: Increasing professional effectiveness.* San Francisco: Jossey-Bass.

Asch, S. (1956). Studies of independence and conformity: A minority of one against a unanimous majority. *Psychological Monographs, 70* (9) No. 416.

Bandura, A. (1965). Influence of models: Reinforcement contingencies on the acquisition of imitative responses. *Journal of Personality and Social Psychology, 1,* 589-595.

Bandura, A. (1973). *Aggression: A social-learning analysis.* Englewood Cliffs, New Jersey: Prentice-Hall.

Bandura, A. (1977). *Social learning theory.* Englewood Cliffs, New Jersey: Prentice-Hall.

Bandura, A. (1983). Psychological mechanisms of aggression. In R. J. Green & E. Donnerstein (Eds). *Aggression: Theoretical and empirical reviews.* NY: Academic Press.

Bandura, A. (1986). *Social foundations of thought and action: A social cognitive theory.* Englewood Cliffs, New Jersey: Prentice-Hall.

Bandura, A., & Walters, R. (1963). *Social learning and personality development.* NY: Holt, Rinehart and Winston.

Barone, D.F., Maddux, J.E., & Snyder, C.R. (1997). *Social cognitive psychology: History and current domains.* NY: Plenum Press.

Bateson, G. (1979). *Mind and nature: A necessary unity.* NY: E.P. Dutton.

Bem, D. J. (1967). Self-perception: An alternative interpretation of cognitive dissonance phenomena. *Psychological Review, 74,* 183-200.

Bem, D .J. (1972). Self-perception theory. In L. Berkowitz (Ed.). *Advances in experimental social psychology. Vol. 6.* NY: Academic Press.

Berscheid, E., & Walster, E. (1974). Physical attractiveness. In L. Berkowitz (Ed.). *Advances in experimental social psychology, Vol. 7,* NY: Academic Press.

Bolton, R. (1993). *People skills.* Sydney: Simon and Schuster.

Brehm, S., & Kassin, S. M. (1993). *Social psychology.* (2nd ed.). Boston: Houghton Mifflin Company.

Burgoon, J. K., Buller, D. B., & Woodall, W. G. (1989). *Noverbal communication: The unspoken dialogue.* NY: Harper and Row.

Burleson, B. R. (1986). Attribution schemes and causal inference in natural conversations. In D.G. Ellis and W. A. Donohue (Eds). *Contemporary issues in language and discourse processes (pp. 63-86).* Hillsdale, New Jersey: Erlbaum.

Cartwright, D., & Zander, A. (1968). *Group dynamics: Theory and research.* (3rd ed.). NY: Harper & Row.

Coke, J. S., Batson, C. D., & McDavis, K. (1978). Empathic mediation of helping: A two-stage model. *Journal of Personality and Social Psychology, 36,* 752-766.

Cooley, C. H. (1922). *Human nature and the social order* (Rev. ed.). NY: Scribner's. Originally published in 1902.

Courtright, J. A. (1978). A laboratory investigation of groupthink. *Communication Monographs, 45,* 229- 248.

Cragan, J. F., & Wright, D. D. (1991). Small Group Communication Research of the 1980s: A synthesis and critique. *Communication Studies, 41,* 218-239.

Deaux, K., & Wrightsman, L. S. (1984). *Social psychology in the 80s* (4th ed.). Monterey, California: Brooks/Cole Publishing Company.

Dion, K. (1972). Physical attractiveness and evaluation of children's transgressions. *Journal of Personality and Social Psychology, 24,* 207-2 13.

Egan, G. (1994). *Working the shadow side: A guide to positive behind-the-scenes management.* San Francisco: Jossey-Bass.

Festinger, L. (1954). A theory of social comparison processes. *Human Relations, 7,* 117-140.

Festinger, L. (1957). *A theory of cognitive dissonance.* Stanford, California: Stanford University Press.

Forsyth, D. R. (1990). *Group dynamics* (2nd ed.). Pacific Grove, California: Brooks/Cole Publishing Company.

Furnham, A. (1997). *The psychology of behaviour at work: The individual in the organisation.* Hove, East Sussex: Psychology Press.

Glass, D. C., & Singer, J. E. (1972). *Urban stress.* NY: Academic Press.

Goffman, E. (1959). *The presentation of self in every day life.* Garden City, NY: Doubleday Anchor.

Goffman, E. (1967). *Interaction ritual: Essays on face-to-face behaviour.* Garden City, NY: Doubleday Anchor.

Gold, M. (1997). *A new outline of social psychology.* Washington: American Psychological Association.

Gordon, C. (1968). Self-conceptions: configurations of content. In C. Gordon & K.I. Gergen (Eds.), *The self in social interaction.* NY: Wiley.

Granberg, D. (1982). Social judgment theory. In M. Burgoon (Ed.) *Communication Yearbook 6* (pp. 304-329). Beverly Hills, California: Sage.

Hare, A. P. (1976). *Handbook of small group research* (2nd ed.). NY: Free Press.

Heider, F. (1958). *The psychology of interpersonal relations.* NY: Wiley.

Hewes, D. E., & Planalp, S. (1987). The individual's place in communication science. In C.R. Berger and S. H. Chafee (Eds). *Handbook of communication science* (pp.146-183). Newbury Park, California: Sage.

Hovland, C., Harvey, O. J., & Sherif, M. (1957). Assimilation and contrast effects in reactions to communication and attitude change. *Journal of Abnormal and Social Psychology, 55,* 244-252.

Hovland, C., Janis, I., & Kelley, H. H. (1953). *Communication and persuasion.* New Haven, Connecticut: Yale University Press.

James, W. (1890). *The principles of psychology. Vols 1 and 2.* NY: Henry Holt and Company.

Janis, I. (1982,). *Groupthink: Psychological studies of policy decisions and fiascoes* (Rev. ed.). Boston: Houghton Mifflin Company.

Janis, I., & Mann, L. (1977). *Decision making: A psychological analysis of conflict, choice, and commitment.* NY: Free Press.

Jaques, D. (1992). *Learning in groups* (2nd ed.). London: Kogan Page Limited.

Johnson, D. W. (1993). *Reaching out: Interpersonal effectiveness and self-actualization* (5th ed.). Englewood Cliffs, New Jersey: Prentice Hall.

Johnson, D. W., & Johnson, F. P. (1997). *Joining together: Group theory and group skills* (6th ed.). Boston: Allyn and Bacon.

Kelley, H. H., & Thibaut, J. W. (1978). *Interpersonal relations: A theory of interdependence.* NY: Wiley-Interscience.

Laughlin, P. R., & Jaccard, J. J. (1975). Social facilitation and observational learning of individuals and cooperative pairs. *Journal of Personality and Social Psychology, 32,* 873-879.

Lewin, K. (1935). *A dynamic theory of personality.* NY: McGraw-Hill.

Lewin, K. (1948). *Resolving social conflicts: selected papers on group dynamics,* NY: Harper.

Lewin, K. (1951). *Field theory in social science.* NY: Harper.

Littlejohn, S. W. (1996). *Theories of human communication* (5th ed.). Belmont, California: Wadsworth.

Luft, J. (1969). *Of human interaction.* Palo Alto, California: National Press.

Lumsden, G., & Lumsden, D. (1993). *Communicating in groups and teams: Sharing leadership.* Belmont, California: Wadsworth.

Martin, L., & Tesser, A. (Eds). (1992). *The construction of social judgments.* Hillsdale, New Jersey: Erlbaum.

McGuire, W. J., & McGuire, C. V. (1981). The spontaneous self-concept as affected by personal distinctiveness. In M. D. Lynch, A. A. NoremHebeisen, & K. J. Gergen (Eds). *Self-concept: advances in theory and research.* Cambridge, Massachusetts: Ballinger.

McKnight. J., & Sutton. J. (1994). *Social psychology.* Sydney: Prentice Hall Australia.

Mead, G. H. (1934). *Mind, self, and society.* (C.W. Morris, Ed.). Chicago: University of Chicago Press.

Mohan, T., McGregor, H., Saunders, S., & Archee, R. (1997). *Communicating! Theory and practice* (4th ed.). Sydney: Harcourt Brace.

Napier, R.W., & Gershenfeld, M.K. (1993). *Groups: Theory and experience* (5th ed.). Boston: Houghton Mifflin.

O'Keefe, D. J. (1990). Social judgment theory. In D. J. O'Keefe. *Persuasion: Theory and research* (pp. 29- 44). Newbury Park, California: Sage.

Olson, J. M., Herman, C. P., & Zanna, M. P. (Eds.) (1986). *Relative deprivation and social comparison: The Ontario symposium.* Hillsdale, New Jersey: Erlbaum.

Petty, R. E., & Cacioppo, J. T. (1986). *Communication and persuasion: Central and peripheral routes to attitude change.* NY: Springer-Verlag.

Piliavin, J. A., Dovidio, J.F., Gaertner, S.L., & Clark, R.D. III. (1981). *Emergency intervention.* NY: Academic Press.

Planalp, S. (1993). Communication, cognition and emotion. *Communication Monographs, 60,* 3-4.

Pollock, D., & Cox, J. R. (1991). Historicizing 'Reason': Critical theory, practice and postmodernity, *Communication Monographs, 58,* 170-178.

Ricoeur, P. (1981). *Hermeneutics and the human sciences: Essays on language, action, and interpretation.* Translated and edited by J. B. Thompson. Cambridge: Cambridge University Press.

Robinson, V. (1993). *Problem-based methodology: Research for the improvement of practice.* Oxford: Pergamon Press.

Robinson, V. (1998). *Enhancing practice based learning through critical dialogue.* Workshop prepared for the University of Technology, Sydney, 12 March, Sydney.

Rogers, C. (1961). *On becoming a person.* NY: Houghton Mifflin Company.

Roloff, M. E. (1981). *Interpersonal communication: The social exchange approach.* Beverly Hills, California: Sage.

Rymer, R. (1993). *Genie: An abused child's flight from silence.* NY: Harper Collins.

Schachter, S. (1964). The interaction of cognitive and physiological determinants of emotional state. In L. Berkowitz (Ed.). *Advances in experimental social psychology. Vol. 1,* NY: Academic Press.

Scholtes, P. (1993). *The team handbook: How to use teams to improve quality.* Madison, Wisconsin: Joiner and Associates.

Schön, D. (1983). *The reflective practitioner: How professionals think in action.* Boston: Basic Books.

Schön, D. (1987). *Educating the reflective practitioner: Toward a new design for teaching and learning in the professions.* San Francisco: Jossey-Bass.

Schön, D. (Ed.). (1991). *The reflective turn.* NY: Teachers College Press.

Seta, J.J. (1982). The impact of comparison processes on coactor's task performance. *Journal of Personality and Social Psychology, 42,* 281-291. Shattuck, R. (1980). *The forbidden experiment: the story of the wild boy of Aveyron.* NY: Farrar, Strauss & Giroux.

Shaw, M. E. (1971). *Group dynamics: The psychology of small group behaviour.* NY: McGraw Hill.

Shaw, M. E. (1981). *Group dynamics: The psychology of small group behaviour* (3rd ed.). NY: McGraw Hill.

Shaw, M. E., & Costanzo, P. R. (1982). *Theories of social psychology* (2nd ed.). NY: McGraw-Hill.

Sherif, M. (1935). A study of some social factors in perception, *Archives of Psychology, 27,* No. 187, 1-60.

Sherif, M. (1936). *The psychology of social norms.* NY: Harper & Row.

Sherif, M., & Hovland, C. I. (1961). *Social judgment.* New Haven, Connecticut: Yale University Press.

Sherif, C., Sherif, M., & Nebergall, R. (1965). *Attitude and attitude change: The social judgment-involvement approach.* Philadelphia: W. B. Saunders.

Siebold, D. R., & Spitzberg, B. H. (1981). Attribution theory and research: Formalization, review, and implications for communication. In B. Dervin and Voigt, M. J. (Eds.), *Progress in communication sciences.* Vol. 3, pp. 85-125.

Snyder, M. (1974). Self-monitoring scale. Retrieved March 4, 2008, from http://pubpages.unh.edu/~ckb/SELFMON2.html .

Snyder, M. (1974). The self-monitoring of expressive behaviour. *Journal of Personality and Social Psychology, 30,* 526-537.

Snyder, M. (1980). The many me's of the self-monitor. *Psychology Today, 13,* March, 34.

Snyder, M., & Gangestad, S. (1986). On the nature of self-monitoring: matters of assessment, matters of validity. *Journal of Personality and Social Psychology, 51*(1), 125-139.

Sperber, D., & Wilson, D. (1986). *Relevance: Communication and cognition.* Cambridge, Massachusetts: Harvard University Press.

Spitzberg, B. H., & Cupach, W. K. (1988). *Handbook of interpersonal competence research.* NY: Springer-Verlag.

Stewart, J. (Ed.) (1990). *Bridges not walls: A book about interpersonal communication* (5th ed.). NY: McGraw-Hill Publishing Company.

Sullivan, H. S. (1953). *The interpersonal theory of psychiatry.* NY: Norton.

Tennant, M. (1997). *Psychology and adult learning* (2nd ed.). London: Routledge.

Thibaut, J. W., & Kelley, H. H. (1959). *The social psychology of groups.* NY: Wiley.

Triplett, N. (1897). The dynamogenic factors in pacemaking and competition. *American Journal of Psychology, 9,* 507-533.

Tyson, T. (1989). *Working with groups.* Melbourne: The Macmillan Company Pty Ltd.

Williamson, D. L. (1982). *Group power: How to develop, lead and help groups achieve goals.* Englewood Cliffs, New Jersey: Prentice-Hall.

Wilson, G. L., Hantz, A. M., & Hanna, M. S. (1995). *Interpersonal growth through communication* (4th ed.). Madison, Wisconsin: WCB Brown & Benchmark Publishers.

Videos

CRM Productions (1991). *Groupthink* (Rev. ed.). NY: McGraw Hill Films.

Review Questions

Read the following statements and indicate whether they are True or False.
1. The social psychology of adult learning is concerned with how adults learn from social contexts whether others are present or not.
2. Adults' perceptions of how others are evaluating their behaviour does not affect an adults' capacity to learn in a social situation.
3. Social learning theory as proposed by Bandura (1983) emphasises learning from the example of others known as 'modelling'.

4. According to social learning theory, adults may learn to perform a skill in a particular way by observing others but do not always reproduce the behaviour because of personal preferences and environmental influences.

5. Adult learning is affected by a person's resourcefulness which in turn is influenced by attitudes learnt in the social environment.

6. The social psychology of adult learning should explain learning in terms of both psychological factors such as values and motives and social influences such as roles and relationships.

7. Social psychologists are interested in the study of people's motives because motives are founded in unlearned needs and are not amenable to shaping from the social environment.

8. Social psychologists have shown that in a group a majority can influence a minority to conform to perceptual judgments of visual stimuli as well as opinions.

9. In a group a minority will resist a majority pressure to conform if the majority view is obviously incorrect.

10. Groups can exert a pressure towards conformity on members in the following ways: internalisation, identification and compliance.

11. Individuals are more likely to learn and change their attitudes and behaviour if they have been part of a group discussion process where norms have been formed collaboratively.

12. In the social cognition approach to adult learning researchers are interested in concepts such as knowing, meaning and understanding but not to the extent of inferring internal processes of cognition.

13. Experienced adult educators and expert practitioners are ideal models for any adult to learn by social comparison.

14. Adults can learn complex tasks most effectively by comparing their own performance in competition with other learners.

15. According to social judgment theory, social learning experiences that provide for small increments in knowledge, skills and attitudes are likely to be most effective in changing adults' behaviour.

16. Adults can learn through self disclosure to others in a process of social exchange that involves incremental, symmetrical and reciprocal disclosure with varying breadth and depth.

17. According to social penetration theory there is more penetration at the beginning of a relationship because the rewards of disclosure are perceived to outweigh the costs.

18. Self monitoring is likely to assist adults to learn about themselves including the impressions they make on other people.

19. Adults can learn constructively from self disclosure and feedback in social interactions if they experience mutual respect, acceptance, reduced defensiveness, collaboration and specific advice from an expert who assesses the adults' learning needs.

20. According to the Johari Window Model of self disclosure and feedback, shared experiences help adults to learn by enlarging the Arena and reducing the Façade, Blind Spot and Unknown.

21. Learning conversations provide a means where more experienced practitioners can interact with novices to impose their views in direct and constructive ways.

22. Adult learning can be negatively affected by influences from the structural properties of groups such as norms, communication patterns, size and composition including expertise and gender.
23. Research from social psychology on group dynamics has shown that cohesiveness can lead to conformity and 'groupthink' where learning may be based on inadequate information and lack of testing of shared assumptions thus leading to poor decisions.
24. Cohesive groups can try to overcome potentially negative effects on learning, arising from a tendency to strive to seek agreement and to reach consensus prematurely, by encouraging critical evaluation and devil's advocates and by inviting visitors to the group to prevent isolation.
25. Effective learning groups are depicted as being cooperative, participative, innovative and cohesive with a range of strategies for dealing with conflict, decision making, problem solving and evaluation of the group learning process.

Answers

1T	2F	3T	4T	5T	6T	7 F	8T	9F
10T	11T	12F	13F	14 F	15T	16T	17T	18T
19F	20T	21 F	22T	23T	24T	25T		

Exercises and Essay Questions

1. Social learning theory ... takes into account that human learners do not depend as much as other animals do on trial and error in order to discover what is reinforcing. Humans are markedly more capable of learning from observation and explicit instruction. (Gold, 1997, p. 146).

Explain how adults learn from the social environment by commenting on the quotation and by discussing a range of theoretical perspectives in the social psychology of adult learning outlined in this chapter. Give examples from your own learning for each theoretical perspective.

2. Use the guidelines on self disclosure, feedback and the learning conversation given in this chapter to conduct a learning conversation with a partner. Rotate the roles so that you both give feedback to each other on an aspect of each other's performance or skill development. Video the two learning conversations. Replay the videos and discuss how you both followed the guidelines to give direct feedback to each other, to check your own implicit theories of practice with each other and to learn collaboratively. Write a summary of the learning you gained from this exercise including what you did well and what you would do differently.

3. Review the research findings from the social psychology of group dynamics given in this chapter. Give examples of these findings from your own experience of learning in groups. Suggest how you could minimise the negative effects on your learning from some of these influences. Suggest how these research findings can be used to facilitate your learning in a group.

4. Use the following quotation as a basis for discussing the advantages and disadvantages of learning in a group context. Illustrate your answer with examples where your own learning in groups was either facilitated or hindered and suggest reasons why this occurred. Explain how you could facilitate learning in a group

where you are a member by applying research findings on group dynamics and strategies for enhancing learning in a group. Discuss any sources of support and potential problems for implementing your suggestions in the group.

Although cooperative groups outperform individuals working alone, there is nothing magical about groups. There are conditions under which groups function effectively and conditions under which groups function ineffectively. Simply placing people in groups and telling them to work together does not in and of itself promote productivity. (Johnson & Johnson, 1997, p. 18)

Self Assessment of Personal Contributions for Facilitating Learning in a Group

For each item given below circle a number to indicate your usual abilities or tendencies when you are participating in a learning group. Select three or four items that you would most like to change. Draw an arrow showing in which direction you would like to change. Write a personal action plan for developing in each chosen area.

Alternatively, answer these items with a particular group in mind.

1. Ability to express my own personal goals to the group.

0   1   2   3   4   5   6   7
Very unsatisfactory   Very satisfactory

2.   Ability to clarify and negotiate group goals.

0   1   2   3   4   5   6   7
Very unsatisfactory   Very satisfactory

3.   Ability to express thoughts clearly in the group.

0   1   2   3   4   5   6   7
Very vague   Very clear

4.   Ability to present ideas and have them accepted in the group.

0   1   2   3   4   5   6   7
Very low   Very high

5.   Ability to listen with understanding of others' ideas and meaning.

0   1   2   3   4   5   6   7
Very low   Very high

6.   Ability to listen with understanding to others' feelings (empathy).

0   1   2   3   4   5   6   7
Very low understanding Very high understanding

7.   Ability to express emotions and to be willing to express emotions in the group.

| 0 | 1 | 2 | 3 | 4 | 5 | 6 | 7 |

Not very open   Very open

8.   Ability to help the group to make progress on the task.

| 0 | 1 | 2 | 3 | 4 | 5 | 6 | 7 |

Very low   Very high

9.   Ability to help to relieve tension in the group.

| 0 | 1 | 2 | 3 | 4 | 5 | 6 | 7 |

Very low   Very high

10. Tendency to accept responsibility on behalf of the group.

| 0 | 1 | 2 | 3 | 4 | 5 | 6 | 7 |

Very low   Very high

11. Tendency to dominate in the group.

| 0 | 1 | 2 | 3 | 4 | 5 | 6 | 7 |

Very low   Very high

12. Ability to involve and encourage others to contribute.

| 0 | 1 | 2 | 3 | 4 | 5 | 6 | 7 |

Very low   Very high

13. Ability to contribute to discussions to reach consensus.

| 0 | 1 | 2 | 3 | 4 | 5 | 6 | 7 |

Very low   Very high

14. Ability to use a range of problem solving strategies in the group.

| 0 | 1 | 2 | 3 | 4 | 5 | 6 | 7 |

Very low   Very high

15. Tendency to ignore and avoid conflict in the group.

| 0 | 1 | 2 | 3 | 4 | 5 | 6 | 7 |

Very low   Very high

16. Ability to discuss conflict and antagonism in the group.

| 0 | 1 | 2 | 3 | 4 | 5 | 6 | 7 |

Very low   Very high

17.   Ability to express affection and warmth in the group.

| 0 | 1 | 2 | 3 | 4 | 5 | 6 | 7 |

Very low   Very high

18. Tendency to trust others in the group.

0	1	2	3	4	5	6	7

Very suspicious   Very trusting

19. Ability to think creatively in the group.

0	1	2	3	4	5	6	7

Seldom contribute ideas   High idea production

20. Ability to interact well with every one in the group.

0	1	2	3	4	5	6	7

Very low   Very high

Now that you have completed the questionnaire, what have you learned about your participation in learning groups? How can you apply this learning?

As an adult educator, what do the results of the questionnaire indicate to you about how to facilitate learning in groups? How can you apply this learning in adult education practice?

Using the Questionnaire for Feedback and Group Learning
You can use this questionnaire to receive feedback on your abilities and tendencies from other group members and to give feedback to other group members on their contributions. The results could be used to discuss improving the functioning of the group so that members' learning is facilitated. You could write a group action plan for improving the functioning of the group to meet agreed learning goals.

About the Author

Dr Shirley Saunders is a Senior Lecturer, Faculty of Education, University of Technology, Sydney. She has research and teaching interests in the areas of interpersonal communication, group and team communication and communication within systems such as modern organisations. She has worked for over thirty years in communication education and training in the tertiary sector. She is co-author of T. Mohan, H. McGregor, S. Saunders, & R. Archee (1997). *Communicating! Theory and Practice* (4th ed.). Sydney: Harcourt Brace and T. Mohan, H. McGregor, S. Saunders, & R. Archee (2008). *Communicating as professionals* (2nd ed.). Southbank, Victoria: Thomson.

Shirley Saunders
University of Technology, Sydney

IAN R. CORNFORD

4. SOCIAL LEARNING

The Prevalence of Social Learning

An enormous amount of learning occurs through interactions with those around us.
Very frequently we observe other people and model what they do. This is the
essence of what is known as social learning. In some societies the word for "teach"
and the word for "show" are synonymous (Reichard, 1938). Social learning and the
factors which are involved in learning in social and physical contexts have received
a great deal of attention from researchers and educators over the past decade. This
has been because of dissatisfaction with conventional formal school learning and
because there has been increased recognition that much important learning occurs
in setting such as workplaces, in shops and everyday activities of a social nature.
Probably much more learning occurs in places not conventionally considered as
sources of learning and education than in formal education settings such as school,
TAFE and university classrooms.

Despite the fact that the importance of social interaction on learning and
development has been recognised for a long time, there have been few theories
which have been satisfactory in attempting to explain social learning at all or most
age levels. In the following sections some of the earlier theories and more recent,
fashionable theories are considered briefly before a more exhaustive coverage of
Bandura's analyses of factors involved in observational learning. Overall,
Bandura's model appears to provide more substantial insights and bases for
implementation for educators and those engaged in training in work settings than
other theories.

A HISTORICAL PERSPECTIVE: SOME MORE INFLUENTIAL THEORIES

Piaget's Genetic Epistemological Theory

From the 1920s until his death the Swiss researcher Piaget developed a theory of the development of intelligence and cognitive functioning based on a series of genetically determined stages (see the chapter by Collis in this text). In this theory there is a strong emphasis upon social interaction (see De Vries, 1997). Piaget not only observed children at play and interviewed them; he also presented them with intellectual tasks and recorded their answers. From this data he identified four stages of intellectual development - the sensorimotor, preoperational, concrete operational and formal operational stages. Piaget argued that these stages were fixed, invariable and age related, although there were some slight age differences in normal learners.

This cognitive developmental theory centred on social interaction has been attacked from a number of positions, especially in relation to the invariability of stages and fixed sequencing of subcomponents as proposed by Piaget (see Kuhn, 1997; Metz, 1995, 1997). Research findings indicate that the tasks which Piaget established as critical indicators for attainment of the formal operational stage of development cannot be accomplished by many adults. A good overview of Piaget's theory and the problems for it revealed by research may be found in Gage and Berliner (1992) or McInerney and McInerney (1994).

Vygotsky's Social-Cognitive Approach

Vygotsky (1978), who developed theories in the 1930s to explain the links between socialisation, language, and the development of behaviour and cognitive processes in children, was initially influenced by Piaget's early work (Wertsch, 1985).

Vygotsky's theories fell out of favour in the USSR and it was not until the late seventies that there were significant efforts to disseminate his work beyond the borders of Russia. Central to the theory are concepts of self-verbalisation, proximal development and scaffolding of younger children through interaction with carers. The zone of proximal development involves the concept that the child can be encouraged to develop skills which are to close to their immediate capability and may realistically be attained with help from a parent or teacher. In this it is close to the concept of readiness which has been a feature of teacher education since the work of Gesell (1926) established norms of what behaviour and thinking could be expected of average children as they developed physically and intellectually. Scaffolding refers to the process whereby parents or teachers support children as they attempt to learn behaviour beyond their immediate capability and progress to the next stage of development and achievement as expected by society.

The importance of self-verbalisation in the process of internalisation of language, concepts and values in early child development is not in doubt, but the relevance of Vygotsky's work for adolescent and adult learners has not been established. For example, scaffolding seems to be entirely dependent upon an individual's motivation and willingness to be coached or mentored as an inferior being. Many adult or late adolescent learners are not inclined to accept a learning role in which they are not viewed as of equal status even if deficient in knowledge.

Key elements in many adult learning theories are the need for independence and control in learning. By adolescence, normal learners have developed an effective symbol and language basis for effective functioning, hence many aspects of Vygotsky's theory of language internalisation for self-control and effective action do not appear relevant. Vygotsky himself appears to have distinguished between children and adults developmentally, but also indicated similarities between these groups in terms of thinking (see Frawley, 1997, p. 30).

Several researchers have challenged aspects of Vygotsky's theory. For example Schunk and Zimmerman (1997) drew upon social cognitive theory to challenge the assumption by Vygotsky that modelling leads to passivity. They also stressed the importance of the reciprocal interactions between behavioural, environmental and personal variables other than self-verbalisation in development, with behavioural, environmental and personal variables necessary to explain adolescent and adult actions and thinking. Wertsch's (Wertsch, 1985; Wertsch & Tulviste, 1992) writings provide a good introduction to Vygotsky's work apart from Vygotsky's (1978) own accounts. Also useful is Frawley's (1997) book which places Vygotsky's work into historical context by critiquing a number of philosophical and psychological theories of knowledge acquisition.

Situated Learning

Recently a range of theorists have again focused upon the importance of learning in social context. Billett (1996) has claimed that situated learning represents the means of reconciling cognitive and socio-cultural influences. However, there are numerous theories of situated learning which have quite radically different views on a range of issues important for learning (e.g., see Billett, 1996; Brown, Collins, & Duguid, 1989; Greeno, 1997; Lave, 1988). The extreme position (e.g., Lave, 1988; Lave & Wenger, 1991) denied the existence of transfer and holds that learning is only attained through specific physical cues and thus reflects the older, behavioural psychology position (Voss, Wiley & Carretero, 1995). Many situated learning theorists highlight the obvious difficulties in obtaining transfer, and the problem of school learning separated from real-life applications, but fall relatively short on detailed analyses of processes involved in actual learning in cultural contexts.

A major problem for the situated learning theorists is that most do not assume fixed knowledge structures and so cannot account in any satisfactory way for memory (Renkl, Mandl & Gruber, 1996). Several researchers (e.g., Cornford, 1996; Voss, Wiley, & Carretero, 1995) have indicated that, in addition to the social and contextual factors operating in learning, there is a need to consider the learning processes of individuals. More recent work by Collins (1997), one of the seminal researchers in situated learning, has moved away from the position of Lave (Lave, 1988; Lave & Wenger, 1991) to consider deliberate teaching for transfer as an important part of educational practice. Other situated learning theorists like Billett (1996, 1998) have attempted to remedy the lack of adequate consideration of individual learning. Billett's (1998) latest statements took a decidedly developmental psychology approach to explaining learning through life history, but still did not explain the processes which are involved in the acquisition and storage of knowledge.

Bandura's (1977, 1986, 1997) model analysing the factors involved in observational learning successfully reconciled individual, cognitive, social and behavioural elements of learning. What is more this model involved detailed analyses of learning processes. This theory in its earlier versions substantially predated Lave's theorising (Lave, 1988; Lave & Wenger, 1991) but has been ignored consistently by Lave and also by Billett (1996, 1998). This is unfortunate since, even its earlier 1977 form, Bandura's theory represents an important step in reconciling a range of theories in the one model. Elements of cognitive, information processing, social, and behavioural psychology theories are reconciled in a model embodying what is essentially a constructivist approach to learning where individuals makes choices and are actively engaged in making meaning of the world surrounding them.

Bandura's Social Learning/Social Cognitive Theory

Although imitation was of interest earlier this century, S*ocial Learning and Imitation* by Miller and Dollard, published in 1941, appears to have been the first serious attempt to analyse modelling processes. This involved young children and was done from the perspective of drive reduction which marked a departure from associationist behavioural psychology. However, this work did not consider issues of adaptation of modelling, and it was not until Bandura and Walters' (1963) seminal work on modelling processes affecting children and adults that more complex and satisfactory explanations of social learning emerged.

In earlier writings, Bandura (Bandura & Walters, 1963; Bandura, 1977) used the term social learning to describe his theory. Since then he has decided that social cognitive theory better described his intent and concerns (Bandura, 1986, 1997). Bandura's current research interests are centred upon self-efficacy and cognitive processes which underlie successful human thinking and performance. While recognising that Bandura's theories have developed beyond modelling, it was decided to retain the earlier terminology of social learning as a chapter heading.

The reasons for this are that Bandura's social cognitive theory, with its emphasis upon self-efficacy, extends well beyond the concerns of this chapter. It is also considered that the interests of many vocational and adult educators focus upon performance and that the earlier accounts of the theory placed more emphasis upon this. Other researchers, such as Krumboltz (1994), have also chosen to emphasise the social learning aspects and retain these descriptors. An additional reason for choosing the social learning nomenclature is that the more recent situated learning and social cognitive theorists (Lave, 1988, 1990; Lave & Wenger, 1991) have claimed that many cognitive psychological theories have neglected the physical and social contexts. Bandura's theory quite specifically took into account social, cognitive and physical aspects of learning and this chapter is in part an attempt to redress this limited understanding.

The main focus of this chapter is to explain Bandura's model of the component processes governing observational learning (Bandura, 1977, p. 23; 1997, p. 89). There are some slight differences between the earliest and more recently published accounts of the observational learning model. The version presented in this chapter (see Figure 4.1) is an adaptation, redressing the balance towards the performance elements as in the first account. Before considering factors affecting observational learning, let us consider the vital role which models and observational learning play in the learning of behaviour and attitudes, abstract rules governing social interaction, change of self, and the development of important self-regulatory processes.

THE IMPORTANCE OF MODELLING IN SOCIAL COGNITIVE THEORY AND IN THE DEVELOPMENT OF SELF PROCESSES

The foundation of social cognitive theory is belief that there are complex interactions between the individual, the behaviour and the environment, with each of these variables contributing to the individual's cognition and behaviour. In this view of learning and behaviour, modelling is of very great importance and seen as an environmental factor.

Not only does modelling explain the acquisition of a wide range of observable behaviours, but it is seen as important in learning the abstract rules which underlie effective behaviour. There is ample research which demonstrates that even young children are quite capable of deducing and transferring rules and concepts that underlie modelling events (Rosenthal & Zimmerman, 1978; Zimmerman & Rosenthal, 1974). It is possible to deduce the rules governing sporting games or of codes of conduct in informal social settings, which lack formal rules, through observation. Behaving in the correct way or saying the right things in social situations is dependent upon this ability to deduce the rules operating. In effect civilised social conduct is dependent upon recognition of complex rules derived from complex behaviour and adherence to these codes of conduct.

Modelling through observational learning is also considered of very considerable importance in developing self-regulation and positive beliefs about self-efficacy. Self-efficacy is the belief that one is likely to succeed. Many social cognitive researchers consider that these self processes are key issues in the development of effective learning and performance (e.g., Bandura, 1997; Schunk, 1989; Zimmerman, 1989). Zimmerman and Bonner (in Schunk & Zimmerman, 1997) have conceptualised four distinct levels in the ultimate development of self-regulatory behaviour in students. These are an Observational Level, an Imitative Level, a Self-controlled Level and, ultimately, a Self-regulated Level. In this model there is a gradual movement from social sources to self sources. Models, verbal description, and social guidance and feedback are viewed as essential components in the two earlier levels. While the last two levels involve the development of self-control and self-regulatory processes, models, verbal description, and social guidance and feedback also must be considered important in the gradual development of these later levels.

Change, Possible Selves and the Importance of Models

Any learning of behaviour, or of attitudes and values, is dependent upon having some conception of what that may involve. Without some model which provides evidence of the very existence of the form of behaviour or values, then the learner is left without any guidance. Without conception of the possible, change cannot take place. A critical concept in changing behaviours, ideas or attitudes thus is that of possible selves (Markus & Nurius, 1986). It is only possible to direct energies towards change if you can conceptualise what that change may be or involve. Without an alternative idea, taking steps to bring about change is not possible.

In the present climate in which change is advocated in business and education to produce greater efficiency, it is necessary to be able to move beyond vague generalisations and rhetoric to be able to conceptualise in some considerable depth what is involved in translating good ideals or vague slogans into concrete, effective action. Closing of the gap between the ideal and the real is dependent upon much more concrete formulations of series of activities and it is here that having models who are already performing in the desired ways is invaluable in assisting to develop the changed behaviours. A great deal of policy making by governments and politicians in economic and educational matters involves borrowing ideas and practices already adopted in other countries.

Markus and Nurius (1986) indicated that there can be both positive and negative aspects to possible selves. From viewing others and making social comparisons we make judgments about whether we wish to have certain abilities or qualities. Equally from viewing others we make judgments about what we certainly do not want to be like. Together the positive and negative possible selves provide the motivation to pursue certain avenues and avoid others, and they cover all aspects of mature personality and behaviour.

The possible selves that are hoped for might include the successful self, the creative self, the rich self, the thin self or the loved and admired self, whereas the dreaded possible selves could be the alone self, the depressed self, the incompetent self, the alcoholic self, the unemployed self, or the bag lady self (Markus & Nurius, 1986, p. 954).

Few individuals deliberately engage in self-destructive behaviour by consciously emulating the less successful. Human beings are very much inclined only to select those models whom they believe are effective performers (Bandura, 1977, 1997). The viewing of positive models also provides the means by which certain objectives can be accomplished. If individuals have to imagine and develop every single step in achieving a goal then this requires a great deal of trial and error learning. Such trial and error learning takes a great deal of time and hence is not very practical in most work situations, either in formal education settings, where there are both content and processes to be learned in relatively short time frames, or business and industry where efficient performance is a major consideration in producing profit. In formal learning situations or in the workplace demonstrations are often provided to ensure the effective learning of the modelled processes and avoid the inefficiency that would accompany trial and error.

Some Common Effects of Model Observation

Any theory which attempts to explain social learning must be able to provide explanation for a range of naturally occurring human behaviours and explain how modelling can result in a number of different effects. In attempting to explain learning from modelled behaviour it is necessary to be able to explain why some forms of behaviour are modelled and others are not. We are surrounded by models of all types displaying a variety of behaviours and different sets of values. But only some of these behaviours and values are selected for adoption by individual learners. Apart from the facilitation of learning resulting from observation of new behaviour, factors which must be explained by any theory for it to be regarded as satisfactory include inhibition/disinhibition effects and creative adaptations.

Inhibition refers to the effect of observation of models causing the individual not to engage in certain forms of behaviour. Disinhibition is to throw off caution and engage in a form of behaviour previously considered not appropriate (Bandura & Walters, 1963; Schunk & Zimmerman, 1997). A common example of inhibition is when car drivers slow down on the road after seeing a police officer with a notebook in his or her hand talking to another driver. Disinhibition effects are important in explaining crowd behaviour, such as soccer hooliganism where normally sensible individuals engage in generally socially unacceptable behaviour, or the inhumanity of people to each other under war conditions. With inhibition and disinhibition, the environmental factors, particularly the potential of punishment or reward respectively from those in the social context, tend to be important factors.

New forms of behaviour are frequently learned by young children from observing models. Bandura's theory recognised that models can take a number of different forms. Bandura, Ross and Ross (1963) showed that aggressive behaviour could be learned equally effectively from viewing real-life models, human models on film and cartoons. In this experiment the preschool children displayed precisely imitative behaviour in attacking an inflated doll. However, it is usual for the individual, especially more mature adults, to adapt or modify modelled behaviours rather than reproduce the identical behaviour observed. The selection of behaviours for adoption is not haphazard, but is often very carefully considered by the individual learner, and the model advanced by Bandura posits an active and adaptive learner.

What is considered of great importance in modelling is that there are quite important creative adaptations of what is observed. Bandura (1977) in fact indicated that modelling is the appropriate terminology since the concept of imitation does not really accurately represent the complexity or creativity of what occurs. Individuals often attempt to be creative and improve what they have observed as well as to adapt responses to slightly different circumstances. In one experiment involving trainee teachers all practising the same introduction topic twice in separate microteaching sessions, no two individuals performed in exactly the same ways although they saw each others' performances and attempted to adhere to the general principles for effective performance of introductions which they had been given (Cornford, 1991). Such adaptation of rules and forms of behaviour amounts to transfer of learning, with such transfer of learning explained by the interaction of factors in Bandura's (1977, 1986, 1997) observational learning model.

Creative adaptations are important for the individual in solving problems encountered in day-to-day living and work. The ways in which individuals may use fashion magazines in order to gain ideas how to dress more stylishly in what are the new fashions of the day provides a good example of adaptation and creative problem solving. For example an individual may see a photo reproduction of someone wearing green but, knowing that green is not a colour which suits their hair and complexion, may purchase a garment of an identical style but in a colour which is more flattering to them. Alternatively there may be some features of a design or different pieces of apparel which are taken and used and combined with other, different features to suit a particular purpose.

Figure 4.1 *Bandura's Model of Processes Governing Observational Learning.*

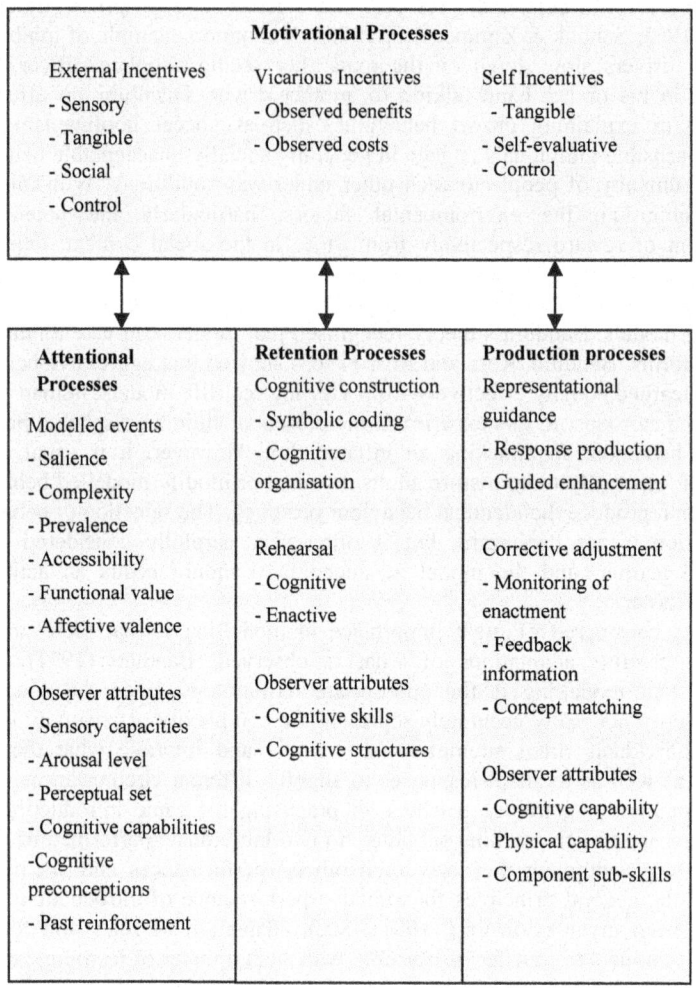

Adapted from Bandura (1977, 1986, 1997)

The Observational Learning Model

Bandura's (1977, 1986, 1997) model analysing factors involved in observational learning, which is represented in Figure 4.1, explained what occurs when an individual sees a model performing some type of skill or action, attempts to learn from this situation and tries to reproduce the modelled behaviour. The model observed may be a real life model, but equally in an information age the model may be a symbolic model. That is to say the model may be in cartoon form or represented by line drawings. For example dance steps are often shown using numbered feet and arrows. These are of course symbols with many similar examples available in texts books, particularly those which illustrate how to perform skills such a cross stitch, golf, etc. In an age in which television is in almost every home there can be considerable learning from movies or television series which may involve fictional characters as well as real ones. The radio, another common form of media, also provides models which may be imitated. There is considerable evidence that media mediated models have considerable impact and there are many in the community who are influenced by media models, especially younger children and adolescents.

The observational learning model takes four sets of factors into account in explaining the processes of matching one's own behaviour to that of a model. These four groups are Attentional Processes, Retention Processes, Production Processes and Motivational Processes. In each of the sets of processes it is necessary to take into account both what the model brings to the learning situation and what the observer brings to the situation. The Attentional Processes are concerned with explaining how the learner selectively extracts information from the modelled event or a range of modelled events. Attention and focus upon a model or event in physical or social context is necessary for information to be acquired by any individual. The information processing model with its subcomponents of sensory input, short term or working memory and subconscious long term memory underpins Bandura's model. At the Attentional Processes phase all three information processing elements are brought into play in various ways.

Just focusing upon aspects of a model is of course not sufficient for learning to have said to have taken place. Information must be retained in long term memory if it is going to be available for future reference, hence the importance of the Retention Processes. Bandura's model also took account of the processes involved in converting the images and information stored in memory into some kind of physical performance via Production Processes. In Production Processes the importance of a range of practice and feedback variables are clearly established. A further, overarching set of considerations are the Motivational Processes in the model. Motivation is a very important factor in initial skill learning, but also in the maintenance of skill standards and in improvement of skills over time (Cornford, 1996). It is probably most appropriate to view motivation processes underlying or strongly influencing all the Attention, Retention and Performance Processes. The importance of motivation in learning more generally is explored in another chapter in this text (Russell, 1999).

Attentional Processes: Modelled Events

Salience
In observing a modelled event the salience or distinctiveness of the act is a very considerable importance. Unless the modelled act and subcomponents can be distinguished from other events and information in the surrounding social and physical context, there is little chance of the individual being able to recognise the information as new and separate from existing knowledge. Without this, there will be no inclination to learn it as new if it is not perceived and conceptualised as such.

Many fine distinctions in codes of conduct and manners are not all that distinctive which explains why individuals fail to perceive cues and respond to them in appropriate ways. Novice learners frequently fail to notice certain cues. Discrimination training in which novices are taught to identify basic stimuli and cues prior to more complex skill training can facilitate identification of important signals or components and thus acquisition of the complex skills (Cornford, 1991).

Key cuing phrases are often used by good teachers. These can be statements like: "Observe what happens when I press the button" or "Look closely at how this arm moves" or "Pay attention now and watch what happens here". In some cases, with modelled events which are particularly rapid or difficult to see, the teacher will describe what the individual needs to look for. Subsequent to the event, teachers often check that there has been accurate and correct observation of key features by the asking of specific questions to ensure that students have noticed what they were supposed to notice and can identify what occurred. Where the teacher has described the difficult event there may be efforts to ensure that observers can describe the event in their own words to ensure that mere parroting back of the teacher's words is not taking place.

Complexity

The complexity of the modelled event will affect how much of the event is actually observed, processed and retained. Long and complex procedures generally will not be accurately perceived or learned from observation of just one performance. This is on account of the limitations of short term or working memory and its capacity to hold more than the seven plus or minus two units of information (Sweller, 1993). Contributing to the problem is the fact that the individual is unlikely to be able to chunk or group together more than this number of pieces of information, which is the means whereby the limitations of short term or working memory are usually transcended, because of the newness of the information to the observer. Where similar events have been observed before, the previous learning will serve as a basis upon which to attach more of the relevant pieces of information which together will constitute all the pieces of the learning jigsaw.

Generally complex skills are learned over numerous viewings. Practice and feedback subsequent to the initial observation coupled with repeated observations is an important part of teaching strategy. [See the section on Retention Processes below and also the chapter on Skill Learning and the Development of Expertise (Cornford, in this text).]

Prevalence

The prevalence or number of opportunities to be able to observe the performance of a modelled event will play a role in the effective acquisition of the information contained in the event. If a skill such as eating with a spoon is frequently observed by a child then this behaviour will be fairly easily acquired. What may not be acquired as information on the first exposure is likely to be acquired on subsequent observations. With a skill such as bread making, where there are very few opportunities to observe in a modern age because most bread making occurs in factories, it is likely that effective learning to reproduce the skill will be imperfect, even using printed recipes. Bandura (1977) noted that there are instances of no trial learning, where the individual is exposed to the modelled event only once and can successfully reproduce the skill from that one exposure. This appears to be atypical of most learning situations and is almost certainly restricted to simple responses and where the sub-skill components already are firmly established in the individual's repertoire (Cornford, 1996).

Accessibility

An important consideration is how easy it is to gain access to a modelling event to enable learning to take place. Access to different models, particularly live models, is largely determined by associational networks, especially those developed because of social class. Social class differences exist in many aspects of human activity, especially in codes of manners. Class-based differences in many aspects of child rearing practices involving socialisation and enculturation have been well documented and recognised for many years (e.g., see Mussen, Conger & Kagan, 1964). For example, differences exist in terms of use or non-use of more elaborated codes of speech and delayed gratification. Because individuals from the different social classes rarely get the opportunity to observe models engaged in interpersonal relations and codes of conduct over extended periods, they seldom have the opportunity to learn other forms of thinking and behaviour. Instead they continue to exhibit those practices which are accessible to them and which they have learned.

The accessibility of an event which may be important for learning and human functioning may be restricted because of wider social values and attitudes other than just class-based ones. There are a whole variety of taboos which are attached to human performance and functioning in our society generally. Mature adults in relationships are expected to be able to perform in sexually adequate ways yet, in our society because of cultural ideals of privacy and the sense of the inappropriateness of younger people being knowledgeable in this area, teenagers are not permitted to watch older, more experienced individuals engaged in love making. The result is a great deal of trial and error learning and many unhappy marriage partners. A role for sex therapists has developed for those who experience extreme dysfunction. Toilet training is another area of human functioning which is complicated by a sense of privacy and cultural taboo. Babies and young children would be more likely to learn effective toileting behaviour if parents were less inclined to close the bathroom door when performing what are normal body functions, performed by every human being, which involve very complex skill learning for that stage of development (Mussen et al., 1964).

Currently there is a great deal of interest in the development of cognitive skills (Weinstein & Meyer, 1991), metacognitive skills (Sternberg, 1998), and attitudes (Schunk & Zimmerman, 1997). However, one of the major problems encountered in developing these skills and attitudes is that cognitive and metacognitive skills are largely invisible. This is because cognition by its very nature is internal, personal and invisible unless individuals choose to make their thinking obvious through words or deeds. Cognitive modelling, which incorporates verbalisation of the models' thoughts and reasons for performing as they do with modelled explanations and demonstrations, has been proven to be effective in the learning of a range of coping skills (Meichenbaum, 1977). Research on the behaviour of teachers indicates that few teachers take steps to verbalise and model aloud their own thinking processes for the benefit of students (e.g., Moely, Hart, Santulli, Leal, Johnson, Rao, Burney, & Pechman, 1985).

Functional Value

Functional value refers to the perceived value or usefulness of a modelled event to the observer. The functional value of a modelled event is of considerable importance in determining whether an individual is likely to pay attention to the event being modelled and subsequently attempt to acquire similar behaviour, attitudes or knowledge. If the model is obtaining some form of reward or gratification from engagement in the activity, and the observer can identify with that model or perceive value in learning the activity, then the observer is more likely to pay attention and attempt to learn from that modelled event. Research indicates that modelled behaviours leading to rewarding outcomes are more likely to be performed than those resulting in punishment (Zimmerman & Koussa, 1979). The importance of the perceived value of an activity or knowledge is particularly well known to most engaged in the teaching of adults or adolescents who will not make efforts to acquire the knowledge or skill unless they can perceive value from so doing.

A modelled event may have functional value although there may be negative consequences flowing from the performance or failure may result in terms of objectives not being attained. From the observed failure an observer may come to understand that other strategies may be necessary to succeed or to avoid punishment. It is possible to learn both what to do and what not to do from observing a model and this information can have considerable functional value.

Affective Valence

Affective valence refers to the degrees of attraction and identification that exist between an observer and a model. It is important in helping to explain why selective adoption or learning of modelled behaviour occurs. Interpersonal attraction leading to adoption of modelled behaviour is consistently utilised by advertisers in their attempts to persuade consumers to purchase their products.

To date much of the research into modelling characteristic likely to promote effective learning has centred upon children (e.g., see Schunk, 1987; Zimmerman & Rosenthal, 1974). Characteristics which are likely to foster identification between observer and model in children and adults include warmth, competence, power and high status (Lefkowitz, Blake, & Mouton, 1955; Lippitt, Polansky, & Rosen, 1952). These characteristics are more effective in prompting the adoption of similar behaviour than those of models who have less prestige or display less effectiveness.

Humans seem almost genetically programmed to learn more effective forms of behaviour from observing others to assist them in successful adaptation to their surroundings. More successful individuals whose behaviour leads to success are likely to be adopted as models. Not only is trial and error learning costly in terms of time it can also be particularly dangerous (Bandura, 1977). This is why teachers who deal with dangerous equipment or processes do not allow their students to experiment but provide clear demonstrations and information. As Bandura noted: "People actively seek proficient models who possess the competencies to which they aspire. By their behavior and expressed ways of thinking, competent models transmit knowledge and teach observers effective skills and strategies for managing environmental demands." (Bandura, 1997, p. 88).

Few investigations of models favourably perceived by adults have been undertaken although it has been assumed generally that similarities in terms of sex, age and social status are important considerations in gaining identification. In one of the few studies involving adults, Brown, Brown and Danielson (1975) concluded that friendliness, self-assuredness and confident portrayal, along with credibility and sincerity, are factors of importance. In this study, however, the expertise of the viewers was not controlled.

Schunk and Zimmerman indicated that: "Similarities to models constitutes an important source of vicarious information for gauging one's efficacy." (1997, p. 197). A number of studies have indicated that the likelihood of skill acquisition increases or decreases with an observer's realistic judgement of their ability to learn to perform the skills effectively (Bandura, 1986). This suggests that coping models may be more effective in promoting identification and learning than expert models who may overawe novice learners with their apparently effortless mastery. Studies with child models who voiced fears as well as ways to overcome those fears have demonstrated learning improvements for observers (Schunk, 1987).

Adult also can benefit from exposure to coping models when learning complex skills. Adult learners exposed to coping models, who did not voice fears but gave good, natural but not very polished performances and who were similar in age to the observers, learned introductions to lessons which transferred to natural classrooms from microteaching settings (Cornford, 1991).

However, there is a need for more extensive research on the employment of different types of training models likely to assist adults learners in an age of occupational change. Coping models may only be relevant in early stages of learning since in business there is a need for performance at mastery level. It seems logical to assume that coping models may serve to help initial stages in skill learning by fostering expectations of self-efficacy, but then it may be necessary to expose learners to expert models to further develop their performance to higher levels.

Attentional Processes: Observer Attributes

Sensory Capacities
In Bandura's model of observational learning the observer is not merely a passive recipient of information but is actively involved in selecting, interpreting and storing information. If an observer has limits on sensory capability, on account of genetic defects or injury sustained during or after birth, then this will impose certain limitations on the information which may be perceived through the relevant senses. Teachers who have visually impaired students in their classes use a variety of teaching strategies to help circumvent these problems and use other senses. Different strategies may be required with those with other sensory disabilities.

Arousal Level
The level at which an individual is functioning whilst exposed to a modelled event is important in terms of how much information can be processed by that individual. If a student is asleep on the desk on a Monday after an exhausting weekend playing sport then there is clearly little chance of that student absorbing any information from the modelled event. If the student is awake but drowsy, then not much will be

absorbed either. Hyperactive students or those who are experiencing an abnormally high arousal level will not be able to concentrate and focus upon single pieces of information long enough for them to be attended to and processed in an appropriate way. It is generally accepted in teaching folklore that younger children become more restless on very windy days and are more difficult to teach while in this state. Similarly it may be difficult to teach students who have just returned from vigorous sporting activities. In these cases it may be necessary to plan for individual work which requires little or no social interaction with teacher or classmates, such as working exercises directly from a text.

Perceptual Set

On account of our previous cultural conditioning and experiences we develop individual ways of seeing the world and interpreting what is seen. Teachers need to be aware that there are certain frames of reference which students bring with them to every situation which may cause them to interpret the modelled events in certain ways which may be at odds with what an objective observer may interpret or what the teacher intended. With experience, and an awareness of the values which certain religious and cultural groups impart to their members, teachers can develop strategies to facilitate more conventional interpretations.

Cognitive Capabilities

The cognitive abilities which an observer brings to bear on a modelled event will strongly influence the interpretation which is made of that event and how successful the individual will be in perceiving information, acquiring the essential elements of information, and storing that information. The ability of the learner to select from a range of competing stimuli, and also attend to what may be multiple, relevant sources of information, is an important consideration in relation to salience or the way in which something stands out. In any modelling situation there are multiple sources of information. These include the characteristics of the model, the nature of the task, situational factors which assist or hinder performance, the characteristics of the actions and the effects that they produce. Young children or atypical learners may lack the experience and cognitive skills which would enable them better to attend to all these aspects of the modelling performance (Bandura, 1997, p. 171). For these reasons, it is preferable in many teaching settings to remove any distractions with the potential to compete with the desired modelled performance and to simplify things in initial learning stages to reduce the complexity. In addition, it is appropriate to plan for multiple exposures to the modelled event introducing increasing complexity gradually.

Bandura (1977, p. 29) indicated that maturation and experience are important considerations in the recognition of the existence, acquisition and improvement of sub-skills. Many teachers and trainers experience the problem that normal, novice learners cannot make fine distinctions and observe differences and this is a reason why learning can occur so slowly with novice learners (see Cornford's other chapter in this text). In practice good teachers and trainers cue learners to pay attention and notice what is being displayed or demonstrated (see Bandura, 1977, p. 50).

Cognitive Preconceptions
The individual's past learning can influence the perception of the modelled event in numerous ways since we all draw upon previous learning to interpret and learn from the present situation (Yates & Chandler, 1991). In some instances the previously learned information will be correct and a useful base upon which to construct new knowledge; in other cases it will be incorrect. A considerable body of research has documented how incorrect perceptions of children and adolescents can hinder them in understanding science and mathematics. The existing cognitive structures which have been previously learned can lead to particular interpretations or perceptual sets as well as possible errors in developing skills from a modelled event. In maths there are so called "buggy algorithms", which are incorrect maths problem solving strategies that have been previously learned and which cause students to continue to repeat the same errors in calculation. These incorrect mental models which children or adults have developed prevent them from being able to recognise a mistake and correcting it.

Past Reinforcement
The past learning of the observer, especially the ways in which the individual has been rewarded or subjected to negative reinforcement, lead to the adoption of particular preferences as a result of the previously developed cognitive structures and perceptual set. In the views of many there are differences in learning styles and these result from life experiences and positive and negative reinforcement. These previously acquired preferences many need to be taken into account by teachers and trainers.

Retention Processes: Cognitive Construction

Symbolic Coding
Retention of information in the memory is dependent upon symbolic coding. Appropriate symbols and memories need to be developed from observation of modelled events and stored in memory in order for there to be records which may be drawn upon at a later period. Unless this symbolic coding occurs no record may be created, and access to this previously experienced event will be impossible.

Information derived from a modelled event which is observed is transmitted to the brain via the senses. In complex processes the information is passed through the short term or working memory and is acted upon by the executive system, with this latter process almost certainly involving searches in long term memory to identify the incoming information against existing memory stores (Lindsay & Norman, 1972; Schmidt, 1975). In all of this process what is actually observed is not transmitted directly to the brain: instead what is transmitted are sensory impressions via the nervous system. Logically the observed model or object itself never reaches the brain. In most cases it is far too large to be fitted into someone's head! Thus for humans to process information what is incoming must be converted into symbolic codes, that is representations of the observed event.

There is some argument about the most frequently used and effective forms of symbolic coding. It appears that most symbolic coding in adults is in verbal form, with language and numerical symbols being necessary for employment of abstract thinking without recourse to manipulation of tangible, concrete physical objects.

Visual images appear also to be very important in human thinking and in the use of memory (Paivio, 1969). It seems logical to assume that information from all the senses, while stored in different locations of the brain, become associated and such associations have both symbolic and personal associative value (Lindsay & Norman, 1972). So we can think in terms of an apple pie, with the words symbols, but that concept is usually associated with certain aromas, tastes and personal memories of pleasure from eating a delicious apple pie. Recommendations for effective generation and use of mnemonics, memory aid devices which have a long history of use and proven efficacy, often include the use of verbal codes combined with vivid, unusual visual imagery (Bellezza, 1981; Levin & Levin, 1990).

Cognitive Organisation
In addition to symbolic coding, effective human functioning is dependent upon effective storage and organisation of information (Ausubel, 1968; Anderson, 1995). The development of expertise appears to be largely dependent upon the development of organised systems of knowledge which can be accessed with ease (see Cornford's other chapter in this text). The linking together of information, and associating it or grouping it (chunking) with like or related pieces of information in memory in structured form, seems important. In a series of related experiments, Gerst (1971), Bandura and Jeffery (1973) and Bandura, Jeffery and Bachicha (1974) clearly demonstrated the importance of symbolic coding, structure, and rehearsal to facilitate retention in long term memory, and also the building in of cues to assist retrieval of information from long term memory storage.

Rehearsal: Cognitive and Enactive
The importance of practice or rehearsal in learning is well established (see Cornford's other chapter in this text) and is essential to establish skills in long term memory. The form which rehearsal takes can be cognitive or enactive. Cognitive rehearsal can involve a number of different approaches. One would be repeating information over and over to oneself to ensure the retention of a new word or concept (Weinstein & Meyer, 1991) or mentally "running through" what has to be performed. A more sophisticated form is to visualise or imagine oneself performing in some specific situation (Meichenbaum, 1977). Enactive rehearsal involves actual physical performance as a prelude to a final set of actions.

Enactive rehearsal, that is physical practice is an important aspect of acquisition of performance to match that of a model. Through such physical performance it is possible to match the present performance against the mental model which has been acquired previously. Through practice and feedback there is refinement and development of a performance more closely matching the one observed or desired (Bandura, 1977).

Retention Processes: Observer Attributes - Cognitive skills and structures

As with the Attentional Processes the previous experiences and past learning which the observer brings to the situation will be important. Again the cognitive skills which the leaner possesses and the cognitive structures that already exist will influence the observer's efforts at symbolic coding and cognitive organisation. In turn, both the existing cognitive skills and structures will influence the forms taken and success of cognitive or enactive rehearsal. There is presently some debate concerning the difference between cognitive and metacognitive skills (Schraw, 1998; Sternberg, 1998). Cognitive skills are seen by some as somewhat limited and more procedural, whereas metacognitive skills are more clearly executive system functions involving planning, monitoring and evaluation. While the development of metacognitive skills in skill learning has not been extensively explored, it would appear that planning, monitoring and evaluation would be key elements in effective retention.

Production Processes

Representational Guidance
The process of reproducing the observed modelled event is dependent upon several factors, not least of which is the accuracy of initial observation and the effective coding of the observed data in such ways as to form a coherent mental model or schema to provide guidance (Cornford, 1996). The conception developed may well be a deliberate modification of the original modelled event, yet it will serve the learner as a guide for future reproduction. This model may be subject to still further refinement and conscious, deliberate change as practice takes place.

Corrective Adjustment
It is unlikely that the first reproduction from a mental model of the modelled event will be an exact match. Basic skills take much practice and considerable time before they can be executed effortlessly and correctly. In the practice period, corrective adjustments require monitoring of the enactments, feedback information and conception matching. Feedback can originate from other persons or the individual who monitors his or her own performance. Ultimately individuals have to monitor their own performance, but in early stages of skill learning corrective feedback may be more accurate when it comes from others who are more skilled. With young children learning new words, parents frequently offer feedback through additional modelled performances involving the word or phrase, and will correct the child's pronunciation until a good facsimile is produced. In the process of modifying the behaviour the mental model is changed also. The accuracy of feedback coming from others or the individual will determine the degree to which the performance matches the original model or the individual's adaptation of it.

Observer Attributes
As in relation to Attentional and Retention Processes the past learning and abilities which the individual brings to the Production Processes will be important. A cognitive impairment may have a major influence on the adequacy of the mental model which is formed to govern production while the physical capabilities also can be of great importance in determining the end product. Clearly a major physical impairment is likely to strongly influence physical performance although it may not be considered politically correct to acknowledge this directly. If someone is fitted with an artificial arm it is unlikely that they will be able to break any swimming records against Olympic class swimmers who are fortunate enough to have their own limbs. However, even with normal learners it is important to recognise there are usually modifications of the original modelled performance to

be taken into account because of individual differences in body build and coordination.

Reproduction of observed modelled events will be made much easier when sub-skill components already exist in the individual's previously developed repertoire. In some cases these existing sub-skills will simply become part of a more complex action or set of procedures. Conventional teaching and training curricula contain analyses of skill ordered in such ways that there is a gradual building from not knowing to knowing, with the growing complexity governed by logical or psychological ordering.

Motivational Processes

Types of Incentives

Social cognitive theory distinguishes between acquisition and performance. Motivation is important in both of these areas and at all phases in the observational learning model. Coverage of motivation here is relatively brief since Russell (Chapter 5 in this text) provides a more exhaustive account of relevant factors and theory. There are three types of incentives in acquisition and performance in Bandura's view - external, internal or self-incentives, and vicarious incentives.

External incentives are incentives that are controlled by other persons and not the learner. These external incentives can involve control, social rewards, pleasurable sensory stimulation as well as more obvious and tangible rewards such as the giving of money or objects. External sources of reward were considered very important in earlier behavioural psychology theories. However, what these earlier theorists frequently failed to recognise is that there is an important distinction between compliance and internalisation. Compliance can be obtained by threat or continuation of reward but once the threat or reward stops then the behaviour is likely to cease as well. In social cognitive theory internal rewards and vicarious reinforcement are viewed as more important in the internalisation of values and maintenance of behaviour.

Internal motivation involves the individual making judgements and rewarding him or herself. This form of self-reward will involve various considerations centred around the value of the learning or performance to the individual, including the feelings of satisfaction gained from engagement in the learning or performance of the skill. For teachers and trainers the benefits of having students engage in self-motivation processes are clearly enormous. Much of any teacher's energy is directed towards motivating students to engage in effective learning. However, like developing many aspects of self-regulatory behaviour, this involves skill learning over periods of time. Seeing significant others value learning and self-regulation is likely to cause students to emulate these things. In other words, being able to view models who do these things will assist in the learning of them. Teachers or trainers should be aware that they are teaching abstract concepts and rules for behaviour, with potentially longer term consequences, as well as more easily identifiable performance skills. The reader is directed to the comprehensive accounts to be found in Bandura (1986, 1997) for a fuller consideration of the development of all aspects of self-judgement and self-reward leading to a sense of self-efficacy.

The third form of motivation is vicarious incentives, which is where an individual learns from observing others being rewarded or punished as a result of their behaviour. In this form of reinforcement individuals do not have to experience the rewards or punishment directly themselves. Seeing reward or retribution descend upon someone else is sufficient and can have quite powerful effects. Making an example of one person so that this can be observed by many other individuals has been a favourite tactic of those attempting to control others for good reasons or bad. Invading armies may single out an individual to punish to convey a clear message to other members of the populace. However, the important effects of vicarious learning are not restricted to such rare events as this, but are to be found all around us in day-to-day living and learning activities.

Brown and Inouye (1978) studied the role of perceived competence amongst school children using a peer model comparison. They found that observation of failure of a model of comparable ability had a detrimental effect upon the observer's self-efficacy and persistence. The more the student's self-efficacy was undermined by vicarious failure, the more readily he/she gave up when difficulty was encountered. While it is easy to see younger children as eager to learn from other children whose behaviour is rewarded or punished, adults are no less inclined to learn in this way from observed events. It is intriguing to watch in business organisations how ambitious junior executives soon model themselves upon those who are seen to be rewarded by the management hierarchy and exhibit similar behaviours ranging from work habits to styles of dressing.

Vicarious learning is considered as one of those aspects of social cognitive theory which clearly differentiates it from conventional behavioural psychology theories (Bandura, 1977). In behavioural theories, such as those of Skinner or even Pavlov, learning was seen as dependent upon direct reward or reinforcement of a response. In social cognitive theory, the cognition and judgements made by an individual become the mediating factors which will determine whether there will be learning or not, and what form the learning will take.

Observer Attributes

Since the observer's judgements and thinking are important factors in mediating the effectiveness of external, internal or vicarious forms of incentives, what the observer brings to any observation is of great importance. Bandura (1997) indicated that there are individuals who will have a distinct preference for certain types of incentives. This explains why some individuals are reliant upon external forms of reinforcement while others are strongly self-motivated. Some individuals will start work on set classwork immediately they walk into the teaching room, while others will require specific instructions from the teacher.

Also of importance is the fact that different individuals will have different social comparison biases. In terms of modelling attributes, those who exercise power and are well dressed frequently are seen as models whereas those who are more poorly dressed and exude less of an air of authority are unlikely to be used as models. Hence clothing can serve as an important signifier and source of social comparison, and ultimately bias in decision making. White collar criminals in expensive suits may be more likely to fare much better in courts on fraud charges than those in more humble garb.

The internal standards, which individuals have developed and to which they adhere, will be important in determining whether or not they learn from observed models or perform what has been learned. Moral beliefs and moral codes of conduct can result in decisions not to engage in certain actions even though the observer can see that those actions will bring a reward in that particular social or environmental context. Equally it is true that there are individuals who will continue to engage in certain actions even though they know that others have been punished for so doing. The cases of citizens in occupied countries who hid Jews from the Nazis at great personal risk during the Second World War are an obvious example.

Concluding Comments

Bandura's observational learning model has successfully reconciled elements from a range of theories including information processing, and cognitive, behavioural and social psychology. This model is unique in its ability to explain in convincing ways the factors which operate in what is surely the most frequent type of learning - learning through observation of others. Factors outlined in the model are equally as relevant for understanding learning in formal situations, such as in schools, TAFE and university education classrooms, as in informal situations, such as social gatherings, homes and workplaces where much of our learning occurs. The areas where the model and social cognitive theory more generally have been successfully applied reflect these different learning and social contexts. Bandura's theories have had wide and successful application in areas involving social learning including education (e.g., Cornford, 1991; Zimmerman, 1989), health (Bandura, 1997), organisational management theory (Bandura, 1988; Wood & Bandura, 1988) and career counselling (e.g., Krumboltz, 1994), as well as nursing.

Through its detailed analysis of component processes underlying observational learning, Bandura's model allows teachers, trainers, managers and students of human nature more generally, to gain important insights into factors which must be taken into account in social learning situations. In real life instruction and learning, there needs to be consideration of what is presented, how it is presented, the means of ensuring retention, practice and feedback considerations in tuning the model which guides performance, and motivation, which is so essential to ensure that all the previous planning and efforts have a likelihood of success. Explicit focus upon Attentional, Retention, Production and Motivational Processes in Bandura's model means that these sets of factors, which are usually considered separately in different theories, are brought together in a practical way. While each of these sets of processes can be distinguished, and indeed do involve distinctly separate factors and elements in successful teaching, training and learning, they need to be reconciled. And Bandura's model directs us towards that reconciliation.

The observational learning model serves equally as guide in planning for effective learning and as a means of analysing the successes and failures that we experience in our attempts to influence others and to ensure effective instruction. In this it is far more sophisticated, detailed and satisfactory than a number of the situated learning and situated cognition theories which at present are currently in vogue. The superiority of Bandura's theory and model lies in its building upon the best elements of previous theories and research, a practical realisation that the many elements impinging on human learning in all their complexity need to be united in the one model, and a formidable body of research conducted over three decades which ensures a solid empirical base. Not only have empirical studies been used to develop social cognitive theory but the theory constructed has itself been subjected to rigorous testing through empirical studies (see Bandura, 1997). This stands in decided contrast to many of the presently fashionable situated learning and situated cognition theories which are largely theoretical and lacking any substantial empirical backing.

REFERENCES

Anderson, J. R. (1995). *Cognitive psychology and its implications* (4th ed.). NY: W. H. Freeman & Co.

Ausubel, D. P. (1968). *Educational psychology: A cognitive view.* NY: Holt, Rinehart & Winston.

Bandura, A. (1977). *Social learning theory.* Englewood Cliffs, NJ: Prentice Hall Inc.

Bandura, A. (1986). *Social foundations of thought and action: A social cognitive theory.* Englewood Cliffs, NJ: Prentice Hall.

Bandura, A. (1988). Organizational applications of social cognitive theory. *Australian Journal of Management, 13,* 137-164.

Bandura, A. (1997). *Self-efficacy.* NY: W. H. Freeman & Co.

Bandura, A., & Jeffery, R. (1973). Role of symbolic coding and rehearsal processes in observational learning. *Journal of Personality and Social Psychology, 26,* 122-130.

Bandura, A., Jeffery, R., & Bachicha, D. (1974). Analysis of memory codes and cumulative rehearsal in observational learning. *Journal of Research in Personality, 7,* 295-305.

Bandura, A., Ross, D., & Ross, S. (1963). Imitation of film-mediated aggressive models. *Journal of Abnormal Social Psychology, 66,* 3-11.

Bandura, A., & Walters, R. H. (1963). *Social learning and personality development.* NY: Holt, Rinehart & Winston.

Bellezza, F. (1981). Mnemonic devices: Classification, characteristics and criteria. *Review of Educational Research, 51,* 247-275.

Billett, S. (1996). Situated learning: Bridging sociocultural and cognitive theorising. *Learning and Instruction, 6,* 263-280.

Billett, S. (1998). Ontogeny and participation in communities of practice: A socio-cultural view of adult development. *Studies in the Education of Adults, 30,* 21-34.

Brown, R. D., Brown, L. A., & Danielson, J. E. (1975). Instructional treatments, presenter types, and learner characteristics as significant variants in instructional television for adults. *Journal of Educational Psychology, 67,* 391-404.

Brown, J. S., Collins, A., & Duguid, P. (1989). Situated cognition and the culture of learning. *Educational Researcher, 18(1),* 32-42.

Brown, I., Jr., & Inouye, D. K. (1978). Learned helplessness through modeling: The role of perceived similarity in competence. *Journal of Personality and Social Psychology, 36,* 900-908.

Collins, A. (1997). Cognitive apprenticeship and the changing workplace. Keynote address presented at the 5th Annual International Conference on Post-compulsory Education and Training, Surfers Paradise, Qld, 26-28 November. Published by Centre for Learning and Work Research, Griffith University, Brisbane.

Cornford, I. R. (1991). Microteaching skill generalization and transfer: Training preservice teachers in introductory lesson skills. *Teaching and Teacher Education, 7,* 25-56.

Cornford, I. R. (1996). The defining attributes of 'skill' and 'skilled performance': Some implications for training, learning and program development. *Australian and New Zealand Journal of Vocational Education Research, 4(2),* 1-25.

DeVries, R. (1997). Piaget's social theory. *Educational Researcher, 26(2),* 4-18.

Frawley, W. (1997). *Vygotsky and cognitive science: Language and the unification of the social and computational mind.* Cambridge, MA: Harvard University Press.

Gage, N., & Berliner, D. (1992). *Educational psychology* (5th ed.). Boston: Houghton Mifflin.

Gesell, A. (1926). *The mental growth of the preschool child: A psychological outline of normal development from birth to the sixth year, including a system of developmental diagnosis.* NY: The Macmillan Co.

Gerst, M. (1971). Symbolic processes in observational learning. *Journal of Personality and Social Psychology, 19,* 7-17.

Greeno, J. (1997). Response: On claims that answer the wrong questions. *Educational Researcher, 26(1),* 5-17.

Krumboltz, J. D. (1994). Improving career development theory from a social learning perspective. In M. L. Savickas, & R. W. Lent (Eds.), *Convergence in career development theories.* Palo Alto, CA: CPP Books.

Kuhn, D. (1997). Constraints or guideposts? Developmental psychology and science education. *Review of Educational Research, 67,* 141-150.

Lave, J. (1988). *Cognition in practice: Mind, mathematics and culture in everyday life.* Cambridge: Cambridge University Press.

Lave, J. (1990). The culture of acquisition and the practice of understanding. In J. Stigler, R. Shweder, & G. Herdt (Eds.), *Cultural Psychology* (pp. 309- 327). Cambridge: Cambridge University Press.

Lave, J., & Wenger, E. (1991). *Situated learning: Legitimate peripheral participation.* Cambridge: Cambridge University Press.

Lefkowitz, M., Blake, R. R., & Mouton, J. S. (1955). Status factors in pedestrian violation of traffic signals. *Journal of Abnormal and Social Psychology, 51,* 704-705.

Levin, M. E., & Levin, J. R. (1990). Scientific mnemonomics: Methods for maximizing more than memory. *American Educational Research Journal, 27,* 301-321.

Lindsay, P., & Norman, D. (1972). *Human information processing.* NY: Academic Press.

Lippitt, R. R., Polansky, N., & Rosen, S. (1952). The dynamics of power. *Human Relations, 5,* 37-64.

Markus, H., & Nurius, P. (1986). Possible selves. *American Psychologist, 41,* 954-969.

McInerney, D., & McInerney, V. (1994). *Educational psychology: Constructing learning.* Sydney; Prentice Hall of Australia.

Meichenbaum, D. (1977). *Cognitive behavior modification: An integrative approach.* NY: Plenum Press.

Metz, K. E. (1995). Reassessment of developmental constraints on children's science instruction. *Review of Educational Research, 65,* 93-127.

Metz, K. E. (1997). On the complex relationship between cognitive developmental research and children's science curricula. *Review of Educational Research, 67,* 151-163.

Miller, N. E., & Dollard, J. (1941). *Social learning and imitation.* New Haven: Yale University Press.

Moely, B., Hart, S., Santulli, K., Leal, L., Johnson, T., Rao, N., Burney, L., & Pechman, E. (1985). *The teacher's role in facilitating memory and study strategy development in the elementary school classroom.* Report for the National Institution of Education, Washington DC. New Orleans, LA: Tulane University.

Mussen, P. H., Conger, J. J., & Kagan, J. (1964). *Child development and personality* (2nd ed.). NY: Harper International Reprint.

Paivio, A. (1969). Mental imagery in associative learning and memory. *Psychological Review, 76,* 241-263.

Reichard, G. A. (1938). Social life. In F. Boas (Ed.), *General anthropology* (pp. 409-486). Boston, MA: Heath.

Renkl, A., Mandl, H., & Gruber, H. (1996). Inert knowledge: Analyses and remedies. *Educational Psychologist, 31,* 115-121.

Rosenthal, T. L., & Zimmerman, B. J. (1978). *Social learning and cognition.* NY: Academic Press.

Schmidt, R. A. (1975). A schema theory of discrete motor skill learning. *Psychological Review, 82,* 225-260.

Schraw, G. (1998). Promoting general metacognitive awareness. *Instructional Science, 26,* 113-125.

Schunk, D. H. (1987). Peer models and children's behavioral change. *Review of Educational Research, 57,* 149-174.

Schunk, D. H. (1989). Social cognitive theory and self-regulated learning. In B. J. Zimmerman & D. H. Schunk (Eds.), *Self-regulated learning and academic achievement: Theory, research and practice* (pp. 83-11). NY: Springer-Verlag.

Schunk, D. H., & Zimmerman, B. J. (1997). Social origins of self-regulatory competence. *Educational Psychologist, 32,* 195-208.

Sohlman, A. (1998). The culture of adult learning in Sweden. Paper presented at How Adults Learn Conference, jointly sponsored by the OECD and The United States Department of Education, Washington DC, 6-8 April.

Sternberg, R. (1998). Metacognition, abilities and developing expertise: What makes an expert student? *Instructional Science, 26,* 127-140.

Sweller, J. (1993). Some cognitive processes and their consequences for the organisation and presentation of information. *Australian Journal of Psychology, 45,* 1-8.

Voss, J. F., & Post, T. A. (1988). On the solving of ill-structured problems. In M. Chi, R. Glaser & M. Farr (Eds.), *The Nature of expertise* (pp. 261-285). Hillsdale, NJ: Lawrence Erlbaum.

Voss, J. F., Wiley, J., & Carretero, M. (1995). Acquiring intellectual skills. *Annual Review of Psychology, 46,* 155-181.

Vygotsky, L. S. (1978). *Mind in society: The development of higher psychological processes.* Cambridge, MA: Harvard University Press.

Weinstein, C. E., & Meyer, D. K. (1991). Cognitive learning strategies and college teaching. *New Directions For Teaching And Learning, 45* (Spring), 15-26.

Wertsch, J. V. (1985). *Vygotsky and the social formation of mind.* Cambridge, MA: Harvard University Press.

Wertsch, J. V. (1991). *Voices of the mind: A socio-cultural approach to mediated action.* Cambridge, MA: Harvard University Press.

Wertsch, J. V., & Tulviste, P. (1992). L. S. Vygotsky and contemporary developmental psychology. *Developmental Psychology, 28,* 548-557.

Wood, R., & Bandura, A. (1988). *Social cognitive theory of organizational management.* Working paper 88-027, Australian Graduate School of Management, University of NSW.

Yates, G. C. R., & Chandler, M. (1991). The cognitive psychology of knowledge: Basic research findings and educational implications. *Australian Journal of Education, 35,* 13 1-153.

Zimmerman, B. J. (1989). A social cognitive view of self-regulated academic learning. *Journal of Educational Psychology, 81,* 329-339.

Zimmerman, B. J., & Koussa, R. (1979). Social influences on children's toy preferences: Effects of model rewardingness and affect. *Contemporary Educational Psychology, 4,* 55-66.

Zimmerman, B. J., & Rosenthal, T. L. (1974). Observational learning of rule-governed behavior by children. *Psychological Bulletin, 81,* 29-42.

Review Questions

The following questions are designed to test your understanding of the content of this chapter. Answers can all be checked by referring to the relevant sections.

1. Name the four psychological traditions or areas which are drawn upon in Bandura's observational learning model.
2. Social cognitive theory considers that there are interactions between which three factors in learning?
3. Define possible selves.
4. What is meant by (a) inhibition and (b) disinhibition in social cognitive theory?
5. Why are there often creative adaptations in learning from models?
6. Describe two ways in which learning from a model can contribute to self-regulated learning.

7. Name the four sets of processes which constitute Bandura's observational learning model.
8. What does the salience of a modelled performance involve?
9. Outline the ways in which the complexity of the modelled performance can affect learning.
10. Why is the prevalence of modelled performances an important consideration?
11. What is meant by functional value?
12. What does affective valence involve?
13. What are coping models and how do they differ from expert models?
14. How can a learner's arousal level affect their learning efforts?
15. What is meant by perceptual set and how does this develop?
16. Why is retention of information dependent upon symbolic coding?
17. Distinguish between cognitive and enactive rehearsal, giving one example of each type of rehearsal that you yourself might engage in.
18. What are external incentives?
19. What are internal incentives?
20. What are vicarious incentives?

Exercises

1. Critically analyse a teaching/training session, that you have given which was not as successful as you might have wished, from the perspective of Bandura's observational learning model, acknowledging the strengths but also indicating the weakness which can be improved upon. Outline the steps you would take and the factors you would consider in attempting to remedy the weaknesses in the future.
2. Closely observe an informal learning situation which involves modelling and considerable social interaction, for example in the workplace. Use Bandura's observational learning model, especially Figure 4.1 which outlines all the relevant components, as a checklist to see how many of the factors which Bandura identifies as important are relevant and can be discerned in the situation you have observed.

About the Author

Ian Cornford holds a PhD in Educational Psychology and is a Senior Lecturer in the Faculty of Education at the University of Technology, Sydney. He has a long association with vocational teacher education. His research interests are centred upon the psychology of learning and include effective learning, teaching and training in classrooms and workplaces, transfer of learning and issues in school-to-work transition. Recently he has been involved in research into the effectiveness of competency-based training while currently he is analysing issues in lifelong learning and examining the implications of lifelong learning for policy making and educational practice.

Ian R. Cornford
University of Technology, Sydney

PETER RUSSELL

5. MOTIVATION

The study of motivation has been described as the most important and vexing question faced by psychologists. Essentially, the question is: "Why do people do the things they do?". This question rarely has simple answers because there are dozens of variables and sub-components which make each situation just a little different from the next.

The search for answers about motivation is thousands of years old and Aristotle, Plato and Socrates were no less interested in the role of motivation in learning and purposeful human action than modern researchers. In the 13th and 14th centuries, philosophers and theologians grappled with the concept of the will and its relationship to the human soul. Thomas Aquinas linked the will with the very essence of what it is to be human. The notion of volition was popular in the 19th century and reappears in the most recent literature on the subject.

Today we see the emergence of "motivational experts" – people who claim to (and often can) bend the will of not only individuals but of whole groups of people. Football teams and athletes' coaches pay huge sums to people who can make others behave in extraordinary ways. Similarly, some religious cults can persuade an alarming proportion of those they recruit to sign away their possessions, rights and family loyalties. Relatives of cult converts have been known to pay thousands of dollars to have their sons, daughters, brothers or sisters kidnapped from cults and then tens of thousands for "deprogramming" courses to restore the personality and self-agency of the converts.

The motivational question for adult educators is not so much: "Why do people do the things they do?", but (bluntly): "How do we get people to do some things which they should do?" There are some lessons to be learnt from the professional motivators and the cult recruiters and it would seem possible to transplant some of their methods (without their questionable ethics) into the educational context, but to get a better understanding of what is known and what is yet to be discovered about motivation and learning there are also the outcomes of nearly a century of research and thinking about this fascinating topic.

James A Athanasou (ed.), Adult Educational Psychology, 95–124
© 2008 Sense Publishers. All rights reserved.

This chapter will try to paint a picture of what has been revealed about human motivation and how some strategies seem to be effective in encouraging people to invest effort to learn. It will become clear that it is a very complex topic and that what motivates one person for a particular task may often not influence another. Similarly, a strategy which works in one situation may be useless in another – even with the same person. It will also be evident that the researchers and theorists only rarely agree on even the most basic aspects of motivation.

Surprisingly, this diversity of strategies and theories will show itself to be an advantage for the educator. In the same way that a (good) doctor has a range of treatment approaches and medications to choose from, a teacher or trainer needs an extensive "tool kit", not only for variability, but also so that the special circumstances of the learner, the task and the learning environment can be weighed up and matched to the motivational strategy. An educator, manager or coach who tries to use only one motivational theory all the time is like the lazy mechanic who tries to use a shifting spanner when the right tool is available - skinned knuckles and mangled bolts are not the mark of a professional who can use judgement and knowledge to get the best results.

How This Chapter Is Structured

The chapter is divided into eight sections including this general introduction. The second section will provide an outline of the main elements and influences which have emerged from years of theory and research. The general concepts such as interest, curiosity, persistence, and feelings of control are introduced here.

The third section traces the history of the very different and often competing ideas on motivation which have been popular at various times over the past 80 or so years. What is interesting here is that nearly all of them are still potentially useful and are applied in various circumstances today. Some have been adapted or incorporated into modern views and some have remained the dominant model in specialist fields, such as Maslow's (1954) hierarchy of needs in many management psychology courses.

The fourth section looks at a range of current approaches to motivation. Some are based on the role of thoughts (cognitions), others on emotions or environmental/social influences, and some on other explanations. It is in this section that the richness of the tool kit becomes apparent. A general theme in this chapter is that motivation is an area which needs a diversity of models to adequately inform and guide educational practitioners.

In the fifth section of the chapter a sample of specific research methods and outcomes is described to give examples of the often detailed and painstaking ways in which theories are formed and tested. It is important to see that theories about motivation are continually checked and challenged by researchers who sometimes find that their (or other people's) hunches or speculations are reinforced and sometimes found to be false, or perhaps not as generalised as first thought. For many years motivation lacked adequate research backing although theories were abundant. Only in the last decade has this changed substantially. A look at detailed research also helps to understand how very complex processes are broken down into variables or groups of elements which can be examined, as if through a microscope, and then (ideally) reintegrated into a wider picture. In thinking about this, however, it is also important to know that many theorists don't believe that such a pulling apart and putting back together process is at all reliable or valid!

Section six could be described as the "if we're so smart, why aren't we rich?" part of the chapter. After the previous discussion of theory and models of motivational processes, this part shows how a few well known researchers in the field have attempted to convert theory into practical advice for the people who have to help learners in everyday training situations. Happily, something of a pattern does appear in these "recipes" for promoting and increasing motivation. Also fortunately, there are reasonably clear links between the theoretical principles and the practical suggestions.

Section seven focuses on taking stock of the main themes in motivational theory and what the future might bring in the long quest for a thorough and reliable understanding of what makes people learn. Some researchers believe that there are important gaps in current theory and that without their inclusion in the overall picture, we may be on the road to a dead-end at which a wasteful period of reviving past ideas is all we can look forward to. Others suggest that unless we go back to look at previously abandoned lines of inquiry, research will get bogged down in more and more petty detail. Bernard Weiner (1990), for example, suggested that motivational research had become too preoccupied with the "psychology of the self" and ignored the influence of social variables such as belongingness. This may represent the end of a rather long phase in which a predominantly cognitivist perspective has dominated motivation research and theory. In spite of this, many writers in the field do seem to agree on a general sense of getting somewhere in recent years and are optimistic about the future.

The last section is designed to clarify the preceding parts by posing a sequence of key questions about motivational concepts, models and theories. As well as being a self-checking exercise, the questions help to consolidate and show the patterns and relationships between elements which may have appeared unrelated at their first encounter.

Elements of Motivation

Anyone who is involved in teaching or training would find it easy to write down a list of things which have a role in motivating people. If you were to get ten or more of them to do this (and it's not a bad exercise to try if you get the chance) they would probably come up with a similar range to the one represented in Figure 5.1.

Although they may not use the same terminology, like locus of control or volition, there would be a generally good match between what could be called a "common sense" view of motivation and the components which researchers use to study it.

The advantages to be gained from a more formal study of this important aspect of human behaviour are considerable. A closer look at the diagram shows that research does more than simply try to identify and define the elements - it also tries to find out how they relate and interact with each other. This process of identifying, defining, and looking for and testing patterns is essentially what psychological theorists and researchers do. If the results of the process can be communicated and understood by those whose job it is to help others learn in offices or factories and training rooms, then the real goal of research is achieved.

Figure 5.1 *Variables influencing motivation.*

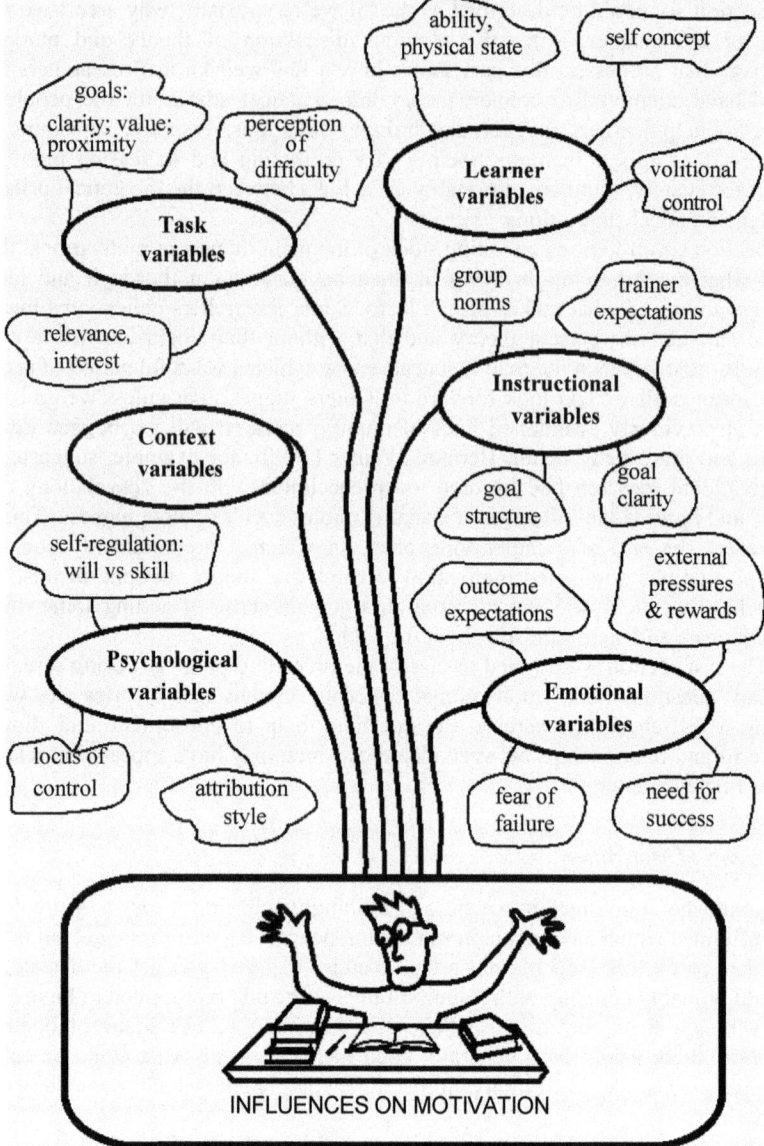

The various theories of motivation often incorporate similar, general elements but vary in how important they are seen to be or how they are believed to influence and affect one another. Before examining some of the major theories in the next two sections, it is worthwhile to look at some of the building blocks or basic concepts in motivation.

What Is the Spring of Action of Human Behaviour?

This is perhaps the most basic question of all. Spring can mean origin (as in the source of a river) or it can imply a storage of energy. Related to motivation, it asks "What makes us do anything?", "Why do we even get out of bed in the morning?", "Why do we suffer boredom if there is too little to do?"

It will be seen in the next section which traces the history of motivation research that changing beliefs about the spring had a strong influence on the major theories. Over at least a century, explanations of the core of motivated behaviour went from innate drives to environmental stimuli and/or rewards, changing to inner (but not necessarily in-born) needs and then more recently to thoughts and perceptions. As the various theories present themselves, it is worthwhile to go back to this basic question about human activity and striving. Theorists can't help becoming blinkered by their own basic philosophical starting point but practitioners can and need to keep a step back so they can apply approaches or strategies which best suit their situation.

Motivation as Investing Effort to Learn

This general way of looking at a person's actions when they are trying (or not trying hard enough) to master a particular skill or understand a course's content is useful to both the educator and the researcher. Investment and effort raise several issues which are features of current views on motivation. In the same way that financial investment has connotations of level of wealth, expecting something back, risk taking and needing accurate knowledge of conditions and time frames, so do models of motivation contain these elements. Figure 5.1 might use terms such as ability and self-concept, outcome expectations, the need for success vs. the fear of failure, goal clarity and proximity and so on, but these theoretical motivation terms are really just factors which most people have observed in everyday life.

Similarly, effort in a general sense has to do with some degree of difficulty and persistence. It is also often linked to applying the best strategy (or way and place of applying the effort). In motivational terminology, and again from the figure, factors such as challenge, threat, volitional control and self-regulation (of strategies) are motivational theory's special terms for everyday aspects of putting effort into achieving goals.

What Happened to Interest and Curiosity?

These important and fundamental aspects of motivation are examined in detail in another chapter of this book. Although it may seem strange at first to separate them, it should become clear that motivated behaviour can have many faces and that research into the field reflects this multidimensional reality. Some researchers have been careful to not lose sight of interest-related variables and others have quite consciously left them out of the equation. Some try to explore the links between things like initial interest and the persistence phases of striving toward goals.

Trudewind, Schneider and Mackowaik (1996) provided a good example of how these concepts have been pulled apart and closely examined. In their study of curiosity they sought to discover what sort of things make people curious and what sorts of other states or feelings go with curiosity. They suspected that a subjective feeling of uncertainty about a task would be a common root of not only curiosity, but also interest, anxiety and motivation generally. Their results in this case were not conclusive, but they did prove to be not alone in their difficulty to show strong and consistent links between successful performance of tasks and initial interest or curiosity. Pintrich and De Groot (1990) found that components such as perceived value, interest and curiosity appeared to have only an indirect influence on performance. To some motivational theorists, they may make initial attempts at the task more likely, but may not always be enough to produce sustained and appropriate effort. In other theories, interest and curiosity remain central to every stage and element of motivation.

The Importance of Both Will and Skill

Being "willing and able" is a pairing of conditions that are so well known to be necessary for successful achievement of goals that the term has become a part of our language. Motivational researchers (e.g., Corno, 1989, McCombs, & Marzano, 1990) have also stressed the need to see motivation as a combination of intentions and abilities. The concept of self-regulation (examined in more detail later) describes motivation as a part of a package of knowledge, emotions, skills and environmental conditions which must all be working properly for real success (see Schunk & Zimmerman, 1994).

The idea that motivation goes beyond incentives and intentions was well put by John Cleese in the training video "You'll soon Get the Hang of It" (1981). The importance of helping trainees convert an initial attempt into sustained and organised effort was highlighted in this video by the point that "Motivation is not one question, but three questions. How do you get them to start learning, how do you get them to keep on learning, and how do you get them to come back tomorrow?"

If this approach is compared to the way a successful athlete's coach operates, it starts to make even more sense. Somebody striving for a goal which is genuinely difficult and which can take weeks or months to achieve needs more than just the wish to succeed. They need to be given "scaffolding" and to be taught skills in persistence and in how to control the resources and environmental conditions which will maintain their efforts. The coach must also break up the final goal into smaller, closer and achievable chunks. As the term suggests, the self-regulated learner is a person who has learnt how to do these things without continual outside assistance.

The Role of the Self-system

A number of models of motivation feature the part played by peoples' thoughts and feelings about themselves while they are trying to select or achieve their goals. Self-system was a term developed to incorporate a number of interpretations related to personal image, effectiveness or value. Although, as mentioned before, some writers on motivation (Munro, Schumaker & Carr, 1997; Weiner, 1990) believed that research has focused too much on this area, it is clear that differences between individuals' feelings about their ability, their well-being and also about the reasons why they have succeeded or failed in the past, must account for some of the differences between their actions.

Terms such as self-concept, self-efficacy, self-worth and self-esteem often mean slightly different things to motivational theorists who try to separate out these variables from other factors such as task difficulty or strategy use (see for example Covington & Teel, 1996; Wilhite, 1990). If motivation is, at least in part, about decisions people make, whether consciously or subconsciously, to try or to give up in a particular situation, then the range of self factors may well influence those decisions in a major way.

The alternative view is that we are not the islands that self-system theorists would appear to be describing. Geen and Shea (1997) suggested that our decisions and perhaps even our self oriented perceptions are determined by "situations in which other people are in close contact" (p. 33). This dimension of social and cultural motivation has too many commonplace aspects of life to ignore. There would, for example, be few other explanations available for the widespread phenomenon of better performance of athletes when cycling or running with others.

How Do the Elements Fit Together?

No single element of motivation described above, nor even the combination of all of them, can fully explain human motivation at present. Unfortunately the same is true for the major theories or models. The elements are like pieces of a jig-saw puzzle and the theories are often like clusters of the pieces, perhaps with missing parts, but nevertheless providing a window into the full picture. A single piece (element) may fit just as neatly into two or more clusters (theories) and, in the end, we may find that there is really more than one picture after all!

By now, though, you have been introduced to some of the terminology of motivational theory and to some of the major elements and variables. This may have already prompted you to think about which may be relevant to your own field. The next section looks at some of the attempts that have been made over the years to put the pieces into wider frameworks.

History of Motivation Theory

Most fields in psychology have been influenced over the years by three main paradigms and motivation is no exception. A paradigm is a general position from which the world is perceived and interpreted. It is a mixture of assumptions, philosophies and experiences which not only determine how to find answers to questions, but also what questions are worth asking. The behaviourist, humanist and cognitivist perspectives have each had their periods of prominence in motivational theory, and as Table 5.1 shows, cognitive approaches have dominated for some time. Table 5.1 represents only a sampling of some better known theories, and they were selected to highlight the variations rather than to trace development in any detail.

Table 5.1 *Examples of motivation theories through the century*

Period	Theorist(s)	Paradigm/ Perspective	Theory Description	Basis of Theory
1920s	Sigmund Freud (1966)	Psycho - analytic	Psycho - analytic	"Battles" between Id. Ego and Super-ego. Basic drives of sex and aggression
1930s	Henry Murray (1938)	Psychoanalytic/ biological	Needs	Viscerogenic (body) and Psychogenic (affiliation, dominance, nurture) needs. Drive reduction mechanisms
1950s	B. Frederick Skinner (1953)	Behaviourist	Conditioning: Stimulus, response, reinforcement	Motivation dependent on prior positively reinforced responses to stimuli or beliefs about reinforcements for current responses
1950s	Abraham Maslow (1954)	Humanist	Hierarchy of Needs (to self-actualisation)	Series of needs from lower order (e.g., food, security) needs to higher, growth (e.g., reaching one's full potential)
1960s	Jean Piaget (1962), Jerome Bruner (1966)	Cognitivist	Competence, Achievement	Action is influenced by thought processes; expectation, curiosity, incongruity, cognitive dissonance
1970s	DeCharms (1972), Heckhausen (1977)	Cognitivist	Causal Attributions	Motivation to achieve and be competent. To be an originator and master of own destiny - requirement of accurate perception of own ability
1980s	Bernard Weiner (1986)	Cognitivist	Causal attributions	Motivation to invest effort in a task depends on how a person has interpreted reasons for past successes and or failures. Attributions to effort are "good", attributions to ability and/or luck are "bad"
1990s	Ames (1992), Zimmerman (1990)	Cognitivist	Goals	Relationships between goals, expectations and perceptions of ability. Self-regulation of cognitions, behaviours and emotional aspects of learning.

Drives and Instincts

The range of explanations is fascinating! Sigmund Freud (1966, translated from 1920s work) claimed that we are motivated to action due to a psychic, primeval energy source with sex and aggression being the predominant channels from the (animal) id within us. The energy source notion was still common in the 1930s and 1940s when basic drives (Hull, 1943) and acquired drives (Miller, 1948) were seen as the innate mechanisms for ensuring survival. Henry Murray (1938) saw needs as having both directional and energetic properties by which the object of the need's satisfaction and the type of effort required to achieve it were included. Although these were a little more genteel than Freud's springs, they were still based on the idea that people were driven by very basic and often in-born forces.

Stimuli, Responses and Reinforcement

An alternative explanation was provided by theorists (e.g., Skinner, 1953; Thorndike, 1913; Watson, 1924) who said that factors in our environment were the source of motivation. The interplay of stimuli and consequent rewards (or punishments) was seen as the mechanism responsible for behaviour change and, more importantly, the interactions could and should be studied using the scientific method in controlled laboratory settings. These conditioning (classical, connectionist and operant) theories, according to Schunk (1996) helped to establish the psychological study of learning and motivation as an objective and experimental science.

The move away from drives and instincts was important at the time due to a wider community belief in the ability of science and engineering to address and solve the world's problems. In the current post-modernist interpretations, the 193 0s and 1940s were the beginnings of technical rationalism - a belief that, if you couldn't see it, touch it, weigh it, smell it, and above all, measure it, it didn't exist! In the 1950s, when Russia won the space-race with the launch of the Sputnik satellite, a "non-scientific" education system in the U.S. was one of the scapegoats of a grieving nation.

In that ideological and political climate, behaviourist models of learning and motivation were at the right place at the right time. School curricula were re-designed and based on behavioural objectives which focused on measurable and observable outcomes of learning. In teaching method, motivation was based on the value of incentives provided by the objectives' clarity of goals and on Skinnerian fixed and variable ratio reinforcement schedules. As a bonus, quality assurance techniques could be applied to analysis of performance as measured against curriculum objectives. Within a relatively short period school education, military training and much of the vocational training systems were firmly based on the behaviourist paradigm. As one might expect, its capacity for accountability and quality control has also made it attractive in an economic rationalist climate and this, some claim, explains its revival (as competency based training) in the 1990s.

Humanism and Self-actualisation

The behaviourist mechanistic and production line methods of education and training certainly appealed to administrators and policy makers. The efficiency of the methods had been demonstrated during the large scale training programmes of the second world war and were refined in the years following when industry was responding to booms in demand, production and, inevitably, training.

It is easy to imagine, however, that many people were uncomfortable with a behaviourist perspective. Teachers of literature or creative arts and adult educators in evening colleges had more trouble than those of science and technology in specifying and encouraging their learning outcomes with objectives and reinforcement schedules. The behaviourist research base in laboratory animals learning mazes and conditioned responses to controlled stimuli was a further insult to educators who saw their role as helping others to be creative and reach their full potential as feeling and thinking human beings.

Whether as a backlash to the popularity of behaviourism or as a parallel development, the 1950s and 1960s also saw a growth in humanism - a paradigm fundamentally opposite to behaviourism. With the general idea that "animals behave and human beings act!", humanist theorists such as Carl Rogers (1959,1963) and Abraham Maslow (1954) emphasised the importance of peoples' choices in behaviour/ action, and how these are central to understanding motivation. To humanists, the spring of action is the need for self-actualisation - the reaching of one's potential in intellect, abilities, and emotionally and spiritually through personal choice. The view that we are controlled by patterns of stimuli and reinforcers was seen as de-humanising and destructive. Interestingly, when inner basic drives were seen as the source of motivation, Gordon Allport (1937) used similar arguments against Freud's (1966) and Murray's (1938) theories. With personal control as central to a humanist paradigm, he described the "functional autonomy of motives" (p. 194) as systems within each individual which are unique and which develop from choices and experiences. Instincts and basic drives, rather than controlling, were seen as having only historical and not functional links to our motives.

Thoughts as Origins of Motivation

Behaviourist and humanist explanations of motivation were clearly different in almost every respect. By the end of the 1950s, behaviourism had a firm power base in education and training contexts (which it has not entirely lost today) and Maslow's (humanist) hierarchy of needs theory was gaining interest and support in management and leadership circles. At the same time there remained a strong wider community loyalty to ideas which could be supported by empirical and statistical evidence. Humanist theory, even at a time of a burgeoning humanist revival and showcased by the 1960s flower power movement, was still greeted by many with an "O.K., but prove it" reaction. The humanist distaste for quantitative, empirical research methods did little to meet that challenge and a paradigm stalemate was the result.

Cognitivist ideas and methods were well placed to fill the gap made by such a stand-off. Their spring of action was, as their title implies, thoughts. They had been contributing to aspects of the motivation debate for some time (e.g., Lewin, 1935, Tolman, 1932) and represented something of a middle ground between behaviourist and humanist traditions. Bernard Weiner, in a 1990 article discussing developments in motivation for the forthcoming edition of the *Encyclopedia of Educational Research,* listed several reasons why the cognitive perspective came to effectively dominate motivational theory from the early 1 960s to the present. Schunk (1996) confirmed this dominance and the reasons for its persistence. These were:
- motivation's parent discipline, psychology, was making a general move away from mechanistic models toward cognition. General, clinical, educational and industrial psychology were experiencing unprecedented popularity in the 1960s, and motivational research was relevant to all of those areas;
- cognitive researchers tended not to make use of animals in experimental designs. As its infra-human basis was a continual source of criticism of behaviourist research, cognitivists' emphasis on human behaviour was seen as not only more credible, but also more likely to be relevant to human problems;
- cognitive research (e.g., Deci, 1975) had cast doubt on the role of rewards in motivation. When it became clear that rewards, if perceived by a learner to be

controlling, could actually be de-motivating, the behaviourist stimulus response-reward construct was challenged. Similarly, if rewards given for easy tasks tended to reduce further effort because they produced perceptions of low ability, the reinforcement mainstay of behavioural motivation theory was weakened;
- the important (and to many people, more interesting) issues relating to success and failure and to achievement strivings became the focus of cognitive motivational research. These aspects were also quite easily studied in the laboratory as well as being common elements in practical learning environments;
- the cognitive approach had the advantage of being able to draw upon earlier drive reduction theory when it seemed appropriate, and Festinger's (1957) cognitive dissonance theory was an example of this more liberal research design. The eclectic approach was more appealing to many researchers who did not want to bound by the exclusive traditions of behaviourist or humanist paradigms;
- the new approach also maintained a more consistent direction. A "grand formal theory" (Weiner, 1990, p. 619) lent itself to a wider range of empirical research paths than existed in (particularly) the behaviourist perspective. Examples of this were expectancy-value theories, slice-in-time construals, or 2 by 2 experimental designs; and
- attention tended to be focused on individual differences and this, for the educational psychologist interested in performance differences between learners, was a refreshing change from generalised interpretations of animal behaviour.

Munro, Schumaker and Carr (1997) added a further justification for the cognitive takeover in that it allowed for cross-cultural study and comparisons. In particular, they said, "it enabled an understanding of cultural phenomena that was more sympathetic to indigenous interpretations than those based on supposedly universal biological, behavioural and psychodynamic processes" (p. ix).

Legacy of the Historical Development

Although the history of motivational research shows an essentially adversarial debate between the various perspectives, it is worth noting that each of them have left their mark on current practices and on new theoretical directions. Freud's psychic energy view may not be clearly represented, but the idea of sub-conscious, perhaps repressed, memories influencing decisions and attributions of successes and failures remains. So also is the importance of drives and drive reduction explanations of motivation. Trudewind, Schneider and Mackowaik (1996) for example, still considered the "curiosity and achievement motive as legitimate descendants of a genetically based competence striving" (p. 9).

Humanist priorities of the 1950s given to choice, personal control and autonomy are still very much a part of modern concepts such as self-determination (e.g., Deci & Ryan, 1991; O'Neill & Drillings, 1994; Vallerand, O'Connor & Hamel, 1995). In adult learning theory (Brookfield, 1985), the central concept of self-directed learning in which control of curriculum, learning activities and assessment is essential, and can be traced back to Rogers and other humanist writers in the 1950s.

Conversely, the behavioural objective, under new names of learning outcomes and assessment criteria has had a re-birth in the competency based training

(C.B.T.) movement of the 1980s and 1990s. Any slippage in adherence to the teaching and assessment of highly specific descriptions of the observable consequences of training was therefore recovered by C.B.T. In these and many other ways current motivational theory has not so much replaced, but has built on, earlier views and traditions.

Current Approaches and Models of Motivation

The common thread running through current motivational theory is cognition. Whether they are thoughts about goals, about expectations of success, about reasons for past successes or failures, or even thoughts about thought (metacognition), motivational theory for the past 40 years has sought to describe how our thinking determines our actions. As a spring or source of motivated behaviour, cognition can be at the beginning of a sequence of other elements or it can be seen as a mediator which works either for or against other variables.

Consider the case of a person who is asked by friends to have a try at learning to water-ski. Until that moment he or she may have been quite content to sit in the boat, enjoying the ride, and watching others take turns skiing. The wish (incentive) to participate could be there, the conditions may be perfect - a warm day, plenty of expert and friendly support, no underlying fear of water or swimming - but why do people so often decline? Clearly there can be a whole range of very simple reasons and these are often given ("too late in the day", "I'd only waste your petrol", "maybe tomorrow", and so on), but what makes one person accept and another refuse?

Assuming that there isn't a prior dislike or disinterest in water-skiing (that the value or intrinsic worth of the activity has already been thought through), cognitive models of motivation look for answers in all stages up to and even beyond successful attainment of the goal. Self-regulation models, for example, address the post-decisional (Corno, 1989) stages when persistence in the face of early failures is required. Alternatively, attribution theory (described in more detail later) deals with the effects of success or failure with one attempt on future attempts at similar tasks. The common characteristic is the role of thoughts in guiding or determining action.

Just as behaviourist models of motivation used machine type metaphors (hence their mechanistic label), Weiner (1992) described cognitive models as frequently using computer metaphors. Cognitivists have replaced behavioural input-output and process-product designs with flow charts and computing terms such as information processing, control processes, sensory registers and rehearsal buffers (see for example Atkinson and Shiffrin, 1968) to show patterns and relationships between thoughts and other aspects of learning and motivation

Figure 5.2 *Flow chart model of the motivational process*

Thought-Emotion-Expectancy-Action Models

Figure 5.2 is a simplified version of attempts to describe the place of thinking in motivation. Although the models it is derived from (e.g., Cannon, 1927; Eccles, 1983; Schachter, 1964) may label the components differently or have many more components and arrange them in different sequences, the simple model demonstrates the flow chart method of representing the interaction of complex components.

To return to the example of the reluctant water skier and remembering that action can also be the decision to withdraw from a situation, it is possible to develop a scenario from the above model. In this sequence, thought is represented at the beginning of the process and includes perceptions, appraisals and conclusions drawn. If the task is judged as valuable and/or pleasurable but difficult and evaluative (others measuring your worth), those thoughts could be expected to produce very different feelings about the task than if it was seen as unimportant, easy and irrelevant to onlookers.

If the initial thoughts produce an emotional response, then the way in which the response is perceived and interpreted becomes important because emotions of excitement and fear produce similar physiological reactions. Butterflies in the stomach, increased heart rate, sweaty palms etc. can be interpreted in positive or negative ways and thoughts, this time stemming from emotions, again influence the motivational process. According to Schachter (1964) and later writers on anxiety (e.g., Sarason, 1990), people label the emotional signs as being due to either threats or challenges and the label, rather than the reality, helps to determine what happens next in the sequence.

At this stage though, our skier, still sitting comfortably in the boat, has not yet made a decision - let alone instigated action. Both the model and theorists going back to Tolman (1932) and more recently Adair (1996), Pekrun (1993) and Wigfield (1994) indicate more cognition based processes operating here. In what could be seen as a little "crystal-ball gazing" our skier has thoughts about the likely outcomes, that is results, of making an attempt. The range of variables and influences in this formation of outcome expectancy has been the basis of a vast amount of theoretical work in motivation and some of these will be evident in other models described in this section. At this point it is sufficient to note that a person's beliefs about their ability must have an effect on how they are going to act. The questions other models examine tend to deal with how those beliefs were formed and how strong and pervasive they can be.

The last element in the diagram - action - is also more complex than it might first appear to be. Genuine motivated behaviour is much more than just "having a go", and this stage is again the focus of various theoretical models with self-regulated learning as one of the most comprehensive. The self-regulation model acknowledges that persistence and skills in selecting and maintaining appropriate strategies are important once the person has committed themselves to an initial effort. Thinking of the skier again, bobbing up and down in the water after falling off for the fourth time, now a little cold and tired with sore hands and arms, wondering why it's not all as easy as it looked - we need to know what makes one person continue and another give up.

During action, according to cognitive theorists, it is still thoughts which influence behaviour. Corno (1986) described the effects of different metacognitive variables in which people monitor their own thinking. With this view being not so much mind over emotion, but mind over mind, it describes how some people monitor their selection of available strategies and are more able to persist by choosing new strategies when inappropriate ones fail. In a similar interpretation, but one developed totally independently and much earlier, Vygotsky (1932, in Harris 1990) stressed the importance of self-speech in maintaining self-control. Like the little steam train in the children's story, saying "I think I can, I think I can, I know I can" repeatedly when climbing the steep hill, self speech is seen to have a powerful effect on preserving initial intentions.

Attribution Theory

One of the things which we might have expected the skier in the thought-emotion-expectancy model to have taken into account when deciding whether or not to have a try would have been past performance on similar tasks. The interesting thing about attribution theory, first discussed by Heider (1958), then Kelley (1971) and more recently by Weiner (1986, 1992) is that it is not so much the string of successes or failures which affect motivation, but the imagined causes of those results.

Imagine a person who has tried several times to learn to play a guitar but has never succeeded beyond the most basic chords and strumming. Their own explanations for their failure may have been that they just don't possess any musical ability or that their fingers are too short to form the chords. Alternatively, they may have believed that the instruments they had were not the right type to learn on or that picking up something like that was a matter of just being in the right place at the right time. A third explanation could have been that they simply didn't try hard enough for long enough to master the skill. Such explanations due to ability, luck or effort are seen to have major implications for future attempts.

Weiner and others suggested that people develop attribution styles (habits) which not only influence their motivation on re-tries of the same task, but which transfer to other areas in learning, employment or, indeed, to life in general. Martin Seligman (1992) calling it explanatory style, based his theory of the personality traits of optimism and pessimism on these often irrational and incorrect ways of attributing causes to events.

Attributions are seen to be important, not only because they affect particular motivational decisions, but also because they influence much more basic perceptions about a person's overall worth and ability to achieve important goals. When the lack of accuracy and irrational formation of some attributions is taken into account, it is no wonder that attribution theory has received so much interest in motivational literature in recent years.

Figure 5.3 *Dimensions of causes of success and/or failure*

	Internal Locus	**External Locus**
Stable	**ABILITY** (Uncontrollable)	**TASK DIFFICULTY** (Uncontrollable)
Unstable	**EFFORT** (Controllable)	**LUCK** (Uncontrollable)

Both Weiner (1986), writing mainly about motivation to learn and Seligman (1992), focusing on optimism, pessimism, helplessness and depression, also pointed out the importance of three other characteristics of attributions - locus (place), stability and controllability. If failure occurs on an important task and it is attributed to lack of effort, the event may not have too serious an affect on future motivation because the cause is within the person's control - next time they can choose to try harder. If, however, the attribution is to a lack of ability, this is not only seen as beyond the person's control and located within them (internal), but also stable (not likely to change over time). An attribution habit or a personality based explanatory style which tends to favour ability as the reason for either successes or failures would not be expected to promote motivation. In the investment of effort view of motivation, such a person would not be expected to equate success with effort and failure with lack of effort. They would be at risk of developing a relatively helpless reaction to life in general unless an uncommonly long string of successes had dominated their experience. Figure 5.3 indicates how other combinations of causes and their dimensions can interact. In each case incorrect attributions, particularly those to internal, enduring or uncontrollable causes can be counter to motivation, particularly if they become a favoured or habitual reaction to events.

The good news about attribution theory is that even entrenched and long term attribution and explanatory habits may be subject to modification by good instructional and feedback methods and/ or coaching programmes. Whether by changing locus of control from pawns to origins (de Charms, 1972), by careful design of feedback methods (Relich, Debus & Walker, 1986) or by teaching metacognitive skills to raise feelings of control over learning (McCombs, 1988), attribution styles do not appear to be as fixed as they were first thought to be. In essence, if they were acquired by a process of learning, as in Seligman's (1975) view of helplessness and depression, then they can be "un-learned" with appropriate techniques derived from an understanding of how they were formed.

Goal Theory and Goal Orientation

Pintrich and Schunk (1996) described goals as things outside of the self but which provide the "engine to move organisms to act" (p. 201). As such, they are the modern cognitive equivalents of the (internal) instincts, drives, habits and needs of earlier theories. Although current goal theories (e.g., Ford, 1992; Locke & Latham, 1990) recognise the importance of expectations, attributions, self-perceptions and social context influences, the striving for goals is their focus and their spring of action. Cognitions in these cases mediate behaviour but are not necessarily its origins.

One way that goal theory accounts for the individual differences evident in the selection of and commitment to goals stems from the basic purpose of engaging in achievement behaviours. Various theorists (e.g., Ames, 1992; Butler, 1992; Nicholls, 1984) have developed different ways of classifying goals according to purposes, but most relate in some way to distinctions between learning vs. performance oriented goals. Learning goals, as the term implies, value the processes and skills used and acquired during learning, and mastery, task oriented and task focused goals are conceptually similar.

Performance goals, conversely, are centred on the completion, results or consequences of tasks. They are also referred to as ego-oriented or ability focused goals. The problem with performance goals is that the underlying purpose for investing effort is one step removed from the material being learned. Instead of striving for understanding or the feeling of acquiring a new skill, the performance goal exists to bolster self-esteem or to protect one's reputation or perceived worth from the point of view of instructors or fellow learners. As motivators, performance goals are still intrinsic (in that they are not focused on clearly external rewards such as money or promotion) but they are not seen as being as valuable as learning goals because they shift attention away from the strategies and processes which are central to genuine learning. Generally, if learning is to be its own reward, striving to attain something which is other than what is being learned is seen as a lower form of motivation within the mastery vs. performance model. Exceptions to this rule, however, must also be considered and Skaalvik's (1997) research is a good example. This indicated that there may be two types of ego orientation - self-defeating and self-enhancing, and that the latter type actually contributes to academic achievement by increasing self-perceptions and reducing anxiety.

Obviously, people do not often behave as simply as the theoretical categories might tempt us to believe. A student could be prompted to start work on a topic because it will be examined at the end of the semester (an extrinsic goal) but soon finds that the material is sufficiently interesting and useful to become quite absorbed in the process of working toward a deep and broad understanding of it (a mastery goal). At the same time he or she may be aware that a sound knowledge of the topic is viewed by others as a sign of very high ability and that many people have difficulty with it (a performance goal). There may even be a motive which relates to being able to avoid harder work on another topic given success on the present one (an alienation goal).

Nicholls, Patashnick and Nolan (1985) used students' descriptions of a "really successful day" to investigate the range of goal orientations which are possible. As well as those which fall clearly into the performance/mastery categories, others such as: to "avoid inferiority" or to show "easy superiority" emerged. Figure 5.4 shows a particularly interesting outcome of the research which indicated that some people may simply enjoy a learning task which keeps them occupied and busy! Such a goal orientation is clearly intrinsic, task oriented and learning focused, but not strictly targeted to mastery of content. Nicholls et al. (1985) referred to these as "task - type 2" orientations to distinguish them from the traditional conceptualisations of mastery goal orientations.

Goal theory and concepts of goal orientation such as the task/ego or the mastery/performance distinctions are useful and are undoubtedly valuable extensions to earlier and simpler intrinsic/extrinsic models. The important thing, well argued by Archer (1994) and reviewed in the next section, is that people may operate under simultaneous goals of different types and they may also alternate between orientations at different stages of working on a task. To judge (for example) extrinsic rewards as inferior to mastery goals may be appropriate in some or even the majority of cases, but to dismiss extrinsic motivators out of hand is an oversimplification of a complex process.

Figure 5.4 *Classification of learning goals according to locus and purpose*

Self-regulation and Self-regulated Learning

The "willing and able" or the "will and skill" dimensions of motivation were briefly described earlier in this chapter. Self-regulation is an approach to the study of performance which gives as much emphasis to the post-decisional aspects of behaviour as it does to the formation of intentions. In one sense it expands the action box in the thought-emotion-expectancy-action model and highlights the skill components of successful learning.

Zimmerman (1989) defined self-regulated learning as the "process whereby students activate and sustain cognitions, behaviours and affects [emotions] that are systematically oriented toward the attainment of their goals" (p. 330). Alternatively, they are "meta-cognitively, motivationally and behaviourally active participants in their own learning processes" (p.330). Together these descriptions give an impression of a person who is thinking consciously, not only about the material being learned, but about how they are going about the learning. They are monitoring and evaluating their reading or other study strategies and they are being

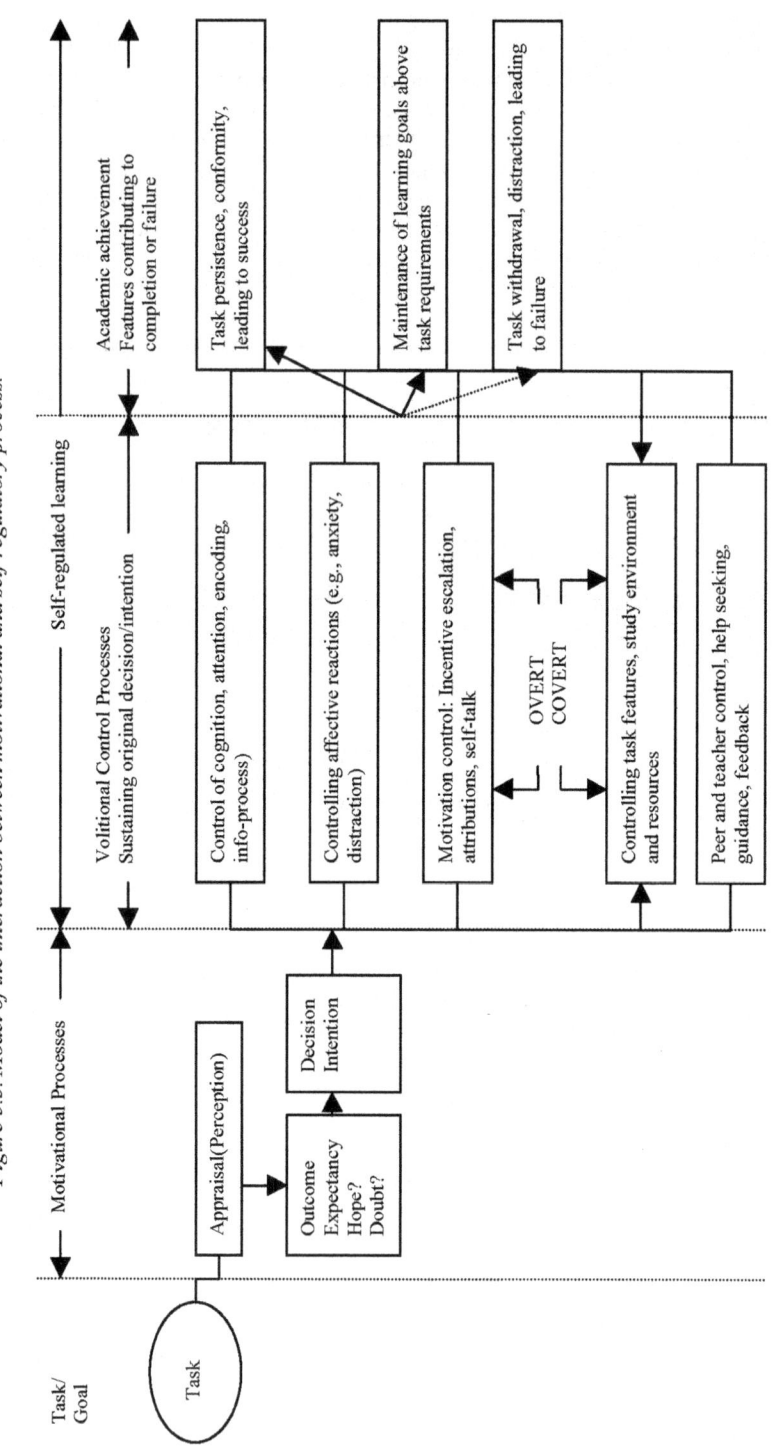

Figure 5.5. Model of the interaction between motivational and self-regulatory process.

disciplined in their attempts to ignore distractions and control themselves and their environment so that learning continues. They are also using well developed skills to manage their feelings when set-backs or boredom threaten to make them give up.

Super-learners you might say? Well, think for a moment about the probability that it takes all those things for anyone to achieve any genuinely difficult goal. Researchers on self-regulation have observed these components rather than invented them, and they are interested in how to help people use them more widely and consistently. A key feature, according to Corno (1989), is how metacognition (thinking about our own thinking) can influence our ability to sustain our initial intentions. This volitional control is seen as a skill which can be learned and improved with correct technique and practice. Similarly, more skilful ways of adapting the learning environment or seeking help, things which natural self-regulated learners are seen to do, are believed to be teachable and able to be improved.

Figure 5.5 combines aspects of Corno's (1989) and Bereiter and Scardamalia's (1989) work on the interplay of intentions, traditional motivational elements, volition, metacognition and goal theory. It represents one way of separating out, but also showing relationships between, the basic motivational processes and the things which self-regulation writers have suggested as providing a more complete picture of eventual achievement.

There are actually several quite different theories of self-regulation, some of which are reminiscent of the major paradigm differences of the 1930s to 1960s. There are operant (behaviourist) views which stress the awareness and monitoring of links between the environment and its reinforcers, there are autonomous/ phenomenological (more humanist) views which stress the role of the self system in self-regulation (see for example McCombs, 1989) and there are social-cognitive models which attempt to bring together all of the above as well as the cognitive aspects (Zimmerman, 1990). This diversity of perspectives within the field can be both a blessing and a curse. Schunk and Zimmerman (1994), though not suggesting that an "omnibus, integrated theory" (p. 312) could or should be developed, do recommend that researchers in self-regulation pay greater attention to ideas from theories other than their own so that differences and areas of convergence can be identified.

Before leaving the topic of self-regulation, two other views of motivation are worth mention because they are sometimes confused with self-regulatory theories. One is that of self-directed learning and the other is self-determination. Although there are fundamental differences between the direction and the determination views, they have in common a focus on who (or what) is in control of learning choices and methods. Self-directed learning (see for example Brookfield, 1985 and Knowles, 1990) has become synonymous with Adult Learning Theory and is based on the assumption that, for adults, decisions about what will be learned, the method of learning and what and how learning will be assessed must be made by the learner rather than the teacher/ lecturer. It is not usually recognised as a psychological theory as it developed independently of the psychological literature and has not, in general, used the usual methods to test and verify its assumptions or conclusions. Self-determination, also stressing personal control, grew out of psychological work in locus of control and other elements of intrinsic motivation (see Deci & Ryan, 1985). Recently applied to the special motivational problems of the elderly by Vallerand, O'Connor and Hamel (1995), it describes four types of motivators which range from high to low in self-determination. These are: intrinsic, self-determined extrinsic, non-self determined extrinsic, and amotivation. The suggestion for elderly people, who may have other life experiences which threaten or erode their perceptions of competence and control, is that motivators can increase or decrease these feelings. According to self-determination theory, the wrong sort of motivators might be well intentioned but may actually worsen feelings of helplessness or depression.

Contributions from Research

As explained in the introduction to this chapter, this section will give samples of results from motivational research which look at specific features of the "big picture theories". Because this is an introductory text, the examples will not feature the complex statistical measures used in the original works, but try to outline the general questions addressed and some of the answers indicated by the results. The purpose is to show how our present understanding of motivation has come from testing assumptions and ideas which theories are based upon.

Motivation and Self-regulation

The first example is a well known and often quoted study by Paul Pintrich and Elisabeth De Groot (1990). They were interested in the assumed links between goal orientation (e.g., mastery vs. performance), aspects of self-regulation (strategy use, anxiety and effort control) and actual performance. They used a common statistical tool - the correlation co-efficient to see which of these variables appeared to go together.

Basically, if two things tend to increase or decrease together when measured in a range of situations or with a number of different people, they are said to be positively correlated. If increases in one tend to go with decreases in the other, they are negatively correlated. High correlations mean the effect is strong and low correlations mean it is weak. The correlation coefficient ("r") can go from minus one (maximum negative correlation), through to zero (no correlation), to plus one (maximum positive correlation). Importantly, correlations do not claim to indicate whether one causes the other because it is always possible that a third unknown factor is influencing them both. Researchers, though being careful not to assume these causal relationships, can make inferences about relationships between variables in complex systems. An example from the Pintrich and De Groot (1990) study was the relationship between learners' anxiety about tests or exams and their performance in those types of achievement measures. Figure 5.6 shows this and some of the other links which correlation calculations indicated. The study produced some expected and some unexpected results when compared with the theoretical model.

Most interesting was support for the theoretical idea that a task's intrinsic value (its interest and importance) does not directly link to successful performance. Just as the motivation - volition - self regulation model (Figure 5.5) in the previous section suggests, there needs to be other intermediate processes operating to ensure eventual successful performance. Fortunately for self-regulation theorists, the study also showed that the combined use of strategy monitoring, goal setting, planning, and effort and persistence management was the best predictor of successful performance. These things are how self-regulated learners are differentiated from others, and if the study did not show them to be more likely to achieve high performance, then the theory would be weakened.

Goal Orientation and Attribution Style

Another study which relates to the models outlined in the previous section was conducted by Jennifer Archer (1994). She wanted to test the theoretical claim that learners oriented to mastery rather than performance goals were more likely to: enjoy their learning, prefer challenging rather than easy tasks, see content as relevant, attribute successes and failures to effort, and use metacognitive strategies. She also wanted to see if mastery goals were more influential than performance goals in generating a positive approach to learning in those cases when learners appeared to be using both goal types simultaneously. Like Pintrich and De Groot (1990), she used correlational methods to see if the relationships suggested by theory were demonstrable. To do this, she asked a total of 859 university students questions about their reasons for learning, their attributions, their task preferences, and perceptions of ability. As a result of statistical analysis of the answers received, several theoretical predictions were supported in that:
— mastery goals were more closely linked to use of effective study strategies than performance goals;
— when mastery and performance goals existed simultaneously, the mastery goals more strongly determined strategy use and a positive approach to learning;
— mastery goals were less associated with students' needs to protect self-worth and self-esteem; and
— mastery goal learners were less likely to attribute success or failure to the level of difficulty of tasks.

As in many studies, however, some of the hoped for evidence for theoretical assumptions was either not obtained (when statistical results are not significant according to rules of probability) or actually contradicted theory. In this case most of the expected links between goals and attributions were not supported at all. Specifically:
— learners following mastery goals did not show a greater likelihood to attribute successes to high effort or failures to lack of effort; and
— learners following performance goals did not show a greater likelihood to attribute successes or failures to low ability or bad luck (in this case, poor teaching).

When unexpected or contradictory results occur in experimental studies the researchers must be very careful to honestly report their failures and offer plausible reasons for them. In this study Archer suggested that either the wording of questions about attributions may have been confusing or that adult subjects have more complex attribution processes than the children other (successful) studies had used.

Figure 5.6 *Diagrammatic representation of causal links between motivational and self-regulated components of performance.*

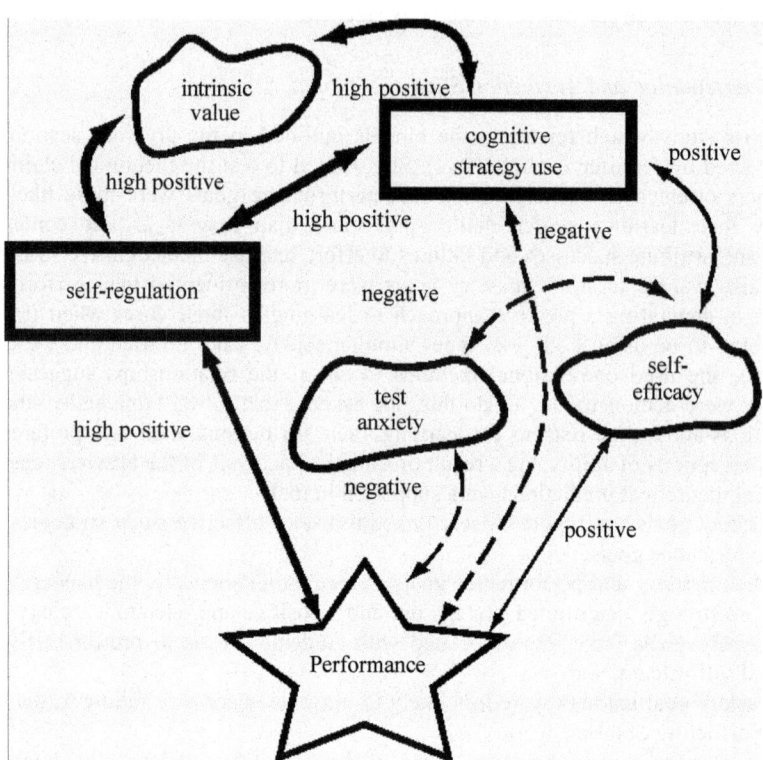

Motivational Strategies

Bernard Weiner, in his chapter on motivation in the 1992 Encyclopedia of Educational Research, was critical of the belief that a "cookbook" could be produced which could tell educators how to motivate students. He claimed that motivational research had actually been hindered by attempts and unrealistic expectations to do this, and that it was simply not possible. Such strong, unequivocal, statements are not common in academic literature and one must think for a moment about why such a respected and key figure in motivational research would be moved to write this.

The statement is, of course, particularly relevant to this section of the chapter because it is here that an attempt is made to turn the theory and research into advice - or a few tips at least - for the practitioner. Weiner's comments served as a warning that motivation is far too complex a field to be solved by a "teachers should..." list of simple procedures. Research and theory can be summarised, maybe even comprehensively, but the range of situations and individuals which educators encounter will always defy simplification. The following attempts at turning theories into teaching procedures and strategies may (at best) work on some of the people, some of the time. Weiner is right that the "all of the people, all of the time" solution probably does just not exist and probably never will.

Socialising Student Motivation to Learn

Jere Brophy has been a prominent researcher and writer on learning and motivation for at least thirty years. Several of his more recent works have contained the theme of socialising learners for either general behaviour (1996) or specific motivational enhancement (1987). The socialising rather than teaching or training approach for motivation is meant to be more multi-faceted than methods which focus on specific aspects such as self-concept, attribution training or goal setting. Brophy (1986, 1987) has provided descriptions of contextual, environmental, course design, teacher behaviour and training strategies which should promote motivation in any learning setting. Many of the theoretical elements discussed in the previous sections of this chapter are represented in such an holistic approach and can span the otherwise disparate theories and paradigms. Brophy (1986) emphasised the need to develop teachers' skills and their commitment to increasing motivation due to his findings that many did not demonstrate these qualities in their everyday dealings with learners.

Design Principles for Promoting Intrinsic Motivation in Instructional Activities

Lepper and Chabay's (1985) and Lepper and Hoddell's (1989) design principles used the dimensions of control, challenge, curiosity and contextualization to incorporate a number of theoretical aspects of motivation into teaching methods (Table 5.2). The emphasis on control and the need to be careful with extrinsic rewards or pressures has links with early criticisms of behaviourist theories and recent self-determination theory (e.g., Deci, 1975, 1996). The challenge dimension relates to goal theory, curiosity includes cognitive dissonance and problem centred learning, and the importance of contextualization draws upon theoretical work on relevance and functionality.

Strategies for Increasing Student Motivation and Achievement

Two years before Bernard Weiner's (1992) criticism of attempts to produce a cookbook for teachers to motivate learners, the American Psychological Association appointed a Task Force on Psychology in Education to "determine ways in which the psychological knowledge base related to learning, motivation and individual differences could contribute directly to improvements in the quality of student achievement." (McCombs & Whisler (1997, p. 2). One of the task force's projects, directed by Barbara McCombs, developed 12 principles about learners and learning which were claimed to be fundamental to all learners, regardless of age, and applicable in a wide range of learning settings. Described generally as Learner-Centred Psychological Principles, they were divided into groups relating to: metacognitive and cognitive factors, affective factors, developmental factors, personal and social factors, and individual differences. The three principles in the affective factors group which related most directly to motivation are summarised in Table 5.3 and provide a useful comparison to the two cookbooks suggested by Brophy (1986, 1987) and Lepper and Chabay (1985).

Although not specific strategies, the principles are intended to be used as criteria for course design and are described as representing the theoretical knowledge base referred to in the American Psychological Association's charter for the task force.

In comparing the three attempts to apply theory and research on motivation to practical situations, it is clear that they have many common elements. It is also clear that promoting motivation is a matter of applying a battery of strategies or principles rather than focusing too much on single fixes. Although theorists can and do often operate within relatively narrow perspectives, educational practitioners need to draw upon a range of views and explanations. The greatest error for the teacher, coach or trainer is to become dedicated to a single model or theory, but neither should they become butterflies, shifting from theory to theory without understanding the underlying assumptions perspectives of each.

Table 5.2 Dimensions and strategies for instructional design

DIMENSION	OBJECTIVE	STRATEGY METHOD	STRATEGY DESCRIPTION
Control	Promote sense of control over activity	Minimise extrinsic constraints Decrease extrinsic constraints over time Minimise salience of extrinsic constraints	Use minimal external pressures and withdraw them as the task becomes more interesting.
Challenge	Provide a continually challenging activity	Use goals with uncertain attainment Set goals of intermediate difficulty Provide multiple goals with multiple levels	Ensure that each student gets feedback on efforts to reach goals which match ability but which are not transparently easy or hard
Curiosity	Provoke curiosity	Highlight areas of inconsistency, incompleteness or puzzlement Pose problems of relevance and inherent interest	Focus on contradictions and gaps in understanding about things which are useful and important to the learner
Contextualisation	Highlight functionality of activity	Present activities in a natural context Use simulations or imagination	Ensure that contextual cues, stimuli and reality contribute to tasks.

Summary and Future Developments

Another look at Figure 1 at the beginning of this chapter may help to bring the range of influences on motivation together. This chapter has attempted to describe the complexity of the field of motivational theory and research but it has also tried to show some of the common themes which have developed over the decades and across the different perspectives. For the educator, an understanding of motivation is important for three general areas of professional practice - course design, diagnosis of motivational problems, and effective responses to problems. For these practical applications both the general thematic trends and the diversity of variables are valuable tools.

The strategy models in the previous section, particularly if looked at together, provide a manageable range of general principles which should be considered when designing courses or, for that matter, learning experiences of any sort. When, on the other hand, a trainer or teacher is trying to identify reasons for specific instances of low motivation, the tendency for researchers to focus on discrete components has had the effect of producing what could be used as a diagnostic check-list. The practitioner can ask: "is it a problem of unclear or too distant goals?", "does this learner attribute failure to lack of ability or bad luck rather than to insufficient effort?", "is there a strong wish to learn the material but is a lack of help-seeking or study skills strategies eroding their ability to persist when the going gets a bit tough?, "have negative expectations of outcomes formed for reasons which are not rational nor real?". Every theoretical model contains elements which can be turned into questions like these to direct the troubleshooting process and when this happens, the elusive meeting of theory and practice can be the result.

Table 5.3 *Motivation-related principles for enhancement of student achievement*

LEARNER-CENTRED PSYCHOLOGICAL PRINCIPLES: (AFFECTIVE FACTORS)
Principle 5. Motivational influences on Learning
The depth and breadth of information processed and what and how much is learned and remembered, are influenced by: a) self-awareness and beliefs about personal control, competence and ability; b) clarity and saliency of personal values, interests, and goals; c) personal expectations of success or failure; d) affect, emotion, and general states of mind; and, e) the resulting motivation to learn.
Principle 6. Intrinsic Motivation to Learn
Individuals are naturally curious and enjoy learning, but intense negative cognitions and emotions (e.g., feeling insecure, worrying about failure, being self-conscious or shy, and fearing corporal punishment, ridicule, or stigmatising labels) thwart this enthusiasm.
Principle 7. Characteristics of Motivation-Enhancing Learning Tasks
Curiosity, creativity, and higher order thinking are stimulated by relevant, authentic learning tasks of optimal difficulty and novelty for each student

Fortunately, after so many years of fragmented and paradigm-limited motivational theory, the field is showing signs of the sort of consolidation and integration which will offer even more to practitioners. Weiner's (1990) call for the 40 year dominance of cognitivist approaches to include group and context influences rather than a preoccupation with the psychology of the self was an example of a widening perspective. Similarly, Schunk's (1996) claim that research needs to extend to the community "that includes schools, homes, neighbourhoods and businesses" (p. 10), remains a welcome new direction for research. In an even wider frame, Munro, Schumaker and Carr's (1997) book on motivation and culture was a reminder that traditional views may need some re-thinking. An argument that they developed highlighted this – they pointed out that while psychologists explain cultures as combinations of the motivations and needs of individual members, anthropologists explain the motivation of each individual as being the consequences of cultural elements. The question is, can they both be right?, or are they both half right?

The future will probably be a combination of continuing examination of identified influences and of totally new directions. Ongoing specific and highly focused research is a necessary part of the incremental growth of understanding in a genuinely complex field. New questions and new contexts are also needed to redress too many years of an adversarial and compartmentalised tradition which decided what the important questions were and how they should be studied. For educators there will remain a rich source of ideas and practical solutions to help people learn and achieve their goals.

REFERENCES

Adair, J. (1996). *Effective motivation.* London: Macmillan.

Allport, G. W. (1937). *Personality: A psychological interpretation.* NY: Henry Holt.

Ames, C. (1992). Classrooms: Goals, structures and student motivation. *Journal of Educational Psychology, 84,* 261-271.

Archer, J. (1994). Achievement goals as a measure of motivation in university students. *Contemporary Educational Psychology, 19,* 430-446.

Atkinson, R. C., & Shiffrin, R. M. (1968). Human memory: A proposed system and its control processes. In K. W. Spence & J. T. Spence (Eds.), *The psychology of learning and motivation* (Vol. 2). NY: Academic Press.

Bereiter, C. &, Scardamalia, M. (1989). Intentional Learning as a Goal of Instruction. In L.B. Resnick (Ed.), *Knowing, Learning and Instruction; Essays in Honour of Robert Glaser.* Hillsdale, NJ: Erlbaum.

Brookfield, S. (1985). *Self-directed Learning.* San Francisco: Jossey-Bass.

Brophy, J. (1986). Socializing student motivation to learn. *Institute for Research on Teaching, report series 169,* Michigan State University.

Brophy, J. (1987). Synthesis of research on strategies for motivating students to learn. *Educational Leadership, 45,* 40-48.

Brophy, J. (1996).Enhancing students' socialisation: Key elements. *Eric Digest,* ED395713.

Bruner, J. S. (1966). *Toward a theory of instruction.* Cambridge, Mass.: Harvard University Press.

Butler, R. (1992). What young people want to know when: Effects of mastery and ability goals on interest in different kinds of social comparisons. *Journal of Personality and Social Psychology, 62,* 934-933.

Cannon, W. B. (1927). The James-Lange theory of emotion: A critical examination and an alternative theory. *American Journal of Psychology, 39,* 106-124.

Cleese, J. (writer and presenter), Jay, A. (writer) & Robinson, P. (director). (1981). *You'll soon get the hang of it* (videorecording). London: Video Arts.

Corno, L. (1986). The metacognitive control components of self-regulated learning. *Contemporary Educational Psychology, 11,* 333- 346.

Corno, L. (1989). Self-regulated learning: A volitional analysis. In B.J. Zimmerman & D.H. Schunk (Eds.), *Self-regulated Learning and Academic Achievement: Theory, Research and Practice.* (pp. 111-141). NY: Springer-Verlag.

Covington, M., & Teel, K. (1996). *Overcoming student failure: Changing motives and incentives for learning.* Washington: American Psychological Association.

de Charms, R. (1972). Personal causation training in the schools. *Journal of Applied Psychology, 2,* 95-113.

Deci, E. L. (1975). *Intrinsic motivation.* NY: Plenum.

Deci, E. L. (1996). Self-determined motivation and educational achievement. In T. Gjesme & R. Nygard (Eds.), *Advances in motivation* (pp. 195- 209). Oslo: Scandinavian University Press.

Deci, E. L., & Ryan, R. M. (1985). *Intrinsic motivation and self-determination in human behavior.* NY: Plenum.

Deci, E. L., & Ryan, R. M. (1991). A motivational approach to self: Integration in personality. In R.A. Dienstsbier (Ed.), *Nebraska symposium on motivation* 1990 (Vol. 38, pp.237-288). Lincoln: University of Nebraska Press.

Eccles, J. (1983). Expectancies, values and academic behaviours. In J.T. Spence (Ed.), *Achievement and achievement motives* (pp. 75-146). San Francisco: Freeman.

Festinger, L. (1957). *A theory of cognitive dissonance.* Stanford, CA: Stanford University Press.

Ford, M. (1992). *Motivating humans: Goals, emotions and personal agency beliefs.* Newbury Park, CA: Sage.

Freud, S. (1966). *The complete introductory lectures on psychoanalysis* (J. Strachey, Trans.). NY: Norton.

Geen, R., & Shea, J. D. C. (1997). Social motivation and culture. In D. Munro, J.F. Schumaker & S.C. Carr (Eds.), *Motivation and culture* (pp. 33-48). NY: Routledge.

Harris, K. R. (1990). Developing self-regulated learners: The role of private speech and self instructions. *Educational Psychologist, 25,* 3 5-49.

Heckhausen, H. (1977). Achievement motivation and its constructs: A cognitive model. *Motivation and Emotion, 1,* 283-229.

Heider, F. (1958). *The psychology of interpersonal relations.* NY: Wiley.

Hull, C. L. (1943). *Principles of behaviour: An introduction to behaviour theory.* NY: Appleton-Century-Crofts.

Kelley, H. H. (1971). *Attributions in social interactions.* Morristown, NJ: General Learning Press.

Knowles, M. (1990). *The adult learner: A neglected species.* Houston: Gulf.

Lepper, M. R., & Chabay, R. (1985). Intrinsic motivation and instruction: Conflicting views on the role of motivational processes in computer instruction. *Educational Psychologist, 20,* 217-230.

Lepper, M. R., & Hoddell, M. (1989). Intrinsic motivation in the classroom. In C. Ames & R. Ames (Eds.), *Research on motivation in education* (Vol.3, pp.73-105). San Diego: Academic Press.

Lewin, K. (1935). *A dynamic theory of personality: Selected papers* (D. K. Adams & K. E. Zener, Trans.). NY: McGraw-Hill.

Locke, E. A., & Latham, G. P. (1990). *A theory of goal setting and task performance.* Englewood Cliffs, NJ: Prentice-Hall.

Maslow, A. (1954). *Motivation and personality.* NY: Harper.

McCombs, B. L. (1988). Motivational skills training: combining cognitive, meta-cognitive and affective learning strategies. In C.E. Weinstein, E.T. Goetsz, & P.A. Alexander (Eds.), *Learning and study strategies: Issues in assessment, instruction, and evaluation* (pp. 141-169). NY: Academic Press.

McCombs, B. (1989). Self-regulated learning and academic achievement: A phenomenological view. In B. J. Zimmerman and D. H. Schunk (Eds.), *Self-regulated learning and academic achievement: Theory, research and practice.* (pp. 51-80), NY: Springer-Verlag.

McCombs, B., & Marzano, R. (1990). Putting the self in self-regulated learning: The self as an agent in integrating will and skill. *Educational Psychologist, 25,* 51-70

McCombs, B., & Whisler, J. S. (1997). *The learner-centred classroom and school: Strategies for increasing student motivation and achievement.* San Francisco: Jossey-Bass.

Miller, N. E. (1948). Studies of fear as an acquirable drive: Fear as motivation and fear reduction as reinforcement in the learning of new responses. *Journal of Experimental Psychology, 38,* 89-101.

Munro, D., Schumaker, J., & Carr, C. (1997). *Motivation and culture.* NY: Routledge.

Murray, H. A. (1938). *Explorations in personality.* NY: Oxford University Press.

Nicholls, J. (1984). Achievement motivation: Conceptions of ability, subjective experience, task choice and performance. *Psychological Review, 91,* 328-346.

Nicholls, J. G., Patashnick, M., & Nolan, S. B. (1985). Adolescents' theories of education. *Journal of Educational Psychology, 77,* 683-692.

Nicholls, J. G., Cheung, P. C., Lauer, J., & Patashnick, M. (1989). Individual differences in academic motivation: Perceived ability, goals, beliefs, and values. *Learning and individual differences, 1,* 63-84.

O'Neill, H. F., & Drillings, M. (1994). *Motivation: Theory and research.* Hillsdale, NJ: Erlbaum.

Pekrun, R. (1993). Facets of adolescents' academic motivation: A longitudinal expectancy value approach. In M. L. Maehr & P. R. Pintrich (Eds.), Advances in motivation and achievement: *Motivation in adolescence* (Vol. 8, pp. 139-189). Greenwich, CT: JAI Press.

Piaget, J. (1962). *Play, dreams and imitation*. NY: Norton.

Pintrich, P. R. & De Groot, E. V. (1990). Motivational and self-regulated learning components of classroom academic performance. *Journal of Educational Psychology, 82,* 33-40.

Pintrich, P. R., & Schunk, D. H. (1996). *Motivation in education: Theory, research and applications*. Englewood Cliffs, N.J.: Prentice-Hall.

Relich, J. D., Debus, R. L., & Walker, R. (1986). The mediating role of attribution and self-efficacy variables for treatment effects on achievement outcomes. *Contemporary Educational Psychology, 11,* 195-216.

Rogers, C. R. (1959). A theory of therapy, personality, and interpersonal relationships, as developed in the client centred framework. In S. Koch (Ed.), *Psychology: A study of a science* (Vol. 3, pp. 184-256). NY: McGraw-Hill.

Rogers, C. R. (1963). The actualising tendency in relation to motives and to consciousness. In M.R. Jones (Ed.), *Nebraska symposium on motivation* (Vol. 11, pp. 1-24). Lincoln: University of Nebraska Press.

Sarason, S. B. (1990). *The predictable failure of school reform: Can we change course before it's too late?* San Francisco: Jossey-Bass.

Schachter, S. (1964). The interaction of cognitive and physiological determinants of emotional state. In L. Berkowitz (Ed.), *Advances in experimental social psychology* (Vol.1, pp. 49-80). NY: Academic Press.

Schunk, D. (1996). Motivation in education: Current emphases and future trends. *Mid-western Educational Researcher, 9,* 5-12.

Schunk, D. & Zimmerman, B. J. (1994). *Self-regulation of learning and performance*. Hillsdale, NJ: Erlbaum.

Seligman, M. E. (1975). *Helplessness: On depression, development and death*. NY: Freeman.

Seligman, M. E. (1992). *Learned optimism*. Milsons Point, N.S.W.: Random House.

Skaalvik, E. M. (1997). Self-enhancing and self-defeating ego orientation: Relations with task and avoidance orientation, achievement, self-perceptions, and anxiety. *Journal of Educational Psychology, 89,* 71-81.

Skinner, B. F. (1953). *Science and human behaviour*. NY: Free Press.

Thorndike, E. L. (1913). *Educational psychology: Vol. 2 The psychology of learning*. NY: Teachers College Press.

Tolman, E. C. (1932). *Purposive behaviour in animals and men*. NY: Appleton-Century-Crofts.

Trudewind, C., Schneider, K., & Macowaik, K. (1996). The common root of curiosity, anxiety, and task motivation: subjective uncertainty. In T. Gjesme & R. Nygard (Eds.), *Advances in Motivation*. (pp. 9- 22). Oslo. Scandinavian University Press.

Vallerand, R. J., O'Connor, B. P., & Hamel, M. (1995). Motivation in later life: theory and assessment. International. *Journal of Aging and Human Development, 41,* 221-238.

Watson, J. B. (1924). *Behaviourism*. NY: Norton. Weiner, B. (1986). *An attribution theory of motivation and emotion*. NY: Springer-Verlag.

Weiner, B. (1990). History of motivational research in education. *Journal of Educational Psychology, 82,* 616-622.

Weiner, B. (1992). Motivation. In M. C. Alkin (Ed.), *Encyclopedia of Educational Research*, (6th ed., pp. 859-865). NY: Macmillan.

Wigfield, A. (1994). Expectancy-value theory of achievement motivation: A developmental perspective. *Educational Psychology Review, 6,* 49-78.

Wilhite, S. C. (1990). Self-efficacy, locus of control, self-assessment of memory ability, and study activities as predictors of college course achievement. *Journal of Educational Psychology, 82,* 696-700.

Zimmerman, B. J. (1989). A social cognitive view of self-regulated academic learning. *Journal of Educational Psychology, 81,* 329-339.

Zimmerman, B. J. (1990). Self-regulating academic learning and achievement: The emergence of a social cognitive perspective. *Educational Psychology Review, 2,* 173-201.

Review Questions

Read the following statements and indicate whether they are True or False.

1. Motivational theories and methods of early this century have been replaced by more modern approaches.
2. Sound motivational strategies can be expected to work in most situations if properly applied.
3. Self-regulation theorists believe that people can be trained to be more effectively motivated.
4. Most motivational theories over the past 80 years were carefully tested and researched before they became popular.
5. High levels of interest and curiosity do not necessarily ensure continuing motivation.
6. Thoughts have been seen as the main determinants of motivation for most of the past 40 years.
7. Behaviourist theories of motivation had the basic individual needs of people as their central issue.
8. Cognitive models of motivation do not include emotions in their explanations of purposeful behaviour.
9. According to attribution theory, self-explanations of successes to high ability are seen to promote motivation.
10. Self-regulated learners seek help more often than non self-regulated learners.
11. A person who tries hard to understand a difficult but interesting concept is said to be working toward a performance-type goal.
12. Two things are negatively correlated if increases in one of them coincide closely with decreases in the other.
13. Self-regulated learning and self-directed learning describe similar approaches and types of learners.
14. Research into motivation in the future is likely to include more social and context variables than it has in recent years.
15. If a person is rewarded for successfully performing an easy task, they will be more likely to attempt more difficult tasks.
16. One reason for the popularity of cognitivist theories of motivation was their ability to encompass cultural issues and differences.
17. 17.Competency based approaches to education and training have their origins in the humanist motivational theories of the 1960s.
18. Maslow's Hierarchy of Needs theory is still taught in some fields as the main (current) theory of motivation.
19. Someone who tries hard so that others will respect and admire them is said to be extrinsically motivated.
20. Metacognition includes thoughts about the selection and monitoring of learning strategies.

Answers

1F	2F	3T	4F	5T	6T	7F	8F	9F
10T	11F	12T	13F	14T	15F	16T	17F	18T
19F	20T							

Exercises

1. Risk-taking. Why do some motivational theorists see investment of effort to learn as "risk-taking"?
2. Causal Attributions. When a person fails to achieve a particular goal, what might be three personal explanations for the failure?
3. Needs. Give an example of a behaviour motivated by a deep biological or physiological need.
4. Self-speech. Give an example of a thought which a person might "carry around in their head" which could decrease their motivation.
5. Volition. Where have you seen someone display a strong control over their initial intention to achieve a goal, even when faced with major obstacles?
6. Goals. Describe a situation in which you had trouble sticking to a project because the goal was unclear.
7. Stimulus/Response. Give an example of a person motivated by a strong environmental stimulus and its contingent reward (other than money).
8. Interest. When has the high interest in, or value of, something not been sufficient to produce sustained motivated behaviour for you?
9. Self-concept. How might a person's opinion of their own abilities influence their decision to try something difficult?
10. Cognitive dissonance. Give an example of a game which relies on cognitive dissonance to motivate the player.
11. Task vs. Ego orientation: (a)How might a typically task oriented person describe a successful day at work? (b) How would an ego oriented person respond?
12. Will vs Skill. Describe an example of a learning or study strategy which, if lacking, could thwart a strong wish to learn.
13. Rewards. When could the offer of a reward for effort actually reduce motivation?

About the Author

Peter Russell is a senior lecturer in education at the University of Technology, Sydney. He has been teaching educational psychology and the theory of teaching and learning to undergraduate and graduate vocational teachers since 1981. Prior to his work in teacher education, he taught radio and television servicing, electronics, and film and television production techniques in New South Wales colleges of technical and further education. His main academic interest is in the areas of self-regulated learning, metacognition, and general motivation.

Peter Russell
University of Technology, Sydney

IRENE STRYDOM

6. EMOTIONS AND ADULTHOOD

As adults we are involved in many activities and experiences every day. We try to make sense of the world around us, we try to survive the many events and demands of the day and most of all we try to interpret our perceptions of daily happenings. Strangely, at the end of the day we best remember the emotions that these events evoked in us. We clearly remember the anxiety, sadness or joy we felt in a particular situation. Then the process of "trying to understand" starts - we want to know why we felt so angry, or why we lost our temper or why a co-worker irritated us so much. In short, we want to understand our emotions and behaviour - this knowledge will empower us not only to develop and acquire new and better coping skills, but have the capacity to become what we should become - to reach our goals with greater ease and poise.

Although the role of emotions in the lives of adults has frequently been emphasised in educational psychology, it is a topic which has received relatively little attention from scholars until the 1990s. Even in the field of psychology, the scientific study of emotions, which some might argue is its most important subject matter, has remained outside the mainstream of psychology. Izard (1991) expressed surprise that anyone can maintain that human beings in relationships and in action in the real world can ever be understood without a thorough study of emotions. The significance of emotions for self confidence, social commitment, creative endeavours, and courageous actions has been recognised by keen observers of the human sphere for as long as there have been written records, yet until the 1980s most of psychology's mainstream scholars ignored them (Izard, 1991). In 1884 William James (Oatley, 1992) titled his famous paper "What is an emotion?", but it is only more than a century later that the psychology of emotions is coming of age.

Despite the increase in research on emotions in recent years, there is still no widely accepted definition of "emotion" (Shaver, Wu & Schwartz, 1992). Historically this term has proved utterly resistant to efforts at definition and there probably is no other term in psychology that shares its non-definability and

James A Athanasou (ed.), Adult Educational Psychology, 125–154

frequency of use (Reber, 1985). Another point which has become clear is that there are still myths surrounding this topic - such as that emotions are dark, destructive forces which have the capacity to destroy our sanity, that emotions are the waste product of intellectual action (Lewis, 1989) and that emotions could be labelled as either positive or negative (Reece & Brandt, 1996). Although reference is made to the positive view of emotions being an integral and inseparable part of being human, the positive role that emotionality - the driving force behind actions, giving colour to our existence - can play in the life of the learning adult is not highlighted enough.

In this chapter different aspects of this complex topic will be discussed. In Part I, the nature of emotions and topics like definitions and theories of the concept will be addressed. In Part I, emotions as organisers of adult behaviour and various factors influencing emotions will also be investigated. Part II consists of a discussion on individual differences in experiencing and expressing emotions, as well as emotional management and the role emotions play in learning.

PART I: THE NATURE OF EMOTIONS

As indicated before, trying to find an acceptable description of "emotions" is a complex assignment. As Fehr and Russell (Clark, 1992) put it, "Everyone knows what an emotion is until asked to give a definition". Definitions vary from brief and vague descriptions to elaborate and complex explanations. The description by Rosch (Clark, 1992) merely stated that emotion is a "fuzzy" category whose members bear family resemblances to each other, and that these categories do not have formal, classical definitions based on essential and sufficient features. At the other end of the spectrum of definitions, the definition given by Sillince (1993, pp. 496) represents the view held by earlier scientists, which explained emotions in more complex terms and emphasised the cognitive dimension of the concept. According to this view, an emotion is an awareness of important internal cognitive transitions. It is either incidentally or comprehensively about transition, and it concerns the construing of various construct subsystems (central constructs, constructs about one's role in relation to others, and constructs about peripheral things) and refers to one's construct system or another's construct system.

Although there is agreement that emotion is a "fuzzy" category and that the cognitive component plays an important role in the awareness of feelings, a more comprehensive view should be reflected here. The following two definitions are representative of many other explanations and are used to suggest a working definition for the purpose of this chapter. These are definitions of Hatfield and Rapson (1990) and Dillard (1993). These definitions manage to incorporate various facets of being human, including the cognitive, the physical (biological), the emotional, the conative (will) and the social (environmental) dimensions. All these facets play a role in the experiencing and expressing of emotions and, in the psychology of education, a definition which disregards the view that emotion is a whole-person experience will probably not be accepted. The two definitions can best be summarised as follows:

Emotions as a System

Hatfield and Rapson (1990) like many other theorists, viewed emotions as a system that activates cognitive, physiological, and behavioural components. No one of the three components can be isolated as all three are crucial to the concept. Each basic or fundamental emotion can be defined in terms of the neurophysiological, expressive, and experiential characteristics it possesses. These are:

- at the neurophysiological level, a fundamental emotion is defined as a particular, innately programmed pattern of electrochemical activity in the nervous system;
- the expressive component consists mainly of a characteristic pattern of facial activity, but may also include bodily responses and vocal expressions; and
- at the experiential level, each fundamental emotion is a unique quality of consciousness.

Dillard's (1993) definition also referred to various facets of being human, but emphasised the role of emotions in adapting to a changing environment. Here the first reference is made to the close relationship between emotion and learning. This definition is explained in the next section.

Emotions as Phasic Responses

Dillard (1993) stated that emotions are complex, yet coherent, phasic responses to ongoing assessments of the person-environment relationship. The function of emotions serves to prepare the individual to make appropriate changes in the person-environment relationship. Emotions are complex in the sense that they are patterns of response to person-environment assessments across four distinct domains: subjective experience, action tendency, expressive behaviour, and physiology. Each of these domains can be explained as follows:

- *Subjective experience:* The person-environment relationship can be favourable or unfavourable to a person. If there is a match between the goals and desires of an individual and the state of the environment, a positive affect results. A mismatch produces negatively valenced feelings.
- *Action tendencies:* Two strategies exist for dealing with the environment, namely active alteration of the environment, and withdrawal.
- *Emotional expression:* Emotionally expressive behaviour probably evolved because it has the potential to enhance the survivability of a species. Individuals can make known their feeling that danger is looming or that something is wrong, or merely state how they experience a situation.
- *Emotions possess a physiological component:* Emotions such as fear and anger function as preparation for mobilization - that is fight or flight. Recent research, however, has established a physiological signature for a limited number of emotions (Dillard, 1993, p.155).

In summary, one can say that emotions can be described as responses to an event in the environment which is assessed by an active cognitive-physiological-behavioural system. Different theories of emotions exist but, before this is explained, it is necessary to make reference of the categories of emotions that can be distinguished.

Categories of Emotions

One can make lists and lists of concepts, all describing specific emotions. One can even go further and produce separate lists to describe concepts closely related to emotions like moods (a relatively short-lived, low-intensity emotional state) sentiments (one's feeling towards some person or idea) and feelings (experiencing a sensory impression). Or one can list all the bipolar emotions like love-hate or pleasantness-unpleasantness. The possibilities are endless, because the categories one can use to organize the different concepts describing emotions can outnumber the number of existing descriptions of emotions.

The solution to this confusing reality - that there are as many descriptions of emotions as there are categories - lies in the suggestion by Lazarus (1991, p. 78) that there is a clear distinction between primary (basic) and secondary (derived) emotions.

Primary emotions arise from circumstances common to all social animals - like attachments, mating bonds, rivalry and predator behaviour (Sillince, 1993, p. 505). Bertocci (1988) referred to primary emotions as unlearned motives like instincts, drives and urges. The following basic emotions are listed by Descartes and Plutchnik (Lazarus, 1991): wonder, love, hatred, desire, sadness, joy, fear, surprise, disgust, anger, anticipation and acceptance. These primary emotions, which are presumably found in all humans and some animals, operate as affect programmes, which arise from common neurophysiological structures and, when set in motion, unfold in more or less the same fashion. The following is also characteristic of primary emotions (Lazarus, 1991):

– Primary emotions are physiologically elemental and pure;
– They are found consistently across cultures and perhaps in some animal species;
– Primary emotions emerge at birth; and
– Primary emotions express the survival tasks of a species, in protecting it from danger, and promoting reproduction, orientation and exploration.

Human self-awareness has led to the development of more complex emotions which are described as secondary emotions, like pity, which requires stepping into someone else's shoes (Sillince, 1993). Many human emotions like guilt, shame, pride, gratitude, nostalgia and regret may be unique to humans and may have emerged based on greater human cognitive and social complexity. Each of these secondary emotions can be seen as a blend of two or more basic (or other) emotions and is therefore more diverse and intricate to define. Secondary emotions only emerge later in life and may be experienced and expressed differently in different cultures.

Theories on Emotions

In order to understand the nature of emotions, different theories of emotions will be discussed. The theories mentioned here will not be discussed in full detail and only the main points of each theory will be highlighted.

Concept Theories
According to these theories, emotion concepts are selected and organised according to predetermined specifications and are represented in different dimensions of emotions like low negative affect or high negative affect. Russell's (1980) model

of emotions and that of Watson and Tellegen (1985) model are examples of this general approach. These broad dimensions of emotions exclude many valuable nuances of each of the hundreds of other emotional concepts that exist, but were not included in the models.

Theories Emphasising that Emotions and Cognitions are Interacting Partners
According to Lewis (1989) emotions and cognitions do not form a linear relationship but affect each other - they are an interplay of complex processes. Livesey (1986) also emphasised the importance of sequential processes and says that an emotional response involves a number of significant processes that constitute a sequence of events characterising the expression of emotion in human beings. These theories do not state that emotions follow cognition or that cognition follows emotion. They emphasise the constant interaction between cognition and emotion during a complicated process of perceiving-interpreting-reacting-feeling.

Combining Theories

Four contemporary views on emotions have evolved during the past few years. Buck (1990) listed these views and stated that these views have at least attempted to bring some degree of order to the conceptual and definitional chaos that characterises this area of research:
– *McNaughton's biological approach to emotion:* In this theory emotion is seen as groups of reactions that have evolved to satisfy some common evolutionary purpose;
– *Morris's theory,* which differentiates between moods and emotions. Morris maintained that mood is capable of altering responses to a wide variety of objects and events, whereas emotion instigates a relatively limited set of responses, and that mood is less intense than emotion;
– *Thayer's theory* of the biopsychology of mood and arousal. Thayer emphasised the importance of the subjective experience of feeling in interaction with thoughts and neurochemical processes and argues that moods are signal systems about general bodily conditions. The activity of two biologically based arousal systems, one of which is experienced as energizing and the other as tension-producing, is also explained in this theory; and
– *Frijda's theory,* which explains how biologically based information (for survival) interacts with other information like personal relationships in a larger social, cultural and historical context. The analytic-cognitive powers of the individual are highlighted in the sense that the individual has the capacity to reason about emotions.
Staats and Eifert (1990) studied the various theories on emotions and suggested that a unified theory of emotion should be accepted as this would create theory bridges, which would unify various concepts and mini-theories. They claimed that their theory of emotions is a general theory that could be useful at a basic level as well as at a human and applied level. Their theory systematically links the studies of the biological foundation of emotion, basic behaviour, basic human learning, personality and psychological measurement, abnormal personality, and clinical treatment. The aim of this theory is to deal with emotion in a unified way, covering all aspects of emotion that are ordinarily left separate. Diverse theories are placed

in a common framework of principles and concepts and a structure is provided which serves as an aid to interpreting discrepant elements in the literature.

This unified model distinguishes among seven levels of theory, each one highlighting a specific area of study. The different levels can be summarised as follows (Staats & Eifert, 1990, pp. 541-559):

- the biological study of emotional responses spells out the basic biological conception of emotion, which is that emotions are central nervous system responses that have to some extent been localised in brain areas such as the hypothalamus and hippocampus (which make up the limbic system). Thus, when humans receive brain stimulation, they will experience some kind of emotion;
- there appears to be an innate as well as a learned aspect to the emotion-behaviour relationship. On the innate side, research has shown that, when a stimulus elicits a substantial emotional response in the individual, this will result in a particular type of facial expression. On the learning side, research has shown that a person generally is attracted to stimuli that elicit a positive emotional response, because positive emotional stimuli are also positive reinforcers - like receiving a good mark will urge the adult to put even more effort into the next assignment;
- in the human learning theory it is important to build theory bridges by means of which the several areas of knowledge can be productively unified. An example is the linkage of emotional learning and emotion-instigated behaviour with the language-cognitive processes and other, essentially human, mechanisms that are responsible for producing, expressing, and communicating emotions;
- there is much valuable knowledge in the fields of personality theory that must be incorporated into a general theory of emotion. Those who consider personality as a causal determinant of emotion will welcome the inclusion of this level in the unified theory of emotion;
- various psychological tests of interests, preferences, values and tests of emotions like fears and phobias, anxiety, depression, stress and anger actually deal with different aspects of the emotional-motivational (emotion-behaviour) repertoire and the interpretation of these tests is part of Staats and Eifert's theory of emotion;
- the unified theory also includes a part devoted to the explanation of abnormal emotions and the abnormal behaviour that is produced; and
- treatment methods directed towards changing emotions have not been properly addressed before and, these are included in the unified model. The emphasis is on treating emotions in order to solve behaviour problems.

Staats and Eifert (1990, p. 542) summarised their multi-level theory of emotion as in Table 6.1.

Table 6.1 Multi-level theory of emotion (Staats & Eifert, 1990)

LEVELS	AREAS AND PHENOMENA OF STUDY
Biological mechanisms of emotion	Neurophysiological foundations of emotions Nature of basic emotional response Bridging biological/behavioural concepts
Basic learning of emotion	Environmental elicitation of emotions Emotion-reinforcement relationship Emotion-behaviour/motivation relationship
Human learning and emotion	Language and cognition in emotion Social cultural human emotional stimuli
Personality and emotion	Individual differences in emotional-motivational repertoire Personality/environment interactions
Measurement of emotion	Tests, psychophysiological indices, behavioural observation
Abnormal behaviour and emotion	Deficit and/or inappropriate emotional-motivational repertoire Person-environment interaction in emotional dysfunctions
Clinical psychology and emotion	Development of treatments for disorders involving inappropriate and deficit emotion

There are a vast number of other theories which explain the arousal of emotions. Table 6.2 summarises a few remaining theories which have not been mentioned yet (Baron & Byrne, 1994, p. 111; Parkinson, 1995, p. 147).

Sharply contrasting views of the nature of emotions exist. Most theories, however, agree that emotions are aroused when human beings react to a stimulus or event and that the interpretation of this has direct implications for human behaviour. It is clear that emotions are easily aroused and that they have the capacity to impede or enhance our reasoning and logical thinking. The implications of this for educational psychology are that adult emotional behaviour is a complex topic which can be understood only if the different aspects of these theories are kept in mind. This background information will help to clarify emotional behaviour and will better explain the role of emotions in the lives of adult learners. Emotions as determinants of adult behaviour will be discussed next.

Emotions as Organisers of Adult Behaviour
On one point almost all emotion theorists agree: there is a definite link between emotion and behaviour. The direct influence emotions have on behaviour can be illustrated by the following two scenarios (Baron & Byrne, 1994, pp. 406-408):
– if a person experiences positive emotions (has pleasant feelings/is in a good mood) an increase in the tendency to assist others in need is noted. If helping others, however, might lead to embarrassment or to spoiling one's present positive mood, some people might reconsider and resist helping others; and
– negative emotions will in some cases urge people to help others and in other cases not. According to the negative state relief model, helping others makes people feel good, and those experiencing a negative mood are inclined to do anything to make them feel better. If the potential helper is, however, so

preoccupied with his own problems and is concentrating on his or her own unhappy circumstances, helping is less likely to occur.

Table 6.2 *Additional theories on emotion*

TYPE OF THEORY	ASSUMPTIONS
Appraisal theory (Lazarus)	Emotions caused by situational evaluation and interpretation
Feedback theory (James)	Emotions caused by feedback of bodily reaction
Systems theory (Barnard & Teasdale)	Emotions as a product of general characteristics of the psychological system
Evolutionary theory (Plutchik)	Emotions as a result of the adaptational history of the species
Sociocultural theory (Averill)	Emotions are cultural solutions to locally defined societal conflicts
Cannon-Bard theory	Emotion-eliciting events cause both a physiological experience and subjective feelings like fear, anger
James-Lange theory	Subjective emotional experiences are the result of automatic physiological reactions
Schachter's two-factor theory	Any form of arousal initiates a search for the causes of these feelings

In these examples specific reference is made to the way emotions influence pro-social behaviour. It is equally important to realise that behaviour can never be unemotional (Blechman, 1990, p. ix). These two factors are interwoven and inseparable - it is therefore impossible to discuss the one without referring to the other. It is important to investigate other facets of this emotion-behaviour relationship and determine the role and place of evaluation, motivation and actual action in this complex process.

Evaluation and Judgement
Put in plain terms, human behaviour starts with a stimulus event, followed by an emotion and specific behaviour. Deci (1996) is adamant that, after an emotion has been aroused, cognitive mediation occurs before behaviour follows. An emotion may energize behaviour, but it is cognitions like goals, values and choices that direct behaviour. Mediators - like goals, values and choices - serve as catalysts between an actual emotion and specific behaviour. What happens is that different emotional states imply characteristic judgements and appraisals, which implies that the adult evaluates what has been sensed or observed (Parkinson, 1995) The personal significance of an event is taken into consideration here and the adult will personalise the event - if it matters - by analysing the consequences and meaning of the stimulus (Reber, 1985, p.235). What come to the fore here are factors like cognitive appraisal (evaluation) and the consequential motivational and action properties.

Motivational and Action Properties
After an emotion has been experienced, evaluated and put into perspective, the adult feels compelled to act. The term "emotion" refers to being moved and this implies that emotion reflects the transformation of how we relate to the world

(Fischer, 1991). The adult wants to act or adapt or change - the motive is to plan action. Motivation refers to the *direction* of possible actions and action reflects a person's *readiness* and ability to bring about changes in the environment. Emotion puts the individual in a state of readiness for focused behaviour that is appropriate to the adaptational agenda activated by appraisal (Parkinson, 1995). Expression flows from this and it provides the basic channels whereby emotional information is communicated - another manifestation of behaviour.

The outcome of action generates a further affective state that feeds back to the generating event and acts to stamp in or register the relationship between that event and the outcome of the particular behavioural response (Livesey, 1986). The result of this intricate process is that it possesses all the factors that will determine future adult behaviour.

Factors Influencing Emotions

There are a number of factors that directly or indirectly, influence emotions.

Temperament

Temperament is regarded by some authors as a specific aspect of the personality which is determined by the individual's physiological structure. It is a person's natural disposition and the beginning of an individual's identity (Reece & Brandt, 1996, p. 235). In the descriptions of this concept, the role nature - for example, inherited attributes - has played in creating temperament, is apparent.

The concise description of temperament is that it is the biological shaper of the personality (Reece & Brandt, 1996). There is then this notion that temperament is characteristic of each adult and that it refers to the speed and way he or she reacts - this is reflected in moods, activities and levels of activation.

There is a school of thought that maintains that certain temperamental characteristics are apparent in children at birth and remain somewhat stable over time - although the shaping of temperament is inevitable (Reece & Brandt, 1996). The moderate stance is that temperament (whether innate or acquired) interacts with social experience. The ways in which parents and other environmental forces treat the developing child, and respond to its temperament, help shape the emotional life (Lazarus, 1991). What remains clear is that temperament is biologically based, that it is reflective of fairly stable individual differences in emotional reactivity, and self-regulating (Saarni & Crowley, 1990).

Adults will, because of their temperament, react differently to a specific event and may implement a certain selection of strategies to cope with their own individual emotions. The speed and the way in which the individual adult will react is determined by temperamental differences like introversion versus extroversion, or low dominance versus high dominance.

Extroverts (directing their energies outward) direct their attitudes and values to the external physical and social environment, while introverts (who tend to shrink from social contact and are preoccupied with their own thoughts) are more interested in their own thoughts and feelings than in intense social and external affairs. Today most theorists doubt that either of these dimensions exists as a singular type. It is accepted that most people exhibit aspects of both temperamental types, although an individual may display behaviour reflective of a dominant temperament style (Reber, 1985). According to this hypothesis, extroverts are more inclined to rapidly release their emotions and may not always want to implement strict self-regulatory measures. Introverts, on the other hand, are less likely to display their emotions so explicitly.

A SOUTH AFRICAN STUDY ON INTROVERSION-EXTROVERSION
A study on the role of temperament and gender in the perception of emotion had interesting results. Fourie & Stuart (1996) reported that gender but not the temperament dimension of introversion-extroversion plays a significant role in the perception of emotion. Contradictory findings in the literature regarding the role of different hemispheres of the brain, especially with regard to the perceptions of various valencies of emotions, were

---

Dominance is the other aspect of temperament that could be mentioned to illustrate the difference in emotional reactions. Adults who are low in dominance tend to be low in assertiveness and to be more willing to compromise (Reece & Brandt, 1996). These adults may keep their feelings to themselves and will probably not let others know how they feel. Any display of their emotions will be a private affair. They will not impose on others and have little intention of claiming their right to expose their inner feelings. Adults who are high in dominance tend to seek to dominate situations they find themselves in, as well as the people around them. They frequently give advice and initiate demands. These adults easily display their emotions and everyone around them knows when they are experiencing emotions like anger, irritation and joy.

A concept closely related to temperament, which really cannot be separated from it, is the "big brother" of temperament, namely personality. The nature of personality has a direct influence on the overall wellbeing of an adult. Extensive research by Costa and McCrae (1984) has indicated a clear correlation between personality and the role emotions play in the wellbeing of adults. It is worthwhile to record some of their findings here:

– an examination of specific facets shows that all the traits of neuroticism, especially anxiety and depression, are related to wellbeing. Individuals who are chronically anxious, hostile, depressed, self-conscious, impulse-driven, and vulnerable to stress are likely to have an unfavourable affect balance and to be dissatisfied with life. Interpersonal warmth leads to greater happiness, but mere gregariousness often does not;
– assertiveness and the predisposition to experience positive emotions consistently correlate with happiness and life satisfaction; and
– individuals who experience dramatic mood shifts are characterised by personality traits like imagination, enthusiasm and openness, whereas less moody adults are rigid, cautious, and closed. An openness to experience seems to have a similar effect on subjective wellbeing. Individuals who are open to experience seek variety and novelty, and have an appreciation for the intrinsic value of experience itself. Such people are likely to be more sensitive than others to both positive and negative experiences and affect.

Subconscious Influences
The subconscious mind is a vast storehouse of forgotten memories, desires, ideas and frustrations and it can have a great influence on behaviour (Neville, 1989; Reece & Brandt, 1996). It contains memories of past experiences as well as memories of feelings associated with past experiences.

It is possible that adults may not remember many important events that occurred earlier in their lives, but these are present in the subconscious mind and can influence adult behaviour. Emotions associated with earlier experiences can surface at any time in adult life and can directly influence current behaviour and emotional states. The content of the subconscious, in some cases, may be incompatible with the conscious attitude and may cause emotional distress in the adult. This last comment corresponds with Freud's view (Freud, 1936) of ego-defence, which states that some cognitive processes are actively stored or ignored to cope with threat and to avoid emotional distress.

Cultural Realities

There is evidence that there are a number of similarities and differences in emotions and in the way they are represented in different culture groups. Some similarities will be mentioned and this section will conclude with some reference to cultural differences in experiencing and expressing emotions.

The similarities in emotion, and in the way they are presented in different cultural groups, are the following (Baron & Byrne, 1994; Heelas, 1996; Russell, 1991; Shaver, Wu & Schwartz, 1992):

– research done in a wide variety of cultures indicates cross-cultural universality with regard to the facial expression of at least six emotions - namely anger, happiness, sadness, fear, surprise and disgust;
– there is also cross-cultural universality of the appraisal preceding certain emotions. In most instances individuals from one culture can correctly name the emotion associated with the interpretive antecedents in another culture group;
– universality is also indicated with regard to individuals' descriptions of specific episodes of emotions like joy, sadness, fear and anger; and
– there is also consensus concerning conceptualization of the emotion domain as a whole. Subjects from different language groups rate the similarity of 28 emotions. In all languages, emotion-related words fell in roughly a circular order in a space definable by two dimensions: pleasure-displeasure and arousal-tranquillity.

The differences in emotions and in the way they are presented in different cultural groups, are the following (Heelas, 1996; Matsumoto 1993; Shaver, Wu, & Schwartz, 1992):

– emotion talk - the way members of a cultural group talk about emotions - differs from culture to culture and this can generate radical differences in emotional experience. This varies from cultural group to cultural group. The emotional vocabulary of some is very limited; other cultural groups go further and discuss differences in how emotions are associated with circumstances, and the differences in the powers ascribed to emotions;
– there are also differences in display rules, the rules that specify who can show what emotion to whom, and when. There is agreement that there are universal emotions and even emotional expressions, but different cultures have different rules about where and when the emotions can be naturally expressed;
– some cultures emphasise particular emotions and tend to refer to certain emotions in various ways. Separate words for anger and irritability may be expressed. Instead of saying that they are sad, Tahitians may say that they are troubled, have no inner push, or feel heavy and fatigued.

Although one recognises the fact that there are differences in the way people of different cultural groups display and talk about their emotions, it is welcoming to know that there are also indeed similarities, and that these may contribute to understanding and fruitful communication between cultural groups. Shaver et al. (1992) very effectively elaborated on this point and as the wording is so illustrative, the following is directly quoted:

> To cultural anthropologists, it may seem reductionist and disrespectful of other cultures when psychologists focus on biologically based human universals in the emotion domain, especially when it is clear that there are cultural differences. While appreciating this view, and agreeing that there may be substantial differences across cultures in the experience and conceptualisation of sub-ordinate-level emotions and in the hyper- versus hypocognition of particular basic emotions, we are also grateful for the communicational advantages of some cross-cultural universality in the emotion domain. People everywhere share many of the same motives, appraisal capacities, emotional reactions, and need to control emotional reactions. These similarities are a large part of what allows people around the world to understand and empathise with each other, despite differences associated with the different cups from which their cultures have drunk. The emerging evidence for cross-cultural similarity in the emotion domain supports Fang Lizhi's "fundamental belief that human nature is universal" (pp. 178 & 183).

PART II: HUMAN EMOTIONS IN THE CONTEXT OF ADULTS' LIVES

In the following section of this chapter, there will be special reference to aspects like individual differences in the emotional lives of adults, the socialisation of emotions, emotional management and the role that emotions play in adult learning.

Individual Differences

Each adult must be considered to have a unique emotional-motivational system, the outcome of remarkably complex experiences, much of which has been generated by the individual's own actions (Staats & Eifert, 1990). Adults learn different emotional responses to the various stimuli surrounding them all the time and these differences become apparent in terms of the stimuli that elicit emotional responses, in the variations in the intensity of the emotional responses, and in the relative intensity of responses elicited by the groups of stimuli.

There is no doubt that emotional development is intertwined with cognitive development, just as emotions are embedded in cognitive processes (Lewis, 1995). It is appropriate to refer at this stage to three theories which have related individual differences in personality and social functioning to differences underlying cognition-emotion interactions. The three viewpoints - biological, cognitive and functionalist - can be summarised as follows (Lewis, 1995, p. 73):
- *Biological viewpoint:* A set of basic emotions guides learning, behaviour and development according to the origin and evolutionary significance of environmental events. Individual differences in personality and social

development derive from dispositional and experiential differences that are encoded in emotional-cognitive structures.

- *Cognitive (constructivist) viewpoint:* Emotions are seen as consisting of cognitive interpretations of affective, motor, and physiological events, mediated by cognitive development. Individual differences in socialisation, goals, opportunities, and interpretations result in variability in people's socio-emotional repertoires, contributing to stable personality patterns over time.
- *The functionalist view* accommodates views from both previous theories and emphasises the role of emotions in organising relations between the organism and the environment by highlighting meaningful contingencies and maximising adaptive behaviour - that is, making appropriate plans to survive. Individual differences in emotion correspond with aspects like developmental capacities, and cognitive and temperamental characteristics.

These theories clearly illustrate that emotion and cognition work together in creating individual differences in the adult's experience, behaviour, learning and, ultimately, the personality. The paradigmatic behaviourist (now called psychological behaviourism) conception of personality clearly illustrates this point (Staats & Eifert, 1990).

The adult's learning experiences (S1) result in the development of the personality repertoires (BBR = basic behavioural repertoires) in the three general areas: emotional-motivational, language-cognitive, sensory-motor. These personality repertoires interact with the adult's present environmental situation (S2) to produce the individual's experience, learning and behaviour (B). These elements may further affect the later situations the adult faces and the personality repertoires the individual has. This illustrates how the adult's later behaviour is determined jointly by the nature of the situation and the nature of his/her personality repertoire (Staats & Eifert, 1990, p. 557). This process can briefly be summarized as: S1 – past learning experiences result in personality repertoires (BBRs) which interact with the adult's current situation (S2) to produce unique behaviour, learning and experience (B) (adapted from Staats, 1996).

That adults respond differently to different stimuli is clear, but what has yet to be addressed is the repertoire of possible emotions to which an adult can resort. It is worthwhile to include here a summary of the emotions adults experience and indicate the role gender plays in this regard. Different emotional styles also deserve to be mentioned as well as emotions and intrapersonal development.

Different Adult Emotions

When one thinks of an emotion, one has a specific concept or vocabulary description in mind. The names of emotion are part of any theory on emotions and, although it is impossible to reflect here all the ideas of the labelling theorists, it is crucial to briefly stand still and at least try to consider some of the ideas on our emotional vocabulary. The names of emotions are linked to abstract and widely shared knowledge structures and the choice of a specific label automatically activates associated situational, physiological and behavioural knowledge (Bellelli, 1995, p. 493).

An example of various descriptions of emotions is illustrated in the research done by Havlena, Holbrook and Lehman (1989). They analysed one hundred and forty-nine verbal descriptions of adult experiences and were looking for important

emotion-related terms. Twenty-eight adjectives were isolated and could be used to describe all but one of the eight basic emotions postulated by Plutchik in 1980. The seven basic emotions that were named, with the corresponding adjectives, are as follows (Havlena et al., 1989, p. 104):
- Joy: Happy, Pleased, Joyful, Enjoying, Proud
- Acceptance: Relaxed, Peaceful, Satisfied, Relieved
- Expectancy: Interested, Aware, Absorbed, Anticipatory
- Sadness: Crying, Sad, Grief-stricken, In pain, Surprised
- Activation: Energetic, Enthusiastic, Exhilarated, Excited
- Anger: Frustrated, Annoyed, Angry, Disappointed
- Fear: Fearful, Horrified.

These basic emotions can be seen as primary human emotions which are needed for physical and psychological survival. Further criteria for a basic emotion are that it is physiologically and expressively distinctive and that it has a biological base (Oatley, 1992; Reber, 1985). Oatley (1992) took the mere verbal description of these emotions a step further by explaining the control signs that correspond with basic emotions. Oatley (1992, p. 55) explained that an emotion occurs when a particular juncture is recognized. Table 6.3 shows five basic emotions, the junctures in action that typically trigger them, and the transition of action readiness that they accomplish. An emotion is experienced when the recognition of one of these triggers is broadcast through the system. The difference in adults' emotional responses becomes apparent when this table is studied.

Table 6.3 Five basic emotions, the junctures that trigger them, and the transition of action

EMOTION	JUNCTURE OF CURRENT PLANS	STATE AND GOALS TO WHICH TRANSITION OCCURS
Happiness	Subgoals being achieved	Continue with plan, modify if necessary
Sadness	Failure of major plan or loss of active	Do nothing/goalsearch for new plan
Fear	Self-preservation goal threatened or goal conflict	Stop current plan, attend vigilantly to environment, freeze and/or escape
Anger	Active plan frustrated	Try harder, and/or aggress
Disgust	Gustatory goal violated	Reject substance and/or withdraw

Other synonyms for basic emotions are fundamental emotions or coarse emotions. Whatever they are called, they serve the same purpose: to enable the adult to respond quickly to an awareness and, according to this interpretation, make adaptations or carry on as before.

Another perspective on the nature of adult emotions is the view by Lazarus and Lazarus (1994) that emotional concepts can be grouped together because they have much in common - although they might differ in meaning. Five groups of emotions can be distinguished with specific emotion-related words categorised under each group:
- the nasty emotions like *anger, envy and jealousy*. These emotions can create tremendous interpersonal and social problems, which threaten not only the

working relationship of the adult with others, but also the very existence of the adult as a member of a subculture or national group;

– the existential emotions like *anxiety-fright, guilt and shame*. These emotions reveal an essential core of the adults' personal worldview and of the way they see their lives. They are universal, powerful and troubling states of mind, which have a significant influence on the adults' daily social lives;

– emotions provoked by unfavourable life conditions like *relief, hope, sadness and depression*. Relief comes about when a negative situation fails to materialise or ends. Hope materialises when the adult feels that a possible negative outcome will not happen. When loss has to be accepted feelings like sadness and depression may surface;

– emotions provoked by favourable life conditions like *happiness, pride and love*. These emotions reveal the uplifting side of the adult's emotional life and protect him/her from melancholy. They also relieve the adult of misery and enhance the quality of life; and

– the empathic emotions like *gratitude, compassion,* and those emotions aroused by *aesthetic* experiences. When the adult receives an altruistic gift the emotion of gratitude is experienced and when another person is suffering, the adult may feel compassion. The adult may also react emotionally to drama, art, music, events in nature and religious experiences. These emotions emphasise the gentle side of the adult's life.

In their categorisations of concepts of emotion, Lazarus and Lazarus (1994, 1991) illustrated the tendency of many emotion theorists to categorise emotions according to two distinctive groups namely positive/negative emotions or pleasant/ unpleasant emotions. Recent research, however, has indicated that individual differences in the basic emotions cannot be reduced to positive and negative affects (Diener, Smith, & Fujita, 1995). To further complicate this issue, the intensity and nature of emotions experienced by males and females also differ. It seems inconceivable to state that specific emotions can be described only as positive or negative, or that specific emotions are experienced most frequently by either males or females. Emotion is such a complex subject that such a reductionist view will not reflect the magic of this elusive construct. To complete the picture of different adult emotions, brief reference will be made to emotions of adult males and females.

Gender Differences in Emotion

One often hears the complaint that women are too emotional and that men are not sensitive enough to the emotions of others. There is no evidence to support the idea that women experience the most prototypical emotions like anger, happiness and disgust more frequently than men do. There is, however, some empirical evidence that women experience some specific emotions like sadness, fear and uncertainty more frequently and intensely than men (Fischer, 1995) - perhaps because they are willing to acknowledge these emotions to a greater degree than men are? Another aspect of this notion of being emotional is that an adult who is sad, crying, or terribly afraid is more likely to be called emotional than someone who is angry. An important characteristic of these "feminine" emotions is the belief that nothing can be done about a negative situation and that one is helpless or powerless.

That gender plays a significant role in the perception and interpretation of emotion has been proved by some empirical investigators (Fourie & Stuart, 1996). The difference in the emotional needs of the two genders also surfaces here. Research by Borysenko (Reece & Brandt, 1996) suggested that women feel men do not take their emotional needs seriously enough and do not respond with support and understanding. Men, again, feel that they need time to give comfort and that support is given by the sincere acknowledgement of the existence of a problem.

The manner of dealing with a very basic emotion, namely anger, also highlights the different ways in which men and women see and handle it. Research does not indicate why, but men are more violent than women. Men see aggression "as a way of imposing control over others and are therefore more likely to regard it as a legitimate means of assuming authority over the disruptive and frightening forces they encounter in life" (Reece & Brandt, 1996: 248). Women again, who suppress their anger or release it explosively often rely on drinking, smoking or eating to calm their feelings. They see aggression as failure of self-control. Researchers find that it is better to engage in physical or mental activity and discuss angry feelings with someone than to indulge in, for example, overeating.

The heart of these differences probably lies in the different ways boys and girls are brought up. Society teaches boys and girls different sets of emotional rules. In many families, males are encouraged to hide their feelings, to appear strong and stable and not to express "female emotions" like sadness - they are also restricted in showing that they hurt (Landman, 1996; Reece & Brandt, 1996). Western society restrains boys from publicly expressing strong emotions and, although girls are permitted a greater emotional range, they are censured and lose face when expressing intense emotions.

The main reasons for possible gender differences in emotion probably lie in the following (Fischer, 1995; Landman, 1996; Reece & Brandt, 1996):
- society scripts boys and girls with different emotional display rules;
- because women experience specific emotions more frequently and more intensely, they have greater experience on this terrain and may know more about the causes, characteristics and consequences of these emotions - they may thus be regarded as "emotional experts"!; and
- emotions have a greater significance to women and women pay more attention to their own and others' emotions.

Variety in emotional experience - not only between women and men, but between different adults as well - can bring excitement and colour to relationships and not only result in confusion and sorrow, as so often happens.

Emotional Styles

According to Magai and McFadden (1995, p. 247), emotions have evolved to assist individuals in coping with threats and in achieving goals. Emotions are the result of perceiving and interpreting an event, and are followed by the implementation of coping mechanisms. It is in these coping mechanisms that differences in adult response styles become apparent. Plutchik and Plutchik (1990, p. 41) defined coping styles as the derivatives of the unconscious ego defences, but Reber (1985, p. 158) stated that it is a conscious, rational way of dealing with the anxieties of life. What is clear is that these coping styles are implemented to facilitate change and adaptation.

Most researchers (Lu, 1996, p. 583; Magai & McFadden, 1995, p. 248; Mikulincer & Orbach, 1995, p. 917) agree that the stable, well-developed/integrated personality has the full repertoire of emotions available and specific emotions are deployed for specific adaptive purposes. Various coping styles have been demonstrated by adults with different personality types, with respect to different emotions. This emphasises the notion that there is a correlation between an adult's inner emotional world and his/her experiences in the outer social world. The following examples are mentioned (Lu, 1996; Magai & McFadden, 1995; Mikulincer & Orbach, 1995):

- *secure* adults regulate inner emotional distress by displaying moderate defensiveness and low anxiety. they have easy access to negative memories, but are not overwhelmed by them;
- *anxious-ambivalent* people are unable to repress negative affects, report high anxiety and are overwhelmed by negative memories;
- *avoidant* people report high levels of defensiveness and anxiety, and a high resistance to negative memories;
- *extroverts* tend to use more direct coping styles than introverts, like addressing a problem immediately;
- *optimistic* adults use various adaptive coping strategies, while pessimism and neuroticism correlate with maladaptive coping strategies;
- *internal locus of control* is associated with active coping rather than with suppression - internal locus of control refers to the person who tends to take responsibility for his/her own actions and who views himself/herself as having control over his/ her own destiny;
- with regard to the experience of sadness, some adults can be characterised as having a *ruminative* (carefully thinking about events) coping style, while others have a *distractive* (analysing events in a disorderly way) coping style; and
- the three styles of coping with anger that can be distinguished are *anger-in* (keeping anger to oneself), *anger-out* (physically or verbally letting go of anger) and *anger-reflective* (thinking about why feelings of anger occurred).

Another way of describing coping styles is by relating the eight basic emotions directly to eight basic coping styles that have applicability to life's problems. The following emotional coping styles are important (Plutchik & Plutchik, 1990, p. 45; Reece & Brandt, 1996, p. 245):

- *Mapping.* Mapping means trying to cope with a problem by getting more information about it. Adults deal with a problem by using their innate curiosity and intelligence to get more information about it. Only then does the adult feel safe to act and react;
- *Avoidance.* Some adults try to cope with a problem by removing themselves from the situation that tends to trigger the problem. Some people may go even further and avoid dealing directly with emotional reactions to a situation. They may suppress their emotions which can lead to a number of mental and physical health problems;
- *Seeking help.* Adults try to address problems by asking for assistance - sometimes on a very informal level, like asking friends and family for help. Adults who seek help do not necessarily see themselves as helpless victims of emotions, and have no intention of capitulating to their emotions;
- *Minimising.* Minimising refers to the idea that the adult can devalue the importance or seriousness of events in his/her life, and that one can choose this

method of coping as a conscious strategy. In some cases, like in a job situation, adults who minimise problems experience less stress. At least minimisation is a more responsible way of coping with problems than giving free rein to one's emotions. Emotional outbursts, especially at the workplace, damage the adult's credibility as they can be seen as a sign of emotional discord. Minimisation is not the same as denial, which simply denies that specific emotions exist;

– *Reversal.* Nearly every adult use this coping style to a greater or lesser degree. Without reversal, meaningful relationships would probably be impossible since the technique is socially effective and helps to handle a wide range of problems. Reversal urges adults to do the opposite of what they feel. Acceptable social behaviour demands that adults state that everything is fine and that they feel great, although they may feel irritated and worried;

– *Blame.* Some adults cope with problems by blaming others. For a while at least the adult may feel that he/she need not take responsibility for the problem, but, in the long run, the person being blamed may feel bad and may develop feelings of resentment. Feelings of resentment can lead to a desire for revenge and a dangerous cycle of blame-resentment-revenge can start;

– *Substitution.* Substitution refers to coping methods that are indirect. In specific situations there are no direct or easy solutions and indirect substitute solutions are implemented to address a complex reality. Some adults may, for instance, survive a boring job by engaging in exciting activities outside the job situation; and

– *Improving shortcomings.* Some adults admit that a problem is created by a weakness in themselves. If they have the insight, the problem can be addressed by mastering new personal, emotional, social and job-related skills and by implementing and refining these.

The adult should be guided in choosing the most appropriate coping style. Two general guidelines in selecting a style are suggested by Plutchik and Plutchik (1990), namely

– choosing a coping style that produces results that are in one's own best long-term interests, and

– choosing a coping style for oneself that does not make the situation worse.

Coping styles are a very personal matter and are deeply integrated with personality and past experiences. Other aspects of emotion also need to be addressed and the next section on aspects of intrapersonal development will conclude this discussion on individual differences in emotions.

Intrapersonal Development

"Why are we on earth?" and "How can I survive painful everyday realities?" These are question many adults ask, and if they ever get answers to their questions, they may be a step nearer to understanding themselves as well as the purpose and meaning of their existence on earth. Practitioners of educational psychology have set self realisation as a goal that should be reached. Every adult has the capacity to realise his/her potential. If there is a discrepancy between the level the adult *is* functioning on and the level he/ she *should* be functioning on, it is likely that the adult is an underachiever in many domains of life, and this may lead to mental ill-health. One should aim for whole-person development, which implies the realisation of different potentialities in the different facets of being human, like realising physical, social, affective, cognitive, normative and conative potentialities. If the adult manages to realise his/her potential, it is logical to assume that he/she will be mentally healthy and will be able to fulfil his/her role as an active and worthy citizen of the community.

With regard to this chapter, reaching emotional goals like emotional control, understanding emotions and dealing appropriately with emotions seem to be important milestones in the personal development of the adult. To reach the emotional goals set by the educational and psychological sciences and by society in general for emotional well-being and perhaps even set by the adult himself/herself, requires a person to acquire skills to solve emotional problems in a creative way very early in adult life. Emotional problem-solving requires emotional openness as well as general intelligence (Mayer & Geher, 1996, p. 89). Some aspects of the emotional lives of adults which are prerequisites for emotional wellbeing, and a crucial part of balanced intrapersonal development, are emotional openness, self-knowledge and emotional intelligence.

As indicated above, emotional problem-solving requires of the adult to be emotionally open. This means that the adult needs to disclose himself and his inner feelings to at least one other person and implies, conversely, that the unhealthy adult does not do so (Gerdes, Moore, Ochse, & Van Ede, 1989). The consequence is lack of self-knowledge, because this can be gained only by sharing inner emotional experiences with others. Self-acceptance is a prerequisite for the acceptance of others. If adults do not accept themselves, the possibility exists that they may, in the words of Lipkin (1996, p. 49), "package [themselves] in a way that will win friends and influence people", because adults could see themselves as being "too fragile and flawed to be exposed to the outside world". The result is that adults wear masks as protection and fail to be the very people they ought to be. The whole idea of unique self-actualisation becomes a dream and an adult who imitates others to survive themselves, is on the way to emotional self-destruction.

Emotional problem-solving also requires of the adult to implement emotional intelligence skills. Emotional intelligence is seen as one of many intelligences that can be classified under general intelligence. Mayer and Geher (1996) referred to the 1920 research results of Thorndike to illustrate that general intelligence can be divided in three divisions of intelligence, namely: intelligence that involves the abstract, analytic, and/or verbal intelligences; mechanical, performance, visual-spatial, and/or synthetical intelligences; and social and/or practical intelligences

Social intelligence has been less studied than the other intelligences and it is only in recent studies that dimensions of this hard-to-understand construct have been addressed. Mayer and Geher (1996) divided social intelligence into two intelligences - namely motivational intelligence and emotional intelligence. They defined motivational intelligence as "understanding motivations such as the need for achievement, affiliation, or power, as well as understanding tacit knowledge related to them and the goal-setting related to them".

Gardner (1993) referred to emotional intelligence as intrapersonal intelligence and Goleman (1996) and O'Neil (1996) saw emotional intelligence as social skills, being able to manage distressing moods well and controlling impulses - remaining hopeful when one has setbacks. Emotional intelligence thus consists of *inter*personal intelligence and *intra*personal intelligence. The link between social and emotional intelligence is clearly illustrated by these recent studies as well as in the following summary, of Gardner's (Goleman, 1996) excellent analysis:

*Inter*personal intelligence is the ability to understand other people: what motivates them, how they work, how to work cooperatively with them. Successful salespeople, teachers, politicians, clinicians, and religious leaders are all likely to be individuals with high degrees of interpersonal intelligence. *Intra*personal intelligence is a correlative ability, turned inward. It is a capacity to form an accurate, veridical model of oneself and to be able to operate effectively in life.

The core elements of emotional intelligence are: being able to recognise emotions; discrimination among these emotions; monitoring one's own and others' emotions; reasoning with emotion and emotion-related information; and processing emotional information as part of a general problem-solving ability (Mayer & Geher, 1996; Mayer & Salovey, 1993).

The positive aspect of emotional intelligence is that the skills that are related to it are virtually all learned (O'Neil, 1996). This implies that the adult who strives for reaching his/her own or society's goals for self-actualisation, also needs to master specific emotional and social skills in order to arrive at emotional well-being. The ability to recognise and effectively process emotions seems to be the key issue here. Adult educational psychology has a key role to play in this yet unexplored field of educational science.

The second point that needs to be clarified under the main heading of Part II, "Human emotions in the context of adults' lives", is the communication and socialisation of emotions.

The Socialisation/Communication of Emotions

As indicated before, there are indications of cross-culture universality with regard to the expression of certain emotions like anger and happiness. It has also been indicated that there are differences in the way different cultural groups talk about emotions and in the way in which they display emotions. There have been further references to emotional coping styles by different personality types. What remains to be discussed are specific aspects of interpersonal communication, like the social nature of the communication of emotions, the expression of emotions and emotional communication in families.

There are definite emotion norms that are passed on from one generation to the next (Landman, 1996) and a good part of socialisation involves transmitting civilisation's command to regulate the expression and to some extent the experience of emotion. Parkinson (1996) felt strongly that this experiencing and expressing of emotions is a social phenomenon. He explained why:

- many of the causes of emotions are interpersonally or culturally defined;
- emotions usually have consequences for other people;
- emotions serve interpersonal as well as cultural functions in everyday life; and
- many cases of emotion are essentially communicative rather than internal and reactive phenomena.

Although not all theorists will agree with Parkinson, one must admit that emotions are not purely a physiological, cognitive or emotional affair and that they are at least in part a social phenomenon, especially when the communication of emotion is taken into consideration. In the theory on the socialisation of emotion, two distinct groups of approaches are identified. Magai and McFadden (1995) called them the first and the second waves of research. The first wave of research refers to the research done by behaviourists and psychoanalysts. In these theories, emotions are described as forces of human ruination which need to be tamed, controlled, restrained or educated by all means. Many theories ignore emotions or disregard them as an impediment to intellectual processes. The second wave of research deals with ideas from the functionalist and cognitive approaches. These theories explain the expression and socialisation of emotion. They also emphasise the adaptive qualities of emotions and the central role they play in the regulation of individual and interpersonal behaviour. Emotions are no longer seen as the source of all human misery and in need of vigorous subjugation. Emotions are developed, not tamed.

What is the purpose of this communication of adult emotions? Dillard (1993) said that there are three types of emotional communication and that each one serves a particular purpose. They are:

- *Emotion-motivated communication.* From this point of view emotion precedes, and is the basis of message-making. There is action and conveying a message involved;
- *Emotion-manifest communication.* The expressive domain is involved in the sense that information is given on the internal state of the adult. The purpose here is to reveal emotions; and
- *Emotion-inducing communication.* This type of communication occurs when a message generated by a person elicits an affective response in another person - the purpose being to generate an emotion in another person.

Communication of emotions implies that information on emotion is transferred from one person to another. In order to have meaningful communication the persons involved need to share a code by which the emotional information can be analysed and interpreted. The adult needs to master particulars of this code, as interpreting emotions is a crucial part in the process of communicating emotions.

Facial Expressions

An example of this common code used in the communication of emotion is the interpretation of facial expressions. Measuring facial behaviour and making judgements about faces are two ways that researchers use to establish whether facial expressions signal specific emotions. Indications are that the face can provide accurate information about "positive" versus "negative" emotions and that correct information (judgements made) can be derived from studying facial behaviour (Ekman, O'Sullivan, & Matsumoto, 1991). But the research by Russell, Fernandez-Dols, Manstead, & Wellenkamp (1995) emphasised that the face provides information relevant to emotion, but does not signal a specific emotion. A situation, rather than facial information, provides clues to the emotion experienced. Be this as it may, there is enough evidence to suggest that human emotions are reflected on the face and that facial expressions can give clues on the inner emotions of people (Baron & Byrne, 1994). Cicero's statement two thousand years ago, that "the face is the image of the soul", is probably correct.

Expressing Emotions

To be able to interpret the state of other people's souls objectively and correctly, the adult needs to be exposed to situations in which he/she is trained to interpret facial and other non-verbal communication clues. Cornelius (1984) stated that, although facial expression and bodily movements are important features in the expression of emotion, a variety of behaviours that are rendered meaningful as expressions of emotion by their interpersonal and social context are equally important. Most important is the social context in which an emotion will be expressed; social contexts include societal norms that stipulate the *way* emotion should be expressed, the *situation* in which it should or should not be felt, and *cultural attitudes* towards a particular emotion (Fischer, 1991).

These societal norms can also be described as emotion rules, which guide adults in their relationships. Emotion rules are defined as rules according to which feelings may be judged as being appropriate to accompanying events (Fischer, 1991). These rules are normative and indicate the contexts in which particular emotions should be felt and how they should be expressed. The five emotion rules which Hochschild (Fischer, 1991) distinguished are as follows:

- the first rule links the antecedent event with the *type* of emotion, like sad or angry. for example, a person would not feel sad when accusing another person of an illegitimate action;
- rules of *intensity, duration,* and *place* refer to the relation between the perceived antecedents and the different characteristics of an emotional reaction. it is not appropriate, for example, to be terrified of a little cat (intensity), or to grieve for just one day over the death of a loved one (duration), or to express one's delight about passing an exam in the presence of someone who has failed (place); and
- rules of *time* refer to the limits within which a certain event may still evoke emotional reaction. for example, feeling elated about something that happened a year ago is not considered to be very normal.

If an adult obeys these cultural rules, he/she probably has control over his/her emotions. The true self of the adult is exposed in this way. If the adult is in contact with his/her true self, this may contribute to emotional and spiritual wellbeing. But not all theorists support this notion. The impulsive theory states that the true self is threatened if emotional expression is controlled and that only impulsive reactions show one's real personality (Lasch, 1978). That the expression of emotion is a personal and cultural affair is evident from the many prescriptions by society as to how the individual should or should not express emotion. This section on the communication of emotion will be concluded by a brief reference to the communication of emotion in families.

Communication of Emotion in Families

As indicated before, many factors influence the communication of emotions. As most adults belong to families, it is appropriate to investigate briefly the effect that emotional communication in the family has on the emotional shaping of the adult.

There is no doubt that the adults' style of expressing emotion is influenced largely by the families they grew up in (Halberstadt, 1984). Children who grow up in families where everyone is encouraged to talk about emotions, are more likely to understand and handle emotions in later life (Dunn, Brown, & Beardsall, 1991).

Families shape the children's future way of experiencing and expressing emotions. The direction that family communication takes influences the children's' later expressiveness of emotion as adults. Examples of communication styles (not necessarily as constellations of characteristics that go together) in families are (Plutchik & Plutchik, 1990): placating, blaming, being unusually reasonable, and being congruent; being dramatic, attentive, dominant, relaxed, or open.

Few adults are aware of their own communication style and the way in which it might influence people around them. What is true is that each adult, by implementing a particular communication style, takes part in scripting young minds and that influence will be visible in many adults' lives in years to come.

Emotional Management

Emotion, once described as a wild steed to be controlled by rationality, is now seen as the source of creativity (Robinson, 1996). Gone are the days when emotions were seen as destructive forces. As stated before, emotions need to be developed, not tamed. As many of the emotions we experience are legitimate and genuine, it is unwise to suggest that all are negative. Borysenko (1987, p. 163) said: "The only negative emotions are emotions that you will not allow yourself or someone else to experience. Negative emotions will not harm you if you express them appropriately and then let them go... Bottling them up is far worse". The need for emotional equilibrium seems to be the key concern here. There is a need for the adult not to fixate so intensely on a specific range of emotions that he/ she ignores the expression of other equally important emotions.

This is easier said than done, because the life of the adult learner is plagued by stressors that trigger acute emotions. Stressors include not only life events that involve change (like the Holmes and Rahe Schedule of Recent Experience), but also continuing demanding environmental conditions in which no change occurs (Cohen, 1983; Santrock, 1986). Other stressors that are distinguished are (Cohen, 1983; Doerr, 1995):

- acute, time-limited events, like awaiting a medical examination;
- stress event sequences, in which a particular event initiates a series of stress events that occur over an extended period of time, like bereavement or even a job transition;
- chronic intermittent stressors like situations that occur and reoccur periodically, such as conflict with in-laws; and
- chronic stress situations, like a chronic disability.

Like emotional responses, stress responses can occur on physiological, psychological, or social levels (Cohen, 1983; Lazarus & Lazarus, 1994). Physiological responses include changes in the automatic nervous system as well as hormonal and immunological responses. It is also a well-known fact that psychosomatic disorders, common infections, heart disease and cancer may directly or indirectly be linked to continual emotional distress. Psychologically, changes can be seen in negatively toned affects, motor-behaviour reactions and alterations in adaptive performance. On the social level, outcomes include antisocial behaviour and difficulties in meeting role requirements. The ideal situation is that adults should preferably experience positive emotions since hormones resulting from these positive emotions (like relief, happiness, pride and love) may be secreted, which could promote bodily equanimity and thereby protect against illness and disease or help cure them.

No wonder then, that many adults fall prey to their life circumstances and find it difficult to survive emotionally and physically. How can the adult reach emotional equilibrium? Is it possible to stay emotionally fit in a modern technocratic society? The answer does not lie in a high-tech computer program or in a quick-fix checklist. It lies in a few common-sense principles advocated by personal leadership, self-management and self-governance theories. The message these theories portray is: take charge. The main principles of these theories are (Borgelt, 1997; Covey, 1993; Knowles, 1990; Lazarus & Lazarus, 1994):

- master emotional problem-solving skills. Evaluate a situation and, if it is worth the effort, gather more information and see what actions should be taken;
- master emotion-centred coping strategies. If there is nothing to be done to change a situation or others' behaviour, internal and private strategies should be applied to relieve emotional distress. Emotion-centred coping consists of what the adult tells himself/herself in an effort to gain control. Hopefully this changes thinking about what is happening from a threatening to a more benign or positive appraisal;
- adults are not emotional yo-yos and need to practise emotion-revealing skills by implementing self-governance. The core element of self-governance is self-knowledge. The adult needs to know if strict emotional control is important to him/her, compared with the need to readily express emotions. The tendency to function at one of these poles cannot be considered to be right or wrong. When interaction with other people takes place, it would be ideal to be flexible and move along this continuum - according to personal needs, the needs of others and according to situational demands. Emotional flexibility is an emotional goal which each adult should strive to reach;
- acquire personal leadership skills by setting goals and by putting into place strategies to reach those goals. The adult should ask: what emotional goals need to be reached? What needs to be done to reach those goals?; and
- practice communication skills. Effective two-way communication demands that the adult capture both *content* and *intent.* The adult needs to learn to speak the languages of *logic* and *emotion.*

Chances are that some adults may not be able to master all these emotional skills and may need more trained help to reach emotional balance. This in itself may emotionally burden the adult as feelings of shame, failure and embarrassment may surface during the process of seeking help. There is comfort, though, in the fact that the adult who is willing to take this risk portrays valuable qualities, like the ability to admit that a problem exists and having an admirable insight in personal matters. This in itself holds a good prognosis for adults who have stumbled emotionally.

The Role of Emotions in Learning

In this chapter, frequent references were made to the role emotions play in various aspects of the lives of adults. There is virtually no aspect of being adult in which emotions do not feature. Emotion can be seen as the motivational power behind many physical, social, mental and cultural activities. Not one but every facet of being adult is influenced by emotions. Although there were earlier references to adult behaviour, learning and emotion, it is important to add to this information an illustration of the interrelatedness between emotion and learning. The theory of Boekaerts (1993) will be referred to for this purpose.

In their broadest sense, learning strategies are implemented to adapt to a changing environment. When an event occurs, the adult responds by evaluating it. More judgements follow and if the adult is convinced that the event poses a threat or will benefit the adult, an emotional response will surface. In the course of time, adults learn how to effectively and objectively evaluate these events and threats. The adult also learns to understand the dynamics of the human-environment relationship better, and learns to correctly interpret human emotions which have been evoked by this relationship. A more complex explanation of the learning process is presented in the model of Boekaerts (1993).

The model assumes that learners have the intention to learn. An intention to learn can be defined as the willingness to put effort into accomplishing the learning goals or relevant subgoals. The aim of the model is to describe appraisals and the way they affect behavioural intentions. Appraisals are seen as ongoing comparison processes between task or situational demands and personal resources to meet these demands. With regard to learning and emotion, the following aspects of the model are relevant:
– even when the learner is not aware of it, learning activities trigger a network of highly specific connotations (current concerns) with their concomitant positive and negative emotions (active readiness changes); and
– even when the learner cannot make them explicit, appraisals are continuously being made.

Learning and emotion facilitate change - changes in both the behaviour and emotional response potential of the adult. Without these changes, adults will not be able to adapt to a changing environment and will suffer tremendous emotional stress.

In Conclusion

Emotion-provoking situations urge the adult to tap from possible emotional responses the one which is more or less in line with the stimulus. These emotions are part of a coping system which is intended to create emotional balance and ensure appropriate behavioural responses. What is to be considered appropriate behaviour depends largely on familial conditioning as well as cultural influences. The main task of the adult is to implement emotional skills that will not only help him/her to survive his/her own personality, but also to understand and correctly interpret and handle others' emotions.

REFERENCES

Baron, R. A., & Byrne, D. (1994). *Social psychology. Understanding human interaction.* Boston: Allyn & Bacon.
Bellelli, G. (1995). Knowing and labeling emotions. In J. A. Russell, J. Fernàndez-Dols, A. S. R. Manstead, & J. C. Wellenkamp (Eds.), *Everyday conceptions of emotion. An introduction to the psychology, anthropology and linguistics of emotion* (pp. 491-504). Dordrecht: Kluwer Academic.
Bertocci, P. A. (1988). *The person and primary emotions.* NY: Springer-Verlag.
Blechman, E. A. (1990). *Emotions and the family.* Hillsdale, NJ: Lawrence Erlbaum.

Boekaerts, M. (1993). Being concerned with well-being and with learning. *Educational Psychologist, 28*, 149-167.

Borgelt, T. (1997). Are you someone's yo-yo? *Career success, 10*, 24-26.

Borysenko, J. (1987). *Minding the body, mending the mind.* NY: Bantam Books.

Buck, R. (1990). Mood and emotion: A comparison of five contemporary views. *Psychological Inquiry, 1*, 330-336.

Clark, M. S. (1992). *Emotion. Review of personality and social psychology.* Newbury Park: Sage.

Cohen, F. (1983). Stress, emotion, and illness. In L. Temoshok, C. Van Dyke & L.S. Zegans (Eds.), *Emotions in health and illness. Theoretical and research foundations* (pp. 31-35). NY: Grune & Stratton.

Cornelius, R. R. (1984). A rule model of adult emotional expression. In C. Z. Malatesta & C. E. Izard (Eds.), *Emotion in adult development* (pp. 213-233). Beverly Hills: Sage.

Costa, P. T. (Jr), & McCrae, R. R. (1984). Personality as a lifelong determinant of wellbeing. In C. Z. Malatesta & C. E. Izard (Eds.), *Emotion in adult development* (pp. 141-157). Beverley Hills: Sage.

Covey, S. R. (1993). *Principle-centered leadership.* London: Simon & Schuster.

Deci, E. L. (1996). Making room for self-regulation: Some thoughts on the link between emotion and behavior. *Psychological Inquiry, 7*, 220-223.

Diener, E., Smith, H., & Fujita, F. (1995). The personality structure affect. *Journal of Personality and Social Psychology, 69*, 130-141.

Dillard, J. P. (1993). Emotional communication, culture and power. *Journal of Language and Social Psychology, 12*, 153-161.

Doerr, D. C. (1995). Coping with the emotions of job transition: A model for presentation to clients. *Journal of Career Development, 22*, 10 1-107.

Dunn, J., Brown, J., & Beardsall, L. (1991). Family talk about feeling states and children's later understanding of others' emotions. *Developmental Psychology, 27*, 448-455.

Ekman, P., O'Sullivan, M., & Matsumoto, D. (1991). Confusions about context in the judgement of facial expression: A reply to "The contempt expression and the relativity thesis". *Motivation and Emotion, 15*, 169-176.

Fischer, A. H. (1991). *Emotion scripts. A study of the social and cognitive facets of emotions.* Leiden: DSWO.

Fischer, A. H. (1995). Emotion concepts as function of gender. In J. A. Russell, J. Fernàndez-Dols, A. S. R. Manstead & J. C. Wellenkamp (Eds.), *Everyday conceptions of emotion. An introduction to the psychology, anthropology and linguistics of emotion (*pp. 457-474). Dodrecht: Kluwer Academic.

Fourie, J.C., & Stuart, A. (1996). The role of temperament and gender in functional hemispheric asymmetry and the perception of emotion. *South African Journal of Psychology, 26*, 52-62.

Freud, S. (1936). *Inhibitions, symptoms and anxiety.* London: Hogarth.

Gardner, H. (1993). *Frames of mind: The theory of multiple intelligences.* NY: Basic Books.

Gerdes, L. C., Moore, C, Ochse, R., & Van Ede, D. (1989). *The developing adult.* Durban: Butterworths.

Goleman, D. (1996). *Emotional intelligence.* London: Bloomsbury.

Halberstadt, A. G. (1984). Family expression of emotion. In C. Z. Malatesta & C. E. Izard (Eds.), *Emotion in adult development* (pp. 235-252). Beverley Hills: Sage.

Hatfield, E., & Rapson, R. (1990). Emotions: A trinity. In E.A. Blechman (Ed.), *Emotions and the family* (pp. 11- 33). Hillsdale, NJ: Lawrence Erlbaum.

Havlena, W. J., Holbrook, M. B., & Lehman D. R. (1989). Assessing the validity of emotional typologies. *Psychology and Marketing, 6*, 97-112.

Heelas, P. (1996). Emotion talk across cultures. In R. Harré & W. G. Parrott (Eds.), *The emotions. Social, cultural and biological dimensions* (pp. 17 1-199). London: Sage.

Izard, C. E. (1991). *The psychology of emotions.* NY: Plenum.

Knowles, M. (1990). *The adult learner.* Houston: Gulf.

Landman, J. (1996). Social control of 'negative' emotions: The case of regret. In R. Harré R., & W.G. Parrott (Eds.), *The emotions. Social, cultural and biological dimensions* (pp. 89-116). London: Sage.

Lasch, C. (1978). *The culture of narcissism.* NY: Norton.

Lazarus, R. S. (1991). *Emotion and adaptation.* NY: Oxford University Press.

Lazarus, R. S., & Lazarus, B. N. (1994). *Passion and reason. Making sense of our emotions.* NY: Oxford University Press.

Lewis, M. (1989). What do we mean when we say emotional development? In L. Cirillo, B. Kaplan, B., & Wapner, S. (Eds), *Emotions in ideal human development* (pp. 53-75). Hillsdale, NJ: Lawrence Erlbaum.

Lewis, M. D. (1995). Cognition-emotion feedback and the self-organization of developmental paths. *Human Development, 38,* 7 1-102.

Lipkin, M. (1996). How to be you. *Style, April,* 49-50. Livesey, P.J. (1986). *Learning and emotion: A biological synthesis.* Hillsdale, NJ: Lawrence Erlbaum.

Lu, L. (1996). Coping consistency and emotional outcome: Intra-individual and inter-individual analyses. *Personality and Individual Differences, 21,* 583-589.

Magai, C., & McFadden, S. H. (1995). *The role of emotions in social and personality development. History, theory, and research.* NY: Plenum.

Matsumoto, D. (1993). Ethnic differences in affect intensity, emotion judgements, display rule attitudes, and self-reported emotional expression in an American sample. *Motivation and Emotion, 17,* 107-123.

Mayer, J. D., & Geher, G. (1996). Emotional intelligence and the identification of emotion. *Intelligence, 22,* 89-113.

Mayer, J. D., & Salovey, P. (1993). The intelligence of emotional intelligence. *Intelligence, 17,* 433-442.

Mikulincer, M., & Orbach, I. (1995). Attachment styles and repressive defensiveness: The accessibilty and architecture of affective memories. *Journal of Personality and Social Psychology, 68,* 9 17-925.

Neville, B. (1989). *Educating psyche. Emotion, imagination and the unconscious in learning.* Melbourne: Collins Dove.

Oatley, K. (1992). *Best laid schemes. The psychology of emotions.* Cambridge: Cambridge University Press.

O'Neil, J. (1996). On emotional intelligence. A conversation with Daniel Goleman. *Educational Leadership, 54,* 6-11.

Parkinson, B. (1995). *Ideas and realities of emotion.* London: Routledge.

Parkinson, B. (1996). Emotions are social. *British Journal of Psychology, 87,* 663-683.

Plutchik, R. (1980). *Emotion: A psychoevolutionary synthesis.* NY: Harper & Row.

Plutchik, R., & Plutchik, A. (1990). Communication and coping in families. In E.A. Blechman (Ed.), *Emotions and the family* (pp. 35-5 1). Hillsdale, NJ: Lawrence Erlbaum.

Reber, A.S. (1985). *Dictionary of psychology.* London: Penguin.

Reece, B. L., & Brandt, R. (1996). *Effective human relations in organizations.* Boston: Houghton Mifflin.

Robinson, D. N. (1996). Aristotle on the emotions. In R. Harré & W.G. Parrott (Eds.), *The emotions. Social, cultural and biological dimensions* (pp. 21- 23). London: Sage.

Russell, J. A. (1980). A circumplex model of affect. *Journal of Personality and Social Psychology, 39,* 116 1-1178.

Russell, J. A. (1991). Culture and the categorization of emotions. *Psychological Bulletin, 110,* 426-450.

Russell, J. A., Fernàndez-Dols, J., Manstead, A.S.R., & Wellenkamp, J. C. (1995). *Everyday conceptions of emotion. An introduction to the psychology, anthropology and linguistics of emotion.* Dordrecht: Kluwer Academic.

Saarni, C., & Crowley, M. (1990). The development of emotion regulation: Effects on emotional state and expression. In E. A. Blechman (Ed.), *Emotions and the family* (pp. 53-73). Hillsdale, NJ: Lawrence Erlbaum.

Santrock, J. W. (1986). *Life-span development.* Dubuque: Brown.

Shaver, P. R., Wu, S., & Schwartz, J. C. (1992). Cross-cultural similarities and differences in emotion and its representation. In M. S. Clark (Ed.), *Emotion. Review of personality and social psychology* (pp. 175-2 12). Newbury Park: Sage.

Sillince, J. A. A. (1993). There is more to emotion than goal attainment. *Genetic Social and General Psychology Monographs, 119,* 491-513.

Staats, A. W., & Eifert, G. H. (1990). The paradigmatic behaviorism theory of emotions: Basis for unification. *Clinical Psychology Review, 10,* 539- 566.

Staats, A. W. (1996). Behavior and personality: Psychological behaviorism. NY: Springer.

Watson, D., & Tellegen, A. (1985). Toward a consensual structure of mood. *Psychological Bulletin, 98,* 219- 235.

Review Questions

Read the following statements and indicate whether they are True or False.

1. Emotion and cognitions form a linear relationship.
2. A stimulus is a prerequisite for an emotion to occur.
3. Emotion has no biological or physiological base.
4. Emotions are cultural solutions to locally defined societal conflict.
5. Behaviour can never be unemotional.
6. We are slaves of our emotions and are in a sense victims of what happens around us.
7. Temperament can be described as the biological shaper of the personality that reflects stable individual differences.
8. People who are chronically anxious, hostile and depressed are not necessarily prone to having unfavourable affective balance.
9. Some cognitive processes are actively ignored to avoid emotional stress.
10. There are no differences in the way males and females see and handle emotions.
11. Social intelligence and emotional intelligence are synonymous.
12. Emotions need to be tamed and controlled at all costs.
13. Emotion rules serve no purpose and can be ignored.
14. Families shape adults' way of experiencing and expressing emotions.
15. Mastering emotional problem-solving skills is a way to help adults take charge of their emotional lives.

Answers

1F	2T	3F	4T	5T	6F	7T	8F	9T
10F	11F	12F	13F	14T	15T			

Exercises

1. Describe in your own words the concept "emotion".
2. What is the difference between moods, sentiments, temperament, emotions and feelings?
3. What are the assumptions on which the evolutionary theory of emotion is based?
4. Explain the influence culture has on the experience and expression of emotions.
5. Explain how emotion and cognition work together in creating individual differences in the adult's experience, behaviour and learning.
6. Why is the face regarded as the image of the soul?

Practical Assignment

Make a one-day observation of your closest friends around you. Keep record of the different *emotions* they express and the *way* in which they express those emotions. In your opinion, are the expressions of emotions appropriate? Why do you say so? You can use the following table to assist you in executing this task.

EMOTIONS OBSERVED
DISPLAYING OF EMOTIONS
EVALUATION OF OBSERVATION

Ask a friend to join you and compare notes at the end of the day.

Now that you are aware of the emotions of other people, what about compiling an emotional landscape on which you record the emotions you experienced during the day. It could look like this:

TIME 06:15
ACTIVITY TV wakes me up - take a shower
EMOTION Feel drowsy and tired - afraid - not in the mood for that Psychology test

If you have the courage, keep this record for a few days and see if any emotional patterns emerge. Do you feel that change is needed? What are you going to do about it?

About the Author

Irene Strydom is a senior lecturer in Educational Psychology at one of the largest distance education universities in the world, namely the University of South Africa. This university is situated in Pretoria in the Gauteng Province. More than 128000 students from all over the world study at this university and follow courses in one of six faculties. Irene Strydom's fields of expertise are life-skills education, gifted child education, adult education and remedial education. Research projects that have been done include developing a life-skills programme for underachieving gifted students as well as research on the decision-making skills of professional adults. Numerous articles have been published in South African journals. Irene Strydom is currently involved in the training of educational psychologists at the honours, master's and doctoral levels.

Irene Strydom
University of South Africa

MARY AINLEY

7. INTEREST AND LEARNING: FROM ATTRACTION TO ABSORBING INTEREST

In this chapter the concept of *interest* will be examined from a number of perspectives. Interest is a term that is used widely in discussion of education and it is broadly assumed that for learning to take place a student must have some interest in what they are doing. The language of education which speaks of lifelong learning, or, self-regulated learning assumes that the learner has a genuine interest in, and is committed to the progress of their learning. However, the term interest is used in a variety of ways in educational literature. Sometimes it has the same general meaning as everyday usage; sometimes it has a more specialised meaning.

The perspectives which are included in this chapter start with some examples of behaviour which illustrate interest in learning as it might be seen among participants in an adult education class. These participant perspectives are then translated into the language of the psychological study of interest. Following this introduction to the language of interest as used in the psychological literature, background theories and research which have contributed to the current state of interest research are outlined; in particular, theories of curiosity and intrinsic motivation. Key issues of definition and how to specify the critical indicators of interest are examined. To set these issues into the context of adult education, interest as a motivation for participation in adult education is considered with special attention to its part in reasons for enrolling in adult education programs. The maintenance and development of interest through participation in adult education programs will also be discussed.

James A Athanasou (ed.), Adult Educational Psychology, 155–179
© 2008 Sense Publishers. All rights reserved.

Participant Perspectives

> Alex has turned up to your class because she needs to complete this unit to qualify for her certificate. She has a ticket for the pop concert later that evening and would much rather have gone to the pub with her friends to have a drink before the concert. But, she has come to your class and will meet up with them at the concert.

> Peta is also taking your unit to qualify for her certificate. She arrives at the class early every week, has always completed the work set from the previous class and is keen to discuss it with everyone.

> You, the instructor for this class, have been discussing the course with some colleagues at a recent PD seminar and have decided to try a different approach to your usual teaching style. You are going to have the class generate some key principles by working through a series of client problems. You normally would have started the class by presenting a summary of the principles and then provide some case examples.

The participant perspectives described in this hypothetical scenario each highlight a different aspect of the concept of interest as it relates to learning. The keen enthusiastic student (Peta) comes ready to be involved and participate in the class. Such students bring with them a continuing interest in the subject they are undertaking. They are ripe to engage with the material the instructor presents. The likelihood of them participating and working with the content of the lesson is extremely high. And just as certain is the fact that they will go away having extended their knowledge and understanding.

On the other hand, Alex has attended out of obligation, quite likely she has denied herself the pre-concert drinks because she is afraid that if she misses the class this will be just the night that something critical for the exam is given. She is well aware that there are penalties which will have to be faced if she fails to gain the certificate at the end of the course. She is only doing the course because she has to and on this particular evening other activities have a much higher priority. Her attitude to what you are about to require of the students in class is one of resigned tolerance. The likelihood that she will engage with the material and extend her knowledge and understanding is relatively low. She brings little or no continuing interest to the content being taught in your classes.

But student interest in learning does not only depend on the attitudes and orientations which students bring to the class. The way in which you have structured the activities for the class time this evening is an additional factor. Half an hour into the class Alex and Peta are observed to be engaged in animated debate over the meaning of the client profile you have given them to work on together. You are congratulating yourself on the changed outcome a little bit of restructuring of the class material has managed to achieve. You mentally note that Alex appears to be caught up in the problem you gave them and despite herself, really seems to want to develop a solution. She hasn't looked at her watch for at least 20 minutes. They are surprised when you say that time is up, and as they leave the room you hear them planning to meet before the next class. It has not been unknown for you to feel at the end of a lesson that everyone even Peta has been turned off by a class which proved to be more than usually dull and lifeless. But this evening's class has been different.

These perspectives can be translated into the language of *interest* as used by the interest researcher.

Perspectives from the Psychology of Interest

A wide variety of meanings of the term interest can be found in research which has explored the role of interest in learning and development. Reviewing this research Krapp, Hidi, and Renninger (1992) described three separate ways and these ways of looking at the meaning of interest as a psychological concept have become a key reference point for discussions of interest (e.g., Pintrich & Schunk, 1996).

> Three major points of view are reflected in interest research: (1) interest as a characteristic of the person (interest as a personal trait or disposition), (2) interest as a characteristic of the learning environment (interestingness), and (3) interest as a psychological state (active interest, aroused interest). Both individual interest, in the sense of relatively stable preferences, and interestingness can bring about experiences and psychological states in an individual that are generally referred to as interest. Typical characteristics of this state might include increased attention, greater concentration, pleasant feelings of applied effort, and increased willingness to learn... (Krapp et al. 1992, p. 9)

It is useful to consider the ways in which these three viewpoints are present in the classroom behaviour described in our evening class scenario. The third type described by Krapp et al. (1992), interest as a psychological state, will be outlined first.

Interest - The Psychological State
This refers to the active state of being interested in the learning task, a state which can be observed by others especially the instructor. In the quotation above Krapp et al. (1992) described the typical characteristics as "increased attention, greater concentration, pleasant feelings of applied effort, and increased willingness to learn". What have you observed?

> Half an hour into the class Alex and Peta are observed to be engaged in animated debate over the meaning of the client profile you have given them to work on together (increased attention, greater concentration and pleasant feelings). You are congratulating yourself on the changed outcome a little bit of restructuring of the class material has managed to achieve. You mentally note that Alex appears to be caught up in the problem you gave them and despite herself, really seems to want to develop a solution (greater concentration, increased willingness to learn). She hasn't looked at her watch for at least 20 minutes (increased attention, greater concentration). They are surprised when you say that time is up, (increased attention, greater concentration) and as they leave the room you hear them planning to meet before the next class (increased willingness to learn).

The features of behaviour which you have observed represent some of the classic behavioural indicators that a student has become interested in the task. Interest then refers to the psychological state of being interested in a specific task or object, a state characterised by "increased attention, greater concentration, pleasant feelings of applied effort, and increased willingness to learn" (Krapp et al., 1992, p. 9). The other two ways of viewing *interest* relate to what are thought to be the precursors of the active state. One perspective looks to individual dispositions as the basis of interest, the other looks to contextual or situational factors.

Individual Interest - the Disposition of the Student
This is sometimes also referred to as personal interest. Using the term interest in this way puts emphasis on the fact that there is a connection or relatedness between the individual student and the course content which existed before, and goes beyond their participation in the class and enrolment in this course. They have enrolled in the course primarily because it is it is about an area which they have enjoyed over an extended period of time. It may have been a passion they developed in secondary school, or something they learned to love working with a relative during childhood. Whatever the background the content of your course is something they know about, feel is important to them, and are keen to develop further. Peta fits this description. A very different picture is presented by Alex who is constrained through employment requirements to be there and to participate at least to the level of passing the exam at the end of the unit. She claims no personal interest in the course content beyond wanting to gain the qualification. Between the levels of personal interest displayed by Peta and that of Alex there are of course many possibilities, and over the years of taking your course you have probably encountered most of that variety.

Situational Interest - the Interestingness of the Task
This perspective on the meaning of interest suggests that it is the specific character of the learning task, or the way in which it is presented, which arouses student interest. This viewpoint proposes that situations, and this includes learning tasks, by their very nature vary in the degree to which they arouse interest. In short, learning tasks differ in their degree of interestingness. In the scenario described above both Alex and Peta are actively engaged in the lesson - their behaviour represents an active state of interest. This was to be expected of Peta who has a strong individual interest in the course. But why is Alex so interested? It may have come about as a reaction to some feature of the way you presented the task to them. It may have been because some of the client profiles you presented contained some personally significant theme or themes which caught Alex's attention. The fact that most of the other students have also shown increased attention and greater concentration suggests that both the content of what you have presented and the way you have structured it can be described as having specific properties which generate these outcomes. The task can be described as having high situational interest.

In summary, these are the three main ways that the construct interest has come to be used in the literature on the psychology of learning - the psychological state of interest; individual or personal interest, the disposition of the learner; and, situational interest, which is a function of properties of the task.

Background Theory - Curiosity and Intrinsic Motivation

A number of different research programs have contributed to the present state of interest research. Two closely related lines of research will be described to show how they have influenced contemporary theory on the nature of interest. The first concerns research on curiosity, the second concerns research on intrinsic motivation. Both lines of research owe a lot to the early work of Berlyne (1960) who was one of a number of researchers challenging the dominant primary drive theory of motivation. His contemporary, Harry Harlow (1953) demonstrated that laboratory animals would work for the opportunity to manipulate mechanical puzzles and not just for rewards which were associated with primary drives. These researchers considered how laboratory animals and humans might undertake activities where the reward seemed to be the activity itself.

For both of these areas, curiosity and intrinsic motivation, the theories and research findings can be organised into those which look for an understanding of the arousal of the motive, curiosity or intrinsic motivation, in terms of specific situational factors, and those which look to describing the occurrence of curiosity or intrinsic motivation in terms of an individual disposition or trait.

Curiosity: The Situation
Berlyne (1960) undertook a broad program of research into the nature of curiosity. He described curiosity as a motive which when aroused leads to exploratory behaviour. His basic model of behaviour suggested that exposure to certain types of stimuli will alter the person's level of arousal (increase curiosity) and this change in arousal will be associated with specific forms of behaviour. A novel event will increase arousal (curiosity) and the person will engage in exploratory behaviour. The exploratory behaviour will increase their information about that stimulus event and thereby reduce arousal, or expressed another way, satisfy their curiosity. Increased arousal was inferred from observations of increased attention being paid to the stimulus. The attention paid to certain stimuli was then the key to identifying the impact of these stimulus properties.

The main body of Berlyne's experimental work was concerned with identifying the critical set of stimulus characteristics which would arouse curiosity. The properties he identified included such attributes as novelty, incongruity, and ambiguity. What is common to these attributes is that exposure to them will attract attention, that is, increase arousal. A novel object or situation is by definition one that is not familiar to the person. The relation between person and stimulus is one characterised by uncertainty. According to Berlyne curiosity is the motive, the feeling of being puzzled which is aroused by exposure to a novel object. A person will approach and explore the object and in the process find out about it. That is, they gain information or knowledge which will reduce the feeling of being puzzled and thereby satisfy the curiosity. In the same way the incongruous stimulus is one that catches attention because there seems to be something not quite right about it. The feeling that there is something not quite right about it is an increase in the curiosity motive. Exploratory behaviour allows the person to sort it out. The ambiguous stimulus catches attention because the observer is being pulled in different directions and is not sure what the right meaning is. Again there is a feeling of being puzzled, an increase in arousal, or, an increase in the curiosity motive. Exploratory behaviour allows the person to overcome their uncertainty. In each case, increased curiosity or increased arousal is followed by exploration and information seeking. It is through expanding their knowledge of the stimulus event that the person's feeling of being puzzled (the curiosity motive) will be satisfied.

In his experiments Berlyne used relatively simple stimuli such as random polygons and incongruous shapes (Berlyne, 1957; 1958; 1963), prose material about invertebrate animals (Berlyne, 1954) and literary quotations attributed to well known authors (Berlyne, 1962). For example, in an experiment using incongruous shapes (Berlyne, 1957), incongruity was manipulated by putting together stimulus patterns with characteristics the viewer had been trained to see as incompatible - the head of an elephant on a lion's body.

Curiosity according to Berlyne (1960) refers to the arousal which stimuli high in collative variability (that is, novelty, incongruity, ambiguity) generate. The exploratory behaviour which follows increases their knowledge of the object and so reduces arousal, or, satisfies curiosity.

Later writers extended this model by describing in more detail the nature of the underlying psychological processes. Hunt (1963; 1971) coined the phrase "motivation inherent in information processing" and focused on the cognitive uncertainty generated by puzzling and novel experiences. This view, like Berlyne's, stressed the importance of the character of the situation, but gave more attention to describing what was happening in cognitive terms. Puzzling, incongruous, ambiguous and novel objects are experienced that way because the information received by the person does not quite fit their known and familiar cognitive categories. The person experiences uncertainty over the meaning of the stimulus and seeks further information about the object thereby reducing their uncertainty. The newly acquired information in turn brings about changes in the learner's cognitive categories or structures.

These models of behaviour link information seeking to the arousal properties of certain types of stimuli and in this way are similar to models of situational interest which link the aroused state of interest to properties of the situation or context of the person. Hidi's work on situational interest looks at interest as it relates to learning and development in this way (Hidi, 1990; Hidi & Baird, 1986). It suggests that for understanding and promoting learning it is important to be able to describe tasks in terms of their different levels of situational interest. Hidi suggested that there are two separate ways in which the character of the situation may arouse interest in the learner. It might be aroused by specific structural components of the task (factors similar to Berlyne's collative variability: novel, unexpected, surprising stimuli etc.), or, it might be aroused through associations between elements of the task and aspects of the person's values, preferences or goals. Hidi argued that within this second area there are themes of universal personal significance which arouse interest; human activity, intensity factors, and life themes. Much of the experimental work supporting Hidi's theory of situational interest has been accumulated through research into children's processing of text materials. An example of a sentence shown to have high text-based interest (high situational interest) used in one of her studies is "Adult wolves carry food home in their stomachs and bring it up again or regurgitate it, for the young cubs to eat - the wolf version of canned baby food." Another "A canary can also bluff by playing dead. A frightened canary may go limp in someone's hand" (Hidi & Baird, 1983). It is thought that the life and human activity themes in these sentences arouse instant connections between the reader and the text, that is, they activate the state of interest.

All of this amounts to the fact that the human system can't help but respond to certain types of inputs - the surprising, incongruous, ambiguous and unexpected will always get a response. Using these properties together with personally significant content themes (e.g., themes of life, death, sex) will generally catch attention and if used skilfully what catches attention may be moved into more focused attention. The content of the client profiles in the earlier scenario appear to have operated in this way for Alex.

> Half an hour into the class activity Alex and Peta are observed to be engaged in animated debate over the meaning of the client profile you have given them to work on together. You are congratulating yourself on the changed outcome a little bit of restructuring of the class material has managed to achieve. You mentally note that Alex has been caught up by the problem you gave them and despite herself, really seems to want to develop a solution. She hasn't looked at her watch for at least 20 minutes.

Curiosity: The Disposition

Another line of theory and research following Berlyne's (1960) development of the curiosity construct, adopted a trait or dispositional approach. These researchers sought to explain individual differences in responses to novel, incongruous and ambiguous stimuli. This approach views curiosity as a characteristic way of relating to new experience, an individual's general way of reacting to novelty. For example, Beswick (1971) described the individual disposition of curiosity as differences in behaviour directed towards seeking, maintaining and resolving conceptual conflicts. Not everyone confronted with the same novel event seeks further knowledge and information about it. The outcome of this line of research has been the development of measures of curiosity as a disposition or trait. One scale following this approach is the Two Factor Curiosity Scale (Ainley, 1987; 1998), which distinguishes two styles of approach to novelty, breadth-of-interest curiosity and depth-of-interest curiosity. These individual curiosity styles are defined in terms of both the type of stimulus events which are approached and the style of approach. Breadth-of-interest curiosity refers to the tendency to approach novel thrilling and daring activities in order to sample the experience. Depth-of-interest curiosity refers to the tendency to approach novel and puzzling phenomena in order to understand what they are about. These are independent curiosity dimensions. In any group of individuals a range of combinations of these two dimensions will usually be present.

This line of research into curiosity has a lot in common with the interest researchers who have viewed interest as an individual disposition or orientation. Both suggest that the general orientation towards learning which the individual brings to a course of study is an important factor in the degree to which they become involved and expand their understanding. When applied to Peta and Alex, the individual differences approach would predict Peta to be more likely to become actively involved with the learning material and to be more likely to demonstrate a higher level of learning.

Intrinsic Motivation

Another body of research that has grown out of Berlyne's (1960) work on curiosity has developed around the distinction between intrinsic and extrinsic motivation. In its simplest form this is a distinction between finding the rewards for an activity within the activity itself and finding the rewards for an activity outside of the activity. This concept is very similar to curiosity, and a parallel literature has developed. Although it is rare for situations to be solely one of intrinsic or extrinsic motivation, it is often the case that one is stronger than the other. Complementary emphases on situation and disposition can also be seen in the research and theory on intrinsic and extrinsic motivation.

In adult education the distinction between intrinsic and extrinsic motivation has been used in the formulation of Houle's (1961) typology of students. Houle separated goal-oriented learners (those who wish to achieve relatively clear learning objectives), activity-oriented learners (those who want an activity, the course provides the opportunity and the course content is secondary), and, the learning-oriented (those whose prime focus is the course content). The basic difference between these categories is the student's position on the purpose, goal or value of the course they are undertaking. Take for example the learning-oriented student; they value the course content as an end in itself. This is the classic intrinsic motivation pattern. On the other hand the goal-oriented learner views the product, the goal, or the outcome as the main focus of their involvement. The course content is a necessary means to achieve this end. For this type of learner the balance is tipped in favour of extrinsic motivation. In the same way the balance is in favour of extrinsic motivation for the activity-oriented learner. The course is providing a vehicle to achieve other ends.

When Houle's typology has been applied (e.g., Courtney, 1992) it has generally been found that most learners have a combination of motives. The student who is doing a course because they need the certificate at the end to move them along in their career may also value the time spent learning about, exploring, or investigating the content of their classes. Nevertheless, the intrinsic versus extrinsic motivation typology is a useful way of describing the relative importance of different motives.

Intrinsic Motivation: The Situation

A large body of research has reported on specific ways in which learning tasks (i.e., the situation) can be structured to increase intrinsic motivation and this has been summarised in a paper by Lepper and Hodell (1989). The questions asked in this research include characteristics of both learning tasks and settings, and focus on identification of features which will maximise the arousal of intrinsic motivation. Most of the research has been carried out with primary and secondary students but the general pattern of the findings is informative for those working in the area of adult education. Lepper and Hodell (1989) suggested that there are four important features of learning tasks and settings: challenge, curiosity, control, and fantasy. Attention to these features can capitalise on arousal of intrinsic motivation. These four factors will be described briefly.

Challenge

The critical issue here is the structure of the learning task in relation to the student's prior learning and competence. Challenging tasks are those that build on the knowledge and skills which a student has already achieved and require progress into an area just beyond their present level. This is often described in terms of presenting tasks of intermediate difficulty or complexity. A task which is too easy (i.e., the student has already mastered the knowledge, skills and competencies) is likely to be met with the reaction "I have done this all before". The student is not moved to engage with that task for its own sake. If extrinsic rewards are strong the task may however be taken on, but enthusiasm for the task itself will be low.

On the other hand, a task which is too hard (i.e., has no clear point of contact with the student's current level of knowledge and skills) is likely to be avoided because most students quickly recognise that the task is beyond them and is likely to end in failure. Activities that are directed at intermediate levels of difficulty challenge students. There are immediate connections between features of the task and the student's existing skills, and the task requires an extension of those existing skills. Engagement with the task and a successful outcome feed back to the student as feelings of increased competence and self-efficacy.

Curiosity
Whereas the issue of challenge emphasises the relation between task complexity and student competence, curiosity refers to task features which maximise the chances of that task being experienced as novel, puzzling, incongruous or ambiguous. Again for the strongest effects task characteristics should be aimed at an intermediate level. Low levels of novelty, incongruity, or ambiguity make it highly likely that the task will be coded as something familiar. Too much novelty, incongruity, or ambiguity will mean that there is no point of contact between the student's present knowledge and features of learning task and if the student has any choice this task is likely to be avoided.

Control
The widespread use of computers in education have made it increasingly clear that tasks which give the learner some active control over the direction of their learning will activate intrinsic motivation and the learner will be more likely to report interest in that task. This aspect of intrinsic motivation has been researched extensively as one of the potential advantages of the individual pacing of instruction which is possible with interactive computer technologies (see Lepper & Cordova, 1992).

Fantasy
Using simulation techniques in learning utilises the role fantasy plays in the arousal of intrinsic motivation. Fantasy elements which allow the student to actually put themselves into the situation have been shown to be associated with higher levels of intrinsic motivation. The learning is then more likely to become personally meaningful and important.

As these examples demonstrate there is a lot in common between the task features which have been described as important for the arousal of situational interest and the psychological principles recommended by educational psychologists for structuring a learning task to increase its potential to arouse intrinsic motivation. Which of these is employed by a teacher will depend both on the particular instructional purposes and the setting. It is also important to reiterate that with most learning tasks there will be a combination of intrinsic and extrinsic motivational components. Rarely is it one or the other and even while undertaking a specific learning task the balance of these motives may change.

Intrinsic Motivation: The Disposition
From the individual differences perspective theorists such as Richard deCharms (1968; 1984) and Edward Deci (Deci & Ryan, 1985) have looked at intrinsic motivation in terms of what deCharms has called "personal causation" and Deci

"self-determination". Both are looking at the intrinsic/extrinsic difference as one of control over learning and being in control means that the learner is taking responsibility for their own learning. Although both the course curriculum and the instructor may set the broad parameters for learning, the student who takes responsibility for the management of their own progress, monitors what they are achieving and makes decisions about when and how to go beyond the minimal course requirements, can be said to be in control of their learning, or, to be intrinsically motivated. This is what is meant by self-determination as used in Deci's theory and by being an "origin" rather than a "pawn" in the terminology used by deCharms. On the other hand the learner who only does what they are instructed to, and only when instructed to, is not assuming any control over their own learning. They are extrinsically motivated. Like a pawn they are letting their learning be dictated by some other person or authority.

In his later writings Deci and colleagues (1992; 1998; Deci, Ryan, & Williams, 1996; Ryan & Deci, 2000) suggest that a more productive way to think of intrinsic and extrinsic motivation is as a continuum marked by different levels of internalisation of goals. At the intrinsic motivation end of the continuum the person's behaviour can be described as autotelic, meaning engaged in for its own sake. At the extrinsic motivation end of the continuum learning activities are performed to achieve goals which are outside of the activity itself, for example, to gain the award, or, to satisfy the number of schooling hours required by the apprenticeship. Between these extremes are behaviours which may develop the character of intrinsically motivated activities, although they started out under the control of external incentives. For example, a person enrols in a course because they have to complete it to get a particular qualification and as a result of their participation in the course they come to value the knowledge and skills they have been learning. No longer are they learning just to get the certificate. They want to master the skills they have discovered.

Ryan and Deci (2000) refer to a process of moving from external regulation (i.e., regulation by extrinsic motivation) through a progression of introjection, identification and integration. What started as externally regulated goals and values for learning have progressively been taken over by the student as their own goals and values for learning. At the first level this may have been to gain approval from others (introjection). It may then have developed to a point where the student endorses as their own what were originally external goals (identification). The final step involves the student incorporating the formerly external goals into their own internalized goal structure (integration). Once integrated these goals cannot be distinguished from the goals of the intrinsically motivated learner.

From this brief overview of theory and research on both curiosity and intrinsic motivation it is possible to see close relationships with the shape of current research on interest. In curiosity the relation between learner and the novel event is described in terms of uncertainty, or being puzzled, a feeling that something important is not quite clear. The intrinsic motivation viewpoint emphasises the learner's active engagement with their learning task. Both perspectives acknowledge that features of the learning context can influence this relation. Both perspectives acknowledge individual differences in the likely occurrence of active engagement between learner and task. Despite obvious differences in emphasis these approaches all direct attention to the character of the relation between person and learning task a point very clearly articulated by Valsiner (1992):

"Interest", then, is not in the object, nor in the mind of the child, but it emerges as a result of processes that link the two in irreversible time. (p. 33)

Understanding Interest - Current Issues

What then are some of the key research issues in the development of our understanding of the psychology of interest? Two issues will be described here to demonstrate current research directions. The first will look at how interest is defined and why this is an important concern, the second will describe some of the behavioural indicators which have been identified.

Defining Interest

One important goal for the study of interest is to settle on an agreed meaning (or, set of meanings) for the term. Because interest is a word used widely the range of meanings it carries presents a problem when scientific discourse requires clear, unambiguous definition. The three ways in which the term has been used as described by Krapp et. al. (1992) are now widely used in theory and research.

A number of important issues to do with the meaning of the term will be considered here: (i) personal versus general and shared meaning; (ii) having "general interest in" versus having "a personal interest in"; and, (iii) invoking interest as both cause and outcome.

The first of these issues (personal versus general and shared meaning) has been described clearly by Valsiner (1992). When a person claims to have an interest, for example, "I am interested in international politics", that person is using the term to refer to their unique experience. Valsiner called this the personal sense of "interest". If we describe another person's interest, for example "Anthony is interested in vintage cars", we are using the term to convey a shared meaning of the experience. In doing so we prune back the very personalised meaning to a common core that we assume can be applied equally well to a group of people (i.e., those who are vintage car devotees).

An important challenge for the researcher is to observe and understand the range of personal meanings of interest and to derive a general meaning which preserves the essential character of those experiences. This is being done in research which is trying to isolate the essential components of experience which justify inclusion in the category "interest". Some progress has been made and this can be seen in the findings on indicators of interest. The results of this work will be taken up in a later section.

A second issue in the use of the term "interest" can be seen in the ambiguity of meaning in the following two situations. Two people are explaining why they are making enquiries about a course on 'Managing Accounts for Community Co-operatives'. The first person states that they have enquired out of "general interest", the second states that they have enquired because they have a "personal interest" in money management systems. In the first case the meaning of the term "general interest" is ambiguous and could mean a number of different things: for example, "I heard about it from a friend and thought I might find it useful" or "I am an economics graduate and anything to do with money management is sure to be of interest". Contrast these with the statement of a "personal interest": for example, "I have been running co-op accounts for years and would like to keep abreast of the latest techniques". The personal interest statement identifies a specific object which the person knows something about and values. It implies a relationship with the object (or class of objects) which has some extension across time. The object of interest with the general interest statement is non-specific and does not imply anything about its extension across time. There is an important difference here in the level of specificity of the relation between person and object.

Close examination of the character of the language used is critical for the interpretation of research findings concerning interest. For example, research into reasons for enrolling in adult education courses generally have provided those surveyed with an "interest" category. Often the term is qualified as either "general interest" or "personal interest". If only one of these is provided the meaning of the term is not precise and interpretation of the results is unclear. However, if both categories are provided personal interest conveys the meaning, "I am really keen about this area of study", while general interest conveys the less committed, "It sounds interesting and I might look into it".

The distinction being made here is very similar to what Renninger (1992) referred to as the difference between "interest" and "attraction". Following her use of the term, interest would only be applied in situations where the person has a firm knowledge base about the object of study and also values it highly; for example "It is a subject I have read a lot about and want to study further". If knowledge is low and value high, Renninger would refer to it as an "attraction", for example, "I don't know much about it but it sounds intriguing". Following this perspective, surveys of reasons for enrolling in adult education courses offering "personal interest" as a category are more likely to draw responses consistent with Renninger's definition of "interest". However, attraction could not be ruled out. Surveys which present a category of "general interest" are likely to be more equivocal being endorsed by some students as an "attraction" and others as an "interest". The critical difference in character of these two experiences is then lost.

A third important issue in the definition of the term "interest" is its status as cause or effect, antecedent or outcome. Like a number of other psychological variables the term interest is used as both cause and effect, the antecedent condition and the outcome. The danger is that descriptions and explanations become circular. For example, consider the following exchange.

"Why is Leon so interested in that new computer?"

"Well, he has always been interested in computers."

The second statement is not an explanation of why Leon is interested in the computer; it merely describes this as one of a more extended set of similar patterns of behaviour. However, it does allow some prediction of future behaviour. Knowing the way he has reacted to similar objects in the past allows prediction to future behaviour. It does not explain why Leon is interested in the new computer. This is very similar to the issue grappled with by the curiosity researchers - Berlyne (1960) looked for an explanation of why people approach novel, incongruous or ambiguous objects in terms of arousal, Hunt (1971) in terms of cognitive uncertainty. These theories explain the selectivity or the direction of behaviour by giving an account of the particular psychological processes brought into play when the person is exposed to a puzzling event. In the same way it is the task of contemporary interest researchers to identify those psychological processes which operate when interest, whether individual or situational, is aroused.

Indicators of Interest

Valsiner (1992) drew attention to the importance of acknowledging that there is a difference between a specific individual's experience of interest and the common core which can be generalised. One perspective gives attention to the characteristics of the personal experience; the other is concerned with isolating those characteristics of behaviour which are available to an external observer as indicators of interest. What then are the characteristics of behaviour observable by others which indicate that a student is interested in the task, or, finds the task interesting?

As was pointed out earlier in this chapter Krapp et al. (1992) have suggested that "increased attention, greater concentration, pleasant feelings of applied effort, and increased willingness to learn" (p.9) are the typical features of the state of active interest (see also Krapp & Fink, 1992). These were identified in the behaviour of Alex and Peta in the hypothetical classroom scenario.

> Half an hour into the class Alex and Peta are observed to be engaged in animated debate over the meaning of the client profile you have given them to work on together (increased attention, greater concentration and pleasant feelings). You are congratulating yourself on the changed outcome a little bit of restructuring of the class material has managed to achieve. You mentally note that Alex appears to be caught up in the problem you gave them and despite herself, really seems to want to develop a solution (greater concentration, increased willingness to learn). She hasn't looked at her watch for at least 20 minutes (increased attention, greater concentration). They are surprised when you say that time is up, (increased attention, greater concentration) and as they leave the room you hear them planning to meet before the next class (increased willingness to learn).

Taking these in turn, "increased attention" and "greater concentration" refer to features of student behaviour which can be observed in the way the student goes about a task. In the example given here, the amount of time spent actually working on the task was a significant indicator. There was no mention of Alex being distracted by other things going on around her, or even by her plans for later that evening. It would normally be expected that someone who wants the class to be over so that they can get on with the real business of the evening would be frequently checking the time. But Alex had not glanced at her watch for at least 20 minutes. Basically what is involved here is an assessment of the degree to which the student is focused on the task. Measures such as time and response to distraction can be used to index such engagement. Other ways of measuring attention and concentration would be to listen in on what Alex and Peta were saying during this class time; to analyse the content of their discussion. This might consist of recording the amount of conversation directed to the actual task and the amount which concerned non-task issues. Another indicator might be the type of questions being asked of each other.

Krapp et al. (1992) also referred to "increased willingness to learn". It is important to note that this involves making an inference about the student's intentions and highlights that interest involves some element of self-initiated activity. The active state of interest presupposes some choice about the level of participation with a specific learning activity. The student chooses to increase or extend their level of involvement. In the example above the two students are choosing to meet prior to the next class. Identification of student interest therefore relies on detecting choice for the activity of interest. Persistence (see Prenzel, 1992) is another way of referring to these same attributes of interest (increased attention, greater concentration, and increased willingness to learn).

A further component of the experience of interest is the affective or emotional aspect, "pleasant feelings of applied effort". The cognitive emphasis of theories of curiosity and intrinsic motivation in the 1970s (e.g., Beswick, 1971; Day, 1971; Hunt, 1971) commonly accorded positive affect a place in the behaviour which was being described but saw its role as a 'by-product' of the information seeking which brought about resolution of cognitive conflict and uncertainty. More recent theories dealing with constructs of interest (e.g., Krapp, 1994; Krapp & Fink, 1992) treat positive affect as an essential part of the psychological state of interest. The same is true for the related constructs of intrinsic motivation (e.g., Deci, 1992; Sansone & Morgan, 1992). Studies using the depth-of-interest subscale of the Two Factor Curiosity Scale (Ainley, 1998) have shown emotions of excitement, enjoyment and surprise to be associated with a general interest in learning.

Athanasou (1998) has taken this further in a study which has investigated the relative importance of cognitive, value, and emotional components in the criteria used by tertiary students to identify interest. In this study young adult students were presented with a number of profiles of information about other students' classroom reactions. Each profile consisted of the ratings which a particular student had made of their own experience at a specific point in a lesson. The issues to be rated were chosen to represent three components thought to be essential to the experience of interest (see Schiefele & Krapp, 1996): cognitive (e.g., skills, knowledge), value (e.g., effort, desire) and emotional (e.g., satisfaction, happiness). For each profile the participants in Athanasou's study were asked to estimate what their personal level of interest would be if the information they were reading was their experience. In effect, participants were being asked to imagine themselves as the person in the profile and report their psychological state of interest. In this way it would be possible to identify particular cognitive, value and emotional components which were consistently associated with higher ratings of interest. The findings suggested the most important indicators were from the emotion and value components. In order of importance they were effort (value), happiness (emotion), desire (value), familiarity (cognitive), importance (value), enthusiasm (emotion), enjoyment (emotion), confidence (cognitive), and excitement (emotion). Hence, the psychological state of interest involves the sense of doing something challenging and worthwhile, something which at the same time is enjoyable.

In our own research program we have been developing techniques that allow access to some of the psychological processes operating when interest is aroused. Using interactive multimedia software we ask students to report on what they are thinking and feeling as they work through a learning task (e.g., Ainley, Corrigan, & Richardson, 2005; Ainley, Hidi, & Berndorff, 2002). What we are finding is that the psychological state of interest is a central feature of being engaged with a learning task. When students report feeling interested in a task they are more likely to persist with the task. In both studies referred to above this has been tested by giving students the opportunity to quit from the task before they have completed it. Those who choose to quit have generally been students who have reported very low interest in the task. The tasks used in our research studies have included reading popular culture and popular science text passages (see Ainley et al., 2002; 2005), and tasks that require development and presentation of an argument on a topical issue (Ainley & Patrick, 2006). The findings of this research suggest that experiences of the psychological state of interest are about affect and emotion and that these experiences function to support continued involvement with the learning task. Other emotions, both positive and negative, may occur in combination with interest but once the experience of interest has been triggered it is likely that the student will persist with the task. From this research we understand more of what is happening when "Alex and Peta are observed to be engaged in *animated* debate over the meaning of the client profile..." and can predict with some confidence that both are likely to persist until they achieve a satisfactory solution.

Interest as a Motivation of the Clients of Adult Education

Surveys of participant's reasons for enrolling, reports on course and sector outcomes, and, retrospectives on adult education (e.g., Claydon, 1988; Parliament of the Commonwealth of Australia, 1991; Peters, 1994) all consider important aspects of student motivation. It is not hard to find some mention of interest in most. Together these documents provide some important insights into the varied character of interest as it relates to adult education. Two particular features will be explored here: (i) the place of interest as a reason for enrolling in an adult education course, and, (ii) changing levels of interest as they have been observed during and at the end of adult education courses.

Interest as a Reason for Enrolling in Adult Education

A sample of participants from a diverse range of adult education courses have been assembled for a teleconferencing session and are asked: What was the main reason you had in mind when you enrolled in your present course? The following reflects the diversity which might result.

> **Ray** (enrolled in a 6 week travel orientation course with the Council of Adult Education): "Well, I hadn't really thought much about it but one day as I was opening the paper a glossy brochure fell to the floor and on the front was a picture of a Greek island. It looked good and when I turned the page and read about this travel course I thought I would give it a go. I have always wanted to go to Greece but it will be a long time before I can afford it, and this seemed like a good idea."

> **Carla** (undertaking apprenticeship studies at a TAFE college): "I enrolled in the course because it was a part of my apprenticeship. I wanted an apprenticeship and was lucky enough to get one so this is what goes with it."

> **Jo** (enrolled in a Neighbourhood House course on Using Computers to Manage a Budget): "I enrolled in the course because I wanted to do something and this sounded interesting. Besides it might give me a few skills which I can use some day.... But to be honest, the real reason was the fact that I am new in the area and this seemed like an easy way to get to meet people."

> **George** (undertaking a Summer School course in ancient Chinese philosophy): "I enrolled in the course because summer is the only time I can get away from my business. I have had a lifetime passion for ancient philosophy. Last year I managed to

find a course which introduced me to early Japanese philosophers and now I want to extend this and see how different they were from the mainland philosophers."

Although hypothetical this sample does represent something of the variety of reasons which prompt enrolment in adult education courses. Each respondent has been tagged to a specific type of course, not because this represents the only type of reason for adults undertaking these courses but because it highlights the diversity of settings through which adult education takes place.

What is the picture which emerges from the formal reports, surveys and research on reasons or motives for undertaking adult education?

It is not uncommon for researchers reporting on the reasons behind course enrolment (e.g., Claydon, 1988; Courtney, 1992; Cross, 1981) to refer to the typology developed by Houle (1961) distinguishing goal-oriented learners, activity-oriented learners, and, the learning-oriented. It is important to note that this typology distinguishes the relative value of course content as an end in itself (learning oriented), as a means to an end (goal oriented) and, providing the setting for other purposes to be achieved (activity-oriented). Before looking at the findings of the reports and surveys it is useful to explore how this typology relates to the distinctions between individual, situational, and active interest.

Using Houle's typology the group assembled for the teleconference would most likely be classified as:

Ray wants to find out about the course content, travelling in the Greek Islands, so here the main motivation is learning-oriented.

Carla wants to get the apprenticeship qualification and passing this course is necessary to achieve that, so here the main motivation is goal-oriented.

Jo has taken the course to meet people. This would be classified as activity-oriented. Reference to acquiring some useful skills indicates there is also an aspect of goal-oriented motivation, and in addition there is a hint that the specific content was important (learning-oriented).

George wants to find out about the course content, ancient Chinese philosophers, so here the main motivation is learning-oriented.

How do these reasons line up against the distinctions between individual interest, situational interest and interest as psychological state?

Both Ray and George have been classified under Houle's typology as being learning-oriented. Their reasons suggest that their course enrolment was a behavioural expression of a personal or individual interest. However, the specific pattern of interest, especially the strength or intensity of that interest, and how it influenced their decision to enrol was quite different. For George this course was one step in a strategy to pursue his interest (his passion). Over the years he has been a keen participant in a number of courses all with an ancient philosophy focus. For Ray the course also relates to a personal interest. However, as far as we can tell this interest is less well-developed than George's interest. Ray is unlikely to speak of it as a passion. His interest was aroused and acted upon because of the attention grabbing quality of the brochure which slipped to the floor from the newspaper. What we don't know is whether Ray would have acted on this personal interest if it had not been focused by the chance encounter with the brochure.

An important implication of this knowledge about personal or individual interest is the style of participation the instructor can expect. No matter what happens in class and how poorly prepared the presentation it is unlikely to diminish the work George will put in. However, Ray has acted upon this personal interest because of a chance encounter with an attention arresting brochure (a combination of dispositional and situational factors). Continued involvement with the course content may well depend on the degree to which the class content and activities maintain and develop the attention triggered by the brochure (situational interest).

The instructor becomes a critical player in the development of individual interest. In their recent model of the development of individual interest, Hidi and Renninger (2006) emphasize the role of the instructor to provide conditions that will support and maintain the initial triggered situational interest allowing it to become a well-developed individual interest. Hidi and Renninger describe four phases on the way to a well-developed individual interest and as interest develops dependence on the supportive role of the instructor decreases. The first level of development is the triggered situational interest, Ray's chance encounter with the travel brochure. When he enrols in the travel orientation course the experiences the instructor provides in those classes can be critical for influencing whether this triggered interest is maintained. The second level of Hidi and Renninger's model refers to a maintained situational interest. In his first classes Ray was introduced to features of travel in Greece that confirmed all the excitement of his initial expectations. The triggered situational interest was maintained and becomes an organized system of experience and information that is charged with excitement and pleasure. By now Ray is seeking out other avenues of information and experience of Greek culture. He has organized a meal at a traditional Greek restaurant for his friends and has enquired about a class to learn conversational Greek. These activities were not suggested by the instructor but when Ray talked about what he was doing the instructor commended his initiative. In this way the triggered interest progresses to a maintained situational interest, an emerging individual interest and becomes a self-sustaining well-developed individual interest.

Carla does not have a strong personal interest in the classes. Successfully gaining the certificate at the end of the course is the strongest factor in her attendance and participation. Knowledge that this course has not been taken out of personal interest also carries implications about the likely level of engagement with the learning tasks which make up the course. The instructor will have to give a lot of attention to class presentation and organisation, situational interest factors, if she is going to trigger Carla's interest and involvement with the course content beyond the minimum level required for passing the exam.

Jo also has enrolled in her course for reasons other than personal interest in the course content. As with Ray the advertising material for the course has aroused interest and to be maintained may depend on the skill of the instructor in structuring the class experiences. More importantly if the primary purpose of meeting some new people in the area is not being satisfied through social interaction in the class, the content will have to be well structured and well presented to trigger and maintain her interest and lead to learning new skills.

So how important is interest as a reason for adults enrolling in adult education courses?

Research Findings: Interest and Reasons for Enrolling

A typical finding of the research in this area is that personal interest is one of a number of major reasons for participation in adult education. However there are marked differences across the variety of forms of adult education in the ranking of personal interest as a major reason for enrolling.

Although conducted some time ago, an investigation (Peters, 1994) of the outcomes of adult education conducted through the Victorian Council of Adult Education (CAE) illustrates some of these patterns.

Survey questionnaires were distributed to a stratified random sample of adults who had enrolled in CAE courses between 1990 to 1992. These adults had enrolled in a variety of courses including Victorian Certificate of Education - Return to Study, Community Programs, Creative arts, Liberal Studies, and Basic Education Courses. Of interest here are the questions which were asked about reasons for attending CAE courses. A list of reasons was supplied and the respondents were asked to circle their reasons for enrolling. The form of the survey allowed for multiple reasons but also asked for an indication of which was the major reason.

The categories with the highest number of responses were personal interest, leisure skills, and personal growth. Together these categories accounted for almost 72% of the total responses to the survey. The next most chosen reason was the work related category. The same pattern was seen in the major reason for enrolment.

The prominence of specific reasons was found to vary according to age and gender of the respondents. CAE enrolment statistics for 1992 showed that approximately 52% of participants were below 45 years of age. Age analyses compared those aged 44 years and less with those aged 45 years and over. When Peters (1994) analysed the reasons for participation by age he found that the work related category was more frequently chosen by the younger age group, approximately 65% of the work related reasons were given by the 44 years and under group. This younger group also accounted for 58% of personal growth responses and 29% of personal interest responses. Clearly there are important age differences in the balance of reasons for participation in CAE courses.

Analysis of these same data according to the gender of the participants indicated that personal interest was the major reason for enrolling for approximately 35% of all the females in the sample and 28% of the males.

Peters (1994) cautioned that these findings which were based on a stratified sample across a range of courses need to be interpreted as a general pattern across CAE participants. Specific specialist courses may show different patterns. He cited a fashion industry program which drew participants from the 26 to 40 years age group many of whom were unemployed. In the case of this one specific course the major reasons given were to get work in the industry and start their own business (59%), and to improve skills (27%).

The reasons for participation were varied and many participants had a number of reasons which combined in their decision to enrol in Council of Adult Education courses. Personal interest (a disposition or orientation to want to find out about the particular subject) is clearly a major reason behind many enrolment decisions. However, this conclusion should be interpreted in the light of the earlier comments made about the need for clearer definition of the term interest in research studies. In this study the participants were given a list of possible reasons for enrolling, one of which was listed as "for mental stimulation or personal interest". The linking of personal interest and mental stimulation sets the context as one of engagement in the learning for its own sake rather than being a means to some other end as was expressed in some of the other reasons presented, for example, "to meet people", "to lead on to further education", "to improve work prospects". However, this form of expression has not allowed for the distinction emphasised by Renninger (1992) between attraction and interest. A tick in the box alongside "for mental stimulation or personal interest" indicates that the course content was seen as valuable but does not necessarily imply any level of prior knowledge.

A very different picture of reasons behind participation in adult education and one where interest was distinguished as a factor associated with *not* enrolling is presented in a study by Henry and Basile (1994). Some detail of this study will be given as it illustrates the complexity of the relationships between reasons for enrolling and the type of course being undertaken.

The study was concerned with participants in a formal adult education program conducted in a university setting.

> The program offers approximately 250 non-degree, non-credit courses each quarter in areas such as professional and technical training, and personal enrichment. There are 4000-5000 enrolled in a typical year and a comparable number of people who call for information about the course offerings but do not take a course. (Henry & Basile, 1994, p.74)

They presented a model of factors which might contribute to the decision to enrol in these courses including:
– reasons for enrolling (e.g., general interest, job related, meet new people, hobby, recent major life changes),
– sources of information (e.g., mailed brochure, media, friend, co-worker, supervisor),
– course attributes (e.g., type, length, location, instructor etc.)
– deterrents (e.g., distance/travel time, parking, child care, course fees, spare time etc.), and,
– institutional reputation (e.g., attitude toward program, image of program, experience with program etc.).

Their aim was to determine which of these factors distinguished between those who actually enrolled in a course and those who made formal enquiries but did not enrol. The course participant group completed a questionnaire during a class session, and copies of the questionnaire were mailed to the non-participant group.

Analysis of the responses identified six variables that distinguished participants from nonparticipants, those who enrolled from those who had made formal enquiry but had not enrolled. These are listed in order of significance and the direction of the association is shown.
– Meet people and get out of the house (negative)
– General interest in a course (negative)
– Paying your own fees (negative)
– Brochure sent to work (positive)
– Major life changes in the past year (negative)
– Institutional deterrents (negative) (Henry & Basile, 1994, p.77)

These are the variables which showed the greatest difference between the group who decided to enrol and the group who enquired about the course but did not enrol. Where a factor is listed as being negative, this response was more likely to

173

occur in the group who had made a formal enquiry about the course but decided not to enrol. Most of the factors significantly associated with decision to enrol were negative.

Where a factor is listed as positive, this response was more likely to occur in the group who actually enrolled. Only one of the factors was reported to be positive - brochure sent to work. This meant that those potential students who had received the brochure advertising the course in their workplace were more likely to be among those who decided to enrol.

The results indicated interest to be the second strongest factor distinguishing between the participant and non participant groups, and most importantly this association was negative.

> There was a substantially larger number of nonparticipants than participants who were motivated to call for information based on a general interest in a course. The suggestion is that while a general interest is initially a motivation, it is a weak one and leads to nonparticipation. In essence, simply having a general interest in a course does not compel enrolment. (Henry & Basile, 1994, p.78)

In this study the motivation questions were presented as a list of reasons for considering enrolment (general interest, job related, meet new people, hobby, recent major life changes) and the form of statistical analysis which was used required dichotomous variables so each of the variables tested in the model was coded as either present or absent. In this set of possible responses the only one which suggested a focus on the content of the course is "general interest". The authors stated that the "general interest" category was used to cover the sort of reasons which can be grouped as learning for its own sake. However, in this form the study is not able to distinguish "It sounds good I will make some enquiries about it" from "This is something I would really find challenging" and so illustrates something of the ambiguity of meaning of the term interest when used in this way. In Renninger's (1992) terms this form of question does not make any distinction between personal interest and attraction.

The findings of these two very different studies serve to illustrate the complexity of making generalisations about the reasons why adults undertake further education courses. The two studies which have been detailed here were concerned with different forms of adult education, many of the nonparticipants in Henry and Basile's (1994) study took up less formal and less costly alternatives. Responses to questions about reasons for enrolling may highlight different emphases when the research includes those who enquired about a course and did not enrol as well as course participants. However, from the point of view of understanding the place of interest in reasons for enrolling (or considering course enrolment) the research would benefit from clearer definition of the basic interest variable.

Participation and the Development of Interest

It was suggested earlier that questions concerning the development of interest are key questions for our general understanding of the role of interest in learning. Under what conditions will arousal of interest in a specific object of study lead to a more enduring personal interest? When a student becomes actively interested in some aspect of course content, have they been started on a path which can develop into a personal interest? Again any answer will need to take into account the wide range of courses which come under the adult education umbrella. A number of examples will be presented here to illustrate the possibility (rather than the probability) of this happening.

Reports on different parts of the adult education sector often include direct comments from the course participants to convey something of the experience for the learner which has not necessarily been captured in the statistics. One such source is a report (Claydon, 1988) on the development of the U3A (University of the Third Age) movement. From his participation in the formation and development of U3A courses Claydon argued that central to the U3A experience was desire for "extension and active adjustment". Using Houle's (1961) typology to classify the responses from informal questioning of U3A participants, Claydon suggested that the profile of the U3A member was a person of mature years who is motivated by a desire to learn often in combination with other purposes. Learning-oriented and activity-oriented responses were more frequently reported than were goal-oriented responses.

The following brief quotations capture the flavour of responses of U3A participants to questions about learning experiences.

What started as therapy... became and absorbing interest.

I needed some way of maintaining purpose in my life. I found that what I am learning is interesting enough to give me that - I want to know it.

I study some subjects just to open up the 'chance' interest - not necessarily to gain new human relationships or social contact. (Claydon, 1988, pp. 103-105)

Clearly for some of the participants' strong personal interests have developed out of the interesting learning experiences.

People appeared to come to a particular course because it was the sort of thing they thought might interest them if they got to grips with it. After a while it seemed to dawn upon those who persisted with the course that this factor of interest forges a common link. The class contained people who had known each other for years yet this new link changed that social bond. It created a community of shared meaning. (Claydon, 1988, p.105)

While the U3A movement is by no means typical of all the adult education sector reports like this do suggest that there are many examples of interests being developed, maintained and extended. We need to find out more about the ways in which this happens and the circumstances which make it more likely to happen. Achievement of these goals will depend on the success of work which is developing more effective ways of identifying and measuring interest, and appropriate research designs for observing its origins and development.

Constructing the Setting: The Educator's Challenge

There are two general messages for the educator from our current state of understanding of the psychology of interest. Firstly, there are ways in which the learning environment can be structured, ways in which learning tasks and materials can be presented, so that student interest is triggered. Once triggered the challenge for the educator is to be able to provide conditions which will maintain and develop interest and thereby support further learning. How this is done will of course vary according to characteristics of the specific course content as well as the student population. One certain characteristic of the student population will be the fact that they all come to the course with different combinations of goals and different levels of personal interest in the course content.

This leads into the second message; what starts as an attraction or general interest can develop into an absorbing personal interest. We know that this happens and are beginning to understand more of how it happens. Contemporary research into the psychological processes involved when a person becomes interested in a task, or, has a personal interest in an issue promise to fill out more of this detail.

REFERENCES

Ainley, J., Batten, M., Collins, C., & Withers, G. (1998). *Schools and the social development of young Australians*. Melbourne: ACER.

Ainley, M.D. (1987). The factor structure of curiosity measures: Breadth and depth of interest curiosity styles. *Australian Journal of Psychology, 39*, 53- 59.

Ainley, M.D. (1998). Interest in learning and the disposition of curiosity in secondary students: Investigating process and context. In L. Hoffmann, A. Krapp, K.A. Renninger, & J. Baumert (Eds.), *Interest and learning. Proceedings of the Seeon-Conference on Interest and Gender*. IPN-Schriftenreihe Kiel: IPN

Ainley, M., Corrigan, M., & Richardson, N. (2005). Students, tasks and emotions: Identifying the contribution of emotions to students' reading of popular culture and popular science texts. *Learning and Instruction, 15*(5), 433-447.

Ainley, M., Hidi, S., & Berndorff, D. (2002). Interest, learning and the psychological processes that mediate their relationship. *Journal of Educational Psychology, 94*(3), 545-561.

Ainley, M., & Patrick, L. (2006). Measuring self-regulated learning processes through tracking patterns of student interaction with achievement activities. *Educational Psychology Review, 18*, 267-286.

Athanasou, J.A. (1998). Perceptions of interest: A lens model analysis. *Australian Psychologist, 33*, 223- 227.

Berlyne, D.E. (1954). An experimental study of human curiosity. *British Journal of Psychology, 45*, 256- 265.

Berlyne, D.E. (1957). Conflict and information-theory variables as determinants of human perceptual curiosity. *Journal of Experimental Psychology, 53*, 399-404.

Berlyne, D.E. (1958). The influence of complexity and novelty in visual figures on orienting responses. *Journal of Experimental Psychology, 55*, 289-296.

Berlyne, D.E. (1960). *Conflict, arousal and curiosity*. NY: McGraw-Hill.

Berlyne, D.E. (1962). Uncertainty and epistemic curiosity. *British Journal of Psychology, 53* (1), 27-34.

Berlyne, D.E. (1963). Complexity and incongruity variables as determinants of exploratory choice and evaluative ratings. *Canadian Journal of Psychology, 17*, 274-290.

Beswick, D.G. (1971). Cognitive process theory of individual differences in curiosity. In H.I. Day, D.E. Berlyne, & D.E. Hunt (Eds.). *Intrinsic motivation: A new direction in education*. Toronto: Holt, Rinehart and Winston of Canada.

Claydon, L.F. (1988). The mature student and learning. In D.E. Graves (Ed.) *Proceedings of the First National Conference on Lifelong Learning*. Melbourne: U3A.

Courtney, S. (1992). *Why adults learn: Towards a theory of participation in adult education*. London: Routledge.

Cross, K.P.(1981). *Adults as learners*. San Francisco, Calif.: Jossey-Bass.

Day, H.I. (1971). The measurement of specific curiosity. In H.I. Day, D.E. Berlyne, & D.E. Hunt (Eds.), *Intrinsic motivation: A new direction in education*. Toronto: Holt, Rinehart and Winston of Canada.

de Charms, R. (1968). *Personal causation: The internal affective determinants of behavior*. NY: Academic press.

de Charms, R. (1984). Motivation enhancement in educational settings. In R. Ames & C. Ames (Eds.), *Research on motivation in education* (Vol. 1, pp. 275-310). NY: Academic Press.

Deci, E.L. (1992). The relation of interest to the motivation of behavior: A self-determination theory perspective. In K.A. Renninger, S. Hidi, & A. Krapp, (Eds.), *The role of interest in learning and development*. Hillsdale, NJ: Lawrence Erlbaum.

Deci, E.L. (1998). In L. Hoffmann, A. Krapp, K.A. Renninger, & J. Baumert (Eds.), *Interest and learning. Proceedings of the Seeon-Conference on Interest and Gender*. IPN-Schriftenreihe Kiel: IPN

Deci, E.L., Ryan, R.M., & Williams, G.C. (1996). Need satisfaction and the self-regulation of learning. *Learning and Individual Differences, 8,* 165-183.

Deci, E.L., & Ryan, R. M. (1985). *Intrinsic motivation and self-determination in human behavior.* NY: Plenum.

Harlow, H. (1953). Mice, monkeys, men and motives. *Psychological Review, 60,* 23-32.

Henry, G.T., & Basile, K.C. (1994). Understanding the decision to participate in formal adult education. *Adult Education Quarterly, 44*(2), 64-82.

Hidi, S. (1990). Interest and its contribution as a mental resource for learning. *Review of Educational Research, 60,* 549-571.

Hidi, S. & Baird, W. (1983). Types of information saliency in school texts and their effect on children's recall. Paper presented at the National Reading Conference, Austin TX.

Hidi, S. & Baird, W. (1986). Interestingness - A neglected variable in discourse processing. *Cognitive Science, 10,* 179-194.

Hidi, S., & Renninger, K. A. (2006). The four-phase model of interest development. *Educational Psychologist, 41*(2), 111-127.

Houle, C. (1961). *The inquiring mind.* Madison: University of Wisconsin Press.

Hunt, J. McV. (1963). Motivation inherent in information processing and action. In O. J. Harvey (Ed.), *Motivation and social interaction: Cognitive determinants* (pp. 35-94). NY: Ronald.

Hunt, J. McV. (1971) Towards a history of intrinsic motivation. In H. I. Day, D. E. Berlyne, & D. E. Hunt (Eds.). *Intrinsic motivation: A new direction in education.* Toronto: Holt, Rinehart and Winston of Canada.

Husen, T. (1995). *The learning society.* London: Pergamon.

Krapp, A. (1994). Interest and curiosity. The role of interest in a theory of exploratory action. In H. Keller, K. Schneider, & B. Henderson (Eds.), *Curiosity and exploration.* Berlin: Springer-Verlag.

Krapp, A. & Fink, B. (1992). The development and function of interests during the critical transition from home to preschool. In K.A. Renninger, S. Hidi, & A. Krapp, (Eds.), *The role of interest in learning and development.* Hillsdale, NJ: Lawrence Erlbaum.

Krapp, A., Hidi, S., & Renninger, A. (1992). Interest, learning and development. In K. A. Renninger, S. Hidi, & A. Krapp (Eds.), *The role of interest in learning and development.* Hillsdale, NJ: Lawrence Erlbaum.

Lepper, M.R. & Cordova, D.I. (1992). A desire to be taught: Instructional consequences of intrinsic motivation. *Motivation and Emotion, 16,* 187-208.

Lepper, M.R., & Hodell, M. (1989). Intrinsic motivation in the classroom. In C. Ames & R. Ames (Eds.), *Research on motivation in education* (Vol. 3, pp. 73-105). San Diego: Academic Press.

Parliament of the Commonwealth of Australia. (1991). *Come in Cinderella: The emergence of adult and community education.* Report by the Senate Standing Committee on Employment, Education and Training.

Peters, L. (1994). *A study of outcomes for students participating in adult education at the Council of Adult Education.* Melbourne: CAE.

Pintrich, P.R., & Schunk, D.H. (1996). *Motivation in education: Theory, research, and applications.* Englewood Cliffs, NJ: Prentice Hall.

Prenzel, M. (1992). The selective persistence of interest. In K.A. Renninger, S. Hidi, & A. Krapp, (Eds.). *The role of interest in learning and development.* Hillsdale, NJ: Lawrence Erlbaum Associates.

Renninger, A. (1992). Individual interest and development: Implications for theory and practice. In K.A. Renninger, S. Hidi, & A. Krapp, (Eds.), *The role of interest in learning and development.* Hillsdale, NJ: Lawrence Erlbaum Associates.

Ryan, R. M., & Deci, E. L. (2000). Intrinsic and extrinsic motivations: Classic definitions and new directions. *Contemporary Educational Psychology, 25*, 54-67.

Sansone, C., & Morgan, C. (1992). Intrinsic motivation and education: Competence in context. *Motivation and Emotion, 16*, 249-270.

Schiefele, U., & Krapp, A. (1996). Topic interest and free recall of expository text. *Learning and Individual Differences, 8*, 141-160.

Valsiner, J. (1992). Interest: A metatheoretical perspective. In K.A. Renninger, S. Hidi, & A. Krapp, (Eds.), *The role of interest in learning and development.* Hillsdale, NJ: Lawrence Erlbaum Associates.

Review Questions

The following questions are designed to test your understanding of the content of this chapter. Answers can all be checked by referring to the relevant sections.

1. What are the typical characteristics of the active state of interest?
2. Distinguish between individual or personal interest and situational interest.
3. According to Berlyne curiosity is the motive and exploratory behaviour the outcome. What specific stimulus characteristics have been found to arouse curiosity?
4. Cognitive theorists (e.g., Hunt) explained curiosity in terms of cognitive uncertainty. Describe what is happening, according to this theory, when a person encounters something ambiguous.
5. Describe how the trait approach to curiosity is different from Berlyne's theory of curiosity.
6. Describe the essential characteristics which distinguish intrinsic motivation from extrinsic motivation.
7. Name and describe the three types of learners identified by Houle (1961).
8. For each of Houle's three types of learners indicate what balance of intrinsic and extrinsic motivation is typical.
9. What difference in meaning of 'interest' is suggested by the following statements? Student 1: "I enquired about the course on computer animation out of general interest." Student 2: "I am interested in animation and want to find out about the course on computer animation."
10. Both students enrol in the course. What will the difference in their interest mean for the way they participate in the course?

For the following questions you need to have a specific learning task in mind.

11. Challenge, curiosity, control, and fantasy have been shown to be important features of the way learning tasks are structured for arousing intrinsic motivation. Describe how you might go about using these characteristics in the way you structure a specific learning task.
12. Describe some examples of student behaviour which would be appropriate indicators that students are interested in the learning task you have designed for them.
13. What specific student actions would be indicators that you have triggered interest in the subject and that this is developing into a personal interest?
14. What might you do to support the triggered interest to develop into a strong personal interest?

15. Extend your knowledge of the character of student interest in your course or subject by seeking out a recent survey of the reasons given for student enrolments in your course(s). What is the balance of intrinsic and extrinsic motivation, and, individual interest behind these enrolments?

About the Author

Mary Ainley is an Associate Professor in Psychology in the School of Behavioural Science at the University of Melbourne. She has had involvement at all levels of education including some time as Chair of one of the former Regional Councils of Adult, Community and Further Education in Victoria. Her major research interests concern investigation of the psychological processes that are involved in curiosity, interest, and various forms of engagement with learning. She has collaborated extensively with Dr. Suzanne Hidi of the University of Toronto on developing measures of the active state of interest in order to further understanding of the roles of individual and situational interest in the development and maintenance of student learning.

Mary Ainley
University of Melbourne

GERARD J. FOGARTY

8. INTELLIGENCE: THEORIES AND ISSUES

Of all the areas of psychology, intelligence is probably the most controversial. At the same time, it is also one of the oldest areas of the discipline, dating back to the 1880s with the work of Francis Galton on individual differences in sensory functioning. It is impossible to capture in a single chapter the immense body of theorising and research that has been devoted to the topic of intelligence. The aims of this chapter are considerably more modest: (a) to give a brief historical overview of the area; (b) to show how developments in the field are tied to the methodologies used to study intelligence; (c) to describe current approaches to intelligence; and (d) to introduce the reader to some of the main controversies in the area. This chapter will trace the developments of the construct, from Spearman's (1904) early conceptions of intelligence as mental energy to the much broader conceptions of modern day theorists. The chapter will also deal with the wider social context and the implications of our understanding of intelligence for society in general. As will be seen, it is not an easy construct to understand but it cannot be ignored because, along with personality, it is one of the most fundamental aspects of the human psyche.

Why Is Intelligence Such an Important Topic?

What sets the area of mental abilities apart is the perceived importance of these abilities in our daily lives. We accept that we are physically stronger or weaker than other people, but few of us care much that someone is stronger or weaker than we are. It doesn't make a great deal of difference to our lives. In the cognitive domain, however, we are constantly compared with others; we compete with each other at a cognitive level for the best courses at universities, the best jobs, and for the best partners in life. Gottfredson (1997) stated "...no other ability has been shown to have such generality or pervasiveness of effect as does intelligence" (p.6).

James A Athanasou (ed.), Adult Educational Psychology, 181–208
© *2008 Sense Publishers. All rights reserved.*

The ancient Greeks were aware of the concept of intelligence, the Chinese before them, and every culture since. Former Australian Prime Minister, Bob Hawke, used the term "clever country" to describe his vision of what kind of a nation he thought Australia should become. Newspapers, particularly the Sunday variety, often contain stories on some new wonder drug or some new training programme that can increase intelligence. The popular media is also fascinated by displays of intelligence: children who can perform amazing computational feats, quiz show marvels who can recall facts with astonishing speed, musical and artistic prodigies, and so on. However, if we are to heed the advice of our former leader, and aspire to be clever, we must begin with some understanding of what the term means. As we shall see, it tends to mean different things to different people.

Definitions of Intelligence

A satisfactory definition of intelligence has always proved elusive. A symposium of 17 experts in the field convened by the editor of the *Journal of Educational Psychology* in 1921 to discuss the meaning of intelligence came up with almost as many interpretations as there were experts present. Intelligence was variously described as "ability to learn" (Buckingham), as "the power of good responses from the point of view of truth or fact" (Thorndike), as "the ability to carry on abstract thinking" (Terman), as "the ability of the individual to adapt himself adequately to relatively new situations in life" (Pintner), as "involving two factors - the capacity for knowledge and the knowledge possessed" (Henmon), as "the capacity to acquire capacity" (Woodrow).

Carroll (1993), to whom the author is indebted for the above information, reported that a similar symposium was convened in 1986 by Sternberg and Detterman to update the findings of the 1921 symposium. Twenty-five experts at the 1986 symposium came up with almost as many views of intelligence. Intelligence was described as "a quality of adaptive behaviour" (Anastasi), as "the end product of development in the cognitive-psychological domain", as "a societal concept that operates in several domains - academic, technical, social, and practical" (Carroll), as "error-free transmission of information through the cortex" (Eysenck), as "acquired proficiency" (Glaser), as "mental self-government" (Sternberg). Carroll (1993) reported that "the symposium did not produce any definitive definition of intelligence, nor was it expected to" (p. 36). This second symposium did, however, reflect some of the newer views of intelligence, such as metacognition (the ability to understand and control oneself), emphasising the fact that views of intelligence are changing over time.

In a recent review of human abilities, Sternberg and Kaufman (1988) threw the definitional problem wide open by reminding us that non-Western views of intelligence may differ quite markedly from those expressed above. The Western emphasis on speed (see later sections of this chapter), for example, is not shared by many cultures. Questions of definition become more difficult if one moves beyond the human sphere to consider whether or not intelligence is something that is shared with other species. The Greek philosopher Anaxagoras believed that all animals have intelligence, but humans were superior. Aristotle arranged the animal species in a hierarchy with man at the top. During the middle ages, Christian theology dominated thinking about such issues and the doctrine of special creation replaced the view of continuity in nature. The doctrine separated animals and humans by the presence of a soul in humans and by the human's capability for reason. The emergence of Darwin's theory of evolution in the late 19th century brought humans and animals together again on the same continuum. Darwin stated that the difference between the mind of a human and that of the highest animal was one of degree and not of kind. Two books bearing the title "Animal Intelligence" were published in the 19th Century.

Contemporary views of intelligence in animals are more flexible. Herman and Pack (1994) reported on a number of research programmes studying the behaviour of pigeons, chimpanzees, rats, and dolphins. These programmes have demonstrated that dolphins can remember lists of sounds and show the same primary and recency effects as humans; pigeons can reliably place classes of objects in different perceptual categories; vervet monkeys use different vocalisations to refer to four different types of predators; dolphins can learn to understand sequences of human commands where understanding depends on the meaning of words and word order; a variety of different species can learn various counting tasks; wild chimpanzees appear to actually tutor their young in the art of nut-cracking; different animal species can show "deceitful" behaviour; for example, feigning injury to lure predators away from young.

The list goes on. How these various displays of apparently intelligent behaviour relate to the concept of intelligence is still problematical. To keep matters as uncomplicated as possible, this chapter will leave the definition of intelligence open and deal only with research relating to human intelligence. The origins of that research date back to the end of the 1800s.

Theories of Intelligence

There are too many theories of intelligence to cover in a single chapter but some have been much more influential than others. These will be summarised in the following section.

Spearman's One-factor Theory
The figure normally associated with the origins of the concept of intelligence is Francis Galton who, in the late 1 800s, was using tests of sensory discrimination to measure intellectual ability, often judged at that time by teachers' ratings. The idea of using such simple tests would strike many people today as being naive but Galton was anything but naive. Howard (1991) reported that at the age of four he wrote this letter to his sister:

My Dear Adele,

I am four years old and can read any English book. I can say all the Latin substantives and adjectives and active verbs besides 52 lines of Latin poetry. I can cast up any sum in addition and can multiply by 2, 3, 4, 5, 6, 7, 8, 9, 10, 11. I can also say the pence table. I read French a little and I know the clock.

Quite clearly, Galton did not suffer from a lack of intelligence himself! The logic of using sensory measures was sound enough. All information comes to use via the senses and the quality of our mental processes will depend to some extent on the quality of the sensory input. It followed, therefore, that those with better sensory discrimination processes could well have better quality mental processes as well. Logic notwithstanding, Galton's simple tests did not discriminate between so-called "intelligent" and "non-intelligent" people. Nevertheless, his views were influential and most of his contemporaries followed his lead in exploring intelligence through basic sensory functions. Charles Spearman, one of the leading figures in the history of intelligence, began his illustrious career using these same sensory discrimination tests.

The first real breakthrough in the field of intelligence stemmed from a practical problem in the French education system. Following the introduction of universal education in this country, there was a need to identify students who had learning difficulties. Alfred Binet was given the task of developing psychological and physical diagnostic procedures for determining retardation and he took the unusual step of developing a thirty-problem test that measured several abilities related to intellect, such as judgement and reasoning. The break from measures of sensory ability was important because, unlike the earlier sensory tests, scores on Binet's test did correspond with other ratings of intelligence. The popularity of Binet's tests - they were soon used in other countries as well - proved to be a much-needed stimulus for research on the nature of intelligence itself. In one of those accidents of history, about the time that Binet published his test (1904), one of the major figures in the field of intelligence, Charles Spearman, began publishing articles on his theory of intelligence. As Brody (1992) put it, "Spearman provided a theory and Binet provided a test" (p. 8).

Spearman was an English engineer and army officer who became interested in psychology late in life. He proposed a theory of intelligence that became known as the two-factor theory (Spearman 1904, 1927). In keeping with his engineering background, Spearman saw intelligence as comprising a central pool of energy that was required for all cognitive tasks. This was the first of his factors, a general factor that he labelled 'g'. In addition to the general factor, each task has something unique to itself, a specific factor. Spearman likened the second of his factors to engines, with an engine for every task. Thus, when a person attempts a mathematical problem, it is 'g' that provides the energy for the operation and a specific mathematical engine that is responsible for the execution of the task. People differ in the amount they have of each and it is these differences that explain the variation we observe between individuals on cognitive tasks.

Spearman's two-factor theory of intelligence has been extremely influential because he developed techniques for measuring the extent to which a test measured 'g' - its "loading" or "saturation". Some tests measured it very well, others hardly at all. Spearman knew, for example, that 'g' could not be measured very well by tests of sensory discrimination, as Galton had tried to do. It could be measured by tests of comprehension, memory, and reasoning. Spearman recognised that the best predictors of academic ability were tests that required the "eduction of relations and correlates" which he defined as follows:

> The eduction of relations ... when a person has in mind any two or more ideas ... he has more or less power to bring to mind any relations that sensibly hold between them.

> It is instanced whenever a person becomes aware, say that beer tastes something like weak quinine ... or that the proposition " all A is B' proves the proposition "Some A is B".

The eduction of correlates ... when a person has in mind any idea together with a relation, he has more or less power to bring up into mind the correlative idea.

For example, let anyone hear a musical note and try to imagine the note a fifth higher ...(Spearman, 1927, pp. 165-166, cited in Brody, 1992).

The problem was that Spearman was describing processes that could not be observed directly. What he could observe directly were the scores that people were obtaining on tests that he was developing to measure 'g'. He could also observe, as others had done before him, whether there was any correspondence between scores on tests of 'g' and academic achievement. One of Spearman's major criticisms of earlier work on intelligence was that it did not use quantitative indices of the degree of relationship between different measures. Spearman was the first to actually use correlations as the raw data upon which a theory of intelligence is based. For those who may be unfamiliar with the concept of correlation, a brief description follows.

A correlation coefficient can take values from 1.00 to -100. A correlation of 1.00 between any two tests means that they are perfectly related. If you knew how well a person performed on one test, you would know how well they performed on the other. For example, if a child topped the class on the first test, a correlation of 1.00 necessarily implies that the child tops the class on the other test. A correlation of -1.00 also indicates a perfect relationship but this time in an inverse manner. Thus, if a child came top of the class on one test that same child would necessarily be at the bottom of the class on the other test. The actual index of correlation is usually somewhere between these perfect extremes. The closer the index is to 1.00 or -1.00, the stronger the relationship between the variables. The closer to zero, the weaker the relationship, until at 0.0 there is no relationship at all between the variables.

For Spearman, the correlations among the tests he used were the data his theories had to explain. One thing struck Spearman quite forcibly: there were no inverse correlations among his cognitive measures. He used the term "positive manifold" to describe the tendency for all cognitive tasks to be positively correlated. To observe that two tests are positively correlated is one thing, to explain it is another. One explanation for the observation of a correlation is that performance on the two tests is driven by the same underlying ability. In fact, this is one of the foundations of theory building in the field of individual differences, of which intelligence forms a part. Spearman's observation that all cognitive tests are positively correlated led him to claim that despite obvious differences in the content of the tests (e.g., some measuring word knowledge, others spatial ability), they all rely to some extent upon 'g'. Thus, to a very large extent, Spearman's two-factor theory was driven by his attempt to explain the phenomenon of positive manifold. He did so by stressing the importance of a dominant single factor. As I mentioned earlier, the specific factors were added to the theory to account for differences due to unique operations called for by each test.

It is important to recognise the empirical basis for Spearman's theory. There is no doubting the fact that cognitive tests do tend to be positively correlated. Where subsequent theorists have differed from Spearman is in their accounts of what it is that all tests have in common and how much emphasis should be placed on the general factor. Spearman's description of 'g' as mental energy was disputed by one of his contemporaries, Godfrey Thompson, who argued that there was a large set of independent bonds or units in the mind. Any test of ability samples some of these bonds. The correlations that Spearman explained in terms of sharing a central energy source were explained by Thompson as tasks sharing the same bonds. Thus, if two tests sample a large number of bonds, by the laws of chance some of these will be the same and it is the sharing that accounts for the observed correlations. Thompson explained the obvious individual differences in intelligence by claiming that each individual possessed only a subset of the universe of bonds and that individuals differed in the number of bonds or units of intelligence they possessed (Brody, 1992).

Other accounts of the tendency for all cognitive tasks to be positively correlated have arisen over the years. For the most part, they have followed Spearman's lead in looking for a single entity that is shared by all cognitive tasks. Hunt (1980), for example, likened the concept of attention to that of 'g'. As Hunt knew, however, the comparison did not help to clarify the nature of intelligence because attention is just as elusive a concept as intelligence. An alternative interpretation of 'g' is that it reflects the ability of the individual to organise processing strategies to face new kinds of mental problems. This account of intelligence is reflected in the work of information processing theorists who stress the importance of metacognition as a component of intelligence (e.g., Sternberg, 1979). What follows from metacognition are planfulness, self-monitoring, and inventiveness, each of which can be thought of as hallmarks of intelligent behaviour.

In a similar vein, it has been suggested that the primary difference between persons of normal intelligence and the mentally retarded lies in the degree to which people are able to develop and use information processing strategies (Belmont, Buttefield, & Ferretti, 1982). They postulated a process called "Executive Functioning" which monitors and controls these strategies. Detterman (1982) pointed out that executive functioning is analogous to the general intelligence factor since its effects should be evident in every sort of mental test or cognitive task.

More recent research on intelligence has also been used to support Spearman's notion of a central factor of intelligence. Brody (1992) reported on research that relates individual differences in intelligence to measures of the overall metabolism of the brain. Interestingly, these studies still rely on correlational data. The research shows a high negative correlation between a measure of energy expenditure of the brain and scores on a test of abstract reasoning ability. In other words, more intelligent people do not expend as much energy on the task. "These findings may be viewed as providing support for a contemporary version of Spearman's theory of mental energy" (Brody, 1992, p. 12). A number of modern researchers have gone one step further than this and are searching for the basic processes that constitute 'g'.

The debate between Spearman and Thompson is characteristic of other debates that have occurred in the history of this branch of the discipline of psychology. The problem with correlational data is that different interpretations are always possible and both Spearman's and Thompson's theories were able to account for the data generated by early studies of intelligence. Before long, however, it became evident that Spearman's theory of a single factor of intelligence that accounted for all observed correlations among tests could not be correct. The need for mass testing of recruits during the First World War had given the testing movement a lot of impetus and many new tests had been developed. It soon became increasingly obvious that groups of tests tended to have more in common with each other than their 'g' loadings suggested they would. A set of spatial tests, for example, which might not be very good measures of 'g', tended to be highly correlated with each other. The same could be said for groups of verbal tests, numerical tests, and so on. As the data accumulated, it became clear that Spearman's two-factor theory of intelligence could not account for the data. The only possible explanation was that tests could be correlated for reasons other than their dependence on 'g'.

Thurstone's Theory of Primary Mental Abilities
Spearman was aware of the evidence accumulating against his two-factor theory but he continued to emphasise the importance of the general factor. The real challenge to his theory came in the person of U.S. psychologist, Thurstone (1938), who used his own versions of the new technique of factor analysis to demonstrate that there was not one underlying ability but a number of independent abilities. In order to understand the basis for his challenge, a brief introduction to factor analysis is necessary.

Mention was made earlier of the fact that correlations are the data upon which early theories of intelligence were based. When there are many tests in a study, however, there are also very many correlations. A study that includes 10 intelligence tests will generate 45 inter-test correlations. Many studies of intelligence contain far more than 10 tests. To overcome the problem of trying to analyse so many correlations simultaneously, Thurstone (1947) developed a technique known as multiple factor analysis (MFA). MFA is a mathematical tool that detects patterns of correlations among the tests in the study. Most textbooks describe factor analysis as a technique that is mainly used to reduce a large set of variables to a smaller underlying set of dimensions. One of the requirements of a successful factor analysis is that the underlying dimensions explain most of the intercorrelations among the input variables. The details of how it does this need not concern us here but it is important to have some understanding of how factor analysis works. Consider the following example.

Table 8.1 *Descriptive statistics and correlations among cognitive variables (N = 126)*

Tests	M	SD	R1	R2	R3	V1	V2	V3	S1	S2
R1		3.01	1.00							
R2	9.02	3.76	.73	1.00						
R3	11.34	3.68	.58	.51	1.00					
V1	5.33	1.68	.35	.31	.27	1.00				
V2	10.22	4.18	.36	.39	.34	.56	1.00			
V3	10.51	4.08	.28	.22	.39	.51	.54	1.00		
S1	6.63	2.89	.30	.24	.12	.10	.32	.21	1.00	
S2	11.37	3.68	.26	.32	.16	.22	.30	.19	.50	1.00
S3	14.19	3.75	.36	.37	.20	.16	.39	.27	.54	.62

Here are some data that I collected many years ago on three measures of reasoning ability (R1 to R3 in 8.1), three measures of verbal ability (V1 to V3), and three measures of spatial ability (S1 to S3). The means, standard deviations, and correlations are presented in Table 8.1.

To those not familiar with statistics, Table 8.1 contains the names of the nine tests in the first row and in the first column. The means and standard deviations of the tests are shown in columns two and three. The remainder of the table is a correlation matrix, showing the type of data that formed the basis for much of the research on the nature of intelligence. Boxes have been drawn around the correlations among each of the three subsets of tests so that they will stand out more clearly.

If you examine the correlations among all of the tests, one feature is immediately apparent: they are all positively correlated. These positive correlations illustrate the phenomenon that Spearman labelled *positive manifold*. However, if you look closely within each box you can see that the reasoning tests are more highly correlated among themselves than they are with the other tests in the battery. The same is true of the verbal and spatial tests, suggesting that there must be factors other than 'g' that cause tests to be correlated. In the present instance, it looks very much as though the data are suggesting that all the tests have something in common because they are all correlated. In addition, the data suggest that reasoning tests have something else in common amongst themselves that helps to explain their higher inter-correlations. The same is true for the verbal and spatial tests.

It was data sets like this that prompted Thurstone to develop his model of separate mental abilities. Using his own version of MFA, Thurstone analysed correlations obtained from large batteries of tests and concluded that there was not a single factor of intelligence but a set of primary mental abilities. With the dataset shown in Table 8.1 (Fogarty, 1984), it is possible to illustrate how he reached this conclusion. Using a modern factor analysis program on a laptop computer, the output shown in Table 8.2 was obtained.

Factor analysis is essentially a data reduction technique: it is designed to find an underlying set of factors that can explain performance on a set of observed variables. In this case, the observed variables are the nine tests administered to 126 people. If Spearman was correct, only one underlying factor ('g') would be needed to explain the correlations among the nine tests. If Thurstone was correct, a number of factors would be needed to explain the correlations. We can see from Table 8.2, that the output from factor analysis suggests that three factors are needed to explain performance on these tests and the correlations among them.

Table 8.2 *Factor analysis of reasoning, verbal, and spatial tests using varimax rotation*

Tests	Factors		
	1	2	3
R1	**.878**	.210	.177
R2	**.736**	.258	.179
R3	**.586**	.006	.301
V1	.233	.001	**.685**
V2	.211	.295	**.699**
V3	.145	.146	**.688**
S1	.140	**.637**	.111
S2	.112	**.715**	.140
S3	.185	**.802**	.154

The tests themselves are listed in the first column. The numbers in the next three columns indicate the extent to which a particular test depends on each of the three factors. Thus, the first reasoning test (R1), depends very much on Factor 1 because it has a high loading of.878 on this factor. It has low loadings on Factors 2 and 3, so does not depend very much on these two factors. We need to look at what other tests are loading on this factor to suggest what it might represent. Tests R2 and R3 are the only other ones that have high loadings on Factor 1, so we can call it a reasoning factor. Test R1 was actually a Number Series test, R2 a Letter Series test, and R3 a test called Sets. All three are known to measure reasoning ability, so it is not surprising to us that they group together in a factor analysis.

The last three variables (S1, S2, and S3) were all different kinds of spatial test. We can see that performance on these three tests depends very much on individual differences on Factor 2, and very little on the other two factors. We can feel quite safe declaring that Factor 2 represents spatial ability. Test V1 was a Spelling test, V2 a Scrambled Words test, and V3 a Hidden Words test. All three have high loadings on Factor 3 and low loadings on Factors 1 and 2, so we can say that performance on all three of these tests is driven by the same underlying factor. Because it is quite obvious what the three tests have in common, we can also suggest that Factor 3 represents verbal ability.

Set out in this way, the results of a factor analysis might appear trivial and uninformative. Select three tests of reasoning ability, three tests of verbal ability, and three tests of spatial ability and then subject the resulting inter-correlation matrix to factor analysis and one should hardly be surprised that the analysis identifies three underlying factors corresponding to the ones used to select the tests in the first place. True enough, but turn the clock back to the late 1920s and early 1930s when terms such as "verbal ability" had no empirical basis and it is possible to see what a powerful tool factor analysis was to researchers in this field. By constructing tests that used different content and different processes, forming correlation matrices among the tests, and then subjecting the matrices to factor analyses, theorists were able to gain an impression of how many underlying factors were needed to account for variations in performance on cognitive tasks.

Thurstone placed great reliance on the techniques of MFA to refine his model of intelligence. From the data collected in studies involving a large number and variety of cognitive tests (56 in his first study), Thurstone (1938, 1947) concluded that intelligence was made up of seven independent primary mental abilities which were labelled S (Space), P (Perceptual Speed), N (Number Facility), V (Verbal Relations), W (Word Fluency), M (Memory), and I (Induction - i.e., reasoning). The number of abilities is not actually crucial to Thurstone's theory. It really does not matter if the true number is more or less than seven, what was important in Thurstone's early formulation of his Primary Mental Abilities (PMA) theory is that the abilities were described as independent, implying that you could be strong in one ability area and very weak in another. Not surprisingly, Spearman hotly disputed this point of view. Spearman had certainly realised that it was possible to identify factors other than 'g' but it was a long step from this position to one in which 'g' was ignored completely and abilities were said to be numerous and independent.

As has been the case so often in this field of psychology, the reason for the differences between these two contrasting views of intelligence had its roots in the methodology employed. Spearman used a technique of factor analysis that highlighted the importance of what was common to all tests, whereas Thurstone used a technique that maximised the chances of tests arranging themselves into independent groups. The three factors shown in Table 8.2 were obtained by a technique known in factor analysis as "orthogonal rotation". The mechanics of this technique need not concern us here but we can note that the factors that come out of such an analysis are bound to be uncorrelated. A different technique of rotation allows factors to be correlated. This technique is recommended by many researchers because it does not impose constraints on the factors: they can be uncorrelated or correlated.

In order to see the effect that different techniques of factor analysis can have, the data shown in Table 8.1 were reanalysed, this time allowing the factors to be correlated. The resulting factor analytic solution was much the same as that shown in Table 8.1. If anything, this second solution was even easier to interpret than the first. The important difference between the two solutions is that the second solution produced a factor intercorrelation matrix showing that the correlation between Factor 1 and Factor 2 was .395, between Factor 1 and Factor 3 the correlation was .512, and between Factors 2 and 3, the correlation was .354. This was the important fact that Thurstone had overlooked in this early work: it is possible to factor analyse a correlation matrix so that tests form groups that measure primary mental abilities, rather than a single general factor of intelligence, but these primary mental abilities are themselves correlated. The proponents of the single factor theory of intelligence were quick to claim that the cause of the correlation among these abilities was 'g'. The arrangement implied by this suggestion is shown in Figure 8.1.

Figure 8.1 *Depiction of relationships between tests, primary factors, and a general factor.*

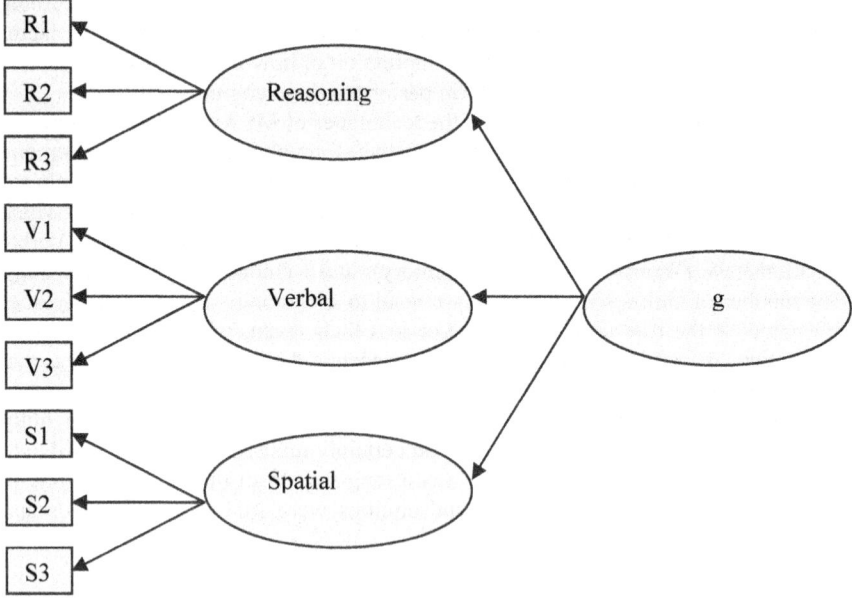

Figure 8.1 shows that performance on tests used by Fogarty (1984) is driven by individual differences on the underlying reasoning, verbal, and spatial abilities. Performance on these abilities is in turn driven by individual differences in 'g'. Quite obviously, models of this type can be extended to include a larger number of tests and primary abilities. Such models represent a compromise between the positions of Spearman and Thurstone. They indicate that it is possible to have both primary mental abilities and a general factor of intelligence. The exercise that we have just completed with a subset of the author's own data was a re-enactment of analyses that were being conducted by a number of psychologists in the late 1930s and early 1940s. Eysenck (1939) re-analysed Thurstone's data using factor analytic techniques that did allow the 'g' factor to emerge. He found strong evidence for both a 'g' factor and for the same primary mental abilities that Thurstone had found. Cattell (1941) indicated that Spearman's theory and Thurstone's theory might be reconciled by postulating the existence of a hierarchical structure of ability. A number of very influential hierarchical models emerged in the 1940s, 50s, and 60s.

Hierarchical Models of Intelligence
The first well-acknowledged hierarchical model of intelligence was proposed by Phillip E. Vernon, a colleague of Spearman's. Vernon (1950) described a structure which placed 'g' at the top of an inverted tree-like figure. Immediately below 'g' were two other broad abilities, v:ed (verbal-educational) and k:m (spatial-mechanical-practical). Branching out from each of these were narrower group factors. For example, verbal ability was viewed as a narrow group factor located under the v:ed broad group factor and spatial ability was a narrow group factor under the k:m group. More specific abilities were located at a lower level still. Although, his model allowed various kinds of group factors, some broader than others, Vernon still felt that 'g' was the major determinant of individual differences in performance on cognitive tasks.

At about the same time that Vernon was developing his hierarchical theory of intelligence, another major figure emerged who was to initiate the work that led to what is now widely regarded as the dominant model of intelligence in the world today. Raymond Cattell was a student of Spearman's who moved to the U.S. and commenced work on both factor analysis and theories of intelligence. Like Vernon, Cattell believed that there was more than one higher-order factor. His view was that there were two kinds of intelligences: "fluid" (General Fluid: Gf) and "crystallised" (General Crystallised: Gc). Fluid intelligence was measured by tests that were assumed to measure the biological capacity of the individual to acquire knowledge. Reasoning processes were an important part of this ability. Crystallised intelligence, was defined by tests that were assumed to measure the influence of schooling and acculturation. Tests of general knowledge and vocabulary measure Gc. Thus, in a sense, crystallised intelligence represents the store of an individual's knowledge and skills whereas Gf represents the processes that helped the individual to acquire these knowledge and skills. The model proposed by Cattell bore some similarities to the model put forward by Donald Hebb (1949), who suggested that there are three kinds of intelligence: Intelligence A, that which we are born with, representing our innate potential; Intelligence B, representing the functioning of the brain as a result of the development that has occurred; and

Intelligence C, representing measured intelligence. The first two of these are similar to Cattell's fluid and crystallised intelligences.

It was not until 1963 that Cattell gave a more complete account of his theory. In doing so, he was careful to look for more than just statistical evidence that the structure he proposed was valid. Gf was said to have a more biological basis than Gc. Indeed, it is defined by one author as "one's native, biologically endowed ability" (Howard, 1991, p.38). Thus, in the early stages of life, Gf helps to shape Gc. Later in life, as the brain began to deteriorate, Gf shows a decline. That is, it becomes harder for people to engage in the abstract reasoning processes that form the basis of some kinds of knowledge. Gc, on the other hand, is less affected by physical deterioration of the brain and certain types of knowledge can continue to develop virtually throughout one's lifespan.

Cattell was not the first to propose a distinction between two broad abilities of this type but his theory generated predictions, such as age-related decline in Gf, that were supported by empirical findings. His theory also attracted capable adherents, such as his student John Horn, who were able to take the model to new levels of development. Horn (1985) maintained the distinction between Gf and Gc but reinterpreted their meaning somewhat, especially Gf. Horn did not believe that Gf was a biological ability factor and he did not believe that there was a causal pathway leading from Gf to Gc, even early in life. Instead, both Gf and Gc are characterised by processes of reasoning, concept formation, and problem solving. The main difference is that Gf depends relatively little on the effects of formal education and cultural experiences (Stankov, Boyle, & Cattell, 1995).

The complexity of the Gf/Gc model has increased considerably since the first description by Cattell (1963). Figure 8.2 shows how the model looked to Horn (1985). The model is not exactly as depicted by Horn, it has been simplified somewhat to suit our purposes, but captures the main features of Gf/ Gc theory. A quick glance over this model shows how it seeks to explain much of what is already known about intelligence. To begin with, it is a hierarchical model. Notice, however, that there is no 'g' at the top of the hierarchy. Horn has a particular aversion to the notion of a general factor of intelligence, especially because of the way in which the concept of ' g' has been used to promote racist views. We will return to this controversy later in the chapter. As Carroll (1993) pointed out, however, if 'g' is ignored or denied, the theory does not really have an explanation for the correlation (about.50) that exists between Gf and Gc. Brody (1992) raised this same criticism.

The centre of Figure 8.2 contains circles enclosing the main second-order factors. Notice that there are nine broad second-order factors in this model and that they are not shown in an inverted tree-like structure but rather in something that bears more resemblance to a chart. The left hand side of the chart shows a vertical line depicting the sequence of development from infancy to adulthood whilst the right hand side shows another vertical line representing the complexity of the processes at each level. Gf and Gc appear at the top of the hierarchy and they are characterised by what Horn calls "deep processing" operations. Spearman's eduction of relations and correlates exemplify the types of cognitive processes one would find at this level.

Figure 8.2. Representation of Horn's theory of intelligence (adapted from Horn, 1985).

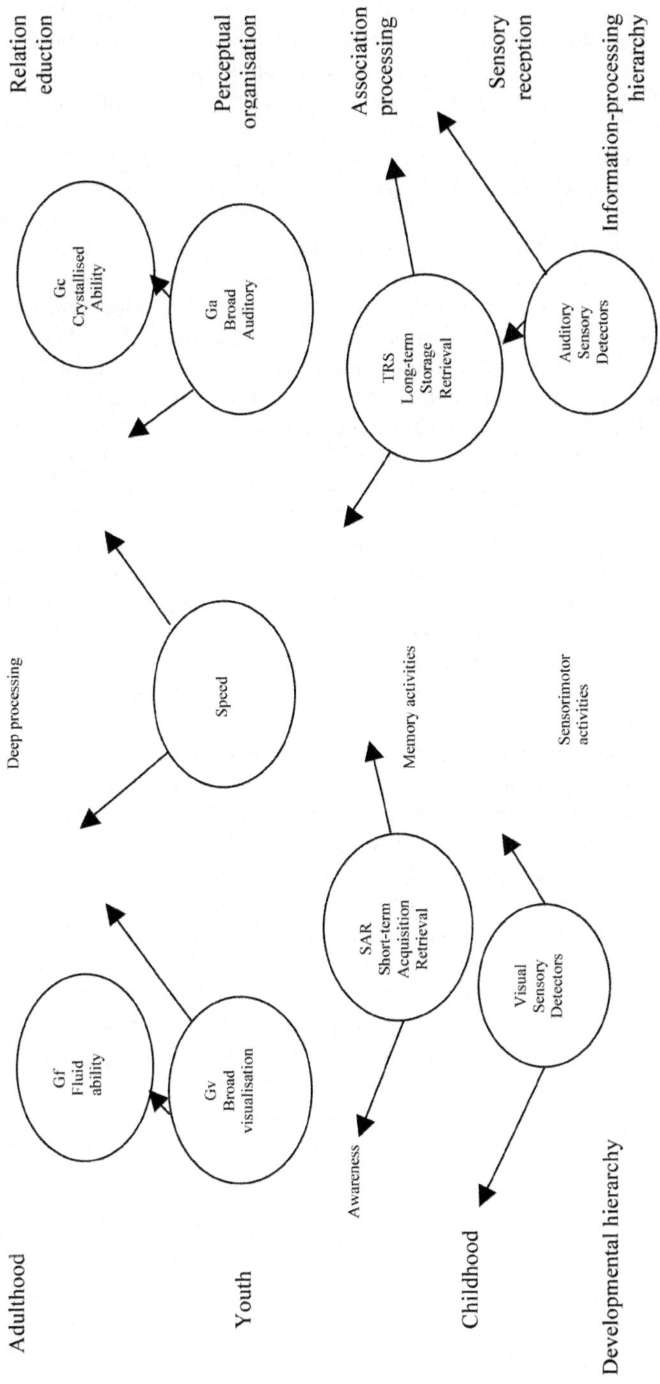

At the next level down, we find the various perceptual organizational processes: visual abilities, auditory abilities, and processes related to speed of information processing. The placement of these second-order factors below Gf and Gc implies that they are less complex and that in a developmental sense, we master these abilities before we master the Gf and Gc abilities. Short term and long term memory functions are found about midway down the chart. The description of these functions as "Association Processing" refers to the type of mental operation that is predominant at this stage of development, forming associations among facts, ideas, and so forth. At the very bottom level, are the sensory functions, the very sort of thing that Galton was assessing 100 years earlier in a vain attempt to measure intelligence. The model shows why these attempts were unsuccessful: the complex functions that we now know to be more central to intelligence are at the top of the hierarchy, whilst the sensory functions are at the bottom. Horn assumed that there would be little correlation among measures taken at the bottom of the hierarchy and substantial correlations among measures taken at the top. Galton did indeed find that sensory discrimination measures failed to correlate with teachers' ratings of intelligence. Binet, who sampled tasks from the top of the chart, found impressive correlations between his measures and measures of intelligence. The chart, however, also partially supports the logic of Galton's quest. Galton looked at sensory measures because he thought that good quality sensory input would lead to good quality mental processes. Horn's chart suggests that good quality input is a necessary but not sufficient condition for good quality mental processes. The input has to be processed and organized as it makes its way up the information processing hierarchy. Detection is just the first of the steps and there is no guarantee that someone who is good at this level will also be good at the other levels.

There are problems with Horn's model but it does accommodate many of the empirical findings noted in the literature. It also has the desirable characteristic of being an open model, one that invites further developments. The inclusion of perceptual organisation factors, for example, led to the recognition of the auditory organisation factor that appears in Figure 8.2 (Stankov & Horn, 1980). Stankov, a student of John Horn's who has worked for many years now at the University of Sydney, reasoned that if there can be spatial abilities, then there should also be auditory abilities. Obvious examples occur in the field of music but Stankov discovered a range of other tasks, some of them involving distortions of speech that depend on this factor. Work of this kind has great importance in areas where auditory abilities are a matter of life and death (e.g., aircraft cockpits). Stankov and his colleagues are now actively exploring the bases of individual differences in other sensory domains, notably touch. Indeed, the model has already been extended through the inclusion of a tactile-kinaesthetic ability that has much in common with broad visualisation and fluid intelligence (Roberts, Stankov, Pallier, & Bradley, 1997). Roberts and his co-workers used tasks that required participants to identify objects by shape and texture, to perform a bead memory test blindfolded, to detect letters and figures traced on their fingers, and a variety of other tactile tasks. Their findings suggest other ways in which intelligence can be assessed, perhaps less culturally biased methods. Research has been active on other aspects of the Gf/Gc model as well. Attempts have been made to determine the status of other supposed factors such as attention (Stankov, 1983), the ability to divide one's attention (Fogarty, 1987; Fogarty & Stankov, 1982), the status of mental imagery ability (Burton, 1998), factors relating to cognitive style (Fogarty & Burton, 1996), and some very interesting recent work on cognitive speed factors (Roberts & Stankov, 1998). The results of this work will extend the model further. Carroll (1993) in his extraordinary review of factor analytic studies of human cognitive abilities had this to say about the Gf/Gc model:

> The Cattell-Horn model, as summarised by Horn (1985, 1988), is a true hierarchical model covering all major domains of intellectual functioning. Numerous details remain to be filled in through further research, but among available models it appears to offer the most well-founded and reasonable approach to an acceptable theory of the structure of cognitive abilities. (p. 62).

Figure 8.3 *Representation of a radex model of intelligence.*

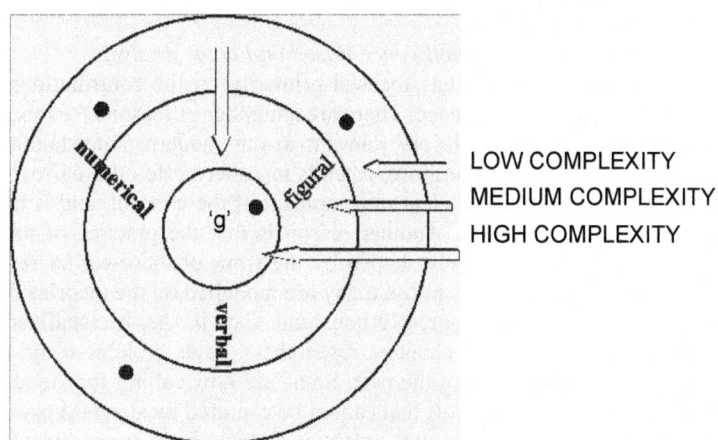

Other Models of Intelligence

There are other models of intelligence that are also based on factor analysis or modifications of factor analysis. One of the most interesting of these is Guttman's radex theory (Guttman, 1954) in which he ordered ability tests in two ways, according to their complexity and according to their content. The first of these orderings is called a simplex, in which a proper ranking is possible. The second is called a circumplex, where proper ranking is not possible but where contents may still be displayed by ordering them in a circular way. It is possible to combine these two orderings in what Guttman called a radex where more complex tests are located towards the centre of a series of concentric circles representing increasing complexity, and where the various content areas are shown as sectors. A rather crude representation of a radex is shown in Figure 8.3. The concentric circles do not mark any clear borders but are shown to reinforce the impression of increasing complexity as one moves to the centre. Similarly, the content areas shown are not meant to represent the sum total of all contents possible. Rather, they show different types of content and illustrate the notion that tests employing a particular type of content will be found in the same sector. Four hypothetical tests, represented as black dots, are shown in the diagram. One test is located towards the centre of the radex. We know from its location at the centre that such a test would be a good measure of 'g'. Because it is in the figural sector, we can see that this imaginary test employs figural or pictorial items. There is another dot in the figural sector but in the outer circle. We can tell from its location that it would not be a good measure of general intelligence.

Snow, Kilonem, and Marshalled (1984) demonstrated that Guttman's model is compatible with the hierarchical model of intelligence derived from factor analysis. They were able to locate a large number of well-known measures of intelligence on a two-dimensional configuration, similar to that shown in Figure 8.3. These researchers believed that the radex models proposed by Guttman provide a generally more useful perspective on cognitive abilities and their relations than does factor analysis. They concluded that "The radex thus emerges as the most general theoretical model to date on both substantive and methodological grounds" (Snow et al., 1984, p.88).

Summary of the Theories of Intelligence Based on Factor Analysis
Up to this point, the chapter has focused primarily on the contributions of early workers in the field of intelligence. There are a number of reasons for this. The first is that this early work is still very relevant to our modern understanding of the concept of intelligence. Furthermore, it tends to concentrate on a narrow range of themes, it shows a reasonably clear development of the concept, and is thus easier to explain in a limited space. Another reason is that the practice of intelligence testing today is still very largely shaped by the work of these earlier researchers. Some of the most popular tests in use today are modelled on the theories developed by Binet, Spearman, Thurstone, Vernon, and Cattell. As we shall see in the concluding sections of this chapter, researchers have broken away from the relatively narrow approaches of the past. Some are now calling for the recognition of different intelligences, the sort that cannot be captured by standard psychometric tests. Developmental psychologists, such as Piaget, have long argued that we should spend more time looking at the processes by which all children come to think intelligently, rather than focusing on why they differ among themselves. There is also new interest in the neural and biological bases of intelligence, prompted by developments in medical technology that allow us better insight into neural processes. Researchers have argued that to base the concept of intelligence solely on the interpretation of patterns of correlation obtained from batteries of cognitive tests leads to a neglect of many important aspects of mental ability. Some of the alternative approaches are described in the next section.

Gardner's Multiple Intelligences
Gardner (1983) put forward some interesting ideas about the nature of intelligence in his book *Frames of Mind*. Gardner argued that our views of intelligence should be informed not only by work with "normal" children but also by studies of gifted children, of experts in various domains, of valued abilities in different cultures, and by individuals who have suffered types of brain damage. Gardner rejected the idea that there is a general ability that acts as a kind of "super ability". Instead, there are several relatively independent intelligences which he defined as a set of problem

solving skills in a given domain. In order for something to be considered an "intelligence", Gardner listed a set of eight criteria that had to be met. These are as follows:
- potential isolation by brain damage. In other words, if it can be demonstrated that a particular ability is affected by localised brain damage and other abilities are not affected, then this criterion is satisfied;
- the existence of idiot savants, prodigies, and other exceptional individuals. Idiot savants are otherwise handicapped individuals who exhibit a high level of development in a particular ability. Gardner argued that if people can be exceptional in one area but only average or below average in others, then it constitutes evidence that the ability in question may be a separate intelligence.
- an identifiable core operation or set of operations. For example, the ability to discriminate between tones is characteristic of musical ability;
- a distinctive developmental history, leading to a stage of expertise;
- an evolutionary history and evolutionary plausibility. Gardner felt that intelligences have evolved and that we should be able to trace their evolutionary history, or see evidence of it in other species. For example, rudimentary forms of linguistic intelligence can be seen in other species and the evolutionary value is clear;
- support from experimental psychological tasks. For example, if it is claimed that two intelligences are separate, then it should be possible to demonstrate in a laboratory setting that tasks drawn from each of the intelligences do not interfere with each other (c.f. Fogarty, 1987);
- support from psychometric findings. In other words, there should not be large correlations between tasks drawn from the different intelligences; and
- susceptibility to encoding in a symbol system.

By looking for evidence of the conjunction of all these criteria, Gardner was able to arrive at a set of seven distinct intelligences. They are as follows:
- *Linguistic.* The traditional verbal ability. Gardner was at pains to stress that although important for success, people could manage without being adept at linguistic intelligence. Einstein, unlike Galton, could not recite poetry and slabs of Latin at the age of four; indeed it is said that he did not speak his first words until four, and it is certainly recorded in many places that he preferred to think in images.
- *Spatial.* Again, a traditional psychometric ability that refers to the ability to visualise spatial arrangements and to manipulate and transform them.
- *Logical-mathematical.* The type of intelligence is tapped by many conventional intelligence tests (e.g., IQ tests). Gardner described this intelligence as involving both a love of dealing with ideas and the power to follow very long chains of mathematical reasoning. It is not hard to see why this intelligence has been highly valued in Western societies.
- *Musical.* The power to understand the music of others, to reproduce it, and to compose one's own. Music has three essential elements: pitch, timbre, and rhythm. Those high in musical intelligence can integrate these well (Howard, 1991). Although many researchers dispute that music is a separate intelligence, there is no doubt that it does not correlate highly with traditional measures of intelligence, hence the need to create new measures to predict musical achievement (e.g., Fogarty, Buttsworth, & Gearing, 1996).

- *Interpersonal.* Involves understanding and "getting on with" other people. The term "social intelligence" is often used to describe this same intelligence. John Horn developed measures of social intelligence as an indicator of crystallised intelligence. Gardner, on the other hand, believed that it is an intelligence in its own right.
- *Intrapersonal.* This intelligence has to do with how well we understand ourselves, our motivations, moods, strengths and weaknesses. At first glance, this may seem a rather unimportant intelligence, but some interesting Australian work on self-knowledge will be discussed later in the chapter.
- *Bodily-kinaesthetic.* This pertains to body movements, sense of balance, hand-eye coordination, and so forth.

The critics of Gardner's theory pointed out that it is difficult to see how all these seven intelligences meet his eight criteria (e.g., Brody, 1992). They also pointed out that if subjectivity enters into the decision about what are intelligences and what are not, there may be a very large number of these indeed. The theories developed on the basis of factor analysis and related methods may be difficult for many to comprehend, but they were based on empirical data. Thus, the factors derived from the psychometric literature are well-established. Gardner's theory, on the other hand, appears to have both an empirical and a subjective basis. Gottfredson (1997) warned "Labelling other abilities and traits as other 'intelligences' creates only the appearance, not the reality, of multiple equally useful abilities" (p. 6). Despite these reservations, the theory has generated a lot of interest and stimulated research in relatively neglected areas.

Sternberg's Triarchic Theory

Robert Sternberg's (1985) triarchic theory proposed that there are three fundamental aspects of human intelligence - analytic, creative, and practical. Analytic intelligence is what is typically measured by intelligence tests. Problems testing this type of intelligence usually (a) have a single correct answer, (b) come with all the information needed to solve them, and (c) have little intrinsic interest. Practical problems, in contrast, tend to (a) require a definition of the problem, (b) be poorly defined, (c) have several solutions, (d)require everyday experience, and (e) require motivation and personal involvement. Sternberg was not the first to make a distinction between analytic and practical intelligence, Neisser (1976) had done so much earlier, but research supporting the distinction did not emerge until the 1 980s and 1990s. Ceci and Liker (1986) in a study of expertise in betting on horse races, found that handicappers used quite complex interactive models with as many as seven variables. Despite the seemingly obvious reliance of this type of ability on mathematical skills, level of performance was not correlated with IQ scores. There are other examples of complex skills being displayed in the workplace by people who do not score well on IQ tests. One criticism of these examples, however, is that they involve highly learned skills. In separate writings, Sternberg has emphasised the importance of coping with novel (what he called "nonentrenched") situations as a hallmark of intelligence. Ackerman (1988) has shown that intelligence plays a smaller and smaller role as a task ceases to be novel and becomes more automatic. It is sometimes difficult to say whether people displaying high levels of skills in a workplace situation are displaying practical intelligence or highly overlearned skills. Motivation is also a major consideration.

Whilst there may be some question about the status of practical intelligence, there is no disputing the status of what Sternberg called "creative intelligence". The notion of creative ability has existed for a long time. Research has shown that creative people tend to (a) be experts in their field, (b) have the capacity to think differently about problems, and (c) be motivated by intrinsic (e.g., satisfaction) rather than extrinsic (e.g., money) rewards. Anastasi and Urbina (1997) reported that correlations between tests of intelligence and creativity tend to be low, although an average or above average intelligence is necessary but not sufficient for creativity to emerge. Unfortunately, it is very difficult to measure creativity and Sternberg's recognition of creative intelligence in his model has not really taken us any closer to understanding its nature.

Piaget's Theory
Most people today are familiar with the theories of cognitive development put forward by Swiss psychologist, Jean Piaget. As stated earlier, Piaget (1972) was not interested in individual differences in intelligence but in the means by which all children learn to act in an intelligent manner. His theory was constructed primarily on the basis of observational data. The four stages of cognitive development described in this theory give an insight into what he considered intelligence to be:
- *Sensori-motor.* A stage lasting up to the age of two during which the child is capable of very limited cognitive operations, mostly sensory in nature;
- *Pre-operational.* Lasting from two to seven years during which the child starts to develop a sense of concepts such as number and weight, but still only in a limited way. Everything is taken very literally;
- *Concrete operations.* The child is no longer so dominated by the appearance of things and is capable of a range of operations but is still not capable of abstract thought; and
- *Formal operations.* From 11 years onward the child is increasingly capable of abstract thought. Piaget mentions the grasp of concepts such as probability as an indication that people have reached this stage. Many statistics lecturers would claim that some students never reach the formal operational stage!
It is interesting to compare this sequence with those shown on the left and right hand sides of Figure 8.2, which depicts Horn's version of the theory of fluid and crystallised intelligence. The two versions of the development of intelligence are not dissimilar. Both show a developmental sequence wherein humans begin by dealing with sensory data, move to a stage where they form associations, and then ultimately progress to abstract levels of thinking. However, it would be a mistake to think of Piaget's model purely in terms of this progression from sensory perception to abstract thought. His model is rather complex and incorporates an explanation of how we actually acquire information and develop knowledge structures. The driving force behind intellectual progression is the struggle to make sense of our experience. We do this by building schemas, mental models that represent our view of the world. Once a schema is formed it can be used to *assimilate* new information. If the information is incompatible with the schema, we may be forced to alter the schema itself and restore equilibrium through a process that Piaget labelled *accommodation.* This is how learning occurs. At the same time, children are acquiring an increasingly complex range of cognitive operations, to the point where as adults we are capable of thinking about thinking itself.

Piaget's views changed the way people thought about intelligence, especially the intelligence of children, and had a big impact on curriculum design in many countries. His account of intelligence certainly represented a different point of view to the one being espoused by the factor analysts, who were developing their theories on the basis of individual differences observed in performance on cognitive tests.

Biological Approaches to Intelligence
In recent years, one of the fastest growth areas in psychology has been the search for biological foundations for psychological constructs. Stankov, Boyle, and Cattell (1995) provided a succinct summary of these developments in the field of intelligence. A brief review follows.
- *Brain Size.* There is no doubt that brain size is related to degree of intelligence across species, although not within species. Absolute brain size is not important but the ratio of brain size relative to body size does give a good indication of the intelligence of the species. A person living today has a brain almost four times as large as one of our human ancestors who lived more than three million years ago (Di Lalla & Patrick, 1994). In the process of evolution, the cortex became more and more convoluted. The human brain is three times as large as that of a chimpanzee, yet has only 1.25 times as many neurons. The distinguishing characteristic of the human brain is the very large number of interneuronal connections, many of which have formed over the past three million years. The cause of this extraordinary change in our brain structure is undoubtedly related to increased tool use, increased complexity of social systems as humans ceased to be hunter-gatherers and started living in larger and larger communities, and increased dependence on written and spoken language. Individuals with more complex brain structures were more likely to survive and reproduce, passing on these physical characteristics to the next generation. Despite the obvious connection between brain size and intelligence across species, however, there is very little evidence suggesting that within-species variation can tell us much about intelligence, the correlations are too weak (Stankov et al., 1995). Even where the correlations are more robust (e.g., Willerman, Schultz, Rutledge, & Bigler, 1991), it is impossible to say what these correlations mean.
- *Biochemistry and intelligence.* There have been reports of successful attempts to increase intelligence by nutritional means. Stankov cited one study that showed an increase of about four IQ points in children as a consequence of an intervention that assured a normal daily intake of vitamins and minerals. However, there is no reliable evidence that children already enjoying a normal intake of the same substances will show an increase in IQ (to use this term as a synonym for measured intelligence). Temporary boosts can be obtained by the use of stimulants, such as caffeine, but these substances will not have long-term effects.
- *Neural efficiency and intelligence.* Brain imaging techniques now allow us to observe metabolic processes in the brain during the performance of cognitive tasks. It is early days yet for this kind of research but the evidence so far suggests that higher intelligence is associated with faster and more efficient neural activity (Stankov et al., 1995; Sternberg & Kaufman, 1998). That is, intelligent people don't have "more brains", they have "more efficient" brains. Eysenck (1967) was the first modern theorist to push this view strongly.

Progress is likely to be slow in this research area because recording techniques are still somewhat unsuited to measuring things like speed of neural transmission and the imaging technique itself is very expensive.
- *Health, age, and intelligence.* There is not much evidence of the effects of poor health on intelligence. Stankov and co-workers at the University of Sydney have found that there is a definite decline in fluid intelligence abilities with aging but that "higher mental functions seem to be largely spared the effects of transitory physical illness" (Stankov et al., 1995, p.24).

Modern Trends in the Study of Intelligence
One modern trend has already been mentioned, the tendency to search for biological correlates of intelligence. Two other trends are worth mentioning. The first has to do with a general opening up of the field of intelligence. Over the years, many abilities have been suggested but, for the most part, research has focused on what has often been called analytical intelligence. In recent years, the field has expanded and researchers are now looking at the relationship between intelligence and personality (e.g., Sternberg & Ruzgis, 1994; Stankov et al., 1995). Stankov et al. (1995) concluded that both normal and abnormal personality traits can influence cognitive abilities but that the mechanism and the extent of its influence are unclear. Ackerman and Heggestad (1997) have thrown the net wider to include intelligence, personality, and interests. They found evidence that the three traits work in tandem with ability level and personality dispositions determining the probability of success in a particular task domain, and interests determining the motivation to attempt a task. Further research of this type will help to elucidate how a broad range of constructs, such as values, combine with intelligence, personality, and interests to determine behaviour.

A second encouraging trend in intelligence research has seen the continuing cross-fertilisation between the fields of cognitive psychology and individual differences. Hunt (1978, 1980) started this trend when he began to search for the basic processes involved in verbal ability. Following Hunt, cognitive psychologists began to use some of their experimental tasks, developed to measure very specific processes, as a way of shedding light on the factors identified by those working within the psychometric tradition. This has led to research in the area of cognitive speed and the use of very basic speeded tasks to measure intelligence. Researchers in South Australia (Vickers, & Smith, 1986; Nettlebeck, 1987) have developed a task called inspection time that reliably correlates with measures of intelligence. The IT task involves the discrimination of a very briefly presented stimulus and is said to measure the effective speed of intake of stimulus information. Deary and Stough (1996) have claimed this research programme as a success story in the reductionist approach to human intelligence. On a much broader level, but still inspired by cognitive theory, Stankov and Crawford (1997) have been working on the concept of self-confidence and studying its relationship with human abilities. They concluded that "There exists a separate self-confidence trait that is tapped by confidence ratings from diverse cognitive measures. This trait may be viewed either as an aspect of metacognition and therefore close to human abilities or as part of the interface between abilities and personality" (Stankov & Crawford, 1997, p. 11).

These research programmes are helping to clarify the nature of intelligence but the reality is that there are not a lot of people working within the psychometric tradition, either here in Australia or overseas. One reason for the relative lack of researchers is undoubtedly the complexity of the psychometric method for many aspiring students. Another reason is the controversy that has from time to time surrounded the area. This chapter will close with a brief consideration of these issues.

Issues and Controversies in Intelligence

Unfortunately, the field of intelligence is as well known for its controversies as for its contributions to understanding human behaviour. Some of the controversies have attracted widespread publicity. This section will touch on the main controversies and relate their origins to work discussed earlier in this chapter.

Improvement in Intelligence

The issue of whether intelligence test scores can be improved over the span of an individual's life is a complex one. At a general level, intelligence is like everything else: use it or lose it, as the popular saying goes. Given the right circumstances, obviously some improvement is possible, but it depends on what type of intelligence one is talking about. Crystallised intelligence can certainly go on improving, until late in life it seems. Fluid intelligence, on the other hand, appears to suffer a decline before one has reached middle age. Life habits (e.g., drug abuse) can accelerate the decline.

One of the most interesting findings to emerge in relation to changes in intelligence occurs at the population, rather than the individual, level. It has been observed in a large number of Western cultures that intelligence test scores have been rising steadily since they were first measured on a large scale in the 1930s. The effect is very powerful - at least 15 IQ points per generation for tests of fluid intelligence (Flynn, 1987). Our children are scoring much better than we did at the same age. Explanations are not easy to come by but suggestions include increased schooling, better nutrition, and a host of improved environmental factors.

The Role of the General Factor

Perhaps the most contentious issue in the history of research on intelligence has been the role of the general factor. Spearman and Thompson debated whether it existed and researchers since then have debated the importance that should be attached to it. Hierarchical models of intelligence showed that there was no necessary incompatibility between theories that stressed the general factor and theories that stressed primary mental abilities; it just depended where you looked in the hierarchy. Nevertheless, the question of the relative importance of each has always generated fierce debate. The strongest proponent of the importance of 'g' in recent times has been Arthur Jensen (1979, 1980). One of the strongest critics has been John Horn.

One reason so much heated debate has surrounded this question is that some of the proponents of a single-factor theory of intelligence have been associated with research that claims to demonstrate race differences in intelligence. As Stankov put it:

> Although it is not necessarily the case that the single 'g' factor position calls for a value laden view of group differences in intelligence, it just so happens

that those holding a multiple intelligence view (Gardner, 1983; see also Horn & Noll, 1994) appear to be more sensitive in their discussion of racial issues. (Stankov, 1998, p. 55).

Stankov also feared what he saw as a tendency to "mindless reductionism" among some of those who hold the single factor view. In particular, he stressed that emphasising a single factor ignores a large body of evidence pointing to the existence of many factors at different levels of complexity. Such a narrow view overlooks the richness of human cognition.

The problem with attaching too much importance to speed, and hence to the brain, is that there is not a lot that we can do about brain structures. There is a danger that over-reliance on biological explanations of intelligence will encourage us to think of intelligence as something that is immutable. Furthermore, whilst speed and neural efficiency are undoubtedly important aspects of analytical intelligence, and worthy of continued research, it is doubtful that it will play such a leading role in other types of intelligence discussed in this chapter, such as those listed by Gardner.

Race Differences in Intelligence
Along with the issue of the importance of the general factor, questions of race differences in intelligence have always sparked a heated debate. Arthur Jensen and Hans Eysenck separately published extensive data showing that as a group black Americans scored about one standard deviation lower than white Americans on standard tests of intelligence (e.g., Jensen, 1985). That announcement in itself was unlikely to cause a great deal of controversy. Concern, yes, controversy, no. The controversial aspect of their work was the linking of this difference with genetic differences. If the difference has a genetic basis, some governments feel justified withdrawing funding support for programmes designed to improve learning opportunities for disadvantaged people. The 1994 publication by Hernstein and Murray of the extremely controversial book referred to as "The Bell Curve" saw an unprecedented level of discussion on this topic. The authors argued that unintelligent people are a drain on society and that society will eventually form itself into two classes: a privileged intelligent group and an increasingly underprivileged unintelligent group. Such sentiments are often expressed in society but Hernstein and Murray backed their claims with a detailed statistical analysis of research on group differences on IQ scores.

To understand the heat generated by this sort of discussion, it is helpful to return to the points made at the outset of the chapter about the importance of intelligence in our society and the consequences of scientists claiming that intelligence is genetically based. Not many scientists would deny that intelligence is partly determined by genetics but most would also acknowledge that learning experiences play a very important role. Unfortunately, although we have learned much about intelligence, we have not yet found a way to handle the controversies that are a by-product of research in this area. As Rowe (1997) commented, whilst research on intelligence as a property of the mind (information processing, mental self-management) and the brain (speed of neural transmission, brain size, rate of brain metabolism) constitutes perhaps the most active frontier today in the study of intelligence, there has been no comparable sociology of intelligence to explain how the effects of this research reverberate through the social system.

The publication of Hernstein and Murray's book created such an uproar that the American Psychological Association set up a special Task Force under the leadership of Ulrich Neisser to report on factual issues relevant to the debate (Neisser et al., 1996). Some of the findings of the Task Force are summarised below and provide a fitting closing comment on many of the themes raised in this chapter.

- The Task Force concluded that the genetic effects on measured intelligence are substantial but that the pathway by which genes produce their effects is still unknown.
- The environment also exerts a substantial effect on the development of intelligence but, once again, we do not clearly understand what those environmental factors are or how they work.
- The role of nutrition in intelligence is equally unclear. Although it is known that severe childhood malnutrition restricts cognitive development, there is no convincing evidence that dietary supplements in normal populations has any positive effect on intelligence.
- Information-processing speed and psychometric intelligence are related, but we do not yet know how important speed should be to our understanding of the construct of intelligence.
- There are differences between Blacks and Whites on tests of intelligence which do not appear to be due to any obvious biases in test construction and administration, nor to differences in socioeconomic status. At present, we do not know why these differences exist.
- The Task Force also mentioned the range of other abilities not currently sampled by existing tests of intelligence. These abilities include creativity, wisdom, practical sense, social sensitivity, and perhaps others that we do not yet know about. Whilst this situation persists, our understanding of the construct of intelligence is limited.

If these conclusions seem a little weak - a series of confessions about what we do not know - surely that is appropriate. Despite the progress in our understanding of intelligence, we still have a long way to go. The Task Force summarised the situation very concisely in its concluding comment:

> In a field where so many issues are unresolved and so many questions unanswered, the confident tone that has characterised most of the debate on these topics is clearly out of place. The study of intelligence does not need politicised assertions and recriminations; it needs self-restraint, reflection, and a great deal more research. The questions that remain are socially as well as scientifically important. There is no reason to think them unanswerable, but finding the answers will require a shared and sustained effort as well as the commitment of substantial scientific resources. Just such a commitment is what we strongly recommend. (Neisser et al., 1996, p. 97)

REFERENCES

Ackerman, P. L. (1988). Determinants of individual differences during skill acquisition: Cognitive abilities and information processing. *Journal of Experimental Psychology: General, 117*, 288-318.

Ackerman, P. L., & Heggestad, E. D. (1997). Intelligence, personality, and interests: Evidence for overlapping traits. *Psychological Bulletin, 121* (2), 2 19-245.

Anastasi, A., & Urbina, S. (1997). *Psychological testing* (7th ed.). Upper Saddle River, NJ: Prentice-Hall.

Belmont, J. M., Buttefield, E. C., & Ferretti, R. P. (1982). To secure transfer of training, instruct self-management skills. In D.K. Detterman & R.J. Sternberg (Eds.), *How and how much can intelligence be increased?* Norwood, NJ: Ablex Publishing Corporation.

Brody, N. (1992). *Intelligence* (2nd ed.). San Diego, Calif.: Academic Press.

Burton, L. (1998). *A factorial analysis of visual imagery and spatial abilities.* Unpublished PhD thesis, University of Southern Queensland, Australia.

Carroll, J. B. (1993). *Human cognitive abilities: A survey of factor analytic studies.* Cambridge: Cambridge University Press.

Cattell, R. B. (1941). Some theoretical issues in adult intelligence testing. *Psychological Bulletin, 38,* 592.

Cattell, R. B. (1963). Theory of fluid and crystallised intelligence: A critical experiment. *Journal of Educational Psychology, 54,* 1-22.

Ceci, S. J., & Liker, J. (1986). A day at the races: A study of IQ, expertise, and cognitive complexity. *Journal of Experimental Psychology: General, 115,* 255-266.

Deary, I. J., & Stough, C. (1996). Intelligence and inspection time: Achievements, prospects and problems. *American Psychologist, 51,* 599-608.

Detterman, D. K.. (1982). Does 'g' exist? *Intelligence, 6,* 99-108.

Di Lalla, L., & Patrick, C. (1994). Evolution of human intelligence. In R.T. Sternberg (Ed.), *Encyclopedia of Human Intelligence, Vol 1,* 406-412, NY: Macmillan.

Eysenck, H. J. (1939). Primary mental abilities. *British Journal of Educational Psychology, 9,* 260-265.

Eysenck, H. J. (1967). Intelligence assessment: A theoretical and experimental approach. *British Journal of Educational Psychology, 37,* 8 1-98.

Flynn, J. R. (1987). Massive IQ gains in 14 nations: What IQ tests really measure. *Psychological Bulletin, 101,* 171-191.

Fogarty, G. (1984). *Abilities involved in performance on competing tasks.* Unpublished doctoral dissertation, University of Sydney.

Fogarty, G. (1987). Timesharing in relation to broad ability domains. *Intelligence, 3,* 207-231.

Fogarty, G., & Burton, L. (1996). A comparison of measures of preferred processing style: Method or trait variance? *Journal of Mental Imagery, 20,* 87- 112.

Fogarty, G., Buttsworth, L., & Gearing, P. (1996). Assessing skills in a tertiary music training programme. *Psychology of Music, 24,* 154-170.

Fogarty, G. & Stankov, L. (1982). Competing tasks as an index of intelligence. *Journal of Personality and Individual Differences, 3,* 407-422.

Gardner, H. (1983). *Frames of mind: The theory of multiple intelligences.* NY: Basic Books.

Gottfredson, L. (1997). Foreword to "Intelligence and Social Policy", *Intelligence, 24,* 1-12.

Guttman, L. (1954). A new approach to factor analysis: The radex. In P. F. Lazarsfeld (Ed.), *Mathematical thinking in the social sciences* (pp. 258-348). Glencove, IL: Free Press.

Hebb, D. O. (1949). *The organization of behaviour.* NY: Wiley.

Herman, L. M., & Pack, A. (1994). Animal Intelligence: Historical perspective and contemporary approaches. In R. T. Sternberg (Ed.), *Encyclopedia of human intelligence., Vol 1,* 86-96, NY: Macmillan.

Hernstein, R. J., & Murray, C. (1994). *The bell curve: Intelligence and class structure in American life.* NY: Free Press.

Horn, J. L. (1985). Remodelling old models of intelligence. In B.B. Wolman (Ed.), *Handbook of intelligence: Theories, measurements and applications.* NY: Wiley.

Horn, J. L., & Noll, J. (1994). System for understanding cognitive capabilities: A theory and the evidence on which it is based. In D.K. Detterman (Ed.), *Current topics in human intelligence: Vol 4. Theories of intelligence* (pp.15 1-203). NY: SpringerVerlag.

Howard, R. (1991). *All about intelligence.* Kensington, NSW: New South Wales University Press.

Hunt, E. (1978). Mechanics of verbal ability. *Psychological Review, 85,* 109-130.

Hunt, E. (1980). Intelligence as an information-processing concept. *British Journal of Psychology, 71,* 449-474.

Jensen, A. R. (1979). "g": Outmoded theory or unconquered frontier? *Creative Science and Technology, 11,* 16-29.

Jensen, A. R. (1980). *Bias in mental testing.* NY: Free Press.

Jensen, A. R. (1985). The nature of black-white differences on various psychometric tests: Spearman's hypothesis. *Behavioral and Brain Sciences, 8,* 193-263.

Neisser, U. (1976). General, academic, and artificial intelligence. In L.B. Resnick (Ed.), *The nature of intelligence* (pp. 295-346). Norwood, NJ: Ablex.

Neisser, U., Boodoo, G., Bouchard, T. J., Boykin, A. W., Brody, N., Ceci, S. J., Halpern, D. F., Loehlin, J. C., Perloff, R., Sternberg, R. J., & Urbina, S. (1996). Intelligence: Knowns and unknowns. *American Psychologist, 51* (2), 77-101.

Nettlebeck, T. (1987). Inspection time and intelligence. In P.A. Vernon (Ed.), *Speed of information processing and intelligence* (pp. 295-346). Norwood, NJ: Ablex.

Piaget, J. (1972). Intellectual evolution from adolescence to adulthood. *Human Development, 15,* 1-12.

Roberts, R. D., & Stankov, L. (1998). Mental speed and intelligence: A multivariate investigation. Submitted for publication.

Roberts, R. D., Stankov, L., Pallier, G., & Bradley, D. (1997). Charting the cognitive sphere: Tactile-Kinesthetic performance within the structure of intelligence. *Intelligence, 25* (2), 111-148.

Rowe, D. C. (1997). A place at the policy table? Behavior genetics and estimates of family environmental effects on IQ. *Intelligence, 24,* 133- 158.

Snow, R. E., Kyllonen, P. C., & Marshalek, B. (1984). The topography of ability and learning correlations. In R. J. Sternberg (Ed.), *Advances in the psychology of human intelligence,* Vol. 2 (pp. 47-103). Hillsdale, NJ: Erlbaum.

Spearman, C. (1904). General intelligence objectively determined and measured. *American Journal of Psychology, 15,* 201-293.

Spearman, C. (1927). *The abilities of man.* NY: Macmillan.

Stankov, L. (1983). Attention and intelligence. *Journal of Educational Psychology, 75,* 471-490.

Stankov, L. (1998). Intelligence arguments and Australian psychology. *Australian Psychologist, 33,* 53-57.

Stankov, L., Boyle, G. J., & Cattell, R. B. (1995). Models and paradigms in personality and intelligence research. In D. H. Saklofske & M. Zeidner (Eds.), *International handbook of personality and intelligence.* NY: Plenum Press

Stankov, L., & Crawford, J. (1997). Self-confidence and performance on tests of cognitive abilities. *Intelligence, 25,* 93-109.

Stankov, L., & Horn, J. L. (1980). Human abilities revealed through auditory tests. *Journal of Educational Psychology, 72,* 19-42.

Sternberg, R. J. (1979). The nature of mental abilities. *American Psychologist, 34,* 214-230.

Sternberg, R. J. (1985). *Beyond IQ: A triarchic theory of human intelligence.* NY: Cambridge University Press.

Sternberg, R. J., & Kaufman, J. C. (1998). Human abilities. *Annual Review of Psychology, 49,* 479- 502.

Sternberg. R. J., & Ruzgis, P. (1994) (Eds.). *Personality and intelligence.* Cambridge: Cambridge University Press.

Thurstone, L. L. (1938). Primary mental abilities. *Psychometric Monographs, No 4.*

Thurstone, L. L. (1947). *Multiple factor analysis.* Chicago: University of Chicago Press.

Vernon, P. E. (1950). *The structure of human abilities.* London: Methuen.

Vickers, D., & Smith, P. (1986). The rationale for the inspection time index. *Personality and Individual Differences, 7,* 609-624.

Willerman, L., Schultz, R., Rutledge, R. N., & Bigler, E. D. (1991). In vivo brain size and intelligence. *Intelligence, 15,* 223-228.

Review Questions

Read the following statements and indicate whether they are True or False.

1. Experts are the only people who are able to agree what intelligence means?
2. The term 'g' was coined by Francis Galton?
3. Spearman and Thompson differed regarding the importance they attached to the general factor.
4. Thurstone proposed that there were seven primary mental abilities.

5. Thurstone proposed the first hierarchical model of intelligence.
6. Cattell claimed that fluid intelligence (Gf) was biologically linked?
7. Hebb's Intelligence B represented our innate potential.
8. The Gf/Gc model is a hierarchical model of intelligence.
9. Two tests that are correlated are said to rely upon at least one common ability.
10. Factor analysis is a technique that forms the basis of all theories of intelligence.
11. Positive manifold is a term that refers to the tendency for all cognitive tasks to be positively correlated.
12. General crystallised intelligence declines with age whereas general fluid intelligence stays the same or may even increase.
13. Guttman's radex model classifies tests in terms of complexity and content.
14. Gardner subscribed to the view that there is a general factor of intelligence.
15. One of the three basic intelligences represented in Sternberg's triarchic theory was called "emotional intelligence".
16. Piaget did not use correlational methods but was very interested in individual differences in intelligence.
17. Piaget's stage of formal operations marks the point at which a child reaches the level of abstract thought.
18. It is not possible to judge intelligence within species by measuring brain size.
19. 19.Research has shown that dietary supplements will boost intelligence for most people.
20. Differences noted between races on measured intelligence can be attributed to genetic influences.
21. Our children are smarter than we are.

Answers

1F	2F	3F	4T	5F	6T	7F	8T	9T
10F	11T	12F	13T	14F	15F	16F	17T	18T
19F	20F	21T (or false, depending on how well you have argued your case)						

Exercises

1. Think about your own definition of intelligence. Write it down and be prepared to defend it to others.
2. What is your view of the relative importance of a general factor of intelligence? Is it more useful to think of a single factor of intelligence that can explain much of our behaviour? Or to think of the many different factors of intelligence?
3. Are there intelligences not mentioned in this chapter (e.g., emotional intelligence) that should be included in Gardner's list? What other ones can you think of?
4. Do you think that the term "intelligence" is too culturally bound to be useful outside Western Society?
5. Can you think of examples of behaviour in other cultures that would be considered intelligent but not so in our society?

6. Is intelligence a uniquely human quality? Or confined to certain species? Or does it form a continuum throughout the animal kingdom?

7. If intelligence is defined as "adaptation to one's environment", are all species equally intelligent?

8. What reasons can you suggest for the large increase in IQ scores from generation to generation?

9. At the time of writing this chapter, there is a site on the Web that will allow you to complete a short (5 min) intelligence test. There is no guarantee that it will still be around when you read this chapter, but here it is: "http://www.brain.com".

About the Author

Professor Gerard Fogarty completed a BA (Hons, Psychology) degree at the University of New England in 1973. He then completed a Diploma of Education and taught English and History for three years at Cabramatta High School in Sydney's Western Suburbs in preparation for further training as a school counsellor. After completing these teaching years, he enrolled in a PhD at the University of Sydney, working with Dr Lazar Stankov on a thesis that explored aspects of the structure of human intelligence. Professor Fogarty left Sydney University in 1984 to take up a position with the head office of the AMP society where he supervised the development and validation of a new computerised selection system for the 5,000 strong field force of the AMP, a system that includes tests of intelligence, personality, and interests. Professor Fogarty joined the University of Southern Queensland in 1988, where he is still working as Head of the Department of Psychology, and lecturing on statistics and psychological measurement. He has published many articles in the areas of intelligence and the validation of psychological tests.

Gerard J. Fogarty
University of Southern Queensland

E. JAMES KEHOE & MICHAELA MACRAE

9. MODERN ASSOCIATIVE THEORY IN TEACHING AND LEARNING

Associative learning is a basic form of learning in which connections are formed in memory between pairs of events. The example of associative learning that is familiar to many people involves the Russian physiologist, Ivan Pavlov, and his dogs. Pavlov (1927) noticed that dogs in his experimental work would begin to salivate when his assistant, who was the person who fed them, entered the room. Pavlov understood that the dogs had formed an association between the assistant and food, and their knowledge led to an anticipatory physiological response of salivation. Pavlov later trained the dogs to associate the sound of a bell with being fed, and they would duly salivate when the bell was rung.

Although associations between pairs of events may seem simple and even rather trivial, they are, in fact, the foundations of more complex forms of learning. Moreover, the study of associative learning has been able to reveal a surprising amount about the central characteristics of learning. As will be seen in this chapter, the study of associative learning helps answer such important questions as: What kinds of feedback promote the best learning? How can material that is to be learned be presented so that it best grabs the learner's attention? How can a lesson be taught so that the principle behind the lesson transfers to new situations?

James A Athanasou (ed.), Adult Educational Psychology, 209–234

Figure 9.1 Professor I. P. Pavlov was a Nobel Laureate in medicine and physiology. As part of his investigation of digestive processes, he discovered conditioned reflexes, which revolutionised the study of learning and the brain.

The research area known as "associative learning" is vast. Therefore, this chapter will focus on a small number of key topics, namely, the basic principles of association, the role of attention in association, transfer of learning, the distribution of practice, discrimination learning, and the loss of learning. For each of these topics, we explain the experimental origins of the principle and illustrate how the principle may be generalized to the adult education setting. The aim of this chapter is to convey to the reader a contemporary understanding of associative learning, which we hope will provide the reader with principles for analysing particular learning situations in order to implement more effective strategies for teaching and learning.

Basic Principles of Associative Learning

Laws of Contiguity and Frequency
In any learning situation, the formation of an association between two events is based on their occurrence close together in time and space. For example, when someone is trying to learn a French-English vocabulary list, it is natural to write each new French word next to each English word and then to say them one after the other, for example, "la voiture" then "car." This simple idea is known as the Law of Contiguity and was first propounded by Aristotle along with the Law of Frequency, which states that the more often events are paired together, the more strongly associated they will become. All other associative principles rest upon the foundation of contiguity and frequency.

The Learning Curve
Learning is often assumed to be a straightforward process in which 'practice makes perfect'. This popular saying implies that learning occurs at a steady pace over practice sessions, or, in other words, each practice session provides an equal increase in learning. In fact, even on fairly simple tasks, learning typically starts out as a slow, laborious process that becomes progressively faster across practice sessions. If one were to plot the course of this learning on a graph, it would follow an S-shaped curve. For example, Figure 9.2 shows a learning curve for a simple association. The curve represents learning on a task in which the learner heard a warning signal – namely, a weak tone – which was followed by a tactile stimulus – namely, a mild puff of air near the eye. This puff of air reliably caused the learner to blink (Schneiderman, Fuentes, & Gormezano, 1962).

Figure 9.2 *A learning curve for a simple association between a warning signal that was paired with an air puff near the eye. The curve shows a progressive increase in the percentage of occasions on which the learner blinked during the warning signal. (Adapted from Schneiderman et al., 1962.)*

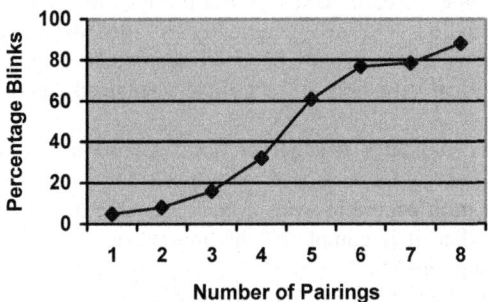

The curve in Figure 9.2 shows the proportion of pairings in which the learner blinked during the warning signal as training progressed. As can be seen, learning followed roughly three stages. First, during the initial pairings, there were relatively few responses to the warning signal. Second, the rate of blinking increased rapidly across pairings. Finally, the rate of blinking reached a plateau, which is also called the "asymptote". Most learning curves are S-shaped, but in situations where the task is very simple and learning conditions are ideal, the initial stage can be very short. The early part of the learning curve that denotes laborious progress is shortened such that the curve represents only the top half of an S shape.

The important implication of the S-shaped learning curve is that "patience makes perfect". It is not simply practice, but also patience, that is required by the learner and teacher. This is true for many relatively simple tasks, and it is certainly true for more complex tasks. It is to be expected that the learning process will require an initial period of practice in which no improvements will be apparent. However, after this initial frustrating stage, the learner will be rewarded with rapid improvement, and finally, a level of expertise will be reached. For complex skills, the plateau that represents expertise is never completely flat; further practice will continue to yield small but important gains (Anderson, 1985, p. 238. See also Cornford's chapter on skill formation in this volume.)

Law of Effect
Like the Law of Contiguity, the Law of Effect states that learning consists of an association between the surrounding cues and one's response to them. However, in addition, the Law of Effect states that such associations will be strengthened only when the cue and the response are followed closely by a reward. The reward itself does not become part of the association, but rather it acts as catalyst in forming the association. Consequently, when the same cue occurs again, it tends to activate the association and elicit the previously-rewarded response. The Law of Effect was introduced by Thorndike (1911), a psychologist. Thorndike's notion that reward could be used to cement associations was inspired by the philosopher Alexander Bain (1855, 1859), who argued that the motive to maximize pleasure and avoid pain is what determines our actions.

Feedback Principles

Thorndike's Law of Effect originally involved simple biological rewards, for example, food, which is a reward with clear-cut motivational significance. However, it has since been recognized that the Law of Effect can be applied to situations in which the "reward" consists of a piece of information for the learner. This kind of information is known generically as "feedback." There are basically two kinds of feedback, which can be used separately or together to promote learning in a practical situation: (1) "critical" feedback, and (2) "instructive" feedback.

Critical feedback indicates whether or not a learner's action has produced a desired result. Suppose, for example, you wish to write a computer-assisted learning module to train people in word-processing. One of the common tasks is to print a document when it is complete. The appropriate response to this cue is to press the "Command" and "P" keys. If this response is correct, critical feedback would be a message like "Correct, your document will now print." Conversely, if the learner presses the wrong keys, the critical feedback would be a message like "Wrong, your document will not be printed."

As may be apparent, critical feedback clearly indicates the success or failure of the learner's action. Conversely, critical feedback gives no explicit guidance as to what a more appropriate response might be. Where there are many possible responses to a situation, being told that one's choice is "wrong" is not very informative. Thus, to learn using only critical feedback, a person may have to try many different possible actions before achieving success.

Learning with critical feedback is traditionally called "trial-and-error" learning. More generally, it can be seen as a form of "learning by discovery", in which the learner must explore the environment and solve the problems it presents. In the psychological laboratory, learning by trial and error has been studied in humans and animals using a technique known alternatively as *"instrumental conditioning"* or *"operant conditioning"*. The most well-known researcher in this area was B. F. Skinner (1938), but the first studies were conducted by Thorndike (1898). In the prototypic experiment, a cat is placed in a "puzzle box," really a modest-sized cage (see Figure 9.3). Just outside the cage, a bowl of food is visible. The cat is allowed to explore the box in any way it likes, but only a single action – pressing a certain latch - opens the cage door and permits access to the critical feedback, namely, a food reward. Over a series of experiences in the box, the cat progressively refines its actions so that it smoothly and quickly opens the latch. The distinguishing feature of this and all instrumental procedures is the contingency between the designated action and the critical feedback, which is known technically as a *"positive reinforcer"*.

Instructive feedback contains explicit instructions as to the desired response to a situation. Consider again how you might train people to print a word-processor document when it is complete. If the person correctly presses the "Command" and "P" keys, instructive feedback would be a message like "Command+P causes your document to print." This message would confirm that the person's key combination was correct. Conversely, if the learner presses the wrong keys, the instructive message would be the same, namely, "Command+P causes your document to print." In this case, the message would effectively coach the learner as to which key combination to use next time.

Figure 9.3 Prof. E. L. Thorndike was among the first to study learning and memory in a scientific fashion. He studied trial-and-error learning in animals using "puzzle boxes" like the one shown in this picture.

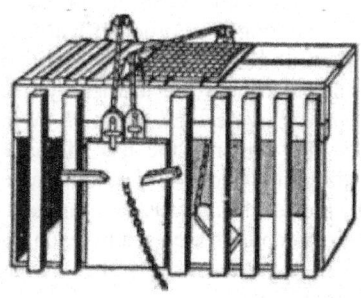

Instructive feedback is simple in the sense that the desired action is demonstrated after each attempt, regardless of whether the attempt was correct or not. It might seem that instructive feedback guarantees successful learning and requires little effort from the learner. However, this is not so, especially for complex tasks. The learner must detect a match or mismatch between their actual performance and the desired performance described in the feedback. Anybody who has attempted to see how their tennis serve differs from that of a professional will understand this problem. For practical purposes, using videos as part of the feedback can be a useful way of helping learners to see how well they conform to the ideal.

The concept of instructive feedback parallels the concept of "cognitive feedback" used in coaching and tutoring. After watching a person perform, a good coach will explain what the person must do to improve their performance next time. Such explanations are a form of instructive feedback and are distinct from statements urging the person to "try harder next time" or "do it better next time." These latter statements can be seen as a form of vague critical feedback.

In the psychological laboratory, a key example of learning with instructive feedback is classical conditioning, which was pioneered by Pavlov and is used widely today in studying the brain mechanisms of learning and memory. As mentioned at the beginning of this chapter, Pavlov's method entailed the presentation of two stimuli to a dog. First, the *conditioned stimulus* (CS) is a relatively innocuous event, for example, the ringing of a "bell." Second, the *unconditioned stimulus* (US) is an event of biological significance to the dog, for example, food in its mouth.

When presented in close succession, the CS acts as a signal for the US. In turn, the US causes a set of inborn reactions known as *unconditioned responses* (URs). Pavlov measured one of those responses, namely, salivation. Across repeated CS-US pairings, the tone CS itself comes to elicit a response that broadly resembles the UR. This learned response to the CS is known as the *conditioned response* (CR). In classical conditioning, the elicitation of the UR by a US effectively acts as instructive feedback in that it either confirms an existing CR or instructs the learner as to the nature of the CR to be learnt.

Feedback Variables
Knowledge of results
In some learning tasks, it can be difficult for learners to perceive their own actions and/or their outcomes. This problem is familiar in learning physical actions, like dancing, tennis serves, or shooting at a target. If learners are uncertain as to what they have done, it is difficult to benefit from either critical or instructive feedback. However, steps can be taken to help the learner by using what has been called either *knowledge of results* or *augmented feedback* (Winstein & Schmidt, 1990). For complicated actions like dancing, the use of large mirrors in studios is a traditional way of providing knowledge of results to a student. Video replays can serve a similar function; the feedback is not as immediate as a mirror but can be repeated as needed. Where computers are used to teach tracking tasks, for example, flight simulation, knowledge of results can be augmented on the display by showing a trace of the learner's actions.

Delay of feedback
As a rule of thumb, feedback of either type is most effective when it is delivered immediately after the learner's attempt to perform the desired action. This rule is a direct application of the Law of Contiguity and is applicable in a variety of situations. Even delays of a few seconds can reduce the amount of learning. In one study, for example, 9-year old children were given training in which they were to press a button when presented with one coloured light but not when presented with two other possible lights. The feedback for a correct response was a red light, and the feedback for an incorrect response was a buzzer. In different groups of children, the delay in presenting the feedback was varied – either 0, 10, or 30 seconds (Hockman & Lipsitt, 1961).

Figure 9.4 *Delays in feedback reduce learning. This figure shows the proportion of correct responses for each of the three groups, which were trained with immediate feedback (0 seconds) or delayed feedback (10 seconds, 30 seconds). (Adapted from Hockman & Lipsitt, 1961.)*

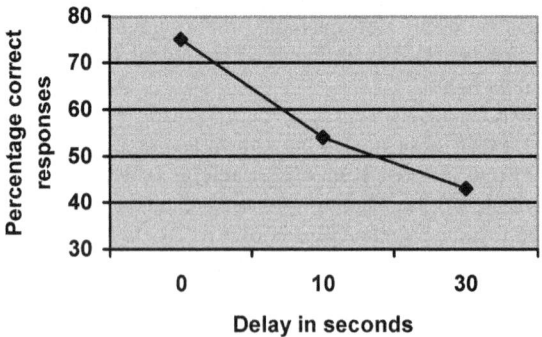

Figure 9.4 shows the proportion of correct responses performed by each of the three groups. As can be seen, the group trained with immediate feedback (0 seconds), showed the highest proportion of correct responses (75%). For groups trained with longer delays, the level of performance declined toward levels near the level that might be expected if the learners were guessing randomly (33%).

The deleterious effects of delaying feedback have been explained in two ways, both of which may be partially true. Some theorists suppose that a short-term memory of the stimulus and/or response can rapidly fade, making it difficult for the feedback to help in forming an association involving the stimulus and response (Gormezano & Kehoe, 1981). Other theorists have contended that, during the delay interval, the learner makes a variety of extraneous responses which compete with the desired response (Spence, 1956).

There is experimental evidence that, in adults, extraneous activity while waiting for feedback can hinder even simple associative learning (Champion & McBride, 1962). University students were required to learn a list of common associations among words, for example, "needle" – "thread." On each trial, the students were given one word as a stimulus and were asked to respond with the other. Either a 2-second or 5-second delay was introduced between the students' response to the stimulus word and the feedback, namely, presentation of the correct word. During the delay, some students read aloud a list of extraneous words that might interfere with learning the target word, for example, "sew", "thimble," "steel." Other students were instructed to continue looking at the stimulus word.

This experiment revealed two findings. First, the students trained with the shorter, 2-second delay showed better learning than the students trained with the longer, 5-second delay. Second, regardless of the delay, the students who read extra words during the delay did not perform as well as students who only looked at the stimulus word. Hence, any delay appears to be deleterious to learning, and, in addition, deliberate extraneous activity does cause additional deficits.

Intermittent feedback
Initial acquisition is fastest and most reliable when appropriate feedback is given after every attempt at the desired behaviour (Schulz & Runquist, 1960; Winstein & Schmidt, 1990). However, as the learner becomes proficient, feedback can be gradually reduced so that it only occurs after a fraction of the learner's attempts. In fact, a reduction in feedback can be beneficial. By reducing the feedback, learners may have to develop skills for monitoring their own performance and resolving any errors that occur. The development of these skills will help learners to perform the task independently and not rely on the feedback supplied by their instructor (Hesketh, 1997; Schmidt, 1991). Provided that feedback occurs occasionally and is not entirely eliminated, intermittent feedback will also improve the retention of learned behaviours over periods without practice (Winstein & Schmidt, 1990).

Use of mixed feedback
Use of mixed feedback, rather than a reliance on one type of feedback alone, appears to be appropriate in many learning situations. At the start of training, instructive feedback that is immediate and frequent can help shape the learner's behaviour in the appropriate direction and reduce frustration over errors. Later in the training process, however, critical feedback that is delivered intermittently may be what is required to keep the learner on the right track. For example, suppose an

apprentice chef is being taught how to chop vegetables finely and quickly with a sharp knife. Early in the training, instructive feedback such as "Chop the pieces so they are just half a centimetre wide" and "Protect the fingers you use to hold the vegetable by curving them slightly towards your hand" would be appropriate. Later in training, critical feedback such as "That's good" or "Do it again, please" would be sufficient.

Starting and Shaping Learning

Traditional depictions of associative learning have given the impression that it is a passive process, in which the learner is merely exposed to events and reacts mechanically. It may seem that the instructor need only set up the right conditions and rigid routine for learning to be assured. In fact, modern conceptions of associative learning require both the learner and instructor to be actively engaged with the environment and with each other, particularly during the initial stages of learning.

At the start of training, there is a multitude of ways that a learner can be exposed to the elements of an association. For simple situations, like a list of technical terms and their definitions, mere presentation of them to the learner might suffice. However, for other situations, like training a person to use a photocopier, the associations between key signals (e.g., "paper out") and their desired responses (e.g., "press the tray release button") can be most effectively introduced by an actual demonstration by the trainer. This process of demonstration, which would be followed by imitation by the learner, is known as "modelling".

Once the key associations have been introduced and the learner has made their first attempts at the desired actions, the learning of most complex tasks requires refinement in both coordinating complex actions and eliminating unnecessary steps. It is common in training complex tasks for the actions to be broken down into a series of steps, and, sometimes, for extra steps to be added specifically for the purpose of training. For example, in training a person to use a photocopier, it might be suitable to have the person initially go through all the possible options, using a checklist containing items such as "paper size indicator, toner supply indicator, number of copies, collating option, etc.". With experience, however, the learner will begin to check only those options that have consequences for their work on a routine basis.

This process of refinement is known broadly as *shaping*. In shaping the learner's actions, there are two things that an instructor should keep in mind. First, shaping occurs by successive approximations. That is, the learner's initial attempts may be awkward and inefficient. However, those attempts, provided they achieve the desired outcome, should be encouraged. The standard of performance desired by the instructor should be raised gradually, depending on the speed of progress. Second, each successful attempt should receive the appropriate encouragement even if the learner needed some assistance in achieving it. For example, suppose the learner forgets exactly where the tray release button is, and, after some time, the instructor is asked to point it out. The learner's final action of pressing the button should still receive the appropriate critical and/or instructive feedback, such as "Right, that's the tray release."

The process of shaping forms the early and middle portions of the learning curve. As the learner reaches a useful level of competence, the natural forms of feedback intrinsic to the task will ordinarily become sufficient to correct errors and produce further refinements. At this stage, the role of the instructor diminishes, and the instructor becomes more a source of advice to the learner rather than a source of immediate modelling, prompts, and feedback.

Attention in Learning

In any educational setting, there are numerous events that could become associated with each other. Fortunately, we only learn what we notice, and this limitation prevents us from being overwhelmed by the huge number of associations. This process has been studied extensively under the heading of "selective attention." Even the most mature learner has a limited capacity for attending simultaneously to several events. Accordingly, the goal of the educator is to direct the attention of the learner to the relevant material and away from tangential material.

Engagement of Active Attention

Learning situations can be designed to actively engage the learner's attention. As compared to rote memorization, storage of an association in memory is far easier when learners are actively engaged with the material. Naikar (1992) investigated the role of active attention when workers in a printing firm were trained to use computers for the first time. In her study, some workers were simply given a list of procedures to memorize. The procedures entailed a set of associations between certain problems that could arise in using the computer and the appropriate corrective action. A second group of workers was given the same list plus a brief explanation of each item. A third group of workers was given only the list of procedures, but they were also asked to generate their own explanations for each item. When tested later, this third group showed far better recall than the other two groups. In fact, making the attempt to generate the explanation appeared to be the important factor in promoting better learning. This was the case regardless of whether the learners' explanations were correct or not. Hence, by being asked to generate an explanation, the learners appeared to have attended more closely to the relevant material and thereby established stronger associations.

Prompting and Blocking

Trainers often attempt to assist learners by giving them prompts for the appropriate action at the appropriate time. Consider the situation shown in Figure 9.5. In this situation, a driving instructor is teaching a trainee to release the clutch at the right time, that is, when the engine reaches an appropriate number of revs in order to put the car into motion. The trainee is told that he may use the sound of the engine as the cue for releasing the clutch. However, as a prompt, the instructor tells the trainee, "release the clutch now."

According to the Law of Contiguity, the prompt should ensure that the cue of the correct engine sound will become associated with the trainee's response of releasing the clutch. Unfortunately, prompts can "block" learning. Learners often attend to the prompt and ignore the additional cue that is to be learned. By depending on the prompt, the trainee fails to learn the new association and, in the absence of the instructor, will fail to identify the correct engine sound for releasing the clutch.

The ability of an old association to block learning of an added new association has been found in a large variety of studies with animals, children, and adults. It might be thought that increasing the intensity of the added cue would divert the attention of the learner away from the more familiar cue. However, making the added cue more prominent has had little positive effect in preventing blocking. Learning theorists have concluded that, in cases of blocking, the familiar cue elicits the desired response, while the novel, added cue provides no new information. No additional learning will occur to the new cue, no matter how attention-grabbing it is.

The Use of Prompts as Instructional Feedback

Prompts block learning when they are simultaneous with the new cue. However, if they are presented after the learner makes an attempt to perform correctly, prompts will not divert the learner's attention and thus can help learning. As you may already see, this use of prompts converts them to a form of instructional feedback.

Using a prompt as feedback would come after initial instruction. For example, in the case of the trainee driver, the instructor would first tell or even show the trainee the correct sequence, emphasizing the correct engine sound and the correct way to release the clutch. Thereafter, the instructor would ask the trainee to press on the accelerator and wait for the trainee to release the clutch, perhaps only intervening when the trainee has revved the engine too much. Depending on the timing of the trainee's release, the feedback would entail basically a repetition of the original instruction, namely, "release the clutch when the engine sounds like so..." In practice, the feedback could be tailored to inform the trainee whether they should wait until the engine revs are higher or lower, depending on the timing of their last attempt.

Transfer of Training

As a goal of education or training, the learner should be able to apply their new knowledge and skills to situations beyond the classroom. This ability is known generally as transfer of training. It is the practical counterpart to our subjective feelings of "understanding." In fact, the ability to generalize our learning to new situations is the useful test that our feeling of understanding is correct.

In the basic type of transfer study, there are two groups of learners. One group receives training in a particular task, for example, learning to name major electronic parts ("transformer, resistor, capacitor, switch, etc.") when presented on a table. The other group would do some other, unrelated activity. Then, both groups would receive a test for immediate *transfer,* for example, they would both be asked to name the same electronic parts when in place on a circuit board. Transfer would be said to occur if the first group could name more parts than the second, untrained group.

Figure 9.5 An example of blocking in a practical training situation.

Figure 9.6 *A generalisation gradient for spatial location. This figure shows the proportion of children that responded to different lights arranged in a horizontal string. They were originally trained to respond to Light 6. (Adapted from Tempone, 1965.)*

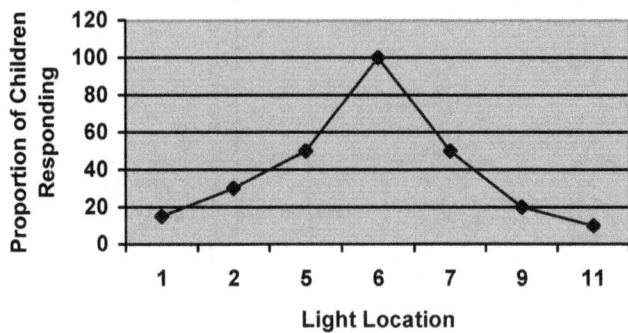

The most common form of immediate transfer is known as *stimulus generalization*. In stimulus generalization, responses acquired to one set of cues are applied to new cues depending on their physical similarity to the original set. Stimulus generalization can occur with both simple and complex cues. The simplest kind of generalization occurs when the cues vary along one, basic physical dimension. For example, in one study (Tempone, 1965), children were trained to press a button when the centre light in a string of lights came on. Subsequently, they were tested by turning other lights on. Figure 9.6 depicts the results, in which the vertical axis shows the proportion of children that pressed the key, and the horizontal axis shows the position of the light in the string. As can be seen, all the children (100%) pressed in response to Light 6, which was used in training. About half the children (50%) responded when either Light 5 or Light 7 was turned on. A smaller proportion of children responded to lights that were more distant to Light 6. This result is known as a *generalization gradient* for spatial location.

A more complex but perhaps more familiar example of stimulus generalization occurs when a learner has to apply a mathematical formula to a problem in which the symbols have been changed. Suppose students had learned this formula: $(x+y)^2 = x^2+2xy+y^2$. Later they were tested with the original item "$(x+y)^2$" and a test item "square (b1+b2)". Studies have shown that about 93% of students will respond correctly to the original item but only 72% will respond correctly to the test item even though it is mathematically identical to the original item. The change in the physical appearance of the formula causes a failure to generalize for some students.

Another form of immediate transfer occurs when a rule that has been learned is applied in a variety of situations that are physically dissimilar. For example, in a course on computing skills, a student is taught some basic trouble-shooting skills to use when a computer isn't working. The student is taught that if the computer can't be switched on, the first thing to do is check the sources of power: Is the computer plugged in to a power point, is the power point switched on, or has there been a general power outage? The following semester, the student is presenting a seminar as part of another course, and has trouble with an overhead projector. The student uses the same set of troubleshooting skills as for a computer and remembers to check the sources of power first. In this situation, the student is able to ignore the superficial differences between an overhead projector and a computer, and instead can identify where a general rule may be applied.

Not all transfer is immediate. Transfer of previous learning can appear gradually during learning in a new situation. This form of transfer is known variously as non-specific *transfer* or *learning to learn,* which is defined as a progressive increase in the speed of learning across a series of tasks that may differ dramatically in their physical appearance but are similar in their solution (Ellis, 1965, p. 32). Another researcher aptly concluded, "... learning to learn transforms the organism from a creature that adapts to a changing environment by trial and error to one that adapts by seeming hypothesis and insight" (Harlow, 1949).

Learning to learn has been demonstrated in wide variety of situations. For example, the number of repetitions needed for adults to learn a list of word syllables decreases by about 50% with practice over a series of a dozen different lists (Meyer & Miles, 1953). Similarly, the acquisition of abstract concepts, like "pick the odd item" can be improved by learning a series of tasks in which the goal is to choose the odd item from a set of objects.

Figure 9.7 A set of learning curves that show learning to learn in a series of 56 simple problems. Each curve shows the average percentage of correct choices across the six trials in each group of problems. The rate of learning improves across problems. (Adapted from Harlow, 1949.)

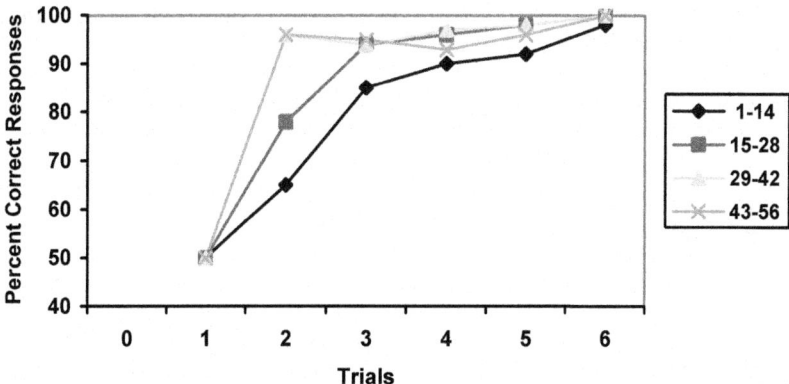

Learning to learn is most easily seen in young children. Figure 9.7 shows a set of learning curves that demonstrate learning to learn in children. They were given a series of discrimination problems. These problems can be viewed as a simple form of concept learning. In each problem, the children were given six opportunities to choose between two objects, for example, two different coloured blocks. In technical terms, each of these opportunities is called a *trial.* If children chose the "correct" block, they were rewarded with a toy. If they selected the other block, there was no reward. After the six trials with one problem, the children were then given another problem using completely different "junk" objects, for example, two different shapes. In all, the children were given 56 problems of this type. Each of the learning curves shows the average percentage of correct choices for Problems 1-14, 15-28, 29-42, and 43-56, respectively.

For each problem, the children had to make a guess at the "correct" object on the first trial. Thus, the learning curve for each problem always starts at 50% correct for Trial 1. After the first guess, an adult would find it easy to choose the correct object on Trials 2, 3, 4, 5, and 6. However, for a child, it can be seen that for the early problems (1-14), their second choice was correct only about 68% of the time, and their third choice was correct only about 88% of the time.

For the children, the process of learning during the early problems was very much one of trial and error. However, as they accumulated experience with discrimination problems, the shape of the curve changed, because learning accelerated. For Problems 15-28, the children's second choice was correct about 82% of the time. By the final set (Problems 43-56), the children were solving the problems like an adult. On Trial 2 of this final set, the children chose correctly nearly 100% of the time.

The process of learning to learn is only partially understood. On early problems, the children appeared to learn simply an association between the particular correct object and the response of choosing it. However, as seen in later problems, the learning in this phase had a wider effect beyond the specific object-response associations. The children were also acquiring an association between the abstract structure of the problem and an abstract response pattern that can be called a "strategy." In this particular case, the children acquired a strategy called "Win-Stay, Lose-Shift." This means that when the children did choose the correct object and won a reward, they would stay with that choice on later trials. Conversely, if the children chose incorrectly and did not win the reward, they would shift their choice to the other object on later trials (Levine, 1959).

Figure 9.8 *Retention curves for relearning (List A) and learning to learn (List B). The figure shows the reduction in the time required to learn the two lists compared the original acquisition of List A. (Adapted from Bunch, 1936.)*

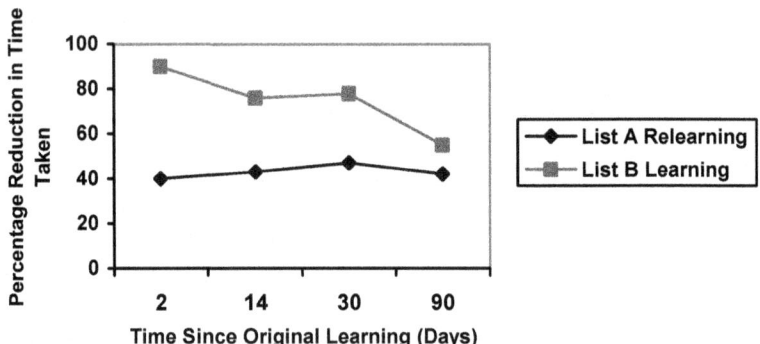

Learning to Learn Is Not Forgotten
Learning to learn in adults is a robust phenomenon that depends on mechanisms which are independent of the original associations. Although retention of specific associations tends to decline rapidly, the amount of general transfer is constant

over many weeks. For example, Bunch (1936) trained groups of university students in a list of associations, each entailing a letter-digit pair (List A). They were then tested either for learning a new list of letter-digit associations (List B) or for relearning of the original list (List A). The intervals between the original learning session and test session varied from 0 to 90 days. Learning to learn was readily apparent. In comparison to a group of students who did not participate in the original learning, the experienced students made fewer errors, took less time, and required fewer trials to master the second set of associations in List B. Figure 9.8 shows this reduction in the time required to learn List B for each of the retention intervals in the experienced students. Regardless of the retention interval, there was about a 40% reduction in the time required, indicating that learning to learn was retained over long periods of time without further practice.

In contrast to the fixed nature of learning to learn, many of the specifics of List A were forgotten. The second curve in Figure 9.8 shows the reduction in time required to relearn List A. As can be seen, students who only had two days between the original learning and relearning showed substantial retention; there was a huge, 91% reduction in the time to relearn List A. However, students who had waited 90 days before relearning List A showed only a 56% reduction in the time they took.

Negative Transfer

Transfer from one task to another is not always beneficial. Previous learning can interfere with new learning. This kind of interference is called *"negative transfer."* It often occurs when the new task has similar cues to an old task but requires a different kind of action from the learner. Most adults have encountered this form of transfer when they are driving an unfamiliar car. Cars do not consistently have the direction indicator lever and the windscreen wiper lever on the same side of the steering column. Consequently, it is possible to find oneself trying to signal a direction change using the windscreen wiper. Elsewhere in this book, Pithers discusses this form of negative transfer in more detail in his section on forgetting and interference.

Both positive and negative transfer can occur in the same situation. For example, in switching to an unfamiliar car, the negative transfer is usually transient, while the positive transfer of previously-learned driving skills will quickly predominate. Thus, learning to drive an unfamiliar car will be far faster than learning to drive one's first car.

The relative strength of negative and positive transfer can vary with time, and this variance can be seen even in animals. Bunch (1939) examined transfer in groups of rats. They were trained first to turn right to obtain a reward in a maze. Then, they were trained to turn left to obtain the same reward. The interval between the two tasks was varied from 0 to 28 days. At the shorter retention intervals, there was negative transfer from the right-turn habit to the left-turn habit. That is to say, the rats took longer to learn the new habit compared to the old habit. However, when there was a two- to four-week period between the training sessions, positive transfer appeared. The rats took less time to learn the new habit. Thus, as the specifics of the first habit were forgotten, the positive effects of learning to learn made themselves felt.

James Kehoe & Michaela Macrae

Practice with Variability
In the educational context, it is possible to capitalise on both immediate and general transfer by providing students with a variety of examples of a problem with the same structure. Variety in problems helps students either to discover the underlying principle or to apply a known principle in different situations. Elsewhere in this book, Pithers discusses the relative merits of discovery learning, in which the student must identify the general principles based on multiple examples, versus expository learning, in which the students are given the general principles for solving the type of problem. In either case, varied examples are needed so that the student can learn to notice the structural similarities of problems that are otherwise superficially different.

Halpern (1998) has provided an illustration of how varied examples can be used in teaching the skills of critical thinking to adults. The principle being taught was the concept of "sunk costs", in which prior spending forms the basis for decisions about the value of further spending. A popular saying which expresses this concept is "beware of throwing good money after bad." Halpern suggested giving students three different examples of this principle. The first example was one in which a friend proposes to spend $500 to repair a beat-up old car, because the friend has already spent hundreds of dollars on previous repairs. This justification for spending even more money is a "sunk costs" argument, because it doesn't take any notice of whether the car in its current state is worth the further expense. The second example was one in which a politician advocates further spending on a missile system because billions had already been spent on its development. In the third example, a friend is planning to marry his long-term girlfriend because they have already spent so much time together.

Common to each of these examples is the notion that past expenditure justifies spending more in the present. In fact, the people making the decisions would be better off if they focused on the future, considering what would be gained by further spending of their money or affection. Halpern (1998) emphasised that, after practice with varied examples, it is this conceptual structure that becomes represented in the learner's memory and is recalled whenever the "sunk costs" type of argument is made. In this way, the transfer of skills can become independent of the content of the particular problems at hand.

Table 9.1 *Rates of learning to type under four different practice schedules*

Practice Schedule	Mean Hours to Criterion	Mean Days to Criterion
1 hour per day	45	45
1 X 2 hours per day	51	25
2 X 1 hour per day	56	28
2 X 2 hours per day	65	16

Note. Criterion was 70 accurate keystrokes per minute

224

Distribution of Training

In colloquial terms, the Law of Frequency is expressed as "practice makes perfect." However, there is an important corollary to that basic principle, namely, that practice spaced out over time produces better learning than the same amount massed into a short period of time. This effect has been seen in two different ways that have important practical implications. Elsewhere in this book, Pithers and Cornford also both discuss distribution of practice in memory and skill acquisition.

Amount of practice per day

As a rule of thumb, it is more efficient to spread out training over several days. For example, Baddeley and Longman (1978) have demonstrated the value of distributed practice when they helped postal workers learn to type so that they could use new sorting machines that were being introduced in their workplace. In the learning to type program, the workers were divided into four groups. One group had the most widely distributed practice: a single session of one hour of practice per day. Another group had two, one-hour sessions per day. A third group had only one session, but it was two hours long. Finally, the fourth group had the most massed practice, in which they received two sessions per day, each two hours long.

Table 9.1 shows the average number of hours that each group practised typing until they reached a level of 70 correct keystrokes per minute. The group that received one hour of practice per day required the fewest hours of practice, on average 45 hours. The second and third groups, which had a total of two hours of practice per day, required more hours to achieve the same level, averaging more than 50 hours. Finally, the highly massed group, which received a total of four hours of practice per day, required 65 hours of training to reach the same level of competence.

The table also shows the total number of days needed by each group to achieve 70 correct strokes per minute. As can be seen, the highly massed group needed the fewest days to achieve that level. Accordingly, if a trained group of people is needed in a short timeframe, massed practice yields the desired result, but at the expense of needing a substantially greater number of hours of training. If there is no pressing need, distributed practice is less expensive in terms of the total hours of practice.

Distribution of practice within a training session

In educational settings, students are often expected to attend to more than one topic during a class. It is traditional to deal completely with one topic and then move on to another. This organisation can be seen as a form of massed practice. Evidence from laboratory studies with adults indicates that, for at least some forms of drill, it is advisable to intermix the material within a class. This intermixed form of organisation allows the learner to benefit from spaced practice.

Evidence for the benefits of intermixed practice was found in a study in which students were given lists of common words to memorize. Some words were presented only once, some were presented twice together, and others were presented twice but separated by 2 to 40 other items (Melton, 1970). When the students were asked to recall the list, only 20% of words that had been presented once were successfully recalled. The words that had been presented twice together were recalled about 28% of the time, thus indicating that repetition was beneficial.

Furthermore, the words that had been presented twice but separated by other items were recalled even better. In the best case, two words that were separated by 40 other items were recalled nearly 50% of the time. Thus, spaced repetition produced the best recall. This finding is particularly surprising, because it might be thought that insertion of other items, which themselves were words, might have interfered with the storage in memory of the two main words.

Although few education classes entail rote learning of lists, the same principle of intermixed practice can be extended to other activities. A traditional piano lesson might contain a 1 0-min block on one piece, a 10-min block on another piece, and a 10-min block on technical work (e.g., scales). The intermixing principle suggests that breaking the session into 5-min blocks, in which one rotates twice through the two pieces and technical work, should produce faster learning and better retention. Finally, for instruction in cognitively more complex skills, the use of reviews, summaries, and/or quizzes towards the end of each class could have the same effect as spaced repetition.

Although the beneficial effects of spaced practice are well known, there is no widely-accepted explanation of why it works so well. Traditionally, theories have focused on the possibility that the storage of associations depends on a period of silent rehearsal which helps their consolidation in brain pathways. However, this explanation does not appear to be adequate for two reasons. First, the intermixing of practice on different topics within a class session would seem to prohibit the learner from taking time to rehearse material. Second, many laboratory experiments have attempted to manipulate rest periods between successive items in simple tasks, on the assumption that longer rest periods should be conducive to more rehearsal and better consolidation. However, there is little evidence that such rest periods within a training session have the desired positive effect. Instead, it may be the case that intermixed practice is beneficial because it changes attention from one set of material to another, thus refreshing the person's interest after their attention has waned.

Discrimination Learning

The associative basis of conceptual categorisation is *discrimination learning*. In general, discrimination learning involves at least two associations, in which one cue is associated with one response, and another cue is associated with a different response. A basic type of discrimination learning is seen when children learn to attach different names to different colours. The earliest stage of this learning often entails some degree of inaccuracy. For example, a child may call all colours "blue," and then gradually learn to associate the correct colours with their corresponding words. The continued refinement of discriminations along basic sensory dimensions like colour can extend into adulthood, say, amongst interior decorators and painters.

For adults, many discriminations entail a combination of a large number of cues. For example, wool classers must learn to attach different labels to wool samples depending on their texture, strength, colour, density, and so on. The acquisition of some discriminations demands that the learner perceive the relationships among some basic features. For example, in learning to read Chinese, the learner must recognize the combination of strokes that make up each character, and learn to associate particular characters with particular spoken words. Similarly, learning the names of different people demands the association of their names to the arrangement of their facial features.

Conditional discrimination is a special type of discrimination learning. In this type of problem, people learn to use one cue to determine their response to a second cue. The first cue is often called the *context,* and the second cue is called the *target stimulus.* A familiar example of a conditional discrimination is seen in self-monitoring, in which people vary their response to, say, a painful stimulus depending on the social context. If someone hits their thumb while using a hammer, their verbal expletive may differ dramatically depending on who else is present – their best friend or their grandparents.

Physical contexts can also act as conditional cues. It is common for business travellers to learn to use both right-hand drive cars, in countries like Australia, Britain, and Japan, and left-hand drive cars in countries like the United States, France, and Germany. At first, most drivers experience confusion in a number of situations where left-right mistakes are possible, such as turning into the correct lane at an intersection. However, the process of conditional discrimination allows them to resolve the confusion and learn to react in the correct way in each context. See Cornford's chapter in this volume for further discussion of context and skill application.

Differential outcomes

One way of helping learners to notice the different cues in both ordinary discriminations and conditional discriminations is to use differential outcomes. Results from laboratory studies have shown that the learning of discriminations among symbols can be speeded up by using different rewards for each symbol-response association. Suppose, for example, one wished to train a person to administer cardiopulmonary resuscitation (CPR) to accident victims. An important part of CPR is to check the victim's breathing, airways, and pulse. Each combination of symptoms requires a different response. This diagnostic procedure can be viewed as a discrimination learning problem. In traditional training, critical feedback is used in which the learner is told whether their response was correct or not. Thus, if the learner administers heart compression to a victim who has no heartbeat, then they are told that they are correct. Similarly, if the learner administers mouth-to-mouth resuscitation to a victim who has ceased breathing, they are also told that what they did was correct. This type of feedback does produce appropriate learning, but the use of different kinds of feedback yields even faster learning with fewer errors. In general, the critical feedback can be supplemented with augmented knowledge of results, for example, a distinctive heart-beat sound for the heart compression action versus a distinctive breathing sound for the mouth-to-mouth resuscitation. Distinctive forms of verbal feedback could also be used.

Loss of Associative Learning

Three students return to a course in car maintenance after the summer holidays. The first student is not very interested in the course, and so has not practised her skills at all over the break. The second student is keen to eventually work as a mechanic and so has practised over the break by trying to tinker on her own car, but with no-one else there to remind her what to do. The third student also practised her skills over the break, plus she was taught some additional 'short cuts' by her older brother. On the first day of classes, all three students are tested on what they recall from the previous school year, and they all fail.

These three students can be understood as displaying three different examples of associative loss. The most familiar form of associative loss is forgetting, in which skills that are not practised are lost over time, as in the case of the first student. However, there are other forms of associative loss. Associative loss can occur despite continued practice, if feedback is not available. For example, the second student might have found that, even despite her attempts to practise, her memories of the course became increasingly inaccurate in the absence of the teacher's feedback. Finally, in cases where retraining has occurred, associative loss is encouraged as old associations are replaced by new associations. Thus, the third student might have found that the new "short cuts" she learned over the holidays replaced the old associations that were required for her to be proficient as a car mechanic. The following sections discuss the various forms of associative loss in more detail, and present illustrative experimental examples.

Figure 9.9 *Retention curve for a complex skill. This figure shows the likelihood of the patient's survival if a worker attempted to perform cardiopulmonary resuscitation (CPR) after varying periods without practice. (Adapted from McKenna & Glendon, 1985.)*

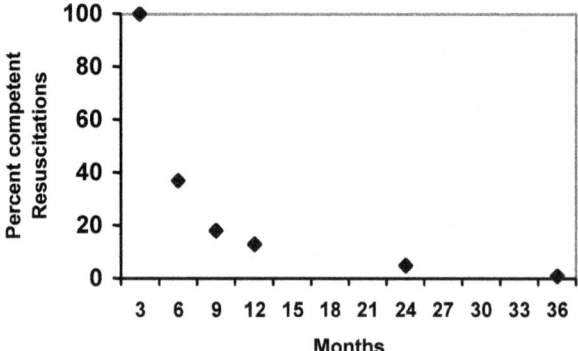

Retention Loss: Forgetting
The rates at which forgetting occurs have been found to vary considerably depending on the nature of the task. For continuous motor tasks, like bicycle riding, retention is nearly perfect over years without practice. Often, only a few minutes of practice are sufficient to completely recover one's former level of skill. For other kinds of simple associations there can be initial losses which then stabilise. For example, Bahrick (1984) studied the retention of Spanish-English associations over intervals ranging from 1 year to 50 years. He found that recall decreases to 75% correct in 1 year and to 45% correct in 2 years. Thereafter, however, the declines are slight. Even after 50 years, people were still able to recall 40% of their Spanish-English vocabulary. For complex skills, however, almost complete forgetting can occur within months. McKenna and Glendon (1985) examined the loss of skills required for successful CPR by first-aid workers in

factories and offices. In this study, 215 workers were trained to a level of proficiency that would virtually guarantee the survival of a revivable patient. Based on tests with a realistic dummy, Figure 9.9 shows the likelihood of the patient's survival if a worker attempted to perform CPR after varying periods without practice. As can be seen, there is substantial forgetting in the first 3 months after training, and, by 12 months, the patient's survival rate would drop to about 13%. By the end of three years, the patient would not be expected to survive at all.

Maintenance Loss: Extinction

As described in the example of the student who tried to practise her car mechanics skills with no corrective feedback, the ability to retrieve an association can decline when appropriate feedback is suspended, even in the face of continuous practice. This type of loss was first discovered in studies of learning with animals. If, for example, an animal was trained to press a small lever to obtain a food reward, it would learn to press the bar frequently and rapidly. However, if food no longer follows the lever press, animals do not persist for very long, and the lever press response will gradually cease. This specific type of loss is called *extinction* of a response.

Although the traditional depiction of extinction involves the disappearance of a response, in humans, extinction can also appear as a loss of accuracy or a loss of organisation in a complex response pattern. For example, one recent study examined the maintenance of breast self-examination for cancer (Jones, et al., 1993). Over a six-month period following initial training, the women were sent monthly reminders to conduct the breast self-examination and report on it. However, no feedback was given regarding their examination technique. At periods of one week and six months after training, each woman's technique was assessed in a variety of ways.

Although all women were proficient at the end of training, many showed declines in their proficiency despite their continued practice. Among other things, there was a decline in the proportion of the breast that was examined. At one week after training, an average of only 73% of the breast was being examined, and at six months after training, only 63% of the breast was being examined. Thus, in the absence of feedback, there was a loss of accuracy in performance.

Deliberate Loss: Counterconditioning

As in the example of the student who learned car mechanics "short cuts" from her brother, there are occasions in which one wishes to replace an old association with a new association. In the laboratory, this form of learning, in which associations are dramatically changed, is called *counterconditioning*. In everyday life, it is common to encounter situations in which a familiar person changes their name, which requires their friends to extinguish the association between their old name and their face, and to replace it with the new name. Similarly, we are bombarded with attempts by corporations to change their image often by changing their name, as when, say, *Telecom* became *Telstra*.

In this era of rapid technological change, most workers will find that, at some point, they will undergo retraining in which new technology will alter their old methods for doing their job. The introduction of computers into virtually every facet of modern work is the most noticeable example. Even road crews laying down bitumen have been retrained to use computers to get the proper mix of stone and tar depending on the air temperature and humidity. Similarly, improvements in occupational health and safety also require changes in well established habits, for example, in methods used for safe lifting of heavy objects.

Reversal of Associative Loss: Savings

Superficially, associative loss suggests that the underlying association has been completely destroyed. However, closer investigations have revealed that the association is largely preserved, and what is lost temporarily is the ability to retrieve it. In some cases, retrieval will show *spontaneous recovery* if the person stops trying to retrieve the association and does something else for several hours or even a day. In many other cases, it is possible to recover a lost association with a small amount of refresher training. The generic name for this rapid recovery is *savings*. In theoretical terms, it has been frequently suggested that all cases of associative loss indicate that an old association has been submerged by a newer association. These theories are reviewed in greater detail in this volume by Pithers in his discussion of forgetting.

A familiar example of savings is seen in the result of feeding pet dogs from the dinner table. A dog will acquire the habit of begging if it is frequently given scraps directly from the dinner table. With patience, ignoring the begging and refusing to give the dog any further food will extinguish the behaviour. However, if on a future occasion a morsel of food accidentally drops from the table, the dog will rapidly reacquire its old habit and begin begging again.

Savings are most obvious when refresher training is used after total forgetting or complete extinction. Refresher training can also be put to good use in preventing associative loss before performance declines below an acceptable level. In the previous example in which women were taught to conduct breast self-examination, some of the participants were given an instructional tape to listen to while practising at home. Listening to this tape once per month prevented part of the loss seen in women who did not have the tape. After six months, those women who used the tape to refresh their technique were more proficient in all aspects of the examination than women who did not use the tape (Jones et al., 1993).

Even a single session of refresher training can be helpful in preventing forgetting over long periods. A key skill for merchant marine cadets is watchkeeping on the bridge of a ship. In one study, the cadets were given initial training plus a brief refresher course six months later. When tested at nine months after initial training, these cadets showed smaller declines in their skills than another group of cadets who did not receive the refresher training (O'Hara, 1990).

Conclusions and Guidelines

In this chapter, our aim was to introduce the reader to useful concepts and principles that have been discovered in the study of associative learning. In this section, we summarise nine guidelines that should improve the design and delivery of adult education.

- *The S-shaped learning curve.* Patience makes perfect. The effects of initial instruction and practice may not be apparent in a student's performance. However, with appropriate repetition, performance will improve.

- *Feedback.* Feedback is crucial to initial acquisition of any type of knowledge or skill. Instructive feedback is particularly useful early in training, and critical feedback becomes more useful as the student gains proficiency.
- *Active attention.* People only learn what they notice. People best learn when their attention is actively engaged through interaction with the teaching material. One useful method for engaging the learner's attention is to ask them to generate explanations and/or extensions to the material.
- *Two kinds of transfer of training.* Immediate transfer is the most obvious type of transfer, as when learners have their facts and skills available "at their finger tips" in a variety of situations. Learning to learn is equally important. It provides the foundation for solving new problems with increasing efficiency, thus enabling learners to adapt more readily to the changing demands of their environment.
- *Distribution of training.* Learning is most efficient when training is spread out over time. This can be achieved by distributing a fixed amount of training on a topic over several days and by intermixing different kinds of material on a topic within a training session.
- *Conditional discriminations.* A little knowledge can indeed be a dangerous thing. There is a tendency for students to apply a new skill uniformly in all situations. In fact, the appropriate application is usually context-dependent. As students become proficient, they should be given explicit instruction as to the contexts in which a new skill is appropriate and also the contexts in which it is not.
- *Differential outcomes.* Learning of simple and conditional discriminations can be enhanced if the learner's responses to different situations receive distinctive forms of feedback.
- *Associative loss.* The continued performance of learned behaviour also needs
- some feedback. Without feedback, well-learned skills can deteriorate, despite the learner's best attempts to practise.
- *Refresher training.* Associative loss can be prevented by periodic feedback in the form of refresher training. Even if there has been substantial loss, refresher training can capitalise on savings, leading to rapid recovery of the lost skill.

REFERENCES

Anderson, J. R. (1985). *Cognitive psychology and its implications* (2nd ed.). New York: W. H. Freeman. Baddeley, A. D., & Longman, D. J. A. (1978). The influence of length and frequency on training sessions on the rate of learning to type. *Ergonomics, 21,* 627-635.

Bahrick, H. P. (1984). Semantic memory content in permastore: Fifty years of memory for Spanish learned in school. *Journal of Experimental Psychology: General, 113,* 1-29.

Bain, A. (1855). *The senses and the intellect.* London: Parker.

Bain, A. (1859). *The emotions and the will.* London: Parker.

Bunch, M. E. (1936). The amount of transfer in rational learning as function of time. *Journal of Comparative Psychology, 22,* 325-337.

Bunch, M. E. (1939). Transfer of training in the mastery of an antagonistic habit after varying intervals of time. *Journal of Comparative Psychology, 28,* 189- 200.

Champion, R. A., & McBride, D. A. (1962). Activity during delay of reinforcement in human learning. *Journal of Experimental Psychology, 63,* 589-592.

Ellis, H. (1965). *The transfer of learning.* NY: Macmillan.

Gormezano, I., & Kehoe, E. J. (1981). Classical conditioning and the law of contiguity. In P. M. Harzem & M. D. Zeiler (Eds.), *Advances in analysis of behavior Vol. 2. Predictability, correlation, and contiguity* (pp. 1-45). NY: Wiley.

Halpern, D. (1998). Teaching critical thinking for transfer across domains: Dispositions, skills, structure training, and metacognitive monitoring. *American Psychologist, 53*, 449-455.

Harlow, H. F. (1949). The formation of learning sets. *Psychological Review, 56*, 51-65.

Hesketh, B. (1997). Dilemmas in training for transfer and retention. *Applied Psychology: An International Review, 46*, 317-339.

Hockman, C. H., & Lipsitt, L. P. (1961). Delay-of reward gradients in discrimination learning with children for two levels of difficulty. *Journal of Comparative and Physiological Psychology, 54*, 24-27.

Jones, J. A., Eckhardt, L. E., Mayer, J. A., Bartholomew, S., Malcarne, V. L., Hovell, M. F., & Elder, J. P. (1993). The effects of an instructional audiotape on breast self-examination proficiency. *Journal of Behavioral Medicine, 16*, 225-235.

Levine, M. (1959). A model of hypothesis behavior in discrimination learning sets. *Psychological Review, 66*, 353-366.

McKenna, S. P., & Glendon, A. I. (1985). Occupational first aid training: Decay in cardiopulmonary resuscitation (CPR) skills. *Journal of Occupational Psychology, 58*, 109-117.

Melton, A. W. (1970). The situation with respect to the spacing of repetitions and memory. *Journal of Verbal Learning and Verbal Behavior, 2*, 1-21.

Meyer, D. R., & Miles, R. C. (1953). Intralist-interlist relations in verbal learning. *Journal of Experimental Psychology, 45*, 109-115.

Naikar, N. (1992) *Facilitation of learning: The generation effect*. Honours thesis, The University of New South Wales.

O'Hara, J. M. (1990). The retention of skills acquired through simulator-based training. *Ergonomics, 33*, 1143-1 153.

Pavlov, I. P. (1927). *Conditioned reflexes: An investigation of the physiological activity of the cerebral cortex* (G. V. Anrep, Trans.). London: Oxford University Press.

Schmidt, R. A. (1991). Frequent augmented feedback can degrade learning: Evidence and interpretations. In G. E. Stelmach & J. Requin (Eds.), *Tutorials in motor neuroscience* Dordrecht: Kluwer Academic Publishers.

Schneiderman, N., Fuentes, I., & Gormezano, I. (1962). Acquisition and extinction of the classically conditioned eyelid response in the albino rabbit. *Science, 136*, 650-652.

Schulz, R. W., & Runquist, W. N. (1960). Learning and retention of paired adjectives as a function of percentage occurrence of response members. *Journal of Experimental Psychology, 59*, 409-413.

Skinner, B. F. (1938). *The behavior of organisms*. NY: Appleton-Century-Crofts.

Spence, K. W. (1956). *Behavior theory and conditioning*. New Haven, CT: Yale University Press.

Tempone, V. J. (1965). Gradients of stimulus generalization as a function of mental age. *Child Development, 36*, 229-235.

Thorndike, E. L. (1898). Animal intelligence: An experimental study of the associative processes in animals. *Psychological Monographs, 2*, 1-100.

Thorndike, E. L. (1911). *Animal intelligence*. NY: Macmillan.

Winstein, C. J., & Schmidt, R. A. (1990). Reduced frequency of knowledge of results enhances motor skill learning. *Journal of Experimental Psychology: Learning, Memory, and Cognition, 16*, 677-691.

Review Questions

Read the following statements and indicate whether they are True or False.

1. An association between an object and its name is most quickly learned if seeing the object and hearing its name are close together.

2. Improvements in performance will start to appear right after the first time an association is practiced.

3. Forgetting represents a loss of memory that can never be recovered.

4. Critical feedback is always better than instructive feedback.

5. Thorndike's Law of Effect requires contiguity of a stimulus, response, and a reward.
6. The use of videos in training is useful for providing instructive feedback
7. In Pavlov' classical conditioning method, the conditioned stimulus (CS) acts as critical feedback.
8. Early in acquisition, feedback should be delayed to enable learners to think about their answer.
9. Late in acquisition, intermittent feedback can be useful to help students learn to monitor their own performance.
10. When a person can no longer retrieve an association, relearning will take just as long as original learning.
11. Modelling and imitation can be an effective way to help someone to start learning a skill.
12. Learning is best done when the learner is passively receives the new material.
13. Prompts to the correct action by an teacher can block a student from acquiring a new association between a situation and the correct response.
14. Learning to learn is like stimulus generalisation in that both appear immediately when a person is starting to learn in a new situation.

The following questions are designed to test your understanding of the content of this chapter. Answers can all be checked by referring to the relevant sections.

1. List the similarities between classical and instrumental conditioning. List the differences.
2. List the kinds of transfer and their characteristics.
3. List the different types of feedback and their characteristics.
4. List the types of associative loss.

Answers

1T2F	3F	4F	5T	6T	7F
8F9T	10F	11T	12F	13T	14F

Exercises

1. A student who shows potential for being a good electronic technician is having difficulty in learning to solder small parts to a printed circuit board. Suggest a sequence of activities that might help the student to improve this skill. What feedback provisions would you recommend?
2. Students in an office skills course need to acquire skills in data entry, phone reception, word-processing, and data-base management. How would you schedule the instruction and practice sessions to maximise learning?
3. You have been asked to select a computer-based training package for a unit in small engine repair. Several packages are available. In terms of the principles you have read in this chapter, what features of the packages would be important for engaging the students' attention in the learning task.
4. For a complex task like computerised book-keeping, discuss whether training should ensure that every piece of knowledge and every sub-skill be available for immediate transfer to the actual book-keeping job. If not, what should the objectives for transfer and retention be?

5. The starting of learning can be difficult. Some people claim that exploration and discovery produce the best learning. Other people claim that careful guidance during the early stages of learning is useful. What

6. principles might you use in designing learning activities that will help shape the appropriate pattern of behaviour in a new skill?

7. Suppose you want to design training exercises that require recognition and classification of different sorts of events. For example, air traffic controllers have to learn to identify and report different kinds of aircraft, their altitude, speed, and direction amongst the "clutter" on a radar screen. How would you go about helping the trainees to discriminate amongst the alternatives and correctly label them?

Acknowledgement

This research was supported by Australian Research Council Grant A79600502.

About the Authors

E. James Kehoe studied at Lawrence University (B. A., 1971) and The University of Iowa (M. A. 1973, Ph.D., 1976). Since 1977, he has been at The University of New South Wales, where he is currently a Professor of Psychology. He has published research on basic associative learning in animals, the neural bases of learning, associative processes in early reading, and implications of associative theory for clinical psychology. He teaches courses in behavioural neuroscience and training in organisations.

Michaela Macrae has a B.Sc. (Psychology, Hons, I) from The University of New South Wales. She is currently completing her PhD in the neuropsychology of human navigation and its relation to memory processes. She also continues research in associative learning and its neural bases.

E. James Kehoe and Michaela Macrae
University of New South Wales

R. T. PITHERS

10. MEMORY AND RETRIEVAL: IMPLICATIONS FOR TEACHING AND LEARNING

It is the initial session with a new Stage 2 class and a teacher or trainer decides to start by revising some of the essential concepts and practices that the students have learned during Stage 1 of their course. Like most good practitioners they attempt to motivate and make the learners active by asking a series of questions about these issues. Answers to these questions, however, are either forgotten or mixed up and confused and they quickly discover that over the vacation period the student's remembrance of the knowledge and skills previously covered has suffered. While these students are apt to blame last year's teacher for this loss and, no doubt, blame this teacher for a similar failure next year, much of this loss is due to a failure to remember.

Remembering is a major problem for the student and the teacher alike. Most teachers are especially concerned with first, how much of the knowledge and skills taught will be remembered over time and second, with whether the student can use and apply the knowledge and skills not only as a basis for future learning as in the example just used but also to their workplace outside of the training room. Both of these problems are related because students cannot transfer knowledge or skill to higher subject levels or to their workplace, if they cannot remember what it is that they have initially learned. Teachers and trainers, therefore, should try to maximise their student's memory of whatever is taught and learned.

James A Athanasou (ed.), Adult Educational Psychology, 235–260

What Is Learning?

Learning may be examined in two ways: (a) the way in which behaviour changes as a result of experience - termed acquisition and (b) the way in which, given a fixed level of performance, performance is retained over an ensuing period of time without practice - termed memory. If there was no retention of what is practised then there could be no improvement with practice during acquisition. This is because learning depends on the culmination of the effects of practice over periods of time without practice.

Memory is not observed but inferred from changes in an individual's performance following certain conditions of practice, for instance, a learner's recall of the safety features associated with a particular work task. Research evidence has indicated that most forgetting takes place soon after learning, whether or not the learned material is verbal or perceptual-motor in nature. It is important for teachers and trainers, therefore, to discover the causes of failure to remember and of errors in remembering and try to reduce these effects. Nevertheless, as remembering is based to a large extent on the degree and quality of the initial learning and what follows, any techniques that influence these factors will affect whether and the extent to which the learner remembers.

What Is Memory?

The term 'memory' as it appears defined in most English dictionaries denotes a variety of different meanings. It can be used in about a dozen different ways in the language from the notion of a reservoir for perceived information through to notions of process. A typical definition is that memory is some sort of mental faculty for retaining impressions. Definitions such as this one, however, do not help the memory researcher and theorist because they are clouded by a rich, hazy fabric of colloquial everyday language.

Memory is, no doubt, a unitary term but in the literature on memory it is used to describe a quite complicated process and sub-systems. These sub-systems are seen to have different storage durations ranging from less than one second up to a complete lifetime. Their capacities for storage of information vary from very small to a capacity that allows for living and, perhaps, expertise in a range of different workplace domain areas. In short, memory:
– contains all of that knowledge, skill and attitudes that allow human functioning whether it be successful or unsuccessful; this is our worldly knowledge;
– is linked to what and how we learn. Learning is concerned with registering sensory information, encoding or making sense of it and then storing the useful, relevant bits; and
– is obviously concerned with forgetting and how some memories are disrupted or "lost", although sometimes only briefly, whilst others appear to be dispensed with altogether.

In this sense, methods of the retrieval of memories such as recognition and recall are valuable cues to memory. These methods measure what has been retained; what has been forgotten can then be inferred from the evidence obtained.

Thus retention is inevitably linked closely with forgetting. The retrieval cue given allows tests of memory to be classified in terms of:

Recall, Recognition and the Relearning

Recall
The learner has to remember the appropriate information as happens, for example, when a teacher asks a student "What are the uses of a Cross-cut File?" or "Describe two methods of conflict resolution".

Recognition
This method asks the learner to indicate the items that have been previously learned. Recognition was thought to be a more sensitive measure and gave superior performance when compared to recall. This, if true, is probably because new as well as old stimuli (anything noticeable that impinges on a sense receptor) are preserved and extra cues are provided for recall. Students, being aware of this difference, notoriously rely on less preparation for multiple-choice tests than for set exam questions or recall type assessment tests.

Nevertheless, recognition, is subject to false alarms or guesses which need to be accounted for and a correction for guessing applied. Research in signal detection theory, where accuracy of recognition is assumed to vary in strength and not on an all-or-nothing basis, has shown that the supposed superiority of recognition over recall is not all pervasive and in fact can be reversed, especially under the influence of a number of similar distractor items. Furthermore, there is a relationship between recall, recognition and frequency which stipulates that highly frequent words are better recalled than less frequent words but are less well recognised (Baddeley, 1997, p. 199).

Relearning (savings method)
Here the learner relearns the original material (even though the learner cannot recall or recognise the original material) after a given period without any practice. This procedure is sometimes referred to as the 'Savings Method' because it often takes less practice trials than it took initially to relearn the material.

In conclusion, apparently, all of the foregoing indicates that the ability to remember material depends on the means of retrieval. What is important, therefore, are the particular nature of the retrieval cues to evoke particular memories. Furthermore, what and how can be remembered will depend on how well learned the material was in the acquisition or practice stage of learning.

The Course of Memory

Ebbinghaus (1885/1964) initially examined the course of memory by learning nonsense syllables (e.g., "buk", "zed"). After learning each list he made measures of retention after various elapsed times. He devised over 600 nonsense syllables and over the course of his studies he learned over 1,200 lists each containing 13 syllables. An example of his findings is shown in Figure 10.1.

Figure 10.1 A typical retention curve, after Ebbinghaus, 1885.

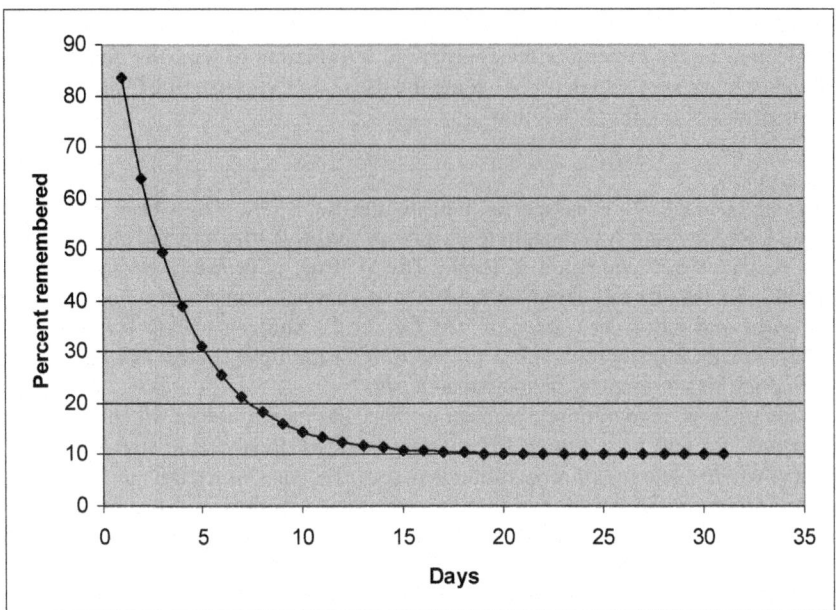

Most retention curves follow the course shown in Figure 10.1, namely, negative acceleration to an asymptote. Notice that performance deteriorates and most is forgotten very quickly soon after initial learning ceases.

Ebbinghaus (1885/1964) was aware that recognition and recall of everyday memories were strongly influenced by relevant prior experience, knowledge and motivation. This is why his experimental approach utilised nonsense syllables. The use of the unknown items minimised the effect of relevant past experience on present learning. This methodological procedure allowed Ebbinghaus to study, in a controlled way, learning and memory not confounded with prior learned knowledge, skills and attitudes.

Since the time of Ebbinghaus up to the present day, memory researchers have tended to study the acquisition of predominantly verbal material in laboratories under controlled conditions to try to discover what factors strengthen learning and what factors, during and after learning, are associated with forgetting. This basic procedure continues to this day. It usually involves having the individual learn a list of unrelated material and then asking them to reproduce the learned material by free recall at various times after acquisition practice has ceased.

Memory and Everyday Events

A recent facet of research and theorising on memory has been to examine the nature of everyday memory. This may be seen somewhat as a contrast to the more controlled scientific laboratory studies of human memory such as Ebbinghaus' research, that have predominated in the memory literature. For instance, Stein,

Ornstein, Tversky and Brainerd (1997) have argued for the ecological validity of the everyday events approach to memory research. Their book examined such issues as the role of emotion and trauma in everyday memory, perceptual and verbal processes and the intriguing area of memory in eyewitness testimony all of which includes the social context of remembering. Cohen's (1996) book puts forward a similar case and is concerned with memory in the "real" world.

Research reported by these workers, however, has shown a very mixed pattern of memory across different individuals and situations. In some circumstances adults can accurately recall real-life events, especially those of relevance to their own physical and psychological being (Ceci & Bruck, 1993). For instance, it has been observed that if an event is personally significant because it is stressful and it is meaningful, it can be accurately remembered (e.g., Bower, 1992)

Nevertheless, different researchers have shown how adult everyday memories are later not remembered with accuracy (e.g., Loftus & Doyle, 1987). In such cases, errors in memory predominate in stressful conditions. Research has shown that eyewitness suggestibility, after the witnessed event, can lead to quite serious errors in the accuracy of the recalled memory of the original event. This finding, of course, has serious implications for "facts'" within legal testimony. The ability of the individual to infer causal relations, prior knowledge, the potential for prior interpretations and the strength of emotional reactions such as anxiety and stress apparently all have a part to play in the accuracy of recall or recognition of everyday events (e.g., Stein, Ornstein, Tversky & Brainerd, 1997).

The apparent confusion about the conditions and factors underlying the accuracy or the inaccuracy of everyday memories, of course, often requires a return to more controlled experimental research where the variables and their effects can be examined more closely. This has led some theorists to contend that the study of memory for everyday events is not the most useful way of understanding memory processes and the factors or variables that might be implicated in or indeed be the cause of effective and accurate learning, memory functioning and retrieval. It is not the writer's intention here to pursue this interesting, ongoing debate only to point out that memory for everyday events is a developing area in memory research.

Indeed, memory for everyday events such as the recognition of faces, past emotional events, memory for stories, dreams, music, childhood memories, lying and deception and so on are of less relevance in a chapter written for teachers and trainers than they are for public policy. In an educational or training context the material to be learned is usually verbal or perceptual-motor by nature, it is planned, structured and usually presented or facilitated in semi-formal ways using a variety of teaching methodology. The process ensures the learners' attention, covert and/or overt practice. This is the sort of context to which we will soon turn.

Theories of Memory

Memory can be thought of, at one level, as a reservoir for storage of personal information. Other workers in the field, at another level, have preferred to conceive of memory differently. These researchers see it rather as a system or series of systems in the human brain which process incoming sensory information in different ways and perhaps, by different means.

There are three main classifications of theories of memory. The first, structural theory, focuses on the structure of memory. For instance, the number of stores (e.g., Sensory memory; Short-term memory; Long-term memory), what information is contained in which store and how the information is transported between the stores. The best example of this theory is the Atkinson and Shiffrin (1968) model.

A second classification of memory theories is the functional approach. Here, levels of processing are of more importance than the structure of memory. Memory performance here depending on the level or depth of processing at the time of the acquisition and encoding of the incoming sensory information (e.g., Craik & Lockhart, 1972). The focus is more on varied language-based memory tasks and is flexible about the type of verbal material learned.

Thirdly, a structural-function classification has been proposed to deal with those theories which focus on learning non-verbal material. Verbal and non-verbal memory systems or so it is supposed, are accessed differently by verbal and non-verbal material, which have different effects on memory. Engelkamp and Zimmer (1996) have argued that this type of multi-model approach is a more valuable one than a unitary memory system approach. They argue that this theory can more readily account for the available research evidence. For example, a research finding that shows that a person's memory performance after "enacting" or actually performing a task (e.g., combing their hair) was superior than after simple verbal instruction to "comb your hair". This finding remained the case even after the subject simply watched someone else comb their hair. The researchers argued that this is because different types of information are encoded and processed in partially independent subsystems, when the learner is actually engaged in a task. These workers stated that such findings cannot be explained by established structural or functional theories of episodic memory alone. Episodic memory refers to our memory for biographical experience.

The proponents of the structural theory or model of human memory postulate that there might be no unitary memory but rather two component subsystems, namely short-term memory (S TM) and long-term memory (LTM). These models do account for many established facts about, for instance, the temporary storage of the short-term memory store and the fact that free recall has separate short-term and long-term components. But these theories have run up against a number of other problems (see Baddeley, 1997 for a review). Nevertheless, for the sake of simplicity of understanding for the reader of this chapter it is proposed, at least initially, to use the concepts of STM and LTM to help organise and report on some very useful research evidence about memory of significance to teachers and trainers.

The Sensory Store and Attention

Sensory information appears to be stored very briefly unless it is attended to quickly. Structural theories of memory (e.g., Atkinson & Shiffrin, 1968) see this as the first subsystem in information processing. Visual or iconic sensory information is stored for less than one second, whilst auditory (echoic) information for no more than a few seconds (e.g., Neisser, 1967). Unless further processed, the incoming sensory "event" is lost.

Not much more will be written here about this facet of memory as it is of less interest to teaching practitioners than long-term memory. Suffice to say that this may be the first important stage in our later memory of transient sensory information, that is if it is immediately attended to and further processed in short-term or working memory.

Short-term or Working Memory

Short-term or working memory refers to the temporary storage of information for only a few seconds. In long-term memory material may be stored for days or years. It is not clear yet whether these are two separate processes or part of one memory system. Peterson and Peterson (1959) found that a great deal of forgetting takes place very shortly after a single exposure to a stimulus item (e.g., nonsense syllable, verbal item). In such a case forgetting is virtually complete after only 18 seconds. For example, consider the case of trying to recall a telephone number given to you only once after a few seconds have elapsed.

Without reciting and processing the information as it is received most people cannot retain more than about 7 ± 2 chunks (e.g., single figures, letters, nonsense syllables or words) after a single exposure (Miller, 1956). Furthermore, short-term memory is easily disrupted by distractions of attention (Brown, 1958).

Miller (1956) found that with seven "chunks" of learned verbal material perfect recall was only achieved about 50% of the time. This finding indicated that the capacity of STM or working memory as it has been otherwise termed, is actually less than seven chunks. Broadbent (1975) has since shown that its capacity was more likely, in practice, to be about four chunks. Studies have tended to show that even with this restriction a large variety of cognitive activities such as problem solving, concept formation and decision making are still possible in practice. Nevertheless, there remains the problem that skilled experts, in their roles in the workplace, require access to a vast amount of information very quickly.

This hypothesised short-term subsystem of memory, termed "working memory" for the foregoing reason, is seen to describe the alliance of temporary memory systems that plays an important role in many cognitive tasks humans engage in such as thinking, reasoning, judging, learning and evaluating. Working memory or STM has been seen by some workers in the field to involve different systems to those used in the memory subsystem said to be involved with our long-term memory storage (Baddeley, 1997).

Is relatively quick retrieval of memories really just a short-term memory process, controlled by the same processes as LTM? Is STM or working memory a unique subsystem? All of this is still neither clear nor understood (see Bjork & Bjork. 1996).

Baddeley (1986, 1996) has argued that there are other working memory paradigms that appear to rely on visuo-spatial encoding. Research exploring the short-term memory for visual imagery led Baddeley to the related proposition of a "Visual sketchpad" concept. Visual information, or so it is theorised, is coded in terms of what and where, respectively in short-term storage by this complex mechanism. If concurrent visual or spatial activity is inconsistent with the original information in the "sketchpad" then performance or so it is predicted, will be disrupted.

Numerous workers who have written chapters in Gatherole's (1996) book have shown the importance but complexity of theoretical models needed to account for the short-term storage of information be it verbal or visual, how it develops, operates and degrades with accidental "damage". Indeed continuing research in the area of working memory remains an important contribution to memory research in total.

In brief, short-term memory is probably mediated by a short-term visual or auditory trace of a stimulus and by at least a covert response to the stimulus. Nevertheless, remembering quickly is a problem because: (a) only one presentation of the item occurs (i.e., only one practice trial is given); (b) no immediate overt response occurs and (c) no reinforcement and knowledge of results is presented. Teachers and trainers need to improve these conditions with a view to getting the stimulus item or "chunks" into long-term memory (LTM).

Long-term Memory

Long-term memory involves memories lasting over long time periods or even, perhaps, for a lifetime. Inspection of the retention scores of learners exposed to the verbal teaching-learning occurring as a result of a lecture show the same type of retention curve found by Ebbinghaus (1885). For instance, McLeish (1968) measured immediate and delayed recall of lecture material and found that overall, whereas approximately 40% of the material taught was remembered immediately after the lecture, a short-term delayed recall resulted in only 17% of the material being remembered. Of course, the issue for lecturers or demonstrators is how might the students' memory for this material or its retrieval be improved, either during its acquisition and encoding or later after acquisition practice during the lecture has ceased.

The storage of learned or practised material in LTM is assumed to involve associations or connections where material or items are related to each other or subsumed within a wider or more inclusive context. Information is also linked to issues in the context in which it is learned. Thus one major problem for the later retrieval of memories from LTM may be a shortage of retrieval cues that are related to the memory required and previously stored in LTM.

This associative system has further problems. One is that other related information has been stored or will be stored in the future, which may interfere with or inhibit the retrieval of the material or item which is now required to be recognised or recalled. Furthermore, sometimes learning new information will actually facilitate rather than inhibit recall of prior memories. These are rather useful findings for those engaged in teaching or training and the inhibition or enhancement of material to be retrieved from LTM are issues about which more will be said shortly.

It has already been mentioned that LTM may not be a single entity but rather, it is argued by some workers, to be comprised of several components (see Squire, 1987). For instance, studies of amnesic patients, as well as other research, shows that these patients cannot recognise or recall past events but otherwise perform quite normally on a wide variety of tasks (Squire, Knowton, & Musen, 1993). Findings such as these have led some researchers to postulate as part of LTM a declarative and a non-declarative memory.

Declarative and Non-declarative Memory
Retrieval from declarative memory is thought to be conscious and explicit with subjects aware that retrieval of information is going on, whilst retrieval from non-

declarative memory appears, or so it is argued, to be slower, more inflexible but more reliable and, perhaps, unconscious.

Non-declarative memory is said to involve some perceptual-motor skills and cognitive procedures that enable the individual to operate normally in their environment. It is thought by some memory theorists that these habits can be learned without awareness and are independent of declarative memory (e.g., Squire et al., 1993). Squire et al. have used rather tentative evidence from amnesic patients and the brain function of animals to support the concept of non-declarative memory. This concept, however, is a very difficult one to test in a scientific behavioural sense, although Squire et al. (1993) argued that there is neurophysiological evidence for its support.

Episodic and Semantic Memory
Episodic and semantic memory are the two most well known forms of so called declarative memory. Episodic memory is thought to be a part of LTM responsible for our capacity to acquire new information and relate this to ourselves and our environment. Semantic memory refers to our general world knowledge. Both of these concepts involve conscious retrieval of information.

Some memory workers have made even more distinctions between different parts of LTM but these are usually based on the assumption that different types of learning (e.g., conditioning, skills, habits, procedural learning) require different types of LTM. This is really quite questionable if, as recent research in learning has shown, there is only one type of learning based on two major principles: practice and reinforcement. In this sense classical conditioning, human instrumental learning and the less experimentally artificial, trial-and-error learning are best seen as ways of arranging learning situations, depending on whether the response required is to be elicited or has been already emitted (i.e., has some current learned strength). These procedural variables or the different types of learned material such as knowledge or skills, therefore, are not conceptually likely to involve different types of learning.

As an example, episodic and semantic memory apparently, become dissociated in amnesic patients; episodic memory can be completely absent while retrieval of semantic memories remains possible. Squire et al. (1993) suggested that there may be many types of LTM systems such as those they say are involved with skills, habits, conditioning and priming (the facility for identifying perceptual stimuli based on recent practice with the stimuli). The problem then remains that the list of types of LTM is dependent on showing that there are many conceptually different types of learning and this has not been shown. For example, habits simply involve very well established associations which are so well practised or learned, that they are very dominant when elicited by particular cues in the environment. Otherwise, one faces the problem of proposing a new LTM system as underlying every new awkward fact when it is encountered (Roediger, 1990).

There may, in fact, be many memory subsystems but they are best viewed as theorised models, analogies or even metaphors that have been devised to help organise and classify various research findings to aid theorising and our understanding. In this sense they help simplify a very complex process and entity but in the end, perhaps, wrongly. Nevertheless, the facts gathered through much research evidence about such things as learning, retention and forgetting remain and it is to these that we shall mostly turn in the remainder of this chapter.

Forgetting: Some Theories

Ebbinghaus (1885) originally gave three possible reasons to explain forgetting. One reason involved what is today known as interference theory. This is that new learning interferes with prior learning and vice versa. Secondly, he assumed a decay of the memory trace over time much as soil might be eroded away in time by the elements. Thirdly, he reasoned that in some cases the memory might "crumble" into parts which were forgotten, rather than the notion of a more general memory loss over time.

There is subsequent evidence to support all three of these early explanations, although the complete explanation of forgetting is still unresolved (see Baddeley, 1997). Certainly, however, interference effects can be a very powerful cause of most forgetting, especially in teaching-learning. Interference effects may act in a proactive or retroactive way.

Proactive Interference

Proactive interference occurs when learning one activity interferes with the memory of something learned afterwards. Evidence indicates that as with other acquisition conditions such as overlearning, variables operating prior to acquisition most affect retention because they affect the final level of learning during practice. An example may occur at a party when the names of individuals learned first get confused with the names heard and remembered later.

Retroactive Interference

In this case, learning a new activity may interfere with the memory of a previously learned activity. For example, see the Appendix which is a class exercise to demonstrate the effects of retroactive inhibition using a list of nonsense syllables followed by various tasks. In the previous party example, now it is the names of individuals learned last which get confused with the names heard first. The type of interference in operation really depends on what the learner is asked to remember. For instance, interference is likely to be greatest in trying to remember the middle part of imperfectly learned verbal material, because here both proactive and retroactive interference effects are likely to be at work. The interfering effect of the new activity interpolated between the end of acquisition and the retention test is greatest when that material is similar but requires different responses to that already learned (as in the class exercise).

For instance, Barnes and Underwood (1959) found that during learning, first-list responses weakened as second-list responses were learned. In another experiment, Jenkins and Dallenbach (1924) tested the number of nonsense syllables recalled for students at the end of various set time periods: (a) after sleep and (b) after a period of normal waking activity. More was forgotten after waking activity than after the corresponding period of sleep and these workers concluded that forgetting was not a result of the decay of old impressions but was due to the interference or inhibitions of the old by the new material. Interestingly, Minami and Dallenbach (1946) found a similar result with cockroaches by having them learn to avoid a dark section of their cage and then making half the group inactive by putting them on their skeletal backs in a narrow space with a velvet soft lining so as to reduce their activity and, therefore, any competing incidental learning. Interference effects apparently, are not unique to humans alone. The major cause of forgetting due to proactive and retroactive inhibition is probably the learning of new responses which compete with those learned and required in the retention test.

Interference Effects and Some Hints for Teaching Practice

Retention is reduced if students learn a similar type but different material after or before (i.e., retroactively and proactively) they learn given verbal or skill-based material. As in the case of the results of the class exercise, the greater the similarity of the *different* material or concepts the greater can be the interference.

As an example, in an accounting procedures subject, students often become confused because many of the common words used now have specialised meanings. For instance, although there are specialised cost systems (e.g., standard cost system, absorption cost system, process cost) these can be combined into one complete but different costing system. Alternatively, consider teaching to students the meaning of "debt" "debtor" and "debit" in the one practice session.

The major question for teachers, then, is how to overcome these sources of inhibition. As one of the major sources of forgetting is proactive inhibition (Underwood, 1954) teachers should:

– carefully consider the entering behaviour of their students such as what previous associations do the student bring to the new learning. For instance, consider the problems the vocational teacher or trainer has at the beginning of every year learning sets of new student names;

– point out sources of proactive and retroactive inhibition for individual students and discriminate them from new, similar subject matter;

– attempt to analyse the task and the learnable steps and procedures made explicit; interference is reduced when material is structured and organised;

– actively present the tasks or "chunks" of material to reduce proactive and retroactive interference. For example, as found in the class experiment, if already completed, dissimilar stimuli with responses held constant (or even varied responses) aid retention. Teachers and trainers should, therefore, use as much variety as is possible in teaching similar types of material, e.g., use different colours, symbols, concrete illustrations, drawings as well as verbal explanation;

If the original material is well practised then the less the degree of interference that can be expected.

Anderson and Neely (1996) use the particularly good example of the power of confusion by interference in trying to remember where your car has been parked in a large multi-storage shopping centre carpark. This is usually a particularly good test of memory. Here memory failure or forgetting occurs predominantly by interference. All of the parking rows look similar and the available cues cause confusion and failure to retrieve the exact cues needed for car location. Research on interference has been particularly useful in generating explanations of forgetting or memory retrieval failure.

These authors stressed the idea that interference effects emerge from competition for access to memory between likely retrieval cues. This is a principle, they argue, which research evidence indicates has much generality and explains much forgetting. It is the notion that forgetting occurs because new memories can and do compete with older, already retrieved memories. This is a cause of retrieval failure or, alternatively, the retrieval of an incorrect or irrelevant remembrance.

Remembering to do everyday things, called prospective memory, is also influenced by interference effects but it appears to be more dependent on motivational factors. These memories are also influenced by the way the memory of the event is embedded in a social context. There are also theories of motivated forgetting or repression based on anxiety, fear and guilt such as those of Freud but they will not be canvassed here. In any case, they are almost impossible to test scientifically.

Retrieval Failure as a Cause of Forgetting

Sometimes something forgotten and unable to be recalled one day comes back quite spontaneously the next. Forgetting, perhaps, universally may also be due to the failure of the individual's retrieval system because the necessary cues for retrieval have not been presented (Tulving & Pearlstone, 1966). Sometimes, therefore, providing an individual with proper retrieval cues greatly facilitates recall, a fact that teachers and trainers are often aware of during a questioning session. Nevertheless, much of the available evidence dealing with the retention of verbal and perceptual-motor skill indicates that learning would be permanent and forgetting just an artefact, if only information retrieval from memory could be ensured.

In addition, Tulving (1974) argued that remembering is a product of information from acquired information ("memory traces" he called them) and retrieval information. Hence strong memory traces may be accessed by relatively weak retrieval cues and vice versa. The implication for teachers or trainers: strengthen the 'memory traces' during the acquisition phase of learning or the retrieval cues during remembering or, better still, strengthen both.

Remembering Using Effective Retrieval Cues

The processes of memory, therefore, can be thought of as involving three stages. Encoding is the acquisition stage of learning. Storage is maintaining information overtime, whilst retrieval is about accessing the stored information.

Much research evidence has shown that firstly, maximising the psychological similarity of the stimulus conditions during acquisition and processing between the study and the test improves retention; see Roedinger and Guynn (1996) for a review. Here the same or similar cues are used during encoding and for retrieval; this is the so-called encoding-specificity principle. Secondly, cue distinctiveness is important. Cues or stimuli that stand out from their background or from other similar events; cues that are novel are likely to be remembered and used for later retrieval of specific memory material. Thirdly, if a cue is overloaded with varied information and therefore, memories, the recall of any single piece of that information is likely to be weaker.

These research findings have direct implications for teachers and trainers. These are: (a) maximise the similarity of the stimulus conditions during encoding or the acquisition of learning to those to be used later during the memory test; (b) the effectiveness of a retrieval cue will be determined by firstly, its novelty or distinctiveness and secondly, whether it is "overloaded" with other related memories.

Acquisition Conditions: Retention effects

Practice Effects
Dempster (1996) and Baddeley (1997) have provided very useful reviews of the research evidence on the effect of practice or encoding conditions during the acquisition of learning upon subsequent remembering during the memory phase.

In studies of the effect of practice variables on memory, initial practice experience must be equated and kept constant and only the relevant practice variable varied. When these conditions apply the following findings have consistently emerged.

Frequency of Practice
The opportunity for more than one session of practice during acquisition promotes learning; there is consequently, obviously, more to remember. Within limits, therefore, the teacher or trainer should provide for adequate practice or repetition of the material to be learned. Learning is, after all, defined as a relatively permanent change in behaviour as a result of reinforced practice. These changes are likely to be more permanent if practice is substantial.

The student or trainee should be encouraged to continue to practise the material beyond the initial mastery stage. This technique is called overlearning. To some teachers or trainers it may appear that a student does not learn any more once he or she has a basic mastery of the knowledge or task but that depends on the sensitivity of the measure of learning used (e.g., amount correctly recalled vs speed of response).

Overlearning
Overlearning occurs when a learner is able to recall correctly the material just learned but then continues with the practice. Research evidence indicates that, within limits, increased overlearning results in improvements in retention over long periods of time. Krueger (1929), for example, found that 100% overlearning (twice as many trials given, as was required to reach the criterion of one correct recitation) improved retention beyond a 50% overlearning group which, in turn, was better than a no overlearning group. Retention curves were obtained like those shown in Figure 10.1, except that the remembered performance of the overlearning groups was always superior to the non-overlearning group. This result, however, may really only be an artefact and due to a relatively crude performance measure such as the number of items correctly recalled.

For instance, if a person learns to the criterion of one successful run through a list of 10 words, further practice trials, or overlearning, appear to result in no further increase in performance because a ceiling of performance has been reached *viz.,* 10 out of 10 correctly recalled. If speed of response is the measure of performance, however, then further improvement is observed during overlearning because a higher performance ceiling is established. This suggest that the effects of overlearning on retention may reflect sheer acquisition performance.

It may be thought that to obtain greater retention a practitioner should simply continue to get the students to overlearn. A problem with this approach is that overlearning can result in boredom and reduced motivation. Teachers and trainers, therefore, should endeavour to provide continuing practice but use variation in examples or reviews. They could split up long practice periods such as might occur in learning a speeded vocational skill with short rest periods. They could use breaks where students listen to related theory or practice another skill where the students use different muscle groups to those initially used. Nonetheless, the use of sheer practice to promote learning and to improve long-term memory is well documented.

Distribution of Practice
Distributing the practice sessions is usually more effective for remembering than using massed practice. Dempster (1996) has reviewed the evidence available and pointed out that it supports the contention that reviews or further practice sessions, not only improve the quantity of learned material but also its quality. Distributed reviews enable the learners to learn more sophisticated encoding strategies based on their developing knowledge and skill with the subject matter content, rather than just the technical details.

Two reviews close in time are not as effective as two that are somewhat spaced over time. Two spaced practice sessions can be up to two times as effective as two "massed" practice sessions; this is a very large practice effect indeed. Longer retention intervals tend to favour the effect more than shorter ones (Dempster, 1996). This effect works in all areas of verbal learning and notwithstanding the method of retrieval such as recognition or recall.

The spacing effect, unfortunately, does not appear to be as dependable in every area and the effect is not as robust in the area of perceptual-motor skills (Dempster, 1996). These effects may be because of the conditions sometimes existing in teaching skills such as poor practice and acquisition. The initial learning may not be supported by enough active practice in the perceptual-motor skills case with consequently, lower levels of immediate reinforcement and feedback. Another reason for this effect may be the poorer structure of the skill-based material to be learned and, therefore, the greater likelihood of interference effects. Teachers or trainers, however, should be cognisant of the length of the practice period the students are likely to face at their workplace.

Retrieval Practice: Review and Assessment
When a previously learned item is retrieved from memory once there is a greater chance of further retrieval, that is the item is more likely to be remembered. This is not simply because of a second practice trial but also because, somehow, the retrieval route to the item is strengthened (Baddeley, 1997).

This effect, together with the distributed practice effect, suggests that teachers or trainers should attempt to expand rehearsal. This means that verbal material or perceptual-motor skill learning should be tested soon after initial practice ceases. If the material is recalled then the delay between retesting should be extended systematically. If the response in the initial test is incorrect then the delay should be shortened. This has proved to be, in practice, a particularly powerful strategy even with the learning disabled (see Baddeley, 1997). These findings run counter to the views of many students and teachers who strongly assume that massed practice and "cramming" is always the "best" procedure to improve memory, especially before an examination.

There is no doubt that reviews and the assessment of previous learned material has clear implications for remembering. The reviews and tests not only provide opportunities for further practice, reinforcement, knowledge of results or feedback on errors. Suffice to say, that they also provide the opportunity for the learners to find and use relevant methods of structuring the information in a variety of meaningful ways. This process is usually attempted between the sessions. Insightful and creative learner behaviour seldom occurs without practice and feedback with relevant material over a reasonably long period.

It is not the purpose here to explore in detail the various theoretical justifications for these findings. They are thought to involve process-type theories about two kinds of rehearsal (i.e., maintenance and elaboration functions in STM) or categorising and encoding functions based on visual character and sound, respectively (e.g., Craik & Lockhart, 1972) which might lead to deeper levels of processing during the reviews. There are even more recent voluntary-attention theory explanations. They suggest that the provision of extra spaced repetitions enhances successful retrieval of earlier material and the encoding process.

There is no doubt, however, about the positive effects on remembering of further testing and review. Nevertheless, in one study of what teachers actually did it was found that they reviewed the previous days learning only 25% of the time and checked on homework only 50% of the time (see Dempster, 1996). Often educational or training programs only have a mid-semester and end-on exam but as Dempster pointed out many teachers think that spaced reviews, tests, and repetitive practice stifles creative work and is a form of meaningless rote learning. In this "commonsense" respect, according to the available research evidence, they appear to be wrong.

All of the foregoing evidence can be applied to other areas of practice such as questioning. For instance, straight after new material is introduced questioning is very useful to strengthen the material in memory and the feedback to help minimise or eliminate errors which left alone only serve to promote interference during retrieval. Questions also serve to increase attention and on-task behaviour, which are vital for remembering taught material. Questions about specific training outcomes can be asked but with an increasing inter-question duration over an extended time period. Studies have shown that memory for material acquired in these ways is reasonably permanent.

Whole or Part Methods of Learning
These methods refer to the issue of how elemental the material to be taught is presented to the learner. In practice, which of these two methods works best appears to depend on the learner characteristics, the nature of the material and the time frame available. The affect of these variables on retention is probably because of the underlying organisation of the material. McGeoch and Irion (1952) reviewed a number of studies in this area and suggested a number of factors that ought to be considered in judging the relative effectiveness in terms of retention of whole or part procedures:
– part methods are advantageous in some learning situations because the material is divided into smaller units. Small units are easier to comprehend and the task is easier to learn and remember;
– whole methods are advantageous in some situations because the materials are learned in their appropriate relationship to each other, so no time is lost in connecting the different parts as would be the case in the part methods;

- the whole method gains in effectiveness when the learner's practice is distributed rather than massed; and
- the whole method tends to work better than the part method with meaningful and highly structured material or with experienced learners.

Active Responding During Learning

Active learning promotes retention more than passive learning so that the teacher or trainer should try to make learners actively respond whenever possible. Trainers should use interactive methods. They should try to get the students to think and answer questions, write or draw, use equipment, manipulate materials, discuss issues, solve problems and research materials. They could go on to put their learned knowledge and skill into practice in the workplace.

Active learners tend to remember material better than passive learners and this is probably because active learning allows greater amounts of practice with the material to be learned. It provides an improved chance of the student organising the material, attending strongly and increasing motivation. Active student responding also provides the practitioner and the students with feedback about the range of individual differences in ability within the group.

Speed of Acquisition and Retrieval

Generally the finding in this area is usually that fast learners remember more than do slow learners (Underwood, 1954). The problem in this sort of study is to make sure that the amount learned initially is the same for both groups of individuals which is a difficult task. Perhaps, one reason why fast learners remember material better is because they find the material more meaningful or organise and sequence it better during acquisition.

Overall, people vary in how much they remember. Those whose knowledge is greater tend to learn better, whether the knowledge is specific or global, probably because more knowledge means more elaborative links and relationships are formed. Nevertheless, intelligence and verbal ability also affect retrieval speed from long-term memory. No sex differences have been found in memory (Bors & Macleod, 1996).

Reinforcement and Feedback

The evidence indicates that positive reinforcement such as teacher comments like "yes", "good", "OK", after a student's correct response results in speedier learning and, consequently, better remembering. This is also the finding for non-verbal acknowledgments such as a smile and for general feedback such as knowledge of results on the number of errors or how well the student is going according to job specifications. If feedback is withdrawn the result is a decrease in student performance and motivation. Delaying reinforcement and knowledge of results, even by a few seconds, results in poorer levels of student retrieval performance (Pithers & Champion, 1979).

Partial or intermittent reinforcement during acquisition practice results in improved remembering of learned material over longer periods of time than does continuous reinforcement. This is an outcome about which most gamblers and teachers alike are well aware.

Guided Discovery vs Expository Learning

Guided discovery learning can be distinguished from expository learning by the fact that in the former case the teacher or trainer presents a build-up of examples and the students are guided to discover the relevant general principle. In expository teaching the teacher first presents or exposes the general principle and then presents the supporting examples. One of the claims of the advocates of discovery learning is that the use of this procedure results in better retention of the material presented and the general principle discovered.

Available research evidence is confusing in this area, although the weight of research indicates that the claim generally can not be supported (e.g., Ausubel & Robinson, 1969; Shulman & Tamir, 1973; Wittrock, 1963). The point to be made for practitioners is this: use whichever method suits your students, level of material and time constraints. Nevertheless, to ensure good retention of that material make sure the material is organised, meaningful, that the students get plenty of practice and obtain feedback and immediate reinforcement.

Memory: Meaning and Organisation

A group of students had to learn in any order the following ten letters - MODGOYOREM. They could recite them until learned or they might rearrange them so as to make them more easily pronounceable - MEMGOODROY. They could further arrange the sequence of consonants and vowels to the pronounceable words - GOOD MEMORY. These two words are now meaningful and are structured as a phase (i.e., adjective-noun). This makes the letters a lot easier to learn and remember. This is the case with all verbal material that is practised, structured and meaningful.

One acquisition condition affecting remembering is the meaningfulness of the verbal material. There is much older evidence available to suggest that meaningful material is remembered better than non-meaningful material (McGeoch & Irion, 1952). Guildford (1952), for example, reported that the retention of nonsense syllables was poor when compared with the retention of factual prose. Poetry, however, was retained even better than both the nonsense syllables and the prose.

Other studies have found, however, when the degree of learning is controlled, that meaningfulness may not be a factor influencing retention after all (Ekstrand & Underwood, 1965; Underwood & Keppel, 1963). In other words, meaningful material may be better retained than non-meaningful material because it is more familiar or better learned in the first place. Nevertheless, meaningful material is organised and learned in large response units connected with mediating responses so that the recall of the larger unit provides internal stimuli for the recall of the components. This organisation probably plays a useful part in improving the retention of meaningful material.

Teachers and trainers should try to provide for as much meaning as possible by mediation, that is use familiar examples of a concept, anecdotes, models, visual or auditory examples. For example, to enable new verbal material to be understood a practitioner should gauge the entering behaviour or the background knowledge of the students to assess their existing cognitive structure, then use pictorial aids, models or verbal illustration which make use of material already familiar to the students. An instance of this procedure is the electrical theory teacher who attempts to explain the abstract concept of the function of Ohm's Law (the relationship between electrical pressure, current flow and resistance) through comparing the pressure and flow electrons moving along a wire to the analogous and already understood example of the pressure and flow of water along a pipe. Nevertheless, the teacher of adults as well as the students, need to realise the limitations of analogy and metaphorical language usage in an explanation.

Landauer (1986) has estimated that we store about 1,000,000,000 facts in memory so that organisation of this amount of material is critical. Baddeley (1997) has summarised the wealth of research findings on organisation, learning and memory. There appears to be little doubt, that in most content-matter domains, organised and meaningful material is easier to learn and remember. Organisation is relevant to (a) the subject matter to be learned,(b) existing long-term memory and (c) organisation of associations between these two. This allows the access of new material from LTM when it is needed.

Organisation that is categorical and laid out in rows and columns is particularly useful (see Figure 10.2). Chunking slabs of material as in planning content for teaching is another way of organising elemental material into larger, relevant, more unified groupings of like material or ideas. Visual imagery also helps as a method of organisation as do instructions to students to organise the material themselves. Mnemonic devices are, of course, based on such techniques.

Figure 10.2 An example of "carnivore" conceptual hierarchy.

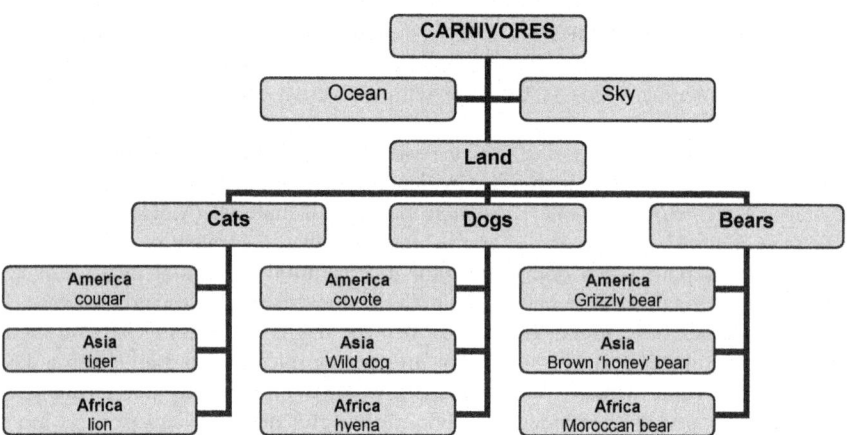

Cooper and Lang (1996) have shown, following a review of visual-spatial memory research, how visual-spatial representations provide a flexible and varied way of coding information during learning. Images preserve structural, relational and sometimes even metric information. They argue that spatial layouts such as a branching tree layout or classification (see Figure 10.2) or instructional resources, preserve much more abstract and hierarchically organised information than do images of single objects or items. They also help to account for more efficient retrieval of the information probably, in part, because of the varied cues available and their learned linkages or connections.

For example, during an automotive trade lesson a brief discussion or demonstration of the general concept of friction might precede a lesson on brakes and materials. In a painting and decorating lesson a general discussion of the four basic painting methods (*viz.,* roller, brush, electrostatic and spray) could precede a lesson on foam-roller application, or during a welding lesson an introduction via the explanation of 'Weldability' (i.e., the welding qualities or various metals) in relation to the various metals and alloys (e.g., carbon steels, alloy steels, heat-treated steels, cold-treated steels) before a lesson on welding medium carbon steel. Visual-spatial representation (i.e., a hierarchical branching-tree organisation) could be developed and used in each of these areas.

Memory for Perceptual-Motor Skills

Long-term Retention of Skills

Most of what has been found out about the retention of verbal material also applies to the retention of perceptual-motor skills. Some skills such as swimming, cycling or walking involve continuous motor activity and appear to be retained better than those involving a host of discrete, less connected responses. Reasons for this difference are that: (a) components of the continuous skill simply are better practised, (b) there may be less interference due to competing responses and (c) the organisation of the skill provides a structure which allows chains of mediating stimuli; these then help in the recall of the next response.

Knowledge and skills are often learned initially to different degrees and so these differences during acquisition will affect the extent of skill retention. Rehearsal of verbal information is also more likely than for spatial or perceptual-motor learning after initial acquisition practice ceases. For an effective memory test, skills have to be tested after initial acquisition and also during post-training generalisation.

As with verbal retrieval, practice after initial learning improves remembering after long delays. Schmidt and Bjork (1992) have also shown in a series of studies that:

– random scheduling of two or more tasks (tasks are intermixed during learning) rather than blocked scheduling where one task is learned, followed by the other, appears to improve the retention of skills;
– intermittent reinforcement and feedback, rather than continuously given after every practice trial, promotes retention; and
– variation of tasks along one dimension during acquisition improves skill generalisation.

Memory: Experts vs Novices

Ericsson and Kintsch (1995) have postulated a long-term working memory. This is based on evidence that skilled experts must maintain access to a vast amount of information including information on context in order to be able to integrate information provided in their new context with that available from past experience in different contexts. This is in addition to short-term working memory which refers only to the temporary storage of information that is processed (e,g., Baddeley, 1986). They argued that information in long-term working memory is stored in stable form but with temporary access to it maintained by retrieval cues in short-term working memory. It would seem that the complexity of memory functioning for those individuals with expertise and therefore, with a large amount of contextual information and metacognitive "wisdom" learned, is much more comprehensive and involved than it was hitherto thought to be.

"Experts" appear to remember better by identifying the problems as members of conceptual groupings, whereas novices tend to categorise by surface similarities. Rapid retrieval from memory is a "hallmark" of expertise (Ericsson & Kintsch, 1995). According to Bors and Macleod (1996) three elements of superior memory encoding involve:
- elaboration with existing knowledge;
- attaching cues to the material to be remembered; and
- overlearning of the mnemonic skills and the new information.

Training Skills for Long-term Retention

Healy and Sinclair (1996) have drawn some further useful conclusions about training skills for long-term retention based on many other research outcomes and their own work. These include ideas such as:
- procedures used during training practice should match those required for later retrieval;
- new information should be related to prior experience;
- the retrieval of spatial information is improved when the information is distinctive;
- the recall of skills learned can be highly specific to the training situation;
- retention is improved if, during initial acquisition or learning, practice is given in retrieving the relevant skilled response procedures that will be later retrieved from memory, for example, through questioning or testing;
- whether to initially use part or more holistic component training is difficult to resolve. It depends on factors like task difficulty and training practice time available. For instance, if the first task or procedure is complex or difficult and cannot be learned correctly within the training session time frame then it would be better to begin with a part of the task or procedure that is easier to learn; and
- finally, overlearning builds "automaticity". This is useful for speeded long-term performance.

Sargent and Unkenstein (1998) have provided a useful summary of some factors that can affect remembering, especially with ageing. The major factors reported include health variables such as the onset of Alzheimer's disease, chronic pain and negative expectations about memory fluctuations which they argue create a self-fulfilling prophecy about our lack of control over our memory ability. High anxiety and poor self-confidence have also been linked with memory 'decline'. Nevertheless, continuation in a variety of cognitive activities which involve thinking and reasoning has been linked with the maintenance of memory ability as long as it is not too speeded, well into the 60s. Of course, the excessive consumption of drugs over time such as alcohol and brain injury have both been linked to memory decline or dysfunction.

Teaching Strategies for Better Remembering

In the literature, strategies for improving remembering are seen to involve quite a range of techniques. These range from external aids to help retrieve everyday memories such as writing things down, using diaries, timers and alarms or coloured paper messages in prominent places to those techniques more applicable to remembering more detailed, taught knowledge, skills and attitudes.

Relevant to the teaching or training domain, the following represent typical techniques written about by many memory workers as aids to remembering:

- *Focus attention.* This technique helps get new information from the sensory store into working memory. It also helps to minimise distractions which may interfere with correct retrieval.
- *Rehearsal, further practice, repetition and self-testing with increasing delays between these events.* Increased frequency of practice helps get new information from short-term memory into long-term memory.
- *Provide reinforcement and feedback.* These procedures help to strengthen the material within LTM store and eliminate errors, respectively.
- *Structure the information.* Grouping like material and 'chunking' is an important technique. The names of the chunks help cue or elicit the elements.
- *Add meaning.* Link the new material to what is known. Make association explicit by, for instance, anecdote, examples or case studies. These help to elaborate the encoding of the new information and provide contextual cues for better later retrieval.
- *Make links or connections with other stimuli.* For example, with colour, sound or smells. These can later help provide extra cues for retrieval.
- *Imagine or visualise the to-be-remembered event.* Picture something, in a novel way
- if possible, and make a connection to the new material.
- *Use logical search techniques.* For instance, having "lost" a set of keys, try to remember where you last had them, or the last room you were in.
- *Use rhymes* for example, "Thirty days hath September...". They provide extra retrieval cues.
- *Develop and teach mnemonics* such as acrostics where the first letter of each item to be remembered is used to make a sentence. For example, "Oh, Be A Fine Guy and Kiss Me" - OBAFGKM - to remember the classification of stellar spectral types in astronomy.

Mnemonic Methods

Bellezza (1996) among others, has shown how important as a psychological tool mnemonic devices can be in education and how they can aid in the development of effective instructional techniques. These devices make use of verbal cues and visual images to cue the retrieval of new material to which they are associated.

The method of loci (well known locations associated with items to be later remembered) and "peg word" mnemonics are based on extrinsic cues that are already in memory and are then associated with the material to be learned. These are organisational devices, other mnemonic types assist in encoding new material for which mental images are impossible such as abstract words or ideas. Here forming a novel visual image of the new word may help with later retrieval but the mental representation must be memorable and, therefore, striking.

Bellezza (1996) argued that these linking memories must be (a) constructible or reliable at both learning and recall; (b) associable or linked to the new material; (c) discriminate one from another and (d) bidirectional or capable of use in either a forward or backward direction (e.g., with method of loci). Mnemonic structure can act as a mental scaffolding that can be dispensed with later in learning as more relevant associations become learned. The point needs to be remembered, however, that the effective use of these techniques requires much practice; the skills must be well learned and they need to be taught to practitioners as well as to their students.

Mnemonics need to be learned during the acquisition and encoding phase so that they can better be later effectively used as extra cues for originally learned material. The term refers to numerous techniques that may be employed to aid retrieval. If the associated material is already well organised, meaningful, easy to learn and possesses novelty, all the better for the ease with which a familiar novel cue will work to help the learner remember the appropriate material. Here are some examples:

- to aid the correct spelling of words containing "e", "i" and "c": "i" before "e" except after "c";
- the word "KCAASE" to remember Bloom's taxonomy of education objectives - Knowledge, Comprehension, Application, Analysis, Synthesis and Evaluation;
- in welding trades, "A goes with Z" helps to remember that Aluminium needs a Zinconated electrode;
- in engineering or a basic physics courses, one way to help learners remember the colour spectrum is by memorising the fictitious name "Roy G Biv" - each letter spells out the spectrum: red, orange, yellow, green, blue, indigo, violet;
- in mathematics, "Bodmas" represents the order of process undertaken in calculation; that is, brackets, of, division, multiplication, addition, subtraction.
- the "ABC" of resuscitation - check for Airways, Breathing, Circulation;
- "INTRO" - helps to remember the major ingredients of an introductory training or teaching session - Interest, Need, Title, Range and Outcomes;
- "Red-Right-Returning" to cue correct channel marker positions when entering port in a Maritime course;
- an example using visual imagery comes from the electrical theory area and is called the "Left hand rule". It indicates the direction of a magnetic field in relation to current flow. The student is taught to visualise their left hand reaching out to take hold of a conductor (e.g., a wire) with thumb extended. Thumb direction will indicate the direction of electrical current flow, whilst curled fingers represent the direction of the associated magnetic field. This visual image, if taught during the acquisition of the electrical theory provides very powerful cues to later retrieval of the correct theoretical electrical information; or
- again in electrical theory a visual representation of the formula for Ohm's Law: where $V = I \times R$ or $I = V R$ or $R = V I$ helps retrieval of the correct formula.

Summary

Memory is a complex concept and it is viewed by theorists and researchers in many ways; whether "memory" refers to a unitary system or to several different functioning subsystems is still a point at issue. For the sake of this chapter memory is discussed in terms of three subsystems: sensory memory, short-term or working memory and long-term memory. This hypothesised classification gives the opportunity to discuss some of the salient theory and research evidence about memory in a more structured and coherent manner.

In brief, the view discussed in this chapter is that a range of factors occurring during acquisition and encoding of verbal or perceptual-motor learning appear to later affect the remembering of that verbal content or the sequence of motor activity. Other factors also play a role in the retention of learned verbal material and skills such as the method of retrieval employed (e.g., recognition or recall), the fading of memory traces as well as interference effects of various types. Interference has been strongly implicated as a cause of forgetting, although modern research evidence indicates that failure to remember may be because of retrieval failure. In this case, learning would be permanent and forgetting merely an artefact, if only information or skill retrieval from long-term memory could be ensured. Implications of the research for teachers and trainers of verbal material and perceptual-motor skills are discussed.

REFERENCES

Anderson, M. C., & Neely, J. H. (1996). Interference and inhibition in memory retrieval. In E. Bjork & R. Bjork (Eds.), *Memory*. San Diego: Academic Press.

Atkinson, R. C., & Shiffrin, R. M. (1968). Human memory: A proposed system and its control processes. In K. Spence & J. Spence (Eds.), *The psychology of learning and motivation*. (Vol. 2, pp. 89-195). NY: Academic Press.

Ausubel, D. P., & Robinson, F. G. (1969). *School learning: An introduction to educational psychology*. NY: Holt, Rinehart and Wintson.

Baddeley, A. D. (1986). *Working memory*. New York: Oxford University Press.

Baddeley, A. D. (1996). The concept of working memory. In S.E. Gatherole (Ed.), *Models of short-term memory*. Hove: Psychology Press.

Baddeley, A. D. (1997). *Human memory: theory and practice*. Hove: Psychology Press.

Barnes, J.M., & Underwood, B.J. (1959). 'Fate' of first-list associations in transfer theory. *Journal of Experimental Psychology, 58*, 97-105.

Bellezza, F. S. (1996). Mnemonic methods for storage and retrieval. In E. Bjork & R. Bjork (Eds.), *Memory*. San Diego: Academic Press.

Bjork, E. L., & Bjork, R. A. (Eds.). (1996). *Memory*. San Diego: Academic Press.

Bors, D.A., & MacLeod, (1996). Individual differences in memory. In E. Bjork & R. Bjork (Eds.), *Memory*. San Diego: Academic Press.

Bower, G. (1992). Emotion and memory. In S. A. Christianson (Ed.), *Handbook of emotion and memory*. Hillsdale, NJ: Lawrence, Erlbaum.

Broadbent, D. E. (1975). The magic number seven after fifteen years. In A. Kennedy & A. Wilkes (Eds.), *Studies in long-term memory*. London: Wiley.

Brown, J. (1958). Some tests of the decay theory of immediate memory. *Quarterly Journal of Experimental Psychology, 10*, 12-21.

Ceci, S. J., & Bruck, M. (1993). The suggestibility of the child witness: An historical review. *Psychological Bulletin, 113*, 403-429.

Cohen, G. (1996). *Memory in the real world*. Hove: Psychology Press.

Cooper, L. A., & Lang, J. M. (1996). Imagery and visual-spatial representations. In E. Bjork & R. Bjork (Eds.), *Memory*. San Diego: Academic Press.

Craik, F. I. M., & Lockhart, R. S. (1972). Levels of processing: A framework for memory research. *Journal of Verbal Learning and Verbal Behaviour, 11*, 268-294.

Dempster, F. N. (1996). Encoding and retrieval practice. In E. Bjork & R. Bjork (Eds.), *Memory*. San Diego: Academic Press.

Ebbinghaus, H. (1885/1964). *Memory: A contribution to experimental psychology*. (H. Ruger & C. Bussenius, Trans.) NY: Dover (original work published in 1885).

Ekstrand, B. R., & Underwood, B. J. (1965). Free learning and recall as a function of unit-sequence and letter-sequence interference. *Journal of Verbal Learning and Verbal Behaviour, 4*, 390-396.

Engelkamp, J., & Zimmer, H. (Eds). (1996). *Human memory: A multimodal approach*. Seattle: Hogrefe and Huber.

Ericsson, A.. K., & Kintsch, W. (1995). Long-term working memory. *Psychological Review, 102,* 211-245.

Gatherole, S. E. (Ed.). (1996). *Models of short-term memory.* Hove: Psychology Press.

Guildford, J. P. (1952). *General psychology.* New Jersey: Princeton.

Healy, A. F., & Sinclair, G. P. (1996). The long-term retention of training and instruction. In E. Bjork & R. Bjork (Eds.), *Memory.* San Diego: Academic Press.

Jenkins, J.G., & Dallenbach, K.M. (1924). Obliviscence during sleep and waking. *American Journal of Psychology, 35,* 605-612.

Krueger, W. C. (1929). The effect of overlearning on retention. *Journal of Experimental Psychology, 12,* 71-78.

Landauer, T. K. (1986). How much do people remember? Some estimates of the quantity of learned information in long-term memory. *Cognitive Science, 10,* 477-493.

Loftus, E. F., & Doyle, J. M. (1987). *Eyewitness testimony. Civil and criminal.* NY: Kluwer.

McGeoch, J. A., & Irion, A. L. (1952). *The psychology of human learning* (2nd ed.). NY: Longmans, Green.

McLeish, J. (1968). *The lecture method.* Cambridge: Cambridge Institute of Education.

Mandler, G. (1962). From association to structure. *Psychological Review, 69,* 415-427.

Miller, G. A. (1956). The magic number seven, plus or minus two: Some limits on our capacity for information processing. *Psychological Review, 63,* 81-97.

Minami, H., & Dallenbach, K. M. (1946). The effects of activity upon learning and retention in the cockroach. *American Journal of Psychology, 59,* 1-8.

Neisser, U. (1967). *Cognitive psychology.* NY: Appleton-Century-Crofts.

Petersen, L. R., & Petersen, M. J. (1959). Short-term retention of individual verbal items. *Journal of Experimental Psychology, 58,* 193-198.

Pithers, R.T., & Champion, R. A. (1979). Differential delay of reinforcement effects in human learning. *Australian Journal of Psychology, 31,* 169-179.

Roediger, H. L. (1990). Implicit memory: Retention without remembering. *American Psychologist, 45,* 1043-1056.

Roediger, H. L., & Guynn, M. J. (1996). Retrieval processes. In E. Bjork & R. Bjork (Eds.), *Memory.* San Diego: Academic Press.

Sargent, D., & Unkentein, A. (1998). *Remembering well.* St Leonards: Allen & Unwin.

Schmidt, R. A., & Bjork, R. A. (1992). New conceptions of practice: Common principles in three paradigms suggest new concepts for training. *Psychological Science, 3,* 207-217.

Schulman, S., & Tamir, P. (1973). Research on teaching in the material sciences. In R. M. Travers (Ed.), *Second handbook of research on teaching.* Chicago: Rand McNally.

Squire, L. R. (1987). *Memory and brain.* NY: Oxford University Press.

Squire, L. R., Knowton, B., & Musen, G. (1993). The structure and organisation of memory. *Annual Review of Psychology, 44,* 453-495.

Stein, N. L., Ornstein, P. A., Tversky, B., & Brainerd, C. (Eds.). (1997). *Memory for everyday and emotional events.* Mahwah, N.J.: Lawrence Erlbaum.

Tulving, E. (1974). Cue-dependent forgetting. *American Scientist, 62,* 74-82.

Tulving, E., & Pearlstone, A. (1966). Availability vs accessibility of information in memory for words. *Journal of Verbal Learning and Verbal Behaviour, 5,* 381-391.

Underwood, B. J. (1954). Speed of learning and amount retained: A consideration of methodology. *Psychological Bulletin, 51,* 276-282.

Underwood, B. J., & Keppel, G. (1963). Retention as a function of degree of learning and letter-sequence interference. *Psychological Monographs, 77,* No. 4.

Wittrock, C. M. (1963). Verbal stimuli in concept formation: Learning by discovery. *Journal of Educational Psychology, 54,* 183-190.

Review Questions

1. Why is it important for teachers and trainers to plan for the process of forgetting?

2. Under what conditions or circumstances are interference effects involved with remembering likely to be severe?
3. What evidence is there to support the contention that failure to remember is primarily because of failure of retrieval?
4. Are there any particular factors or research findings which suggest that the retention of perceptual-motor skills in different from that of verbal material? Discuss this contention.
5. In which ways, during acquisition, can teachers or trainers plan to aid the later retrieval of learned material?
6. Which of the various ideas to promote memory and later retrieval presented in this chapter appear to have most relevance to your subject-matter content, students and context? Why?

Exercise

Interference and Remembering
The following exercise is a useful way of demonstrating the effect of interference (in this case: retroactive inhibition) on remembering. It involves the following steps:
1. Randomly divide the class into equal groups (A & B).
2. All groups learn **List 1,** a list of nonsense syllables (to control for prior experience) for 3 minutes by reading up and down the list.
3. All groups recall as many nonsense syllables as possible in any order — time limit — 1 minute. Make sure that List 1 is now hidden from view.
4. **Group A** now learn **List 2** for 3 minutes. **Group B** now engage in calculating say 15 **maths problems** eg. 2672 ÷ 35; 861 x 18; etc. for 3 minutes.
5. All groups now recall syllables from **List 1** (with lists hidden as well as evidence of their first recall) for 1 minute.
6. Score the number of syllables recalled (**List 1** *only)* and subtract the second recall score from the first.
7. Calculate the mean or average scores separately for both groups.
8. Compare the findings.
9. Discuss reasons for the interference effect, if any, found. Why use two different types of interpolated activity?

The Lists:
 List 1
 VEH; XUB; ZAT; QUJ; MEC; KOD; WUB; CIK; JUH; GEC.
 List 2
 XUL; VUH; YIG; QOD; MIB; KEZ; WAC; XIJ; MUX; GID.

About the Author

Bob Pithers has over 25 years experience in teaching trainers, adult and vocational educators and other training professionals in colleges, universities and in private enterprise. He holds a MA (Hons) and PhD in the psychology of learning. He is an Associate Professor in the Faculty of Education, University of Technology, Sydney. He teaches adult vocational educators and trainers in the subject areas of training-learning, educational psychology, organisational and educational leadership, research methods and adult development. He has presented at many vocational education and training conferences in Australia and overseas. He is the author of the recent book entitled: *Improving Learning through Effective Training.*

R. T. Pithers
University of Technology, Sydney

IAN R. CORNFORD

11. SKILL LEARNING AND THE DEVELOPMENT OF EXPERTISE

Importance of Skills and Expertise

Modern society is very much dependent upon the development of skills and expertise and only functions effectively because individuals with specialist knowledge and skills can apply these quickly and effortlessly. Teachers, engineers, doctors, food technologists, managers, plumbers, electricians, those involved in office administration along with typists, stenographers, professional musicians, and sportspersons all make their contributions to society and its effective functioning. The most talented and creative, who are generally recognised as experts, are essential for ensuring progress and development through their problem solving, innovations and creativity. This applies equally whether their expertise be work-related or centred upon entertainment or cultural activities. While not everyone can make important scientific discoveries, develop new teaching strategies, write new symphonies or successfully implement new systems of management, the effective functioning of our society is dependent upon proficiency in everyday, work-based skills. Only recently the central business district of the New Zealand city of Auckland was plunged into darkness and disarray because of the failure of cables and power supplies, illustrating the importance of basic managerial and maintenance skills.

The learning of skills appears closely linked to human survival. Education by parents, family, school or higher education institutions involves transmission of knowledge and skill from generation to generation to ensure that the same mistakes are not made and that survival is ensured. Getting the skill right and speed of execution can be vital for survival even where commonplace, everyday experiences are concerned. Even crossing the road in Australia, a supposedly simple activity,

James A Athanasou (ed.), Adult Educational Psychology, 261–288

requires degrees of skill in terms of looking to the right, looking to the left, and looking back to the right to ascertain whether there is any coming traffic before then quickly crossing directly across the road in a straight line. Failure to adhere to these simple elements and observe them in the correct order can prove fatal.

Skills and expertise are vital for national prosperity and thus indirectly the maintenance of arts grants, pensions and community services funded by government or local councils. We live in an increasingly competitive world and are being buffeted by ongoing technological, economic and social revolutions as a result of computerisation and the application of new information technologies. In such a world, skills are the key to economic survival. Thurow (1992, p. 275) has argued that "skills are the only source of sustainable competitive advantage" in an age when reverse engineering has become an art form and a wealth of natural resources no long provides the competitive edge that it once did.

A great deal of learning involves skill learning. Apart from the examples involving readily identifiable work-related or occupational skills given above, which are generally taught in the upper secondary school and later in universities and colleges of post-compulsory education, much of the learning which occurs in the earlier years of schooling involves development of skills. These include the skills of reading, writing, and numeracy which are frequently known as the three Rs. All of these, along with socialisation and the development of increasing capacity to adhere to codes of conduct and manners, involve skill learning.

Lack of Understanding of Skill Learning

As Paul Fitts (1964) noted, skill learning has only been of intermittent interest to researchers. At present there appears to be a resurgence of interest in skill development (for example, see VanLehn, 1996; Zimmerman & Kitsantas, 1996, 1997) on account of its importance in effective learning, development of problem solving skills and self-regulation. However, despite the importance of skills and skill learning in everyday functioning, there appears to be little real understanding of skill learning by teachers and trainers in school, TAFE, university and business sectors as judged by the development of courses likely to promote really effective skill learning. This is despite the fact that skills are frequently referred to as important in many educational psychology texts. Teachers and trainers involved in these different educations sectors need to be knowledgeable in order to develop relevant education policies, courses and teaching practices to promote effective skill learning.

The lack of understanding of skill learning and its importance extends well beyond the academic community, teachers and trainers. There is also a generally lack of understanding by business and industry, despite the important role training plays in the development and maintenance of work skills (see Bassi & Van Buren, 1998). Managers and human resource development personnel reveal very little understanding of skill learning and the development of expertise in the training programs which are implemented. For example, in Australia business and industry has a poor history of providing on-the-job training programs which are extensive and which involve extended mentoring or advising to provide longer term feedback on performance, even for managers (Australian Mission on Management Skills Report, 1991; Karpin, 1995).

Australian government bodies responsible for the establishment of policies and educational goals within the wider community also appear deficient in even basic understanding. With their emphasis upon competency-based training, Australian federal government agencies or subsidiary boards and committees connected to the Department of Employment, Education, Training and Youth Affairs (DEETYA) have not displayed any awareness of the time factors involved in effective skill learning or the stages that are progressed through in skill learning and the development of expertise. Research evidence suggests that competency-based modular courses, implemented in TAFE as a result of federal government pressures, are not resulting in students with superior knowledge and skills (Cornford, 1997). These findings are at least partly the result of failure to recognise the need for extensive practice and feedback over considerable periods of time to ensure that skills become securely established.

This chapter briefly considers earlier attempts to categorise skills as performance and cognitive skills, before examining the defining attributes of skill and skilled performance more generally. The basic principles of skill learning are then examined via the skill learning theory of Paul Fitts (1962, 1964, 1968), along with the stages in the development of expertise (Berliner, 1988; Dreyfus& Dreyfus, 1986; Stevenson, 1994). Finally, issues of importance in education for ensuring highly effective skill learning and performance are discussed. Understanding of these theories and issues is important for all teachers, trainers, careers counsellors, human resource development managers, consultants and policy makers involved with change management and the development of more efficient work skills and organisational practices.

Types of Skills

The earlier skill literature reveals a fascination by researchers with the classification of skills into different categories (e.g., see Adams, 1987). Cognitive and performance skills are just two of the many classification categories which have been used by various researchers, with these two categories still used widely today (see Colley & Beech, 1989a; Morrison, 1991). These two categories, however, reflect the dichotomy between body and mind which has bedevilled western science and psychology for hundreds of years (Ainley, 1993). This type of categorisation underlies the sometimes not very productive disputes over the nature of education and training, the value of academic versus practical learning and work, and the role that the schooling system should play in preparing individuals for work (see Stevenson, 1998).

Divisions between the mind and body are not considered particularly useful in helping understand skill learning. Indeed it may well be that this artificial division of cognitive and performance skills has hindered wider understanding of skill development. Several researchers (Colley, 1989; Cornford, 1993; Fitts, 1968) have indicated that there are great similarities in the processes and acquisition of cognitive and performance skills. All skills appear to follow the same learning phases (see Anderson, 1982; Fitts, 1964, 1968; VanLehn, 1996) and appear to have the same defining attributes as outlined in the next section. Additionally, there is evidence that cognitive and performance skills both follow the same Law of Practice (Newell & Rosenbloom, 1981; VanLehn, 1996).

Performance skills are more clearly visible since cognitive skills, by virtue of their nature, occur privately and invisibly in the brain. Yet any critical examination of the concepts of cognitive and performance skills soon reveals that these two categories do not serve as particularly good criteria for the division of skills into different categories. It is not possible to conceive of human performance of any kind without their being some cerebral activity directing and monitoring the performance. Indeed it seems inescapable that some schema or mental model is required to exist in the mind for skilled performance to occur. The more recent major advances in understanding the performances of experts have come about through examination of cognitive processes, particularly those involved in problem solving.

When it comes to examining so-called cognitive skills, with computing a generally accepted example of this categorisation, it is difficult to conceive of skill performance consisting only of cognitive elements. Computers require a keyboard and physical manipulative skills in order to interact with the machine. Frequently combinations of keys are required to achieve certain commands or macros and here considerable physical skill is required to depress the relevant keys at the same time. Both cognitive and performance elements appear inextricably linked in skill performance even though in many situations the performance elements are most clearly noticeable. In any situation where there are attempts to communicate to others, performance skills will be involved.

Defining Skill

The Concise Oxford Dictionary defines "skill" as "expertness, practised ability, facility in doing something, dexterity". Any series of steps of an activity which are required to be repeated, and which require degrees of facility and speed in effective performance, constitute skill or skilled performance. However, the dictionary definition provides but a rough working definition and there appear to be nine defining characteristics of skill and skilled performance across all skill types (Cornford, 1996).

Skill is learned.

The first of the defining attributes is that skill is learned and not something which is an innate or a reflex. With some skills human genetic or developmental factors may influence the acquisition of skill. For example language learning appears to have developmental and genetic aspects with an explosion of language learning occurring around the age of two with normal human infants (Gage & Berliner, 1992). With other skills, involving muscular coordination and the need for strength, physical maturation may be necessary before satisfactory performance can be attained. Even with adults, who possess normal levels of strength, exercises may be necessary to strengthen muscles to carry increased loads or weight. With piano playing there are usually exercises to strengthen required muscles in the fingers and to gain coordination and fine motor control.

Skill involves motivation, purpose and goals.

The second defining attribute of skill is that it involves motivation, purpose and goals. A number of researchers see learning and skilled performance as problem solving activity (e.g., Anderson, 1982; Annett, 1991). Problem identification presupposes motivation, that is purposive behaviour (a) to identify the problem and

(b) to engage in finding a solution. Motivation is important both for initial learning of the skill and then for subsequent practice to attain effective performance. Whether an individual who has acquired a skill will continue to perform to the high levels learned also will depend upon motivation. Many examples of unsatisfactory standards in work performance can be found in individuals who have been trained to quite high levels in initial training sessions yet do not believe that it is necessary to offer high levels of customer service. It is also possible that individuals who are not highly motivated may not continue to produce the skill at all. Many who have learned sports or musical instruments may choose no longer to perform them on account of lack of motivation.

Schemas are required.
A mental model or schema which embodies the components, processes, correct sequencing of components and processes, and the time relations between components and processes needs to exist in memory before a skill can be performed (Colley, 1989; Gott, 1994; Schmidt, 1975). Analyses of skills based on observation clearly reveal that performance is based upon a series of related steps with the sequence and timing of the steps of very considerable importance. For example, it is necessary to undress and turn on the water before attempting to lather soap when taking a shower. If this sequence is not followed the rather surreal situation of the individual trying to use dry soap on a dressed body may occur. The schema or mental model is the representation of these elements in memory and, as we will see later when we look at Fitts' skill learning theory, the existence of the schema or mental model is necessary to explain how individuals can perform automatically on "automatic pilot".

Skills are context specific.
Skilled performance is linked to a specific context. The need for performance of specific skills is signified by specific cues and this is explained in terms of stimulus-response connections in behavioural psychology theories. Stimuli, which act as cues for specific forms of behaviour and skill performance, are important in explaining why individuals engage in appropriate behaviour rather than engage in any of the other wide range of other behaviours which exist in their skill repertoires. The failure of individuals to apply skills in appropriate ways to new settings, with this involving transfer of learning, is explicable in terms of these individuals failing to perceive the cues which signal that this is an appropriate place to apply previously learned skills.

There has been substantial development of policies by different governments around the world to focus upon generic skill development. An example in Australia is the Mayer Key Competencies (Mayer, 1992) which were based upon the UK Core Skills and American SCANS concepts. However, research into aspects of generic skills, for example that by Stasz (1996), has indicated that the skills required in different contexts vary quite considerably in specific details even though the skills in two different work environments may be generically similar.

Skills involve problem solving relevant to the context.
The fifth defining attribute is that skilled performance involves elements of problem solving relevant to the particular context in which the skill is used. Some researchers, such as Anderson (1982) and Annett (1991), viewed skill learning and

performance as problem solving activity. Varying types of problems, ranging from the easy to the more difficult, may need to be solved in the course of performing a skill. In many cases skills are taught as involving particular principles which then need to be applied to settings differing in various ways from those in the initial training examples. For example, basic formulae may be used by a carpenter in calculating the area of a bench top, but the dimensions and measurements which need to be substituted in the formulae will vary. More complex problem solving may be required in gaining access to plumbing or wiring in older dwellings which have had additions or alterations made to them.

Skills involve relative judgements with individual differences in skilled performance evident.
Another defining attribute of skills is that different levels and standards of performance exist among practitioners in any specialist skill or sub-skill area. There are good and poor performances and performers, and we recognise that there are some individuals who are more skilled than others. In everyday living we frequently take this into account, such as when we make decisions as to whom we will employ to perform some service for us, such as building a house or being operated upon. Skill is itself a relative concept in that there are always less and more skilled performances which are used as benchmarks to base judgements about the presence, absence and quality of a skill.

Standards of excellence.
Standards of excellence are integral to judgements about the existence of skill and relative degrees of excellence. Standards of excellence are important in individuals making judgements about their own performance which may vary from occasion to occasion. They are also important in making judgements among various individuals who are performing the same skill.

Skill involves comparable replication.
Skills involve performance which can be comparably replicated or repeated to similar standards by the performer. While the extraordinary shots played by professional golfers and tennis players cannot be repeated exactly, similar levels can be attained on other occasions by truly skilled individuals. Consistency of application over time is an important commonsense indicator of skilled performance. One-off performances, which unfortunately are used in some forms of currently popular competency-based assessment, do not give a true indication of probable consistency and skill levels achieved.

Considerable periods of time are required to achieve high levels of skill.
Very considerable periods of time are required for skill acquisition. There is ample evidence that even seemingly simple skills like stringing pearls or marching require hundreds of thousands of repetitions before high levels of skilled performance can be demonstrated (Kottke, Halpern, Easton, Ozel & Burrill, 1978). Many researchers consider that ten years is a minimum for the development of expertise in a wide variety of specialty fields (Ericsson & Smith, 1991). In terms of practical, real world learning, a recent survey of skilled personnel revealed that 34% of all respondents considered that four or more years on-the-job training was required to

achieve satisfactory levels of work performance with some 8% indicating that ten or more years was needed (Cornford, Athanasou, & Pithers, 1996).

These defining attributes have substantial implications for skill learning and the development of programs intended to foster effective skill learning (Cornford, 1996). We need to teach and train in such ways as to encourage the development of these attributes. Practical aspects of training for superior skill learning and the development of expertise will be returned to later in this chapter. First, however, it is necessary to consider Fitts' (1962, 1964, 1968) skill learning theory, as this provides understanding of the phases in effective skill development.

Fitts' Skill Learning Theory

A number of theories of skill learning have been advanced (see Colley & Beech, 1989b; Sincoff & Sternberg, 1989; Shuell, 1990). However, it is the skill learning theory of Paul Fitts (1962, 1964, 1968) which appears to be the most satisfactory theory to explain the stages involved in the learning of all types of skills. This theory is recognised as the most satisfactory by Annett (1991), while Anderson (1982) and VanLehn (1996) have based their cognitive skill acquisition theories on Fitts' seminal work.

Fitts' theory was developed from interviews with large numbers of highly experienced teachers and trainers involved in such diverse area as aircraft flying instruction, where to be successful learners require considerable cognitive skills, and more obviously physical skills such as swimming, diving, tennis, basketball, soccer and football. From these interviews Fitts developed a theory in which there are three distinct phases. Fitts' (1962, 1964, 1968) terminology to describe these stages varies in different writings as his conceptualisation of the theory developed and changed (Shuell, 1990). The terminology used is in accordance with the last of Fitts' publications in 1968 when he appears to have started to have been more influenced by information processing theory. The three phases are the cognitive phase, the fixation phase and the autonomous phase. For some time in vocational education circles in Australia the fixation phase has been known as the practice-fixation phase. While this varies from Fitts' own terminology, this description is retained as it serves to emphasise the most important process which occurs at this phase.

Cognitive Phase

In the cognitive phase the learner attempts to analyse the skill and to verbalise about it or describe it. Verbalisation would appear as important in identifying elements in the skill and coding these into a form which can be remembered and stored in long term memory (Colley, 1989). Although Fitts did not describe it in these terms, the cognitive phase appears to involve the initial steps to construct a schema or mental model which represents the skill in symbolic form in the mind and which will serve to guide behaviour and later act to assist error detection (Schmidt, 1975).

The first step in the cognitive phase is to gain an overall picture of what the skill involves. Then it becomes a matter of identifying the separate steps or sub-skills which together constitute the skill, the sequence in which they occur and elements of timing. Timing is often a critical factor in many skills. For example it may be very important to wait until glue reaches a particular stage of stickiness before another coat of the glue is applied. Understanding of patterns of rhythm, which involve time intervals and relationships, and their use are important in many skills, for example, dancing, tennis playing, but they are also used in teaching typing and other skills which involve some regular form of movement. Fluid, apparently effortless movement, in harmony with gravity and individual differences in body proportions, typifies expert skill performance. Also gained at this stage are elementary concepts of standards of performance of the skill. Initially these standards of performance are generally very basic but are further refined beyond very crude generalisations of "good" or "bad" during the second phase of skill learning.

Practice-Fixation Phase
The second phase of skill learning is the practice-fixation phase which Fitts (1964) also referred to as the associative phase. What happens at this phase is that the steps or sub-skills become closely linked or associated, hence the use of the earlier terminology "associative phase". Each previous step or sub-skill serves as the stimulus for the next step and thus associative links are formed. Remembering the next steps in a sequence, and the requirements for successful performance of this, are often quite difficult and require considerable concentration and help from a teacher or trainer in the early stages of learning. It is through repetition that these associations and links between steps or sub-skills become fixed in memory. We generally call such repetition practice, and there is little doubt that practice and feedback are the key elements at this stage of skill learning as the overall mental model in the mind becomes more elaborate and sophisticated with more links being established between elements in this model.

In terms of Rumelhardt and Norman's (1978) three types of learning, this practice-fixation phase involves the tuning of the ideas accumulated in the cognitive phase so that the performance of the skill becomes accurate and more fluid. Because short term or working memory can only hold limited amounts of information (see Sweller, 1993), the learning of reasonably long chains of steps or sub-skills requires considerable periods of time. The more complex the skill, the longer it is likely to take to ensure the accurate storage of the chain of steps or sub-skills in long term memory.

Language often remains important at this stage as we talk to ourselves and recall chains of steps or sub-skills in the correct order in order to better integrate these. Prompts and hints derived from instructors are built into our own self-talk as we engage in movement through the different steps or sub-skills. All of these things assist us as to what we need to focus upon specifically as we practise the skill. Slow practice is certainly essential in very early stages in order to ensure that all the relevant steps are present and to get these sub-skills accurate and in correct order. Accuracy is more important than speed at this stage. Although there is a natural tendency for learners to want to build up speed, this tendency needs to be resisted until the sub-skill elements can be reproduced accurately and in correct sequence. The danger at this stage is that incorrect elements may intrude, or some elements may be omitted, and these inappropriate elements then get stamped into long term memory through practice. Should this occur then there is a need for restructuring, the most difficult and frustrating of processes for both teacher and student (Rumelhardt & Norman, 1978). Restructuring is particularly difficult where repetitive physical performance is concerned, such as with incorrect technique in piano playing, golf or typing.

Autonomous Phase
The third phase in Fitts' skill learning theory is the autonomous phase. The chief characteristic of this phase is that the skill tends to be performed automatically. There is increased speed and accuracy. There is also increased resistance to stress and interference from other activities which may be performed at the same time. It is because skills have reached this autonomous phase that two or more skills can be performed at the same time without an apparent decline in quality of performance. The result is that most people can walk and chew gum at the same time! While performance of these two skills may not appear all that important, being able to do a number of things at the same time may have great importance for effective performance in many work settings. Bloom (1986, p. 70), has argued that automaticity provides the "hands and feet of genius".

Fitts appears to have deliberately chosen the word autonomous rather than automatic to describe this phase. "Autonomous" suggests that the individual is very much in control of the performance of the skill in contrast to the earlier practice-fixation phase where very frequently a trainer or teacher has to assist in prompting or monitoring the performance. Certainly during this phase the individual performing the skill is monitoring his or her own performance with the schema or mental model acting as a template against which to measure the ongoing activity (Schmidt, 1975). Although there may not appear to be obvious concentration on performance, skilled performers know when they have made some error. For example good typists know that they have struck an incorrect key because the "feel" is not right for striking that letter as measured against the mental model which exists in long term memory and which is guiding performance even at the autonomous phase.

Being able to perform at an autonomous level overcomes the problems of limited capacity of short term or working memory (Sweller, 1993), thus freeing up more capacity so that there can be concentration upon other aspects of the tasks in hand. These other aspects may involve engaging in another skill while still performing the first, or attending to issues which are known to be problems and may impede the smooth performance of the skill. Pintrich (1990) has made important points about automaticity in terms of teaching. Effective teachers or trainers need to have developed basic teaching skills to the point of automaticity in order that they can concentrate upon reactions of individual students in the course of teaching a lesson. The teacher, by being able to note that Jason or Penny has drifted off, is getting bored and may create disruption in the class, is in a position to adopt an appropriate strategy to involve the student in the lesson without upsetting the flow of the lesson. A well-directed question, or movement near the offender to prompt the putting away of an irrelevant book which is distracting attention from the lesson, only becomes possible where such skills are at an autonomous level and performance can continue while the problem solving action takes place.

The Continuity of the Phases and Overlap
Fitts theory, like all theories which posit a series of stages or phases in development, is open to criticism from those who demand a clear delineation of the

commencement and the end of a phase or stage. Fitts (1964, 1968) himself is clear on the issue: he did not see any phase being discrete or self contained but the phases flowing into one another and overlapping. In Fitts' terms, each phase is broadly descriptive of the learning activities that occur then, and understanding of cognitive, practice-fixation and autonomous phases should serve to guide teachers and trainers in their teaching and development of programs for effective skill development.

While Fitts indicated that there is overlap between phases, each phase of skill learning is most characterised by concentration upon specific types of activities associated with that phase. For example, elementary standards of excellence are learned in the cognitive phase but in the practice-fixation phase these elementary standards are further refined. This occurs because practice and feedback lead to increased discrimination and awareness of ever smaller components of the steps or sub-skills and, through this, the tuning or refinement of the mental model or schema being developed so that it produces more effective performance. Fitts' three phase skill learning theory thus implies that different activities and strategies may be involved or receive more emphasis at some stages than at others. For example, research by Zimmerman and Kitsantas (1997) into the development of self-regulation, indicates that process and outcome goals are more important at different stages in skill learning.

Fitts' skill learning theory helps explain how learning occurs with single skills. When we work in a specialty area we learn large numbers of skills which together contribute to effective performance in that area. Systematic research into the performance and thinking of mathematicians, physics problem solvers, avionics trouble shooters, chess players, radiologists, doctors, nurses and computer programmers has led to the identification of a series of stages in the development of expertise as people work longer in a specialisation, gain more experience, and more knowledge and skills.

What Is Expertise and How Is It Determined?

Expertise refers to levels of excellence which transcend the performance of average individuals. In everyday language an expert is someone who is able to perform better than most people around them. This common language usage also is currently employed by some educational psychologists, for example Sternberg (1998), when they are referring to individuals who are performing at highly satisfactory levels or the development of clusters of skills to such levels.

However, for those seriously involved in the study of what makes an expert and how experts differ from others working in the field, expertise is defined more precisely. These researchers consider that genuine experts are very few in number and must meet certain criteria before being judged as such and selected for study. The first criterion which must be met is that of genuinely superior performance. In some fields it is possible to use objective statistical procedures to identify those persons who perform two standard deviations above the mean or average (Ericsson & Charness, 1994). A standard deviation is a measure derived from a normal distribution which results from the measurement of a large number of individuals on that particular skill or ability. Those who score two standard deviations above the mean are very few in number relative to the total population measured. It is relatively easy to measure athletic performance and identify expertise in this way, but not all specialty performance can be assessed easily like this. For example, it does not seem appropriate to judge the performance of a neurosurgeon by using a stopwatch in the same way you would measure the performance of a long distance runner or sprinter. Survival rates of patients, difficulty of surgical procedures and effective repair or removal of tumours are likely to be of far greater significance than speed of performance.

Experts in professions involving complex skills are frequently identified through surveying their peers or superiors to determine those individuals who are most highly regarded within that particular profession. However, socially adept individuals can engage in self-promotion and the development of professional mystique, thus creating false reputations. In numbers of studies where objective measures have been used, experts have not performed impressively at all. Amongst the least impressive performances have been with economic forecasting (see Johnson, 1988), despite which an enormous faith is placed in such forecasting by governments and politicians. To avoid errors in selection of genuine experts, researchers using the approach of surveying knowledgeable peers usually couple it with more objective measures. For example, Gaea Leinhardt (1986), who conducted important research into teaching mathematics, selected expert teachers by (a) tracing student growth scores on standardised tests over five years and picking teachers whose students' growth scores were in the top 15 percent for the previous three years, (b) asked principals and supervisors to review the list and suggest outstanding math teachers, and (c) visited classrooms, observed and made judgements about teachers who had agreed to participate in ongoing research.

Characteristics of Experts

Much knowledge about expertise is derived from expert-novice comparisons where the performance and strategies employed by experts are compared with those employed by individuals who are relatively new to learning or working in a field. A number of researchers (Dreyfus & Dreyfus, 1986; Glaser & Chi, 1988; Berliner, 1988; Ericsson & Charness, 1994; Sternberg, 1998) have identified the chief characteristics of experts. These characteristics include:
– expertise tends to be restricted to a specific context. There is little evidence that individuals who are expert in one specialty area can transfer those skills to a different field of practice. For example Voss and Post (1988) found that expert chemists approached the solving of problems in political science much the same as novices, describing the problems in very concrete and specific ways although they used abstract logic quite consistently when solving chemistry problems. One of the obvious reasons why experts excel in their specialist domain is that they have extensive, detailed content knowledge of their particular field. For example doctors who have success in diagnosis have a very extensive knowledge of different types of diseases and illnesses and of the different symptoms which may reveal themselves with each of the diseases or illnesses;
– experts have large, rich schemas or mental models which encapsulate not just factual data but also sophisticated conceptualisations at abstract levels. These schemas are developed in such ways that interconnections between different areas of relevant knowledge are clearly represented, both in terms of relationships and causality;

- under time pressure, experts can perform more quickly and accurately than can novices;
- experts spend proportionately more time determining how to represent the problem, that is how they should go about tackling the problem, than they do in searching for and executing a problem solving strategy;
- experts have automatised many sequences of steps in problem solving strategies. the result is that they appear to perform effortlessly;
- experts can more accurately predict the difficulty of solving a problem than can novices;
- experts have specific occupational memories with ability to recall complex details from past instances, especially the atypical or error situations;
- experts carefully monitor their own problem solving activities and the
- processes which they use. this indicates that experts possess more effective metacognitive processes (Sternberg, 1998); and
- experts are highly motivated and proud of their accomplishments;

Stages in the Development of Expertise

Expertise clearly takes many years to develop and in this process five distinct stages have been identified (Berliner; 1988; Dreyfus & Dreyfus, 1986). These five stages in the development of expertise are novice, advanced beginner, competent, proficient and expert.

Generally speaking novices are students or beginning workers; advanced beginners are in the second or third year of their career; around the third year or fourth year they may become competent. The majority of skill learners will probably reach the stage of being competent: a smaller number will become proficient, while a still smaller number of those who are proficient will develop into experts (Cornford & Athanasou, 1995). These stages which are developed from examining real life expert functioning and work in the field of artificial intelligence are useful in identifying learners at different stages and explaining why there are differences in performance. It should be noted that in these stages the qualitative changes over time are as important, if not more important, than the quantity of information acquired.

Novice

The beginner has to learn all the commonplace terms and elements such as the different gears in driving a manual car and what the different road sign symbols are and mean. Beginners seeks all purpose rules to guide their behaviour. These rules are logical, fairly consistent and the beginner typically is locked into these and unable to deal with situations which require more than the application of rules. This is because at this early stage rules are stated in broad terms and hence are context free. Such rules for beginning teachers for example are "never criticise students" and "give praise for right answers".

Advanced Beginner

At this point experience starts to be important. The individual realises as knowledge of different situations is accumulated, that the rules, which are of necessity generalisations, do not adequately cover all situations. At this stage the new teacher starts to recognise that critical feedback to a good student may improve performance considerably and that you may choose not to give praise for a partially correct answer.

Competent
The competent worker exercises greater authority by setting priorities and making plans. At this stage they have come to determine what is important and that the order of priority may change with the circumstances. There is thus a much fuller understanding that rules may need to be varied depending upon the particular context and the circumstances.

Proficient
In the proficient worker intuition or "know-how" becomes important. They may no longer consciously think about adjustments. They notice similarities between events. There is more analysis and decision making with more flexible observance of rules.

Expert
The expert has an intuitive grasp of situations. Performance is fluid and qualitatively different. The knowledge of experts contains fewer rigid classifications of areas of data with there being a mastery of understanding of the interrelationships and linking between the different areas of knowledge.

Benner (1984, pp. 23-4) gave an excellent example from nursing that illustrates the differences between novice and advanced beginners, and competent, proficient and expert nurses in terms of experience and being rule bound.

> I give instructions to the new graduate, very detailed and explicit instructions: When you come in and first see the baby, you take the baby's vital signs and make the physical examination, and you check the I.V. sites, and the ventilator and makes sure that it works, and you check the monitors and the alarms. When I would say this to them, they would do exactly what I told them to do, no matter what else was going on... They couldn't choose which one was more important... They couldn't do for one baby the things that were most important and then go onto the other baby and do the things that were most important, and leave the things that weren't as important until later on... If I said you had to do these eight things... They did those things, and they didn't care if their other kid was screaming its head off. When they did realize, they would be like a mule between two piles of hay. (Benner, 1984, pp. 23-4)

Westerman (1991), in her study of expert and novice elementary school teachers, provided good illustrations of the ways in which the performance and understanding of experts differ from those of novices. She found quite substantial differences between the thinking and decision making of these two groups of teachers on pre-active (lesson planning), interactive (actual teaching) and evaluation stages in teaching. Expert teachers had a good understanding of the curriculum and how different topics interrelated, they related new information to the stages of learning and interests of individual students and they engaged in cognitive task analysis from the perspective of the students. Novice teachers largely were lacking in all these skills.

The novices used specific objectives to develop structured lesson plans, which they seemed unable to adapt to meet student needs, whereas the expert teachers were able perceive the difficulties being faced by students and modify their planned lessons to meet the changed circumstances. Novice teachers typically ignored off-task behaviour, until they could no longer do so, then they tended to interrupt the lesson to correct the behaviour. By contrast, the expert teachers read the signals of potential disturbance and used their voices, body language and well practised management strategies to bring the child back onto the task. Expert teachers also had a greater understanding of the abilities and interests of individual children and were able to use this knowledge to engage or re-engage them in effective learning. Because experts were able to predict possible problems, they were able to develop and implement contingency plans to overcome the problems if and when they arose. Overall, experts had much greater ability to establish realistic goals and be flexible in meeting these than novices. While this research involved elementary school teachers, there is good reason to believe that the findings apply to teachers and trainers more generally.

The Relationship between the Stages in Fitts' Theory and Those in the Development of Expertise

There are both quantitative and qualitative differences between stages in the development of expertise. At each stage there would appear to be increases in the quantity of knowledge over earlier stages. But more important are the qualitative changes. This is especially so from the competent stage onward. Here problem solving abilities are a key element, with much of the problem solving seeming to occur in intuitive ways with experts. This appearance may be given because many processes are performed at an autonomous level without seeming concentration upon elements. In fact most skills are probably performed at an autonomous level at proficient and expert stages. In contrast, at the novice and advanced beginner stages, many, if not all skills are performed at the cognitive and practice-fixation stages (Cornford & Athanasou, 1995). By the competent stage, however, many less complex skills are likely to be approaching an autonomous level of performance, while more complex skills are still developing at the cognitive or practice-fixation levels.

It is important to remember that the stages of skill learning apply to the acquisition of each individual skill, whereas the stages in the development of expertise describe changes which occur as individuals learn clusters of skills relevant to their specialist area. As new skills emerge because of advances in a specialisation, even those at the proficient and expert levels will have to work through the cognitive, practice-fixation and autonomous stages in acquiring those new skills to high levels of performance. An obvious example is with surgeons and the introduction of key-hole surgery, a potentially beneficial operating procedure because it involves less invasive techniques. Problems have emerged and been reported because some surgeons have been operating and using these new techniques with inadequate previous training and practice. The results in some instances have been complications and injury by less effective surgeons.

Bodies of knowledge and skills previously acquired will assist in the learning of new skills, especially where the new skills contains sub-skill components which are identical to previously learned and well practised skills (Bandura, 1977). For example, after individuals have acquired the skill of walking over many years of practice involving an estimated three million steps by age six, they then can be taught to march to parade ground standard in the army in only six weeks with 800,000 steps (Kottke et al., 1978).

Training for the Development of Expertise

The purpose of identifying the differences between the different stages in the novice-expert continuum is to understand how expertise is acquired so that ultimately we know how to teach better. It is desirable that novices, advanced beginners and those at the competent stage can be presented with appropriate experiences to assist in the development of their full potential. Very few individuals develop into experts but there are more who attain proficiency. Many remain most of their working lives at the competent stage, but it would appear most logical to attempt to aim generally for proficiency in training rather than competent, which is only a middle level (Cornford & Athanasou, 1995).

To date, expert-novice comparisons have been a rich source of understanding of skill development generally, but especially for teaching skill development (for example see Leinhardt, 1986; Leinhardt & Greeno, 1986; Sabers, Cushing & Berliner, 1991; Swanson, O'Connor & Cooney, 1990; Westerman, 1991). However, there are still considerable gaps in our knowledge of how experts develop since most of the knowledge gained has been derived from cross-sectional studies that examined different cohorts at different stages of development. What is really necessary is the tracing of the development of expertise in individuals over all stages through longitudinal studies conducted over extensive periods of time. Only then will we start to have a fuller understanding of how experts acquire and structure knowledge. Since expertise is closely linked to specific areas of practice, experts in different areas are likely to employ different types of skills in varying combinations and proportions, quite apart from possessing different factual knowledge bases. This indicates the needs for extensive research in all the different, major occupational skill areas.

At present we know that expertise is rarely taught in formal ways, although Gott (1994) appears to be making considerable progress in the specific area of training in avionics troubleshooting, an area which involves much conceptual analysis and problem solving. The following sections outline factors which have the potential to promote more effective teaching of skills and assist in the development of expertise. In any training for skill learning there are sets of pre-requisite conditions which need to be met to ensure effective learning. These include subject knowledge and teaching ability of the teacher, communication skills, interpersonal relations and establishment of a training environment in which errors are considered as a learning opportunity. A full account of these is beyond the scope of this chapter but more comprehensive consideration of the relevant issues may be found in several sources (Cornford, 1996; Cornford & Athanasou, 1995; Learmonth, 1993).

Teaching Learners about the Stages in Skill Learning and the Development of Expertise

Skill development is very much dependent upon individual motivation and self-regulation. Motivation and self-regulation are necessary for individuals to process new information, develop their own schemas or mental models to guide and monitor future performance, practise to achieve greater mastery of skills, and continue to perform at the highest levels attained (Cornford, 1996). Motivation is also essential for individuals to strive for higher levels of knowledge and skill in order to become proficient or expert rather than remaining content to perform at a merely competent level. Teachers and trainers need to ensure that students understand Fitts' skill learning theory and the stages in the development of expertise. Understanding of the different stages in skill learning and the development of expertise will allow students to better understand their own learning. It is likely that this knowledge will foster increased motivation, prepare them for some of the frustrations and plateauxing, which will occur with extended practice (see below), and permit the development of metacognitive processes, especially planning, problem solving, monitoring and evaluation, which are essential for all forms of learning and skilled performance (Colley & Beech, 1989c; Sternberg, 1998).

Effective practice and feedback are essential for the effective development of skills and progression through the stages in the development of expertise. The following sections outline a range of factors related to effective practice and the construction of appropriate teaching and practice programs by teachers and trainers if high levels of performance are to be attained. While it is highly desirable that learners be made aware of these factors and the issues that surround them, the responsibility for using this knowledge to develop better training programs will largely rest with teachers and trainers who generally can bring to bear more objective judgements than learners. Administrators and managers in education, business and industry too need to be cognisant of these factors and their effects in order to be supportive of teachers when they devise programs which require more than minimal time and resources.

Importance of Practice and Feedback

Modelling and practice
A great deal of initial skill learning is facilitated by the performance of a model or models who reveal or intentionally demonstrate a particular skill. The chapter on Social Learning (Cornford, 1999), which deals with the issue of modelling in learning, should be read in conjunction with this chapter since it has major implications for using the demonstration method, the chief method of instruction for skill learning based on modelling. Following observation of a model or models and initial coding of meaning (Bandura, 1977), practice and feedback become the most important factors in the development of effective skills through Fitts' practice-fixation and autonomous phases. Ultimately, through sufficient practice, proficiency or expertise may develop. Practice is vital for the secure establishment of the developing model or schema in long term memory and so is the feedback which refines or tunes the elements of that mental model and actual performance

(Schmidt, 1975; Ohlsson, 1996). Only through extensive practice, and the gaining of feedback through practice, will the autonomous phase of skilled performance be reached.

Practice variables
The concept of overlearning is an important one in learning and practice although unfashionable at present because of its association with drill approaches to learning. Overlearning is important in ensuring retention of material learned and involves practice beyond the point at which competent performance is achieved (Kreuger, 1929; Spitzer, 1939). Continued practice beyond initial capability to reproduce the knowledge or performance accurately appears to ensure that there is consolidation of knowledge and it probably also ensures the development of feelings of self-efficacy (Bandura, 1997), with success leading to further success.

Practice may involve either massed or spaced practice. Massed practice involves the repetition of the skill for a fixed number of times or repetitive practice within a set time interval. Spaced practice, as the name suggests, involves practice occasions being spread out over a period of time. There appear to be a number of advantages which are associated with spaced practice (Dempster, 1988), not least that this gives the opportunity to critically analyse a performance and plan to improve it on the next practice occasion.

Both massed and spaced practice have their place in the development of a skill practice program, and it is not possible to lay down general rules since the nature of the skill and the training objectives will vary according to a number of factors including the particular phase of skill learning. For example, massed practice may be useful towards the autonomous stage where the training objective may be to train for resistance of stress and fatigue. It may also be useful in initial stages in skill learning to ensure retention of initial learning. In deciding upon the type of practise to be employed, the teacher needs to take into consideration the potential effects of boredom, fatigue and loss of alertness, as well as the possible benefits.

Immediate and delayed feedback need also be considered. The traditional behavioural psychology approach was to follow a response with reinforcement as soon in time as possible so as to ensure that the feedback was connected closely to the original stimulus and response. More recent research indicates that there may be benefits obtained from delayed feedback with certain skills and in certain contexts (Swinnen, Schmidt, Nicholson & Shapiro, 1990; Winstein & Schmidt, 1990). The delay of feedback may well encourage learners to undertake critical analysis of the results from their practice efforts, and compare these with the mental model in their minds which guided their performance. The importance of this in observational learning from modelled events is elaborated further in the chapter on Social Learning (Cornford, 1999).

Deliberate practice
Ericsson and Charness (1994), in a somewhat controversial article, have argued that deliberate practice is more important than ability in the development of expertise. While ability and aptitude are certainly more important than are recognised by Ericsson and Charness, these researchers are partially correct. Too many teachers use judgement of lack of ability in students as an excuse to give up, when more effective teaching and coaching, and development of carefully planned practice sessions, would ensure more individuals are motivated to achieve

277

something like their full potential. Unfortunately many learners discontinue courses or cease practice with damaged notions of self-efficacy before any real mastery is obtained. It is also clear that many individuals do not practice sufficiently and that, if they did more practice, they would be more effective and skilled. The large numbers of individuals in the community with inferior English reading and writing skills are partially the result of incorrect teaching and lack of personally directed practice.

Deliberate practice, in Ericsson and Charness' terms, is intensive, carefully directed practice which occurs over long periods of time. In such practice there is often careful coaching or training by more knowledgeable performers of the skill, and learners focus consciously upon errors and incorrect or unsatisfactory aspects of performance in order to substantially improve them. However, self-direction and self-regulation are essential elements. Ericsson and Charness indicated that most individuals who are regarded as promising in their field are highly motivated and practise to ensure that effective learning results from their efforts. This means that in many cases that practice occurs, when there is choice, earlier in the day when individuals are generally fresher and more alert.

Practising while alert
The effects of stress and body clock and time of day factors on skill performance, practice and learning have been recognised for a long time (Hartley, Morrison & Arnold, 1989; Smith, 1989); and so have the effects of ageing (Salthouse, 1989). Unless learners monitor skill practice very carefully in phases prior to automaticity, errors are likely to creep in. When this occurs the incorrect skill may be inadvertently ground in through practice and then need to be removed. This then necessitates additional time for restructuring and reestablishment of the correct skill elements and sequence (Rumelhardt & Norman, 1978) and can de-motivate the learner. It bears repeating that slow, accurate practice in the early stages is the key to later effective performance.

Plateaux
A major source of frustration for many learners is that at times when they are seriously practising a skill they remain at the same level of performance and do not improve, despite concerted efforts to do so. What is involved is a plateau effect. Although the existence of plateaux is challenged by some researchers (e.g., Fitts, 1968) there is ample evidence to indicate that skill learning is rarely reflected in smooth, continuous, upward learning curves (Shiffrin, 1996). There are also absolute limits to human performance which include physical capacity, and the aptitude and ability of the performer. Limitations on human performance also may be imposed by the technical limits of equipment. In terms of related issues, some decrements in performance is to be expected with age (Ericsson & Charness, 1994), a factor well recognised in many sports.

Typical of patterns of skill learning is a period of initial rapid improvement because the learning is starting from a very low base. After this, learning appears to slow down and frequently levels-off before the performance again improves. It is important that learners come to recognise the formation of plateaux, that is levelling off before higher levels are achieved, as a normal part of skill learning. It is also important that they do not become frustrated but persevere and attempt to discover the cause of a plateau in order to progress again.

There are several causes of plateau effects. These include failure to understand the relative importance of the sub-skill components and get them in the correct order, and not having mastered each subcomponent of the skill sufficiently. In a skill process each sub-skill contributes and serves particular purposes. Probably the most frequent cause of plateaux is not giving each sub-skill component its due consideration. It is human nature to concentrate upon those elements which are easier to perform and neglect those elements which are more difficult or give concern. Unfortunately one weak link in the chain of sub-skills which comprise the skill will reduce the overall effectiveness.

Situated learning and cognitive apprenticeship
Social factors have been recognised as contributing to skill development and learning for some considerable time (Bandura, 1977; Fitts, 1968). Recently, however, social factors in learning have received more attention. Concepts of situated learning (Lave, 1988; Lave & Wenger, 1991) and cognitive apprenticeship (Brown, Collins & Duguid, 1989) have emerged over the past decade, along with renewed interest in mentoring and coaching. All of these concepts or strategies are concerned with more effective learning through modelling superior performers, teaching real-life problems in authentic or real situations, and the development of cognition and performance which approach those of genuine experts or practitioners. In all of these concepts or strategies, knowledgeable individuals are involved in both transmission of the knowledge and the culture which surrounds superior practice.

Culture certainly will determine values placed upon certain skills, and whether formal courses will be established for these and in what educational system, that is in school, TAFE, university or the general community. To date, however, these lines of research have identified the importance of cultural contexts, but the means of social transmission of knowledge have not been satisfactorily analysed and described (Anderson, Reder & Simon, 1996, 1997; Billett, 1994). Bandura's (1977, 1997) model of factors governing observational learning, which is outlined elsewhere in this text (Cornford, 1999), provides a more explicit and satisfactory analysis of the social factors which teachers and trainers need to consider.

Training for self-regulation
A problem in initial skill learning, and also in maintaining effective performance over the long term, is that of the individual being able to perceive performance accurately and gain feedback, even when performing at high levels. Self-reflection is clearly unable to provide totally unbiased, accurate and objective feedback, especially with complex skills which are performed at considerable speed and which involve the performer concentrating closely upon a range of elements at the same time. Beyond the teaching-training setting, continuing feedback from peers or more expert co-workers in many work situations is seen as an important source of feedback (Brown et al., 1989). The problem of obtaining reliable and valid feedback is the reason why many professionals, who would be regarded as experts in sports and the arts, still retain coaches to provided vital feedback to either maintain or improve performance (Ericsson & Charness, 1994).

In the early stages of skill learning, novice learners are often unable to distinguish between correct and incorrect, and good, mediocre and poor examples of their own efforts; hence they need assistance from the teacher or trainer in making appropriate judgements. However, it should be part of the teacher's objective to make the learner independent. In the real world of work no one wants to employ any one who is incapable of self-regulation and who needs to be constantly monitored by a manager or boss to assure that quality is maintained and mistakes are identified and rectified.

Glaser (1996) has identified three interactive phases in what he terms the principles underlying a change in agency. By change of agency Glaser meant the ways in which individual learners moves from considerable dependency upon those around them to self-regulation of performance, with this latter state characterising expert performance. These three phases provide guidance for teachers and trainers in structuring their training so as to move from a very supportive to a self-monitoring and self-regulating situation. The three phases are: (a) external support, which involves early environmental structuring influenced by parental dedication and interests and the support of teachers and coaches; (b) transition, which is characterised by decreasing scaffolding of environmental supports and increasing of apprenticeship arrangements that offer guided practice and foster self-monitoring, the learning of self-regulatory skills, and the identification and discrimination of standards and criteria for high levels of performance; and (c) self-regulation, which is a later phase of competence in which much of the design of the learning environment is under the control of the learner as a developing expert (Glaser, 1996, p. 305).

It is advisable to seek to develop learners' capacity to make judgements about their own and others' work as soon as the teacher considers that the learners are capable of developing this skill. The making of judgements about performance itself involves developing judgment and self-regulation skills as well as improving performance, and, hence, will occur over a reasonably long period of time. While in the very early stages the novice learner may be unable to make fine distinctions, it is the duty of the teacher to guide the learner so that comparisons are made.

Getting the learner to focus upon clearly defined factors is essential as is the setting up of opportunities for the learners to compare their efforts and the superior efforts of the teacher. The teacher needs to point out directly and describe the differences when the learners cannot perceive them, then use similar, parallel examples or models as a basis for questions to determine that the learners have learned and are continuing to make the needed distinctions. Learners should be required to make judgements, describe what they see and use their own words to justify what judgements they have made and why.

Types of Knowledge in Developing Expertise

Understanding of the different types of knowledge involved in skill learning and the development of expertise has the potential to assist teachers and trainers to foster more effective skill development through greater care in task analysis, session planning and presentation.

Declarative and procedural knowledge
Anderson (1982) revived the distinction between declarative and procedural knowledge and made it central to his account of cognitive skill acquisition. Declarative knowledge is factual knowledge or content, whereas procedural knowledge is "how-to-do-it" or process knowledge. These two types of knowledge

have come to be widely cited in the learning literatures but there appear to be limits to their usefulness since the term procedural knowledge may obscure a range of distinctions that need to be made about different types of procedural knowledge. Anderson's theory, whence contemporary use of the terminology originated, has apparent weaknesses in detecting erroneous procedures in the cognitive skill acquisition process. Cognitive skills may not necessarily relate to effective performance of the skills in a problematic, real world context, and there appears to be a need to make a distinction between practical procedural knowledge and theoretical procedural knowledge (Cornford, 1993). Bandura (1997, pp. 25-6) too has noted this problem and argued that procedural knowledge and cognitive skills are necessary but not sufficient for effective performance.

Strategic decision making knowledge
Anderson's distinction between declarative and procedural knowledge has been extended in useful ways by Gott (1994), whose interests have centred on real world problem solving in avionics troubleshooting with state-of-the-art F1 5 aircraft. Gotts' (1994) analysis of the types of knowledge which need to be taught in skill learning expanded declarative knowledge, that is factual information about a particular domain or skill area, to system knowledge, strategic decision factors and strategic knowledge. System knowledge is essentially knowledge about how it works. For example with a computer it might involve knowledge about the need to turn the computer on and how to use a mouse to access commands or indicate where words are to be altered. Strategic decision factors might involve being able to identify and interpret error messages flashed on a computer screen, while strategic knowledge involves knowledge and understanding of what to do about that message and how to overcome the problem. Strategic knowledge in turn leads to procedural knowledge of the steps which must be undertaken to fix the problem. Together, strategic decision factors and strategic knowledge involve "how-to-decide-what-to-do-and-when", while procedural knowledge is essential for carrying out the actual performance.

"How-to-decide-what-to-do-when" skills appear to be the foundation skills in problem solving. These skills, which are important in professional functioning across all occupations, need to be introduced in early stages of skill learning at an appropriate level for the learner. Unless the ever present reality and need for problem solving in skill learning is established early in initial learning, it is likely to be somewhat delayed in development. Hence, it seems important that even novices are taught from the very commencement of training that effective problem solving is important in skilled performance. However, the limitations of novice and advanced beginners in particular must be fully recognised, especially their rigid adherence to rules and their lack of broader, contextually based knowledge. It is inappropriate for learners to be forced to attempt to solve difficult problems way beyond their capability and stage of development since this is likely to be a disincentive to learning. Use of the concept of scaffolding, central to the theories of Vygotsky (1978) and the learning of children, which involves a measured stretching of the learner beyond what he or she already knows by a teacher aware of the learner's ability and stage of development, may be appropriate.

"How-to-decide-what-to-do-when" skills amount to metacognition in skill learning and performance. Metacognition has been recognised as an important area for skill learning and the development of expertise (Colley & Beech, 1 989c;

Sternberg, 1998), but to date there has been no detailed analysis of what specific skills are required in specialist areas and how these may be taught other than through embedding them in the normal process of training for specific skills.

Previous sections in this chapter have outlined a range of different theories and factors which need to be taken into account in effective skill learning and the development of expertise. The following section outlines aspects of a model program which has proven successful in a challenging training area and demonstrates how numbers of the factors and issues covered so far may be brought together as part of a carefully planned, systematic training program for complex skill learning.

A Model Program Using Expert-Novice Comparisons

The Sherlock 2 program, reported by Gott (1994) as being particularly successful in training avionics trouble-shooters, contains a number of elements which have particular relevance for others attempting to develop effective training programs for solving problems and facilitating complex skill performance. Critical factors contributing to the success of the Sherlock 2 program are now outlined.

Cognitive task analysis

Traditionally skill learning has involved behavioural task analysis of the particular skill or task which a teacher or trainer intends to teach to a class. The development of cognitive task analysis procedures (Glaser, Lesgold, Lajoie et al., 1985), which involve analyses of experts' thinking in performing complex tasks and solving problems, has added a cognitive psychology perspective to more traditional behavioural approaches. What results from cognitive task analysis is identification of the thinking skills that need to be taught for a learner to think and solve problems like an expert. Cognitive task analysis led in turn to development of the PARI method (Gott, 1994), which involves pairs of experts confronting problems in their specialist domain. Through the process of problem posing and solution presentation it is possible to conduct task analyses based on a sequence of Precursor-Actions-Result-Interpretation. Results from analyses using the PARI method have formed subject content for programs for teaching avionics troubleshooting via computer-based learning with the intelligent tutoring systems Sherlock 1 and Sherlock 2 (Gott, 1994).

Intelligent tutoring systems

The Sherlock 1 and 2 intelligent tutoring systems have incorporated many of the salient features which have been revealed as important in learning by research into cognitive psychology and intelligent tutoring systems over the past fifteen years (see Polson & Richardson, 1988; Gott, 1994). An extensive review of these factors is beyond the scope of this chapter but a brief outline of the most important aspects of Sherlock 1 and 2 follow since the success is heavily dependent upon the adoption of processes which facilitate effective learning. Sherlock 1 and 2 enable the simulation of the equipment system and also of expert problem solver models with these expert models permitting the student to access feedback of an expert kind at various stages. Probably the most important type of feedback provided is that from the experts. This allows comparison by students of their own efforts with a schematic model of how an expert would have solved the problem.

Instructional features of Sherlock 1 and 2 also include a series of problem solving scenarios graded for difficulty, coaching to allow for supported learning, decision rules for moving students through the scenarios, and methods for conducting post-problem reflective follow-up such as interactions between the coach and student about solutions just generated. Also part of Sherlock 1 and 2 is a student model which records individual progress, including problems solved or not solved, and rules of troubleshooting violated in the student's problem solving efforts. The design of the systems and equipment allows students to manipulate the front panel controls on the equipment, access coaching and participate in the reflective follow-up.

Findings from Gott's research

Avionics troubleshooting involves complex problem solving of faults occurring in state of the art F1 5 aircraft. Usually, when a LRU (line replaceable unit or black box) is removed from an aircraft because of suspected malfunction, it is sent to the workshop for repair or checking. The challenges in problem solving are considerable because complex circuitry and microchips are involved and the problems cannot be seen. Typically expert trouble-shooters only emerge after 8-10 years of on-the-job training. Gott (1994) reported that the specialist programs involving expert-novice comparisons for avionics troubleshooting delivered through Sherlock 1 and 2 have resulted in considerable savings in time and high levels of knowledge. Statistically significant test results indicated that trainees' troubleshooting skills and knowledge, which were also tested for transfer and generalisation, were superior to results from the control groups which experienced traditional training, and approached the high levels of experts in about 5.5 years compared with the usual 8-10.

Of course not every school college or university will have such sophisticated programs and equipment to enable the development of and use of intelligent tutoring systems. However, the processes and procedures employed, with expert-novice comparisons, cognitive task analysis, learning by doing, extensive feedback involving comparison of experts and novices, and relating learning to real work settings, are elements which can and should be incorporated into many skill learning programs.

Concluding Remarks

Skill learning is one of the most important kinds of learning and forms the basis for most of the personal or economic productive activities which are engaged in by human beings. Despite its importance, there appears to be little understanding in the education community or the world of business and industry of what is involved in skill learning and the development of expertise. Or, if there is such awareness, there is very little in the ways of supporting structures and systematic programs to continue to develop skills over long periods of time to indicate commitment to practical application. It is something of an irony that sporting organisations appear to be much more aware of the challenges involved in effective training for skilled performance than those sectors of the society directly responsible for the education and development of individuals for life and productive work. Part of the problem would appear to reside in the lack of understanding by governments and policy makers, whose policy frameworks are necessary for systems to operate effectively and who provide much of the funding.

Effective skill learning, upon which expertness is dependent, requires effective teaching, adequate resources, and a great willingness on the part of learners to persist with practice in order to acquire the attributes which characterise experts. Programs to foster effective, longer term skill development need to be of a considerable duration, adequately resourced, and staffed by well-trained teachers knowledgeable about skill learning and processes in the development of expertise. While the elements and factors conducive to effective longer term skill development are complex, they are not unduly so, and programs like the model described by Gott (1994) illustrate what can be achieved when there is motivation to ensure that existing knowledge is properly applied. If Australia is to become a truly "clever country" there is a need to replace rhetoric with action, money, commitment and knowledge in order that this goal can be achieved.

REFERENCES

Adams, J. A. (1987). Historical review and appraisal of research on the learning, retention, and transfer of human motor skills. *Psychological Bulletin, 101,* 41-74.

Ainley, P. (1993). *Class and skill: Changing divisions of knowledge and labour.* London: Cassell.

Anderson, J. R. (1982). Acquisition of cognitive skill. *Psychological Review, 89,* 369-406.

Anderson, J. R., Reder, L. M., & Simon, H. A. (1996). Situated learning and education. *Educational Researcher, 25(4),* 5-11.

Anderson, J. R., Reder, L., & Simon, H. (1997). Rejoinder: Situative versus cognitive perspectives: Form versus substance. *Educational Researcher, 26* (1), 18-21.

Annett, J. (1991). Skill acquisition. In J. E. Morrison (Ed.), *Training for performance. Principles of applied human learning.* Chichester, UK: John Wiley & Sons Ltd.

Australian Mission on Management Skills (1991). Report (Vol. 1). Canberra: AGPS.

Bandura, A. (1977). *Social learning theory.* Englewood Cliffs, NJ: Prentice Hall.

Bandura, A. (1997). *Self-efficacy: The exercise of control.* NY: W. H. Freeman & Co.

Bassi, L. J., & Van Buren, M. E. (1998). The 1998 ASTD (American Society for Training and Development) state of the industry report. *Training and Development,* January, 21-43.

Benner, P. (1984). *From novice to expert: Excellence and power in clinical nursing practice.* Reading, MA : Addison-Wesley.

Berliner, D. (1988, February). *The development of expertise in pedagogy.* Charles W. Hunt Memorial Lecture for the American Association of Colleges for Teacher Education, New Orleans, LA.

Billett, S. (1994). Review of S. Chaiklin & J. Lave (Eds), Understanding practice. *Australian and New Zealand Journal of Vocational Education Research, 2,* 142-147.

Bloom, B. S. (1986). Automasticity: The hands and feet of genius. *Educational Leadership,* February, 70-77.

Brown, J. S., Collins, A., & Duguid, P. (1989). Situated cognition and the culture of learning. *Educational Researcher, 18(1),* 34-41.

Colley, A. (1989). Learning motor skills: Integrating cognition and action. In A. Colley & J. Beech (Eds.), *Acquisition and performance of cognitive skills.* Chichester, UK: John Wiley & Sons.

Colley, A., & Beech, J. (Eds.), (1989a). *Acquisition and performance of cognitive skills.* Chichester, UK: John Wiley & Sons.

Colley, A., & Beech, J. (1989b). Acquiring and performing cognitive skills. In A. Colley & J. Beech (Eds.), *Acquisition and performance of cognitive skills.* Chichester, UK: John Wiley & Sons.

Colley, A., & Beech, J. (1989c). Epilogue. In A. Colley & J. Beech (Eds.), *Acquisition and performance of cognitive skills.* Chichester, UK: John Wiley & Sons.

Cornford, I. R. (1993). Theories of skill development and research into the development of expertise: some implications for competency-based training. *Conference Papers, After Competence: The Future of Post- Compulsory Education and Training Conference, December 1-3, Brisbane, Vol. 1.* Brisbane, Australia: Centre for Skill Formation, Research and Development, Griffith University.

Cornford, I. (1996). The defining attributes of "skill" and "skilled performance": Some implications for training, learning and program development. *Australian and New Zealand Journal of Vocational Education Research, 4(*2), 1-25.

Cornford, I. R. (1997). Competency-based training: An assessment of its strengths and weaknesses by New South Wales vocational teachers. *Australian and New Zealand Journal of Vocational Education Research, 5(1),* 53-76.

Cornford, I. R. (1999). Social learning. In J. Athanasou (Ed.), *Adult educational psychology.* Wentworth Falls: Social Science Press.

Cornford, I. R., & Athanasou, J. A. (1995). Developing expertise through training. *Industrial and Commercial Training, 27(2),* 10-18.

Cornford, I., Athanasou, J., & Pithers, R. (1996). Career counsellors and the promotion of lifelong learning. *Australian Journal of Career Development, 5(2),* 43-46.

Dempster, F. N. (1988). Informing classroom practice: What we know about several task characteristics and their effect on learning. *Contemporary Educational Psychology, 13,* 254-264.

Dreyfus, H. L., & Dreyfus, S. E. (1986). *Mind over machine.* NY: Free Press.

Ericsson, K. A., & Charness, N. (1994). Expert performance. *American Psychologist, 49,* 725-747.

Ericsson, K. A., & Smith, J. (1991). Prospects and limits of the empirical study of expertise: An introduction. In K. A. Ericsson & J. Smith (Eds.), *Toward a general theory of expertise.* Cambridge: Cambridge University Press.

Fitts, P. M. (1962). Factors in complex skill training. In R. Glaser (Ed.), *Training, research and education.* Pittsburgh: University of Pittsburgh Press.

Fitts, P. M. (1964). Perceptual skill learning. In A. W. Melton (Ed.), *Categories of skill learning.* NY: Academic Press.

Fitts, P. M. (1968). Factors in complex training. In G. Kuhlen (Ed.), *Studies in educational psychology.* Waltham, MA: Blaisdell Publishing Company.

Gage, N., & Berliner, D. (1992). *Educational psychology* (5th ed.). Boston: Houghton Mifflin.

Glaser, R. (1996). Changing the agency for learning: Acquiring expert performance. In K. A. Ericsson (Ed.), *The road to excellence: The acquisition of expert performance in the arts and sciences, sports and games.* Mahwah, NJ: Lawrence Erlbaum Associates.

Glaser, R., & Chi, M. T. H. (1988). Overview. In M. Chi, R. Glaser & M. Farr (Eds.), *The nature of expertise,* pp. xv-xxix. Hillsdale, NJ: Lawrence Erlbaum.

Glaser, R., Lesgold, A., Lajoie, S., Eastman, R., Greenberg, L., Logan, D., Magone, M., Weiner, A., Wolf, R., & Yengo, L. (1985). *Cognitive task analysis to enhance technical skills training and assessment.* (Contract No. F41689-83-C-0029). Brooks AFB, TX: Armstrong Laboratory, Human Resources Directorate.

Gott, S. (1994). Rediscovering learning: Acquiring expertise in real world problem solving tasks. Keynote paper presented at (re)Forming Post-compulsory Education and Training: Reconciliation and Reconstruction Conference, Brisbane, 7-9 December. Published by Centre for Skill Formation Research and Development, Griffith University.

Hartley, L., Morrison, D., & Arnold, P. (1989). Stress and skill. In A. Colley & J. Beech (Eds.), *Acquisition and performance of cognitive skills.* Chichester, UK: John Wiley & Sons.

Johnson, E. J. (1988). Expertise and decision under uncertainty: Performance and process. In M. Chi, R. Glaser, & M. Farr (Eds.), *The nature of expertise,* pp. 209-228. Hillsdale, NJ: Lawrence Erlbaum.

Karpin, D. S. (Chair) (1995). *Enterprising nation: Report of the Industry Task Force on Leadership and Management Skills.* Canberra: AGPS.

Kottke, F. J., Halpern, D., Easton, J. K. M., Ozel, A. T., & Burrill, C. A. (1978). Training of coordination. *Archives of Physical Medicine Rehabilitation, 59,* 567-572.

Kreuger, W. C. F. (1929). The effects of overlearning on retention. *Journal of Experimental Psychology, 12,* 71-78.

Lave, J. (1988).*Cognition in practice: Mind, mathematics and culture in everyday life.* Cambridge: Cambridge University Press.

Lave, J., & Wenger, E. (1991). *Situated learning: Legitimate peripheral participation.* Cambridge: Cambridge University Press.

Learmonth,A. (1993). *Creating a learning environment in the workplace.* Adelaide: National Centre for Vocational Education Research.

Leinhardt, G. (1986). Expertise in mathematics teaching. *Educational Leadership, 43*(7), 28-33.

Leinhardt, G., & Greeno, J. (1986). The cognitive skill of teaching. *Journal of Educational Psychology, 78*, 75-95.

Mayer Committee (1992). *Putting general education to work. The key competencies report.* Australian Education Council and Ministers for Vocational Education, Employment and Training.

Morrison, J. E. (Ed.) (1991). *Training for performance. Principles of applied human learning.* Chichester, UK: John Wiley & Sons Ltd.

Newell, A., & Rosenbloom, P. S. (1981). Mechanisms of skill acquisition and the law of practice. In J. R. Anderson (Ed.), *Cognitive skills and their acquisition.* Hillsdale, NJ: Lawrence Erlbaum.

Ohlsson, S. (1996). Learning from performance errors. *Psychological Review, 103*, 241-262.

Pintrich, P. P. (1990). The implications of psychological research on student learning and college teaching for teacher education. In W. R. Houston (Ed.), *Handbook of research on teacher education.* NY: Macmillan.

Polson, M. C., & Richardson, J. J. (1988). *Foundations of intelligent tutoring systems.* Hillsdale, NJ: Lawrence Erlbaum.

Rumelhardt, D. E., & Norman, D. A. (1978). Accretion, tuning and restructuring: Three modes of learning. In J. Cotton & R. Klatzky (Eds.), *Semantic factors in cognition* (pp. 37-53). Hillsdale, NJ: Lawrence Erlbaum Associates.

Sabers, D. S., Cushing, K. S., & Berliner, D. C. (1991). Differences among teachers in a task characterized by simultaneity, multidimensionality and immediacy. *American Education Research Journal, 28*, 63-88.

Salthouse, T. (1989). Ageing and skilled performance. In A. Colley & J. Beech (Eds.), *Acquisition and performance of cognitive skills.* Chichester, UK: John Wiley & Sons.

Schmidt, R. A. (1975). A schema theory of discrete motor skill learning. *Psychological Review, 82*, 225-260.

Shiffrin, R. M. (1996). Laboratory experimentation on the genesis of expertise. In K. A. Ericsson (Ed.), *The road to excellence: The acquisition of expert performance in the arts and sciences, sports and games.* Mahwah, NJ: Lawrence Erlbaum Associates.

Shuell, T. J. (1990). Phases of meaningful learning. *Review of Educational Research, 60*, 531-547.

Sincoff, J. B., & Sternberg, R. J. (1989). The development of cognitive skills: An examination of recent theories. In A. Colley & J. Beech (Eds), *Acquisition and performance of cognitive skills* (pp. 19-60). Chichester, UK: John Wiley & Sons Ltd.

Smith, A. (1989). Diurnal variations in performance. In A. Colley & J. Beech (Eds.), *Acquisition and performance of cognitive skills.* Chichester, UK: John Wiley & Sons.

Spitzer, H. F. (1939). Studies in retention. *Journal of Educational Psychology, 30*, 641-656.

Stasz, C. (1996) Workplace skills in practice: Understanding the new basic skills. Keynote address at the 4th Annual International Conference on Post-Compulsory Education and Training, Learning & Work: The Challenges, Surfers Paradise 2-4 December, published by Centre for Learning and Work Research, Griffith University.

Sternberg, R. J. (1998). Metacognition, abilities, and developing expertise: What makes an expert student? *Instructional Science, 26*, 127-140.

Stevenson, J. (1994). Vocational expertise. In J. Stevenson (Ed.), *Cognition at work: The development of vocational expertise.* Adelaide: National Centre For Vocational Education Research.

Stevenson, J. (1998). Forging a convergence amongst imperatives for vocational education and training. Keynote paper presented at the Inaugural Australian Vocational Education and Training Association (AVETRA) Conference, Sydney, 16-17 February.

Swanson, H. L., O'Connor, J. E., & Cooney, J. B. (1990). An information processing analysis of expert and novice teachers' problem solving. *American Educational Research Journal, 27*, 533-556.

Sweller, J. (1993). Some cognitive processes and their consequences for the organisation and presentation of information. *Australian Journal of Psychology, 45*, 1-8.

Swinnen, S., Schmidt, R., Nicholson, D., & Shapiro, D. (1990). Information feedback for skill acquisition: Instantaneous knowledge of results degrades learning. *Journal of Experimental Psychology: Learning, Memory and Cognition, 16*, 706-716.

Thurow, L. (1992). The key is in the skills. In *World competitiveness report 1992*, pp. 274-275. Geneva: World Economic Forum.

VanLehn, K. (1996). Cognitive skill acquisition. *Annual Review of Psychology, 47*, 513-39.

Voss, J. F., & Post, T. A. (1988). On the solving of ill-structured problems. In M. Chi, R. Glaser & M. Farr (Eds.), *The nature of expertise* (pp. 261- 285). Hillsdale, NJ: Lawrence Erlbaum.

Vygotsky, L. S. (1978). *Mind in society: The development of higher psychological processes.* Cambridge, MA: Harvard University Press.

Westerman, D. A. (1991). Expert and novice decision making. *Journal of Teacher Education, 42,* 292-305.

Winstein, C. J., & Schmidt, R. (1990). Reduced frequency of knowledge of results enhances motor skill learning. *Journal of Experimental Psychology: Learning, Memory and Cognition, 16,* 677-691.

Zimmerman, B. J., & Kitsantas, A. (1996). Self-regulated learning of a motoric skill: The role of goal setting and self-monitoring. *Journal of Applied Sport Psychology, 8,* 69-84.

Zimmerman, B. J., & Kitsantas, A. (1997). Developmental phases in self- regulation: Shifting from process to outcome goals. *Journal of Educational Psychology, 89,* 29-36.

Review Questions

The following questions are designed to test your understanding of the content of this chapter. Answers can all be checked by referring to relevant sections.

1. Why is holding firmly to the distinction between performance and cognitive skills logically flawed?
2. Describe what occurs in the cognitive phase of Fitts' theory of skill learning.
3. Describe what happens in the practice fixation phase in Fitts' theory.
4. What does autonomous mean? What occurs at this phase in Fitts' theory?
5. Why is the autonomous phase so important for real world functioning?
6. Did Fitts consider that the three stages in his theory are quite distinctly separate or discrete?
7. What does "expert" mean in common language usage? How would serious researchers attempt to identify experts?
8. Much of our knowledge of experts has been obtained through comparisons with what other group?
9. What do you understand by "quantitative" and "qualitative"? Are there both quantitative and qualitative differences between stages in the development of expertise?
10. In what ability area do experts and the proficient most clearly differ from novices, advanced beginners and the competent?
11. Describe the relationship between skill learning and the stages in the development of expertise.
12. What will happen in terms of skill learning theory when experts have to learn new skills?
13. Briefly outline the reasons why students should be taught about the phases and stages in skill learning and the development of expertise.
14. What is the difference between massed and spaced practice?
15. What do Ericsson and Charness (1994) mean by "deliberate practice"?
16. Why is delayed feedback possibly useful or effective?
17. Why is it best to practise while alert?
18. What is a learning plateau?
19. Describe each of the three stages identified by Glaser (1996) in the change of agency leading to self-regulation.
20. What do strategic decision factors and strategic knowledge in combination lead to?

Exercises

1. Carefully examine a syllabus or other document which is meant to serve as a basis for guiding the teaching of a particular set of skills in an occupational specialisation, in relation to the stages in the development of expertise. Critically evaluate how much you can realistically attain in the time frame set for this training.
2. Using your knowledge of your specialty area and the amount of time likely to be taken for someone to become proficient in it, develop a plan for further development beyond initial training. You might like to consider what additional short-duration, off-the-job training and in-service or on-the-job training ideally should be provided to assist learners reach the level of proficiency, assuming that they have the prerequisite potential and ability to achieve this level.
3. Map out a practice plan involving a typical skill that you would teach. Indicate the number of practice sessions which you would like to use, the purpose that these sessions would serve in terms of Fitt's skill learning phases, and also indicate where you would use massed and spaced practice along with the reasons why you would use these forms of practice.

About the Author

Ian Cornford holds a PhD in Educational Psychology and is a Senior Lecturer in the Faculty of Education as well as a Research Associate of the Research Centre for Vocational Education and Training (RCVET) at the University of Technology, Sydney. He has had a long association with vocational teacher education. His research interests are centred upon the psychology of learning and include effective learning, teaching and training in classrooms and workplaces, transfer of learning and issues in school-to-work transition. Recently he has been involved in research into the effectiveness of competency-based training while currently he is analysing issues in lifelong learning and examining the implications of lifelong learning for policy making and educational practice.

Ian R. Cornford
University of Technology, Sydney

KEVIN F. COLLIS

12. ADULT COGNITION: DEVELOPMENT AND CHARACTERISTICS

Any discussion of the topic of adult cognition suggests an initial consideration of at least two factors; the traditions and recent developments which have given rise to cognition as we know it today and the significance of limiting our discussion to the intellectual functioning of the grown ups in our society. It is relatively straightforward to deal with the first factor by looking briefly at the development of epistemology over the long term and then considering some of the highlights of the exponential growth in our understanding in the area during the last fifty years. The second factor is more problematic. The old saying that "the child is father of the man" appears as true in this area as in any other where there is continuous development throughout the life-span. The base modes of intellectual functioning are formed during childhood and adolescence and, because the modes are in their earlier stages of development, they are less complex and involve less static than is the case with the adult. If adult students can gain a clear understanding of the nature of the human cognitive development which has taken place up to the teenage years, it puts them in a good position to see themselves against this time-line and to evaluate their current cognitive level against the elements which have gone to making it up. This approach caters for the known preference of adults to be more interested in the process than in the (declarative) outcome of a learning sequence and also gives them an insight into the cognitive characteristics of their peers. We will begin with a short historical introduction to epistemology, follow up with a fairly detailed consideration of cognition as seen at the earlier stages in the life-span and conclude by drawing attention to some specific aspects of particular relevance to adult learning and teaching.

At least since the time of the philosophers of classical Greece, people in the western tradition of scholarship have been fascinated by epistemology, the question

James A Athanasou (ed.), Adult Educational Psychology, 289–318

of "how we know". In more recent times, one aspect of this age-old quest has become the study of human cognition, a branch of psychology which is concerned with the scientific study of "how we know and learn about the world in which we live". Thus we begin this chapter with a brief look at some of the traditional positions taken on this question of "knowing" during the modern era in order to get a feel for where the approach taken in this chapter fits into the overall scheme of things.

Three distinct epistemological traditions may be identified in western thought during the last three hundred years: *empiricism* as articulated by the British philosophers Locke, Berkeley and Hume in 17th century; *rationalism* as proposed by European philosophers such as Descartes, Leibneitz, Spinoza and Kant at least partly in reaction to the British empiricists; and the *sociohistoric* epistemology of Hegel, Marx, and the modern continental philosophers (Kaufmann, 1980).

According to the empiricist position, knowledge of the world is acquired by a process in which the sensory organs first detect stimuli in the external world, and the mind then detects the customary patterns or "conjunctions" in these stimuli and responds to them. Behaviourist psychology, with its emphases on conditioning of one kind or another supplying the principles for the main learning processes, has its roots in this line of thought. Educational psychologists who have adopted this perspective have tended to see instruction as a didactic process in which the concepts, symbols, and problem solving strategies that need to be acquired are analysed carefully, arranged in logical sequence, and taught in a fashion that involves clear exposition followed by carefully graded practice.

The second epistemological tradition, rationalism, which, along with the sociohistoric view, has tended to dominate the educational reform agenda in the last part of the present century, hypothesises that knowledge is acquired by a process in which the human mind imposes order on the empirical data obtained by the senses, not merely detects patterns pre-existing in these data. Psychologists in this tradition (e.g., Baldwin, 1967; Piaget, 1964) tended to see knowledge as originating in the constructive activity of the child, rather than the exposition or drill provided by teachers and texts. Educational psychologists in this mould see the way to improve educational achievement in the schools as dependent on matters such as, the development of curriculum materials appropriate to the student's existing conceptual levels; the provision of more opportunities for children to discover concepts on their own; to place less emphasis on outcomes and more on the processes by which answers may be generated; and the encouragement of cooperative work.

The third epistemological tradition, the sociohistoric view, proposes that conceptual knowledge has its primary origin in the social and material history of the culture of which the subject is a part, and the tools, concepts, and symbol systems that underpin its daily practices. Psychologists who have held this view (Bruner, 1964) have tended to see education as a process of cultural initiation. Educators who hold this view seem to accept the ideas proposed by the rationalist tradition (constructivists) but tend to go considerably beyond them and to focus on the question of how to create a community of learners who are engaged in the same sort of knowledge building activity as goes on at the leading edge of a discipline.

It seems to the writer that cognitive science has its origins primarily in the first tradition but that much of the effort over the past 40 years has been aimed at integrating the insights of the second (constructivist) tradition with those of the first. Much of the educational progress over that period has reflected this psychological orientation. It is proposed to take account of this development here by describing the point reached in the 1 990s by an outstanding example of the constructivist tradition - an example in which, as the theory grew in the developing field, it was honed at each step by the discipline imposed by its use in professional practice. Let us follow the development of perhaps the most highly rated constructivist theory of cognitive development to be put forward this century; the Piagetian model.

The Development of the Piagetian Model

The 1950s marked the appearance of the basic Piagetian work in English translation and the subsequent intense interest in its usefulness for the classroom and curriculum development which continued well into the 1 960s. In its earliest years, this work concentrated on translating and transforming Piaget's original formulations into terms which could be applied in school contexts. Some of the red-brick universities in the U.K. were at the forefront of this work, with such well-known researchers as Peel (1960) and Lunzer (1965) and their students being major contributors.

Although this work generally accepted the Piagetian formulations, some modifications of the basic Piagetian constructs were necessary to come to terms with the data. In addition, once this new work began to take a form where it was to be used as a basis for classroom or curriculum practice, researchers were compelled to go beyond mere description towards some explication of the phenomena in the new context. An example can be seen in a modification made to some of the criteria for, and nomenclature of, Piaget's stages (Collis, 1975) to handle the data which came out of a series of detailed studies in the learning of school mathematics. In the detailed work on conceptual understanding which was necessary for classroom purposes, it was found that some of the expectations being placed on the children's conceptual understandings were too high. Moreover, there were more powerful explanatory mechanisms for the observed ability of children to handle more abstract elements and more complex operations as they progressed through the mathematics curriculum than had been proposed by the original theory, the concept of Acceptance of Lack of Closure (Collis, 1974) proved to be one of these. These interpretive and descriptive studies, which tried to relate Piagetian constructs to a practical context, were at the cutting edge of research in those days and obviously helped to prepare the ground for the explanatory phase which followed.

The 1970s and 1980s were marked by the development of theoretical standpoints which sought to explain the phenomena of Piaget's stages. Much of this work adopted information processing concepts (Case, 1972; Halford, 1980; Pascual-Leone, 1970) which served the explanatory aim well and assisted in making application of the theory in practice a more rational undertaking. These, and accompanying developments, marked a neo-Piagetian era and led to a questioning of some of Piaget's major tenets, such as the existence of stages and the validity of stopping his developmental sequence at formal operations and the exceptionality of the decalage phenomenon. This last was a concept which Piaget used to explain the situation which occurs when an individual can perform one task at a particular stage of development but cannot perform another task of similar structure until some time later. Biggs and Collis (1982) found that, rather than being the exception in a school context, decalage was the rule. Following this line of thought through gave rise to a taxonomy based on the structural features of a person's response. Called the SOLO Taxonomy (Biggs & Collis, 1982), it provided a way of classifying an individual's responses so that practitioners could have a rational base for evaluating one of the most important outcomes of school learning, the *Structure of the Observed Learning Outcome.*

An important feature of this period, along with the earlier one, was that it focused on the development of cognition. Each stage was seen as a prerequisite for the next higher stage and, in fact, a casual reader could be forgiven for believing that the only purpose for one stage of development was a step along the developmental continuum towards the next stage. This was reflected in the academic side of much of the school curriculum where the aim was clearly to lead students from the idiosyncracies of pre-operational thinking so characteristic of their K2 years, through the unexciting, but very basic, logic of the concrete operational thinking commonly associated with the thought of primary and early secondary school children, and on to the final goal of formal thinking during adolescence and early adulthood.

As the 1980s drew to a close, there appeared the realisation that intelligent functioning has many faces. Sternberg (1985; 1988) and Gardner (1985) are two well known writers on the subject who put forward what appeared at the time to be quite revolutionary ideas. Sternberg proposed a triarchic model of intelligence which sought to integrate three elements of intelligence by relating intellectual functioning to an individual's internal mental components, experiential activity and external contextual components. Gardner put forward a theory of multiple intelligences and has spent much time in examining the educational significance of his ideas. An example of how this change in thinking has been reflected in work that had been broadly identified with the neo-Piagetian position can be seen by considering one important aspect of a paper by Biggs and Collis (1991). In this paper, stages of development become modes of functioning. The notions, that each mode is preparatory for the next higher mode, and that the development of each particular mode was characteristically the cognitive development task of a particular age group, are still there. However, Biggs and Collis pointed out that once in place in its earliest form, each mode continued to develop throughout life and continued to be utilised alongside and together with both the developing and previously developed modes, these were significant insights which have added much to our understanding of human cognition.

This change in orientation is reflected in the thinking on school curriculum during the 1990s. For example, recent writings on curriculum and evaluation in areas such as literacy, numeracy and studies of society (civics) emphasise the importance of fostering intuitive thinking, cooperative learning, and positive attitudes - all of which are characteristics of the ikonic (pre-operational) mode. It could be argued that these elements were always implicit in these areas, alongside the mastery of the skills and substantive content of the underlying disciplines but the difference is that they are now no longer on the fringe. They form part of the core expectations and are expected to be incorporated in any evaluation scheme alongside the traditional items concerned with concrete symbolic and formal manipulation. Incorporation is also the operative word in instruction. Classroom and individual methods for developing a skill based in a particular mode are expected to utilise, consciously and explicitly, modes already included in the individual's repertoire. Piagetian theory not only legitimises this shift in emphasis but appears to provide a basis upon which to build a rational programme for its implementation and evaluation.

This sketch of the three main waves of change in the way in which cognitive developmentalists in the Piagetian tradition have viewed the concepts involved has had its most obvious impact in the instructional materials and procedures utilised in the learning and teaching of the child and adolescent in the pre-school and school (K-12) context. However, the implications of what we have learned over these years have not only broadened our understanding of school based learning but have fundamentally changed the way in which psychologists think about intelligent behaviour throughout the lifespan - from the cradle to the grave as it were! This latter is extremely important for our purposes in this chapter where the orientation is towards adult functioning. Let us examine the modes of intellectual functioning as the theories have been developed over the past decade or so. There are three aspects to be taken up here: a general picture of the mechanism under discussion; a consideration of the nature of each mode of functioning when it first appears in the course of an individual's development and a close look at the implications for adult intelligent behaviour. In this last aspect we are concerned not only with the continued development of the individual modes themselves but also with the power and flexibility given to mature intelligence by the ability to utilise intermodal functioning.

The Cognitive Mechanism Available

During the 80s and early 90s several psychologists (Biggs & Collis,1982; Biggs & Collis, 1991; Case, 1985, 1991; Collis & Biggs 1991; Fischer,1980; Fischer & Pipp,1984; Fischer & Sylvern,1985; Halford, 1982, 1993) had put forward developmental models in respect of cognition which had features which marked them as neo-Piagetian in origin and hence basically compatible with one another. They all regarded cognitive development as a series of hierarchical skill structures which could be grouped into sets of levels or stages incorporating skills of gradually increasing complexity, a skill at a higher level developing directly from specific skills at the preceding level. The processes of development within each level or stage were parallel from stage to stage and involved the capacity to cope with increasingly abstract concepts. These insights formed a sound basis for identifying key elements in an individual's understanding and competence during both the school and the adult years. As the nineties progressed, however, and the full impact of the implications of the work of the previous decade became clear, certain additional points emerged which were highly significant for educational thinking. Three of these are of special interest here. First, the concept of cognitive development as a hierarchy of stages in logical development was softened and, as a result, the importance of the hierarchy in logical thinking as a developmental imperative began to lose its force in educational and psychological thinking. Second, and concomitant with this change, the concept of cognition was broadened to embrace intelligent functioning in all its modes: sensorimotor, ikonic, concrete symbolic, abstract formal and beyond. It was no longer restricted to the intellectual logical mode which reached fruition in abstract formal thinking. Third and last, once each mode of thinking appeared it was regarded as continuing to develop throughout life, alongside both earlier and later developing modes. This last notion added considerable power and flexibility to the concept of cognition as it not only added status to even the earliest developing mode, sensorimotor, but made available the notion of multimodal functioning in cognition which gave access to a whole range of ideas on intellectual functioning throughout the life span. As the Biggs and Collis (1982, 1991); Collis and Biggs (1991) and Collis (1994) formulations are more thoroughly worked out for describing and analysing the conceptualizations alluded to above, especially in practical learning contexts, it is these proposals which are used as the basis for what is described in some detail below.

The Development and Structure of Learning: The Modes

A post-Piagetian theoretical stance and a detailed analysis of responses to questions, of observations recorded in a range of research data and of the development of skills in various contexts, all suggest that there are two phenomena involved in determining the mode of intelligent functioning represented by an individual's response to an environmental cue. The first is the level of abstraction of the elements utilised, and the second is the nature of the operations upon these elements. In the theoretical stance taken by Biggs and Collis (1991) these two fundamental variables together form the basis for distinguishing between the modes. The first four modes are well established in the post-Piagetian literature with a fifth hypothesised by several researchers. The bare essentials of these modes are stated first so that the reader can get a feel for the phenomena:
- *Sensorimotor.* The elements are the objects in the immediate physical environment and the operations involve the management and coordination of motor responses in respect of these objects;
- *Ikonic.* The elements become signifiers (words, images, etc.) which stand for objects and events and the operational side involves the manipulation of these such as is required in making perceptually based qualitative judgments or in oral communication;
- *Concrete Symbolic.* The elements develop from mere signifiers to concepts which are manipulated using a logic of classes and equivalences; both elements and manipulations being directly tied to the empirical world; *Formal.* The elements are abstract concepts and propositions and the operations on them are concerned with determining the actual and deduced relationships between them; neither the elements nor the operations need a real world referent; and
- *Post formal.* The elements are abstract systems of concepts and propositions which are operated upon by a highly flexible strategy of choosing and/or amalgamating the operational techniques used in the first four modes.

While keeping the above outlines of the modes in mind let us proceed to examine each mode in some detail, mode by mode:

Sensori-motor (available from birth)

This is the most elemental of all the modes. It is available from birth and represents the most fundamental way of knowing the world, based, as it is on the physical management and coordination of elements in the immediately available physical environment. The infant's interaction with its environment is perhaps at its most concrete in the early days after birth when its motor responses are directly related

to sensory stimuli. During the first 12 - 18 months of life the child learns, retains and hones quite complex sensori-motor skills. These have been well documented in the Piagetian literature and will not be discussed here. There are three major points to note concerning the development of these skills at this juncture:
- they form the base for movement to the next mode, ikonic, which marks a distinct advance in the individual's way of coping with the environment;
- they lay the foundation for the advanced sensorimotor skills which are learnt in later childhood and adulthood; and
- these sensori-motor skills are now available to contribute to inter-modal functioning as the individual moves through the later developing modes.

The sensori-motor skills of walking, and grasping form the basis for running and catching games of later childhood and early adulthood. The skills learnt at this stage form a sound basis for children's exploration of shapes so necessary in the early stages of geometrical and spatial understandings which become of some significance in the concrete symbolic mode. The form of knowledge in this mode is well described as tacit knowledge because it consists in knowing how to carry out an act without necessarily being able to describe or explain it. At the mature level, it is exemplified in sporting and other basically kinaesthetic activities, such as dance and gymnastics where the exponent knows by the feel during the course of the execution of an act when and how to make any necessary adjustment to the performance. Golfers can carry out a skilled act, without being able to describe it in detail, and know that they have performed it well because it feels right. In fact, introducing modifications to the act by applying the results of information from another mode of functioning may lead, at least initially, to a lower level of performance.

In the early stages of learning the basic skills involved in sailing a boat, flying a light plane and so on, experienced instructors, teaching these skills to novice adults, do their best to ensure that the beginner performs by the practical feel for the activity before allowing or encouraging the use of the later developing modes which are at least one step removed from the direct perception - reaction bond characteristic of this basic mode. In fact, one indication of the move towards the ikonic mode occurs when the child turns the sensorimotor understanding that an object exists regardless of his/her currently experiencing it to an ikonic imaging of it. The latter development being reflected in his/her use of a single word sentence, such as "ball!", as a signifier for the concrete object which may or may not be present at the time. This beginning development in the language area signals the culmination of a number of sensorimotor skill coordinations which enable control over the voicing of recognisable native language units; as well, it marks the beginning of a memory, attached to an imaging ability. These last two developments contribute enormously to the intellectual power required for a successful sortie into the ikonic mode which is the next mode to appear in the developmental sequence.

Ikonic (available from about 18 months)
In this mode the elements become signifiers (words, images, etc.) which stand for objects and events; the operations involve the manipulation of these signifiers to facilitate cognition in three main ways:

- to establish oral communication in the individual's native language - the basic structures being fully in place by the time the child is seven or eight years old for normal individuals;
- to make links between affect and image [cf. 'mythic' stage (Egan, 1984)]. The love of myths and fairy stories in early childhood and the popularity of romantic novels on the one hand and "horror" stories on the other in later life are both illustrations of the strength and validity of this link; and
- to make perceptually based qualitative judgments. This characteristic is a major factor in the many amusing idiosyncrasies described as typical of the reasoning of the pre-school child in the Piagetian literature of thirty years ago (e.g., Ginsburg & Opper, 1978; Phillips, 1969) as well as in forming the basis for much of the intuitive reasoning typical of everyday life in adulthood.

The ikonic mode is the first to enable the "internalization of action" which Piaget (1950) defined as the beginning of thought proper and which Bruner (1964) saw as the stage during which the individual formed internal pictures, images or ikons, to facilitate thinking. The idiosyncrasies of this particular level of functioning in the preschool, preoperational child, mentioned above, is well documented in the Piagetian literature and will not be repeated here. It should be indicated at this juncture that satisfactory development in this mode facilitates movement into the concrete symbolism typical of much important school-based content such as that required in the literacy and numeracy programs. There are three major ways in which this mode contributes to future intelligent functioning by the individual:

- the development of oral communication reaches adult level in terms of its structure and is thus ready to be utilized for the kinds of concrete propositional reasoning so important for developing the literacy skills associated with written communication;
- the high level of imaginative thought, often affect laden, achieved, lays a sound basis for much of the future development in all cognitive areas, both logical and alogical; and
- the tendency to make perceptually-based qualitative judgments, linked with the capacity for imaging and the continuing interest in sensori-motor activities for their own sake, makes a good foundation for the cognitive demands of the concrete symbolic skills especially in their early stages.

At the adult level ikonic thought is evident in aesthetic appreciation in the arts and literature, in fact in all performances, or parts thereof, where affective or value-laden aspects are regarded as important. It is also well documented for its use by mathematicians (Hadamard, 1954) and scientists (Kekule's discovery of the organic ring compounds, preceded by his vision of six snakes chasing each others' tails, for example). The typical description given by mathematicians and scientists of their use of the ikonic mode is that the solution to the problem is imaged in this mode and then later established to the satisfaction of their colleagues in the scientific community by evidence and argument in the concrete symbolic and the formal modes. The ikonic mode is thus not merely pre-symbolic and restricted to early childhood, but continues to grow in power and complexity well beyond childhood. Moreover, it interacts with other modes particularly in the process of problem solving at higher levels. Ikonic thinking leads to a form of knowledge commonly known as intuitive which is highly valued by creative thinkers in both the sciences and the arts.

Concrete-symbolic (available from about 6 years)
In this mode the elements develop from being simply signifiers to concepts and the operations on them become manipulations using a logic of classes and differences, equivalence and substitution (Peel, 1960); both elements and manipulations being directly tied to the empirical world. This mode represents a significant shift in the level of abstraction involved in thinking as the concrete world can now be interpreted through symbolic systems such as written language, maps, musical scores and mathematics. In the case of the last, for example, number operations carried out on paper can refer uniquely to real world happenings.

The unique importance of the concrete symbolic systems stems in large part from the fact that there is a logic and order between the symbols themselves which is mirrored in the real world. This allows for the independent manipulation of the symbols to be linked to operations on their empirical counterparts and vice versa. Mastery of symbol systems involved in such acts as writing, doing mathematics, drawing and reading maps and diagrams, reading musical scores and so on gives us one of our most powerful tools for acting on our environment. The mastery of these systems, and applying them to problems in the real world, must be regarded as a major task for formal education and training in our society. The need for this kind of learned skill, which required some special expertise not readily available in the home, was one of the strong reasons for the development of public schooling in the past couple of hundred years. Learning in this mode leads to declarative knowledge which is demonstrated by an ability to make symbolic descriptions of the experienced world. The ability to function efficiently in the skills of this mode is crucial to operating effectively within our society, not only because it is the mode in which most of the fact-based everyday decision making needs to be carried out, but also because it has become virtually a prerequisite for all levels of employment in our society.

Formal (available from about 16 years)
The elements in this mode become abstract concepts and propositions and the operations on them are concerned with hypothesising and determining the relationships among them; neither the elements nor the operations need an empirical referent. Development in this mode becomes more content specific and increasingly the concern of teachers at the upper secondary and early tertiary levels (Collis & Biggs, 1983). This is the mode where theoretical constructs, not having an empirical referent, are able to be manipulated. Apart from this new and abstract database, the thinking process changes to one involving hypothesis formulation and propositional reasoning. A new dimension is added to thinking because this development allows the individual to consider not only the real but also the possible. The earliest level of thinking in this mode begins to appear in some students, with respect to their particular specialisations, from around 16 years of age and sometimes earlier. This is the commonly expected level for successful entrance to study at the tertiary level (Collis & Biggs, 1983). Collis and Biggs (ibidem) also argue that a bachelor's degree requires a high level of functioning in this mode in the student's major study areas for a minimum passing standard to be achieved at the end of a four year course. This is the mode in which the theoretical knowledge necessary to have a workable grasp of an abstract academic discipline is gained. This mode of functioning is the normal expectation for undergraduate study (Collis & Biggs, 1983) and represents a major development in some

individuals from around Year 9 or 10 in areas of the curriculum in which they show intense interest and some talent. It does not generalise to all thinking and in some individuals may not develop at all.

At this stage the data of thinking become abstract entities, concepts, classes and categories and the reasoning is by means of formulating and testing hypotheses using propositional statements. In mathematics, one easily recognisable ability available for the first time at this level is the ability to operate on the operations in a mathematical statement independently of its content. For example, at the concrete symbolic level, by using a beam balance, students are able to order from heavy to light the weight of various objects made of the same material, (WI, W2...); likewise they are able to order the volume of the same objects for volume measured by displacement (Vl, V2...). What they are unable to comprehend until they can handle the abstractions of the formal level is the relationship $W/V = K$ for a given material. Where the concrete symbolic mode ties the individual to the real world and concretely demonstrable relationships, the formal mode allows consideration of the possible world and possible relationships. This not only widens the horizon for the individual concerned but makes available other formal characteristics of this mode, such as the form of an argument often taking precedence over its content (which may be trivial), the ability to use the formal logic of deduction, and to have a full comprehension of the constraints upon both induction and deduction as strategies for reaching conclusions. In general, the formal mode of thinking is what we expect of a person with professional (as opposed to technical) competence in his or her area of expertise.

Postformal

The characteristics of this mode are not well investigated but it seems safe to assert that one aspect would be further development of the previous modes as well as an ability to bring into play any aspect of the other modes, or their interaction, which might appear relevant or worth consideration in the context of a current problem. Where individuals in the formal mode are able to demonstrate their understanding of a discipline well enough to work within it, the individuals who aspire to the post-formal mode must have an overview of their discipline such that they can challenge its basic tenets and conduct research to advance understanding in the area. The prerequisites for functioning in this mode in a particular discipline area then are twofold:

– an in depth knowledge and understanding of the abstract concepts, categories and constructions of the discipline and the inter-relationships among them - these form the elements of thought which are to be operated upon; and

– the ability to utilise all of the modes in every conceivable way, from the simplest imaginative and/or analogical processing to the most complex interrelational/ intermodal linking, as the modus operandi for the problem-solving operational procedures.

One way of conceiving this mode at its most basic is to consider the way in which the research higher degree students and their supervisors function as they investigate their research problem. We could hypothesise that the successful completion of a Ph.D. by research would indicate at least a moderate level of ability to function in this mode in the discipline or sub-discipline which has been researched. This is the mode in which the high level of research expertise required to make advances in the disciplines through which we have achieved the modern level of understanding and control over our environment. The hypotheses at this stage suggest that this mode is the one in which questioning the bounds of current theory and practice and the establishing of new boundaries and parameters takes place. It is the form of thought institutionalised in postgraduate study and basic research. It is manifested in many fields and is highlighted by remarkable performances in scientific research as well as in literature, music and the arts.

Perhaps this summary description of the modes can be made more user-friendly by a consideration of the basic facts in diagrammatic form (See Figure 12.1).

Figure 12.1 *Modes, learning cycles, and forms of knowledge (adapted from Biggs & Collis, 1991).*

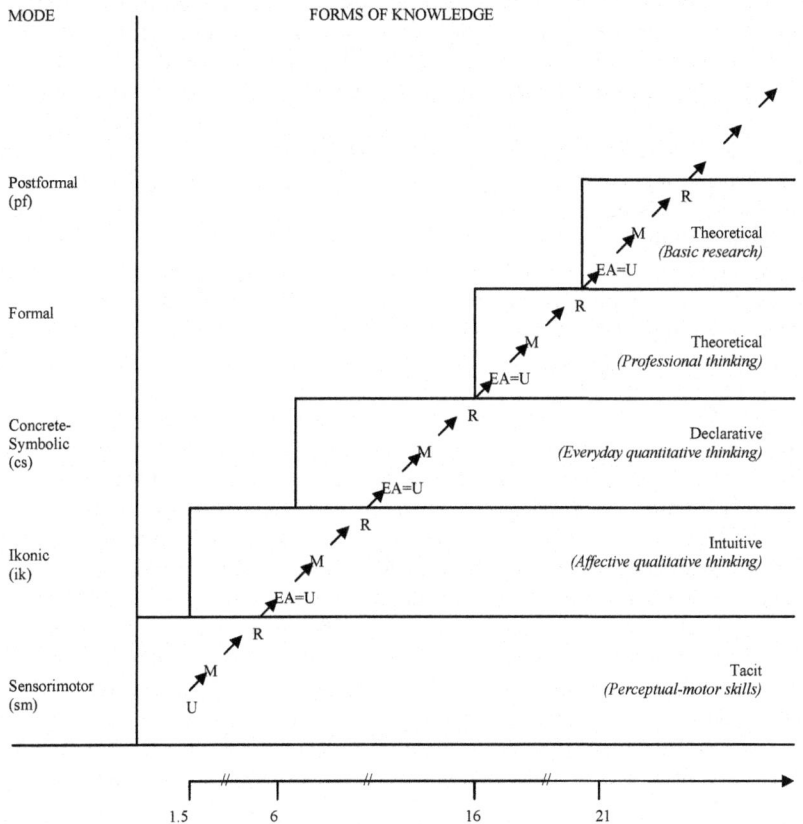

Key: U=Unistructural M= Multistructural R = Relational EA = Extended Abstract

Ages at which modes typically appear are shown on the horizontal axis; the modes themselves are on the vertical axis. It can be seen that the modes progress from concrete actions to abstract concepts and principles and, in direct contrast to Piagetian theory, the emergence of one mode does not replace its predecessor. The modes in fact accrue; the later developing modes existing alongside the earlier modes. The implication of this last statement is twofold and is highly significant when we come to consider adult learning and reasoning:

- as the individual matures physiologically the mode(s) developed earlier continue to develop on the basis of the increasingly mature physical, experiential and intellectual background; and
- as the modal repertoire available increases beyond sensori-motor, functioning in more than one mode in any one episode (i.e., multi-modal functioning) becomes the norm.

The Driving Force or Why Bother?

The development of a new skill within a mode or the acquiring of a new mode clearly involves enormous effort on the part of the individual - an effort which is unlikely to be put in if the individual does not see a significant personal pay-off. Another way of saying this is that there needs to be a motivating force which drives the individual to master the increasingly complex skills required for development both through each mode and, more importantly, from mode to mode. Broadly speaking, this force can be seen as an inbuilt desire to gain control over one's environment, to gain independence vis-a-vis one's own personal space in the world. During infancy this is shown in the high motivation the child has to attain skills such as walking and talking. At later periods in life, skills which the children adjudge to be advancing their control over the world around them are engaged in readily and can be seen as the basis for many play activities. Often one can get an insight into the children's current pre-occupation in this context by examining what they are spending their time in practising. For example, in learning advanced motor skills, such as catching a ball or skipping, children will spend many hours in endless repetition until they have acquired the skill to a level with which they are satisfied. At a later stage the same applies to the more abstract skills, such as arguing for a point of view. Adolescents and young adults will often spend many hours honing these skills in both peer driven bull sessions or with safe adults such as parents. Similar progression can be traced in the development of social skills, which show a sequence of key developmental levels as the individual matures from infancy to adulthood via childhood and adolescence. Again the individual appears to be motivated essentially by the need to improve control over one's personal space, ironically by establishing one's position as a functioning unit in a desirable group. This phenomenon has a high level of significance for teachers.

For learning to take place the learner must adopt a learning set, that is, focus attention on the task and decide to learn. Without some form of motivation learning is unlikely to take place. For the motivation to learn to be intrinsic, and at a high level, it is important for individuals to feel that the activity contributes to their current view of what will empower them vis-a-vis their environment, broadly defined. This last statement applies particularly to those concerned with adult learning. To some extent children can be conned or badgered into a certain amount of school learning even if they cannot see its relevance at the time - this is not a luxury which those in adult education can enjoy. Adults who do not see the relevance of the content or teaching processes of the course over a medium time-frame will be most likely to vote with their feet and move on to areas of greater interest.

A not unrelated phenomenon shows up when we note that individuals in all cultures seem to be able to progress through the first two modes naturally, that is, without the necessity for formally organised instructional procedures. In fact, some societies - the bushman in South Africa for example have survived, both as individuals and as a culture, using only highly developed abilities confined to the sensorimotor and ikonic modes. Of course, informal modelling and showing how is not included in the notion of formal instructional procedures as they are common from infancy onwards in all cultures. The move to the concrete symbolic mode implies both the development of skills that are far from naturally occurring and a much more sophisticated understanding of the idea of control of one's environment. Once this transition has been made however, it appears that progress through the concrete symbolic mode will be much less difficult than making the transition in the first place. The next real difficulty lies in making the move into the formal mode, a development which greatly raises the level of abstractness and complexity of operations required as well as having even less obvious relevance to one's ability to lead an independent life-style.

Cycles of Learning within Modes

Another implication of what has been described so far is that we need to make a distinction between modes of intellectual functioning and the notion of learning a particular skill within a mode.

The former notion refers to the developing ability to understand and work, in increasingly complex ways, with concepts that are more and more abstract. This developing ability can be linked with the Piagetian notion of sequential and hierarchical development of cognition from the sensorimotor stage through to the formal stage. The notion of attaining specific skills within a mode involves treating each skill as an individual entity whose structure of development can be traced independently of other developing skills. This means that individual skills within the same mode may be at different levels of development. For example, reading and arithmetic are both set in the concrete symbolic mode but there is no reason why, in any individual case, achievement in one should not be higher than achievement in the other. In fact, in practice, this disparity (or decalage as Piaget would have called it) is the norm (Biggs & Collis, 1982). Let us look more closely at the notion of cycles of learning within a mode.

The idea of the cycle of learning is common to all of the theorists referenced at the beginning of this chapter; in each theoretical stance it is the notion used to describe the nature of the increasing complexity of structure as a response is developed within each mode. Each theory postulates that there are four distinct levels of functioning using the elements and operations peculiar to that mode. The nature of the elements and operations relevant to the theory being described here have been summarised and exemplified above. A metaphor for the concept of the structure of a learning cycle is shown in Figure 12.2.

The first level represents no use of the relevant elements of the mode and indicates that the individual has not engaged the learning cycle for the skill in question and is designated as prestructural in that context. At the second, or unistructural level, we note the most basic use of one of the elements relevant to the skill being learned; this level simply demonstrates that the individual has entered the learning cycle in the appropriate mode. It can serve as a useful indicator for an instructor in making an assessment of the person's readiness for further instruction in the particular skill involved. The third level of the cycle (termed multistructural) shows up as an elaboration of the unistructural level of response, typically a sequential increase in the information/ number of elements utilised rather than any integrative elaboration of the information/ elements. This level is not simply several unistructural responses strung together but involves at least a moderate ability to control the sequence to enable a meaningful outcome to be achieved. At the fourth level further elaboration takes place. The most significant change seen at this point in the cycle is that the monitoring process involving several elements becomes a thoroughgoing integration of virtually all the elements available to the person in the given context. This enables a fully satisfactory response for the mode in question to be made and is a noticeably high level of response for that mode. The fifth level involves a consolidation of this integration, adds a new dimension made up of relevant concepts and reasoning styles typical of the next mode and in fact soon becomes the first level of the next mode. As an example let us take one of the early concepts learned by a child by age 24 months, object permanence. The learning cycle for this concept takes place in the sensorimotor mode and has been well illustrated using a typical plaything such as a ball. The characteristics of each level of the cycle are set out below:

- *Prestructural*: if the ball rolls out of sight the infant does not look for it but acts as though it no longer exists;
- *Unistructural*: the infant uses only one sense modality, usually sight, to look for the ball that has rolled away; if it is not immediately successful the infant gives up;
- *Multistructural*: if a ball is placed under a cushion in full view of the child, he/she will retrieve it by raising the cushion. However, if, again in full view of the child, the ball is removed from under the original cushion and placed under a nearby cushion, the child continues to look under the original cushion. The child uses more than one sense modality but does not coordinate the information;
- *Relational*: the child solves the problem of sequential displacements, first when he/she sees the displacement; later, even when the displacement is unseen; and
- *Extended Abstract*: in the absence of the ball the child will ask for it, that is, "ball?". This response represents a move to a new mode of functioning and the cycle begins again with this response representing the unistructural stage of the new cycle.

The implication involved when we put together the notion of different modes of intellectual functioning as described earlier and what has been said above about the structure of the cycle of learning within a mode is highly significant for our understanding of how skills of all kinds are learned. A helpful way of linking these notions is through the concept of target mode.

The Target Mode

Any specific skill, or complex of skills, has a target mode: the mode which provides the basic infrastructure for the task concerned. To learn the skill effectively one has to concentrate one's learning time in that mode. Let us take an example which is probably familiar to most readers. Suppose we wish to learn to play the game of golf which, by its nature, is set in the sensorimotor mode because, to be successful, one has to take the set of sensory motor skills one has and adapt

Figure 12.2 *Metaphor for learning cycle (adapted from Biggs & Collis, 1982).*

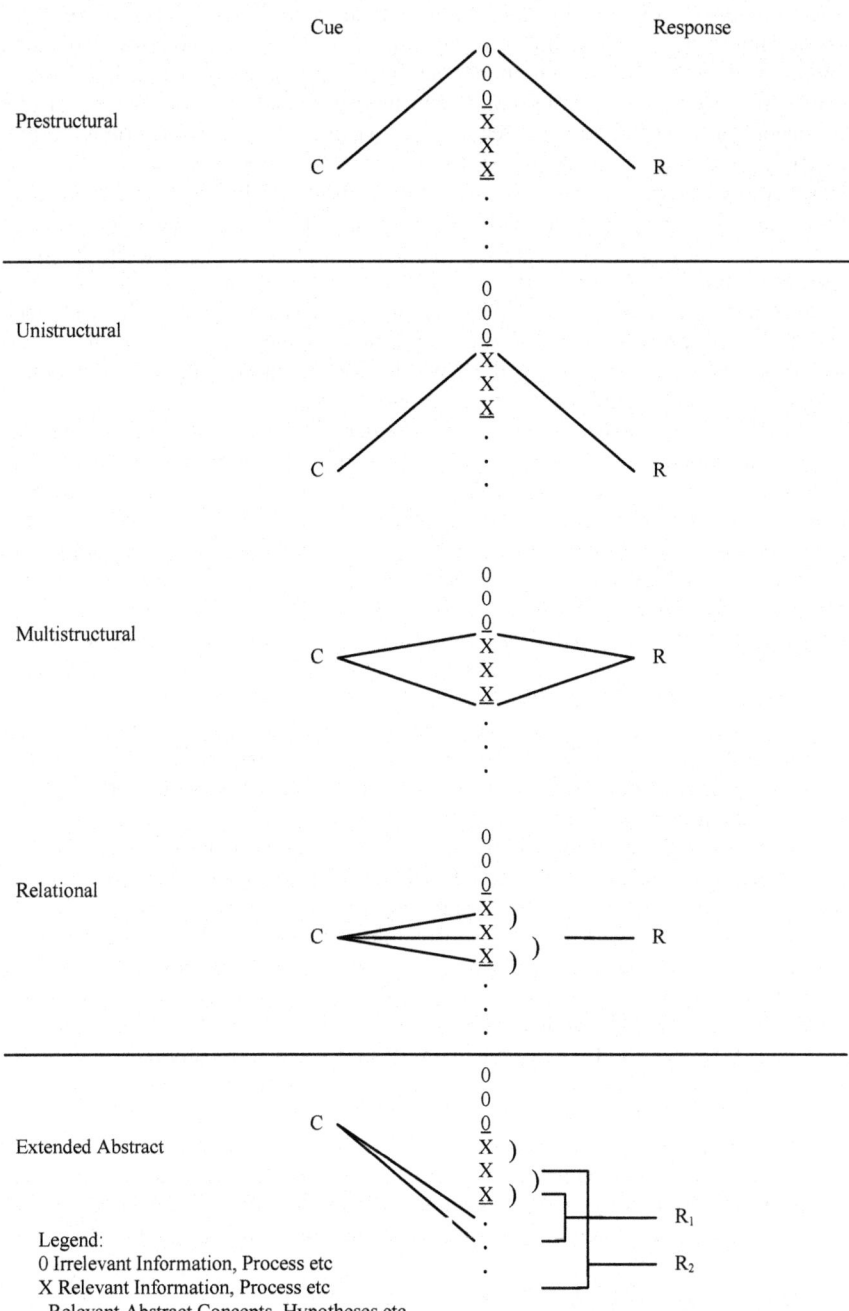

them by training and practice to form a new set of complex coordinations. To achieve this, the individual has to spend most of his or her golf time out hitting the ball (a sensorimotor activity involving tacit knowledge). It is true, as research shows, that reading about how to play (concrete symbolic mode) and imaging oneself striking the ball (ikonic mode) can help improve performance, but the skill itself will only be achieved by practice in the sensorimotor mode. If we consider elementary arithmetic and basic reading and writing for communication as further examples, we note that they belong to the concrete symbolic mode. As the skills involved are concrete symbolic, it follows that most of the learning and practice time must be spent in that mode. Other available modes should be used to supplement instruction, but we need to remember that we learn a concrete symbolic system by practising that system.

In other words, we learn to read by reading, to do arithmetic by doing arithmetic and so on. As already indicated, the target mode is the one in which the task is naturally set, for example golf, sensorimotor; painting, ikonic; elementary arithmetic, concrete symbolic; abstract algebra, formal.

The individual begins to learn a particular skill when it is clear that the appropriate mode has been focused upon and one relevant aspect of the skill has been selected for attention thus exhibiting an engagement with the task of learning the skill at the unistructural level of the cycle of learning. Progress to the multistructural level occurs when several correct or relevant features are brought to the task; that is several of the elements involved in the skill are manipulated independently, often sequentially as in a listing. Apart from a shortish, often temporal sequence, the individual does not have a sufficient overview of the process to be able to integrate the elements into a coherent whole which might bear on a theme, schema or generalisation.

The relational level is attained when the individual has generalised and integrated the available elements of the mode in which the skill is being developed into a coordinated schema; previously independent elements are brought together as a new and higher level skill in that mode.

The extended abstract level is beyond the target mode under consideration and marks the movement of the individual into the next mode. This point in the development of the skill is highlighted by the person's ability to give a high quality performance in the particular skill in question at the relational level together with (more and more successful) attempts to link it in with elements and operations from the next mode. For example, students moving between the concrete symbolic and the formal modes begin by attempting to take in additional abstract features of the context involved and to reason with propositions not as closely tied to reality as previously. This extended abstract level, when thoroughly entrenched, becomes the unistructural level of the next mode.

The description given above matches the global description of development of stages mentioned earlier (Figure 12.1) and, it will be remembered, the development of the structure within each mode is mirrored in microcosm in the many thousands of different skills developed by individuals throughout their life-spans.

Factors in the Development of Modes

Before moving on to the implications that this theoretical stance has for learning and instruction, it would appear useful to bring to the reader's attention, however briefly, five factors which seem to be essential for individuals to develop a particular mode.

Maturation

The different modes tend to appear at different stages of physiological development; the first appearance of certain life skills, such as walking or talking, clustering, as they do, around certain age groupings lends support to this observation. Obvious examples of this clustering occur in the sensorimotor mode skills but careful observation of older students, including adults, reveal the onset of markers for later developing modes as they arise - the ability to pick these up is an important skill which teachers, psychologists and other professionals dealing with people in a learning or "need to understand" context must acquire.

The relational level of a previous mode expands into the following mode. The modes appear in a set sequence viz, sensorimotor, ikonic, concrete symbolic, formal, postformal, each new mode dependent upon the skills developed in the earlier mode(s). More specifically a particular skill with roots in the previous mode requires that those roots be at least the relational level before they can supply entry to the skill in the next mode. For example, the usual way of introducing the study of algebra (a formal mode skill) is to link it to generalised arithmetic (a relational skill in the concrete symbolic mode). The difficulties experienced by some individuals in the early stages of learning algebra can be traced to the fact that either the prerequisite skill, arithmetic, was not available at the relational level, viz. generalised arithmetic, or, if it was, it was not drawn upon by the instructor in the early lessons.

Availability of space in working memory

This is a complex psychological concept which refers to the amount of information that an individual can attend to at any one time. The space to hold information in working memory is limited and thus it is necessary to find ways to utilise the available space most efficiently. One way is to "containerise" the information into a concept or "chunk"; another is to automate some of the operations so that certain "calculating" space is not required. Making space available is a necessary condition for higher level intellectual functioning as the level of abstraction of the elements increases and the operations on them become more complex.

Social support

Cognitive activity has always been both a personal and a social phenomenon. The social aspect has become of major interest in the last couple of decades. Suffice here to point to the importance of the culture, the society and the peer group in determining the valued activities in the area of intelligent behaviour and hence the ones which are most likely to be taken up. In a less ambitious frame we might consider the success of cooperative learning, group problem solving and peer tutoring as stimuli to cognitive activity.

Problem-solving mismatch

The individual's independence within, and mastery of, the environment is closely related to the ability to make accurate predictions of outcomes given certain facts. If there is a mismatch between predicted and actual outcomes in a matter in which the individual has a serious interest there will usually be a strong attempt to resolve that dissonance. In cognitive activity, this often means changing the mode. For example, if one sets out to catch a bus, using intuitive reckoning - a feeling that a bus is due, perhaps - the outcome is likely to be unsatisfactory on many occasions; if one uses the appropriate concrete symbolic reasoning - with a bus timetable say - the outcome is likely to be close to 100% accurate.

Implications for Learning and Teaching

It is clear that learning is most likely to be motivated and teaching most likely successful if the teacher takes account of certain key variables that have been described in the earlier discussion.

The first and most critical task that the teacher or instructor has is to select the *target mode,* that is the basic mode in which the skill to be learned is set. This determines the nature of the learning experiences to be made available and where the bulk of the learning time must be spent. The selection of the target mode also has important implications for the way in which adjacent modes are able to be utilised to complement instruction in the target mode. Let us follow up this last implication. In the course of explaining it, the other matters could well fall into place.

There are basically three ways (Biggs & Collis, 1991; Collis & Biggs, 1991) in which other modes are used to complement instruction in the target mode: (a) a later developed mode is used to facilitate skill learning in an earlier mode (top-down); (b) an earlier developed mode is used to facilitate skill learning in a later mode (bottom-up); (c) instruction in which the target mode lies between earlier and later developed modes (two-way) - these are all examples of multi-modal instruction/learning. To complete the picture we have learning which takes place within the target mode only, unimodal instruction/learning. *Top-down learning.* Perhaps the best examples here are found in the way in which sensorimotor skills are learned at different points in the life span. Adolescents and adults, for example, are much more mature developmentally than infants: their brains and nervous systems are more highly developed and they have also acquired modes additional to the sensorimotor which they are able to use to facilitate learning in the target mode. As Paivio (1986) indicated, the learning of motor skills associated with such sporting activities as skiing can be enhanced by imaging oneself performing the activity (viz. employing the ikonic mode) or, as Fitts (1962) suggested, by reading about the technical aspects of the activity (viz. employing the concrete symbolic mode). The final goal is to perform a skilled action without error and without conscious thought; this involves tacit knowledge. If we look beyond the conditions which are likely to enhance the achievement of a sensorimotor skill at a competent basic level, we will note that the level of use to which the skill is to be put determines the mix of modes which the individual needs to bring together in order to perform at an elite level. Olympic athletes, for example, whose training is focused on performance must continue to hone their skills in almost a unimodal fashion. On the other hand a performing artist such as a dancer, needs to incorporate a strong ikonic flavour to define the performance as a dance rather than callisthenics.

Let us consider, from this angle, the role expected to be played in the community by members of the traditional professional groups, such as doctors, lawyers, engineers or teachers. It was pointed out earlier that the notion of professionalism lies in the formal mode, but in practising the profession multimodality is required. A professional person is expected by the community to give informed advice or take informed action at an empirical (concrete) level guided by a set of theoretical (formal) understandings obtained during their training.

One of the most difficult aspects of professional training is the integration of the practicum with the theory, where the aim is to enable the beginning professional to interpret the formal mode abstractions and propositions of the discipline in a way which is readily understood and put into effect by non-professionals operating at the concrete symbolic and/or ikonic modes in the area. The traditional way of solving the problem is to keep the two apart.

The beginning lawyers, doctors, accountants, engineers, do their basic theoretical training first, followed by a practical, in many cases apprentice-like, period in which the beginning professional works under the supervision of an experienced member of the profession who, in the end, has the responsibility for recommending the registration to full membership of the professional group. The obvious problem of creating a satisfactory link between the theory and the practice has given rise to some dissatisfaction with the traditional training procedures and some institutions have replaced it by a form of problem-based learning in which the content to be learned is presented in context; the content taught is related to an immediate problem as well as to the body of knowledge of which it is a part. This, of course, gives rise to its own set of problems, which the reader might like to consider in terms of the model set out in this chapter.

Bottom-up Learning

The second form of multimodal learning occurs when the target mode is a later developing mode and an earlier developed mode is invoked to assist the learning process. This is the most common type of learning we would expect to find in schools and other formal learning institutions in which symbolic learning is the main aim. Let us examine specifically the implications for teaching content which has the target mode of concrete symbolic.

The aim is to provide declarative knowledge and practice in using this form of knowledge to arrive at the decisions required in everyday living. In this type of situation the "bottom up" strategy requires the teachers to focus on the target mode while invoking earlier developed modes (sensorimotor and ikonic) to give the students a broad base of experience on which to build their concrete symbolic system. In calling on the earlier modes to supplement children's experience in this context, two caveats should be borne in mind. First, the experiences called upon must be real and relevant, not simply experience for the sake of providing contrived concrete examples. Second, the earlier-mode experiences are usually enjoyed by the children who can function very well at those levels and thus there is frequently a temptation to linger too long at this level. This earlier level ability must not be allowed to overwhelm the main aim of succeeding in the target mode. The results of an experimental teaching project may make the point clear.

Mackenzie and White (1982) arranged for three mixed classes of Year 8 and Year 9 students to be given a detailed lesson on coastal geography which addressed 35 objectives. Two of the classes were then taken on an excursion. One of these classes was given the set piece tour with demonstrations arranged by the teacher and directed observations aimed at exemplifying the points made in the lesson. The tour arrangements for the other group required the students to be actively engaged *in situ* in generating the information to be observed and recorded. The important point for our purposes is that the activities engaged in by the latter group, such as wading through a mangrove swamp, tasting leaves for salinity, scrambling over cliff platforms and so on, invoked the use of the sensorimotor and ikonic modes directly in the learning of a concrete-symbolic task.

The results of post-tests on the unit were very interesting. There were no differences between the three classes immediately after the classroom lesson was given at the beginning of the study. However, a post-test carried out three months later, with the excursions intervening, showed that the group who had had the opportunity to incorporate the earlier modes of functioning into their learning recalled 90 per cent of the original lesson, the traditional excursion class recalled 58 per cent, and the third class who had the lesson but no follow-up excursion of any kind recalled 51 per cent. A special test to see if students were able to link their experiences or observations with the facts taught in the lesson showed that the class taught inter-modally was far better at making these links than any of the others. In other words, for longer-term retention, the demonstration type of excursion was little better than no excursion at all. A carefully designed excursion, requiring students to be actively on task in as many modes as are relevant, was very successful in helping students not only to retain material, but to make the connection between their 'formal' knowledge and their experience of the world.

The success of the multiple embodiment and perceptual variability principles suggested by Dienes (1963) for teaching mathematical concepts and the discovery methods recommended by Bruner (1966) can be explained in these terms as special forms of bottom up instruction. The guided discovery technique which grew out of Brunerian ideas seems particularly applicable to some adult instructional situations. The instructor structures the activity for an outcome in the target mode and encourages the students to find the principle(s) involved by actively searching for it themselves; the better examples of the method have the individuals working on self-selected tasks in a group situation, with the instructor acting as guide and provider of information, material and motivation.

Two way instruction
This method of instruction is probably best illustrated in content areas where the target mode is clearly the ikonic; the content is concerned with learning which is associated with the affective, intuitive and imaging ways of understanding the world. In teaching major aspects of the areas such as Religious Studies, Peace Studies and appreciation in the various art forms, Music Appreciation for example, this method of approach to instruction would appear to be most appropriate. As pointed out earlier, ikonic mode knowledge is intuitive, thus, if it is the target mode, the aim of the instruction will be to get the individuals to feel, imagine, and empathise with the content. Suitable activities to help achieve this aim would appear to include appropriate modelling and meditative type regimes together with some input from both the concrete symbolic declarative knowledge domain and the tacit knowledge domain of the sensorimotor mode; the former to provide some facts relevant to the area, and the latter to link in with the kinds of target mode instructional procedures which have been put in place. Assessment of the outcome of the instruction under these conditions is difficult but would probably be

attempted by various measures of attitude, feeling of well-being or changes in these dimensions as appropriate to the aims of the course.

An example of a poor use of the two-way technique may be found by examining the way in which music was once taught in schools. The expressed aim was to develop an appreciation of the art form and not to train competent performing musicians. The children were given experiences in the modes on either side of the (ikonic) target mode; elementary sight reading of music scores in the concrete symbolic mode and basic sensorimotor experiences with simple musical instruments such as drums and triangles and certain vocal exercises, some of which involved singing. The last mentioned came closest to ikonic mode experience which one might expect to have had an effect on the students' appreciation of the art form. The assessment of the course outcomes was made mainly by testing the level of declarative knowledge gained; sometimes account was also taken of some of the sensorimotor skills achieved. It was expected that success in achieving skills either side of the target mode (which were easily tested) gave an indication of success in achieving the skills involved in musical appreciation.

Unimodal learning
The occasions when this form of learning is appropriate would be, or should be, rare as it is a form of learning which does not make use of all the intellectual functioning powers of the individual. The Mackenzie and White (1982) study described above shows that the group who only received the lesson, a unimodal, concrete symbolic experience, recalled the least in the long term and were not good at linking their everyday experiences with the facts about the environment taught in school. An obvious legitimate use of the mode occurs in early infancy where the child has only one mode available. Even in this case, however, we find that it is common for the parents and siblings to interact with it in the ikonic mode. The infant learns to react to affective type stimuli and basic oral communication long before it is capable of functioning at the ikonic level itself.

There are also occasions when instruction is taking place at the upper levels of the concrete symbolic or early formal modes when it is necessary to appeal to examples within the same mode to make a point rather than try to use a supplementary mode. A good example of this is the attempt to get the individual to accept the concrete symbolic generalisation, $3y + 4y = 7y$, by appealing to a number of concrete symbolic examples of the form $3 \times 4 + 2 \times 4 = (3 + 2) \times 4 = 5 \times 4$ instead of falling back on an intuitive (ikonic mode) analogy, 3 apples + 4 apples = 7 apples. It so happens that this analogy is false and, although it may overcome an immediate problem, it soon has the student in trouble. The concrete symbolic examples, however, will serve the student well and, in addition, will make a helpful link to the mathematical axiom in the formal mode. The main danger of unimodal learning is that the knowledge, particularly if it is theoretical (formal mode), may become isolated from the person's everyday experience and so make it difficult for it to be used in making explanations about the world around them. Several studies have shown (Gunstone & White, 1981; Marton, 1981) that university students, capable of handling the concepts of modern physics in university examinations, often return to Newtonian views when asked to explain events in their daily interactions with the environment. They have become quite expert at working within a particular mode, especially in a specific context, but are at a loss to connect it beyond this circumscribed arena to the empirical world beyond.

Summary

The various teaching strategies described above have been around for a long time. Progressive teachers have used inter-modal techniques, often intuitively, for at least the past 50 years. What the type of developmental theory described here has done in the last decade is provide a clear theoretical basis that not only gives explanatory power but also enables the techniques to be shared widely amongst instructors and teachers. A bonus of course is that by taking it out of the realm of intuition and making its elements available in the later developing modes, the processes themselves become open to research scrutiny which will sharpen their impact and improve their conceptualisation.

The key feature, the *sine qua non* of the implications of the theory for practical use in instruction, is the cental focus the instructor must place on the target mode at all times, while encouraging the appropriate use of the other modes as supplements. In the past there have been many examples of failed curriculum innovations because the educators involved did not maintain their focus on the target mode but concentrated on using supplementary modes for the instruction with the belief that this would give the desired outcome. The temptation is particularly high in primary school instruction because the children quite clearly enjoy themselves when working in well established fun modes such as the ikonic and sensorimotor. If they can obtain correct answers as well they are even less motivated to move on to a more demanding mode such as the concrete symbolic where important skills in mathematics and writing for communication are set.

Cuisenaire rods did not live up to the high expectations originally generated for them as the base upon which to build children's early learning in mathematics. An examination of the way in which the material was used shows that the target mode, concrete-symbolic in the case of mathematics, was not the mode upon which the children focused when they were working with the rods. The experiences as the children interpreted them were largely in the ikonic mode. They solved their problems and wrote their quasi mathematical statements by working with visualisations of the colour coding and length sets instead of the numbers *per se*. The children saw the translation from colour code and length set to the number field as a separate teacher-devised activity not necessarily related to what they had done with the rods.

A similar problem arises for mathematics and written expression in school programs which focus their teaching in these areas during the early years almost exclusively on the so-called process method. If the method is used in its purest form the target mode, concrete-symbolic in both cases, is not set up by the teacher, and so the children concentrate their activities in the ikonic mode. In written expression this is represented by excessive emphasis on the "expression" of personal feelings, thoughts and ideas with no attention being given to the communicative conventions which are necessary if others are to read the material without the help of the author. In mathematics it shows in an excessive emphasis on problem solving by imagery, context and social interaction without a systematic focus on the development of the concrete-symbolic system which is mathematics at this level.

An instructor responsible for leading adult groups in discussion sessions, which often form a significant part of the instructional context at this level, must allow the free-ranging type of interaction which occurs in a successful adult group of this kind. This gives the participants the necessary opportunity to engage the various modes of functioning which they have available and which they see as possibly helpful to their learning. But, the instructor must know what the target mode is; provide stimuli for discussion that force attention on this mode; and, as appropriate and necessary, steer the discussion in a direction that is compatible with the target mode outcome desired. In summary, the teacher has the task of deciding on the target mode for a learning episode and then focusing the instruction on that mode while taking care to involve the students actively in relevant supplementary mode experiences.

On the few occasions when the learning episode is to involve one mode only, the teacher must plan the instruction to avoid the temptation to use analogies which will be misleading in the longer term.

With the target mode selected the instructor has the task of guiding the individuals through the intra-modal levels of skill development described earlier (Figure 12.2). First, the skill level of the student within the particular mode has to be considered. Given that the individual has the basic concrete building block for the skill in question, the cycle of learning for the skill has at least three relevant levels - unistructural, multistructural and relational. In general the assumption is that the aim is for the students to raise their level of functioning in the cycle to the point where they are able to respond at the relational level.

However, it is important to point out that recent research into the complex conceptualisations necessary for successful achievement in certain school-based academic content, where the concrete base is not available, show that there may be more than one cycle required to develop a thorough-going concrete symbolic understanding of the area. For example, it appears from studies by the author and colleagues on the development of common and decimal fractions (Watson, Campbell & Collis, 1993; Watson, Collis & Campbell, 1995) and the concept of the measurement of volume (Campbell, Watson & Collis, 1992) as well as on how children come to an understanding of vision in everyday life (Collis, Jones, Sprod, Watson, & Fraser, 1998), that at least one cycle is required to develop a basic concept and another to integrate the understanding involved in order to use the concept effectively in everyday reasoning.

When making instructional decisions while working in the usual classroom situation, that is within the one cycle, the plus one strategy, a teaching notion developed in the context of moral education (Rest, Turiel, & Kohlberg, 1969), would appear to recommend itself in the context of this model. The basic idea is that if the learner indicates performance at a particular level of the cycle, the teacher pitches instruction at the next level up. If the student cannot attain this level immediately with a little help, then more experiences at the current level are indicated. When these have been given the teacher tries again to raise the level of instruction, and so on. A classroom example may make the idea clear. A Year 2 class was asked to write a 'good' (sic) story about a 'refrigerator'. One child wrote: "We have a refrigerator" - a unistructural response in the concrete-symbolic mode. The teacher recognised the level of the response and tried to encourage the child to add to the story to make it into a multistructural response; something like the following, which a class-mate had written: " On Saturday, Mum, me and Grandma went to town and bought a white refrigerator but it would not go properly and so we sent it back to the shop and got another one." The teacher attempted to effect this improvement by asking questions and making suggestions: "What colour is it?", "Where is it kept?", "Where did mother buy it?" and so on. In this case the child did not see the point of adding to the sentence which he had originally constructed. In fact, careful interviewing of the child, revealed an inability to monitor the theme of a personally written communication beyond one statement. If pressed the child simply gave two unrelated "stories"; for example, "We have a refrigerator and on Saturday we went to the football". However, the teacher had at least begun to set up a dissonance between the child's version of a good story and the teacher's. Establishing such a dissonance was critical if the child was to be motivated to try for the next level. The child appeared unable to take up the suggestions that the teacher made at that time and some more experiences were provided at the unistructural level to help automate the elements and operations involved before returning to the 'plus 1' strategy. Happily, six months later the child was performing up to the average multistructural standard of the group.

Conclusion

The background for a large part of this chapter has come out of research studies which were focused on cognitive development during childhood, adolescence and early adulthood; the implications for instruction set out have a similar orientation. It seems important to conclude by focusing on the differences in emphasis between this form of initial educational learning and the learning we usually find associated with adult education. Perhaps this can best be done by examining briefly some ways in which we can expect a mature adult group to approach educational activities. The average adult education group is made up of a number of self-directing individuals who have freely chosen, and very often paid fees, to attend a course. Their reasons for doing this range from having a one-off personal development experience to choosing a course because it forms part of a long term plan for professional advancement. The variety of life experiences represented in the group, the ages of the individuals and the way the group was formed guarantee that there will be a wide range of individual differences in almost every aspect relevant to the course being undertaken. At the same time it is almost equally certain that the people in the group will be alike in their desire to have a course that is student-centred, experience-based, problem-oriented and organised along collaborative lines as much as possible. In short, the students' backgrounds and their expectations lead us to the following principles by which we might expect general adult education to be distinguished from initial education:
- the learner rules the domain rather than the teacher;
- the experience is not seen as a preparation for life but rather as a participation in life; and
- the experience is to be focused on the process rather than the content.

However, closer examination of these three principles reveal that the perceived differences between the levels of learning are quite subtle and appear to be more of degree than of substance with different aspects receiving varying emphasis at different times. It would seem reasonable to suggest that apparent differences may be largely attributed to the view of the world that is obtained from different positions in an individual's life cycle.

Prior to the formal school years, in infancy and the pre-school years, the above three principles clearly apply and it comes as no surprise to find that these are years of rapid development in which there is an incredible growth in the child's ability to function as an independent person within a fairly circumscribed environment. The one big difference from adult learning is that the children of this age have comparatively little experience with the percepts and concepts that they have to deal with; even the physical skills are developed from the selection of and integration and practice with the original primitive sensory and physical elements. As they are going through these learning processes for the very first time they have a unique naivety about the content and process of learning which adults are unable to match.

A similar situation applies during initial education in the formal years of schooling; individuals are still meeting basic concepts and developing fundamental skills for the first time. However the content, processes and skills to be mastered at school have been selected as essential by the society concerned and this in itself makes the educational experience in these years different from both the pre-school and adult level experiences. This group of learners is still relatively naive, especially in the primary school, and thus the individuals, in general, tend to accept the material presented and the way that it is presented as the norm. As long as the school experience serves their major concern for developing their present or future independence within the social situation in which they find themselves and is not beyond the level of modal functioning that they have attained, motivation for learning will usually remain high. The teacher is in command, as it were, but only while these conditions apply - thus in a subtle, but very real, sense the learners may be seen to be in charge of their initial education. This becomes more obvious as the child acquires some concrete symbolic mode declarative knowledge in the early teenage years and realises that he or she now has the intellectual skills necessary to carry on a successful life without further school-based learning. The teachers' task, at this stage, becomes one of presentation and organisation of material and activities which will gradually enable the individuals to take over responsibility for their own learning. Thus the adult learner as ruler of his/her own learning domain is simply an extension of a process which began very much earlier. Both pre-schoolers and adults see education as participation in life and are free to enjoy their educational experiences accordingly. It is during the intervening years, when society sets the agenda for the individual's educational curriculum, that the notion of education as a preparation for life is introduced.

An important factor underlying the individual's world view, and thus important to the way in which the three principles are seen to work in practice, is the nature of the development of the modes of functioning and the kind of knowledge outcome expected in each mode. During babyhood and infancy, children quickly develop the sensorimotor mode of intelligent functioning, the knowledge outcome being survival physical skills. As soon as the sensorimotor mode is far enough advanced to act as a base (approx 1.5 years), the ikonic mode begins to develop and this, with its facilities for memorising, imaging and signifying, leads to intuitive knowledge. This form of knowledge with a strong base in perception and imagination adds great strength to the individual's capacity to learn and to control his/her personal environment. When the children begin formal schooling they are introduced to new modes of intelligent functioning, concrete symbolic being the first and the most important for the individual's personal future well being. Its importance lies in the development of a form of knowledge known as declarative - a form that is firmly tied to the empirical world of concrete facts and concepts. Moreover, a concrete logical process is added to intuition as a means of problem solving which can be applied to the elements of declarative knowledge.

The individuals enrolled in adult education courses will have developed each of these three modes to an advanced level and each mode hosted more and more complex behaviours as the individual gained experience and physical maturity. It is also clear that, as each mode developed, it increased the power of the individual's intellectual functioning by much more than its face value as a new mode because it made available a whole new set of intermodal connections. These developments are especially relevant in distinguishing mature adult learning from initial learning. For example, because of the adult's extensive experience and practice with modal and inter-modal functioning over the years the occasions when they come completely naively to a learning situation will be very rare. Indeed, they will very often find themselves needing to unlearn certain misunderstandings of concepts and procedures learned in their earlier years before being able to move forward in their current higher level studies. In addition, adult education learning in formal courses tends to be pitched at the transition from late concrete symbolic mode to the early formal levels. Thus we find that the concepts being dealt with are abstract or semiabstract, and depend on definition, hypothesis formation and propositional reasoning for their manipulation. The adult students already have a vast store of declarative knowledge and are very familiar with the ways of adding to this if they have the need to do so; they are now more interested in the process that they are going through in obtaining new knowledge than memorising more declarative material.

The developed modal infrastructure, the lack of naivety in educational matters and the nature of the concepts and operational procedures to be learned help to distinguish the application of the three principles in mature adult learning from their application in initial learning.

REFERENCES

Baldwin, A. L. (1967). *Theories of child development.* NY: Wiley.

Biggs, J. B., & Collis, K. F. (1982). *Evaluating the quality of learning: The SOLO Taxonomy.* NY: Academic Press.

Biggs, J. B., & Collis, K. F. (1991). Developmental learning and the quality of intelligent behaviour. In H. Rowe (Ed.), *Intelligence: Reconceptualization and measurement* (pp. 57-76). Hillsdale, NJ: Erlbaum.

Bruner, J. S. (1964). The course of cognitive growth. *American Psychologist, 19,* 1-15.

Bruner, J. S. (1966). *Towards a psychology of instruction.* Cambridge, Mass.: University Press.

Campbell, K. J., Watson, J. M., & Collis, K. (1992). Volume measurement and intellectual development. *Journal of Structural Learning and Intelligent Systems, 11,* 279-298.

Case, R. (1972). Learning and development: a neo-Piagetian interpretation. *Human Development, 15,* 339-358.

Case, R. (1975). Gearing the demands of instruction to the developmental capacities of the learner. *Review of Educational Research 45,* 59-87.

Case, R. (1985). *Intellectual development: Birth to adulthood,* NY: Academic Press.

Case, R. (1991). *The mind's staircase.* Hillsdale NJ: Erlbaum.

Collis, K. F. (1974). *Cognitive development and mathematics learning.* London: Shell Centre, University of London.

Collis, K. F. (1975). *A study of concrete and formal operations in school mathematics: A Piagetian viewpoint.* Melbourne: Australian Council for Educational Research.

Collis, K. F., & Biggs, J. B. (1983). Matriculation, degree requirements, and cognitive demands in universities and CAEs. *Australian Journal of Education, 27,* 41-51.

Collis, K. F., & Biggs, J. B. (1991). Developmental determinants of qualitative aspects of school learning. In G. Evans (Ed.), *Learning and teaching cognitive skills,* (pp. 185-207). Melbourne: Australian Council for Educational Research.

Collis, K. F. (1994). Mathematics and cognition. In H. L. Chick and J. M. Watson (Eds.), *Mathematics and teaching: topics for the professional development of teachers* (pp. 337-370). Adelaide: Australian Association for Mathematics Teachers.

Collis, K. F., Jones, B. L., Sprod T., Watson, J. M., & Fraser, S. P. (1998). Mapping development in students' understanding of vision using a cognitive structural model. *International Journal of Science Education, 20,* 45-66.

Dienes, Z. P. (1963). *An experimental study of mathematics learning.* London: Hutchinson. Egan, K. (1984). *Educational development.* Oxford: Oxford University Press.

Fischer, K. W. (1980). A theory of cognitive development: The control and construction of hierarchies of skills. *Psychological Review, 87,* 477-531.

Fischer, K., & Pipp, S. (1984). Process of cognitive development: Optimal level and skill acquisition. In R. Sternberg (Ed.), *Mechanism of cognitive development.* NY: W.H. Freeman.

Fischer, K. W., & Sylvem, L. (1985). Stages and individual differences in cognitive development. *Annual Review of Psychology, 36,* 613-648.

Fitts, P. (1962). Factors in complex skill training. In R. Glaser (Ed.), *Training, research and education.* Pittsburgh: University of Pittsburgh Press.

Gardner H. (1985). *Frames of mind.* London: Granada.

Ginsburg, H. & Opper, S. (1979). *Piaget's theory of intellectual development* (2nd ed.). Englewood Cliffs, NJ: Prentice-Hall.

Gunstone, R. & White, R.T. (1981). Understanding gravity. *Science Education, 65,* 29 1-9.

Hadamard, J. (1954). *The psychology of invention in the mathematical field.* Princeton, NJ: Princeton University Press.

Halford, G. S. (1980). Toward a redefinition of cognitive developmental stages. In J.R. Kirby and J.B. Biggs (eds), *Cognition, development and instruction.* NY: Academic Press.

Halford, G. S. (1982). *The development of thought.* Hillsdale, NJ: Lawrence Erlbaum.

Halford, G. S. (1993). *Children's understanding: The development of mental models.* Hillsdale, NJ: Lawrence Erlbaum.

Kaufman, N. L. (1980). Review of research on reversal errors. *Perceptual and Motor Skills, 51,* 55-79.

Keats, J. A., Collis, K. F., & Halford, G. S. (Eds.) (1978). *Cognitive development in children and adults - a neo-piagetian approach.* Chichester, UK.: Wiley.

Lunzer, E. A. (1965). Problems of formal reasoning in test situations. *Child Development Monograph, 30,* 19-46.

Mackenzie, A., & White, R. T. (1982). Fieldwork in geography and long-term memory structures. *American Educational Research Journal, 19,* 623- 32.

Marton, F. (1981). Phenomenography - describing conceptions of the world around us. *Instructional Science, 10,* 177-200.

Paivio, A. (1986). *Mental representations: A dual coding approach.* NY: Oxford University Press.

Pascual-Leone, J. (1970). Mathematical model for the transition rule in Piaget's developmental stages. *Acta Psychologia, 32,* 301-45.

Peel, E. A. (1960). *The pupil's thinking.* London: Oldbourne.

Phillips, J. L. (1969). *The origins of intellect: Piaget's theory.* San Francisco: Freeman.

Piaget, J. (1950). *The psychology of intelligence.* London: Routledge & Kegan Paul.

Piaget, J. (1964). *The early growth of logic in the child,* trans. E.A. Lunzer & D. Papert. London: Routledge & Kegan Paul.

Rest, I., Turiel, E. & Kohlberg, L. (1969). Relations between levels of moral judgment and preference, and comprehension of the moral judgment of others. *Journal of Personality, 37,* 225-52.

Sternberg, R. J. (1985). *Beyond IQ: A triarchic theory of human intelligence.* NY: Cambridge University Press.

Sternberg, R. J. (1988). *The triarchic mind.* NY: Viking. Watson, J.M., Campbell, K.J., & Collis, K.F. (1993). Multimodal functioning in understanding fractions. *Journal of Mathematical Behaviour, 12,* 45-62.

Watson J. M., Collis, K. F., & Campbell, K. J. (1995). Visual processing during mathematical problem solving. *Educational Studies in Mathematics, 28,* 177-194.

Review Questions

Read the following statements and indicate whether they are True or False.

1. The behaviourist tradition in psychology teaches that knowledge originates in the constructive activity of the child.
2. The translation of the Piagetian model of cognitive development into English has been a major influence on our understanding of cognition in school - based learning during the past fifty years.
3. The current concept of cognition is restricted to the intellectual logical mode which has abstract formal thinking as its high point.
4. The *sensorimotor* mode represents the most fundamental way of knowing the world.
5. Intuitive thinking is highly valued by artists and scientists alike.
6. The formal mode is the most commonly used mode for everyday decision making.
7. Improving control over our personal space is the basic motivation for engaging in a learning episode.
8. In a learning cycle, a multistructural response is simply a string of unistructural responses.
9. A mismatch between a predicted and an actual outcome is often a trigger for attempting to raise the level of functioning.
10. 10.Adults attempting to learn a new sensorimotor skill, such as skiing, usually engage a top-down learning strategy.
11. 11.The most common type of learning strategy found in schools and colleges can be described as unimodal.
12. An instructor should focus teaching efforts on the mode in which the skill to be learned is based.
13. In a learning cycle, the relational level is the one at which the student first shows an integrated understanding of the topic involved.
14. Principles involved in adult education are completely different from those which apply to earlier age groups.
15. Adults come back to formal education mainly to build up their store of declarative knowledge.

Answers

1F	2T	3F	4T	5T	6F	7T	
8F	9T	10T	11F	12T	13T	14F	15F

Exercises

1. Discuss the statement, "All learning is learning and all teaching is teaching - there is no basic difference between teaching school students and teaching adults".
2. (a) Write a one page commentary (300 words), giving examples as you go, on **three** of the following:

- ikonic mode
- concrete symbolic mode
- formal mode
- post formal mode.
  (b) Write one page (300 words) on what you see as the significance of **each** of the following concepts as they are used in the learning/teaching context:
- target mode
- task analysis.
3. Write an essay of 2000 words (approx) to discuss the factors which are involved in the development of modes. Include examples to illustrate each factor.
4.　　Each of the following have been used to describe a method of instruction, top-down; bottom-up; two-way; unimodal; plus 1 strategy.
   Select three and write up to 300 words on **each** to describe its characteristics. Include two practical examples in each description.
   5. Write an essay of 2000 words (approx) on what you understand by the phrase, "structure of learning".

About the Author

Professor K.F. Collis, BA, MEd, PhD, FAPsS, FACE was born and educated in Queensland, Professor Collis began his working life as a primary school teacher, largely in one-teacher schools in South East Queensland. During the mid 1950s he graduated in Arts from the University of Queensland and moved into secondary school teaching in Mathematics and Physics. After five years he moved into the private system by joining the Hubbard Academy in Brisbane where he was a specialist teacher of pure and applied mathematics and logic for several years. In the latter stages of this appointment he became engaged in action research which set out to investigate how children learned school mathematics. At the same time he completed a BEd degree and a MEd (first class hons) by research with the University of Queensland. In the second half of the 60s he took up a Lectureship in Education at the University of Newcastle (N.S.W.) where he completed a PhD in cognitive development in the department of Psychology and was promoted to Associate Professor. His teaching and research interests are in cognition, evaluation and mathematics and science education. In the late 60s he began research which aimed at giving Piagetian theory classroom meaning, initially using school mathematics as his vehicle. As the work developed over the years, two outcomes began to appear: a modification of the Piagetian model which made it more applicable to the educational context (Collis, 1975) and, on the back of this, a practical, but theory-based, assessment technique, the SOLO Taxonomy (Biggs & Collis, 1982), which is now widely used in school content areas both in school systems and research contexts on a national and an international basis. Both the theory and the practice of these early outcomes have been built on systematically over the 80s and 90s and, indeed, currently form the basis of several research activities both in Australia and overseas. From 1977 until 1995 Professor Collis occupied a chair of Education at the University of Tasmania where he continued to develop his teaching and research interests as well as serving a number of years as

Dean and/or Head of Department. Upon retirement he was made a Professor Emeritus of the University of Tasmania. In 1996 he was given the status of Professor (honorary) in the Faculty of Education, University of Newcastle where he currently spends some time most weeks writing, researching and carrying out consultancies.

Kevin F. Collis
University of Newcastle

RAY W. COOKSEY

13. MAKING JUDGEMENTS AND DECISIONS

Adults are continually confronted with the task of making decisions and rendering judgements in their everyday as well as working lives. It could be argued that judgement and decision making constitutes the major portion of an adult's cognitive activity while awake. A decision involves the making of a specific choice and frequently has an action or implementation aspect to it. A judgement is a cognitive assessment that has an evaluative aspect to it (like/dislike, good/bad, or strong/weak) but not necessarily an action or implementation aspect. Thus, a court magistrate may *judge* a defendant to be guilty of the crime of breaking and entering and then *decide* to sentence the defendant to two years in prison.

In some cases, it may be difficult to distinguish between a judgement and a decision because they occur almost simultaneously. For example, a manager who makes the decision to hire a specific job applicant will most likely also have come to a judgement that this applicant looks best for the job. However, it is usually the case that a judgement is made prior to a decision being reached. Thus, while driving, one might scan ahead to the next intersection and judge that it is safe to go through without slowing down which then leads to a decision not to apply the brakes. The close relationship between judgements and decisions has led behavioural scientists to study them as if they were a single phenomenon – and, for the most part, this has been an appropriate approach.

Adult judgements and decisions can be seen to vary in terms of the degree of mental effort that must be undertaken in order to arrive at them. For example, a judgement regarding whether or not one likes a particular painting in an art gallery will usually involve minimal cognitive effort and can be made fairly quickly (in a matter of seconds) and automatically. Conversely, a decision regarding whether or not to take a new job in Sydney when one lives in Alice Springs may demand a great deal of thought, extensive information gathering efforts and opinion seeking from other relevant people or agencies and may therefore take days or weeks to reach.

Adult decisions can also be seen to vary in terms of the degree to which they impact on other people (including the decision-maker), a characteristic relating to the consequences that may flow from a decision. For example, a decision about which book to read at night really only affects the person making the choice and a wrong decision probably has minimal consequences. On the other hand, the decision to send troops into battle made by a head of state has the potential to affect a great many people including the head of state and there are very severe consequences if the decision is in error.

Figure 13.1. The four interrelated facets of adult judgement and decision making.

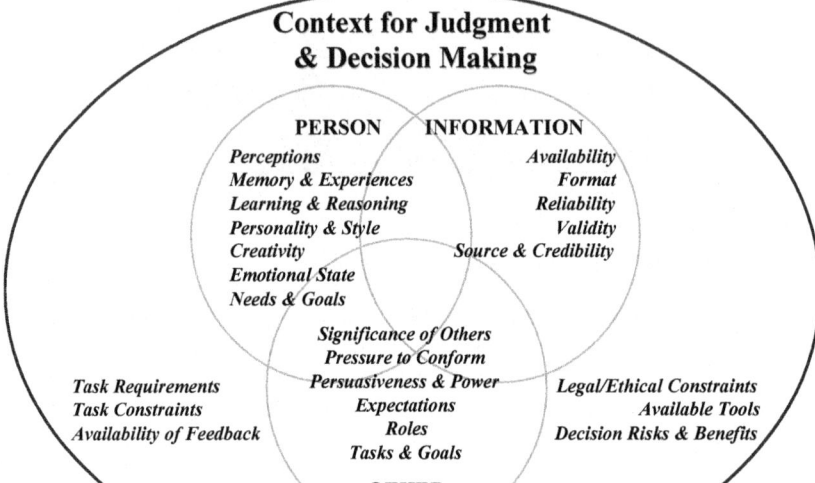

However, no matter how important or trivial a decision is and no matter how narrow or wide its potential impact, there are certain key facets which combine to influence how a person makes a decision or renders a judgement. These four facets are: the *context* in which the decision is being made, the *person* who is making the decision, *other people* who may be involved in making the decision or may be affected by the decision, and the *information* on which the decision is to be based. Figure 13.1 shows how these four facets relate to each other and gives an indication of some key features associated with each facet. Notice that all facets overlap, at least partially, with each other – a representation that is meant to suggest the mutual influence each facet has upon the others and the synergy that the combination of the four facets lends to judgement and decision making. If we restrict our focus to just one or two of these facets, as has often been the case in behavioural research on the topic, we limit our potential to more fully understand adult judgement and decision making.

Context in which the Judgement or Decision Is Made

Adult judgement and decision making cannot be understood without recognition of the critical importance of the decision context. The decision context establishes the conditions under which the decision or judgement must be made. These conditions include: the nature of the decision to be made; any constraints on time or resources which apply to the decision task; the availability of previous feedback from earlier decisions; any legal or ethical constraints that must be factored into the decision or judgement; the availability of any tools or support systems to assist in the decision process; and the potential rewards/benefits and costs/risks associated with making a correct versus an incorrect decision or judgement. Often, the decision context is the primary determinant of the decision processes that are adopted. For example, a very tight timeframe for making an important decision precludes an exhaustive search for information and thorough consideration of all possible options – thus processes that facilitate restricted information search, increased dependence on mental information processing shortcuts, or reliance on previous experiences become more predominant.

The potential rewards/benefits and costs/risks associated with making a correct versus an incorrect decision or judgement coupled with legal and/or ethical constraints is often a very potent determinant of decision outcomes. Hammond (1996, 2007) has reviewed a number of decision-making examples from various fields in order to illustrate this very point. For example, the decision by a jury to declare a defendant innocent or guilty of a crime carries with it certain societal expectations and risks. It is not possible to know a person's guilt or innocence for certain, so a jury must make its best judgement within that context in full knowledge that there is a risk of being wrong no matter which verdict is reached.

Historically, it has usually been the case that a person is considered innocent until proven guilty beyond a reasonable doubt. This translates into an expectation that it is more costly (and therefore more important to avoid) to judge that an innocent person is guilty and therefore decide to imprison them than it is to judge that a guilty person should be declared innocent and decide to set them free. An incorrect judgement of guilty applied to an innocent person creates injustice to that individual whereas an incorrect judgement of innocent applied to a guilty person creates injustice to society. In free and democratic societies, it is considered a more serious wrong to be unjust to an individual than to be unjust to society at large, hence the preference to presume innocence until proven guilty. Societal expectations do change and evolve over time, so it is easy to imagine that in the future this expectation might be reversed, especially where crime rates are exceedingly high. Note that none of this discussion has said anything about how the jurors might go about making their decision. Rather some overarching contextual parameters are established which exert pressures to move the decision in particular directions depending upon the level of decision uncertainty with which society (or the judge) is willing to live ('beyond a reasonable doubt' states this level of uncertainty in verbal form).

Person Who Makes the Judgement or Decision

Considerations about the person are obviously quite central to understanding how judgements and decisions are made. People make decisions or judgements within particular contexts on a daily basis. Much of our understanding of human decision making has come from investigations of the role that various person-related factors play in influencing the decision or judgement made. It is clear from much of this research, whether performed under highly controlled laboratory conditions (see, for example, Kahneman, Slovic, & Tversky, 1982; Lichtenstein & Slovic, 2006) or under more naturalistic conditions (see, for example, Zsambok & Klein, 1997), that perceptual processes, memory processes, learning and reasoning processes, personality variables, creativity, emotional states, and needs and goals all play their part in contributing to the direction a decision or judgement takes.

One important advance in theories of decision making is Hammond's Cognitive Continuum Theory (see Hammond, 1996). Hammond has suggested that human thinking while making a judgement or decision can be characterised along a continuum ranging from *intuitive thinking* at one end of the continuum to *analytical thinking* at the other end. Thinking along this continuum also relates to perceptual information processing and memory processes. Figure 13.2a (adapted from Table 1.4 in Cooksey, 1996) depicts the Cognitive Continuum and highlights some of its essential characteristics. Note that the large middle area of the continuum is termed the region of *quasi-rationality*. Thinking in this region is characterised by a blending of the characteristics of intuitive and analytical thought and can be thought of as the region where 'commonsense' emerges. Decisions are seldom made using either a pure form of intuition or analysis, thus some level of quasi-rational thinking is usually involved. [It is important to note here that Hammond's notions of intuitive and analytical thinking are very similar to Epstein's (2008) proposed modes of experiential and rational thinking respectively. The chief difference is that Epstein did not infer the existence of a continuum nor did he acknowledge quasi-rational modes of thought.]

Hammond's theory also proposes that there are important linkages between the modes of thinking a person will employ to make a decision and the environmental context for the decision task. Thus, he suggests a Task Continuum along which decision or judgement tasks may be placed according to their tendency to induce intuitive, analytical or quasi-rational thinking. Figure 13.2b (adapted from Table 1.6 in Cooksey, 1996) shows the Decision Task Continuum along with some of its more important characteristics. The fact that Cognitive Continuum Theory proposes parallel systems for analysing human thought and the tasks confronted within the decision context permits the prediction that decisions or judgements will be most appropriately made if the mode of thinking applied is the same mode as the task tends to induce. Thus, deciding whether or not one likes a particular painting while strolling through an art gallery is a task which will tend to induce intuitive thinking and, if this is the case, the most appropriate and adaptive judgement will likely be made. However, a mismatch between mode of thinking applied and that which the task tends to induce will tend to lead to inappropriate decisions being made. Thus Hammond suggests, somewhat radically, that there is no single correct mode of thinking (in contrast to the many researchers who extol the virtues of analytical or rational thinking as the only proper mode of thought), correctness is a question of appropriateness to the task at hand.

Figure 13.2. The Cognitive Continuum and the Decision Task Continuum of Hammond (1996).

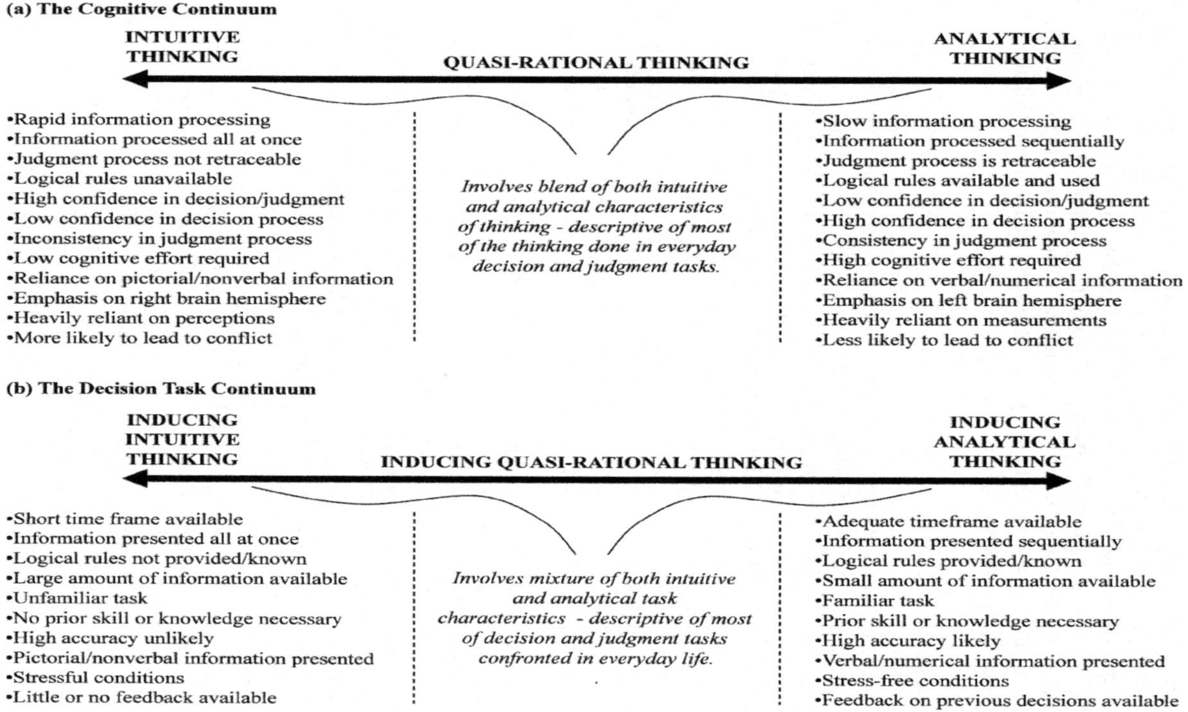

(a) The Cognitive Continuum

INTUITIVE THINKING

QUASI-RATIONAL THINKING

ANALYTICAL THINKING

Involves blend of both intuitive and analytical characteristics of thinking - descriptive of most of the thinking done in everyday decision and judgment tasks.

- Rapid information processing
- Information processed all at once
- Judgment process not retraceable
- Logical rules unavailable
- High confidence in decision/judgment
- Low confidence in decision process
- Inconsistency in judgment process
- Low cognitive effort required
- Reliance on pictorial/nonverbal information
- Emphasis on right brain hemisphere
- Heavily reliant on perceptions
- More likely to lead to conflict

- Slow information processing
- Information processed sequentially
- Judgment process is retraceable
- Logical rules available and used
- Low confidence in decision/judgment
- High confidence in decision process
- Consistency in judgment process
- High cognitive effort required
- Reliance on verbal/numerical information
- Emphasis on left brain hemisphere
- Heavily reliant on measurements
- Less likely to lead to conflict

(b) The Decision Task Continuum

INDUCING INTUITIVE THINKING

INDUCING QUASI-RATIONAL THINKING

INDUCING ANALYTICAL THINKING

Involves mixture of both intuitive and analytical task characteristics - descriptive of most of decision and judgment tasks confronted in everyday life.

- Short time frame available
- Information presented all at once
- Logical rules not provided/known
- Large amount of information available
- Unfamiliar task
- No prior skill or knowledge necessary
- High accuracy unlikely
- Pictorial/nonverbal information presented
- Stressful conditions
- Little or no feedback available

- Adequate timeframe available
- Information presented sequentially
- Logical rules provided/known
- Small amount of information available
- Familiar task
- Prior skill or knowledge necessary
- High accuracy likely
- Verbal/numerical information presented
- Stress-free conditions
- Feedback on previous decisions available

For fairly complex decisions, it may not be clear which mode of thinking will be most productive therefore we will see people move around on the Cognitive Continuum between different modes of thought in pursuit of that which is most productive. This alternation between modes will usually be stimulated by failure to reach a proper decision or judgement using the mode of thought currently being employed. [It should be noted that there is a linkage between Hammond's and Epstein's ideas of intuitive/experiential thinking and analytical/rational thinking in terms of brain function: intuitive/experiential thinking tends to be associated with activity in the right hemisphere of the brain and analytical/rational thinking with activity in the left hemisphere of the brain.]

Rationality

For many, decision making is intimately bound up with the idea of rationality. That is, the decisions or judgements people make should be rational. In terms of the Cognitive Continuum, this means that the 'preferred' mode of thinking for decision making is analytical. For a long time, economists and psychologists accepted this view. This belief that decision making should be rational gave rise to numerous prescriptive schemes for producing rational decisions (see, for example, the various discussions in Brown, 2005, Goodwin & Wright, 2004, and Kleindorfer, Kunreuther, & Schoemaker, 1993). Among such schemes are approaches such as decision analysis, decision trees, Bayesian revision of probabilities, and multi-attribute utility theory. These approaches make the same general sorts of assumptions regarding what counts as a rational decision process. The decision-maker:

- must have all relevant information at hand and must know the available options from which a choice is to be made;
- makes some type of assessment of the likelihood of achieving various outcomes or specific aspects of those outcomes;
- makes some type of assessment of how important or useful each of those outcomes or aspects is to themselves or to some group of interest; and
- mathematically or cognitively integrates this information to arrive at a choice which maximises the expected return to themselves or to some group of interest.

However, more recent research has found that while these approaches may prescribe rational methods for helping people make 'good' judgements and decisions, they often make unrealistic assumptions about both the decision-maker and the information available to make the decision. This means that rational decision approaches are not oriented to reveal how adults actually make their judgements and decisions - there is instead much to be gained from analysing and describing how decisions appear to be made by people using whatever processes and resources they may have to hand. Cognitive Continuum Theory is one coherent move toward this goal; the new developments in naturalistic decision making described in Zsambok and Klein (1997) are another. Importantly, some integrative work by Russo and Schoemaker (1989) has shown that the decision process can be broken into four broad sequential stages without necessarily implying that there is one most rational approach to working through the stages. The four stages are:

- *Decision Framing*: understanding the context of the decision and defining the problem to be addressed;

- *Information Gathering and Intelligence*: gathering high quality information that is appropriate and necessary for making the decision;
- *Coming to Conclusions*: systematically integrating the gathered information to arrive at a final choice or judgement; and
- *Learning from Feedback*: gathering and reviewing information about the outcomes of the decision process and about the decision process itself with a view to reducing future errors and conflict.

Decision Making Styles

A great deal of research has been done to investigate the relationships that may exist between the psychological processes associated with perceptions, values, personality and creativity, and a person's typical approach to making judgements and decisions. This research has resulted in the elaboration of *decision styles*. Several different theories regarding decision styles exist, but it will suit our purposes to focus on the system devised by Alan Rowe and his colleagues (Rowe & Mason, 1987; Rowe & Boulgarides, 1992). Rowe proposed that decision styles describe the ways in which people (especially managers within organisations) tend to operate when making decisions. A decision style synthesises a decision maker's perceptual preferences, value preferences (e.g., preference for being task- or person-focused), and cognitive complexity (tolerance for ambiguity and uncertainty) into a single summation that reflects how the decision maker will tend to interpret the decision context and work within it to achieve a decision outcome. It is important to realise that people do not exhibit just one decision style, but will vary in the extent to which specific styles will dominate in their approach to decision making. Thus, more than one style may be dominant within a single person. While styles will vary in terms of the extent to which a person exhibits them, under conditions of stress and tight contextual constraints (such as short timeframes or severe lack of information), the person will tend to resort to their most dominant style. However, the mark of a mature decision maker is the ability to 'flex decision styles' in accordance with the demands of the decision task and, of course, this capacity would be less likely to be displayed by people with strong authoritarian or dogmatic personalities.

Figure 13.3 displays these dimensions and characteristics of Rowe's Decision Style Model as summarised in Rowe and Boulgarides (1992). Rowe described decision styles as varying along two critical dimensions: *cognitive complexity* (low or high tolerance for ambiguity and uncertainty – the vertical axis in Figure 13.3) and *values orientation* (preference for focusing on task/technical or person/social aspects of a decision task – the horizontal axis in Figure 13.3). The intersection of these two dimensions yields four distinct decision styles: *Directive, Analytical, Conceptual,* and *Behavioural*. Figure 13.3 summarises how each decision style is related to other key psychological processes, behaviours and preferences. The Decision Styles Inventory reported in Rowe and Boulgarides (1992, p. 38) provides a simple method for assessing adult decision style preferences. A key feature of this inventory is its orientation toward providing a profile of style preference strength scores that indicates whether a particular style is very dominant, dominant, back-up or least preferred. A simplified variation of this inventory is provided at the end of this chapter. A close reading of Figure 13.3 should reveal that each

Figure 13.3. Rowe's Decision Style Model loosely adapted from materials and tables in Rowe and Boulgarides (1992, pp. 29, 33, 34, and 35).

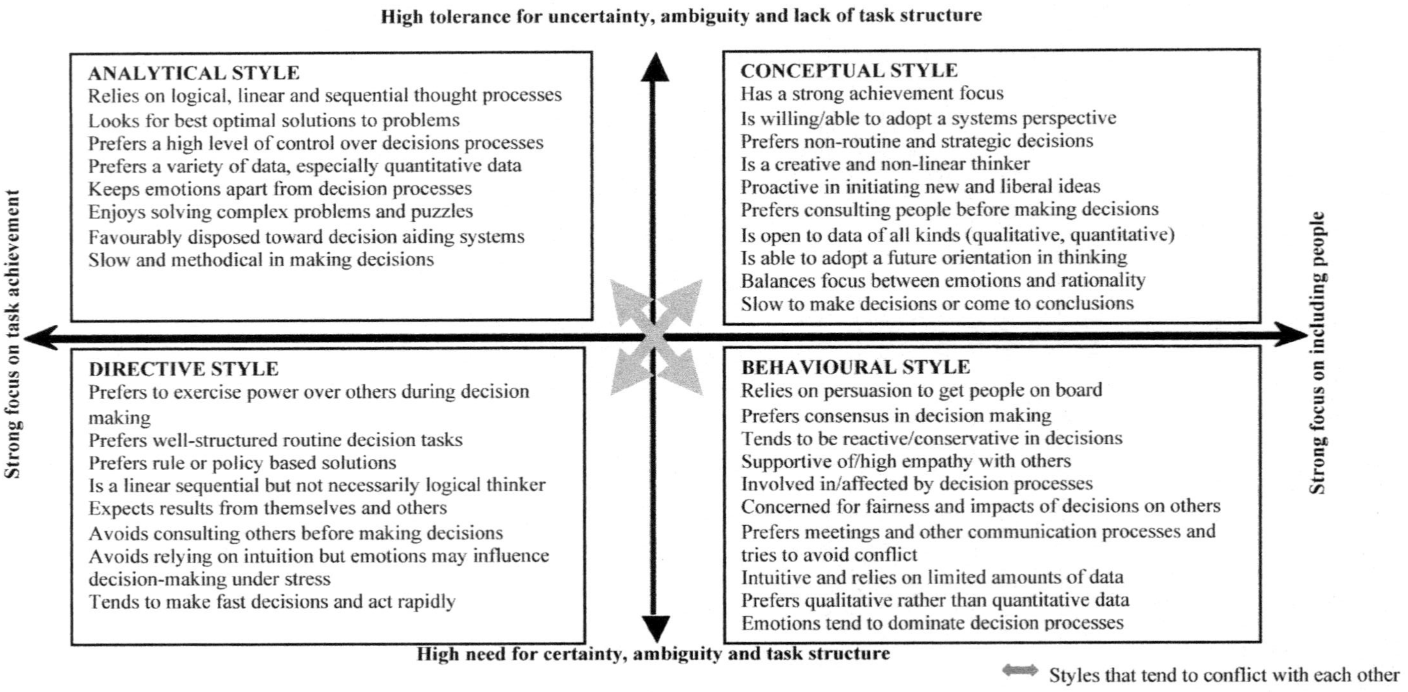

High tolerance for uncertainty, ambiguity and lack of task structure

Strong focus on including people

CONCEPTUAL STYLE
Has a strong achievement focus
Is willing/able to adopt a systems perspective
Prefers non-routine and strategic decisions
Is a creative and non-linear thinker
Proactive in initiating new and liberal ideas
Prefers consulting people before making decisions
Is open to data of all kinds (qualitative, quantitative)
Is able to adopt a future orientation in thinking
Balances focus between emotions and rationality
Slow to make decisions or come to conclusions

BEHAVIOURAL STYLE
Relies on persuasion to get people on board
Prefers consensus in decision making
Tends to be reactive/conservative in decisions
Supportive of/high empathy with others
Involved in/affected by decision processes
Concerned for fairness and impacts of decisions on others
Prefers meetings and other communication processes and tries to avoid conflict
Intuitive and relies on limited amounts of data
Prefers qualitative rather than quantitative data
Emotions tend to dominate decision processes

ANALYTICAL STYLE
Relies on logical, linear and sequential thought processes
Looks for best optimal solutions to problems
Prefers a high level of control over decisions processes
Prefers a variety of data, especially quantitative data
Keeps emotions apart from decision processes
Enjoys solving complex problems and puzzles
Favourably disposed toward decision aiding systems
Slow and methodical in making decisions

DIRECTIVE STYLE
Prefers to exercise power over others during decision making
Prefers well-structured routine decision tasks
Prefers rule or policy based solutions
Is a linear sequential but not necessarily logical thinker
Expects results from themselves and others
Avoids consulting others before making decisions
Avoids relying on intuition but emotions may influence decision-making under stress
Tends to make fast decisions and act rapidly

Strong focus on task achievement

High need for certainty, ambiguity and task structure

Styles that tend to conflict with each other

326

decision style has both advantages and disadvantages; no one particular style would be suitable for all decision tasks.

One interesting benefit of understanding one's own decision style preferences is that this can facilitate an understanding of where potential conflicts may occur between people who have different dominant styles (such as between managers and their subordinates – see grey arrows in Figure 13.3). For example, a manager whose dominant style is Directive will be more likely to conflict with subordinates whose dominant styles are either Conceptual or Behavioural but not with a subordinate who has a dominant Analytical style whereas a manager whose dominant style is Conceptual will tend to have minimal or no conflict with subordinates who exhibit any dominant decision style except Directive. In the context of group decision making, it may be easy to see how group conflict might arise if members have conflicting decision styles. Equally, though, having a diversity of decision styles represented within a group may allow the strengths of one style (e.g., Analytical) to offset the weaknesses of another style (e.g., Behavioural) and vice versa.

Heuristics and Biases

Plous (1993), Beach and Connolly (2005), Newell, Lagnado and Shanks (2007) and Bazerman (2006) have all provided very complete descriptions of the types of mental shortcuts, called *heuristics*, that adults often use when making particular types of judgements or decisions. According to Johnson (1995), mental heuristics can be seen to have roots in our evolution as methods for achieving quick decisions that have good survival potential (e.g., avoiding dangerous animals, spotting food which is likely to be poisonous, and being conservative in approaching something which has hurt us in the past). Reliance on heuristics permits us to impose some degree of certainty (and therefore to obtain some psychological 'control') over contexts which are highly uncertain. In today's world, day-to-day survival is not so much an issue, but coping with the complexities and uncertainties of modern decision contexts is definitely problematic. Thus, heuristics have retained their value as methods for reducing uncertainty and producing quicker decisions than thorough analysis would permit (in this sense, the use of heuristics can be viewed as falling within the quasi-rational thinking region of the Cognitive Continuum).

While heuristics often do result in saving of mental effort, they also have a tendency to lead the person into making *biased* judgements or decisions. Whereas the penalty for biased or erroneous decisions early in our evolution was usually death (e.g., erroneously concluding that an attractive mushroom was safe to eat when it was really fatally poisonous), nowadays, the penalty for biased or erroneous decisions is often measured in dollar costs or in inconvenience to ourselves (e.g., we buy the wrong car) or injustice to others (e.g., we fail to hire a potentially good employee because they remind us of a dishonest employee whom we just sacked). We will review here three of the more well-understood heuristics (along with their associated biases): *representativeness, availability,* and *anchoring and adjustment.*

Representativeness heuristic
The *representativeness heuristic* is a mental shortcut that produces a judgement about some object or event of interest based on the similarity of that object or event

to previous instances or encounters or to some process which the person believes he or she understands. Suppose, for example, that while playing a betting game involving successive flips of a fair coin (where only two outcomes, heads (H) or tails (T), are possible), a person achieves the following outcomes on eight previous throws: THTHHHHH. What would be your guess as to the outcome the person might bet on for the next throw? If you are like the majority of people who are asked this sort of question, your answer is likely to be T. This is because most people have an intuitive understanding of random or chance processes like coin tosses and the last 5 successive outcomes were Hs. Thus, it 'seems' like time for a T outcome because we know the coin is fair and that the outcomes for a random process should have a mixture of H and T results. So, we feel psychological pressure to guess T as the next outcome because that outcome would be more like what one would expect from a random process: the judgement is based on how 'representative' the previous outcomes are of a random coin flip process. However, the truth is that, with a fair coin, on any one coin flip, there is a 50-50 (even) chance of achieving an H or a T outcome, so either bet would have the same chance of being paid. If people were not employing a representativeness heuristic, then 50% of people asked to guess the next outcome would say T and 50% would say H; in reality, it is more like 80% of people will say T and the percentage increases if we make the successive run of H outcomes even longer! This result is called the *gambler's fallacy* and is one of the biases that over-relying on the representativeness heuristic can lead us to. This is where things like the belief in a streak of luck or a 'hot' streak in sports come from. It may be useful to remember this fallacy when you next play Lotto!

The representativeness heuristic can also be seen to operate in routine decisions like those in which strangers say "G'day" to you as you walk downtown. Your memories of previous encounters with people who exhibit certain characteristics (like physical deformities, facial features, modes of dress, and racial differences) can be used to help you decide: you will often end up saying "G'day" to those people who resemble those types of people you have had positive encounters with in the past and tend not say "G'day" to those who don't bear such a resemblance. In many cases, you might be right, but perhaps you can see where we are heading here: over-relying on this mental heuristic may lead us to avoid encounters with certain people merely because they resemble someone we had a negative encounter with before, even if the person really is one we could potentially get along with. This type of bias is what generates prejudice and stereotypes. Often it takes just a single bad encounter for us to form a link in our brains between 'that type of person' and 'that kind of negative or unpleasant behaviour'.

Think about how people become superstitious. If a person walks under a ladder and happens to be hit on the head by a falling object, they may link the two events and change their behaviour so as to avoid walking under ladders in the future. In this case, the person perceives an illusionary causal link between walking under a ladder and getting hit on the head (the outcome is 'representative' of what one would expect if the two events were causally connected) and uses this link to make future judgements – and it often takes only one such occurrence to establish the link (meaning the connection is based on a sample of one observation). However, if we were to do a proper and statistically valid sampling study of many people who walk under ladders, we would most likely find that only a very tiny percentage of those people also have something hit them on the head – hardly evidence for a causal connection!

Availability heuristic

The *availability heuristic* is a mental shortcut that leads us to make judgements based on the ease with which we can recall prior examples of the same outcome in the past. Thus, I may make a decision not to buy a particular car simply because my best friend, whose judgement I value highly, said that she had a very bad experience with that particular brand of car. The fact that I find the source of this information very credible means I may place a great deal of importance on the information she offers. The easy availability and high salience of this information means that I don't have to spend a lot of time thinking about this particular car, I may dismiss it as a viable option immediately. In some instances, this decision may be correct and the heuristic will have done its job. In other instances, it may lead me to an erroneous decision because my friend might only be giving me one bit of negative information, based upon her own selective experiences, which may be contradicted by a wealth of positive information (perhaps statistical test data from sources like *Choice* magazine) attesting to the worthiness of that particular brand of car. Thus, the availability heuristic can lead me to make a biased decision.

Think about how you might judge your personal risk of suffering a heart attack. Your mental estimate of risk might be very different depending upon whether or not you have had some very close relatives or friends die recently of a heart attack. The easier it is to recall previous instances of a particular outcome, the higher our estimate will be of the chances of that outcome occurring again in the future. Sometimes the fact that the media present certain sensational outcomes in vivid and graphic fashion can alter your perceptions of the likelihood of an event (e.g., a passenger plane crash) occurring again, perhaps with you involved this time! These personal estimates of risk based on highly vivid easy-to-recall or imagine information will often be much higher than what would really be the case. Once again, we see the potential for bias arising from dependence on the availability heuristic.

Anchoring and adjustment heuristic

The *anchoring and adjustment heuristic* is a mental shortcut that bases our judgement or decision on establishing an initial impression or position and then incrementally adjusting our position relative to that anchor point until a final judgement or decision is reached. Think about interviewing someone for a job. Research (see Reece & Brandt, 1996) has shown that, within the first four minutes of a job interview, most interviewers have formed a fairly complete impression of the stranger they are interviewing (based on observable surface cues such as the applicant's mode of dress and grooming, speech patterns and accent, eye contact, nervous tics and gestures). This impression provides a solid anchor against which all future information can be gauged. If our initial impression is negative, we will probably be unwilling to or unlikely to significantly revise our impression through the remaining 26 minutes or so of the job interview unless we encounter some overwhelming evidence to the contrary. The converse will likely be true if our initial impression is positive. Thus, the initial anchor position retains a strong attraction for our judgement and we do not tend to stray very far from it. In this sense, the anchoring and adjustment heuristic tells us that our initial anchor is probably close (this is our brain trying to impose certainty on an uncertain world again!) and we don't need to move very far from it without very solid reasons. This tends to result in a bias of conservatism – we fail to move as far from our initial anchoring position as we should given the new information we encounter.

We can see evidence of the anchoring and adjustment heuristic and its associated biases in areas such as the real estate market where property values might be established based on a preliminary estimate by a real estate agent and are then seen not to be sufficiently revised based on new and more complete information about the house. We may also see the heuristic in operation in the courtroom where jurors may be instructed to consider possible verdicts for a defendant in a specific order: from harshest to most lenient or from most lenient to harshest. Evidence shows that whatever the starting point (which establishes the 'anchor'), the resulting decision remains closer to that anchor point than an identical decision made using the reverse ordering. Thus, considering the harshest sentence first will result in an overall harsher sentence for a defendant than considering the most lenient sentence first.

Information on which Decision/Judgements May Be Based

Any judgement or decision is made on the basis of at least some minimal information. The fundamental problem surrounding adult decision-making is *uncertainty* and the primary role of information is to assist in reducing that uncertainty. If there were no uncertainty in the world, there would be no need for masses of information, no need for judgement, and no need for a decision. It is precisely because the environments in which we must operate are awash with uncertain paths to the future, uncertain relationships, and uncertain information, that adults must make judgements and decisions. Risk is a special form of uncertainty entailing the assessment of the chances that a particular undesirable event will occur (e.g., chance of a critical component failing in a nuclear reactor plant; chance of contracting cancer from soil contaminated by toxic wastes; chance of worker injury if safety equipment is not worn). It is important that we come to grips with the concepts of uncertainty and risk in order to understand the fundamental basis for many decision errors.

The critical limiting factor for any person making a decision is that, at the time they must render a judgement or make a decision, they are uncertain (unsure, doubtful, sceptical) of at least the following *three* aspects of the decision problem:

– what the correct decision or judgement should be;
– how their information should relate to the judgement or decision to be made; and
– how good, in terms of quality, their information is.

These three aspects of uncertainty correspond roughly to three questions in the mind of the decision-maker:

– *What is the right decision?* This question focuses our attention squarely on the reason that judgement is needed - the correct answer or course of action is not known at the time that the decision is made. Further, it reflects our doubts as to how we might best go about making the correct decision (procedural uncertainty);

– *What information is important for me to use to make the right decision?* This question focuses on the uncertainty linked to not knowing which information is important for the particular decision to be made; frequently by addressing this question we implicitly consider which values are important in the decision context; and

– *Does the information I have really tell me what I think it's telling me?* This question focuses our attention on the quality of the information we have to deal with in terms of its validity, its reliability, and the credibility of its source(s).

Consider, as an example, the problem of selecting an applicant for a particular job out of a pool of available applicants. Judgement is required since we do not, at the point the selection decision must be made, know who the best applicant will be. Further, out of the wealth of information we may have available on each of the applicants (e.g., years and level of experience, highest education level, letters of reference, past work history, scores on a set of selection tests, impressions formed at interview, lunch time conversations about some applicants with others who knew them, etc.), we are unsure as to which one or more of these bits of information are most useful or predictive of the applicant's likely success in the job. Therefore, we must decide what information we will choose to consider as important which implies employing a set of value judgements to determine what is important for us to emphasise. [Note that this is distinct from knowing which sources of information are objectively most useful for the decision, which gets more directly at the environmental uncertainties involved.] Finally, for each source of information, we are unsure as to its accuracy, consistency, and credibility (are lunch time conversations and letters of reference really accurate reflections of relevant characteristics of a job applicant; do the selection tests employed really measure what they were intended to measure; are interview impressions consistent and valid indicators of the person's future capabilities on the job; and so on).

Representing uncertainty

Historically, uncertainty, whether within the environment or within the mind of the decision-maker, has been characterised using one of two very general concepts: *probability* or *correlation.* These two representations differ in terms of the type of uncertainty they address. *Probability* addresses the question regarding which of several possible outcomes our information is pointing to whereas *correlation* addresses the question of causal ambiguity and redundancy with respect to how different sources of information are related. Thus probability quantifies or characterises the likelihood of a specific outcome (e.g., chance of rain today) and correlation quantifies or characterises the relationship between two types of information (e.g., the relationship between quality of one's personal grooming and his or her intelligence).

The probabilistic representation of uncertainty

The *probabilistic* representation of uncertainty is at least somewhat familiar to many people through vehicles such as media reports of weather forecasts (e.g., 20% chance of rain tomorrow), medical dangers (e.g., 5 times more likely to contract lung cancer if exposed to passive smoking than if not exposed), and social issues (e.g., teenagers have a 35% greater chance of dying in road accidents through drink driving). Probability and risk are typically quantified using a scale ranging from **0.0** (impossibility) to **1.0** (complete certainty) with respect to the occurrence of a particular event. However, behavioural scientists (for example, Anderson, Deane, Hammond, McClelland, & Shanteau, 1981) further distinguish between *objective probability* and *subjective probability*. Goodwin and Wright (2004, Chapter 4) provide a very complete discussion of issues related to the use of probabilities in decision making.

Objective probabilities are based on empirical counting of events and are always quantified on the 0.0 to 1.0 continuum described above. Objective probabilities can be explicitly attached to all decision outcomes under consideration such that (1) the probabilities of different mutually exclusive events can be added (e.g., the probability of rolling a four or a six on a fair die is equal to the probability of a four plus the probability of a six); and (2) the probabilities for all the mutually exclusive and exhaustive events in a set of interest add up to 1.0 (i.e., it is virtually certain that one of the events in the set will occur; e.g., the probability of no rain plus the probability of rain will add to 1.0).

Subjective probabilities are based on human judgement and represent a person's beliefs about the likelihood of events. Philosophers and mathematicians through the centuries have quibbled over fine details in the meaning of subjective probability but what is important for us is the idea that, unlike objective probabilities, subjective probabilities have no necessary link to empirical reality or even to logical sets of events. Subjective probabilities are often not explicitly quantified, but are represented in ordinary language using phrases like "reasonable doubt", "highly likely", "possible", "good chance", or "almost impossible". To illustrate the objective/subjective distinction, consider the following illustration. It would be one thing for a school counsellor to tell a parent that son Johnny had a 30% achievement rate based on an accurate recording and evaluation of the number of assessment tasks he passed or failed through the year (an objective probability of his achievement success). It would be another thing entirely for the counsellor to say that Johnny was fairly unlikely to achieve well at school next year based upon his or her (the counsellor's) perceptions of how Johnny had performed in the past (a subjective probability of achievement success). It would be quite important for the parents to know which form of probability was being put forward by the school counsellor before they decided whether or not Johnny needed to be moved to a school for children with special needs.

The correlational representation of uncertainty
While the correlational representation of uncertainty is less widely known, we implicitly employ such a representation in making many decisions and judgements. *Correlation* is a statistical concept that refers to the extent to which two sets of measures are interrelated or associated. For example, it may be useful to know how the price of automobiles is related to manufacturing quality. Current issues that involve an implicit expression of uncertainty using a correlational representation include: whether there is a relationship between passive smoking and increased risk of heart disease, asthma, or lung cancer; whether uncontrolled access to guns leads to more violent crime, and whether there is a relationship between Australian immigration rates and the unemployment rate for young Australians.

A *positive* association or correlation ($\uparrow\uparrow$) is observed when the quantity of one indicator tends to increase when the quantity of a second indicator increases (e.g., greater exposure to passive smoking is associated with higher risk of lung and heart problems). A *negative* association or correlation ($\downarrow\uparrow$) is observed when the quantity of one indicator tends to decrease when the quantity of a second indicator increases (e.g., lower interest rates for mortgages associated with larger numbers of houses being sold in the real estate market). No association or correlation ($\uparrow\rightarrow$) exists if the quantities of both indicators exhibit no systematic tendency to vary with each other (e.g., interest rate levels for mortgages would have no statistical relationship to a person's level of exposure to passive smoking).

Correlation may be assessed objectively, usually through explicit research efforts, and this results in an explicit quantification along a scale ranging from −1.0 (a perfect negative or inverse relationship: $\downarrow\uparrow$ and $\uparrow\downarrow$) through 0.0 (no relationship: $\uparrow\rightarrow$) to +1.0 (perfect positive relationship: $\uparrow\uparrow$ and $\downarrow\downarrow$). Correlation may also be subjectively assessed through beliefs that a relationship exists (e.g., the belief that a very sloppily dressed person will not make a good executive suggests that grooming quality and the likelihood of becoming a good executive are positively correlated). Note that a subjective correlation assessment is closely related to the bias problem encountered with the use of the representativeness heuristic when single events become causally connected in our brains as a result of our experiences – we then use that 'connection' to help make future decisions (e.g., deciding not to walk under a ladder, to say "G'day" to someone, or not to hire someone).

Quality of information
The quality of information is an ever-present problem for people who have to make a decision or render a judgement. This is because poor quality information will lead to poor quality decisions whereas good quality information will at least have the opportunity to facilitate achieving a good decision. We will see that the concept of information 'quality' for decision-making has several important aspects.

One important aspect of information quality is *validity*. Validity refers to whether or not the information available to us is measuring what it is claimed or believed to measure. Thus, validity bears on the question of how accurate our information is. For example, in making a decision whether or not to purchase a new dessert product which claims to be "No Fat", you may observe that the label on the product says "0 grams of fat". However, it may be the case that this actually means no fat has been added to the product beyond what it naturally possesses. If this is the case, then the measure of "0 grams of fat" is invalid because it does not reflect what you think it reflects. Your decision might be entirely different depending upon which interpretation you attach to this bit of information. Also consider whether or not it is the case that the price of a good reflects its quality. If this is true, then we would say that price is a valid indicator of product quality. However, if this is not true, then price is not a valid indicator of product quality; it may instead be a valid indicator of some other product characteristic (e.g., demand for the product, the prestige value of the brand, or the public image of the retail outlet selling the product, for example).

A second important aspect of information quality is its *reliability*. Reliability refers to whether or not the information at hand is consistent and would therefore be very similar or the same no matter where or when we obtained it. For example, suppose that I read, in two different consumer magazines, that the new Toyota Camry gets 30.1 miles per gallon and 30.4 miles per gallon, respectively, during a standard road test on the same test track. I might then consider this to be reliable information that may be useful in helping me make a purchase decision (since it may be important to me to purchase an economical car). However, I read one magazine that reports 30.1 miles per gallon and another reports 22.7 miles per gallon on the same track under the same conditions. I might then wonder about the reliability of this measure and therefore doubt its utility in helping me decide whether or not to buy the car.

A third important aspect of information quality emerges from the social aspect of gathering information, namely, its *credibility*. This characteristic arises in situations where information is transmitted interpersonally. With socially communicated information, a myriad of factors can influence how seriously we take the information as reported. These factors can be things such as: how close I am to the information provider (e.g., close friend, acquaintance, or stranger); my perception of the provider's expertise in the area they are offering information; the provider's persuasiveness in convincing me of the validity of their information; and my past experience with the person as a provider of useful information for my decisions. Any or all of these factors may play a role in influencing my attentiveness to the information being provided.

The quality of information for decision making is often influenced by various contextual factors. For example, the type of information that is available is a critical determinant of information quality. Psychological information about behaviours, such as aggressiveness or satisfaction, is typically more variable in quality than physically verifiable information, such as automobile mileage or blood pressure. Another contextual factor is the medium of communication, whether by magazine or newspaper, oral conversation, Internet, TV or radio. Other contextual factors include: the form the information takes (e.g., pictorial image versus statistical data versus spoken or written word); the amount of time available for gathering accurate information (as opposed to estimates or guesses); the cost of acquiring "good" information; and the technology available for acquiring "good" information. Limitations in any of these areas may reduce information quality as well as quantity. When this happens, decision quality frequently suffers.

Other People Associated with the Judgement or Decision

Frequently, the judgements or decisions made by a person are made in the context of other people, either those who stand to be affected by the decision or those who are collaborating with the person to actually make the decision. We will focus primarily upon decisions that are made within a group context, whether the group is a family unit (e.g., husband and wife, parents and children), a social unit (e.g., a club or sports team) or a work- or service-based unit (e.g., Board of Directors, department or committee, jury).

One critical question concerns when a decision or judgement should be made by a group as opposed to leaving it in the hands of an individual. People seldom actually consider this question but it is worthwhile pursuing. Generally speaking, a group-based decision is preferable when many competing interests must be addressed in the decision, when the expected outcome from the group exceeds what any one individual could reasonably achieve, when the decision needs wide acceptance, or when the risks of error must be carefully weighed through argument and analysis. However, in many cases, groups do not make better decisions than their individual members would by deciding alone. This is because scant attention is paid to the fact that groups are social interactions that need to be explicitly well handled and managed if they are to produce useful outcomes. Most people have, at one time or another, been involved in a group process which seemed to go nowhere or to be chasing its own tail without achieving anything – certainly a frustrating and wasteful experience. Managing the group decision process requires some understanding of group dynamics.

Group dynamics and self-interest

Group dynamics focus on changes in the behaviour patterns of individuals when they attempt to work together in a group. To make a decision group work effectively, each group member must, in their own mind, evaluate and come to some satisfactory position regarding the following trade-off: how far will they go to meet the group's needs and desires and how strongly do they wish to pursue their own needs and desires. Most groups, whether they be work-related or family-oriented, have to contend with issues of leadership and power (and perhaps politics), communication, expectations (what group members expect from themselves and what they expect from the other members), how clear the group's goals are to each member, expected norms for behaviour within the group (norms are expected ways of behaving and may be reflected in behaviours such as modes of dress, timeliness to meetings, meeting procedures) and how various tasks are to be divided up between the members. Clearly, there is a lot involved in simply making groups function well before they can actually get down to making a decision. If a group spends all of its time arguing about who should lead, or perform which tasks, or which goals to pursue, it will have little capacity or energy left to pursue anything but highly intuitive decision making. When this happens, one individual is better off making the decision him or herself! Good leadership can help the group to negotiate its way through these problems as long as the leader can exhibit behaviours (including decision styles) that meet the group's expectations and needs.

Janis (1989, and earlier, Janis & Mann, 1977) produced a useful schema within which to view group decision behaviour in a realistic fashion. Figure 13.4 summarises Janis' perspective that involves group members treading fine lines of balance between three competing sets of constraining pressures (*egocentric constraints, cognitive constraints,* and *affiliative constraints*) in their pursuit of a quality group decision under uncertain and ambiguous circumstances. Cognitive constraints generally centre on issues arising from the interplay between the Cognitive Continuum and the Decision Task Continuum. Egocentric constraints focus on pressures within each member to meet their own needs. Affiliative constraints focus on internal and external pressures on each group member to meet the needs of the group itself. These constraints, if ignored or left to exert a strong influence, can negatively impact on and even corrupt a group's decision processes, leading to poor and even questionable decisions (you may be able to identify examples where this has occurred in recent media stories about decision making in NASA, local city councils and boards of directors of companies like Enron and HIH). Group decision making must therefore be a well-managed process in order for the balance between these competing constraints to be sensitively and fairly achieved and their power to influence the decision process reduced or at least controlled.

Group decision quality will tend to increase as the quality of the management of group dynamics increases. Certain situational factors, if they can be controlled, will contribute to this achievement. For example, the larger the group, the less likely it will be that it can achieve effective functioning, so groups with more than 3 people but fewer than 8 people will tend to have the best chance of working through their dynamics effectively. Generally speaking, groups that are cohesive (form a common bond, share common goals, and have a strong identity as a *group*) tend to be more effective than groups that are not cohesive (however, we will see later that too much cohesion is also not desirable!). In many cases, a group comprised of members from different backgrounds possessing a variety of skills will be more effective in making decisions, particularly where creative and/or complex rather than simple routine decisions are needed, than a group that has a more homogeneous membership.

Figure 13.4 *Irving Janis' constraints perspective on group decision behaviour (adapted from Janis, 1989, p.16).*

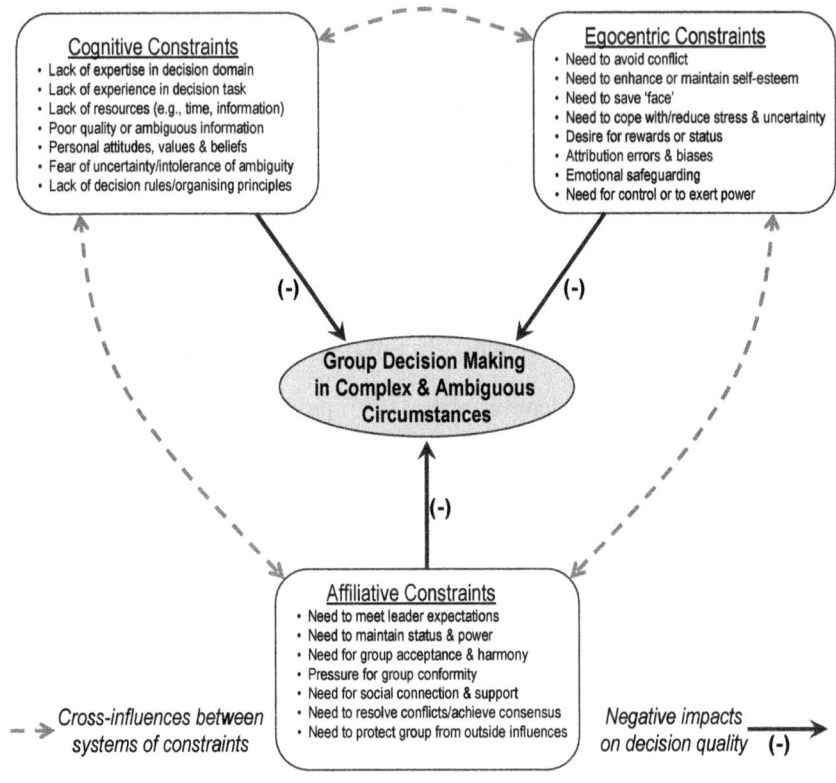

Groupthink
Janis (1983, 1989) is also well known for his identification and subsequent theoretical explanation of a phenomenon of group decision making called *groupthink*. Groupthink is a defective group decision process associated with very highly cohesive groups charged with making potentially high impact decisions (in terms of costs and number of people potentially affected). Janis and others have identified groupthink problems associated with some of the major decision fiascoes

of the 20th century including the Bay of Pigs invasion of Cuba by the USA during John Kennedy's presidency, the fatal launching of the space shuttle Challenger, and the escalation of the Vietnam conflict. However, evidence of groupthink can be seen in less prominent more localised decisions as well.

The characteristics to look for in a group at risk of succumbing to groupthink include: a highly cohesive group; a strong group leader; pressure to achieve a particular solution; an unstructured group process; and a narrow perceived range of possible solutions. This does not mean that all groups exhibiting such characteristics will succumb to groupthink, but their risk is certainly higher. When a group does succumb to groupthink, certain symptomatic behaviours and attitudes can be observed. For example, the group will tend to believe it is on the high moral ground and therefore invulnerable to criticism of its decisions. The group will tend to develop a strong sense of an "us versus them" mentality when considering new information, that is, only information from "insiders" is seriously considered; information from "outsiders" is routinely discounted or ignored.

Groups exhibiting groupthink also tend to bring strong social pressures (e.g., threatened expulsion from the group, marginalising or publicly abusing/ridiculing the offending member) to bear on members who express their dissent from the direction the group is heading. Coupled with this development, certain members of the group may become "self-appointed mind guards" for the leader and act to shield the leader from negative information and opinions which do not agree with the leader's expressed preferences. Group members will also tend to censor (deliberately withhold expression of) their own dissenting opinions and, as a result, the group forms an illusory perception of its own unanimity of perspective (the work of the "mind guards" may also contribute to this perception).

If these symptoms collectively begin to emerge, problems are likely to occur because information search will be very restrictive and selective, all possible options will not be explored, viable options will not be thoroughly evaluated, the status quo will not be challenged, and there will be poor planning for contingencies. It is perhaps easy to see why the groups which are most at risk from groupthink are those highly placed groups that exercise a good deal of power, have strong leadership present, and are prestigious groups to belong to (such as Boards of Directors of companies, Presidential or Prime Ministerial cabinets, executive advisory committees, local government councils, and specially established task forces such as organisational committees for international events such as the Olympics).

It is possible to set up certain group processes to reduce the risk of groupthink. For example, the group leader can encourage the expression of creative and divergent views while deliberately withhold expressing his or her preferred views so that the group will not prematurely converge on his or her preferred view as the way to go. This tactic also effectively sabotages any self-appointed mind guards as well since they don't know what position they are protecting. The group can create a special role of devil's advocate, perhaps rotating this role to different group members at different meetings, whose job it is to critically question every important aspect of the group's thinking and information processing. Information from a diverse range of outside groups can be sought and the group can explicitly plan for contingencies if the final decision is not correct or workable. Finally, the group can set up a final "last chance" review session (perhaps a day or two after making their decision) before implementing their decision in order to critically revisit the decision one more time with respect to its appropriateness. This provides a final opportunity to head off a potentially erroneous decision while affording group members time to cool down from the typical emotional high of achieving a tough decision and regain a more 'rational' perspective.

Common Decision Making Traps

There are several common traps that a person may stumble into if sufficient care is not taken during a decision or judgement process. Russo and Schoemaker (1989) have outlined ten such decision traps that, not coincidentally, happen to integrate many of the issues discussed earlier in this chapter. They did this, not to show how flawed humans are at making decisions, but to indicate where changes might be made to improve the quality of one's decisions and judgements. Figure 13.5 presents a mind map of the ten common decision traps identified by Russo and Schoemaker. Notice that the traps are grouped according to where, in Russo and Schoemaker's system of four decision making stages, each trap is most likely to be encountered.

Often it is the case that stumbling into one or more decision traps occurs because of pressures from competing forces within the decision context, influences of others on the decision process, and/or conflicts between information sources. In short, the traps snare individuals as they slip around between the demands of rational decision processes and the very real experiential demands of simply getting to the point of reaching a decision so that other tasks may be accomplished. The more uncertainty, stress and pressure associated with a decision, the more likely it will be that an individual or a group will fall into one or more of the decision traps.

Making Better Decisions

Regardless of the traps and pitfalls that potentially confront any decision-maker, it is possible to improve human judgement and decision making. It is not hard to see that education and training can potentially play a role in assisting people to improve their decision processes. As a general technique, training can serve to educate people as to the potential traps which await the naive decision-maker, alert them to possible biases in their own decision processes, and suggest possible ways in which they might avoid these limitations (hopefully, this chapter has begun this educational process for you!). If a person must estimate probabilities as a part of some decision to be made, he or she can be taught to produce more accurate estimates, even if they are subjective. Often, people can be taught to learn better from their own experiences; in other words, people can be shown how to benefit more profitably from any feedback which flows from decisions they have made. This clearly has implications for helping decision-makers avoid the final three decision traps described in Figure 13.5.

Figure 13.5. Mind map of the ten common decision traps identified by Russo and Schoemaker (1989)a.

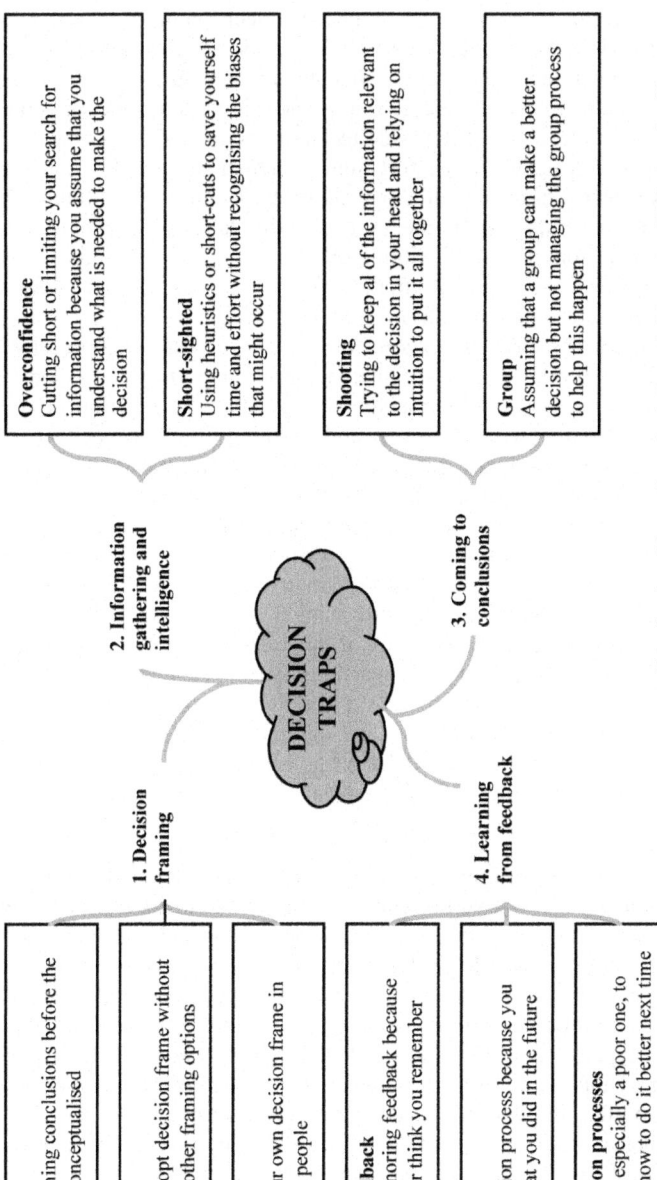

Overconfidence
Cutting short or limiting your search for information because you assume that you understand what is needed to make the decision

Short-sighted
Using heuristics or short-cuts to save yourself time and effort without recognising the biases that might occur

Shooting
Trying to keep al of the information relevant to the decision in your head and relying on intuition to put it all together

Group
Assuming that a group can make a better decision but not managing the group process to help this happen

2. Information gathering and intelligence

3. Coming to conclusions

DECISION TRAPS

1. Decision framing

4. Learning from feedback

Plunging in
Getting information and framing conclusions before the decision has been properly conceptualised

Frame blindness
Using a simple or easy-to-adopt decision frame without thinking about or looking at other framing options

Lack of frame control
Uncritically letting go of your own decision frame in favour of the frames of other people

Fooling yourself about feedback
Incorrectly interpreting or ignoring feedback because you are protecting yourself or think you remember

Not keeping track
Not documenting your decision process because you think you will remember what you did in the future

Failure to audit your decision processes
Not revisiting your decision, especially a poor one, to review it and possibly learn how to do it better next time

aLoosely adapted from a discussion in Russo & Schoemaker (1989), pp. xvi-xviii.

Many specific techniques for improving decision making are procedural in nature - describing an explicit series of steps or procedures for the decision process to follow. Other techniques are technological in nature – employing computer software systems to support the decision-maker in various tasks undertaken during the decision process. No matter what technique or procedure is employed, the goal of any system designed to support human judgement and decision making is to help move decision-making thinking along the Cognitive Continuum away from intuition toward analysis. Some systems will do this by providing a specific rational framework to work within; other systems will do this by helping the decision-maker manage the information that has been assembled and also, perhaps, to help him or her integrate that information to reach a decision. Thus, if we refer back to the four essential aspects of the decision process identified by Russo and Schoemaker (1989), we can see that decision support systems and devices are designed to assist decision-makers during the Information Gathering and Intelligence, Coming to Conclusions, and Learning from Feedback stages.

However, one danger of decision support systems and procedures is that they will often require the decision-maker to frame or structure the decision in a certain specific way, often using highly quantified objective or subjective information. This is so the decision process can be displayed as a decision tree, hierarchical network, or an attribute-alternatives matrix and so that integration, using mathematical computation, of the information can be performed to produce a final recommended choice. The drawback of this requirement of many decision support systems is that it risks leading the decision-maker to give up control over their own framing of the problem and thereby force-fit the problem into a pre-determined structure which may or may not be appropriate. It is therefore important to maintain control over how the decision problem is being framed, and then select the tool or technique that best suits that way of framing the problem.

Creativity

Bazerman (2006) argued that one way to improve people's judgement and decision making is to foster creative thinking at various stages of the decision process. He calls this use of creativity "assumption-breaking" and suggests that it is an essential process for forcing people to think beyond the boundaries of the problem, to consider other ways of framing the problem, and to seek information that goes against one's preferred options or that contradicts what the person believes is true. Often this type of creative thinking takes the form of asking "devil's advocate" or "Doubting Thomas" kinds of questions which then stimulates a process of seeking answers to allay the doubts and concerns. For example, to avoid over-relying on certain mental heuristics, I could ask myself questions like "is there really a relationship between car price and manufacturing quality?", "am I overly relying on past experiences which are easiest for me to remember or visualise?", or "have I sufficiently revised my initial impression of person X in light of the new information I have encountered?". Obviously, creative thinking takes time and mental effort, so the viability of such thinking must be judged within the specific contextual constraints one is working under. However, the gains are frequently worth the extra time and effort, especially if a high risk decision with potential long term effects is being made, and the exercise is typically fun as well. Proctor (2005) provides a rich resource compendium of methods and techniques for stimulating creativity in problem solving and decision making.

Procedures for improving decision-making
I will illustrate two simple decision support methodologies that can be used to help improve decision making. One method is called *Prudential Algebra* and the other is called *Criteria Testing*. There are a large number of other decision support procedures and computer software systems and you can explore by reading some other sources such as Cooksey (1997), Hammond, Keeney, and Riaffa (1998), Hogarth (1987), Brown (2005), Proctor (2005) and Senge, Kleiner, Roberts, Ross, and Smith (1994) or visiting an online resource like http://www.decisionarium.tkk.fi/. One thing to remember is that the purpose of any decision support system is to assist decision-makers, not to replace them!

Prudential Algebra
Prudential algebra (see Hammond et al., 1998, for a description) is a simple procedure for improving decision making, originally invented by Benjamin Franklin in 1772 in a letter written in response to a plea for help from British scientist Joseph Priestley concerning how to make an important decision. The procedure works as well today as it did in Ben Franklin's day and has the chief benefit of forcing one to take a more methodical and analytical look at the decision to be made. Prudential Algebra is a process where the Pros and Cons for each of several possible actions/decisions are listed and evaluated for importance. Write a specific alternative action to take or option to choose from at the top of an A4 page and divide the page into two columns, one column labelled PROS (or UPSIDE) and the other labelled CONS (or DOWNSIDE). Create as many such pages as you have alternatives or options to choose from (a two alternative decision problem is illustrated in Figure 13.6).

Figure 13.6 *Illustration of the Prudential Algebra decision support Procedure A.*

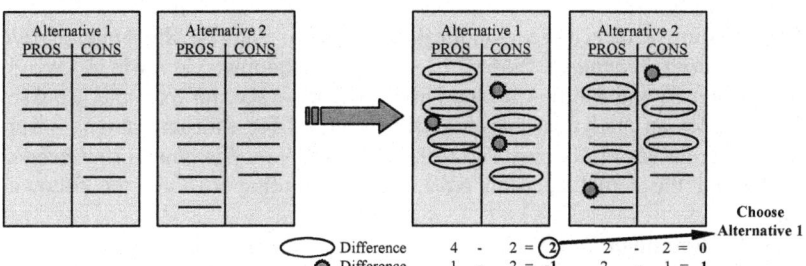

1. For the first alternative, list all of the reasons that would support the choice of this alternative in the PROS column. These reasons may include beneficial consequences, resource implications, and any other criteria that have a positive association with this alternative. In a similar fashion, list all of the reasons that argue against choosing this alternative in the CONS column. Once these two lists have been completed, move onto to consider the next alternative and proceed in the same fashion until *all* alternatives have their PROS and CONS columns completed. Feel free to add to previous lists if subsequent ideas arise.
2. Now, focusing on each alternative in turn, look through the list of PROS and **circle** those reasons that are most important or critical to the decision in your view and **star** those reasons that are of moderate importance; any remaining

reasons in the column can be considered to be of minor or no importance. Do the same for the reasons in the CONS column. Repeat this process for all alternatives.

3. Finally, there are two ways you can proceed from here for each alternative. Procedure A (illustrated in Figure 13.6) is simpler, but less precise; Procedure B is more precise but also more complicated. The final choice of procedure will depend upon your preferences.

– *For each alternative*: Count up the number of **circled** reasons and the number of **starred** reasons in the PROS list and subtract, from these numbers, the number of **circled** reasons and the number of **starred** reasons, respectively, in the CONS list. Notice that more preferable alternatives will tend to have larger positive differences and less preferable alternatives will have very low positive differences, zero differences, or perhaps negative differences. The final choice can be made by comparing the differences obtained from this procedure across the different alternatives. The basic rule is to choose, as the preferred option, that alternative which has the *largest positive difference* for **circled** reasons. If two or more alternatives are tied with respect to **circled** reasons, choose on the basis of the *largest positive difference* for the **starred** reasons.

– *For each alternative*: weight (by quantifying) each **circled** reason in both the PROS and CONS lists as 3, each **starred** reason as 2, and each unmarked reason as 1. Add up all of the numbers in the PROS column and all of the numbers in the CONS and subtract the CONS total from the PROS total. The basic rule is to choose, as the preferred option, that alternative which has the *largest positive difference* between the PROS total and the CONS total.

Criteria Testing.

Criteria Testing (other more complicated variations include the *Simple Multi-Attribute Rating Technique* (SMART – see, for example, Goodwin & Wright, 2004, Chapter 3) and Multi-Attribute Utility Theory – see, for example, Cooksey, 2000) provides an analytical and defensible method for choosing among several possible alternatives or actions. The technique requires a *flip chart* or *whiteboard* for recording the actual decision table. Criteria Testing involves the following steps:

Step 1 - Establish and Weight Criteria for the Decision: In this stage, you must decide which criteria will be used to evaluate each alternative course of action. Try to keep the number of criteria to seven or less. Make sure you have a clear idea of what each criterion means. Write each criterion down the first column of a ruled table as shown in Table 13.1. Finally, decide how important each criterion is to the overall decision by taking 100 points and dividing them up amongst the criteria in accordance with their perceived importance. These points become criteria weights and should be written in a column beside each criterion in the decision table. If you decide that all criteria are equally important, then no weights need be written in the table.

Table 13.1 *Illustration of Criteria Testing for choosing amongst three applicants for an accounting position*

| Criteria | Select an Applicant for an Accounting Position | | | | SENSITIVITY ANALYSIS WITH REVISED WEIGHTS |
	Weight	Applicant A	Applicant B	Applicant C	
Prior Experience	30	50	70	100	25
Accounting Skills	30	90	60	75	25
Interpersonal Skills	15	100	40	65	25
Education	15	90	100	50	25

Recalculate:

- Preference for Applicant A: (30x50)+(30*90)+(15*100)+(15*90) = **7050**   8350

- Preference for Applicant B: (30x70)+(30*60)+(15*40)+(15*100) = 6000   6750

- Preference for Applicant C: (30x100)+(30*75)+(15*65)+(15*50) = 6975   7250

Decision maximizing preference: **Hire Applicant A   Still hire Applicant A**

Step 2 - Develop the Alternatives: Write the various alternatives being considered across the top of the decision table as shown in Table 13.1. Try to ensure that you have a clear understanding of what each alternative entails. While Criteria Testing can theoretically be applied to any number of alternatives, it works more effectively if just a short list of the most viable alternatives is evaluated.

Step 3 - Evaluate Alternatives Against Criteria: There are two methods by which alternatives can be evaluated in the decision table.

- **Rating Method** (illustrated in Table 13.1): Decide, for each criterion, how alternatives will be assessed against it using simple arbitrary 1 to 10 rating scales where 1 anchors the lowest point on the scale (Low, Easy, Short, Bad, Poor, Worst, A Little, etc) and 10 anchors the highest point on the scale (High, Hard, Long, Good, Excellent, A lot, best, etc.). Next, rate each alternative on each criterion using these 1 to 10 scales and write the rating in the appropriate place in the decision table. Use whatever information is to hand to make your ratings.

- **Ranking Method**: In this method, ranks from 1 up to the number of alternatives being assessed are used (e.g., if five alternatives are being assessed, then the ranks used are 1, 2, 3, 4, and 5). For each criterion, decide which alternative is best on that criterion, assign the highest rank (e.g., 5) to it, and write this rank in the appropriate place in the decision table; assign the next best alternative on the criterion the next highest rank (4), and so on down to the alternative which is worst on the criterion which receives the rank of 1. Repeat this ranking process for all criteria.

Step 4 - Aggregate Criteria Evaluations to Reach Final Choice: Irrespective of the method (Rating or Ranking) used in step 3, this aggregation step is run in the same way. If all *criteria were assumed to be of equal importance*, then simply add the criterion scores for each alternative up and write the sum in the appropriate spot in the final column of the decision table. *If the criteria have different importance weights attached to them*, first multiply each criterion score by the appropriate weight for that criterion (shown in parentheses in Table 13.1), then add up all the resulting values and write the weighted sum in the appropriate spot in the final column of the decision table. The decision rule, then, is straightforward: *choose, as the preferred alternative, that which has the **highest** sum or weighted sum in the final column* (see **circled** value in Table 13.1.

Step 5 - Conduct sensitivity analysis: Irrespective of the evaluation method used, it is a good idea to systematically vary some of the numbers in the Table (e.g., vary the weightings of the criteria, as shown at the right-side of Table 13.1). Then recalculate the preferences for each alternative. If your preferred alternative remains the same, then your decision is robust against fuzziness in your numbers. If small changes in your numbers suggest different choices, then your decision is very sensitive to the weights and/or ratings/rankings you used. If this occurs, you will need to try to develop more precision in your numbers. The SMART version of this method provides one such approach to enhancing precision (see, Goodwin & Wright, 2004, Chapter 3).

REFERENCES

Anderson, B. F., Deane, D. H. Hammond, K. R., McClelland, G. H., & Shanteau, J. C. (1981). *Concepts in judgment and decision research: Definitions, sources, interrelations, comments.* New York: Praeger Scientific.

Bazerman, M. H. (2006). *Judgment in managerial decision making* (6th Ed.). New York: John Wiley & Sons.

Beach, L. R. & Connolly, T. (2005). *The psychology of decision making: People in organizations,* Thousand Oaks, CA: Sage Publications.

Brown, R. (2005). *Rational choice and judgment: Decision analysis for the decider.* Hoboken, NJ: John Wiley & Sons.

Cooksey, R. W. (2000). Managerial judgment and decision making, in S.B Dahiya (Ed.), *The current state of business disciplines: Volume 5 – Management II.* Rohtak, India: Spellbound Publications, 2121-2158.

Cooksey, R. W. (1997). *Systems thinking and group problem solving/decision making tools and techniques: A resource collection.* Unpublished compendium, School of Business, Economics & Public Policy, University of New England, Armidale, NSW, Australia. [A copy is available from the author on request.]

Cooksey, R. W. (1996). *Judgment analysis: Theory, methods, and applications.* San Diego: Academic Press.

Epstein, S. (2008). Intuition from the perspective of Cognitive-Experiential Self-Theory, in H. Plessner, C. Betsch & T. Betsch (Eds.), *Intuition in judgment and decision making,* New York: Lawrence Erlbaum Associates, 23-37.

Goodwin, P., & Wright, G. (2004). *Decision analysis for management judgment* (3rd Ed.). Chichester, UK: John Wiley & Sons.

Hogarth, R. M. (1987). *Judgement and choice: The psychology of decision* (2nd Ed.). Chichester, UK: John Wiley & Sons.

Hammond, K. R. (2007). *Beyond rationality: The search for wisdom in a troubled time.* New York: Oxford University Press.

Hammond, K. R. (1996). *Human judgment and social policy: Irreducible uncertainty, inevitable error, unavoidable injustice.* New York: Oxford University Press.

Janis, I. (1983). *Groupthink: Psychological studies of policy decisions and fiascoes.* Boston: Houghton Mifflin.

Janis, I. (1989). *Crucial decisions: Leadership in policymaking and crisis management.* New York: The Free Press.

Janis, I., & Mann, L. (1977). *Decision making: A psychological analysis of conflict, choice, and commitment.* New York: The Free Press.

Johnson, G. (1995). *Monkey business: Why the way you manage is a million years out of date.* Aldershot, UK: Gower Publishing.

Kahneman, D., Slovic, P., & Tversky, A. (Eds.). (1982). *Judgment under uncertainty: Heuristics and biases*. Cambridge: Cambridge University Press.

Kleindorfer, P. R., Kunreuther, H. C., & Schoemaker, P. J. H. (1993). *Decision sciences: An integrated perspective*. New York: Cambridge University Press.

Lichtenstein, S. & Slovic, P. (Eds.). (2006). *The construction of preference*. New York: Cambridge University Press.

Newell, B. R., Lagnado, D. A. & Shanks, D. R. (2007). *Straight choices: The psychology of decision making*, Hove, UK: Psychology Press.

Plous, S. (1993). *The psychology of judgment and decision making*. New York: McGraw-Hill.

Proctor, T. (2005). *Creative problem solving for managers: Developing skills for decision making and innovation*, London: Routledge.

Reece, B. L., & Brandt, R. (1996). *Effective human relations in organizations* (6th Ed.). Geneva, IL: Houghton Mifflin.

Rowe, A. J., & Mason, R. O. (1987). *Managing with style: A guide to understanding, assessing, and improving decision making*. San Francisco: Jossey-Bass.

Rowe, A. J., & Boulgarides, J. (1992). *Managerial decision making*. New York: Macmillan.

Russo, J. E., & Schoemaker, P. J. H. (1989). *Confident decision making: How to make the right decision every time*. London: Piatkus.

Senge, P., Kleiner, A., Roberts, C., Ross, R., & Smith, B. (1994). *The fifth discipline fieldbook*. London: Nicholas Brealey.

Zsambok, C. E., & Klein, G. (Eds.). (1997). *Naturalistic decision making*. Mahwah, NJ: Lawrence Erlbaum Associates.

Review Questions

Read the following statements and indicate whether they are *True* or *False*.

1. The validity of information for making a decision indicates its consistency from one source to another.

2. The fact that I may decide not to go on an ocean cruise because I recently heard about large ferry sinking in Sydney Harbour would indicate I am relying on the availability heuristic.

3. A group whose members constantly seek a range of opinions and information from outside the group in order to converge on a decision would be said to be exhibiting a groupthink process.

4. The Cognitive Continuum is most useful for showing that analytical thinking is the most preferred mode of thinking for decision making.

5. If I were to rely very heavily on my own memory and attempt to integrate the information I have available in my head rather than using a systematic approach, I would be at risk of stumbling into the "Shooting from the Hip" decision trap.

6. Of the four facets of adult judgement and decision making, the decision context is the most critical facet.

7. One important role for a decision support system is to assist the decision-maker in integrating information to come to a decision.

8. Alan Rowe's approach to describing decision styles attempts to describe styles in terms of both values orientation and cognitive complexity.

9. The chief difference between the probabilistic representation of uncertainty and the correlational representation is that correlations focus on associations between indicators whereas probabilities focus on single outcomes.

10. In group decision making, the really tough problem is balancing egocentric, affiliative and cognitive constraints.

11. One key reason that the Decision Task Continuum is such an important concept is that it reflects the idea that decision contexts can actually influence the way we think about decisions and judgements.

12. If I say that it is quite likely that I will need to stay home from work because I have a fever of 40 degrees Celsius, I am employing an objective probability assessment.

13. Suppose that early in the school year, I attend a meeting with my second grade daughter's teacher and come away from the meeting thinking that the teacher is harsh and uncaring. Between this visit and one later in the school year, my daughter periodically tells me that her teacher is great and fun. If, however, after the second meeting with the teacher, I still think she is harsh and uncaring, I would likely be reflecting a bias created by over-reliance on the representativeness heuristic.

14. Rational decision approaches are problematic because they make unrealistic assumptions about people.

15. If I believe that smart people are also good looking, my thinking is implicitly reflecting a positive correlation between intelligence and attractiveness.

16. If I like to be creative and broad-ranging in my thinking, I tend to think about the future rather than the past, and I prefer to focus on people rather than on tasks, I am probably exhibiting a Behavioural decision style.

Answers to Review Questions

1. *False*. Validity refers to aspects of the accuracy of information; that is, does a specific indicator or bit of information measure what it claims to measure.

2. *True*. Recent media exposure to specific events can change the subjective probabilistic expectation of that event occurring in future.

3. *False*. A key symptom of groupthink is observed when a group deliberately does not seek information from outside the group or, when it does have such information, seeks to discount it or devalue it so that the group's decision path toward the preferred choice remains unaffected.

4. *False*. A key feature of the Cognitive Continuum is that it reinforces the idea that there is no one best mode for thinking; what is best is what fits the decision task best.

5. *True*. Heavy reliance on mental juggling of information and intuitive integration of that information is a hallmark of the "Shooting from the Hip" decision trap.

6. *False*. All four aspects of decision making (*context, person, information,* and *other people*) are equally important to consider.

7. *True*. Many decision support systems are designed precisely to help the decision-maker accomplish the task of integrating information to arrive at a preferred choice.

8. *True*. These are the two key dimensions of the two-fold decision style classification system that Alan Rowe described.

9. *True*. Correlations assess uncertainty in relationships between information indicators whereas probabilities assess the likelihood of observing a single specific outcome or event from a set of possible outcomes or events.

10. *True*. This is precisely the point that Irving Janis' framework is trying to make – it shows just how difficult the task of making a group-based decision can be.

11. *True*. This is why the decision Task Continuum is so vital for us to understand – people don't just make decisions, they make decisions within a specific context under specific types of constraints and those contextual parameters and constraints influence the mode of thinking which is most adaptive for making the decision.

12. *False*. The assessment "quite likely" is a subjective probability assessment expressed in verbal terms. The temperature reading of 40 degrees Celsius is numerically precise but does not lead to a probability assessment.

13. *False*. This scenario describes an instance where reliance on the anchoring and adjustment heuristic has produced a biased judgement because an initial (negative) impression of the teacher was formed earlier and this impression was then insufficiently revised upon learning new information (daughter's views).

14. *True*. This is precisely why many people have difficulty accepting rational decision approaches.

15. *True*. A positive correlation measures the tendency for increases on one information indicator to be associated with increases on a second information indicator.

16. *False*. Creativity, broad-based thinking, future-oriented thinking and a preference to focus on people rather than tasks are hallmarks of the Conceptual decision style.

Exercises

Thought Problem.
Try auditing one of your own decisions, preferably a recent major one. In your personal audit, think about how various contextual, personal, group and information factors may have influenced the decision. Think about how the decision might have turned out if you had had more resources or a specific systematic approach available to help support you as you made the decision. If you had to make this decision again, or in the future, consider what you would do differently next time. You could try applying the Prudential Algebra or Criteria Testing to assist in your reflection here.

Locating Decision Problems along the Task Continuum.
For each task listed below, indicate where along the Continuum you would place the task (which means that you feel your thought processes would likely be working in that mode of thinking) by placing an **X** at that point. As you work, think about the types of information you would like to have in order to make the decision; also think about where, in making each decision, you might slip into a decision trap or over-rely on a mental heuristic. [**I** = Intuitive; **Q** = Quasi-rational; **A** = Analytical]

Example Tasks	I	Q	A	Comments
Balancing an account			----------------X	Debits, credits, expenses, assets, liabilities; available analytical rules for balancing accounts reduce the risk of relying on heuristics
Deciding whether or not you like a particular sculpture	X----------------			Rich and dense visual and tactile information, memories of other similar sculptures; risk of relying on representativeness heuristic

Decision Tasks

Deciding on a laundry soap to buy	-------------------		
Choosing which car to purchase	-------------------		
Forming a first impression of a new co-worker	-------------------		
Deciding who to vote for in an election	-------------------		
Deciding which DVD to rent for the evening	-------------------		
Deciding which school to send your child to	-------------------		
Judging the quality of an LCD or Plasma TV	-------------------		
Deciding whether you are pro- or anti-abortion [note this is a moral judgement]	-------------------		
Deciding whether or not to lie to protect a friend [another moral judgement]	-------------------		
Deciding if your child is ill enough to warrant a visit to a doctor	-------------------		

Identify your Decision Style Preferences.
The following task will help you make a preliminary and informal assessment of your most and least preferred decision styles. In this task, you need to think carefully about how you tend to approach decision tasks and judgement problems, either at home or at work. For each statement in the following list, circle the number you think most genuinely reflects the degree to which you feel the statement is like you. [**LL** = Least Like me; **SL** = Slightly Like me; **ML** = Moderately Like me; and **VL** = Very Like me]

	LL	SL	ML	VL
1. I expect quick results from people.	1	2	3	4
2. I make my decisions rapidly.	1	2	3	4
3. I rely on rules to guide my thinking.	1	2	3	4
4. I rely on intuitive thinking.	1	2	3	4
5. I prefer verbal information.	1	2	3	4
6. I enjoy solving problems.	1	2	3	4
7. I try to find the best answer to a problem.	1	2	3	4
8. I prefer numerical information.	1	2	3	4
9. I rely on logical thinking.	1	2	3	4
10. I need to be challenged by decision tasks.	1	2	3	4
11. I take a broad perspective when I decide.	1	2	3	4
12. I am creative in decision making.	1	2	3	4
13. I prefer to look to the future.	1	2	3	4
14. I prefer information in any form, numerical or verbal.	1	2	3	4
15. I like to involve people in my decisions.	1	2	3	4
16. I find it easy to empathise with people.	1	2	3	4
17. I prefer meetings to make decisions.	1	2	3	4
18. I am concerned for people in my decisions.	1	2	3	4
19. I don't like to deal with a lot of information.	1	2	3	4
20. I find it easy to communicate with people.	1	2	3	4

Building your Decision Style Profile.
To score yourself on the informal Decision Style scale, you first need to notice (if you hadn't already) that there were blocks of five questions, each focusing on a different style. Questions 1 to 5 focus on the **Directive** style; questions 6 to 10 focus on the **Analytical** style; questions 11 to 15 focus on the **Conceptual** style; and questions 16 to 20 focus on the **Behavioural** style. To score yourself on each style, simply add up your ratings for the five relevant questions; each score can have a minimum total of 5 and a maximum total of 20. Once you have the four totals, transfer them to the graph below, using a coloured dot to mark each total. Finally, connect the four dots with a line. The tallest peak on the graph will indicate your most preferred decision style and the lowest valley on the graph will indicate your least preferred style. It may be the case that you have two styles at nearly the same high level, in which case you have two dominant styles that you

may switch between as required by the decision context or your own perceptions regarding what appears to be needed.

Your Decision Style Profile

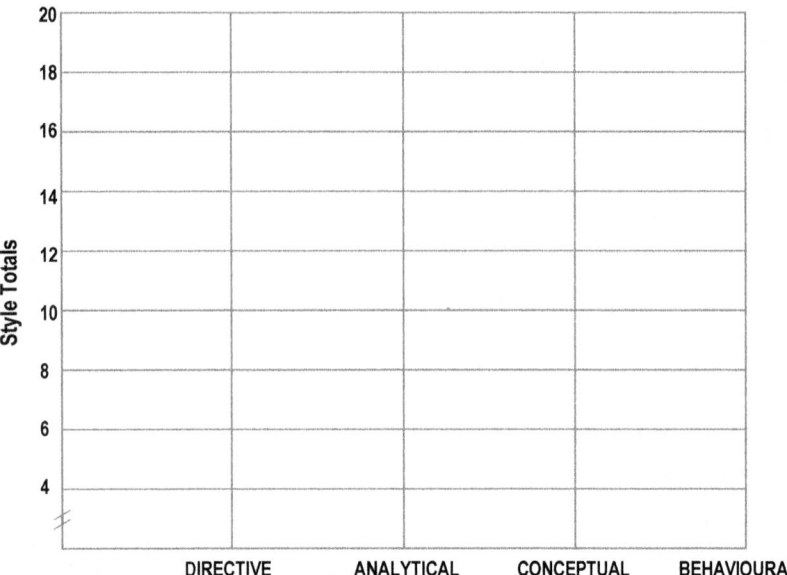

About the Author

Ray W. Cooksey is Professor of Organisational Behaviour and Decision Making in the School of Business, Economics and Public Policy at the University of New England. He has a PhD in psychology from Colorado State University and teaches in the MBA and Bachelor of Business programs at the University of New England. His teaching areas include organisational behaviour, managerial thinking and decision making, organisational research methods, quantitative and qualitative approaches to data analysis and organisational change. His research work focuses on human decision making in organisational, educational and other contexts, chaos and complexity theory applied to organisational behaviour and work performance, and applications of systems thinking and systems theory to organisational processes. He is the author of *Judgment Analysis: Theory, Methods, and Applications*, published by Academic Press in 1996 and *Illustrating Statistical Procedures: For Business, Behavioural and Social Science Research*, published by Tilde University Press in 2007.

Ray W. Cooksey
University of New England

GERARD J. FOGARTY

14. PRINCIPLES AND APPLICATIONS OF
EDUCATIONAL AND PSYCHOLOGICAL TESTING

The main aim of this chapter is to introduce the reader to the concept of testing and to the principles that underpin the practice of educational and psychological testing. The first part of this chapter is devoted to that aim. A second aim of the chapter is to examine applications of testing under the headings of educational, industrial, and clinical. Examples will be introduced from the author's own work to illustrate various applications. A final aim is to discuss some of the issues and controversies that surround the theory and practice of testing. By the end of the chapter, the reader should have an understanding of the techniques used in test validation and should be familiar with some of the main applications of educational and psychological tests.

PART A: TECHNICAL REQUIREMENTS OF TESTS

Definition of Tests

The word "test" refers to any systematic and standardised method of obtaining information about some aspect of human behaviour. The definition covers both educational and psychological tests and, to save space, the term "psychological test" will be used in most places in this chapter. A typical text book definition of a psychological test will usually cover the three defining characteristics (Murphy & Davidshofer, 1988):
- a psychological test is a sample of behaviour;
- the sample is obtained under standardised conditions; and

James A Athanasou (ed.), Adult Educational Psychology, 351–383

– there are established rules for scoring, or for obtaining quantitative (numeric) information from the behaviour sample.

Thus, a psychological test is a sample of behaviour taken under standardised and highly regimented situations. For example, in the case of a paper and pencil intelligence or personality test, there is usually a set of instructions that have to be followed for every administration of the test, a set of instructions to be followed by the examiner regarding scoring and interpretation, and a set of guidelines covering the use of test results. It is important to follow the instructions exactly, whether in the administration, scoring, or interpretation phase. Any deviation from the standard pattern may cause a change in the test-taker's behaviour that might not otherwise have occurred.

Apart from the aspect of standardisation, which is intended to ensure that everyone is treated in the same way, the definition given above also emphasises the fact that any test is just a sample of behaviour. If you grasp that simple fact, you will understand much about testing. The whole point of sampling in any field is to select manageable subsets of elements and draw conclusions about the whole set from the sample. Thus, a quality control inspector may take a fistful of components from a bin at the end of a production line and make inferences about the quality of the whole production process by looking at the components in his or her hand. The assumption underlying the sampling technique is that the characteristics of the whole set will be reflected in the sample. In a highly automated production line situation, where components are manufactured by machines, the sampling process is relatively straightforward. For many aspects of human behaviour, however, obtaining a representative sample of behaviour is usually very difficult. Constructs such as personality, intelligence, motivation, interests, values, and knowledge cannot be observed directly and are extremely complex in their own right. Yet it is mostly constructs such as these that form the subject of educational and psychological testing.

Given the difficulty of the subject matter, it should come as no surprise to learn that an elaborate technology has been built around the practice of testing to ensure that the behaviour sampled reflects the constructs in which we are interested and that the testing instruments themselves are up to the task of accurately sampling this behaviour. The branch of science concerned with the development of educational and psychological tests is known as psychometrics. As the term implies, the main task of psychometrics is to measure psychological entities, such as what we know, how we feel, and what we think. The full range of techniques used by psychometricians to measure these complex processes requires a sound grasp of some maths processes and of statistics. We do not need to worry about the more difficult techniques here. However, some of the basic concepts of psychometrics are straightforward and absolutely essential for an understanding of the principles of testing.

Key Technical Concepts in Educational and Psychological Testing

As stated above, the area of educational and psychological testing has become highly technical and specialised with its own terminology and techniques. The two most important terms are reliability and validity. There is usually no point in administering a test that has low reliability and validity. In order to explain the concepts of reliability and validity, however, we need to backtrack a little and introduce a statistic that is used to assess both reliability and validity and is also used in many other applications of testing. That statistic is the correlation coefficient.

Correlation Coefficients

The psychometric properties of tests are often evaluated in terms of correlation coefficients. A correlation coefficient can take values from +1.00 to -1.00. A correlation of 1.00 between any two tests means that they are perfectly related. If you knew how well a person performed on one test relative to the rest of the group taking the test, you would know exactly how well they performed on the other test. For example, if a person topped the group on the first test, a correlation of +1.00 necessarily implies that the person tops the group on the other test. Conversely, if the person was at the bottom of the first test, he or she would be at the bottom of the other test as well. You would not know the person's score, a correlation does not tell you information about actual scores, but you would know the ranking of the person on the second test. Conversely, a correlation of - 1.00 also indicates a perfect relationship but this time in an inverse manner. Thus, if a person came top of the group on one test that same person would necessarily be at the bottom of the group on the other test. The actual index of correlation is usually somewhere between these perfect extremes. The closer the index is to +1.00 or -1.00, the stronger the relationship between the tests. The closer to zero, the weaker the relationship until, at 0.0, there is no relationship at all between the test scores, or between that test and some criterion measure.

Apart from its role in assessing reliability and validity, which we will get to shortly, the correlation coefficient is extremely important in virtually all areas of psychological testing. Its popularity stems from the fact that the sample of behaviour obtained by administering a psychological test is often not the behaviour that we want to measure but is strongly related to it. Thus, the selection tests that job applicants are required to undertake usually contain tasks and questions that may not be encountered anywhere in the job itself. What is known about the selection tests is that performance on the tests is correlated with actual job performance. Someone who obtains a high score on the test is likely to do well on the job. Conversely, someone who does poorly on the test is likely to be a poor performer in the workplace. In order to be able to make these decisions, there must have been a time when test scores and performance measures were available for a group of employees, so that the correlation between the two could be calculated. From that time onwards, the behaviour sampled by the test was used as a predictor of actual job performance. This situation has many parallels in educational, organizational, and clinical settings. Tests are used so widely because they sample behaviour that is related to behaviour in other settings. It is the correlation coefficient that is used to indicate the strength of this relationship.

Reliability

The reliability of a psychological test is often defined as the extent to which the scores on the test are free from error. That is, test reliability indicates the extent to which individual differences in test scores are attributable to "true" differences in the characteristics under consideration and the extent to which they are attributable to chance errors. For example, if the petrol gauge in your car gave wildly different readings each time you looked at it within a short space of time, you would begin to suspect that it was somewhat unreliable. The differences you are observing are not "true" differences. That is, the tank is not full one minute and half-full the next; these are "error" readings from the petrol gauge and we would say that it is unreliable. Reliability is usually, but not always, synonymous with consistency: the consistency of scores obtained by the same persons when re-examined with the same test on different occasions, or with different sets of equivalent items (Anastasi & Urbina, 1997). The following treatment of reliability theory aims, within the space of a page or so, to give you a basic understanding of its importance in test theory. For a more detailed treatment of this and other technical terms refer to a standard text such as Anastasi and Urbina (1997) or Murphy and Davidshofer (1988).

Reliability is usually assessed by examining aspects of the consistency of scores yielded by a test. Whilst this approach sometimes gives misleading results it has been adopted by most test constructors. Consistency measures of reliability fall into four kinds: parallel forms, test-retest, internal consistency, and inter-rater reliability.

Parallel Form Reliability
If two equivalent forms of a test exist, then it is possible to administer both forms to the same group of people and look at the correlation between them. If the correlation is very high, then both forms may be regarded as reliable. One has to exercise great care to ensure that the two forms are truly parallel with questions expressed in the same form, covering the same content, and containing items that cover the same range and level of difficulty. If one of the versions is less reliable than the other, the correlation between the two of them will be depressed. If the two forms are administered close together, there may also be learning effects that transfer from one test to the next. Another major problem for this kind of reliability is that the effort involved in constructing a single version of a test is often very large indeed and few test producers have the resources to develop parallel forms. Examples of tests with parallel forms include the AL/AQ and ML/ MQ tests of intelligence developed by the Australian Council for Educational Research (ACER). AL and ML both measure linguistic reasoning whereas AQ and MQ both measure quantitative reasoning. The AL and ML forms are parallel, as are the AQ and MQ.

Test-retest Reliability
Test-retest reliability does not require the existence of two versions of a test. Instead, a single test is re-administered to the same group of people after a short interval. Often this type of reliability is called a stability index because it reflects the extent to which individuals held their positions in the group over the two testing periods. High reliability does not mean that people obtain the same score but that they tend to maintain their position within the group. Once again, reliability is assessed by looking at the correlation between test and retest scores. Six weeks is often regarded as a satisfactory interval for establishing test-retest reliability. Much shorter than six weeks and there is the risk that respondents will remember answers given on the first occasion and that practice effects will occur. Much longer than six weeks and there is the risk that life experiences may have changed the scores on underlying traits in the intervening period. Six months is

usually regarded as about the outer limit for test-retest correlations. This form of reliability is suitable for sensory discrimination and motor tests but a large number of educational and psychological tests cannot be administered twice over the short periods of time demanded by test-retest reliability.

Internal Consistency Reliability

Internal consistency reliability is a type of reliability that has some similarities to parallel form reliability. The simplest form of internal consistency reliability is called split-half reliability. Split-half reliability is obtained by dividing the items of a test into two equivalent halves. For example, the first half may consist of the odd numbered items and the second half of the even numbered items. The correlation between the scores from each half is taken as an index of reliability. An alternative method of estimating reliability from internal consistency uses the mean of all the possible split-half reliability coefficients that could result from different divisions of the test. Coefficient alpha is an example of such a coefficient and is probably the most widely used index of reliability.

Inter-rater Reliability

Inter-rater reliability is relevant where interviews, observations, or open-ended questions are used. For example, the author has been involved in research with people with an intellectual disability (PWID). We have been assessing their stress, anxiety, and depression levels. Many PWID cannot complete normal paper and pencil tests so we have used psychologists to conduct interviews with these people and make ratings of stress, anxiety, and depression. It was important to ensure that the psychologists were being consistent in their ratings. We were able to establish this by having three psychologists each interview and rate a small group of PWID. The inter-rater reliability was .87, which is close to the recommended minimum.90. Had the index of agreement been much lower, we would have had to abandon this method of assessment. Similarly, where people are being observed or where open-ended questions are used, an inter-rater reliability check should be conducted. This begins with the construction of an unambiguous coding system for every type of response. At least two raters then independently use the coding system to score a sample of responses and check that there is a high level of agreement.

If correlation indices are used to measure reliability, the index should be above .90 for inter-rater reliability. Apart from inter-rater reliability, there is no set figure for an acceptable level of reliability, although indices below .70 are generally regarded as unacceptable. Many sources indicate a lower bound of .60 for non-professionally developed tests and.80 for professionally developed tests.

Speeded tests - that is, tests which are designed so that most people cannot complete them within the specified time frame - present special problems for estimating reliability. Essentially, measures of internal consistency cannot be used unless one divides the test into sections and administers each section separately. Test-retest or alternate form estimates of reliability are used with speeded tests.

Standard Error of Measurement

The reliability coefficient is a helpful statistic when a judgement has to be made about the usefulness of a particular test. If the reliability is too low, say below.60, the test is probably not suitable for general use. The value of the reliability coefficient, however, is not confined to the situation where a choice has to be made between tests. Having made the choice, the reliability coefficient of the test chosen can also be used to give some indication of the confidence one can have in the score obtained for any individual.

Because the reliability coefficient tells us the extent to which the scores on a test are free from error that is due to imperfect reliability, if you know the reliability of a test it is possible to set a band of tolerance around a given score and make estimates as to the likely error component. The reliability coefficient plays a part in this through the following formula:

$$SEM = SD_t\sqrt{1 - rtt}$$

where SEM = standard error of measurement

SD_t = standard deviation of test scores

r_{tt} = reliability coefficient for the test

The standard deviation (SD) is a measure of how the scores are distributed around the mean or average score on the test. A small SD is an indication that most people have scored close to the mean, a large SD indicates that scores are spread more or less evenly across the whole range. The actual formula for calculating the SD is given below:

$$SD = \sqrt{\sum(x - \bar{x})^2 / N - 1}$$

where x is the mean of the scores

The SEM can be treated in the same way as other standard error estimates: if you take a band plus or minus one SEM on either side of the obtained score, you can be about 68% sure that the true score lies somewhere within this band. Extend that band to include plus or minus 1.96 SEMs, and you can be 95% sure that the true score lies within this band. Thus,

upper boundary = score + 1.96 x SEM

lower boundary = score - 1.96 x SEM

Figure 14.1 *Illustration of a test report that includes standard errors of measurement.*

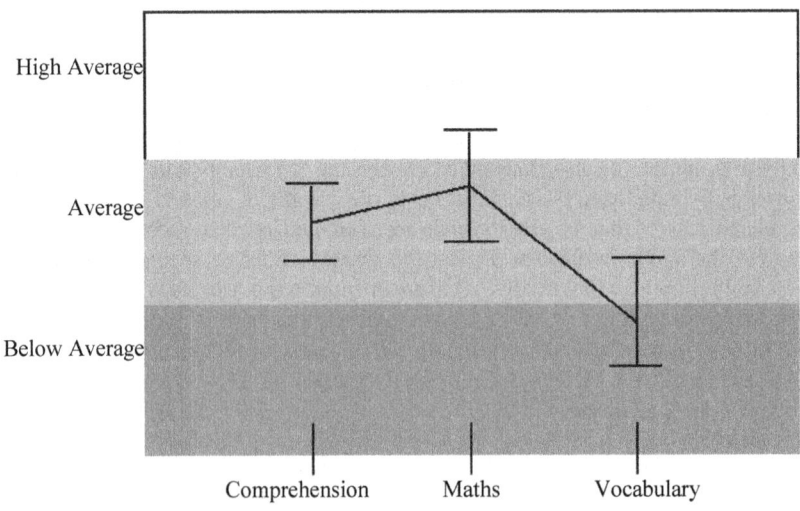

A test with low reliability will have a large SEM, a reliable test, on the other hand, will have a narrow band. An illustration of a test report used by the author that includes SEMs is shown in Figure 14.1.

Test such as the ones shown in Figure 14.1 are very often administered as part of a job selection process. An educator or a supervisor looking at this chart can see what the person actually scored on the Comprehension, Maths, and Vocabulary tests and is also reminded that there is some error in the estimates. The size of the SEM bands gives a direct indication of how much faith we can have in the accuracy of the score. In this figure, the Comprehension test is quite reliable and has a rather narrow SEM. The SEM bands for the Maths and Vocabulary tests are somewhat broader, reflecting a lower reliability estimate for these tests.

The SEM statistic is much used in psychological and educational measurement for the interpretation of individual scores. Most published tests have SEMs listed in the test manuals. Unfortunately, many people still do not know how to interpret them.

Validity

Validity is another important psychometric characteristic of a test and it is often defined by the question: "Does the test actually measure what it is intended to measure?". There are four broad means of establishing a test's validity: content-related validation, face validity, construct-related, and criterion-related. Let's look at each of these in turn.

Content Validity

When constructing tests, the test items should be representative of the behaviour domain to be measured. An arithmetic test, for example, should contain items that are representative of the content area, factorially pure (e.g., not contaminated by other factors such as ability to read instructions), and arithmetic in nature. Test-specifications help to achieve this. These define the content areas, the weightings, and the objectives. Thus, a test at the end of a training course should be related to the material learned in the course and should not overemphasise areas that did not receive much attention in the course.

Face Validity

Face validity refers to the extent to which a test looks as though it measures what it was designed to measure. Whilst face validity has no scientific or technical basis, it must not be overlooked if a test is to be accepted by applicants. For example, if a particular position in a manufacturing firm required numerical skills and a selection test was required to test these skills, it would be wise to use questions that are based on the materials of the workplace. If the firm makes spare parts and employees are required to calculate the prices of different combinations of these parts, it is worthwhile constructing questions that use these examples. There may be existing tests with excellent reliability that ask the same types of questions using different objects (e.g., apples and oranges) but job applicants are more likely to see the relevance of the context-sensitive questions and therefore show greater motivation. Face validity is a weak kind of validity in the sense that it is to do with appearances rather than more fundamental considerations such as whether the test measures what it purports to measure. However, appearances can determine reactions to a test and although it is the weakest form of validity, it is unwise to dismiss face validity as completely trivial.

Criterion Validity

Procedures used to establish criterion validity indicate the effectiveness of a test in predicting an individual's performance in specified activities. Test scores are correlated with actual performance on some independent criterion. The most obvious example would be the relationship between performance on job selection tests and actual performance on the job itself or on a job-related training course. The validation could be concurrent or predictive. In the first situation, validity is established by administering the test to those for whom some criterion measure is already available. In the second situation, validity is established by first testing then matching against the criterion some time later. Thus, if we were to test a group of computer programmers and correlate the results with a supervisor's ratings of work performance, this would constitute a measure of concurrent validity. If, on the other hand, we were to test a group of newly-hired computer programmers and later obtain measures of on-the-job performance for these same people, the correlation between test scores and job performance would constitute a measure of predictive validity. In both cases, a high correlation coefficient would indicate that the test has good criterion validity.

Construct Validity

Construct validity is more abstract than the other forms of validity. It reflects the degree to which a test measures some theoretical construct or trait. To some extent, content validity and face validity also deal with this same aspect of a test and the reader may find the overlapping terms confusing. The terms do overlap but their meanings can be separated. Content validity refers to the material that is included in the tests. A test of mathematical ability should include mathematical questions. A subject matter expert should be able to judge whether or not a test has content validity. Face validity refers to the extent to which the test looks as though it is measuring what it should be measuring. Anyone can make such judgements but they may be wrong and psychometricians do not place much value on face validity, sometimes referring to it in a derogatory fashion as "faith validity". For example, people may expect a test of mathematical ability to contain mostly symbols and equations and to rate it low on face validity if it does not contain a high proportion of such items. However, many mathematical problems can be couched in verbal terms (e.g., word algebra problems) and a test that contains such questions may still have excellent content validity. Unlike content validity and face validity, construct validity cannot be judged by simply looking at a test. Rather it requires the application of statistical techniques to determine what is being measured by the test. Some of the techniques contributing to construct-related validation are as follows:

– *Developmental changes.* Some tests, for example the Stanford-Binet (SB) test of intelligence, assume changes in performance will occur with age. The basis of test construction is that the SB consists of a number of sub-scales, which are like mini-tests assessing different areas of performance, for example, vocabulary, spatial ability, comprehension, and so on. Within each sub-scale, items are grouped according to age bands: a group of items that the typical two-year old can solve, followed by a group that the typical three-year old can solve, and so on, right through to adult level. In this way, the items become increasingly more difficult. The SB is administered on an individual basis with different starting and finishing points for each person. A person will complete an initial test that determines on which level he or she will start. If the person gets these items right and the items right on the next level as well, it is assumed that all of the earlier items would also have been correct and credit is awarded for them. The person then moves through the higher levels of the sub-scale until failing the majority of items at two consecutive levels. It is then assumed that all subsequent items would also be failed and the test is discontinued. Clearly, it is most important that the test constructors have not mixed up the ordering of items. If they have, then the test is invalid. In the case of the Stanford-Binet, the first edition of the test appeared in 1904 and there is an enormous bank of data that can be used to justify the ordering of items.

- *Factor analysis.* In general, this highly mathematical approach involves calculating the correlations among a set of tests and looking for patterns that suggest some tests "go together", so to speak. If such patterns do exist, the tests that "go together" will define a factor and the statistical packages used to conduct factor analyses will show the correlations of each test with its factor. The correlation of each test with its relevant factor is referred to as the factorial validity of a test. Factor analysis can also be applied at the item level where observations of high intercorrelations among sets of items indicate that they are measuring something in common, hopefully what they were intended to measure. Factor analysis is also discussed in the chapter on intelligence, including an example of its application in that field. A brief example follows here.

Table 14.1 *Correlations among Approaches to Studying Inventory Subscales*

Sub-scale	1	2	3	4	5	6	7
Achieving	1.00						
Meaning	.47	1.00					
Comprehension	.42	.52	1.00				
Operation Learning	.42	.43	.41	1.00			
5. Reproducing	-.06	-.11	-.12	.02	1.00		
6. Improvidence	.09	.06	-.08	.03	.38	1.00	
7. Globe Trotting	-.08	-.08	-.17	-.08	.37	.35	1.00

The example comes from research the author conducted with a colleague on the structure of learning styles among adult learners (Fogarty & Taylor, 1997). We used a 30-item test called the Approaches to Studying Inventory (ASI: Entwistle, 1983). The ASI contains seven subscales which, as mentioned above, are like tests within a test. Each of the sub-scales is designed to measure one of seven different learning orientations: Achieving, Meaning, Comprehension, Operation Learning, Reproduction, Improvidence, and Globetrotting. The first four of these measure aspects of what might be called a "deep" approach to learning, the last three measure aspects of a "shallow" approach. In terms of what was discussed above, one might expect that these two underlying constructs would be identified in a factor analysis. The table of correlations among the sub-scales of the test is shown in Table 14.1.

It is quite apparent from Table 14.1 that the four sub-scales measuring a deep approach to learning tend to correlate among themselves and not to correlate with the remaining three sub-scales, which measure a shallow approach to learning. The three sub-scales measuring a shallow approach show the same tendency to correlate among themselves. Patterns of correlations like this suggest that these seven sub-scales are measuring two unrelated constructs, which we can call factors. A factor analysis will tell us whether or not this is the case and just how well each test measures the underlying construct it was intended to measure. Table 14.2 shows part of the output from a factor analysis of the correlation matrix in Table 14.1.

The mathematics used to generate the figures shown in Table 14.2 need not concern us. What is apparent is that the first four sub-scales of the ASI are related to Factor 1 (Deep) and the last three sub-scales relate to Factor 2 (Shallow). This is what Entwistle intended. On the basis of this study, we can say that there is support for the factorial validity of each of the sub-scales of the ASI.

Table 14.2 *Factor Analysis of Approaches to Studying Inventory*

Sub-scales	Factor 1	Factor 2
Achieving	.65	
Meaning	.74	
Comprehension	.67	
Operation Learning	.61	
Reproducing		.61
Improvidence		.64
Globe Trotting		.57

- *Convergent and discriminant validity.* Support for the validity of a test can also be obtained by showing that it correlates highly with variables with which it should be correlated and also by showing that it has no relationship with variables with which it is not expected to have a relationship. The former is called convergent validity, the latter, discriminant validity. In the example reported immediately above, if there was another well-validated measure of deep and shallow processing, it would be possible to test whether the ASI measure of deep processing has convergent validity by examining its correlation with its counterpart. The correlation should be high. Its discriminant validity could be ascertained by checking to see that the correlation between the ASI measure of deep processing is uncorrelated with the measure of shallow processing from the second test (Entwistle argued that deep and shallow constructs are uncorrelated). The same checks could be applied to the ASI measure of shallow processing.
- *Known groups validity.* This aspect of validity is demonstrated by showing that test scores differentiate, in a predictable manner, between groups of test-takers known to differ on the characteristic being measured. Known groups validity is similar in some respects to concurrent validity. Thus, a test of honesty might be expected to discriminate among criminals (low scores), politicians (moderate scores), and clergy (high scores). Similarly, a test of mental toughness might be

expected to differentiate among athletes of various levels. A test developed to measure sex-role perceptions should demonstrate different average scores for groups of males and females. Failure to find expected differences would raise doubts about either the construct of sex-role perception, the construct validity of the test, or both.

Which Type of Validity Is Most Important?

Apart from face validity, it is a mistake to think that one type of validity is more important than another. It depends on the purpose of the test. If the purpose is to select good employees, predictive validity is all-important. If the purpose is to assess performance in a course or training programme, content validity is very important. If the purpose is to develop models of how different constructs relate to each other, construct validity is paramount. In some situations, it will be necessary to demonstrate that all forms of validity are satisfied.

By way of illustration, the author was once involved in the development of a selection test for sales personnel. The early stages of the project required a thorough search of the literature to determine just what aspects of ability, personality, and interests were related to success in sales. When these were determined, the test construction process began. One of the early decisions made by management regarding the test was that it had to "look the part". That is, it had to have face validity, not just in relation to the seeming appropriateness of the questions but also in relation to things like the physical appearance of the test. A second consideration for the test developers was that the questions had to sample various content domains. There was a need for questions on numeracy and literacy skills, some questions on various aspects of personality, such as extraversion and persistence, and quite a range of questions tapping demographic characteristics such as age, previous employment, and so forth. These were issues of content validity. When a draft set of questions had been developed, they were trialled on a group of salespersons that included both high performers and low performers. The aim was to establish the concurrent validity and also the known-groups validity of the test by showing that it discriminated between these two groups. The trial also resulted in valuable feedback about the acceptability of the test (face validity). Finally, the test was included in the selection process, allowing the accumulation of a large dataset that included scores on both the test and later sales performance. The predictive validity could then be established.

In the process of validating this selection test, some of these stages were revisited a number of times during the early years of its operation. The validation process should not stop once the test has been implemented. Circumstances do change and it will be necessary to keep checking all aspects of reliability and validity throughout the lifespan of the test. Test validation is most intensive in the construction and implementation phases, but it is an ongoing activity.

Relationship between Reliability and Validity

Reliability and validity should not thought of as just desirable features of a test, they are both essential. The relationship between the two is best depicted in diagrammatic form. Figure 14.2 shows the relationship using the analogy of a target board.

Example (a) shows what an unreliable test would look like. Example (b) shows what a reliable but invalid test would look like. It is similar to a rifle that has its sights mis-aligned. The high degree of reliability is shown by the consistency of the strikes. The lack of validity is shown by the fact that the missiles are missing their target, the bullseye. For example, a job satisfaction test given to unskilled workers may measure literacy skills rather than job satisfaction if the test is written in complex language. In psychometric terms, the test is not measuring what it was intended to measure. Example (c) is what a valid and reliable test would look like: the missiles hit the mark and they hit it consistently.

Figure 14.2 *The relationship between reliability and validity.*

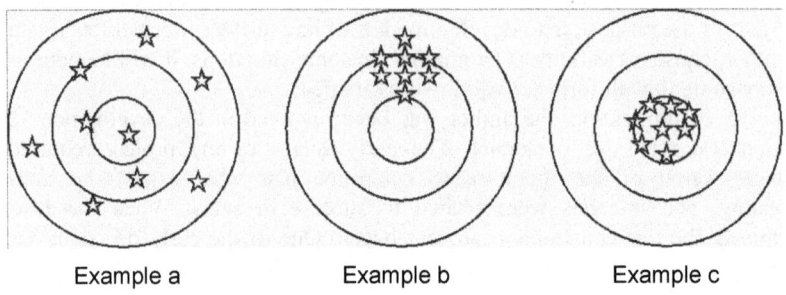

Example a   Example b   Example c

Different Types of Tests and Their Applications

Most psychological tests can be sorted into three general categories (Murphy & Davidshofer, 1988):
– Performance tests in which the test-taker performs some specific task, such as writing an essay, answering multiple choice items, or mentally rotating images presented on a computer screen;
– Behaviour observation tests that involve observations of a person's behaviour within a particular context;
– (c) Self-report measures, in which the test-taker describes his or her feelings, attitudes, beliefs, interests, and the like.
The following paragraphs will expand upon each of these categories.

Tests of Performance
One of the most familiar testing situations is one in which participants are given some well-defined task and asked to do their best within a given time frame. The score is usually the number of items that the participant has scored correctly in that time. Cronbach (1970) referred to this as a "test of maximal performance". To illustrate the nature of a test of maximal performance, Ackerman and Heggestad (1997) gave some rather delightful examples of instructions to early examinees around the turn of the century. For example, they cited the description of test procedures given by Binet and Simon (1911- 1915), the developers of the Stanford Binet intelligence test:

> What should be done [if a child does not respond]? The help of the teacher is often useful. If she is intelligent, she knows what to say to her children to

reassure them and arouse their courage. A caress to one, a reprimand to another and all goes well. [Cited in Ackerman & Heggestad, 1997, p. 220].

Contrast those instructions with the set given for testing US army recruits during the First World War:

When everything is ready E. (sic) proceeds as follows: "Attention! The purpose of this examination is to see how well you can remember, think, and carry out what you are told to do... You are not expected to make a perfect grade, but do the very best you can.

Now, in the army a man often has to listen to commands and then carry them out exactly. I am going to give you some commands to see how well you can carry them out. Listen closely. *Ask no questions.* [Cited in Ackerman & Heggestad, 1997, p. 221]

Both sets of instructions, contrasting though they may be, make it very clear that in these intelligence-testing situations, the individual is expected to demonstrate maximal performance.

Behaviour Observations

Some psychological tests involve observing the examinee's behaviour and responses in a particular context (Murphy & Davidshofer, 1988). Tests of this type usually involve an examiner noting the typical behaviour of the individual in a particular situation. Teachers may make assessment of the social skills of children in classrooms by observing how they behave to other children. Employers in job situations may set up typical job simulations and observe how job applicants handle the work in those situations. Many training situations involve highly structured observations by trainers of trainees undergoing particular tasks. Trainee teachers are subjected to regular inspections in a classroom. These situations are a lot less standardised than those described earlier but provided that the instructors are using a checklist of behaviours and recording the student's behaviour using some standardised format, then it is a testing situation. Reliability is usually assessed by checking inter-rater agreement.

Self Reports

The final class of test includes a variety of measures that require the examinee to report or describe his/her feelings, attitudes, beliefs, values, opinions, or physical or mental state (Murphy & Davidshofer, 1988). Many personality inventories take this form. It is a very efficient form of data collection and large numbers of respondents can be tested at the same time. Self-report techniques do have a number of drawbacks, which will be dealt with later in this chapter.

Interpretation of Test Scores

Whatever the form of test, the result will be a score or rating of some kind. The score or rating can provide two types of information. One type is the relative standing of the individual in relation to his or her peers. Such measures are called norm-referenced. A second type of measure that can be obtained from tests of maximal performance reflects the degree to which the individual has mastered the skills that characterise the domain being tested. Such scores are called criterion-referenced. Other names used for this type of reference framework include content-, domain-, and objective-referenced.

Criterion-referenced Testing

A very simple example will suffice to illustrate the difference between the two treatments of a test score. A driver's licence test is a criterion-referenced test. The score obtained does not indicate how well you went compared with everyone else who sat the test but how well you can drive. Thus, the emphasis is on what you can do. The driver's test is a very simple format, you either pass or fail. Some criterion-referenced tests have many levels. Criterion-referenced testing became popular in the 1970s, especially in the field of education. The advent of computerised instruction systems made it relatively easy to test what an individual knows and to adapt instruction accordingly. Repeated testings indicate the level of mastery attained and the learning modules that should be presented next. At no stage is there any comparison with other individuals, the focus is entirely upon what the learner knows and what the learner can do. A score in this context reflects the level of attainment. Anastasi and Urbina (1997) commented that this form of test score interpretation is best suited for basic skills where instructional objectives can be arranged in an ordinal hierarchy, the acquisition of more elementary skills being a prerequisite for the acquisition of higher level skills (p. 77). Beyond the basic skill level it is extremely difficult to arrange skills in such an ordered sequence and norm-referenced testing, or a combination of norm-referenced and criterion-referenced testing, is more appropriate.

Norm-referenced Testing

A much more common form of norms employs a quantitative approach to show the position of an examinee in relation to his or her peer group. The crudest of these simply indicate whether someone is above or below average. For example, an individual may be described as above average on a test of intelligence, or neuroticism, or self-confidence, or whatever it is that is being measured. A more elaborate and quite common scheme uses five intervals corresponding to the top 10%, the next 20%, the middle 40%, the next 20%, and the bottom 10% of the population. University grading systems often use schemes like this.

Percentile scores represent an improvement on the five-fold classification scheme. Percentile scores use a scale numbering from 1 to 100 to tell us where an individual is located on a test. Thus, a percentile score of 45 indicates that 45% of the population obtained this same score or a lower score. A percentile score of 99 means that 99% of the population were equal to or below this score. Percentiles are easy to understand and are found in nearly all test manuals. Unfortunately, they are somewhat distorted near the ends of the distribution. That is, a small difference in raw scores in the middle of the distribution can lead to a big difference in percentile scores whereas the same difference towards the tails of the distribution may result in only one or two percentile points difference.

To overcome this problem, psychologists and educators frequently use norms that are based on the normal frequency distribution. There are four main types of norms based on this distribution: z scores, quotients, stens, and stanines (see Anastasi & Urbina, 1997, pp. 61- 66). Z scores report an individual's scores in terms of how many standard deviations the score is from the mean. The formula is easy enough: simply subtract the mean from the score and divide the result by the standard deviation. In virtually all cases, this will result in a z-score that ranges somewhere between -3.00 and +3.00. Z scores are not often used because they can be negative as well as positive and many people do not like dealing with negative test scores! To overcome this problem, some test manuals use quotients. A quotient is a standard score with the mean set at 100 and the standard deviation set at 15. IQ scores are always reported in this form. A raw score is obtained on the test and then converted to an IQ score on the basis of tables given in the test manual. The term "IQ" comes from Intelligence Quotient and is a leftover from earlier times when intelligence was assessed by forming a ratio between mental age and chronological age. The ratio is no longer used but IQ has come to stand for scores on tests of general intelligence. T scores are similar to IQ scores, but are based on distribution with a mean of 50 and a standard deviation of 10. Sten (standard ten) scores are based on a distribution that has a mean of 5.5 and a standard deviation of 2, with 10 discrete scores being possible. The decimal point has made sten scores somewhat unpopular. Stanines (standard nine) scores are based on a distribution with a mean of 5 and a standard deviation of 2, with nine discrete scores being possible. They can be obtained from z scores by multiplying the z score by 2 and adding 5. Stanine scores are used in many test settings. Both stens and stanines operate by banding together scores in a specific region of the distribution and using the same number to represent all scores falling within that band.

Constructing and Validating a Test

This final section on technical matters will attempt to bring together much of what has already been discussed by tracing the development of a test in which the author has been involved. The description will cover all aspects of the development process, from the rationale right through to the point where publication of a test manual is possible.

Overview of Test Development Process

Test construction involves first deciding the broad domain to be covered by the test. Once it is clear what has to be covered by the test, the process of item construction begins. The idea is to develop as many items as possible because some of them will not pass the various filters. The first filter is normally a group of experts who will make judgements about the face and content validity of the items. Some will be discarded at this point. Surviving items are generally tested with a representative sample drawn from the population for whom the test is intended. This testing will make it clear whether there are any major problems with intelligibility, clarity, and appropriateness of items. If the test is one of maximal performance, pre-testing will help to ascertain whether the items are too easy or too difficult for the intended population. Figure 14.3 shows examples of tests that are (a) too easy, (b) too difficult, and (c) of an appropriate difficulty level.

Figure 14.3 shows what are often referred to as item-person maps. The dotted line in the middle represents a difficulty continuum with low difficulty and low ability at the bottom of the line. The "People" line represents the ability range of the people taking the test whilst the "Items" line represents the range of difficulty of the items. Item difficulty can be something as simple as the proportion of people who made an error on the item (typically this is not how it is measured but it will do for our purposes). The item-person map shown in example (a) indicates that the items are too easy for this population. In example (b) they are too hard. There would not be any point in giving either of these tests to the populations sampled here. In example (a) everyone would get all the items right and in example (b) everyone would get every item wrong. Example (c) shows the type of item-person correspondence test constructors are trying to achieve.

Figure 14.3 Diagrams depicting suitability of test difficulty.

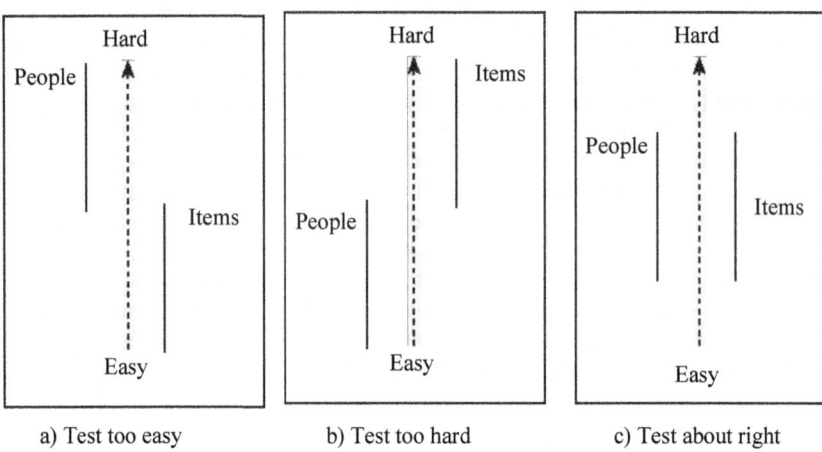

a) Test too easy   b) Test too hard   c) Test about right

Item-person maps can also be constructed for self-report tests where there are no right or wrong answers but where people have to judge the extent to which they agree or disagree with statements posed in the items (e.g., Tenenbaum & Fogarty, 1998). It is just as important in these situations to ensure that some of the respondents agree with the statements and some disagree. If all respondents find it too easy to agree with the statements (or to disagree), everyone will end up with almost the same score, and that is a highly undesirable situation in testing. After all, one of the aims of any test is to discriminate among individuals. This is not possible if everyone has close to the same score. A technique known as Rasch analysis is particularly useful for making these kinds of analyses (Tenenbaum & Fogarty, 1998).

If the test for students passes these preliminary filters, it is time to use it with a larger sample. The reliability of the test can then be assessed. Some further item changes may be required after these analyses. The final stages of test validation will involve checking relationships between scores on the test and external measures (concurrent and possibly predictive validity) and also checking whether the test appears to be measuring the constructs it was intended to measure (construct validity).

An Example of Test Development and Validation
To clarify the process of test development further, consider the steps involved in the validation of a test intended to measure stress in people with an intellectual handicap (Bramston & Bostock, 1994; Bramston & Fogarty, 1995; Fogarty & Bramston, 1997).

- *Initial item construction.* Original items for this test were derived from 89 adults with mild intellectual disabilities who took part in one of 22 brainstorming groups set up across two Australian states. Participants discussed what aspects of their day-to-day lives upset, bothered, worried, and stressed them. Twenty-four people who worked closely with people with intellectual disabilities completed similar brainstorming exercises and their responses were added to the pool of ideas. After duplications were removed, 60 stressors remained that were then worded into interview questions. The test was then tested widely among adults with mild intellectual disabilities and reviewed for content and clarity of item wording by a panel of six people consisting of academics (2), teachers in the disabilities field (2), and parents of adults with intellectual disabilities (2). Based on their responses and the trials, the items were revised and the test reduced to 31 items.
- *Test administration.* The resulting Lifestress Inventory is a self-report test administered by interview. Respondents are asked to acknowledge if any of the stressful events listed in the test had occurred in the last fortnight (e.g., "Have you argued with anyone recently?"). To counter any tendency towards acquiescence, the stressful option was "yes" for half the items and "no" for the remainder. If the stressful option was indicated by the response, the respondent was asked to rate how stressful the event currently was by pointing to a spot on a 4- point scale. The rating clearly set out the numbers "1-4", written descriptors from "not stressful" to "a great deal of stress", and graphic representations of each point using buckets with varying amounts of water in them. Normally the graphic representation would not be necessary, but with this population extra care was taken to ensure that they understood what was required of them. The interviews were conducted by one of two interviewers, both aged in their late 30s, one male and one female. Both were experienced clinicians and familiar with the test. It had already been established that the inter-rater reliability for trained interviewers was.87. Respondents were helped to feel at ease and then asked if they would simply say whether certain events or issues had occurred in their life within the last two weeks. The interviewers were required to verify subject responses with the prompt "Tell me more about that", so that unreliable responses could be detected and scored accordingly. The interviews generally took about 15 minutes each.
- *Validation of test structure and cross-validation.* The next stage (Bramston & Fogarty, 1995; Fogarty & Bramston, 1997) involved the analysis of the data, including a factor analysis that identified three sub-tests of the Lifestress Inventory: general worry, interpersonal concerns, and concerns with coping. Another study was then conducted to refine weak items and to confirm the construct validity.
- *Further validation and refinement of test.* The next part of the validation work consisted of yet another administration of the test to a different sample, this time a clinical psychologist also interviewed respondents and ratings of stress were collected from their work supervisors for the purposes of concurrent validation.
- *Production of test manual.* The last stage involves the production of a test manual that will contain a complete description of the test, psychometric data relating to reliability and validity, and tables showing typical scores for males and females and different age groups. In other words, norms will be constructed

so that it is possible to tell whether a particular score is high or low in relation to the general population of people with an intellectual disability.

If the above process seems rather exhaustive, it is a reminder that it is an extremely painstaking process to put together a test that is reliable and valid. Such projects should not be undertaken lightly.

PART B: APPLICATIONS OF TESTING

It is not possible to describe the full range of testing applications in one book, let alone in a chapter, but it is relatively easy to identify the main types of test in current use and to describe some of the purposes for which they are used. The three main types of test to be considered here are tests of intelligence, tests of achievement, and tests of personality.

Tests of Intelligence

Modern intelligence tests can be classified into two categories. The first category contains what are called individual tests of intelligence. The best known of these are the Stanford Binet, now up to its fourth edition, and the Wechsler Adult Intelligence Scale (WAIS-III), the fourth version of which has just been released in Australia. Both of these take anything up to 2 hours to administer, although the time taken is typically less. Test items cover a range of abilities employing both verbal and non-verbal item types. Test takers may be asked to give the meanings of words, to complete a series of numbers, to recall a list of numbers, and so on. Both tests yield overall estimates of intelligence (IQ) and estimates of a range of specific abilities. Because they are administered in an interview situation, both tests are capable of yielding a lot of clinical information as well. The Fourth Edition of the Stanford Binet can be used with both adults and children. The WAISIII is similar in format and style to the Stanford Binet but comes in different versions: (a) an adult version (WAIS-III); (b) a children's version (WISC-III); and (c) a preschool version (WPPSI). Both the Stanford Binet and the Wechsler tests are updated from time to time, with new revisions subjected to thorough validation procedures. There are other individual tests of intelligence, some that are arguably more reliable and more valid for certain purposes, but none that would match the Stanford Binet or the Wechsler tests in terms of popularity.

The second category consists of the group tests of intelligence. These tests were first developed to handle the very large number of soldiers recruited into the US army during the First World War. Results helped with placement and classification decisions. Most group tests of intelligence now yield scores on a broad range of abilities, such as vocabulary, numerical ability, spatial ability, memory, reasoning, and many others. Testing has become a much commercialised enterprise and major test publishers offer a variety of group tests of intelligence. Examples of some ones include the Differential Aptitude Test (DAT: Bennett, Seashore, & Wesman, 1989) and the Australian Council of Educational Research (ACER) Advanced Tests AL-AQ and BL-BQ (ACER, 1982). Such tests can be administered to many people at the same time, scoring is generally easy, and norm tables can be compiled without any great difficulty. For this reason, there tends to be many more group tests than individual tests. Some group tests of intelligence have also been developed for special populations, such as those with language difficulties or hearing or sight impairment.

Applications of Tests of Intelligence

Intelligence tests, whether group or individual, have been in widespread use since the start of this century. They were developed initially for use in educational settings but quickly found their way into occupational and clinical settings.

Tests of Intelligence in Clinical Settings

Tests of intelligence are routinely used in clinical settings. Level of intellectual functioning provides insights into general level of health. The fact is that a lot of the problems that are referred to a psychologist or psychiatrist either have their origins in intellectual weaknesses or can be better understood following a diagnosis of the individual's intellectual strengths and weaknesses. Invariably, the tests used are individual tests, such as the Stanford Binet or one of the Wechsler tests. A major use of intelligence tests in clinical settings is in neuropsychological assessment, where the aim is to assess possible brain damage as a consequence of trauma, usually caused by a car accident.

Tests of Intelligence in Educational Settings

Intelligence tests were originally developed to measure learning potential, something that they still do very well. The author has for many years used measures of numerical ability, verbal comprehension, vocabulary, and abstract reasoning to predict educational achievement. There is no doubt that tests such as these give a fairly accurate indication of success in various subject areas. That is, they have good predictive validity. Used in conjunction with measures of actual academic performance, intelligence tests can help guide people towards appropriate career choices. Although not as popular as they were in the 1950s and 1 960s when most school children underwent IQ testing, intelligence tests are still very much part of the educational environment. They are used as the basis for awarding scholarships, for gaining entrance to some prestigious courses (especially in the United States), and they are widely used for diagnostic assessment where learning difficulties are suspected.

Tests of Intelligence in Occupational Settings

The role of intelligence testing in occupational psychology was summarised in a review by Hunter (1986) who pointed out that although intelligence testing has not been as successful in the occupational field as the educational field, it nevertheless predicts a reliable proportion of job performance, and it does so better than alternative measures, such as interviews or personality assessment. The relationship between intelligence and job performance, however, depends very much on the individual's familiarity with the job. In the early stages when there is a lot of learning occurring, tests of intelligence predict performance quite well, probably because performance is closely linked with the ability to learn rapidly. Once the individual has settled into the job, however, the strength of the relationship between intelligence and job performance starts to decrease. In jobs which impose variable demands and where learning is constantly occurring, intelligence tests will prove more useful for predicting performance.

Furthermore, there are many occupational settings where the tasks are quite complex and in these situations intelligence tests can be useful. Indeed, with the increasing complexity of modern day work situations, it is possible that the predictive validity of intelligence tests will increase in occupational settings. The introduction of automation is a familiar scene everywhere in the workplace. Tasks that were once performed by manual labour are now being completed by a machine. As this happens, the job requirements are shifting from physical strength and motor coordination to cognitive dexterity. In Reich's (1991) terms, we are moving from a world of doers to a world of symbol analysts. The new technologies devalue experience and increase the value of the ability to learn (Hunt, 1995), precisely the sort of thing that is predicted by tests of intelligence. However, the trend is not completely in the direction of greater complexity. Some jobs that formerly required cognitive skills no longer do so because a machine (e.g., a calculator) now takes care of the cognitive work. Time will tell whether intelligence becomes more or less important in the workforce of the future. For a thorough analysis of this issue, see Hunt (1995).

Tests of Achievement

For most people, the most commonly experienced tests are the ones that we sit as students in educational institutions or as adults seeking professional or trade qualifications. These so-called achievement tests are designed to measure the effects of a specific programme of instruction or training (Anastasi & Urbina, 1997). They usually take the form of either free-response questions such as essays, or objective questions such as the popular multiple choice format. A problem with many achievement tests is they are never standardised or validated in the manner suggested in this chapter. It is not hard to see why: most people who construct achievement tests have neither the time nor the expertise to undertake the necessary analyses. Free-response format tests, for example, should really be checked for inter-rater reliability to make sure that different subject matter experts rate the answers in the same way. For reasons mentioned above, this rarely happens. Multiple choice tests are a different story: software is readily available to score these tests and at the same time give valuable feedback about questions that are unreliable and therefore decreasing the reliability of the whole test. If a test is unreliable, it cannot be valid. Unfortunately, it is probable that some constructors of achievement tests do not even use test specifications when selecting questions for inclusion. At the very least, the specifications should take account of the objectives, the content areas covered, and topic weightings.

Having said this, there are excellent examples of achievement tests that are properly standardised and validated. The Progressive Achievement Tests (PAT) published by ACER are widely used in Australia to measure a student's level of attainment in key academic areas such as vocabulary, comprehension, and mathematics. Test norms are available, so it is possible to see how a student compares with other students throughout Australia. Tests like this can be extremely helpful for designing curricula and making decisions about which students can be directed to extension classes and which ones might benefit from supplementary work.

Personality Tests

In terms of widespread usage, the assessment of personality ranks second only to intelligence and achievement testing. There are two basic forms of personality testing: self-report measures and projective techniques such as the Rorschach and the Thematic Apperception Test. The Rorschach, better known to most people as the inkblot test, is one of the earliest forms of personality assessment, having first made its appearance in 1921. The test presents a series of 10 stimulus cards to the test taker, who is required to state what he or she can see in the card. The theory upon which the test is based claims that the way a person perceives and interprets the test material reflects fundamental aspects of his or her psychological functioning, including personality. The Thematic Apperception Test (TAT) also makes use of pictures, but employs them in a different way. A series of 19 pictures and one blank card is shown to the test taker who is asked to make up a story about each picture. In the case of the blank card, the task is to imagine a picture on the card and then tell a story about it. The rationale underlying the use of the TAT is much the same as that for the Rorschach; there is an expectation that people will project much of themselves into the stories they tell. However, although projective techniques are powerful tools for personality assessment they are not used by many practitioners. They take a lot of time to administer and a lot of training before reaching a reasonable degree of proficiency. Self-report methods of personality assessment have proven to be much more popular.

As the term implies, self-report tests rely upon the test-taker responding to a set of standard statements by indicating whether they agree or disagree with the statements (if the answer is a simple yes-no) or choosing a number to indicate the extent of their agreement or disagreement with the item. There are so many self-report forms around these days that it is extremely unlikely that the reader has not encountered this form of test before.

In the development of self-report personality inventories, several approaches have been followed in formulating, assembling, selecting, and grouping items. Among the major procedures in current use are those based on (a) content validation, (b) empirical criterion keying, and (c) factor analysis.

- *Content-related validation.* These personality inventories are generally formed from lists of known problems which the individual can then tick as affecting them or not affecting them. This is the technique used in the development of the Lifestress Inventory described earlier in this chapter.
- *Empirical criterion keying.* This method builds upon the previous method but takes a more statistical approach, looking for items that separate "normal" from "abnormal" response patterns. In a purely hypothetical example, if it became known that schizophrenics showed a fear of clocks, an item assessing attitude to clocks could be included in a test designed to detect schizophrenia. It is not important that we have no idea why clocks might inspire fear in this group. The important thing is that people with the disorder have the fear whilst others don't, so empirical criterion keying would suggest that such an item could be included. The best known example of a personality test developed through the use of empirical criterion keying is the Minnesota Multiphasic Personality Inventory (MMPI). The MMPI is a very long self-administered test, comprising numerous sub-scales. The sub-scales were developed empirically by criterion keying of items, the criterion being traditional psychiatric diagnosis. The latest revision of

the MMPI has resulted in it being separated into two forms, the MMPI-2 and the MMPI-A (for use with adolescents). The California Psychological Inventory (CPI) is another very well-known instrument that was based on the MMPI. It consists of 434

- items to be answered true or false. Half of these items came from the MMPI. The CPI has been widely used in industry as well as in clinical practice.
- *Factor analysis.* As mentioned earlier, factor analysis is a technique for detecting patterns of correlations among test scores that indicate underlying dimensions that are responsible for scores on the test. Factor analysis can be used to help select items for inclusion in a personality test or to identify how many dimensions underlie tests developed by either of the first two methods. Cattell's Sixteen Personality Factor Questionnaire (16 PF) was developed using this method. The so-called Big Five Factor Model (Costa & McCrae, 1991), perhaps the dominant model of personality in occupational testing settings, was also based on factor analysis. The big five personality factors are:
  - *Neuroticism* (N): indicates an individual's level of emotional stability, ranging from calm and even-tempered up to maladjustment and emotional distress.
  - *Extraversion* (E): indicates a person's degree of sociability and preference for interacting with people.
  - *Openness* (O): measures openness to experience, and is related to divergent thinking and creativity. Low scorers tend to be conventional and conservative.
  - *Agreeableness* (A): measures how a person views others. Low scorers tend to be competitive while high scorers favour cooperative interactions with others.
  - *Conscientiousness* (C): indicates a person's ability to control impulses and desires. High C is associated with strong will and high need for achievement, while low C is associated with a more lackadaisical approach to life.

Applications of Personality Testing

The two traditional areas for the application of personality tests have been clinical settings and occupational settings. Recently, personality tests have become popular in the new field of sport psychology, where they are used to gain insights into factors that affect performance.

Personality Testing in Clinical Settings

Personality testing has a long history in clinical settings, where it has obvious relevance to the analysis of personality disorders. Perhaps the most common use of personality tests stems from the profile that can be obtained following their administration. A profile is a line linking an individual's scores on various parts of a test. Figure 14.1 showed a profile on an ability test. Similar profiles can be constructed for personality tests. The resulting pattern can be inspected for signs of abnormality. A single high or low score on its own may not indicate any problems but a combination of test scores may well be indicative of particular syndromes, such as schizophrenia.

These forms of profile analysis have not lived up to expectations for two main reasons. Firstly, variations among subtest scores could arise from a variety of circumstances, only some of them pathological. Secondly, the diagnostic categories that provided the criteria for profile analysis are themselves subject to debate. For example, what does it mean to say that a particular pattern indicates schizophrenia when schizophrenia itself is not a clearly defined condition? Profile analysis may tell us something about group characteristics but it is prone to error when applied to individual cases. A more fruitful approach is to treat the pattern information as a source of hypotheses that can be tested against the wealth of other data collected in individualized testing.

Personality Testing in Occupational Settings
Personality testing also has a very strong tradition in job selection testing where the 16 PF and more recently the Five Factor Inventory, a measure of the big five personality factors (NEOFFI: Costa & McCrae, 1991), have proved very popular. This popularity continues despite evidence that personality tests do not predict job performance very well, even for sales positions (Hunter, 1986). Robertson and Smith (1989) reported a validity coefficient as low as. 15 in personnel selection testing. In contrast, the coefficient for ability tests ranges between.25 and.45.

The use of personality testing in occupational settings is not confined to selection testing, it has also proved very popular as an aid in training courses. The Myers Briggs Type Indicator (MBTI) is one of the best known personality tests because it is used so often in workshops on career decision making, team building, conflict resolution, time management, relationship counselling, and a number of other applications. The MBTI is based on the theory of psychological types proposed by Carl Jung. Psychological types represent combinations of two or more traits or attributes that are stable and shape the way individuals think and behave. The MBTI classifies people into 16 types and one of the reasons for its success lies in the fact that all types are seen as being valuable with each having particular strengths and weaknesses. There are many clones of the MBTI that also seek to describe people in terms of types. They are frequently used in management courses. Such type indicators can be extremely valuable in workshop settings where they serve as a basis for discussion of the different perspectives individuals may have on work situations, home life, and so on. For career selection purposes, there are as yet no data to support claims that knowledge of type (or personality) is a useful in predicting job performance.

Personality Testing in Sport Settings
The latest field of psychology to embrace personality testing in a big way is sport psychology. Much of the testing centres on what is now known as "sport personology" - the study of personality characteristics as determinants of sporting success. As in occupational testing, the findings so far have not been very promising. When the personality profiles of elite athletes are compared with those of novice athletes, there are differences. Elite athletes are more aggressive, more focused, less anxious, and so on, but individual differences on these traits do not predict who is going to be an elite athlete. That is to say, the tests of personality have concurrent validity but poor predictive validity. Talent identification programmes have grappled unsuccessfully with this problem for years. Perhaps more situation-specific personality tests will help to improve the predictive validity

of personality tests in both occupational and sports settings. There is no doubt that serious attempts are now being made to develop personality tests that are suited to sports situations. Ostrow (1990, p. 8) has included a graph which shows a quite steady increase in the number of sports-specific tests since 1975. The proportion is now close to 45%. As one might expect, given the nature of sport, these new tests are primarily in the areas of anxiety, motivation, mental skills, and specific sporting factors such as team cohesion (Fogarty, 1995).

Tests of Vocational and Career Interests

Another category of test that has proved to be very popular in educational and occupational settings is the career interest inventory. The best known of these are the tests based on Holland's model of career decision making. The Self-Directed Search (SDS) is the most popular of these tests and has an Australian version which is in widespread use in this country. Holland (1985) believed that the most productive approach to career decision making involved an investigation of the individual's personality type. He proposed a six-category typology: Realistic (R), Investigative (I), Artistic (A), Social (S), Enterprising (E), and Conventional (C). He believed that this six-category system could be used to not only describe the major types of people but also to describe the work environments they are likely to encounter in Western society. Holland's assumption was that people seek environments that allow them to express their interests, and by knowing something about their general orientation we are in a better position to judge where they will be happiest working. Holland's tests, or derivatives of them, are widely used in educational and occupational settings to assist with career decision making.

Miscellaneous Tests

There are many more test types than can be described here, some of them adapted to particular situations. Areas not covered in this chapter include stress (e.g., Osipow and Spokane, 1987), values (e.g., Schwartz & Bilsky, 1987), decision styles (e.g., Driver, Brousseau, & Hunsaker, 1990), learning styles (Entwistle, 1983), and perhaps it is better to stop here because the list could go on and on. The reader is referred to a text devoted exclusively to psychological testing, such as Anastasi and Urbina (1997), for an overview of virtually the whole testing domain. For information on tests available here in Australia, the best place to approach is the Australian Council for Educational Research (ACER), which has a number of test catalogues containing descriptions of individual tests, including details of what qualifications you need to administer the tests and suitable areas of application.

Computerised Testing

It would be a mistake to conclude this chapter leaving the reader with the impression that tests are available only in paper-and-pencil format. Testing was one of the earliest areas within psychology to benefit from computer applications with standardised, objective-type personality tests being particularly well-suited to automation (Bartram & Bayliss, 1984). Initially, interest focussed on automated scoring but later expanded to include the computerised administration of existing pencil-and-paper tests. Currently, almost every facet of personality testing has been computerised, from test design and development, through item generation and analysis, to test interpretation and report generation. In a typical computerised test presentation, individual questions or stimuli are presented on a monitor attached to the computer, a set of limited responses is offered, and test-takers record their selected response via a keyboard or some other interface. The advantages of this form of administration over conventional administration are well-documented in several reviews (e.g., Bartram & Bayliss, 1984).

The move from paper-and-pencil tests to computer-based formats, however, represents a major shift in the way tests are administered and it is important that research is conducted to check the equivalence of the two methods. Work has already started in this area, especially on the equivalence of paper-and-pencil versus computerised presentation. Reviews of these studies report conflicting findings, with many uncontrolled variables influencing the outcomes (e.g., Burke & Normand, 1987; Webster & Compeau, 1996). The author's own experience with this form of testing is that it does not appear to make a noticeable difference and that test manuals developed on the basis of paper-and-pencil tests are still applicable to computerised versions of tests (Fogarty, 1998).

One of the major benefits of computerised assessment is undoubtedly the increased efficiency of administration made possible by software that adapts the presentation of items for each user. Thus, when assessing abilities there is no need to present a whole lot of easy items to a very capable person. It is a waste of time. Similarly, there is no need to present a lot of difficult items to a person who has no chance of solving them. In a traditional paper-and-pencil test, everyone is given the same instructions, the same items, and the same time in which to complete the test. In an adaptive, computerised test situation, the algorithms built into the software can quickly estimate a person's level of cognitive functioning on the ability being measured, rather than the person's total score. Such an estimation is possible because the difficulty level of each item is known beforehand and the test can draw upon a large bank of items covering all possible ability levels. A typical test scenario is presented in Figure 14.4.

If you can imagine that the higher items are more difficult you can see that each time the person is correct, a more difficult item is selected. When the item is incorrect, the computer selects an item from an easier level. In the oversimplified representation shown in Figure 14.4, the person's ability level is somewhere near to the levels assessed by items 3, 5, and 7. Above that level, the items are incorrect. Below that level and the items are correct. In actual practice, it is not quite this easy, but the principle is clear. At some point, performance will alternate between success and failure. The test is then ended and the level at which this occurred is reported as the ability estimate for that individual. Adaptive tests are not new in psychology and education, many individually administered tests are adaptive (e.g., the Stanford Binet), but computers allow whole groups of people to be tested simultaneously. In some cases, testing time is halved because fewer items have to be presented. Adaptive computer testing can be used with other types of test (e.g., personality), but so far their application has mostly been with intelligence and achievement tests.

Apart from test administration, computers are increasingly being used to write test reports on the basis of scores collected during a computerised administration of the test or entered by the test administrator. There is a real question mark hanging over the issue of the lack of flexibility of reports written by a computer. Such reports are based on test scores only and omit the large amount of data that can be collected in a face-to-face testing situation. When using tests of maximal performance, for example, a clinician can report the amount of effort put into the test, a computer cannot. In personality testing, many signs of abnormality may be evident in the person's bearing and manner, things that are not available to the computer that generates the report. It may be some time before there is good research data on the validity of computer generated reports. Certainly they should be supplemented by other reports from the training officer, psychologist, or whoever arranged the test.

Figure 14.4 *Illustration of possible sequence of items in an adaptive computerised test.*

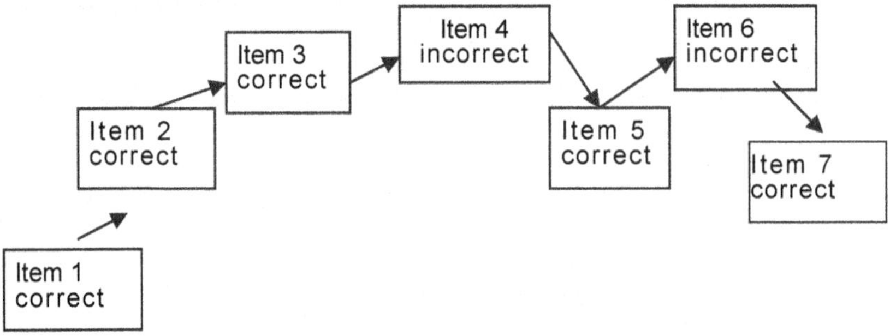

PART C: LIMITATIONS OF TESTING AND CONTROVERSIES

Up to this point, the chapter has emphasised the positive aspects of testing but there are negative aspects that should also be mentioned before closing. The chief limitation of testing is implied in the definition mentioned at the outset of the chapter: tests provide samples of behaviour. As such, they should never be interpreted as yielding completely accurate descriptions of people. They are accurate up to a point. The degree of accuracy is reflected in the psychometric properties discussed in the first section of this chapter. Even a test with excellent psychometric properties, however, will yield trustworthy data only if the individuals undertaking the test understand what is required of them and are motivated to answer the questions properly.

The fallibility of test results has resulted in some strong criticisms of the practice of psychological testing. There are two main areas of controversy, the first has to do with test users, the second with the tests themselves.

Problems Relating to Test Users

Most examples of test misuse relate to test users. Problems relating to test users can be summed up under the following headings (Anastasi & Urbina, 1997):
  – *User qualifications and professional competence.* The introduction to the technical aspects of testing at the start of this chapter has probably left some readers wondering how much training is required before one can be considered competent to administer tests. The answer is that the amount of training depends on the type of test with some tests such as the MMPI requiring a high level of

training and others, such as tests of decision styles, requiring less training. Virtually all forms of testing, however, require a basic knowledge of psychometrics. Following reports by a special panel of the U.S. National Academy of Sciences set up to investigate testing practice (Wigdor & Garner, 1982a, 1982b), much more attention is now paid to the qualifications of test users. Most test publishers now have categories of usage, with sensitive tests restricted to professions such as psychologists who complete the appropriate training, usually at postgraduate level. Less sensitive tests can be used by teachers, personnel managers, training officers, and other professionals. These people may have some university training but the majority will undertake private training courses run by their companies or by the test publishers. There are two main reasons for restricting test usage: (a) to ensure that the test is administered and interpreted by a qualified user and that the test is properly used, and (b) to prevent general familiarity with the test content, which would invalidate the test (Anastasi & Urbina, 1997, p. 10).

- *Responsibilities of test publishers.* The publishers have to make sure that they do not sell restricted tests to people who lack the training or qualifications to use them. In Australia, a lot of responsibility is placed on the publishers and distributors of tests to make sure that tests do not fall into the wrong hands. The main distributors in this country are the Australian Council for Educational Research, The Psychological Corporation, Science Research Associates/London House, and private companies such as Saville Holdsworth. The first three of these publish catalogues that show quite clearly the level of training required for each test listed. The Psychological Corporation, for example, uses a three category system. Level A tests require basic professional qualifications, such as those gained through a Bachelor of Education. Level B tests require a specialist professional qualification, such as physiotherapy. Level C tests require advanced training in psychometrics, such as that provided through a Masters degree in psychology. Private companies, such as Saville Holdsworth, run their own training courses which are open to everyone, for a fee.
- *Protection of privacy and confidentiality.* Given the nature of constructs being assessed by educational and psychological tests (e.g., personality, ability, achievement), there has always been a concern about leakage of test results to people who may use the results inappropriately. For example, an employer who refused a promotion to an employee because he or she had learned from an outside source that the employee had a high score on neuroticism. Such incidents were not uncommon in the early days of testing. The issue of privacy and confidentiality is now covered by statements in the code of ethics for psychologists and statements about Testing Standards. For non-psychologists, the threat of legal action helps to keep matters in check.
- *Communicating test results.* As you have seen, testing can envelop itself in a shroud of technical terms that imposes a barrier between the general public and test administrators. Some of the controversy surrounding test usage has stemmed from basic misunderstanding of what testing is all about. More attention is now being given to communicating test results in an intelligible form for parents, teachers, and others who may need to view reports.

Problems Relating to Tests

Problems relating to the tests themselves include the following:
- Self-report inventories, of which there are a great number, are too open to faking. People can often see what are socially desirable responses and may choose to respond in a "socially desirable" way, especially if a job is at stake. Lie scales - questions designed to trap people who are trying to project a favourable image - are often used to overcome this problem but the evidence indicates that lie scales are not all that effective.
- It is unfortunate that so many tests are constructed that do not meet the rigorous guidelines discussed above. The problem is worse in some areas than in others. New fields of education and psychology tend to suffer from a rash of poorly constructed tests. The field of sport psychology is an excellent example of over-zealous test development. Fogarty (1995) reviewed the situation in this field and reported a large number of tests developed for the purpose of a single study but then used in applied settings without any evidence of reliability or validity. Many of these tests are not worth administering.
- Fortunately, most fields of education and psychology are well developed and offer a variety of tests for which there is abundant psychometric information. Sources such as the Buros Mental Measurements Yearbook (MMY) offer critical reviews of nearly all commercially available psychological, educational, and vocational tests published in English. Test manuals that accompany commercial tests also contain a lot of valuable psychometric information that can be used to help evaluate a test. In fact, one could almost say that if a test does not have a manual, it may not be a good idea to use that test. Look for one that has the important psychometric information described above and one that, hopefully, is reviewed positively in publications such as the MMY.
- Various forms of bias can occur in tests, especially tests of ability and achievement, such that the tests tend to favour one group over another. The debate on bias has been most bitter in the U.S. where it has been known for many years that significant black-white differences exist on tests of intelligence. If such tests are used to select employees, obviously white applicants are going to have a better chance of success. However, the debates on bias in the 1970s made it clear that bias does not exist simply because one group scores better than another on the selection test. Job performance differences must also be taken into account. Bias exists if it can be shown that the equation used to predict job performance on the basis of test results is different in certain important ways for the two groups. The issues surrounding the debate are too technical to introduce here, suffice it to note that a great deal of research has failed to show evidence of bias. It seems that where tests predict such outcomes as job performance or academic achievement, they do so equally well for most cultural minorities. The emphasis has now switched from looking at the relationship between test scores and job performance, which seems to be the same for all groups, to looking at other criteria that might lead to more members of the lower-scoring group being selected.

Conclusion

There is no doubt that despite the criticism testing may have attracted from some quarters, it is here to stay. If anything, its popularity appears to be growing as the search for information continues to drive our society. It is to be expected that people will seek to know more about themselves and about each other. If testing is to become as safe and dependable as we would like it to be in the fields of clinical psychology, organizational psychology, and education then the tests themselves must be valid and reliable and test users must be well-trained in the principles and ethics of testing. The first of these considerations can be handled by ensuring that tests are evaluated and that psychometric data are published in independent sources such as the Buros Mental Measurements Yearbooks, as well as the test manuals. The World Wide Web will play an important role in disseminating this information. Much information on tests can already be obtained from this source. Professional bodies, test publishers, and legislators need to ensure that people are competent to use whatever tests they employ in their work. Potential users will require sources of objective guidance on what to buy, training will be available from a number of sources (not just the test distributors), and the interests of test-takers will be protected.

Tests have been criticised from various quarters over the past few decades, and such criticism has led to improved testing practices. The criticism has not, however, uncovered any basic weaknesses in theory or methodology. Indeed, one of the main reasons tests are criticised is simply because they can be criticised - they are open to review. Psychological tests do not provide a basis for making completely accurate decisions about individuals. In reality, there is no method which guarantees complete accuracy. However, a special panel of the National Academy of Sciences in the United States concluded that psychological tests generally represent the best, fairest, and most economical method of obtaining information which is necessary to make sensible decisions about individuals (Wigdor & Garner, 1982a, 1982b).

REFERENCES

ACER (1982). ACER Advanced Tests: AL-AQ and BLBQ. *Catalogue of tests and materials.* Melbourne: ACER.

Ackerman, P. L., & Heggestad, D. D. (1997). Intelligence, Personality, and Interests: Evidence for overlapping traits. *Psychological Bulletin, 121,* 219-245.

Anastasi, A., & Urbina, S. (1997). *Psychological Testing* (7th ed). Upper Saddle River, NJ: Prentice Hall.

Bartram, D., & Bayliss, R. (1984). Automated testing: Past, present and future. *Journal of Occupational Psychology, 57,* 221-237.

Bennett, G. K., Seashore, H. G., & Wesman, A. G. (1989). *Differential Aptitude Tests: Australian Manual.* NSW, Australia: The Psychological Corporation.

Bramston, P., & Bostock, J. (1994). Measuring perceived stress in people with intellectual disabilities: The development of a new test. *Australia & New Zealand Journal of Developmental Disabilities, 19,* 149-157.

Bramston, P., & Fogarty, G. (1995). Measuring stress in the mildly intellectually handicapped: The factorial structure of the Subjective Stress Test. *Research in Developmental Disabilities, 16,* 117-131.

Burke, M. J., & Normand, J. (1987). Computerised psychological testing: Overview and critique. *Professional Psychology: Research & Practice, 18,* 42-51.

Costa, P. T., & McCrae, R. R. (1991). *Manual of Revised NEO Personality Inventory and NEO Five-Factor Inventory.* Odessa, FL: Psychological Assessment Resources.

Cronbach, L. J., (1970). *Essentials of psychological testing* (3rd ed.). NY: Harper & Row.

Driver, M. J., Brousseau, K., & Hunsaker, P. (1990). *The dynamic decisionmaker: Five decision styles for executive and business success.* NY: Harper & Row.

Entwistle, N. J. (1983). *Styles of learning and teaching: An integrated outline of educational psychology for students, teachers, and lecturers.* Chichester: John Wiley.

Fogarty, G. (1995) Some comments on the use of psychological tests in sport settings. *International Journal of Sport Psychology, 26,* 161-170.

Fogarty, G. (1998). Response bias in computerised tests. *South Pacific Journal of Psychology* (in press).

Fogarty, G., & Bramston, P. (1997). Validation of the Lifestress Inventory for people with mild intellectual handicap. *Research in Developmental Disabilities, 18,* 435-456.

Fogarty, G., & Taylor, J. (1997). Learning styles among mature-age students: Some comments on the Approaches to Studying Inventory (ASI-S). *Higher Education Research and Development, 16,* 321-330.

Holland, J. L. (1985). *Making vocational choices: A theory of work vocational preferences and work environments* (2nd ed.). Odessa, FL: Psychological Assessment Resources.

Hunt, E. B. (1995). *Will we be smart enough: A cognitive analysis of the coming workforce.* NY: Russell Sage Foundation.

Hunter, J. E. (1986). Cognitive ability, cognitive aptitudes, job knowledge, and job performance. *Journal of Vocational Behaviour, 29,* 340-362.

Murphy, K. R., & Davishofer, C.O. (1988). *Psychological testing: Principles and applications.* Englwood Cliffs, NJ: Prentice-Hall.

Osipow, S. H., & Spokane, A. R. (1987). *Manual for Occupational Stress Inventory: Research version.* Odessa, FL: Psychological Assessment Resources.

Ostrow, A. C. (1990) *Directory of psychological tests in the sport and exercise sciences.* Morgantown: Fitness Information Technology, Inc.

Reich, R. (1991). *The work of nations: Preparing ourselves for 21st century capitalism.* NY: Knopf.

Robertson. I. T., & Smith, M. (1989). Personnel selection methods. In M. Smith and I. Robertson (Eds.), *Advances in selection and assessment* (pp. 89-112). NY: Wiley.

Schwartz, S. H., & Bilsky, W. (1987). Toward a universal psychological structure of human values. *Journal of Personality and Social Psychology, 53,* 550-562.

Tenenbaum, G., & Fogarty, G. (1998). Application of the Rasch analysis to Sport & Exercise Psychology measurement. In J. Duda (Ed.) *Advancements in Sport & Exercise Psychology Measurements,* pp. 409-421. Morgantown, USA: Fitness Information Technology.

Webster, J., & Compeau, D. (1996). Computer-assisted versus paper-and-pencil administration of questionnaires. *Behavior Research Methods, Instruments, & Computers, 28,* 567-576.

Wigdor, A. K., & Garner, W. R. (1982a). *Ability testing: Uses, consequences and controversies, Part 1: Report of the Committee.* Washington, DC: National Academy Press.

Wigdor, A. K., & Garner, W. R. (1982b). *Ability testing: Uses, consequences and controversies, Part 2: Report of the Committee.* Washington, DC: National Academy Press.

Review Questions

Read the following statements and indicate whether they are True or False.

1. Reliability coefficients reflect the extent to which a test measures what it purports to measure.

2. Face validity is the most important aspect of validity.

3. A test is acceptable for use if it is either reliable or valid. It does not need to be both.

4. A correlation coefficient of -1 .00 between two tests means that the tests are unrelated.

5. The standard error of measurement is useful for interpreting individual test scores.

6. If I said that someone had a stanine score of 3 on a test, I would be using relative
7. norms to assess performance rather than some external criterion.
8. Convergent discrimination refers to the extent to which a test correlates with other variables with which it could be expected to correlate.
9. A percentile score of 23 means that a person has scored exactly 23 on a test that is marked out of 100.
10. IQ scores are based on a distribution that has a mean of 100 and a standard deviation of 15.
11. Item-person maps are useful for judging whether the items in a test are suitable in difficulty level for a particular test population.
12. The Stanford Binet is a group test of intelligence.
13. Individual tests are easier to administer and score.
14. Neuropsychological tests are designed to assess brain damage.
15. Holland's model of career interests is based on four basic personality types: Realistic, Social, Investigative, and Enterprising.
16. Cattell's 16 Personality Factors model of personality is based partly on factor analysis.
17. The so-called big five personality factors are neuroticism, extraversion, openness, agreeableness, and conscientiousness.
18. Profile analysis is a technique for looking at patterns of correlations among test scores.
19. The biggest problem with the use of tests of intelligence in occupational selection is that they are biased against minority groups.
20. Research findings indicate that people respond quite differently to tests that are presented by computer.
21. The tendency to respond in a socially desirable way can be a problem with self-report inventories.

Answers

1F	2F	3F	4F	5T	6T	7T	8F	9T
10T	11F	12F	13T	14T	15T	16T	17F	18F
19F	20T							

Exercises

1. Do you think measures of intelligence taken in early childhood would predict academic performance in adult years? Explain.
2. What problems do you foresee with computers not only administering tests but also scoring and interpreting them?
3. On the basis of your own experience, draw up a list of problems related to testing and make suggestions as to how these problems may be rectified. Base your answer on your own personal experiences or, if necessary, your imagination.
4. If you were about to apply for a job, would you feel comfortable if you learned that the selection process included tests of personality and intelligence?

5. Assume that you are working in the personnel section of a small firm and have been asked to prepare selection criteria for a computer programmer's position, what tests would you consider using?
6. There is a site on the Web that allows you to complete a personality test and then obtain feedback. Another site allows you to test your IQ. Whether they will still be there when you read this, I do not know. Perhaps there will be other sites. Here are the addresses: Personality test: http://www.onlinepsych.com/ home.html/; Five-minute IQ test: http://www.brain.com/

Comments on Exercises

1. One would have to question the reliability of measures of intelligence in early childhood. Even if you considered the measure to be both reliable and valid, it is not likely that measures taken so far apart, especially when the first measure was taken during early childhood, will be strongly related. Although many parents take delight in seeing signs of great intelligence in their very young children, the effects of schooling, motivation, and opportunity will combine with innate potential to determine eventual learning achievements. The length of time itself is not the only consideration: measures of intelligence taken in early adulthood will still be strongly related to measures of learning taken in mid-adulthood. Rather, the enormous changes in intellectual development between childhood and adulthood will weaken the relationship.
2. Points to consider include the following:
   – Can any computer programme capture the enormous complexity of individual test results? Will the reports be too stylised?
   – Will the highly impersonal nature of human-computer interaction dissuade people from responding accurately? [Actually, the evidence suggests that some people are more inclined to reveal personal details to a computer than to another person]. (c) What happens if something goes amiss during the testing process when a computer is running the test? (d) Will the people reading the report have any idea of how it was generated? Or how it can be explained? (e) Will the test results and reports be confidential if they are stored on computer disk?
3. Possible problems include: (a) Were you aware of the purpose of testing? (b) Were you asked if you were willing to participate? (c) Did you find out your results? (d) Could you understand the results? (e) Was the testing harmful to you in any way (e.g., prospects)? (f) Were the results treated in a confidential manner?
4. You should feel more comfortable if you can be assured that the test is reliable. If it is reliable, you can have some confidence that the score you obtain is about what you would normally obtain on such a test. You should also feel more comfortable if it is valid. Not only should it measure what it was designed to measure but these processes must be related to job performance. There have been some successful lawsuits in Australia involving disgruntled job applicants suing test administrators because the test used in the selection process was not related to job performance.

5. What would you need to measure? Possibly programming skills. Are reliable and valid tests already available? Yes, there are some. How do you find out about them? Do you need to construct your own test? What else could you measure that might be related to performance in a programming position? Possibly interests. Programmers work a lot with machines, not a position well suited to people who want to spend most of their time working with other people. What about personality variables? Could you justify the inclusion of any tests you choose in a court of law if an applicant claimed that they were unrelated to the position advertised? Do you need to use tests at all?

About the Author

Professor Gerard Fogarty completed a BA (Hons, Psychology) degree at the University of New England in 1973. He then completed a Diploma of Education and taught English and History for three years at Cabramatta High School in Sydney's Western Suburbs in preparation for further training as a school counsellor. After completing these teaching years, he enrolled in a PhD at the University of Sydney, working with Dr Lazar Stankov on a thesis that explored aspects of the structure of human intelligence. Professor Fogarty left Sydney University in 1984 to take up a position with the Head Office of the AMP society where he supervised the development and validation of a new computerised selection system for the 5,000 strong fieldforce of the AMP, a system that includes tests of intelligence, personality, and interests. Professor Fogarty joined the University of Southern Queensland in 1988, where he is still working as Head of the Department of Psychology, lecturing on statistics and psychological measurement. He has published many articles in the areas of intelligence and the validation of psychological tests.

Gerard J. Fogarty
University of Southern Queensland

15. INTRODUCTION TO PSYCHOMETRICS

The case of Rasch models

Educational psychology has developed rapidly in the last few decades; partly thanks to the widespread use of robust test construction models and techniques. The principles and the applications of educational and psychological testing are successfully addressed elsewhere in this book, in the chapter *Principles and Applications of Educational and Psychological Testing*. That chapter introduces the reader to the concepts and principles of testing, illustrates various practical applications and finally goes on to cover the fundamental issues of validity and reliability.

This current chapter aims to extend the knowledge the reader has already gained and introduces the reader to the concept of psychometrics and then goes on to present a family of psychometric models that is, the Rasch models. The next sections illustrate the practical application of a simple Rasch model on empirical data for purposes of scale construction and evaluation. The reader has the opportunity for hands-on-experience by replicating the analyses presented using the analysis software that can be used in conjunction with this chapter. Finally, the chapter ends with a word of caution by discussing issues related to the use and abuse of psychometric models in practice.

Although the chapter is psychometrics-oriented, it is not heavily technical. The purpose is only to familiarise the reader with the fundamental concepts of psychometrics and to offer further references to those wishing to proceed with technically heavier material. The software aims to make the book more practical through hands-on-experience but the aim is not to develop expert psychometricians.

James A Athanasou (ed.), Adult Educational Psychology, 385–418
© *2008 Sense Publishers. All rights reserved.*

The pedagogical approach of the chapter will be somewhat instrumental, avoiding too much jargon, mathematics and details that might deter the novice readers; instead it focuses on giving the average reader the opportunity to apply a model, generate some results and study them to draw some conclusions. It is hoped that this introductory text will win the minds and the hearts of some people and encourage them to further study psychometric models using more technical material.

DEFINITIONS

Before proceeding with the main body of the chapter, it is important to present some operational definitions which will assist the author and the reader to establish a common language.

Test

We adopt the definition of test that has been given elsewhere in the book. Therefore, for the purposes of this chapter, test refers to systematic and standardised methods to obtain information about some aspect of human behaviour or state of mind that is, knowledge, ability, attitudes etc (Fogarty, G. J., this book). The use of the term covers both educational and psychological tests, unless clearly otherwise stated. For the purposes of this chapter, this definition also covers the term "questionnaire".

Psychometrics

Psychometrics is a field of study which deals with the theories and techniques of educational and psychological measurement, for example, the measurement of knowledge, abilities, attitudes, and personality traits. Although the field of psychometrics is interested in individual differences, studying differences between groups of individuals is also very common in the international literature and in practice. Psychometric research and practice elaborates, among other things, on issues like the construction of tests, the establishment of measurement procedures, and the development and refinement of measurement theories.

The borders between psychometrics and other closely related fields are not always clear. For example, Silva (1993) argued that the "nucleus of [...] psychometric approach resides in the so called test theory" (p. xiii) and she opposed those that confuse psychometrics with the totality of "scientific psychological assessment". Since such a discussion is beyond the scope of this chapter, the interested reader is encouraged to visit http://en.wikipedia.org/wiki/Psychometrics for more information about psychometrics and its history of evolution.

In the heart of psychometrics there reside various psychometric models and theories, that is, statistical models and theories that attempt to describe the way people are expected to behave under specific well-described conditions and under certain (usually strictly described) assumptions. Among the most prominent of those theories is the Item Response Theory, part of which is the family of Rasch models which is the focus of this chapter. More detail on the Rasch models is presented below.

Educational and Psychological Measurement

In the previous paragraphs, we defined psychometrics using the term "measurement". This term needs to be defined as well. One of the earliest definitions of measurement is "the assignment of numerals to objects or events according to some rule" (Stevens, 1946). In this chapter, educational and psychological measurement means, in practical terms, to quantify and express with numbers the knowledge, abilities, attitudes and personality traits of people. For example, educational measurement takes place when people are examined on the Test of English as a Foreign Language (TOEFL) exams and have their responses scored and statistically processed and then their results published using a specific scale.

Item Response Theory and the Rasch models

Item Response Theory consists of a large number of competing and/or complementary statistical models which aspire to describe/model some measurement process. According to Molenaar (1995), item response theory is built around the central idea that the probability of a certain answer (or a certain observation, reaction) when a person encounters a question (or a task, a statement) may be estimated by using some specific pieces of information regarding the characteristics of the question (or task, statement) and the person. Deeper discussion of this fundamental issue is postponed until later in this chapter, but the clarification is necessary in order to give to the reader a first glance about the mathematical nature of item response theory.

The Rasch Model represents a family of item response theory models which share a common characteristic: they all have their origins in the Rasch model as inspired and described by George Rasch in 1960 (Rasch, 1960). This chapter will tap only the Simple Model, which is mathematically more tractable and conceptually easier to digest. Although unusual for a psychometric chapter, we will only present the bare minimum of maths and equations. Instead, the focus of the chapter will be to convey as much information as possible through illustrations, tables and text.

At this point, we may need to acknowledge a fact of life: a number of researchers and psychometricians do not agree that the Rasch Model should be categorised as an item response theory model and they have a number of arguments to support their thesis. However, we will not delve into this discussion. For the purpose of an introductory text such as this, it is important to position the reader into a context where he/she will feel more comfortable, without confusing arguments. If the reader wants, he/she may get involved into deeper discussions regarding the nature and the philosophy of psychometrics using additional material such as Alagumalai, Curtis and Hungi (2005).

Rasch Analysis Capable Software

There are a large number of software packages that can handle analysis involving various Rasch models. Each of the software packages has its own advantages and disadvantages. Some packages are fast and can handle very large datasets, other packages can handle very complex Rasch models and other packages are more user-friendly using a windows-based interface but may be slower or may not be able to handle very large datasets. More information on the different Rasch analysis capable packages may be found on the internet simply by Googling the keywords "Rasch analysis software".

The Analysis package used for the Rasch analysis examples of this chapter belongs to the latter category: user-friendly using a windows-based interface but probably a bit slower or not capable of handling very large datasets. However, this is the category of packages that are mostly well-suited to teaching Rasch models to novice readers.

The Analysis software was written and is maintained by the author of this chapter. He has used this software for several years to teach Rasch models to postgraduate students at the University of Manchester, UK. The software may be reached at the page http://www.relabs.org/software.html from where a manual may be downloaded as well. All the datasets used in the examples of this chapter are also included in the package and will become available when the software is installed. They may also be downloaded as separate files from the same web page. It is advisable to visit the page every now and then to download updated versions of the manual, more examples, papers, and datasets. The software and the manual are under the freeware license, that is, anyone may use or distribute them (with no modifications) for free to anyone, provided this is not done for profit. It is important, however, to acknowledge, as happens with all software, that the users must read and agree with all terms and conditions of the use of the software before downloading, installing and using it. Also, regarding the screenshots of this chapter, it is important for the reader to know that most software does not remain unchanged across time. Usually, all software packages undergo minimal or larger changes/upgrades, therefore, future versions may look slightly different.

KEY TECHNICAL CONCEPTS OF THE RASCH MODEL

The field of psychometrics is based on a number of psychometric models that is, statistical models used to describe human behaviour under specific conditions and under specific assumptions. Modelling human behaviour is a very difficult thing to do, however, because humans are very complex organisations and their behaviour may be the result of a very large number of interacting factors.

Therefore, trying to predict human behaviour always involves statistical (i.e. probabilistic) instead of deterministic[1] models. For example, when a person attempts to give a response to a question, you can never be sure about the outcome: even a very able student may give an incorrect response to an "easy" question because of carelessness, fatigue, a sudden illness or other factors. At best, we may be able to say that a specific person has x% chance to give a correct response to a specific question under certain conditions but we can never predict the outcome (right or wrong response) for sure.

It would be reasonable, though, to assume that the more difficult a question is, the smaller the probability of a given student to give a correct response. And our experience from our school life also advises us that the less difficult a question is, the higher the probability of a specific person to give a right response. Is it possible, however, to quantify this relationship between the ability of a person and the difficulty of a question? And if possible, how can the probability of a correct response be estimated?

In order to estimate the probability for a correct or an incorrect response to a question, various researchers have developed some technical jargon. We will call the Rasch scale, a conceptual ruler on which we imagine that we can place both the difficulties of the question and the abilities of the persons. Imagine that this scale extends from minus infinity to plus infinity and represents the dimension, ability, trait etc (generally speaking any quantity) we want to measure.

Figure 15.1 *A common conceptual 'Rasch scale' on which to place the ability of persons and the difficulty of questions (from Athanasou and Lamprianou, 2002).*

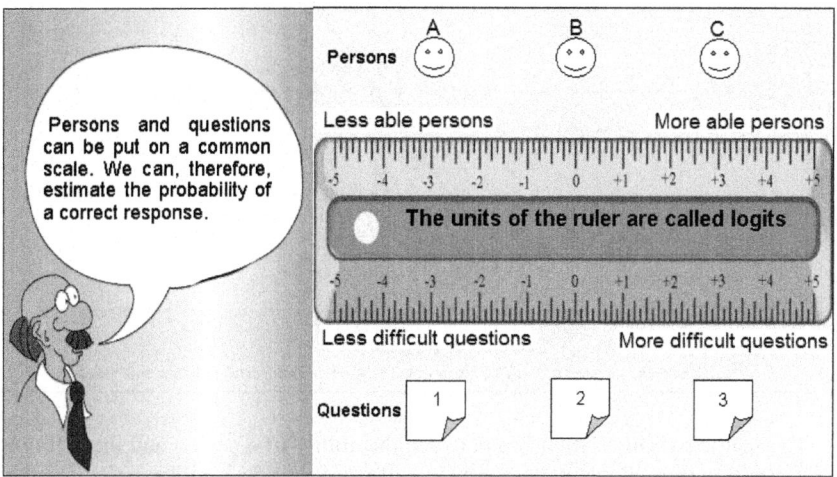

Imagine that it is possible to measure the ability of persons and the difficulty of questions using a common metric, in the same way in which we can measure the length of a pair of trousers or the height of a person. Imagine also that we can place the ability measure of a person and the difficulty measure of a question on this common metric or Rasch scale. Therefore, we can directly compare the ability of persons and the difficulty of questions.

Where a person's ability is larger than the difficulty of the question, then we would expect this person to have a good chance to give a correct response. For example, in Figure 15.1 person C has an ability measure which is larger than the difficulty measure of question 2; therefore, we would expect person C to have more than 50% chance to give a correct response to question 2. Later on, in this chapter, we will explain in detail how we decided that person C has more than 50% chance to give a correct response on question 2.

Figure 15.2 *The Item Response Function estimating the probability for a correct response comparing the ability of the person and the difficulty of the question (ability=difficulty).*

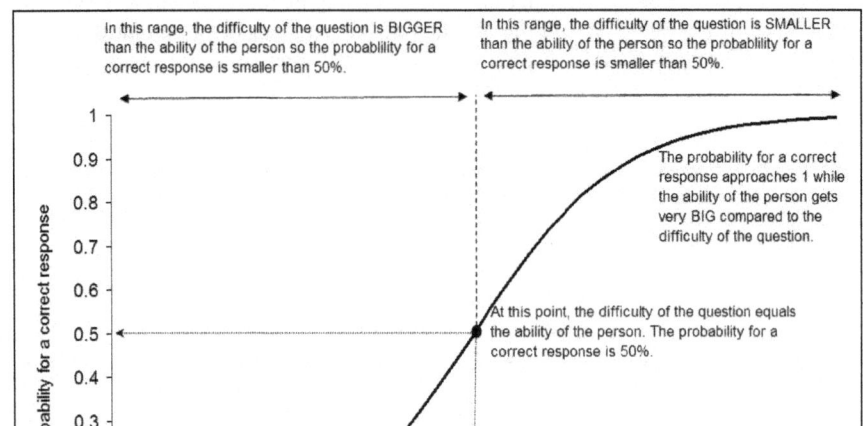

The Rasch scale on which we place both the question's difficulty and the person's ability

The mathematical relationship between the ability of a person and the difficulty of a question that allows us to compute (estimate) the probability for a correct or incorrect response is usually called the *Item Response Function*. The actual formulation of the item response function is not of interest at the moment, it is however useful to depict it graphically (see Figure 15.2).

Figure 15.2 makes the interpretation of the relationship between the ability of a person and the difficulty of a question easier. The x-axis (the horizontal ruler) shows the Rasch scale, on which we may place both the ability of the person and the difficulty of the question. The discrepancy between the ability and the difficulty governs the probability for a correct response which is shown on the y-axis (vertical axis). When the ability of the person equals the difficulty of the question the probability of a correct response is 50%.

Figure 15.3 also illustrates the relationship between the ability of the person and the difficulty of the question. The difference between Figure 15.2 and Figure 15.3 is that in the latter case the ability of the person is larger than the difficulty of the question, therefore, the probability for a correct response is larger than 50%. Notice that the ability of the person in Figure 15.3 is larger than the difficulty of the question by 1 Rasch unit (1 logit). In fact, the probability for a correct response is now around 73%, suggesting that an increase in the ability of the person by 1 logit may increase his/her success chance by around ½ of what it was (from 50% to 73% in this case).

Figure 15.3 *The Item Response Function estimating the probability for a correct response comparing the ability of the person and the difficulty of the question (ability>difficulty).*

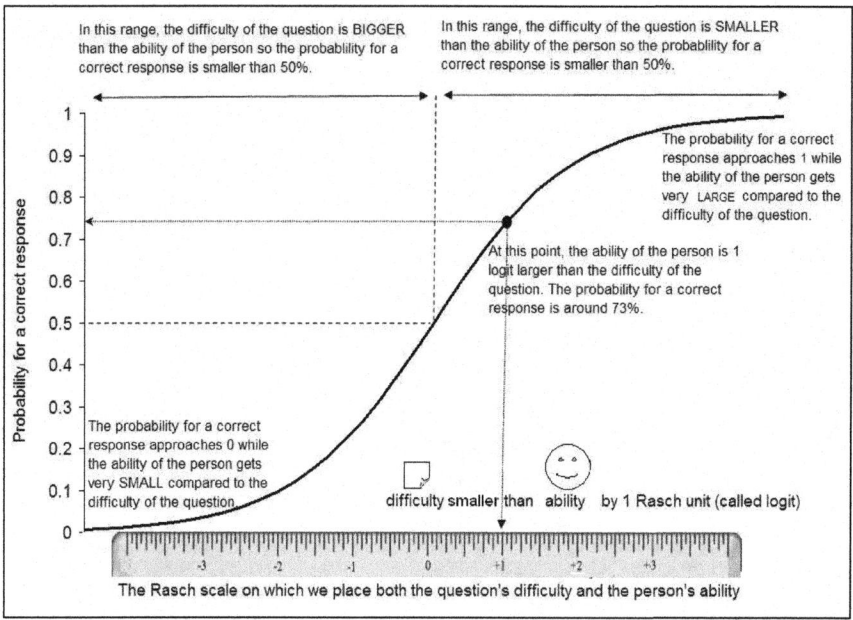

The Rasch scale on which we place both the question's difficulty and the person's ability

Figure 15.4 again illustrates the relationship between the ability of the person and the difficulty of the question. The difference between Figure 15.2 and Figure 15.4 is that in the latter case the ability of the person is smaller than the difficulty of the question, therefore, the probability for a correct response is smaller than 50%. In fact, the probability for a correct response is now around 27%, suggesting that a decrease in the ability of the person may decrease his/her success chance to give a correct response. In the case of Figure 15.4, the ability of the person is smaller than the difficulty of the question by 1 Rasch unit. Compare (contrast) the two figures (Figure 15.3 and Figure 15.4) to see how the probability of a correct response changes while the ability of the person changes in relation to the difficulty of the question.

Figure 15.4 *The Item Response Function estimating the probability for a correct response comparing the ability of the person and the difficulty of the question (ability<difficulty)*

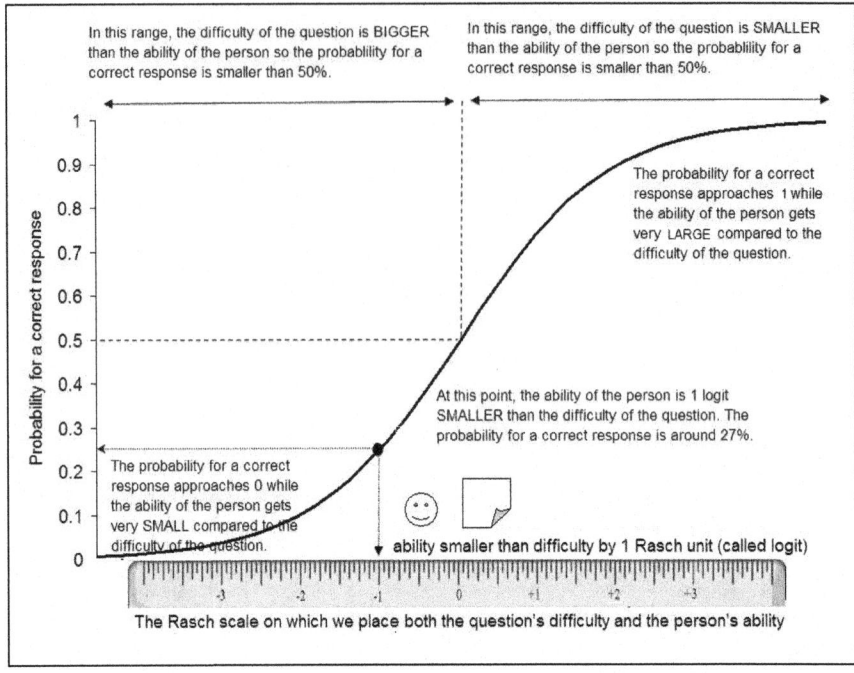

Table 15.1 *The relation between a person's ability, a question's difficulty and the probability of a correct response*

If a person's ability	then the probability of a correct response
is larger than a question's difficulty	is larger than 50%
is smaller than a question's difficulty	is smaller than 50%
equals a question's difficulty	equals 50%
While a person's ability gets	**then the probability of a correct response**
bigger than a question's difficulty	increases
smaller than a question's difficulty	decreases

Table 15.1 was constructed to summarise the findings of Figure 15.2, 15.3 and 15.4. In summary, Table 15.1 says that while a person's ability gets larger, his/her chance to answer a specific question correctly also gets larger. Also, while the ability of a person gets smaller, his/her chance for a correct response also gets smaller.

The equation that describes the relationship is given below

Probability for a correct response=Function (Ability-Difficulty)   (1)

Using mathematical terms, this relationship may be expressed as below

$$P\{\chi = 1/\theta, \delta\} = \frac{e^{\theta - \delta}}{1 + e^{\theta - \delta}}$$

(2)

where θ is the ability of a person, δ is the difficulty of a question, χ is the response of the person (either right=1 or wrong=0) and $e = 2.718$ (approximately). From now on, we shall represent persons' abilities with θ s and δ s will represent the difficulties of questions.

The above equation of the Rasch model gives the probability of an examinee of ability θ to obtain the correct answer of a question with difficulty δ. This probability ranges between zero and 100 percent. For example, on the Rasch scale (ruler) of Figure 15.1, the second person on the figure has an ability of 0 units (θ=0 logits) and the difficulty of the third question is +3 units ($\delta = +3$ logits). The probability that Person B gives a correct response rather than an incorrect one (i.e., $x = 1$ rather than $x = 0$) to question 3 may be computed as

$$P\{\chi = 1/\theta = 0, \delta = 3\} = \frac{e^{0 - 3}}{1 + e^{0 - 3}} = \frac{e^{-3}}{1 + e^{-3}} = \frac{0.05}{1 + 0.05} = 4.7\%$$

Apparently this person has a very small probability of giving a correct response to this question. In the case where a question is just right for a person (in any case that ability equals difficulty such as $\theta = \delta = 1$ or $\theta = \delta = 0$ or $\theta = \delta = -1.4$), there is a probability 50% for a correct response. This is illustrated below:

$$P\{\chi = 1/\theta = 1, \delta = 1\} = \frac{e^{1 - 1}}{1 + e^{1 - 1}} = \frac{e^0}{1 + e^0} = \frac{1}{1 + 1} = \frac{1}{2} = 50\%$$

At this point it should be emphasised that 'ability=0' does not mean that a person does not know anything, in the same way as 'temperature=$0^o C$' does not mean 'no temperature at all'. It should be explained that the ability scale extends from minus infinity through zero to plus infinity and that ability zero is sometimes conceptualised (although it is not entirely correct) as the ability of a person who answered half of the questions correctly, or, the ability of a person of 'average' ability (regarding the property we measure using the test). In the same way, a question of zero difficulty does not mean 'no difficulty at all'. It just means that an item with 'difficulty=0 logits' is probably an item of 'average' difficulty or an item that has probably been answered correctly by half the persons that took the test. Although these explanations are not entirely correct, they will be useful for the time being.

Surely, one of the main objectives of the Rasch model is to estimate the question and the person parameters (difficulties and abilities respectively). However, it is also important to estimate the degree of uncertainty by which these parameters are estimated. It is not possible to use empirical data to compute the true values of abilities and difficulties with perfect accuracy. This is especially true for people: random responses, careless errors, sudden illnesses, atypical schooling, the unreliable human nature and other factors may contribute to the imprecision by which ability parameters are estimated. The index which shows the degree of unreliability for ability and difficulty estimates will be called Standard Error (S.E.). It is important to mention that every estimate must be accompanied by its standard error; otherwise the reader does not know how much trust to put to an estimate. In this chapter, we will always include in tables the standard errors of estimates when we present the results of Rasch analyses. Very large standard errors of the question difficulty estimates, for example, may mean that we cannot say for sure which question is more difficult than the other.

A PRACTICAL EXAMPLE: APPLICATION OF THE SIMPLE RASCH MODEL ON ADULTS' TERTIARY ASPIRATIONS DATA

Since the fundamental concepts of the Rasch model have been defined, it is time for the first numerical example. The aim of this section is to introduce the reader to his/her first application of the simplest Rasch model on empirical data. At the same time, we aim to establish the meaning of the fundamental concepts that have been introduced in the previous sections through examples.

The Dataset

The dataset consists of the responses of 474 adults to a questionnaire investigating their aspirations for university degree studies. All of the adults are secondary school graduates but none managed to follow further studies. Each of them was individually presented with a list of 49 university degree programs, each one leading (upon graduation) to a specific profession (e.g., mathematics, civil engineering, nursing etc). The adults were instructed to declare their preference for any number of these university degrees, for example one might choose to tick civil engineer, mathematics, and nursing studies. In other words, they were asked to tick any of those degree programs they would like to follow, if they had the chance. At the same time, they were instructed to leave blank (not to tick) the degree programs that did not interest them. Depending on their academic qualifications, they might be awarded a place in higher education, based on their preferences, so they had every legitimate reason to complete the questionnaire honestly and carefully.

Not all people, however, responded to the same questionnaire. A small group of people were administered a shorter version of the questionnaire, which included only 42 (instead of 49) degree programs. This happened because these people did not satisfy the criteria for all degree programs on the list (but it is beyond the scope of this chapter to give more explanations about this). As a result these people were not presented with 7 out of the 49 degree programs and they did not have the opportunity to express their desire to follow or not to follow them.

When the data was coded, the result was a 474 by 49 matrix with zeros and ones (350 cells in fact were blank because 50 of the persons were administered a questionnaire with only 42 degree programs). If a person had ticked a specific degree program, then he/she received a '1' in that cell of the matrix. If a person did not tick a degree program, then he/she received a '0' in that cell of the matrix. If a person did not have the opportunity to respond to a degree program, the cell remained blank.

To make things clearer, please use the Analysis software to open the file studies.txt[2] (or to import the file studies.xls[3]). The screen should look like the screenshot in Figure 15.5.

Figure 15.5 *The content of the file studies.txt when opened in the Analysis package.*

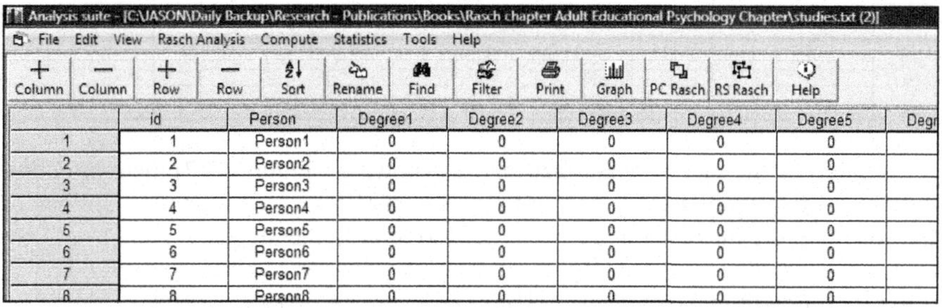

	id	Person	Degree1	Degree2	Degree3	Degree4	Degree5	Degr
1	1	Person1	0	0	0	0	0	
2	2	Person2	0	0	0	0	0	
3	3	Person3	0	0	0	0	0	
4	4	Person4	0	0	0	0	0	
5	5	Person5	0	0	0	0	0	
6	6	Person6	0	0	0	0	0	
7	7	Person7	0	0	0	0	0	
8	8	Person8	0	0	0	0	0	

The spreadsheet of Figure 15.5 illustrates the nature and the content of the file *studies.txt*. The first column shows the number of the rows in an increasing order. The second column carries the name 'Person' and contains the names of the persons that took part in the study (ranging from 'Person1' to 'Person474'). The rest of the columns carry names that depict the order by which each of the degree programs happened to be presented on the questionnaire (for example, Degree26 is 'Nursing Studies' and it happened to be presented as the 26th item on the questionnaire). Instead of using the code-names Degree1 to Degree49 we could have used the actual name of each of the degree programs, but for the purposes of this example this is not necessary.

The content of the columns 'Degree1' to 'Degree49' is either 1 (i.e., the degree program was ticked) or 0 (i.e., the degree program was not ticked) or blank. If you scroll down, to the 100th row and to the 43rd column, a whole set of cells are blank: these show the 'non-administered' or 'missing' nature of those cells because the persons from Person100 to Person149 did not have the opportunity to respond to questions Degree43 to Degree49 (see Figure 15.6).

The unpopularity of each of the degree programs (i.e., the frequency of zeros rather than ones) may be investigated using a simple procedure. Go to the main menu at the top of the Analysis software, click on 'Statistics' and then select 'Traditional'. A new window will appear in front of the sheet (see Figure 15.7). Select the variables with names 'Degree1' and 'Degree46' and click on the arrow heading to the right. The variables will move to the box to the right. Check the box 'Frequencies Tables' at the bottom of the window and then click on 'Run Statistics'.

Figure 15.6 *'Not-administered' variables in the data sheet.*

	Degree39	Degree40	Degree41	Degree42	Degree43	Degree44	Degree45	Degree46	Degree47	Degree48	Degree49
96	0	0	0	0	0	0	0	0	0	0	0
97	0	0	1	1	1	1	1	1	0	0	0
98	0	0	0	0	0	0	1	0	0	0	0
99	1	1	0	0	0	0	0	0	0	0	0
100	0	0	0	0							
101	0	0	1	1							
102	0	0	0	0							
103	0	0	0	0							
104	0	0	0	0							
105	0	0	0	0							
106	0	0	0	0							
107	0	0	0	0							
108	0	0	1	1							
109	0	0	0	0							

Ignore, for the moment, the fact that (as shown on Figure 15.7) there are other options on the window. For more information about the menus and the options of the software, the interested reader will need to refer to the manual.

Figure 15.7 *Generating a table of frequencies for the two variables.*

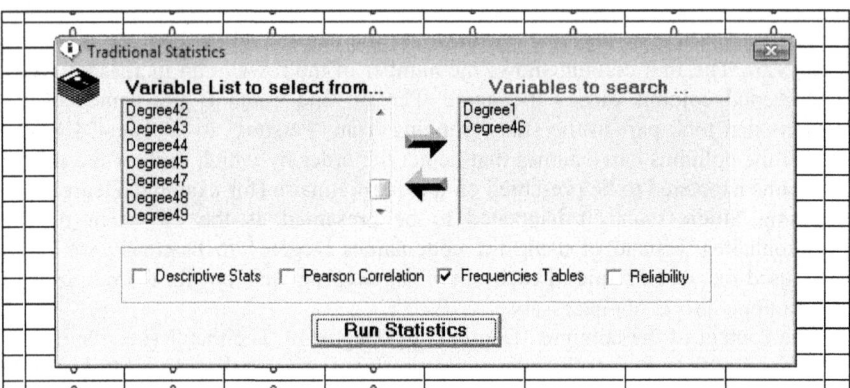

Figure 15.8 shows the results for the variables Degree1 and Degree46. There were no missing cases for the variable Degree1 (blank cells are depicted using the term 'Mi') because all persons had the opportunity to provide a response: not ticking a degree program in this case means 'I do not wish to study it'. Degree1 was ticked by only 35 persons (a score of 1), a percentage of around 7% and almost 93% (N=439) did not tick it (a score of 0). We assume that the more persons that tick a degree program, the more popular this program is among the respondents. The fewer the people that tick it, the more unpopular it is.

Apparently, Degree1 was not very popular among the respondents in this dataset since most of them chose not to tick it. In terms of Rasch measurement we would expect this degree program to have a very large unpopularity statistic (i.e., the program was difficult for the respondents to endorse) and we would place it at the right part of the Rasch scale; somewhere near question 1 in Figure 15.1 for example.

Figure 15.8 *Table of frequencies for the variable 'Degree1'.*

```
Variable Name: Degree1
=========================================================================
   Grade         N          %         Cum%      Valid%     Valid Cumul.%
=========================================================================
    Mi            0          0          0
     0          439       92.62       92.62      92.62        92.62
     1           35        7.38        100        7.38         100
=========================================================================


Variable Name: Degree46
=========================================================================
   Grade         N          %         Cum%      Valid%     Valid Cumul.%
=========================================================================
    Mi           50        10.55      10.55
     0          397       83.76       94.3       93.63        93.63
     1           27        5.7         100        6.37         100
=========================================================================
```

However, Figure 15.8 shows the frequency table for the variable Degree46 as well. There were 50 persons who did not have the opportunity to provide a response to this variable (indicated by the code 'Mi' which means 'missing'). This makes the direct comparison between the popularity of the degree programs difficult. For example, how can we compare the 7.4% popularity of Degree1 with the 5.7% popularity of Degree46, if we know that 50 of the respondents did not even have the chance to tick the latter? One might reasonably ask if it is likely that the popularity of the two degree programs might be the around the same levels, had all the persons been administered the same questionnaire.

Similarly, it is not possible to compare the degree of the divergence of the interests of the persons since they were not all presented with the same questionnaire. For example, Person1 and Person100 both ticked only one degree program that is, Degree26 (which incidentally is a Nursing degree program from a medical school). Does this information help us to say whether the two persons have the same divergence of academic interests? Person100 was only presented with 42 out of the 49 degree programs and ticked one program only, a ratio of $\frac{1}{42}$. On the other hand, Person1 ticked only one in 49 programs, a ratio of $\frac{1}{49}$. Had Person100 been presented all options, one might ask, is it possible that he/she would make additional ticks on the questionnaire?

A similar procedure may be followed to produce tables of frequencies and other statistics for all the variables in the sheet[4]. That way, we can compare between the variables and identify those degree programs which were more or less popular, although the existence of missing responses (i.e. not administered) makes our work much harder. Thankfully, there is hope: the Rasch model promises to help us solve this problem by generating popularity/unpopularity indices for the degree programs that are directly comparable. Also, the Rasch model promises to generate indices for all persons that are directly comparable even if they completed different questionnaires. It is true, however, that the Rasch model can successfully deliver these promises only if specific assumptions hold, but we will save this discussion for later because it may sound a bit technical. The aim of the next section is to apply a simple Rasch model on the data and interpret the results.

Application of the Simple Model on a Dataset

The application of the simple Rasch model on this dataset will help us to model mathematically the response patterns of the persons to the questionnaire. We will estimate a single index for each person to indicate his/her variability of interests for university degree programs. We will call this index 'range of interests for further study' in the sense that the larger the number of degree programs a person ticks, the more divergent his/her interests are for further study. Also, the smaller the number of degree programs a person ticks, the narrower the range of his interests for further study.

For example, if a person ticks only one degree program, then this person gives us the message that he/she is very selective about their further studies: even if universities gave him/her access to other degree programs, they would probably turn them down. Therefore, such a person has a small (narrow) range of interests for further studies. On the other hand, a person who is very eager to proceed to higher education no matter what the exact nature of the degree program will be, would be expected to tick a larger number of degree programs, indicating that he/she is not very selective that is, such a person has a larger range of interests for further studies.

At the one extreme, a person selecting no degree programs at all on the questionnaire shows that he/she is not interested in further studies. A person selecting all the degree programs on the list indicates that he/she has a huge range of interests and a desire for further studies of any kind no matter what the nature of the study is. For each one of these two types of persons, the Analysis software will produce a 'range of interest (for further study)' index which will be placed on the Rasch scale of Figure 15.9 but it will be extreme in magnitude and very imprecise. In fact, all the persons and all the degree programs with zero (no ticks) or full (all ticks) scores are special cases and we usually drop them from Rasch analysis. An informal discussion of the issue may be found at http://www.rasch.org/rmt/rmt122h.htm for the interested reader, but it may be a bit technical.

A similar idea holds for the degree programs. In the case of this example, we will construct a Rasch estimate for every degree program which we will call 'unpopularity[5]' index (i.e., the 'difficulty' of a degree program to be endorsed by the persons that responded to the questionnaire). A degree program is less unpopular if more people choose to tick it. Such a program would probably have a negative unpopularity Rasch estimate (i.e., negative unpopularity means that the program is popular) and we would probably locate it at the left part of the Rasch scale of Figure 15.9. On the contrary, a degree program is more difficult to be endorsed (i.e., is more unpopular) if fewer people choose to tick it; therefore, we would probably place its 'difficulty to be endorsed' (unpopularity) estimate at the right part of the Rasch scale.

Figure 15.9 *A common conceptual 'Rasch scale' on which to place the range of interests of persons and the unpopularity of degree programs.*

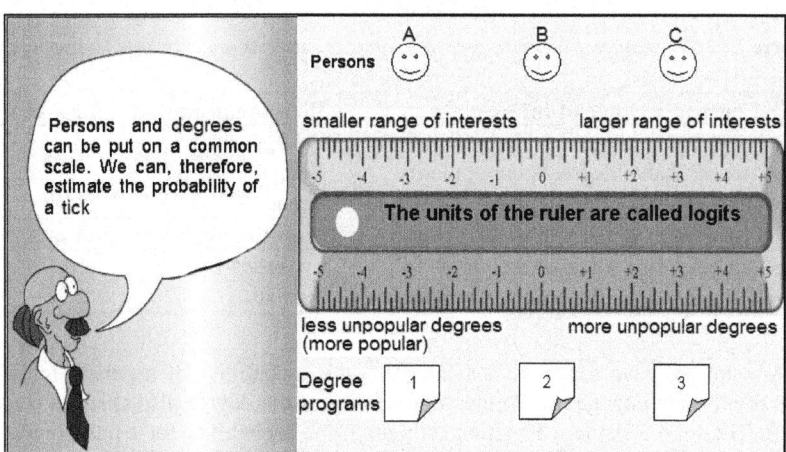

Therefore, the main aim of the simple model is to estimate an unpopularity index for every degree program and a 'range of interests' index for each person. This is based on the fundamental assumption that the wider (the larger) the range of interests of a person for further study, the larger the number of the degree programs he/she will tick. Also, a second fundamental assumption is that the more unpopular a degree program is, the smaller the likelihood that the people will tick it. A third assumption is that the likelihood that a person will tick a degree program is exclusively governed only by the range of interests of that person and the unpopularity of the degree program; not by any other external factor (such as external pressure by peers, boredom, indifference to complete the questionnaire) – this is the assumption of uni-dimensionality. A fourth assumption is that the persons have ample time to respond to the questionnaire honestly, for example, without trying to fake their responses to please the researcher or to randomly tick degree programs. A fifth assumption is that the responses of a person to the previous questions do not affect his/her responses to the next questions, for example, if a person has ticked a specific degree program this will not affect his/her behaviour when considering the next degree programs (whether he/she will tick the next programs) – this is the assumption of local independence. These assumptions are very important, and if a researcher feels that one (or more) of those are harshly violated then running a Rasch model may become a risky business. In such situations, the results will need to be studied very carefully before publishing them because they may not be valid. Also, in such a situation or when in doubt, the novice researcher is encouraged to seek some help from a more experienced Rasch practitioner.

As we mentioned above, the main aim of the simple model is to estimate an unpopularity index for every degree program and a range of interests (for further study) index for each person. We hereby make the following statement, trying to paraphrase Table 15.1 by generating Table 15.2 which is more suitable in the context of this example. The difference between those two tables is that in the latter, we do not talk about persons' ability and questions' difficulty any more, but about (a) a person's range of interests and (b) a degree program's unpopularity.

This is important to keep in mind when we interpret the results of the Rasch analysis.

Table 15.2 *The relation between a person's range of interests and a degree's unpopularity*

If a person's range of interests	then the probability for a tick
is larger than a degree's unpopularity	is larger than 50%
is smaller than a degree's unpopularity	is smaller than 50%
equals a degree's unpopularity	equals 50%
While a person's range of interests	**then the probability for a tick**
gets bigger than a degree's unpopularity	increases
gets smaller than a degree's unpopularity	decreases

A graph may be drawn to indicate how the probability of a person to tick a degree program changes while the unpopularity of the degree also changes (Figure 15.10 The Item Response Function estimating the probability for a tick comparing the range of interests of a person and the unpopularity of a degree (range of interests > unpopularity).

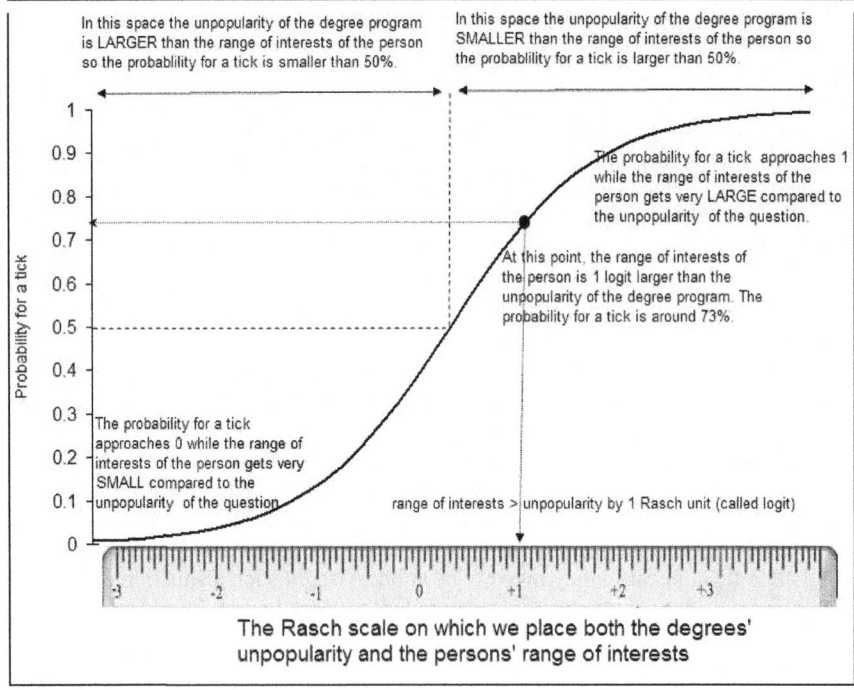

The Rasch scale on which we place both the degrees' unpopularity and the persons' range of interests

In order to produce the Rasch analysis we need to indicate to the Analysis package which of the variables (degree programs) we would like to include in the Rasch analysis. We can do this by clicking on the "PC *Rasch*" button on the toolbar (see Figure 15.11).

Figure 15.11 *How to initiate a Rasch analysis.*

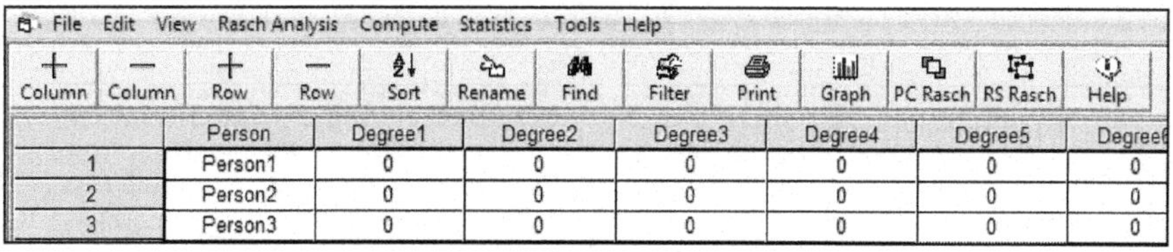

	Person	Degree1	Degree2	Degree3	Degree4	Degree5	Degree6
1	Person1	0	0	0	0	0	0
2	Person2	0	0	0	0	0	0
3	Person3	0	0	0	0	0	0

File Edit View Rasch Analysis Compute Statistics Tools Help

Column — Column — Row — Row — Sort — Rename — Find — Filter — Print — Graph — PC Rasch — RS Rasch — Help

As soon as you click on the 'PC Rasch' button, Analysis will present you with a window which will ask you to indicate which of the variables (i.e., degree programs) should be included in the analysis. Click on each of the columns 'Degree1' to 'Degree49' and then click on the arrow facing to the right to pass them (one by one) to the other box. Ignore any other variables for the moment. Then click on the button 'Run Rasch Analysis' at the bottom of the window.

). This is similar to the graphs presented by Figure 15.2, Figure 15.3 and Figure 15.4 although it is better suited in the context of this specific practical example. Notice how the terms 'ability' and 'difficulty' were changed to 'range of interests' and 'unpopularity'. The rest of the concepts and the way to read the graph remains the same as in Figure 15.2, Figure 15.3 and Figure 15.4. Notice, also, that since the range of interests of the person is larger than the unpopularity of the degree program (by 1 Rasch logit), the probability of a tick is well above 50%.

A secondary aim of the simple model is to estimate an uncertainty index (the standard error as we call it) for each persons' range of interests and for each degree programs' unpopularity. This is necessary because in real life we can never be sure what the exact index of each person or degree program would be, had we administered the questionnaire to a similar but different group of people. This holds true even if we had administered the same questionnaire again to the same people; we would still expect some responses of some people to change for a number of reasons. We will say more about the uncertainty indices (hence, standard errors) later on in this section.

Figure 15.10 *The Item Response Function estimating the probability for a tick comparing the range of interests of a person and the unpopularity of a degree (range of interests > unpopularity).*

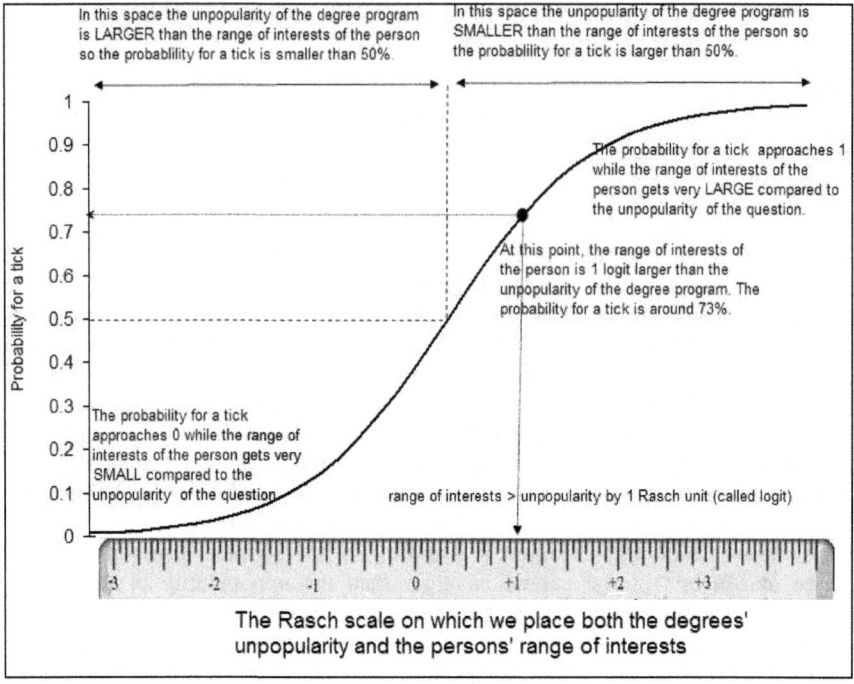

In order to produce the Rasch analysis we need to indicate to the Analysis package which of the variables (degree programs) we would like to include in the Rasch analysis. We can do this by clicking on the "*PC Rasch*" button on the toolbar (see Figure 15.11).

Figure 15.11 How to initiate a Rasch analysis.

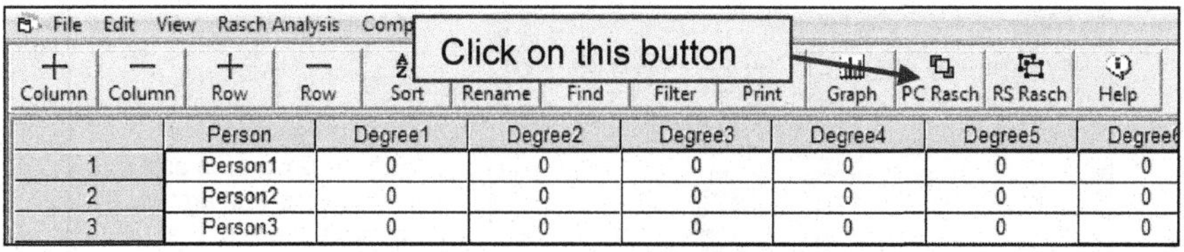

	Person	Degree1	Degree2	Degree3	Degree4	Degree5	Degree6
1	Person1	0	0	0	0	0	0
2	Person2	0	0	0	0	0	0
3	Person3	0	0	0	0	0	0

As soon as you click on the 'PC Rasch' button, Analysis will present you with a window which will ask you to indicate which of the variables (i.e., degree programs) should be included in the analysis. Click on each of the columns 'Degree1' to 'Degree49' and then click on the arrow facing to the right to pass them (one by one) to the other box. Ignore any other variables for the moment. Then click on the button 'Run Rasch Analysis' at the bottom of the window.

The screen should look very similar to the one shown in Figure 15.12[6]. Make sure that you copy all the degree programs to the right box because if you leave any of them behind, they will not be included in the analysis. But notice, also, that you should not include any of the other variables, like 'id' or 'Person', because they may make the software crash. The reason of the possible crash is that the specific software can only handle variables representing numeric values of a specific range (from 0-9).

Just after clicking on the 'Run Rasch Analysis' button, a 'Please Wait' message will appear on the screen while the software prepares the output of the analysis. For the specific dataset, the analysis should not take more than a few seconds on a standard modern computer. After a while, a new (vertical this time) toolbar should appear at the right of the working sheet (Figure 15.13). You may use this toolbar to view the results of the Rasch analysis, including information about the estimates of the persons and the degree programs. These issues will be addressed in the next section.

At this point, it is important to mention that the exact procedures and algorithm to estimate the parameters of the persons and the questions will not be presented in this chapter for a number of reasons. First of all, they are technically heavy, and it is possible that they may discourage some people from further study. Also, it is unlikely that they will be interesting to everybody, so we will leave it to the most motivated readers to seek more information about the estimation techniques in www.rasch.org .

Figure 15.12 *How to indicate the degree programs to be included in the Rasch analysis.*

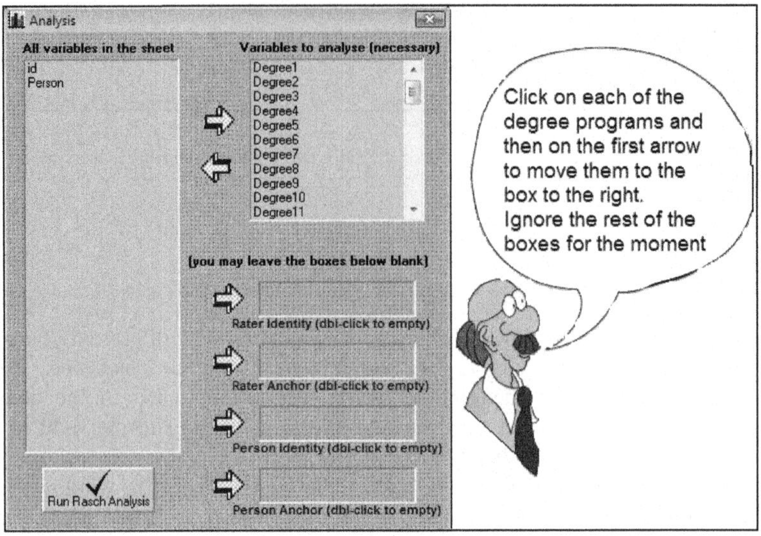

Interpretation of the Results of the Simple Rasch Model

Clicking on the first icon of the toolbar with the label "Scale" will produce a graph which illustrates the distribution of the unpopularity indices of the degree programs and the distribution of the persons' 'range of interests' index. Figure 15.14 illustrates the fact that the estimates of the degree programs (with the red colour and the legend 'Degrees %') are spread on a scale from -3.5 units (Rasch logits) to +3 units (Rasch logits). Each bar shows the percentage (%) of degree programs on each level of the scale. In this case, (since there are 49 degree programs in the statistical analysis), each of the programs represents around 2% of the total. Therefore, the first red bar represents 1 degree program, having an estimate in the range from -3.75 to -3.25 logits.

Figure 15.13 *The toolbar negotiating the output of the Rasch analysis.*

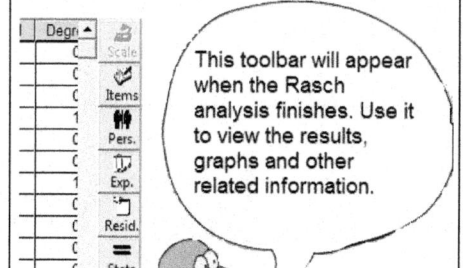

A large percentage of the degree programs are found to the right of the scale, indicating that these were rather unpopular. The massive majority of the degree programs are scattered around the centre of the scale but far to the right of the range of interests of the persons, indicating that most of the degree programs were indeed unpopular. It seems that the distribution of the person estimates is shifted to the left compared to the distribution of the unpopularity estimates of the degree programs. Indeed, very few programs have unpopularity indices that overlap with the range of interests of the persons; we may therefore suggest that in most of the cases, the probability of a 'typical' person to tick a 'typical' degree program is rather small. This is in accord with the small % of ticks, as found in Figure 15.8.

On the other hand the majority of the persons (the green bars with the legend 'Persons %') are found to the far left of the scale, indicating that they have small ranges of interests: these persons were very selective, probably ticking only one or two degree programs. Very few of the persons have estimates around the centre of the scale (and none beyond it), indicating that overall, the persons were selective on which degree studies they would wish to follow if they had the chance. More specifically, the percentage of people to the far left of the scale (more than 30%) is so large, that we might assume that these people might be a group with some special common background characteristics, for example they might be adults with very specific goals in their life, aiming for a specific profession through a specific university degree.

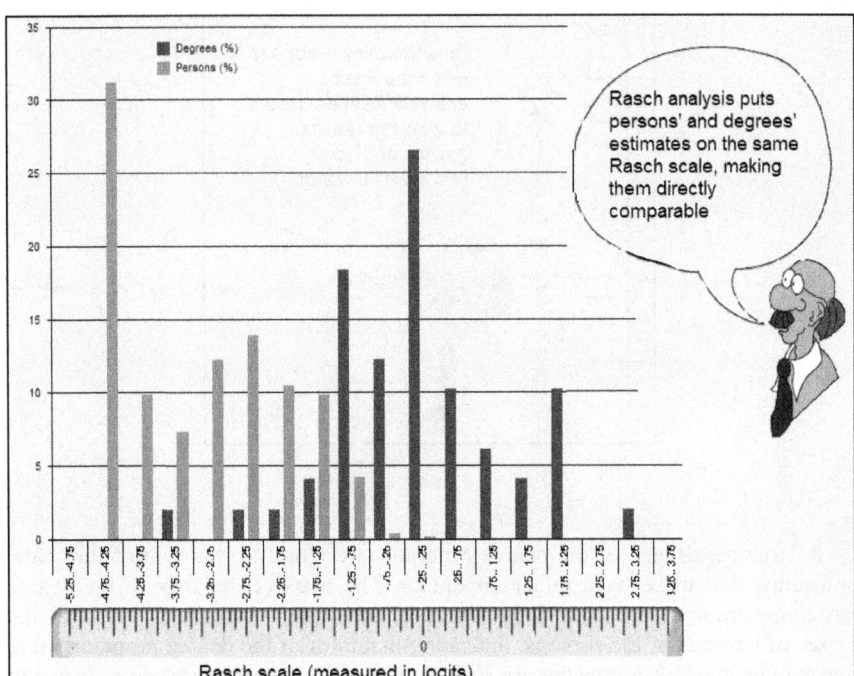

We can close the graph by clicking on the 'Exit' button on the window of the graph. Do not worry that you may need the graph later; you may make the graph visible again by clicking on the 'Scale' button of the toolbar. Check the manual to see how you can copy the graph or the data behind the graph and paste them into MS Excel or MS Word for further processing.

Clicking on the "Items" button on the toolbar to the right will produce the Rasch statistics of the degree programs (Figure 5.15). The first column of the table shows the name of the degree program, the second column the number of persons that had the opportunity to respond to this program (i.e., do not forget that not everybody was administered the same questionnaire), the third column shows the number of persons that actually selected each one of the degree programs and the fifth column (skip the fourth column for the moment) shows the % of the persons that chose each of the degree programs (i.e., the number of persons who ticked a degree program divided by the total number of persons who had the opportunity to do so, multiplied by 100).

Figure 15.15 *The Rasch statistics of the degree programs.*

Name	Count	Score	MaxPoss	%Achieved	Estimate	StdErr	InMSQR	OuMSQR
Degree16	474	53	474	11.18	-0.61	0.16	0.85	0.54
Degree17	474	43	474	9.07	-0.36	0.17	0.93	0.69
Degree18	474	12	474	2.53	1.09	0.3	0.95	0.59
Degree19	474	11	474	2.32	1.18	0.31	0.96	0.62
Degree20	474	6	474	1.27	1.81	0.41	0.94	0.35
Degree21	474	8	474	1.69	1.51	0.36	0.93	0.36
Degree22	474	6	474	1.27	1.81	0.41	0.95	0.41
Degree23	474	5	474	1.05	2	0.45	0.94	0.34
Degree24	474	7	474	1.48	1.65	0.38	0.93	0.31
Degree25	474	59	474	12.45	-0.75	0.15	0.87	0.67
Degree26	474	246	474	51.9	-3.28	0.11	2.25	2.69
Degree27	474	83	474	17.51	-1.22	0.13	0.75	0.54
Degree28	474	71	474	14.98	-1	0.14	0.71	0.41
Degree29	474	90	474	18.99	-1.34	0.13	0.77	0.55
Degree30	474	18	474	3.8	0.65	0.25	0.99	1.09
Degree31	474	73	474	15.4	-1.04	0.14	0.75	0.47
Degree32	474	53	474	11.18	-0.61	0.16	0.8	0.5
Degree33	474	72	474	15.19	-1.02	0.14	0.77	0.55
Degree34	474	62	474	13.08	-0.82	0.15	0.76	0.44
Degree35	474	78	474	16.46	-1.13	0.13	0.77	0.51
Degree36	474	19	474	4.01	0.59	0.24	1.02	0.88
Degree37	474	19	474	4.01	0.59	0.24	1.01	0.88
Degree38	474	15	474	3.16	0.85	0.27	0.98	0.78
Degree39	474	19	474	4.01	0.59	0.24	1	0.79
Degree40	474	18	474	3.8	0.65	0.25	0.99	0.72
Degree41	474	37	474	7.81	-0.17	0.18	1.07	0.93
Degree42	474	36	474	7.59	-0.14	0.18	1.07	0.99
Degree43	424	32	424	7.55	-0.17	0.19	1.04	0.82
Degree44	424	23	424	5.42	0.21	0.22	1.02	0.69
Degree45	424	31	424	7.31	-0.13	0.2	1.03	0.82
Degree46	424	27	424	6.37	0.03	0.21	1.02	0.86
Degree47	424	25	424	5.9	0.12	0.21	1.17	1.36
Degree48	424	25	424	5.9	0.12	0.21	1.18	1.38
Degree49	424	57	424	13.44	-0.89	0.15	1.38	2

For example, 474 persons had the opportunity to tick the program Degree25 but only 59 did so, a percentage of 12.45%. On the contrary, 424 persons had the opportunity to tick the program Degree49 but only 57 did so, a percentage of 13.44%. The percentages ranged from 51.9% to 0.42%, showing that there is much variability in the popularity of the degree programs.

The difficulty of Degree49 to be endorsed by the respondents (i.e., unpopularity) was estimated to be -0.89 Rasch logits and the difficulty of Degree25 was estimated to be -0.75 Rasch logits. This information is shown in the sixth column (carrying the caption 'Estimate'). The important issue here is that the percentages of the persons that ticked the two programs are not comparable (because they are based on a different sample of people); however, their Rasch 'unpopularity' estimates are directly comparable because they are purposefully built on the same Rasch scale by the software. The unpopularity Rasch estimates of the degree programs ranged from 2.93 logits (only 2 ticks out of 474 persons) to -3.28 logits (246 ticks out of 474 persons). This shows a spread of 2.93-(-3.28)=6.21 logits with a standard deviation of 1.22 logits. Large positive estimates indicate huge unpopularity (e.g. Degree6) and large negative estimates indicate huge popularity (Degree26).

The next column (with the caption 'StdErr' or standard error) shows the uncertainty around which the unpopularity estimate of the degree programs was computed. While this gets larger, the uncertainty around the estimates also gets larger. As we have already mentioned earlier in the chapter, in practical settings, we can rarely estimate quantities with a 100% certainty (if we use data from a sample instead from the whole population). Therefore, for the purposes of this chapter, the computation of standard errors is always a necessary task. We should keep in mind that the smaller the standard error is, the more confident we are that we estimated accurately the unpopularity of a degree program to be endorsed by the persons.

There are two major factors affecting the uncertainty by which we estimate the unpopularity of the degree programs. The first is the sample size that is, the number of persons that had the opportunity to tick or not to tick a degree program i.e. the number of people who completed the questionnaire. From the 49 degree programs, 7 were administered to 424 persons and 42 were administered to 474 persons. Everything else being equal, the standard errors of the degree programs that were administered to 474 (instead of 424) persons should be slightly smaller. Also, everything else being equal, the standard errors of the degree programs that were administered to the same number of persons should be the same (indeed, they are: compare the standard errors of Degrees 36, 37 and 39 for example).

The second factor is the value of the unpopularity index itself: when it yields substantially extreme values (either towards the left or the right edge of the Rasch scale), the information contained in the dataset is not appropriate to estimate such values properly. Therefore, a degree program which is only ticked by one out of the 474 persons, for example, has a very large unpopularity and we would place its unpopularity index at the far right of the Rasch scale; the standard error of its estimate however will be far larger. This is reasonable because, in real life, if we repeated the same research again, the same degree program would most likely not be ticked only by one person: the next time we repeat this research (with a similar but different sample), we would expect that the degree program might be ticked by 2 persons or by nobody (or by any other number of persons). Therefore, the uncertainty around the unpopularity estimate in such a case is very large.

Figure 15.16 illustrates the factors affecting the standard errors of the estimates explicitly. Each one of the bubbles represents the standard error of the unpopularity estimate of a degree program. Larger bubbles indicate a larger standard error. A bubble is located on the horizontal axis, according to the value of the unpopularity estimate, for example a bubble representing a very unpopular degree program will be at the far right side of the Rasch scale. Vertically, the bubbles lay on two different groups: those encountered by 424 persons and those encountered by 474 persons. Notice that (a) the bubbles of the degree programs encountered by 474 persons are slightly smaller than the bubbles of the degree programs encountered by 424 persons, for those bubbles that lay on the same place on the horizontal axis (Rasch scale), of course; and (b) the bubbles of the degree programs at the left of the scale are substantially smaller than the bubbles of the degree programs at the far right of the scale, because there is a better match between the estimates of the persons and the estimates of the programs (compare the two graphs in Figure 15.16).

Figure 15.16 *Factors affecting the standard errors of the Rasch estimates.*

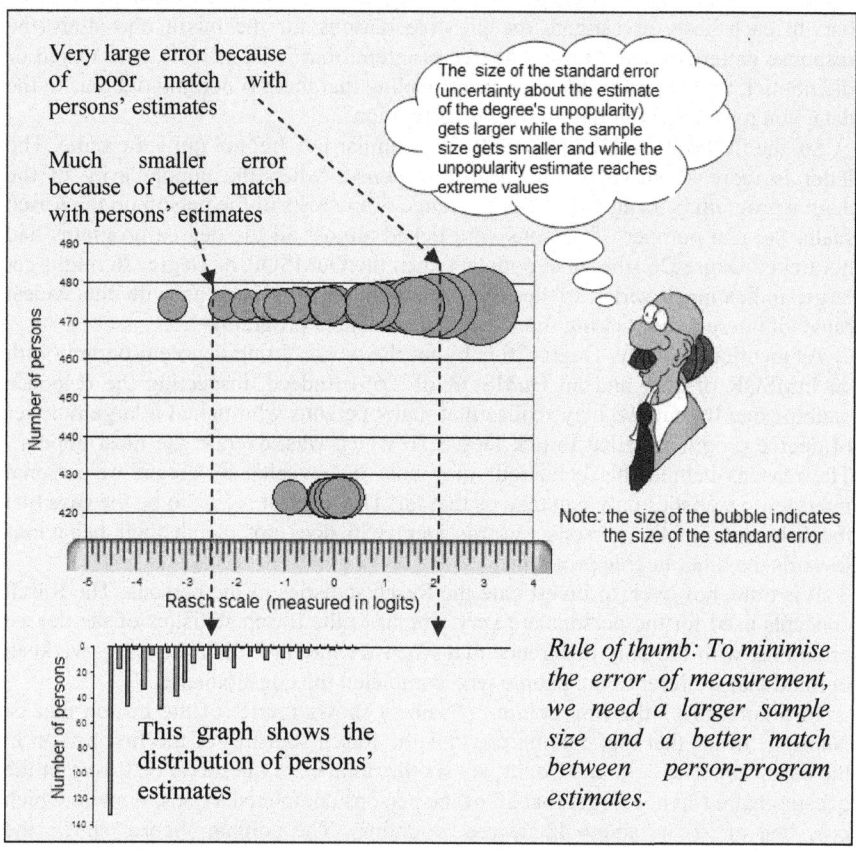

The last two columns of Figure 15.16 are the Infit and the Outfit Mean Squares (labelled as InMSQR and OuMSQR). These two statistics have a very similar role: they aim to inform us about the quality of our Rasch model. They can warn us about unexpected and surprising observations in the dataset that deviate from the overall pattern of the responses of the persons to the questionnaire. The possible values of these statistics are from 0 to infinite, although 1.0 is the expected value. The more InMSQR and OuMSQR deviate from 1.0 (towards larger values), the worse the fit between the data and the Rasch model. So, by visually inspecting Figure 15.15, it is easy to spot that Degree26 (with an InMSQR of 2.25 and an OuMSQR of 2.69) has the worse model-data fit among the 49 degree programs. In fact, there is too much difference between Degree26 and the next worse fitting degree program which is Degree49 (Degree49 has an InMSQR of 1.38 and an OuMSQR of 2.0). Conventional rules of thumb say that when the fit statistics are well beyond the ('psychological threshold') value of 1.3, then we should investigate the source of the aberrance more carefully. We will do so later.

At this point we should mention another very good practice to investigate model-data fit. The method instructs us to sort the elements (either persons or degree programs) in descending order of fit statistics, starting from the one with the worse fit, to the one with the smallest first statistic. Start your investigation from the one with the worse fit (larger fit statistic), and work towards the bottom of the list. In each case, investigate the possible reasons for the misfit and study the response patterns related to this degree program, that is investigate who ticked or did not tick the program. When you start feeling that there is nothing dubious in the data, you may stop your data-model investigation[7].

So, the InMSQR and the OuMSQR do a similar job, but not quite the same. The latter is more sensitive to unexpected responses when the unpopularity of the degree program is located far from the range of interests of the person on the Rasch scale. So, if a number of persons who ticked almost all the degree programs had not ticked Degree26 (the most popular), then the OuMSQR of Degree26 might get large, indicating a series of unexpected responses (the persons with the widest range of interests not ticking the most popular degree program).

As mentioned above, Degree26 is by far the worse fitting degree program (with an InMSQR of 2.25 and an OuMSQR of 2.69). Indeed, inspecting the response patterns one by one we may realise that many persons who ticked a large number of degree programs failed to tick Degree26 which was, overall, the most popular. The reasons behind this behaviour may only be revealed by means of personal interviews; statistics only can take us that far! However, it seems to be the case that the behaviour of the persons towards Degree26 does not match their behaviour towards the other degree programs.

It is time, however, to investigate the Rasch statistics of the persons. The Rasch concepts used for the persons are very similar to the Rasch statistics of the degree programs, with the only difference that when we interpret their meaning, we keep in mind that we refer to the people who completed the questionnaire.

In Figure 15.17 the first column ('Name') shows the ID of the person that is, Name=1 means that this column presents the Rasch statistics of the first person in the datasheet. The column 'Count' shows the number of questions that were in the questionnaire (do not forget that 50 of the persons completed a questionnaire which only had questions about 42 degree programs). The column 'Score' shows the number of degree programs that were ticked by the person that is, the first person only ticked on one degree program. The column '%Achieved' (ignore the 'MaxPoss' column for the moment) shows the percentage of the degree programs ticked by each person ('Score'/'Count'X100) that is, for the second person the %achieved is 3/49X100=6.12%.

Figure 15.17 *The Rasch statistics of the persons.*

Name	Count	Score	MaxPoss	%Achieved	Estimate	StdErr	InMSQR	OuMSQR
1	49	1	49	2.04	-4.54	1.04	0.68	0.09
2	49	3	49	6.12	-3.3	0.63	1.26	1.3
3	49	9	49	18.37	-1.86	0.4	1.05	0.69
4	49	5	49	10.2	-2.66	0.51	0.77	0.51
5	49	5	49	10.2	-2.66	0.51	1.48	2.97
6	49	1	49	2.04	-4.54	1.04	0.68	0.09
7	49	6	49	12.24	-2.43	0.47	0.81	0.56
8	49	2	49	4.08	-3.77	0.76	1.19	0.94
9	49	6	49	12.24	-2.43	0.47	1.15	1.21
10	49	1	49	2.04	-4.54	1.04	0.68	0.09
11	49	1	49	2.04	-4.54	1.04	0.68	0.09
12	49	5	49	10.2	-2.66	0.51	0.71	0.4
13	49	6	49	12.24	-2.43	0.47	1.1	0.62
14	49	4	49	8.16	-2.95	0.56	1	1.12
15	49	7	49	14.29	-2.22	0.44	1.06	0.81

The column 'Estimate' refers to the 'range of interest for further study' for each person and is a Rasch statistic which is comparable between all persons, no matter whether they completed the shorter or the longer version of the questionnaire. This statistic is measured in Rasch logits and helps us to place the persons on the Rasch scale, in the same way as we did for the degree programs. Larger values indicate a person with a wider range of interests (that is, a person who ticked many degree programs) and smaller values indicate a person with a narrower range of interests (that is, a person who ticked a smaller number of degree programs).

At this point it is interesting to indicate that persons who ticked the same number of degree programs but completed different questionnaires also received different Rasch estimates from the Rasch model. The Rasch model recognised that it is not possible to compare the response behaviour of persons who completed different questionnaires, so it adjusted the estimates of persons in such a way so that they become directly comparable (Figure 15.18). The way to read the figure is really intuitive: follow a horizontal line (such as the one shown on the figure) from the y-axis until you meet the star-points of the graph. The horizontal line shown on Figure 15.18 is the value '11 ticks' on the y-axis. Then, follow the vertical lines from the point where the horizontal line meets the star-points down to the x-axis: the first line crosses on the -1.56 logits range of interests and the second line crosses on the -1.34 logits range of interests. Although the difference that is -1.56-(-1.34)=-0.22 logits, is not huge, it is indicative of the fact that the raw score (the number of ticks or even the percentage of degree programs ticked) are not comparable between the persons; that is why we needed the Rasch model, to generate comparable estimates.

The column 'StdErr' shows the magnitude of the standard error of the persons' estimate that is, the uncertainty with which the 'range of interests' of persons where estimated. It is the same concept that was discussed for the degree programs; however, it is interpreted in the context of the range of interests of the persons. The persons that completed the longer questionnaire indeed have slightly smaller standard errors of estimate, provided their range of interests is about the same.

The last two columns are the familiar fit statistics which we discussed in the context of the degree programs. The same issues hold for the persons as well. For example, the OuMSQR for a given person would be inflated if that person had ticked only one degree program e.g. Degree23 (the most unpopular) but missed Degree26 (the most popular). That would indeed be a surprise because in a previous section we 'agreed' on the basic assumptions of the Rasch model, and these assumptions say that it is more likely for a person to tick a degree program if the program is more popular. So, if the observed responses of a person are very different from his/her expected responses, we call his/her response pattern as 'misfitting the Rasch model'.

Figure 15.18 *The persons' Rasch estimates and the number of degree programs they ticked.*

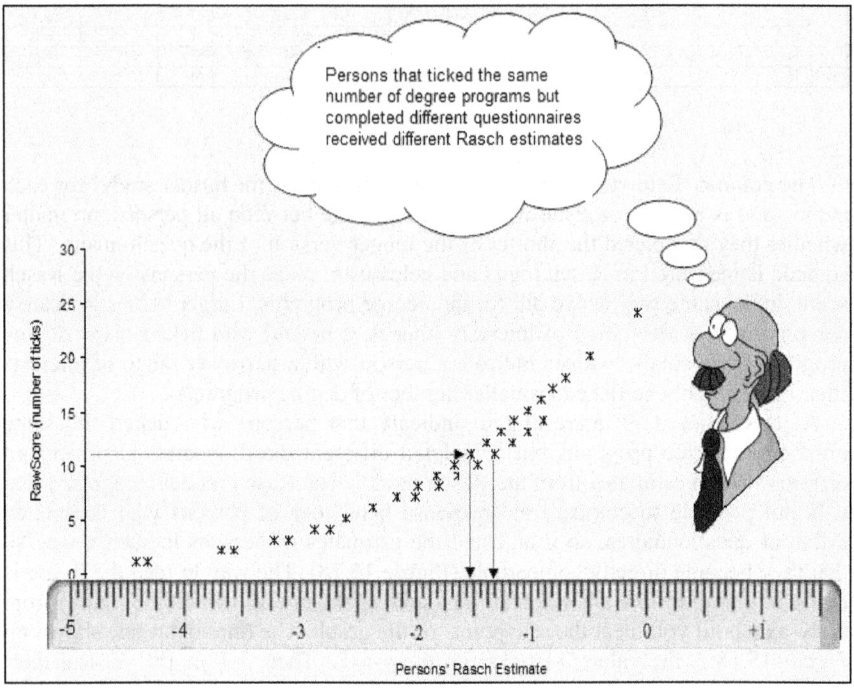

In fact, the Analysis software estimates the expected response of every person on every degree program for us and saves this information in a sheet which we can open and view at any time. Click on the button "Exp." on the toolbar, to open the sheet with the expected ticks of the persons that is this sheet shows the probability that a person would tick a specific degree program. The screen should look like the sheet of Figure 15.19. The first column carries the label 'Examinee' but refers to the persons that completed a questionnaire. The second column shows the estimate of their range of interests, and the next two columns show the InMSQR (carries the label 'Exam Infit') and the OuMSQR (carries the label 'Exam Outfit'). Then, ignore (for the moment) a few columns carrying other labels and focus on the columns with labels 'Degree1', 'Degree2' etc. Each of this column shows the probability that a person would tick each of the corresponding degree programs. Since these cells represent probabilities for a tick, they can take values from 0 to 1. For example, Figure 15.19 shows with arrows the probabilities that Person3 will tick Degree1 and Degree7. It is easily deduced that the least unpopular (i.e., more popular) degree program of the two, which is Degree7, has a higher probability to be ticked by Person3.

Figure 15.19 *The persons' expected ticks, according to the Rasch model.*

Examinee	Exam Ability	Exam Infit	Exam Outfit	Degree1	Degree2	Degree7	Deg
1	-4.54	0.68	0.09	0.01	0.01	0.02	0.
2	-3.3	1.26	1.3	0.04	0.04	0.06	0.
3	-1.86	1.05	0.69	0.15	0.16	0.22	0.
4	-2.68	0.77	0.51	0.07	0.08	0.11	0.
5	-2.66	1.48	2.97	0.07	0.08	0.11	0.
6	-4.54	0.68	0.09	0.01	0.01	0.02	0.
7	-2.43	0.81	0.56	0.09	0.09	0.14	0
8	-3.77	1.19	0.94	0.02	0.03	0.04	0.
9	-2.43	1.15	1.21	0.09	0.09	0.14	0
10	-4.54	0.68	0.09	0.01	0.01	0.02	0.
11	-4.54	0.68	0.09	0.01	0.01	0.02	0.

Person3 with a range of interests of -1.86 logits had a probability of 15% to tick Degree1 (unpopularity of -0.1 logits) and a probability of 22% to tick Degree7 (unpopularity of -0.61 logits)

$$P\{\chi=1\}=\frac{e^{-1.86-(-0.1)}}{1-e^{-1.86-(-0.1)}}=\frac{2.718^{-1.76}}{1-2.718^{-1.76}}\approx 15\%$$

$$P\{\chi=1\}=\frac{e^{-1.86-(-0.61)}}{1-e^{-1.86-(-0.61)}}=\frac{2.718^{-1.25}}{1-2.718^{-1.25}}\approx 22\%$$

The figure also shows two numeric examples of the equations used to compute the expected ticks for each person. To extend the discussion a step further, comparing the observed responses (whether a person indeed ticked a degree program) with the expected responses (the probability estimated by the Rasch model that a person will tick a degree program) we may spot unexpected responses. For example, the actual responses of Person3 on Degree1 and Degree7 were 'Not Ticked' and 'Not Ticked' (that is, '0' in both cases). Therefore, in the first case, the residual (i.e., the difference Observed-Expected) was 0-0.15=-0.15 and in the second case the Residual was 0-0.22=-0.22. That means that Person3 had a 15% chance to tick Degree1 but he/she did not tick it. The residual is not large, and this is not considered to be an unexpected response. Since the probability for a tick was small, it is reasonable to say that Person3 behaved according to the expectations of the Rasch model. There are, however, cases where Persons have generated highly unexpected response patterns.

Figure 15.20 *The persons' expected ticks, according to the Rasch model.*

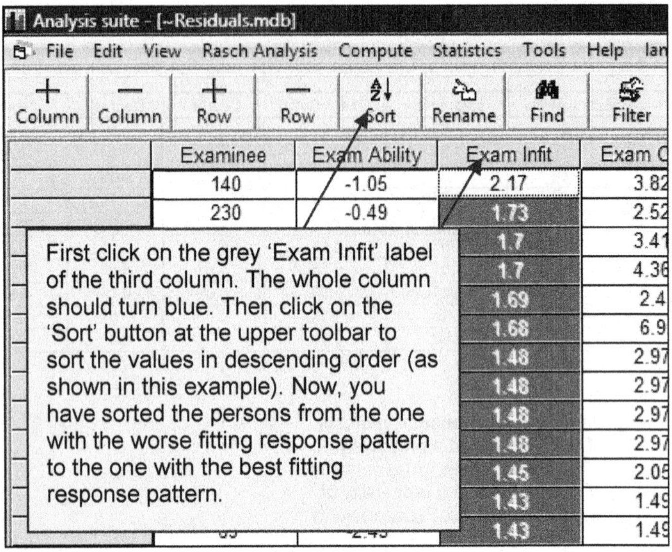

Examinee	Exam Ability	Exam Infit	Exam O
140	-1.05	2.17	3.82
230	-0.49	1.73	2.52
		1.7	3.41
		1.7	4.36
		1.69	2.4
		1.68	6.9
		1.48	2.97
		1.48	2.97
		1.48	2.97
		1.48	2.97
		1.45	2.05
		1.43	1.49
		1.43	1.49

First click on the grey 'Exam Infit' label of the third column. The whole column should turn blue. Then click on the 'Sort' button at the upper toolbar to sort the values in descending order (as shown in this example). Now, you have sorted the persons from the one with the worse fitting response pattern to the one with the best fitting response pattern.

The software also estimated the probabilities of Person140 and Person230 to tick any of the degree programs on the questionnaire. These are the two persons who generated the most misfitting response patterns according to the magnitude of their InMSQR. It is not necessary, however, to compute the residuals by hand, as we did in the example above with Person3. The Analysis software computes all the residuals for you and stores them in a sheet which you can view at any time. You may open the sheet by clicking on the 'Resid.' button on the toolbar. Let's study a couple of interesting cases of persons with atypical and unexpected response patterns: (a) Person140 (completed the short questionnaire; ticked 13 programs; has a range of interests estimate of -1.05 logits; a Standard Error of estimate of 0.38; and InMSQR=2.17 and OuMSQR=3.82) and (b) Person230 (completed the long questionnaire; ticked 20 programs; has a range of interests estimate of -0.49 logits; a Standard Error of estimate of 0.33; and InMSQR=1.73 and OuMSQR=2.52).

Click on the 'Resid.' button to open the sheet with the residuals (the 'Residual Matrix' as is more technically known). Click on the 'Exam Infit' label of the third column and then click on the 'Sort' button on the upper toolbar, as shown on Figure 15.20. Person140 has generated the most misfitting (unexpected) response pattern according to the magnitude of his/her InMSQR (as shown on Figure 15.20 and Figure **15.21**). You may scroll to the right to observe his/her residuals on each of the degree programs. For example, he/she ticked Degree23 which was the most unpopular one, therefore he/she has a residual of 0.95 (very large with a maximum possible residual of 1): his/her expected score was 0.05 (5% probability to tick it) and his/her observed score was '1' (i.e., 'tick'), so his/her residual is 1-0.05=0.95. Along the same lines, he/she failed to tick Degree26 which was the most popular one, therefore he/she has a residual of -0.90: his/her expected score was 0.90 (90%

probability to tick it) and his/her observed score was '0' (i.e., 'no tick'), so his/her residual is 0-0.90=-0.90.

As Figure **15.21** shows, both Person140 and Person230 have very large residuals, either positive or negative. It is not important to investigate which of those are positive and which are negative. The sign of the residuals is not important and usually there is a balance between the positive and the negative residuals. The important issue here is the absolute value of the residuals: aggregating too many large residuals, for example, larger than 0.7 (i.e., 0.8) or smaller than -0.7 (i.e., -0.8) is a strong indication of a misfitting response pattern. This is an undesirable situation. In the cases where a person has accumulated too many large residuals, such as the case of the persons 140 and 230, the estimate of their range of interests may not be valid (i.e., may not be believable).

Figure 15.21 *The persons' residuals, according to the Rasch model.*

Examinee	Degree20	Degree21	Degree22	Degree23	Degree24	Degree25	Degree26	D
140	0.95	0.93	0.95	0.95	0.94	-0.43	-0.9	
230	0.91	0.88	0.91	0.92	0.9	0.44	-0.94	
310	0.97	0.96	0.97	-0.03	-0.04	-0.31	-0.85	
121	0.97	-0.03	-0.03	0.98	0.97	0.75	-0.81	
185	0.87	0.83	0.87	0.89	0.85	0.34	-0.96	
267	0.98	0.98	0.98	0.99	0.98	-0.19	-0.74	
77	-0.01	-0.02	-0.01	-0.01	-0.01	-0.13	-0.65	

Conclusion

This chapter aimed to introduce some theory and a practical application of the Rasch model on empirical data. The main message to the reader is that the Rasch model can be a valuable statistical tool in the hands of academics, researchers and practitioners. For example, the Rasch model may be used, and has often been used, to build new psychological theories or confirm existing ones.

Unfortunately, the Rasch models are sometimes not only used, but abused, in the hands of researchers and practitioners. The routine use of Rasch models on any type of dataset can be a risky business. It is advisable that the Rasch analyst gets to know his/her dataset and investigate whether it fulfils the fundamental assumptions discussed earlier in this chapter.

There is a wealth of freely available or commercial Rasch-capable software. The user is encouraged to download and try a specific free software package (i.e., the Analysis package) for the purposes of this chapter. However, other researchers have published very successful and popular introductory Rasch books based on other packages (such as Bond & Fox, 2001).

This chapter did not aim to develop expert Rasch users. We have just managed to scratch the surface and we did not have the opportunity to dig deep in the goldmine of Rasch models. We have also presented only one, the simplest, of a large family of complex Rasch models. The interested reader is encouraged to visit a popular web page which is a useful source of freely available Rasch-related material www.Rasch.org. Having said the above, we hope that students, practitioners and academics in the area of adult psychology will find this chapter a good starting point in their endeavours for new statistical tools to assist them in their job.

NOTES

[1] Models which assume that there is only one possible result

[2] Use the File → Open menu. From there, locate the file studies.txt and click OK.

[3] You will find the studies.xls and the studies.txt files in the folder where you installed the Analysis software. Alternatively, you may download it from the web page www.ReLabs.org/IntrPsych . Open the studies.xls file through MS Excel to view the content. Alternatively, use the Analysis package. Remember that this is a MS Excel file, you cannot read it directly: you will need to use the 'Import' facility from the File → Import → Excel file menu.

[4] The procedure is demonstrated in more detail in Acrobat pdf files which you can download from www.ReLabs.org/IntrPsych.

[5] The reason why we chose to construct an unpopularity index, instead of a popularity index will be made clearer later on.

[6] The reader should keep in mind that, as happens with all software, future versions may look slightly (or a lot) different. Therefore, consulting software's manual before using it, is always a good idea. The screenshots used in this chapter come from version 3.1 of the Analysis package.

[7] You may use the same strategy when investigating the model-data fit of the persons.

Acknowledgement

This work has been adapted from an earlier publication and reproduced with permission.

REFERENCES

Alagumalai, S., Curtis, D. D., & Hungi, N. (2005). Applied Rasch measurement: A book of exemplars. The Netherlands: Springer.

Athanasou, J. A., & Lamprianou, I. (2002). *A teachers' guide to assessment*. Tuggerah, Australia: Social Science Press.

Bond, T. G., & Fox, C. M. (2001). Applying the Rasch model: Fundamental measurement in the human sciences. New Jersey: Lawrence Erlbaum Associates.

Molenaar, I. W. (1995). Some background for Item Response Theory and the Rasch model. In G. H. Fischer & I. W. Molenaar (Eds), *Rasch models: Foundations, recent developments and applications* (pp. 3-14). New York: Springer-Verlag.

Rasch, G. (1960). Probabilistic models for some intelligence and attainment tests. Copenhagen: The Danish Institute of Educational Research. (Expanded edition, 1980. Chicago: The University of Chicago Press).

Silva, F. (1993). *Psychometric foundations and behavioural assessment*. New York: Sage.

Stevens, S. S. (1946). On the theory of scales of measurement. *Science*, 103, 677-680.

Review Questions

1. Give an informal definition of the Rasch model, as was presented in this chapter.
2. Explain the main assumptions of uni-dimensionality and local independence.
3. What is the role of the standard errors of the ability and difficulty estimates?
4. How do we investigate the quality of our Rasch analysis?
5. Should we apply the Rasch model on any dataset?

Answers to Review Questions

1. Answer: A probabilistic model which describes the relationship between a person's parameter (e.g., ability) and a question's parameter (e.g., difficulty); this relationship governs the responses of the person when encountering a question.

2. Answer: Uni-dimensionality demands that the likelihood of an observation (e.g. a correct response to a question) is exclusively governed by the parameter of a person (e.g., ability) and the parameter of the question (e.g., difficulty). Other factors should not affect the likelihood of a correct or incorrect response to a question. Local independence, on the other hand, demands that the responses of a person to the previous questions do not affect his/her responses to the next questions.

3. Answer: It is a fact of life that when we use data from a sample, we can never be 100% precise about the person abilities and the question difficulties we estimate. Therefore, we need to answer the question: "If we had a similar but different sample of data, how different our results could be"? Thus, we use special statistical techniques to investigate the margin of error of our estimates, to know how much trust to put on them. It is always preferable for the standard errors to be as small as possible.

4. Answer: Among other things, we tend to investigate the model-data fit in the form of fit statistics. In this chapter, we investigated the model-data fit using the Infit and the Outfit Mean Squares. Large values for persons and questions may indicate issues in our data that deserve further investigation. In the case of persons or questions with large Infit and Outfit Mean Squares, we may need to use the residual matrix (the table of residuals) to identify the extent and the source of the unexpected responses.

5. Answer: The Rasch model may be applied on a wide range of datasets and in fact, it has been used on all sorts of datasets in the area of education and psychology. However, whenever it is used, it is strongly advisable to investigate whether the fundamental assumptions of the Rasch model indeed hold. If the model-data fit is less than satisfactory, or if the researcher suspects that the assumptions of the model do not hold, then it is possible that the Rasch model may not be appropriate for the dataset (and vice versa).

About the Author

Iasonas Lamprianou has a special interest in educational measurement and has obtained a PhD with the title "Optimal Appropriateness Measurement in the context of the One Parameter Logistic Model" (University of Manchester, UK). He has taught advanced statistical modelling (Item Response Theory analysis) at a postgraduate level at the University of Manchester, Faculty of Education. In the last five years Iasonas has worked as a consultant to many assessment organisations like the Qualifications and Curriculum Authority (UK), the National Assessment Agency (UK), the Assessment and Qualifications Alliance (UK), the University of Manchester (UK), the Agha Khan University Examination Board (Pakistan), the University of Malta, the Cyprus Testing Service and others. He has successfully applied advanced statistical models and published in diverse disciplines such as: educational measurement (e.g., *Journal of Educational Measurement, Journal of Applied Measurement, International Journal of Testing*), computing (e.g., *Computers & Education*), medicine (e.g., *Injury*), psychology (e.g., *Australian Journal of Educational & Developmental Psychology, Australian Educational and Developmental Psychologist*), physical education (e.g., *Physical Education and Sport Pedagogy*), vocational education (e.g., *International Journal of Vocational Education and Training*) and professional development (e.g., *Journal of In-service Education*).

Iasonas Lamprianou
The School of Arts and Education Sciences, European University – Cyprus
& School of Education, University of Manchester, UK

About the Editor

James A. Athanasou was born in Perth in 1948 and came to the Maroubra area of Sydney in 1953 where he still lives. He completed his schooling at the Maroubra Junction Primary and Maroubra Bay High schools. He went on to complete his undergraduate studies at the University of New South Wales majoring in History and Philosophy of Science as well as Psychology and then postgraduate studies at the University of Sydney and the University of New England, where he obtained his PhD in the Centre for Behavioural Studies in Education. Jim spent most of his career in the New South Wales Public Service, serving as Senior Counsellor in the Youth Counselling Service, Principal Executive Officer for the Commerce and Industry Training Council, Deputy Director of the Vocational Services Branch and Government Recruitment Agency, and finally Chief Project Officer in the former Department of Further Education Training and Employment. He came to the School of Adult and Vocational Education at the University of Technology, Sydney as a lecturer in measurement and evaluation in 1991 and is now Associate Professor in the Faculty of Education.

Most recently Jim is the author of *Evaluating Career Education and Guidance* (ACER Press), co-author with Iasonas Lamprianou of *A Teacher's Guide to Assessment* (Social Science Press), editor of *Adult Education and Training* (David Barlow Publishing) and co-editor of the *International Handbook of Career Guidance* (Springer). In 1989 he developed the *Career Interest Test* (now used on www.myfuture.edu.au). Since 1995 he has been editor of *PHRONEMA,* the Annual Review of St Andrew's Greek Orthodox Theo-logical College and since 2000 has been editor of the *Austral-ian Journal of Career Deve-lopment*. He has been Visiting Fellow at the Universitat der Bundeswehr, Muenchen, Vrije Universiteit Brussel and the University of Illinois Urbana-Champaign. Jim is a registered psychologist, a member of the Australian Psychological Society and a Fellow of the Career Development Association of Australia.

He teaches in the areas of educational and vocational psychology as well as assessing learning. He is married with four children and his spare time interests include religion, reading, classical music, walking, crosswords and gardening.

INDEX

9 789087 905538